Creating Web Pages
All In One Desk Reference
For Dummies

Cheat Sheet

D0534117

Web Page Do's and Don'ts

A successful Web site doesn't just happen by accident. To create a Web site people will want to visit over and over again, keep the following time-tested guidelines in mind.

Do:

✔ **Do offer something useful on every page.** Avoid creating pages that are just steps along the way to truly useful information.

✔ **Do let your individuality show.** Find out what other Web sites similar to yours have to offer. Don't create a "me too" Web site that offers nothing but information that is already available elsewhere. Instead, strive for unique information that can be found only on your Web site.

✔ **Do make it look good.** Yes, substance is more important than style. But an ugly Web site turns people away, whereas an attractive Web site draws people in.

✔ **Do proof it carefully.** If every third word in your Web site is misspelled, people will assume that the information on your Web site is as unreliable as your spelling.

✔ **Do provide links to other sites.** Some of the best pages on the Internet are links to other Web sites that have information about a particular topic. But don't just slap up an URL; add a concise description of what your readers can expect to find when they surf off to another page.

✔ **Do keep it current.** Internet users will not frequent your site if it contains old, out-of-date information.

✔ **Do publicize it.** Few people will stumble across your Web site by accident. If you want people to visit your Web site, you have to publicize it. Make sure that your site is listed in the major search engines, such as Yahoo! and Lycos. Also, you can promote your site by putting its address on all your advertisements, correspondences, business cards, e-mails, and so on.

Don't:

✔ **Don't pack your pages with unnecessary images, sound files, Java applets, or other gew-gaws.** Multimedia files make your pages download more slowly — so if you use them, make sure your users find them worth the wait.

✔ **Don't tie your Web page to a certain browser.** Exploiting the cool new features of the latest and greatest Web browser, whether it's Microsoft Internet Explorer or Netscape Navigator, is a good idea. But don't do so at the expense of users who may be using the *other* browser.

✔ **Don't make hardware assumptions.** Remember that not everyone has a 21-inch monitor and a high-speed cable-modem connection to the Internet. Design your Web site so that it can be used by the poor sap who is stuck with a 14-inch monitor and — gasp — a 28.8 Kbps modem connection to the Internet.

Creating Web Pages All In One Desk Reference For Dummies

Cheat Sheet

Web-safe Colors

When it comes to adding color to your Web page, not all colors are created equal: some appear differently in different browsers. Here are the 14 standard "Web-safe" color names — guaranteed to appear the same in all browsers — along with their corresponding hexadecimal designations.

Color	Hex #	Color	Hex #
Black	#000000	Green	#008000
Silver	#C0C0C0	Lime	#00FF00
Gray	#808080	Olive	#808000
White	#FFFFFF	Yellow	#FFFF00
Maroon	#800000	Navy	#000080
Purple	#800080	Teal	#008080
Fuchsia	#FF00FF	Aqua	#00FFFF

Bare-bones HTML reference

HTML defines dozens and dozens of *tags* — special keywords, surrounded by angle brackets, that tell browsers how to display the content of your Web page. Here are the most indispensable, in the order they're most likely to appear in your pages:

HTML syntax	Description
<HTML></HTML>	Defines a Web page (an HTML document).
<HEAD></HEAD>	Defines the heading of a Web page.
<TITLE></TITLE>	Defines the title of a Web page.
<IMG></IMG>	Adds an image to a Web page.
<SCRIPT></SCRIPT>	Adds a script, such as a JavaScript script, to a Web page.
<BODY></BODY>	Defines the body of a Web page (most HTML code goes between these tags)
<P>	Creates a paragraph (line break).
<FORM></FORM>	Defines an HTML input form (all form elements go between these tags)

Hungry Minds™

For Dummies: Bestselling Book Series for Beginners

 ™

BESTSELLING BOOK SERIES

References for the Rest of Us! ®

Are you intimidated and confused by computers? Do you find that traditional manuals are overloaded with technical details you'll never use? Do your friends and family always call you to fix simple problems on their PCs? Then the For Dummies® computer book series from Hungry Minds, Inc. is for you.

For Dummies books are written for those frustrated computer users who know they aren't really dumb but find that PC hardware, software, and indeed the unique vocabulary of computing make them feel helpless. For Dummies books use a lighthearted approach, a down-to-earth style, and even cartoons and humorous icons to dispel computer novices' fears and build their confidence. Lighthearted but not lightweight, these books are a perfect survival guide for anyone forced to use a computer.

> *"I like my copy so much I told friends; now they bought copies."*
>
> — *Irene C., Orwell, Ohio*

> *"Quick, concise, nontechnical, and humorous."*
>
> — *Jay A., Elburn, Illinois*

> *"Thanks, I needed this book. Now I can sleep at night."*
>
> — *Robin F., British Columbia, Canada*

Already, millions of satisfied readers agree. They have made For Dummies books the #1 introductory level computer book series and have written asking for more. So, if you're looking for the most fun and easy way to learn about computers, look to For Dummies books to give you a helping hand.

Hungry Minds™

Creating Web Pages
ALL-IN-ONE DESK REFERENCE
FOR
DUMMIES®

Creating Web Pages
ALL-IN-ONE DESK REFERENCE
FOR
DUMMIES®

by Emily Vander Veer, Doug Lowe, Eric Ray,
Deborah Ray, Damon Dean, Camille McCue,
Emily Weadock, Joyce Nielsen, Mariva Aviram,
Stephen Lockwood, and Madhu Siddalingaiah

Hungry Minds™

Best-Selling Books • Digital Downloads • e-Books • Answer Networks • e-Newsletters • Branded Web Sites • e-Learning

New York, NY ◆ Cleveland, OH ◆ Indianapolis, IN

Creating Web Pages All-in-One Desk Reference For Dummies®

Published by
Hungry Minds, Inc.
909 Third Avenue
New York, NY 10022
www.hungryminds.com
www.dummies.com

Library of Congress Control Number: 2001092902

ISBN: 0-7645-1542-X

Printed in the United States of America

10 9 8 7 6 5 4 3 2 1

1B/QZ/RR/QR/IN

Distributed in the United States by Hungry Minds, Inc.

Distributed by CDG Books Canada Inc. for Canada; by Transworld Publishers Limited in the United Kingdom; by IDG Norge Books for Norway; by IDG Sweden Books for Sweden; by IDG Books Australia Publishing Corporation Pty. Ltd. for Australia and New Zealand; by TransQuest Publishers Pte Ltd. for Singapore, Malaysia, Thailand, Indonesia, and Hong Kong; by Gotop Information Inc. for Taiwan; by ICG Muse, Inc. for Japan; by Intersoft for South Africa; by Eyrolles for France; by International Thomson Publishing for Germany, Austria and Switzerland; by Distribuidora Cuspide for Argentina; by LR International for Brazil; by Galileo Libros for Chile; by Ediciones ZETA S.C.R. Ltda. for Peru; by WS Computer Publishing Corporation, Inc., for the Philippines; by Contemporanea de Ediciones for Venezuela; by Express Computer Distributors for the Caribbean and West Indies; by Micronesia Media Distributor, Inc. for Micronesia; by Chips Computadoras S.A. de C.V. for Mexico; by Editorial Norma de Panama S.A. for Panama; by American Bookshops for Finland.

For general information on Hungry Minds' products and services please contact our Customer Care Department within the U.S. at 800-762-2974, outside the U.S. at 317-572-3993 or fax 317-572-4002.

For sales inquiries and reseller information, including discounts, premium and bulk quantity sales, and foreign-language translations, please contact our Customer Care Department at 800-434-3422, fax 317-572-4002, or write to Hungry Minds, Inc., Attn: Customer Care Department, 10475 Crosspoint Boulevard, Indianapolis, IN 46256.

For information on licensing foreign or domestic rights, please contact our Sub-Rights Customer Care Department at 212-884-5000.

For information on using Hungry Minds' products and services in the classroom or for ordering examination copies, please contact our Educational Sales Department at 800-434-2086 or fax 317-572-4005.

For press review copies, author interviews, or other publicity information, please contact our Public Relations Department at 317-572-3168 or fax 317-572-4168.

For authorization to photocopy items for corporate, personal, or educational use, please contact Copyright Clearance Center, 222 Rosewood Drive, Danvers, MA 01923, or fax 978-750-4470.

Hungry Minds™ is a trademark of Hungry Minds, Inc.

Hungry Minds, Inc., gratefully acknowledges the contributions of these authors and contributing writers: Emily Vander Veer, Doug Lowe, Eric Ray, Deborah Ray, Damon Dean, Camille McCue, Emily Weadock, Joyce Nielsen, Mariva Aviram, Stephen Lockwood, and Madhu Siddalingaiah. Emily Vander Veer's developmental and technical skills, along with her keen awareness of our readers' needs, served to make this book an invaluable resource. Thanks also to Bill Helling, Constance Carlisle, Jodi Jensen, and Nicole Haims for breathing life into this series of books.

Publisher's Acknowledgments

We're proud of this book; please send us your comments through our Hungry Minds Online Registration Form located at www.dummies.com.

Some of the people who helped bring this book to market include the following:

Acquisitions, Editorial, and Media Development

Project Editor: Paul Levesque

Acquisitions Editor: Steve Hayes

Copy Editors: Christine Berman, Rebecca Huehls

Technical Editor: Dennis Short

Editorial Manager: Constance Carlisle

Permissions Editor: Laura Moss

Media Development Specialist: Megan Decraene

Media Development Coordinator: Marisa Pearman

Media Development Manager: Laura VanWinkle

Media Development Supervisor: Richard Graves

Editorial Assistants: Amanda Foxworth, Jean Rogers

Production

Project Coordinator: Nancee Reeves

Layout and Graphics: Joyce Haughey, Jackie Nicholas, Jacque Schneider, Brian Torwelle, Erin Zeltner

Proofreaders: Arielle Carole Mennelle, John Greenough, Andy Hollandbeck, Charles Spencer, Susan Moritz

Indexer: Liz Cunningham

General and Administrative

Hungry Minds Technology Publishing Group: Richard Swadley, Senior Vice President and Publisher; Mary Bednarek, Vice President and Publisher, Networking; Walter R. Bruce III, Vice President and Publisher; Joseph Wikert, Vice President and Publisher, Web Development Group; Mary C. Corder, Editorial Director, Dummies Technology; Andy Cummings, Publishing Director, Dummies Technology; Barry Pruett, Publishing Director, Visual/Graphic Design

Hungry Minds Manufacturing: Ivor Parker, Vice President, Manufacturing

Hungry Minds Marketing: John Helmus, Assistant Vice President, Director of Marketing

Hungry Minds Production for Branded Press: Debbie Stailey, Production Director

Hungry Minds Sales: Michael Violano, Vice President, International Sales and Sub Rights

Contents at a Glance

Cartoons at a Glance

By Rich Tennant

"I have to say I'm really impressed with the interactivity on this car wash Web site."

page 9

"Maybe it would help our Web site if we showed our products in action."

page 189

page 261

"What do you mean you're updating our Web page?"

page 355

"Give him air! Give him air! He'll be okay. He's just been exposed to some raw HTML code. It must have accidently flashed across his screen from the server."

page 105

"Just how accurately should my Web site reflect my place of business?"

page 611

"Well shoot - I know the animation's moving a mite too fast, but dang if I can find a 'mosey' function anywhere in the toolbox!"

page 683

"MIDTOWN WHERE'S THE DANG DOOR?!"

page 435

"FRANKLY, I'M NOT SURE THIS IS THE WAY TO ENHANCE OUR COLOR GRAPHICS."

page 515

"OK, I think I forgot to mention this, but we now have a Web management function that automatically alerts us when there's a broken link on The Aquarium's Web site."

page 763

Cartoon Information:
Fax: 978-546-7747
E-Mail: richtennant@the5thwave.com
World Wide Web: www.the5thwave.com

Table of Contents

Introduction

The Web is long past novelty, if-you've-heard-about-it-you-must-be-a-geek status. (I know this because a long-distance friend of mine — a friend so technology-phobic she bakes bread by hand, not trusting those newfangled grocery store bakeries — recently told me she'd found inexpensive plane tickets on a travel Web site, and would I be so kind as to make up the bed in my spare bedroom?) Everyone, it seems, either has a Web site or is putting one together.

The trouble is, if you want to join in the fun (and profit) and don't happen to be a Web developer by trade, you may have trouble deciding exactly where to start. HTML! HTTP! XML! Java! JavaScript! Just trying to figure out what all these strange-sounding acronyms *mean* can give you a headache — let alone trying to figure out which acronyms you really need to understand and which you don't.

If any of this sounds familiar, relax and heave a sigh of relief: You've come to the right place. This book begins with a minibook (called, appropriately enough, *Creating Web Pages*) that introduces you to the wonderful world of the Web, helps you decide what kind of Web site you want to focus on creating, and outlines the steps you need to take to go from your great idea to a live Web site.

The rest of the book is organized into concise *minibooks*, each of which tackles a specific aspect of Web development — everything from adding graphic images and sounds to your Web pages to turning a simple home page into a full-fledged e-commerce site. You don't need to read through all of them all at once; just pick the one that corresponds to the feature you most want to add to your site and go from there.

This book isn't useful just for folks new to the Web, though. Even if you're an old hand at creating Web pages, chances are you may need a reference that covers one or more Web-related topics you may be unfamiliar with — topics such as the powerful meta language called XML (eXtensible Markup Language), for example, or the Java programming language. Here, too, you've come to the right place: The book you're holding contains reference minibooks on these languages as well as the more accessible and popular JavaScript scripting language.

Because you (like me) may learn best when you perform tasks as you read along, the CD that comes with this book contains a handful of the most popular Web-development tools on the market. To cement your understanding of the concepts I present in this book, all you need to do is pop in the CD, install one or more of the development tools you find there, and try out the examples I provide in each minibook.

Creating a Web site is one of the most creative, communicative endeavors in which you can engage. Whether you're interested in creating a personal home page for your own enjoyment, or developing a multimedia-rich e-commerce site for your boss, you can use the tips and examples in this book to create an interactive work of art that folks all over the planet can access and enjoy.

About This Book

The *Creating Web Pages All-in-One Desk Reference For Dummies* is intended to be a reference for all the great things (and maybe a few not-so-great things) that you may need to know when you're creating or expanding a Web site — from designing a cool-looking page to creating multimedia effects and e-commerce capability. Of course, you could go out and buy a book on each of these Web-development-related topics, but why would you want to when they're all conveniently packaged for you in this handy reference? The *Creating Web Pages All-in-One Desk Reference For Dummies* doesn't pretend to be a comprehensive reference for every last detail of all things Web. Instead, this book shows you how to get up and running fast so that you have more time to do the things that you really want to do. Designed using the easy-to-follow *For Dummies* format, this book helps you get the information you need without laboring to find it.

The *Creating Web Pages All-in-One Desk Reference For Dummies* is a big book made up of several smaller books — *minibooks,* so to speak. Each minibook begins with a parts page that includes a contents at a glance that tells you what chapters are included in that minibook. Useful running heads (the text you find at the very top of a page) point out the current topic being discussed on that page. And who can overlook those handy thumb tabs that run down the side of the page and show the minibook number and chapter title and number? Finally, for your convenience, a small index is located at the end of each minibook, in addition to the regular full-length index at the end of the entire book.

How to Use This Book

This book acts like a reference so that you can locate what you want to know, get in, and get something done as quickly as possible. In this book, you can find concise descriptions introducing important concepts, task-oriented topics to help you realize what you need, and step-by-step instructions, where necessary, to show you the way.

At times, this book presents you with specific ways of performing certain actions. For example, when you must use a menu command, you see a command sequence that looks like this:

File⇨Print

This simply means that you use the mouse to click open the File menu and then click the Print command. If you look closely, you can see some underlined letters. Those letters are the keyboard hot keys for the command in case you prefer to use the keyboard instead of the mouse. To use a keyboard hot key, first press the Alt key and release it, and then press the underlined letter. In the case of the File⇨Print example, you press Alt, release it, press the F key, and the File menu opens. Then you press the P key to activate the Print command from the File menu, and the Print dialog box opens. Easy, huh? In this book, we include hot keys for all menu command sequences.

Sometimes, we tell you about keyboard shortcuts. These shortcuts are key combinations such as

Ctrl+C

When you see this shortcut, it means to press and hold down the Ctrl key as you press the C key. Then release both keys together. (Don't attempt to type the plus sign!)

Names of dialog boxes, menu commands, and options are spelled with the first letter of each main word capitalized, even though those letters may not be capitalized on your screen. This format makes sentences filled with long option names easier for you to read. (Hey, we think of *everything!*)

Just one more thing: When you're asked to click or double-click something, this book assumes that your mouse settings have not been changed from the default. So, when you're told to click, use the left mouse button. When you need to use the right mouse button (to display a shortcut menu, for example), you'll be specifically told to *right-click*. Be sure to make the mental adjustments to these instructions if, for example, you're left-handed and have reversed your mouse buttons.

Who Are You?

Although making too many assumptions about readers (or anything else, for that matter!) can be a dangerous thing, it's very possible that you fit into one or more of the following categories:

✦ You've surfed the Web for awhile and are now contemplating creating your very own home page — but don't know where to start.

✦ You've already put up a home page and are interested in expanding it to create a full-fledged personal Web site.

✦ You're a small-business owner who wants to hop on the e-commerce bandwagon.

✦ You're studying Web design, Web marketing, or e-commerce at school and could use a practical, hands-on reference book like this one.

✦ You work for a company that has its own Web site, and part of your job is (or soon will be) helping to create, improve, or expand your company's site.

✦ You're interested in landing a high-paying job working as a Web site developer.

✦ You're already a crackerjack Web developer, but you could use a good, solid reference book to consult when you know *what* you want to do — but can't remember the specific details for how to go about doing it.

What this book *doesn't* assume (despite the title) is that you are a dummy. Unfortunately, Web development tools and technologies — most of which seem to be created for geeks in the first place — change faster than the scenes in a music video. Creating Web pages can be downright confusing and intimidating, even for software professionals, and you probably don't have time to devote to learning every single aspect of Web design from the ground up. If you want to help yourself — to get started creating Web pages as quickly and easily as possible — this is the book for you.

How This Book Is Organized

Each of the minibooks contained in *Creating Web Pages All-in-One Desk Reference For Dummies* can stand alone: Each has its own contents and index. The first minibook provides a quick-and-dirty overview of the Web site creation process, covering the basics you should know to help you get the most out of the rest of the stuff in the book. The remaining minibooks cover just about everything you ever wanted to know about creating pages. Here's a brief description of what you find in each minibook.

Book 1: Web Page Basics

This minibook presents an overview of the Web page creation process: why you might want to create Web pages, how to go about designing top-notch pages, what steps you need to take to publish your site so that everyone connected to the Web can view it. Here you also find a list of the elements common to all attractive, professional-looking sites — elements you can easily incorporate into your own efforts using the information you find in the rest of the book.

Book II: HTML

All Web pages are written in a special markup language called HTML. While you may find yourself using a graphical HTML editor — such as FrontPage or Dreamweaver — that shields you from the nitty-gritty details of HTML, you may prefer to create your pages from scratch using a simple text editor and the HTML knowledge you find in this minibook. (The HTML details you find in this minibook may also come in handy if you decide to tweak the HTML code generated by your graphical HTML editor.)

Book III: FrontPage 2002

FrontPage 2002, from Microsoft, is several Web-creation tools all rolled into one: It's an HTML editor you can use to create Web pages, an image editor you can use to create Web-friendly graphic images, and a Web site publisher you can use to publish your pages on the Web (in other words, make your pages accessible to everyone hooked up to the Internet running a Web browser). This minibook walks you through the process of creating and publishing a Web site using FrontPage 2002.

Book IV: Dreamweaver

Macromedia Dreamweaver is another popular Web creation tool. Like FrontPage 2002, Dreamweaver allows you to create and publish Web pages with point-and-click ease. Using Dreamweaver, you can also incorporate cool animated effects into your pages.

Book V: Multimedia: Creating Graphics, Sound, Animations, Video, and Java Applets

For those who want to add a bit of visual or aural interest to their Web pages, this minibook has the answers. Here you find how to create your own graphic images, sound files, Java applets, and animated effects from scratch. You also find out how to make sure your multimedia additions are optimized for viewing and listening over the Web — as well as a frank discussion of when multimedia *isn't* a good choice for your Web site.

Book VI: JavaScript

This minibook introduces you to the JavaScript scripting language, a special programming language that allows you to access and work with the components of a Web page to make your Web pages interactive. Here you find out how to create popular JavaScript effects such as mouse rollovers (push buttons that change their appearance in response to a user's mouse movement) and intelligent forms (input forms that alert users when incorrect information is entered).

Book VII: Flash 5

If you're interested in creating animated effects for the Web, you'll want to know more about Flash 5. From Macromedia, Flash 5 is a popular, powerful tool for creating graphic images and turning those images into animations. In this minibook you find out how to use Flash 5 to create animations, slide shows, and more — all optimized for the Web.

Book VIII: Adding E-Commerce Capability

E-commerce, or electronic commerce, is one of the fastest-growing uses of the Web. Whether you want to sell your homemade cookies to cookie aficionados across town or your company's product line to customers all over the world, this minibook presents your e-commerce options. And, because e-commerce is more than just software, this minibook also lists the latest approaches to Web marketing and fulfillment.

Book IX: XML

XML (short for *eXtensible Markup Language*) has an awful lot of developers excited because it defines a way to exchange data over the Web without falling prey to the limitations HTML (and browsers) impose. In this minibook, you find out what XML is and how you use it; you also find out what tools are available to help you create your very own XML applications.

What's on the CD?

The CD that comes with this book is packed with useful software applications you can use to begin creating your own Web pages right away. Here you find HTML editors, programs that help you create multimedia files (such as graphics, animations, and sound files), and much more. For details on exactly what's included, refer to the appendix, "About the CD."

Also on the CD: For your convenience, we've placed the significant URLs that appear throughout this book on a handy file on the CD. You can access this links list by double-clicking the Links.htm file on the CD. After you open this file, you can click whatever link interests you and go immediately to that Web site.

Icon Alert!

As you flip through this book, cute little pictures — called icons — in the margins draw your attention to important information. You'll discover the following icons in this book:

This icon points out tidbits of information that save you time and help you perform a task more easily.

Just a reminder . . . This information may be worth keeping in mind.

Watch out! This icon warns you of things likely to go wrong — the glitches that most often occur when you create Web pages — and helps you sidestep those annoying glitches.

This icon appears beside in-depth, nerdy, technical guru-type stuff you may want to skip over or read later.

This icon alerts you to where the applications on the companion CD are mentioned in the book.

You see this icon when we reference another fine book you might want to check out — one that provides additional details on the topic at hand.

Book I

Web Page Basics

The 5th Wave   By Rich Tennant

"I have to say I'm really impressed with the interactivity on this car wash Web site."

Contents at a Glance

Chapter 1: Creating a Successful Web Site

In This Chapter

✓ Understanding the different kinds of Web sites

✓ Determining what to include on your Web site

✓ Creating a Web site step by step

✓ Finding space for your Web site

Web sites are many things to many people. To some, a Web site is an electronic business card; to others, an online storefront; to still others, a classified advertisement or a family photo album. The trick to creating a successful Web site is to figure out what a Web site is to *you* — and then to build your site and publish it (make it available on the Web) by following a few simple steps.

Web Site Basics

Although the steps you take to create and publish a Web site are pretty straightforward, the geeky terminology surrounding the Web can make the whole process seem downright confusing. Here's an overview of the different kinds of sites you can create, followed by a description of the "big picture" — in other words, a description of what you need to do to turn your great idea into a live Web site that people all over the world can view and enjoy.

Different kinds of Web sites

The following sections describe three very broad categories of Web sites. The Web site that you intend to publish probably falls into one of these three categories.

Personal home pages

Just about anyone with access to the Internet can create a personal home page. The simplest personal home pages contain basic information, such as your name, information about your family, your occupation, your hobbies, and any special interests you may have. You can also throw in a picture. Oh, and links to your favorite pages on the Web are also commonly included in personal home pages.

More elaborate personal home pages can include pictures from your last family vacation, the first chapter of your soon-to-be-published novel, or anything else you think others may be interested in.

If you're looking for a job, you should also include your résumé on your personal home page.

Company Web sites

More and more companies are joining the Web bandwagon. Even mom-and-pop pizza parlors are putting up Web pages. The simplest corporate Web pages provide basic information about a company, such as a description of the company's products or services, phone numbers, and so on.

A more elaborate corporate Web site can include any or all of the following:

✦ An online catalog that enables Internet users to see detailed information about products and services. The catalog may include pictures and, if you want, prices.

✦ Online ordering, which enables Internet users to actually place orders over the Internet.

✦ A customer survey.

✦ Lists of frequently asked questions about the company's products or services.

✦ Online support, where a customer can leave a question about a problem he or she is having with a product and receive an answer within a day or two.

✦ Articles and reviews of the company's products.

✦ Press releases.

✦ Biographies of company employees.

Special interest Web sites

Many of the most interesting Web sites are devoted to special interests. For example, if you're involved with a youth soccer league, you may want to create a Web page that includes team rosters, schedules, and standings. Or, if you are one of those festive neighbors who decorates his house with 100,000 lights at Christmas, create a Web page that focuses on Christmas decorating. The list of possible topics for a special interest Web site is limitless.

Creating a Web site: An overview

Although you don't have to be obsessively methodical about creating a Web site, following these three basic steps helps ensure that you end up with a site you're proud to call your own (in the least possible amount of time).

✦ **Step 1: Planning your Web site.** Taking a bit of time up front to decide exactly how you want your site to look and behave can save you loads of time, as you see in following section, "Planning Your Web Site."

✦ **Step 2: Creating Your Web pages.** A Web site is a collection of Web pages. And although all Web pages must be created in a special language called *HTML* (which stands for HyperText Markup Language), you have several options besides becoming an HTML guru and typing all of your HTML code into a text editor by hand. The section, "Creating Your Web Pages," later in this chapter, describes some of those options.

✦ **Step 3: Publishing Your Web pages.** Before anyone hooked up to the Web can view your Web site, you must first *publish* it — that is, you must first have copied your Web pages to a Web server. In the section, "Publishing Your Web Pages," later in this chapter, you find out how to do that.

Planning Your Web Site

Start by making a plan for your Web site. If all you want to do is create a simple, one-page "Here I Am" type of personal Web site, you don't really need to make a plan. But for a more elaborate Web site, you should plan the content of the site before you start creating actual pages.

One good way to plan a Web site is to sketch a simple diagram on paper showing the various pages you want to create, complete with pictures and arrows showing the links between the pages. Or, you can create an outline that represents your entire site. You can be as detailed or as vague as you want — but in general, the more detailed your plan, the less time you spend later when you actually begin building your site.

Creating Your Web Pages

You can take a couple of different approaches to creating the pages that will make up your Web site: You can hand-code the site from scratch, using a text editor, or you can use a point-and-click graphical editor that generates HTML code for you. Either approach works just fine — and you can always choose one approach, work with it awhile, and then switch to the other approach later if you change your mind.

From scratch, using a text editor

If you dream in Boolean, feel free to fire up NotePad and start banging away HTML code from scratch. You have to learn the intricacies of using HTML codes to format your Web pages, but you gain satisfaction from knowing you did it the hard way! (You also have complete control over every aspect of your Web pages — something you don't always have when you use a graphical Web page editor.) Book 2, "HTML," introduces you to the HTML basics you need to get started creating HTML code from scratch.

Using a graphical Web page editor

On the other hand, if the mere thought of "programming" gives you hives, you can use a simple Web page editor to create your Web pages. (Chapter 2, "Building Your First Web Site," shows you a free Web-page-creation tool in action.) Or, you can purchase inexpensive programs for creating complete Web sites. Two of the best known Web site development programs are Microsoft FrontPage 2002 and Dreamweaver, both of which are included on the CD that comes with this book. (For more information, check out Book 3, "FrontPage 2002," and Book 4, "Dreamweaver," respectively.)

Beyond HTML: Adding nifty features

After you have your basic site up and running, you may want to get fancy and add some cool extras — features such as

✦ **Images, sound, animations, and Java applets** (Book 5, "Multimedia: Creating Graphics, Sound, Animations, Video, and Java Applets")

✦ **Interactive images and forms that automatically check user input for errors** (Book 6, "JavaScript")

✦ **Movie clips** (Book 7, "Flash 5")

✦ **Credit card handling** ("Book 8, "E-Commerce")

For those of you who like to keep up on the cutting edge of things, Book 9, "XML," shows you how to use one of the latest Web-related "meta" language (*XML*, or Extensible Markup Language) to create your very own specialized markup language, complete with semantic definitions called *vocabularies*. Using a combination of XML and a few other tools, you can create your own HTML-like markup tags and your own language processor — in effect, creating a means for extending HTML or exchanging non-HTML data over the Web in a standard, civilized way. For example, some folks in the automobile industry are using XML to enable automobile parts producers and buyers to exchange automobile-related data quickly and easily over the Web.

Publishing Your Web Pages

After your Web pages are complete, it's time to publish them on the Internet. First, you have to find a Web server that will host your Web pages. The following section, "Finding space for your Web site," gives you ideas for finding a Web server. Next, you copy your Web pages to the Web server. Finally, you can publicize your Web site by cataloging it in the major search services.

Finding space for your Web site

Before Web surfers can see your Web pages, you must transfer the pages to a *Web server*. A Web server is a computer hooked up to the Internet running special Web server software. The following sections give you some ideas about where to find a Web server to host your Web pages.

Internet Service Providers

If you access the Internet through an Internet Service Provider (ISP), you probably already have space set aside on their server to set up a home page. Most ISPs give users a small amount of disk space for Web pages included in their monthly service. The space may be limited to a few megabytes, but that should be enough to set up several pages. You can probably get additional disk space if you need it for a modest charge.

Your ISP should be able to give you step-by-step instructions for copying your Web pages to the ISP's Web server.

Online services

America Online (AOL) is the leading online service. (AOL recently joined forces with CompuServe, the other major online service.) AOL lets you publish your own page — up to 2MB of disk space.

Free Web host

If you can't find a home for your Web page at your Internet Service Provider or your online service, consider using a free Web host to host your Web site.

The best known, free home page service is Yahoo! GeoCities, which hosts well more than 1 million home pages. Each free Web site can use up to 15MB of disk space. The only limitation is that you must include a banner advertisement at the top of your Web page and a link to the GeoCities home page at the bottom of your page. (For $4.95 per month, you can eliminate the advertising and increase your space allotment to 25MB.) You can find Yahoo! GeoCities at `geocities.yahoo.com`.

Many other free home page services are available, although most cater to specific types of home pages such as artist pages, churches, chambers of commerce, and so on. You can find a good directory of free home page services by going to Yahoo! (www.yahoo.com) and searching for *Free Web Pages*.

Publicizing your Web site

Just publishing a Web site doesn't ensure that any visitors will find it. To make your presence on the Web known, you must publicize your site. Chapter 7, "Publicizing your Web site," describes the ins and outs of getting the word out about your site. Depending on the type of site you're creating, your online publicity plan might include registering your site with search engines, advertising your site (both online and off), and getting other people to link to your site from theirs.

Elements of a Successful Web Site

A successful Web site doesn't just happen by accident. To create a Web site people will want to visit over and over again, keep the following time-tested guidelines in mind.

✦ **Offer something useful on every page.** Too many Web sites are filled with fluff — pages that don't have any useful content. Avoid creating pages that are just steps along the way to truly useful information. Instead, strive to include something useful on every page of your Web site.

✦ **Check the competition.** Find out what other Web sites similar to yours have to offer. Don't create a "me too" Web site that offers nothing but information that is already available elsewhere. Instead, strive for unique information that can be found only on your Web site.

✦ **Make it look good.** No matter how good the information at your Web site is, people will stay away if your site looks as if you spent no more than five minutes on design and layout. Yes, substance is more important than style. But an ugly Web site turns people away, whereas an attractive Web site draws people in.

✦ **Proof it carefully.** If every third word in your Web site is misspelled, people will assume that the information on your Web site is as unreliable as your spelling. If your HTML editor has a spell-check feature, use it. Otherwise, proof your work carefully before you post it to the Web.

✦ **Provide links to other sites.** Some of the best pages on the Internet are links to other Web sites that have information about a particular topic. In fact, many of the pages I have bookmarked for my own use are pages of links to topics as diverse as hobby electronics, softball, and backpacking. The time you spend creating a directory of links to other sites with information similar or complementary to your own will be well spent.

+ **Keep it current.** Internet users will not frequent your site if it contains old, out-of-date information. Make sure that you frequently update your Web pages with current information. Obviously, some Web pages need to be changed more than others. For example, if you maintain a Web page that lists the team standings for a soccer league, you have to update the page after every game. On the other hand, a page that features medieval verse romances doesn't need to be updated very often, unless someone discovers a previously unpublished Chaucer text hidden in a trunk.

+ **Don't tie it to a certain browser.** Exploiting the cool new features of the latest and greatest Web browser, whether it's Microsoft Internet Explorer or Netscape Navigator, is a good idea. But don't do so at the expense of users who may be using the *other* browser, or at the expense of users who are still working with an earlier version. Some people are still using browsers that don't even support frames. Make sure that any pages in which you incorporate advanced features of the newer browsers work well with older browsers as well by testing your pages in as many different browsers as possible. (For more information on creating Web pages that look great in different browsers, check out "Detecting browser plug-ins" in Chapter 8 of Book 6, "JavaScript.")

+ **Don't make hardware assumptions.** Remember that not everyone has a 21-inch monitor and a high-speed cable-modem connection to the Internet. Design your Web site so that it can be used by the poor sap who is stuck with a 14-inch monitor and — gasp — a 28.8 Kbps modem connection to the Internet.

+ **Publicize it.** Few people will stumble across your Web site by accident. If you want people to visit your Web site, you have to publicize it. Make sure that your site is listed in the major search engines, such as Yahoo! and Lycos. Also, you can promote your site by putting its address on all your advertisements, correspondences, business cards, e-mails, and so on. For more information about publicizing your site, check out Chapter 7, "Publicizing Your Web Site."

Organizing Site Content

Organizing your site's content can mean the difference between creating a great site and a site that visitors click away from screaming in frustration. The following sections describe several popular ways to organize the information on your Web site.

Sequential organization

In sequential organization, you simply organize your pages so that they follow one after another, like the pages in a book, as shown in Figure 1-1.

Figure 1-1:
Sequential
organization.

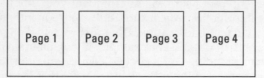

On each page, provide navigation links that enable the user to go to the next page, go to the previous page, or return directly to the first page. You implement navigation links using HTML links and anchors (both of which I describe in Chapter 3 — "Adding Internal and External Links" — of Book 2, "HTML"), but you can also make them more descriptive than a plain underlined text link. For example, you can create navigation links that look like right and left arrows (for "next" and "previous" pages, respectively).

One of the most popular ways to arrange navigation links is the *navigation bar*. A navigation bar is a strip of navigation links that runs either across the top or bottom of a page, or vertically, along the left-hand side of a Web page. You find more information about navigation bars in Chapter 3, "Exploring the Essential Elements of Web Page Design."

Hierarchical organization

In hierarchical organization, you organize your Web pages into a hierarchy, categorizing the pages according to subject matter. The topmost page serves as a menu that enables users to access other pages directly (see Figure 1-2).

On each page, provide a navigation link that returns the user to the menu.

Figure 1-2:
Hierarchical
organization
with one
menu level.

If you want, you can include more than one level of menu pages, as shown in Figure 1-3.

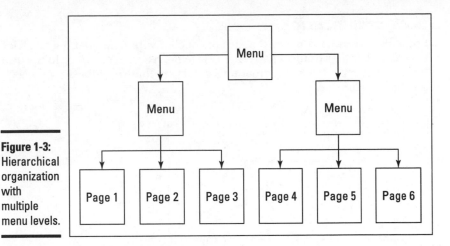

Figure 1-3:
Hierarchical organization with multiple menu levels.

However, don't overdo the menus. Most users are frustrated by Web sites that have unnecessary menus, each containing only two or three choices. When a menu has more than a dozen choices, however, consider splitting the menu into two or more separate menus.

Combination sequential and hierarchical organization

Many Web sites use a combination of sequential and hierarchical organization, in which a menu enables users to access content pages that contain sequential links to one another, as shown in Figure 1-4.

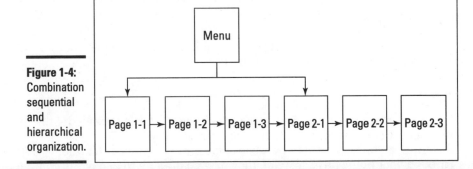

Figure 1-4:
Combination sequential and hierarchical organization.

In a combination style of organization, each content page includes a link to the next page in sequence in addition to a link back to the menu. The menu page contains links to the pages that mark the start of each section of content pages.

Web organization

Some Web sites have pages that are connected with links that defy a strict sequential or hierarchical pattern. In extreme cases, every page in the site is linked to every other page, creating a structure that resembles a web, as shown in Figure 1-5.

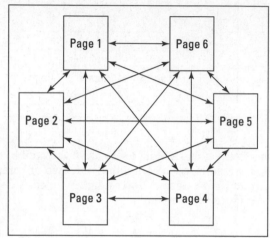

Figure 1-5:
Web
organization.

Web organization — where every Web page links to every other page in a Web site — is a good style of organization if the total number of pages in the web is limited and you can't predict the sequence in which a user may want to view the pages.

What to Include on Every Page

Although every Web page should contain unique and useful information, all Web pages must contain the following three elements.

Title

Place a descriptive title at the top of every page. The title should identify not just the specific contents of the page but also the Web site itself. A descriptive title is important because some users may not enter your site through your home page. Instead, they may go directly to one of the content pages in your site. In addition, many users *bookmark* pages for quick access at a later date — and a bookmarked page titled "My Home Page" doesn't exactly encourage repeat visits. (A page titled "Sarah Bellum's Definitive Guide to Lemurs," on the other hand, helps users remember why they bookmarked your page in the first place.)

Navigation links

All the pages of your Web site should have a consistent set of navigation links. At a minimum, provide a link to your home page on every page in your site. In addition, you may want to include links to the next and previous pages if your pages have a logical sequential organization. Figure 1-6 shows examples of navigational links at the `www.dummies.com` Web site.

Figure 1-6:
The navigational links on the www.dummies.com site include TECHNOLOGY, MONEY, LIFESTYLE, and HEALTH.

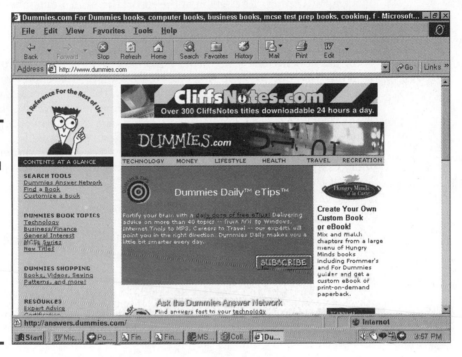

Author and copyright information

Every page should also include author credits and a copyright notice. Because users can enter your site by going directly to any page, placing the authorship and copyright notices on only the home page is not sufficient.

What to Include on Every Web Site

Although every Web site is different, you can find certain common elements on most Web sites. The following sections describe the items you should consider including on your Web site.

Home page

Every Web site should include a home page that serves as an entry point into the site. The home page is the first page that most users see when they visit your site (unless you include a cover page, as described in the next section). As a result, devote considerable time and energy to making sure your home page makes a good first impression.

Place an attractive title element at the top of the page. Remember that most users have to scroll down to see all of your home page. They see just the top of the page first, so you want to make sure that the title is immediately visible.

After the title, include a site menu that enables users to access the content available on your Web site. You can create a simple text menu, or you can opt for a fancy graphics-based menu in which the user can click on different parts of the image to go to different pages. However, if you use this type of menu, called an *image map,* be sure to provide a text menu as an alternative for users who don't want to wait for the image map to download or who have turned off graphic downloads altogether. For more information about image maps see "Carving up Graphics with Image Maps" in Chapter 4, "Working with Graphics, Sounds, and Video."

Here are a few other goodies you may want to include on your home page:

✦ **An indication of new content that is available on your Web site.** Users who return to your site often want to know right away when new information is available.

✦ **The date your site was last updated.**

✦ **A copyright notice.** You can include a link to a separate copyright page where you spell out whether others can copy the information you have placed on your site.

✦ **A reminder to bookmark the page so users can get back to the page easily.**

✦ **A hit counter.** If users see that 4 million people have visited your site since last Tuesday, they automatically assume that yours must be a hot site. On the other hand, if they see that only three people have visited since Truman was president, they'll yawn and leave quickly. If your site isn't very popular, or if you're going for a strictly professional look, you may want to skip the hit counter.

Avoid placing a huge amount of graphics on your home page. Your home page is the first page on your Web site most users see. If it takes more than 15 seconds for your page to load, users may lose patience and skip your page altogether. As a simple test, try holding your breath while your home page downloads. If you turn blue before the page finishes downloading, the page is too big.

Cover page

A cover page (sometimes called a *splash* page) is displayed temporarily before your home page is displayed. Cover pages usually feature a flashy graphic logo or an animation. In most cover pages, the user must click the logo or some other element on the page to enter the site's home page. Or, the page can be programmed so that it automatically jumps to the home page after a certain amount of time — say 10 or 15 seconds — has elapsed.

Many users are annoyed by cover pages, especially those that take more than a few seconds to download and display. Think carefully about whether the splashy cover page actually enhances your site or is more of an annoyance.

Site map

If your site has a lot of pages, you may want to include a site map. A site map is a detailed menu that provides links to every page on the site. By using the site map, a user can bypass intermediate menus and go directly to the pages that interest him or her.

Contact information

Be sure your site includes information about how to contact you or your company. You can easily include your e-mail address as a link right on the home page. When the user clicks this link, most Web browsers fire up the user's e-mail program, ready to compose a message with your e-mail address already filled in.

This should go without saying, but just in case, if you decide to include contact information, make sure you're diligent in reading and responding to the comments your visitors e-mail you. (This goes double for those of you contemplating a commercial Web site.)

If you want to include complete contact information, such as your address and phone number, or if you want to list contact information for several individuals, you may want to place the contact information on a separate page that can be accessed from the home page.

Help page

If your Web site contains more than just a few pages, consider providing a help page that provides information about how to use the site. The help page can include information about how to navigate the site, as well as information such as how you obtained the information for the site, how often the site is updated, how someone would go about contributing to the site, and so on.

FAQ

Frequently Asked Questions (FAQ) pages are among the most popular sources of information on the Internet. You can organize your own FAQ page on any topic you want. Just come up with a list of questions and provide the answers. Or solicit answers from readers of your page.

Related links

At some sites, the most popular page is the links page, which provides a list of links to related sites. As the compiler of your own links page, you can do something that search engines such as Yahoo! cannot: You can pick and choose the links you want to include, and you can provide your own commentary about the information contained on each site.

Discussion group

A discussion group adds interactivity to your Web site by allowing visitors to post articles that can be read and responded to by other people who visit your site.

Troubleshooting Web publishing

The following points summarize the most troublesome aspects of creating high-quality Web pages.

✔ **Too many Web browsers.** Different Web browsers display Web pages differently. Each new version of the two most popular Web browsers — Netscape Navigator and Microsoft Internet Explorer — adds new HTML features. Unfortunately, in their efforts to get ahead of one another, both Netscape and Microsoft put the notion of *compatibility* in the back seat. Whenever you use a new HTML feature, you have to make sure your page looks good no matter which browser the user views your page with.

✔ **Different screen sizes.** Some users have computers with puny 14-inch monitors that are set to 640 x 480 resolution. Others have giant 19-inch monitors that run at 1,280 x 1,024. Your pages look different depending on the display resolution of the user's computer. A good middle-of-the-road approach is to design your pages for 800 x 600.

✔ **Different connection speeds.** Some users are connected to the Internet over high-speed T3 lines or cable modems, which can send megabytes of data in seconds. Others are connected over a phone line at 28.8 Kbps, which downloads large graphic files at a snail's pace. To compensate for lack of speed, some 28.8 Kbps users set up their browsers so that graphics are not automatically downloaded. That means your pages should not be overly dependent on graphics.

Chapter 2: Building Your First Web Site

In This Chapter

✔ Registering with a free Web host

✔ Creating and publishing your first Web page

✔ Using a free Web site creation tool

✔ Viewing your first Web page

Nothing helps give you a feel for how a process works better than walking through each of the steps yourself! In this chapter, you see how to create, publish, and view your first Web page using the free graphical Web editor available from Yahoo! GeoCities, a free Web host.

Registering with a Free Web Host

You have many options when it comes to finding space for your Web site. (Chapter 1 describes several of these options.) In this chapter, I show you how to register and create a site with Yahoo! GeoCities, one of the most popular free Web hosting services around.

Other free Web hosting services at the time of this writing are Angelfire (angelfire.lycos.com), Tripod (www.tripod.lycos.com), and WebJump (www.webjump.com).

To register with Yahoo! GeoCities:

1. **Type** geocities.yahoo.com/home/ **into your browser's address field and press Enter.**

The Yahoo! GeoCities home page appears, as shown in Figure 2-1.

Figure 2-1:
Yahoo!
GeoCities is
one of many
free Web
hosting
services.

2. **Click the Sign me up! link on the Yahoo! GeoCities home page, as shown in Figure 2-1.**

   The Welcome to Yahoo! window appears (see Figure 2-2).

Figure 2-2:
You use this
sign-up form
to register
for free Web
hosting
services
with Yahoo!
GeoCities.

3. **Fill out each field following the instructions provided on the form; then click the Submit This Form button located at the bottom of the form.**

   A Welcome to Yahoo! GeoCities window, part of which is shown in Figure 2-3, appears.

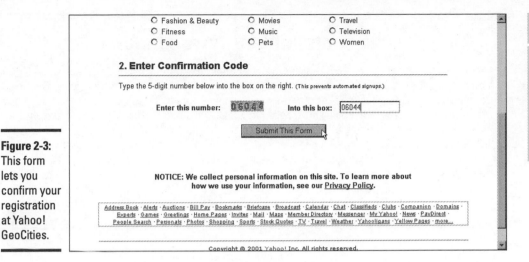

Figure 2-3:
This form
lets you
confirm your
registration
at Yahoo!
GeoCities.

4. **Fill out each field following the instructions on this new form, and then click the Submit This Form button located at the bottom of the form (as shown in Figure 2-3).**

    A "congratulations" message appears (see Figure 2-4).

Figure 2-4:
When you
see this
message,
you know
your
registration
has been
successfully
completed.

When Yahoo! GeoCities finishes processing your registration, you receive an e-mail message reminding you of your Web page URL, ID, and password for future reference. If you lose this information, you won't be able to access your account (or the Web page creation tools), so either file this message somewhere where you can find it later, or print it out and tuck it in a safe place next to your computer.

No such thing as a free lunch?

As you may suspect, "free" Web services aren't *completely* free. Most free Web services don't charge you setup or hosting fees, but they do require you to display advertising messages on your site. Although you may be able to restrict the types of advertising the Web services display on your site (for example, you may request family- or environmentally-friendly messages), the Web service always has the last word.

One more thing to consider when choosing a service: free providers such as Yahoo! GeoCities typically reserve the right to pull the plug at any time. In other words, you may wake up one morning to find out the free provider you were relying on has decided to stop offering its services! For that reason, you may want to choose a for-pay provider if you're creating a business-related or other gotta-be-available-24/7 Web site. (Hey, you get what you pay for, right?)

Using a Free Web-Site-Creation Tool

Most free Web services provide their own graphical Web site creation tools to make creating your first Web pages quick and easy.

Most free Web services don't restrict you to using their Web site creation tools; instead, they allow you to create Web pages using any tool you like. If you choose not to use their built-in tools, however, you need to take an extra step to transfer your Web pages to your free site host — typically by using a transfer utility based on *ftp* (File Transfer Protocol).

As you become more and more skilled at creating Web pages, you may want to switch to a more sophisticated tool such as FrontPage 2002 or Dreamweaver, both of which you can find on the CD that comes with this book.

In the following steps, you see how to use the Yahoo! PageWizards Web tool available free when you register with Yahoo! GeoCities to create a simple Web page. First, I show you how to choose a look, or *theme,* for your Web page; then I show you how to add content — text, links, and a picture.

To use Yahoo! PageWizards to create a simple Web page, follow these steps:

1. **Type** `geocities.yahoo.com/home/` **into your browser's address field and press Enter.**

The Welcome page shown in Figure 2-5 appears.

Figure 2-5:
Yahoo!
GeoCities
Welcome
page.

2. **Type your previously registered ID and password into the Yahoo! ID and Password fields, respectively; then click Sign in.**

   (The previous section describes how to register an ID and password with Yahoo! GeoCities.)

   The Yahoo! GeoCities window, shown in Figure 2-6, appears.

Figure 2-6:
After you log
in, you can
create your
Web pages
by clicking
the Yahoo!
Page-
Wizards link.

3. **Click the Yahoo! PageWizards link, as shown in Figure 2-6.**

   A Yahoo! GeoCities – PageWizards window appears, offering the selection of page themes (see Figure 2-7).

Figure 2-7:
The Yahoo!
Page-
Wizards tool
offers a
selection
of page
themes.

4. **Click any of the theme links shown in Figure 2-7 (for example, you can click Fun D'Mental).**

   A theme is a named set of characteristics — color, layout, and so on. A window titled Yahoo! Quick Start Web Page Wizard appears (see Figure 2-8).

   Themes are sometimes referred to as *styles* or *templates*.

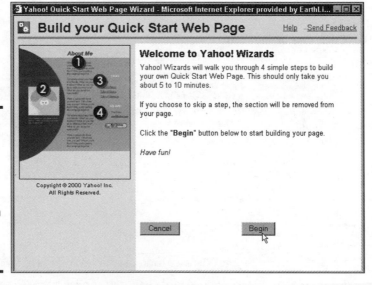

Figure 2-8:
The Yahoo!
Quick Start
Web Page
Wizard is
ready for
you to begin
building
your Web
page.

To see what your Web page looks like at any stage of the building process, click the Preview button located near the bottom of the Yahoo! Quick Start Web Page Wizard window.

5. **Click the Begin button located at the bottom of the screen (refer to Figure 2-8).**

    The screen shown in Figure 2-9 appears.

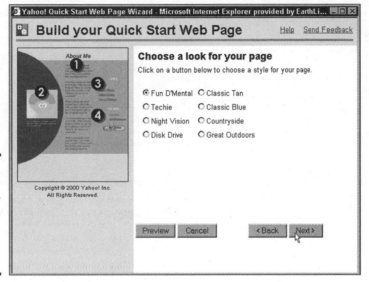

Figure 2-9:
Choosing a look for your Web page is as easy as clicking a button.

6. **Click one of the radio buttons shown in Figure 2-9 to choose a theme (style).**

    For example, you can choose Fun D'Mental, Techie, or Night Vision. (If you wait a few seconds after clicking a style button, a preview of that style appears on the left-hand side of the screen.)

    Does this step sound familiar? It should. You chose a theme, or style, for your Web page in Step 4. Unfortunately, Yahoo! Quick Start Web Page Wizard requires you to specify the style you want for your Web page again! If you want, you can use this opportunity to change your mind and select a different style.

7. **Click Next.**

    The screen shown in Figure 2-10 appears.

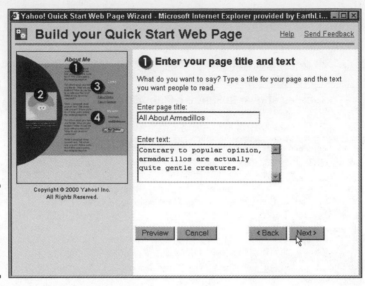

Figure 2-10:
Adding a page title and content (text).

8. **Type the text you want to appear at the top of your Web page into the Enter Page Title field (refer to Figure 2-10). Type the text you want to appear in the middle of your Web page into the Enter Text field.**

9. **Click Next.**

The screen shown in Figure 2-11 appears.

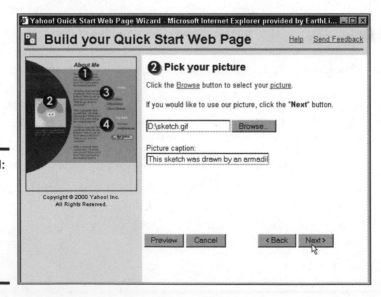

Figure 2-11:
Adding a picture to your Web site, complete with a caption.

10. **Add your own picture to your Web site by typing the fully-qualified name of an image file in the field next to the Browse button (refer to Figure 2-11).**

A fully-qualified file name includes both the filename and the directory in which that file resides on your computer: for example, `c:\photos\ralph.gif` is the fully-qualified filename of a file (`ralph.gif`) located in the `photos` directory, which is located in turn on the `c:` drive.

Don't know whether you have any image files stored on your computer? Pretty sure you have image files, but can't remember where you put them? Not to worry! To search your computer directories for an image file, you can click the Browse button shown in Figure 2-11.

The kinds of image file formats that work best in Web pages are JPEG, GIF, and PNG files. (For the skinny on using images in Web pages, check out Chapter 4.)

To use a picture ready-made by GeoCities, just click Next. (The ready-made picture is the goofy-looking cartoon face you see next to the big 2 in Figure 2-11, but hey — if you don't happen to have a picture file of your own on hand, a goofy-looking cartoon face may be better than nothing!)

11. **Type a few words of descriptive text in the Picture Caption field.**

The screen shown in Figure 2-12 appears.

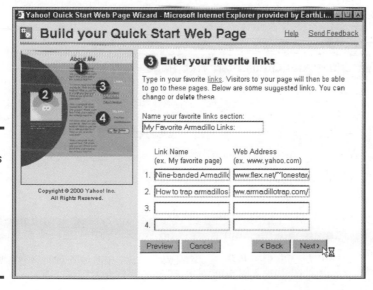

Figure 2-12: Adding links from your Web page to other Web pages makes the Web go 'round.

12. Add links from your Web site to others by typing a descriptive name for the link in the Link Name field and the URL of the link in the corresponding field marked Web Address (refer to Figure 2-12). If you want, you can also type a heading for your link section in the field called Name Your Favorite Links section.

13. Click Next.

The screen in Figure 2-13 appears.

Be cautious when adding deep links to commercial sites. (A *deep* link is a link to a URL two or more directories deep. For example, `www.dummies.com/tips/index.html` is a deep link because it contains two backslashes. `www.dummies.com` is not.) Why the caution? Two reasons: 1) Deep links are more likely to change or disappear than shallow links, and 2) As crazy as it sounds, companies are becoming more and more litigious and bringing lawsuits against folks who deep link to their sites. The rationale is too bizarre to go into here; suffice it to say that when in doubt, ask permission to deep link to a commercial site.

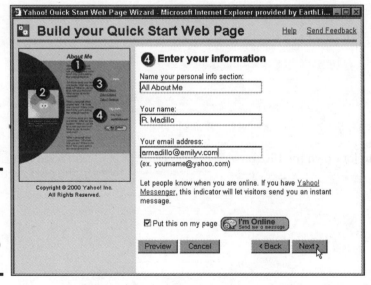

Figure 2-13: Adding contact information to your Web site.

14. Add contact information to your site by typing your name and e-mail address into the Your Name and Your Email Address fields.

Adding contact information to your Web site is a good idea, especially if you're creating a business or community-oriented site.

15. Click Next.

The screen shown in Figure 2-14 appears.

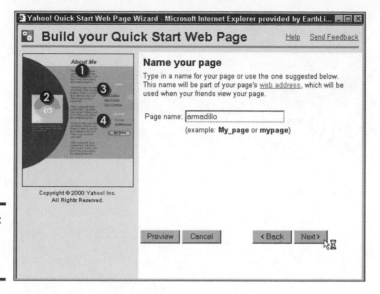

Figure 2-14:
Naming
your Web
page.

16. **Name your page by typing a short, descriptive name into the Page Name field (refer to Figure 2-14).**

17. **Click Next.**

(Don't bother adding an .htm or .html suffix; Yahoo! GeoCities Quick Start Web Page Wizard adds the appropriate extension for you.)

The congratulations screen appears (see Figure 2-15), complete with the URL of your brand spanking-new Web page. As the wizard suggests, take a second to jot down the URL on a piece of scratch paper. (You need this URL to view your new Web page, which I show you how to do in the next section.)

Out of sight, out of mind

Online Web creation tools like the one demonstrated in this chapter save your Web page files directly to their Web server. What this means is that your Web page is available on the Web as soon as you create it. But this also means that you don't have a copy of the file saved on your own computer, which — depending on how paranoid you are — may be a problem, and may not.

Web creation tools that you install on your own machine work differently. In the case of a Web editor such as FrontPage 2002, for example, you save your Web pages files to your own computer, then transfer, or upload, those files to a Web server in a separate step. Although this approach requires a bit more work on your part, you can be sure you have a copy of your file saved on your own machine in case you need it.

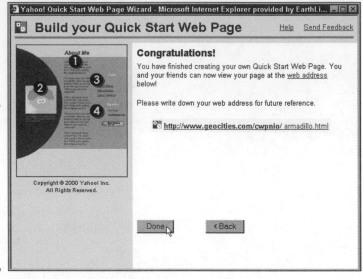

Figure 2-15:
Yee-haw!
The Web
page is
completed
and ready to
view at the
URL listed
on the
screen.

Viewing Your First Web Page — Live

To view your newly created Web page, type the URL (Uniform Resource Locator) of your Web page into your browser's address field and click Return.

Figure 2-16 shows a newly-created Web page as it looks loaded into Microsoft Internet Explorer.

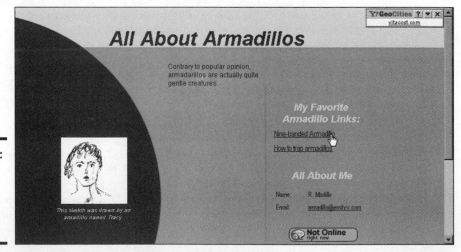

Figure 2-16:
Loading
your first
Web page
into a Web
browser.

Chapter 3: Exploring the Essential Elements of Web Page Design

In This Chapter

✔ **Starting an HTML page**

✔ **Adding headings and titles**

✔ **Formatting text**

✔ **Creating lists and tables**

✔ **Specifying page and background settings**

✔ **Adding navigation tools and links**

*Y*ou can think of HTML as a kind of primitive word processing language for Web pages. HTML defines a bunch of directives, or *tags,* you use to surround individual Web page elements to tell the browser how to display those elements. For example, if you want to display a paragraph in italics, you surround that paragraph with the beginning and ending HTML italic tags ⟨I⟩ and ⟨/I⟩. Book 2, "HTML," describes what you can do with HTML in detail; this chapter gives you a quick overview of the most essential, most popular features to get you up and running in record time.

HTML Basics

HTML defines two types of tags: beginning tags and ending tags.

- ✦ **Beginning tags,** as you may guess, tell a Web browser to begin some kind of formatting process. For example, ⟨B⟩ tells a Web browser to begin displaying text in bold font.

- ✦ **Ending tags** tell a Web browser to stop a particular formatting process. Ending tags are identical to beginning tags except for one tiny detail: Ending tags sport a backslash just after the opening angle bracket, like this: ⟨/B⟩

The following HTML code snippet shows you how the beginning and ending tags look in a typical HTML file:

```
This text will appear in regular font.
<B>This text will appear in bold font.</B>
This text will appear in regular font.
```

Most HTML tags come in the beginning-ending pair, but not all.

Now that you're familiar with beginning and ending tags, you're ready to take a look at the bare-bones tags that virtually all HTML documents contain:

```
<HTML>
<HEAD>
<TITLE>Your title goes here</TITLE>
</HEAD>
<BODY>
The body of your document goes here.
</BODY>
</HTML>
```

Here's an explanation of each of these tags:

✦ <HTML>: This tag should always appear as the very first thing in an HTML document. It tells the browser that the file is an HTML file.

✦ <HEAD> **and** </HEAD>: These tags mark the section of the document called the *header,* which contains information that applies to the entire document.

✦ <TITLE> **and** </TITLE>: These tags mark the document title. Any text that appears within the <TITLE> and </TITLE> tags is used as the title for your HTML document.

✦ <BODY> **and** </BODY>: These tags mark the beginning and ending portions of your document that is displayed by the browser when the page is viewed. In most HTML documents, a lot of stuff falls between the <BODY> and </BODY> tags.

✦ </HTML>: This ending tag should always be the last tag in your document.

Adding Text

To add text to an HTML document, you place the text you want to add between the beginning <BODY> and ending </BODY> tags:

```
<BODY>
```

All of the text for this Web page goes right here. You can surround this text with many different HTML tags to format it attractively.

```
</BODY>
```

You typically include many HTML tags in a Web page; not just the required tags, which I describe in the preceding "HTML Basics" section, but also a handful of formatting tags to make your Web page look attractive. With all those angle brackets (<...>) lying around, you may find yourself accidentally slipping text inside an HTML tag. If that happens, you may be surprised when you try to load your Web page and the text doesn't display! So, for example, the following text does *not* appear on the screen when the HTML snippet is loaded:

```
<BODY Text inside tag declarations is NOT displayed
    onscreen.></BODY>
```

Instead, make sure text falls between tags:

```
<BODY>Text placed properly between tag pairs IS displayed
    onscreen.</BODY>
```

Aligning text

HTML doesn't give you many options for aligning text. By default, text is left aligned on the page. But you can use the <CENTER> tag to specify text to be centered, as in the following example:

```
<CENTER>This text is centered.</CENTER>
```

For more precise control of text alignment, use the text-align style property. It gives you four text-alignment options: left, right, center, and justify. The following example creates a right-aligned heading using the <H1> tag:

```
<H1 STYLE="text-align: right">This heading is right
    aligned.</H1>
```

In the preceding HTML code, double quotes (") surround the value assigned to the STYLE attribute of the <H1> tag. You can assign values to tag attributes — a process some folks refer to as *defining an attribute inline* — for many HTML tags. Just remember that when you do, you need to include the double quotes.

For more information about using the STYLE attribute to create different display styles, see Book 2, "HTML," Chapter 8, "Developing Style Sheets."

Specifying headings

Don't fill your Web pages with a constant stream of uninterrupted text. Instead, use headings and paragraphs to organize the content on each page. The HTML heading tags make creating headings that break your text into manageable chunks easy.

You can include up to six levels of headings on your Web pages by using the HTML tags <H1>, <H2>, and so on through <H6>. The following snippet of HTML shows all six heading styles in use:

```
<H1>This is a heading 1</H1>
<H2>This is a heading 2</H2>
<H3>This is a heading 3</H3>
<H4>This is a heading 4</H4>
<H5>This is a heading 5</H5>
<H6>This is a heading 6</H6>
<P>This is a normal text paragraph.</P>
```

Figure 3-1 shows how this HTML appears when displayed in Internet Explorer 5.

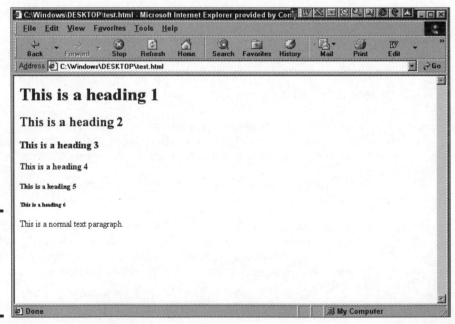

Figure 3-1: Six levels of headings plus one normal text paragraph.

Each Web browser uses its own point sizes for displaying the various heading levels, and most browsers use huge type for the highest heading levels — <H1> and <H2>. Fortunately, you can override the browser's type size by using styles as described in Chapter 3 of *Creating Web Pages For Dummies*, 5th Edition.

Changing text appearance

In addition to changing font face, size, and color (see "Changing fonts" later in this section for details), you can make text appear bold or italicized.

Bold

You can use the <B> tag to format your text in boldface type. Add a <B> tag immediately before the text you want to appear in boldface. Then, turn the boldface off by adding a </B> end tag. For example:

```
This is <B>bold</B>.
```

Italic

You can use the <I> tag to format your text in italic type. Add an <I> tag immediately before the text you want to appear in italic. Then, turn the italic typeface off by adding an </I> end tag. For example:

```
This is <I>italic</I>.
```

Changing fonts

HTML has two tags that let you control font settings: <FONT> and <BASEFONT>. The <FONT> tag lets you control font settings for an individual block of text, whereas the <BASEFONT> tag sets the default font used for a document. Here are the most important attributes of the <FONT> and <BASEFONT> tags:

Many HTML tags come in pairs, but not all. <BASEFONT>, for example, contains only the beginning tag; no corresponding </BASEFONT> tag exists.

+ FACE: Sets the typeface.
+ SIZE: Gives the type size on a scale of 1 to 7, where 7 is the largest and 1 is the smallest. The default size is 3.
+ COLOR: Sets the color of the text. (For more information about using this attribute, see also the section "Adding Color" later in this chapter.)

Here is a snippet of HTML that sets the typeface used for text on a Web page:

```
<BODY>
<BASEFONT SIZE=4 COLOR=BLACK FACE="Times New Roman">
```

```
<P>This is normal body text using the font set by the
   BASEFONT tag.</P>
<H1><FONT FACE="Arial">This is a heading</FONT></H1>
<P>After the heading, the text reverts to the BASEFONT setting.
</P>
</BODY>
```

Figure 3-2 shows how this HTML appears when displayed in a Web browser.

Because the stock fonts that ship with operating systems vary, good programming practice dictates that you include at least a couple of font choices every time you specify a font face. For example, the following HTML snippet tells a Web browser to look first for the Helvetica typeface (which comes installed with Macintosh computers) and, if Helvetica can't be found, to look for the Arial typeface (which comes installed with Windows computers.) Make sure you separate typefaces with commas, as shown in the following line of code; you can specify as many typefaces as you like.

```
<FONT SIZE="2" FACE="helvetica, arial, sans-serif">
```

Figure 3-2:
Using the
FONT and
BASEFONT
tags to
modify the
appearance
of text.

This is normal body text using the font set by the BASEFONT tag.

This is a heading

After the heading, the text reverts to the BASEFONT setting.

Both the `<FONT>` and `<BASEFONT>` tags have been superseded by an even better method of setting fonts and other typographical options: style sheets. For more information about how to use styles, check out Book 2, "HTML," Chapter 8, "Developing Style Sheets."

Creating line breaks

HTML ignores line endings in an HTML document. As a result, you can't insert line breaks just by pressing the Enter key when you create an HTML document. For example, the following lines of text in an HTML document will produce just one line of text rather than two:

```
HTML ignores
line endings.
```

To force a line break, use a `<BR>` tag where you want the line break to occur, as in this example:

```
HTML ignores<BR>
line endings.
```

Many HTML tags come in pairs, but not all. `<BR>`, for example, contains only the beginning tag; no corresponding `</BR>` tag exists.

Adding Color

You can specify colors in various HTML tags. For example, `<BODY>` has a `BGCOLOR` attribute that lets you specify the background color for your page. Or, you can use the `COLOR` attribute in a `<FONT>` tag to set the text color.

Standard HTML defines 14 color names that you can use to set a predefined color. The easiest way to set color is to use one of these color names. For example, to create yellow text, you could use a `<FONT>` tag:

```
<FONT COLOR=YELLOW>This text is yellow.</FONT>
```

For more precise color control, you can specify a color by using a six-digit hexadecimal number to indicate the exact mixture of red, green, and blue you want to use; kind of like mixing paint from a palette containing globs of red, green, and blue. The first two hexadecimal digits represent the amount of red, the next two represent the amount of green, and the last two are for blue. A value of 00 means the color is completely absent, and FF means the color is completely saturated. The entire six-digit color string must be preceded by a pound sign (#).

Hexadecimal numbers are made up of the digits 0 through 9 and the letters A through F. For example, 14, 3F, B9, and AC are valid hexadecimal numbers.

Here are the 14 standard HTML color names along with their corresponding hexadecimal color strings.

Black	#000000	Green	#008000
Silver	#C0C0C0	Lime	#00FF00
Gray	#808080	Olive	#808000
White	#FFFFFF	Yellow	#FFFF00
Maroon	#800000	Navy	#000080
Purple	#800080	Teal	#008080
Fuchsia	#FF00FF	Aqua	#00FFFF

Both Internet Explorer 6 and Navigator 6 support additional color names. But to be compatible with as many browser versions as possible, stick to the 14 standard names.

Watch out for color combinations that result in illegible text! For example, avoid maroon text on a purple background or green text on an olive background.

Changing the Background

When creating Web pages, you don't have to settle for white: You can use colors and images to create an interesting, attractive background.

One caveat, though: Don't make the mistake of using a garish background image that makes your page almost impossible to read. If you want to use a background image for your pages, choose an image that doesn't interfere with the text and other elements on the page. By the same token, if you'd rather use a background color, select a neutral color such as white, light gray, or one of those infamous earth tones: These colors help your visitors read your text without eye strain.

Setting the background color

To set the background color of your Web page, follow these steps:

1. **Create the following <BODY> tag at the start of your document:** `<BODY BGCOLOR=>`.

2. **Type a color name or a hexadecimal color value for the** `BGCOLOR` **attribute into the tag you created, then insert the text for your Web page and add a closing </BODY> tag. For example:**

```
<BODY BGCOLOR="white">
           The body of your Web page goes here
</BODY>
```

This tag sets the background color to white.

For more information about using color, see the "Adding Color" section earlier in this chapter.

Using a background image

To use a background image for your Web page, follow these steps:

1. **Create the following <BODY> tag at the start of your document:** `<BODY BACKGROUND=>`.

2. **Type the name of the image file you want to use or the background as the** `BACKGROUND` **attribute value:**

```
<BODY BACKGROUND="bgpic.gif">
```

This tag uses the file bgpic.gif as a background picture.

The background image repeats as many times as necessary to completely fill the page. Avoid background images that use loud colors or bold designs; such images can overpower the text on your page, rendering your page next to unreadable.

For more information about creating and using images, check out Chapter 4, "Working with Graphics, Sounds, and Video."

Creating Visual Interest with Horizontal Rules

Horizontal rules are horizontal lines you can add to create visual breaks on your Web pages. To add a rule to a page, you use the `<HR>` tag. You can control the height, width, and alignment of the rule by using the `SIZE`, `WIDTH`, and `ALIGN` attributes. For example:

```
<HR WIDTH="50%" SIZE=6 ALIGN=CENTER>
```

Many HTML tags come in pairs, but not all. `<HR>`, for example, contains only the beginning tag; no corresponding `</HR>` tag exists.

In this example, the rule is half the width of the page, six pixels in height, and is centered on the page.

Many Web designers prefer to use graphic images rather than the `<HR>` tag to create horizontal rules. Because different Web browsers display the `<HR>` tag differently, using an image for a rule enables you to precisely control how your rule appears on-screen. To use an image rule, follow these steps:

1. **Type an `<IMG>` tag where you would normally use an `<HR>` tag to create a horizontal rule:**

```
<IMG>
```

2. **Type the name of the graphic file that contains the image rule in the `<IMG>` tag's SRC (shorthand for *source*) attribute:**

```
<IMG SRC="grule1.gif">
```

3. **Add a `WIDTH` attribute that specifies the number of pixels you want the rule to span or a percentage of the screen width:**

```
<IMG SRC="grule1.gif" WIDTH="100%">
```

4. **Follow up with a `<BR>` tag to force a line break:**

```
<IMG SRC="grule1.gif" WIDTH="100%"><BR>
```

Organizing Information into Lists

Using HTML, you can create two basic types of lists for your Web page.

✦ **Bulleted lists:** More formally known as unordered lists. In a bulleted list, each item in the list is marked by a bullet character (typically a dot).

✦ **Numbered lists:** More formally known as ordered lists. Each item in a numbered list is marked by a number. The Web browser takes care of figuring out which number to use for each item in the list.

HTML also lets you create several other types of lists, known as menu lists, directory lists, and definition lists. Because these types of lists are not as commonly used as bulleted and numbered lists, they aren't described here.

Bulleted lists

A bulleted list (more properly called an unordered list) requires you to use three tags:

✦ <UL> marks the beginning of the unordered list.

✦ <LI> marks the start of each item in the list. No corresponding </LI> tag is needed.

✦ </UL> marks the end of the entire list.

Here is a snippet of HTML that sets up a bulleted list:

```
<H3>The Inhabitants of Oz</H3>
<UL>
<LI>The Scarecrow
<LI>The Tin Man
<LI>The Cowardly Lion
<LI>Munchkins
<LI>The Wizard
<LI>The Wicked Witch of the West (WWW)
<LI>Glenda
</UL>
```

Figure 3-3 shows how this list appears when displayed in a browser.

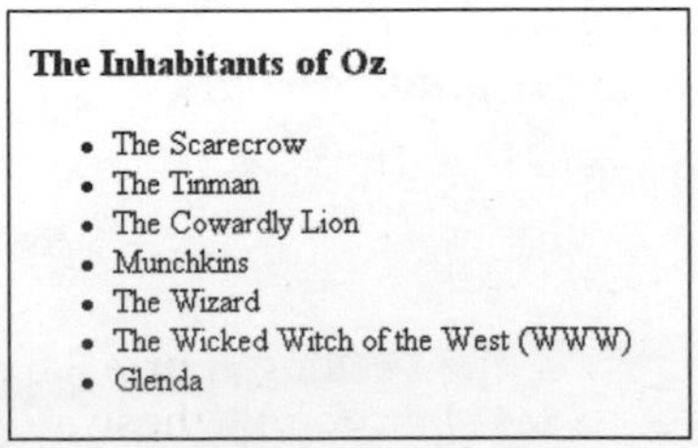

Figure 3-3:
You use
<UL></UL>
to create a
bulleted list.

The Inhabitants of Oz

- The Scarecrow
- The Tinman
- The Cowardly Lion
- Munchkins
- The Wizard
- The Wicked Witch of the West (WWW)
- Glenda

Numbered lists

A numbered list (more properly called an ordered list) requires you to use three tags:

✦ <OL> marks the beginning of the ordered list.

✦ <LI> marks the start of each item in the list. No corresponding </LI> tag is needed.

✦ </OL> marks the end of the entire list.

Here is an HTML snippet that creates a numbered list:

```
<H3>The Inhabitants of Oz</H3>
<OL>
<LI>The Scarecrow
<LI>The Tin Man
<LI>The Cowardly Lion
<LI>Munchkins
<LI>The Wizard
<LI>The Wicked Witch of the West (WWW)
<LI>Glenda
</OL>
```

Figure 3-4 shows how the numbered list appears when displayed in a browser.

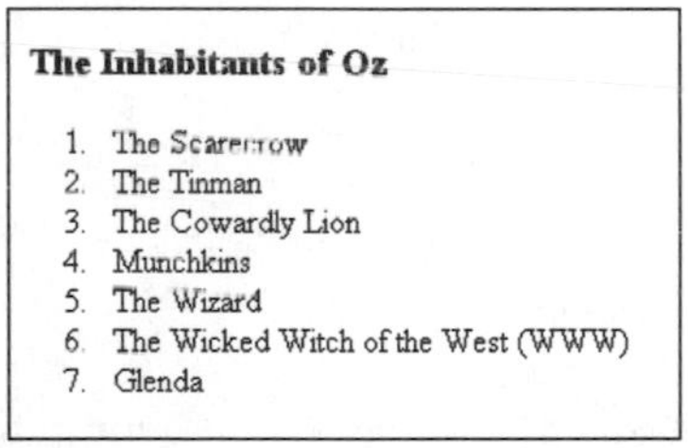

Figure 3-4:
You use
<OL> and
</OL> to
create a
numbered
list.

The Inhabitants of Oz

1. The Scarecrow
2. The Tinman
3. The Cowardly Lion
4. Munchkins
5. The Wizard
6. The Wicked Witch of the West (WWW)
7. Glenda

Creating Links

Links are an integral part of any Web page. Links let your reader travel to a different location, which can be a part of the same HTML document, a different page located on your Web site, or a page from a different Web site located elsewhere on the Internet. All the user has to do to be transported to a different page is click the link.

Using text links

A *text link* is a portion of text that someone viewing your page can click to jump to another location. To create a text link, follow these steps:

1. **Determine the address of the page you want the link to jump to.**

2. **Type an <A> tag at the point on the page where you want the link to appear.**

In the <A> tag, use an HREF attribute (*http reference URL*) to indicate the address of the page you want to link to. For example:

```
<A HREF="http://www.dummies.com">
```

3. **After the <A> tag, type the text that you want to appear in your document as a link:**

```
<A HREF="http://www.dummies.com">The Official For
Dummies Web Page
```

4. **Add a closing </A> tag:**

```
<A HREF="http://www.dummies.com">The Official For
Dummies Web Page</A>
```

The text that appears between the <A> and </A> links is called the *anchor*. The Web address that appears in the HREF attribute is called the *target*.

The anchor text is displayed on the Web page in a special color (usually blue) and is underlined so that the person viewing the page knows the text is a link.

If the target refers to another page at the same Web site as the page the link appears on, you can use just the filename as the target. For example:

```
<A HREF="emerald7.html">See the Wizard</A>
```

When a user clicks the See the Wizard link, the HTML file named emerald7.html appears on-screen.

Using graphic links

A *graphic link* is a graphic image that a user can click to jump to another page or a different location on the current page. To create a graphic link, follow the procedure described in the previous section. But in Step 3, instead of typing text for the link, type an <IMG> tag that identifies the image file to use for the link in its SRC attribute. For example:

```
<A HREF="emerald7.html"><IMG SRC="emerald.gif"></A>
```

In this example, the graphic image file named emerald.gif appears on-screen. If a user clicks it, the browser displays the emerald7.html page.

Linking within the same page

To create a link that simply moves the user to another location on the same page, follow these steps:

1. **Create the following <A> tag at the start of your document: <A NAME=>.
   Make up a name for the section you want to link to ("Here," for example) and type it into the <A> tag you created, as follows:**

   ```
   <A Name= "Here">
   ```

2. **Immediately follow the <A> tag with an </A> end tag.**

   The finished product looks like this: <A NAME="Here"><A/>

3. **Create a text or graphic link to that section by typing the section
   name, preceded by the # symbol, in the HREF attribute of a link.**

Here is a snippet of HTML that creates a link that jumps to the location
named "Here":

```
<A HREF="#Here">Go over there!</A>
```

Using Tables

Tables are a basic HTML feature frequently used for two distinct purposes.
The first is presenting information in a tabular format, in which it is obvious
to the user that a table is being used. The second is controlling a Web document's page layout, in which the user is (or at least should be) unaware that
a table is being used.

Creating a table requires you to use some very complicated HTML tags. For
that reason, setting up a table using an HTML editor such as Microsoft
FrontPage 2002 is often easier.

For the lowdown on Microsoft FrontPage 2002, check out Book 3.

Creating a basic table

The following steps explain how to set up a basic table in which the first row
contains headings and subsequent rows contain data:

1. **Type a set of <TABLE> and </TABLE> tags in the Web document where
   you want the table to appear:**

   ```
   <TABLE>
   </TABLE>
   ```

2. **Add a BORDER attribute to the <TABLE> tag to create a border and
   establish its width in pixels. For example:**

   ```
   <TABLE BORDER=6>
   </TABLE>
   ```

3. **Create the first table row by typing a set of** <TR> **and** </TR> **tags between the** <TABLE> **and** </TABLE> **tags:**

```
<TABLE BORDER=6>
<TR>
</TR>
</TABLE>
```

This first row will hold the headings for the table.

4. **For each column in the table, type a** <TH> **tag, followed by the text you want to display for the heading, followed by a** </TH> **tag. Place each of these heading columns between the** <TR> **and** </TR> **tags:**

```
<TR>
  <TH>Web Feature</TH>
  <TH>Love It</TH>
  <TH>Hate It</TH>
</TR>
```

5. **Create additional rows for the table by typing a** <TR> **and** </TR> **pairs of tags. Between these tags, type a** <TD> **tag followed by the text you want to appear in each column in the row and then a** </TD> **tag.**

For example, here are the tags and text you would type to add a row to show that 62 percent of Web users love tables and 38 percent hate them:

```
<TR>
  <TD>Tables</TD>
  <TD>62%</TD>
  <TD>38%</TD>
</TR>
```

Putting all of this together, here is the HTML for a table with four rows including the heading row:

```
<TABLE BORDER=6>
<TR>
  <TH>Web Feature</TH>
  <TH>Love It</TH>
  <TH>Hate It</TH>
</TR>
<TR>
  <TD>Tables</TD>
  <TD>62%</TD>
  <TD>38%</TD>
</TR>
<TR>
  <TD>Frames</TD>
  <TD>18%</TD>
  <TD>72%</TD>
</TR>
<TR>
  <TD>Style Sheets</TD>
  <TD>55%</TD>
```

```
<TD>45%</TD>
</TR>
</TABLE>
```

Figure 3-5 shows how this table appears when displayed in a Web browser.

Figure 3-5:
A three-column, four-row table.

Web Feature	Love It	Hate It
Tables	62%	38%
Frames	18%	72%
Style Sheets	55%	45%

Using a table for page layout

You can use tables to set up a neat layout for the text and other elements that appear on your Web pages. The following procedure shows you how to set up a simple layout that provides for a page header area at the top of the page, a sidebar area on the left side of the page, and a main text area in the central portion of the page.

1. **Determine the dimensions of the layout you want to use. Be sure to allow for empty "gutter" areas in your layout.**

Figure 3-6 shows the layout used for this example.

Figure 3-6:
Table layout including page header, sidebar area, and main text area.

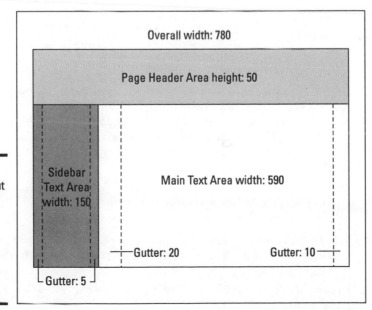

2. **Type a set of** `<TABLE>` **and** `</TABLE>` **tags to begin the table that will establish your page layout. In the** `<TABLE>` **tag, use the** `WIDTH` **attribute to set the overall width of your page layout in pixels. Also include the attributes** `BORDER=0`, `CELLSPACING=0`, **and** `CELLPADDING=0` **so that the table will not have borders or extra space between the cells.**

   The `<TABLE>` tag should look like this:

   ```
   <TABLE BORDER=0 CELLSPACING=0 CELLPADDING=0 WIDTH=780>
   ```

3. **Create a row for the page header area by adding the following tags between the** `<TABLE>` **and** `</TABLE>` **tags:**

   ```
   <TR>
   <TD BGCOLOR=YELLOW HEIGHT=50 COLSPAN=6>
   <H1>Page Header Area</H1>
   </TD>
   </TR>
   ```

   Use whatever color you want for the background color (`BGCOLOR`) and set the `HEIGHT` attribute value to the height of the page header area you want to provide for your layout. `COLSPAN`, which is short for *columns to span*, specifies how many columns you want the page header to run across.

4. **Add a set of** `<TR>` **and** `</TR>` **tags to use for the second table row, which will contain the six columns required to set up the gutter and text areas for the sidebar and main text portions of the page layout.**

5. **Between the second set of** `<TR>` **and** `</TR>` **tags, add a set of** `<TD>` **and** `</TD>` **tags for each of the three columns used for the sidebar area, similar to these:**

   ```
   <TD BGCOLOR=SILVER WIDTH=5 HEIGHT=600
   VALIGN=TOP> </TD>
   <TD BGCOLOR=SILVER WIDTH=150 VALIGN=TOP>Sidebar
   Area</TD>
   <TD BGCOLOR=SILVER WIDTH=5 VALIGN=TOP> </TD>
   ```

   Set the background color (`BGCOLOR`) to the color you want to use for the sidebar background and set the `WIDTH` value to the width your layout calls for. Also, use `VALIGN=TOP` so that any text you place in the columns will be aligned with the top of the cell rather than the middle. And, for the first column only, use a `HEIGHT` attribute in the `<TD>` tag to set the overall height of the page.

   The text for the first and third columns uses a   (non-breaking space) character as a placeholder for the gutters. For the second column, Sidebar Area is used as a placeholder.

6. **Add three more pairs of** `<TD>` **and** `</TR>` **tags to create the columns for the main text area and its two gutter areas, similar to these:**

   ```
   <TD BGCOLOR=WHITE WIDTH=20 VALIGN=TOP> </TD>
   <TD BGCOLOR=WHITE WIDTH=590 VALIGN=TOP>Main Text
   ```

```
Area</TD>
<TD BGCOLOR=WHITE WIDTH=10 VALIGN=TOP> </TD>
```

The HTML for the entire layout should look something like the following:

```
<TABLE BORDER=0 CELLSPACING=0 CELLPADDING=0 WIDTH=780>
<TR>
<TD BGCOLOR=YELLOW HEIGHT=50 COLSPAN=6>
<H1>Page Header Area</H1>
</TD>
</TR>
<TR>
<TD BGCOLOR=SILVER WIDTH=5 HEIGHT=600
VALIGN=TOP> </TD>
<TD BGCOLOR=SILVER WIDTH=150 VALIGN=TOP>Sidebar
Area</TD>
<TD BGCOLOR=SILVER WIDTH=5 VALIGN=TOP> </TD>
<TD BGCOLOR=WHITE WIDTH=20 VALIGN=TOP> </TD>
<TD BGCOLOR=WHITE WIDTH=590 VALIGN=TOP>Main Text
Area</TD>
<TD BGCOLOR=WHITE WIDTH=10 VALIGN=TOP> </TD>
</TR>
</TABLE>
```

7. **Save the file and test the layout it creates using your Web browser. Adjust the settings if necessary until the layout looks just the way you want it to.**

   Figure 3-7 shows how the layout appears in Internet Explorer 5.

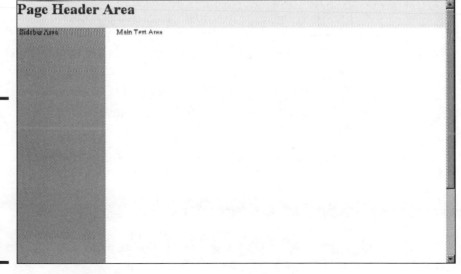

Figure 3-7: Table example including page header, sidebar area, and main text area.

8. To create a document based on the layout, open the file and save it under a new name. Then, replace the Page Header Area, Sidebar Area, and Main Text Area placeholders with the text and other page elements you want to appear in these areas.

Creating Navigation Bars

A *navigation bar* is a collection of text or graphic links that enables users to easily work their way through a series of pages on your Web site. The navigation bar appears in the same place on every page in the site so that the user can easily find it.

You can create a navigation bar in several ways. The most common is to create a table, placing a link in each cell of the table. An alternative is to create a single GIF image for the entire navigation bar and then use that image in an image map. For more information about how to do this, take a peek at Chapter 4, "Working with Graphics, Sounds, and Videos."

Deciding what to include in a navigation bar

Depending on the site, a navigation bar can include some or all of the following links:

+ **Home.** Takes the user to the site's home page.

+ **Next.** Takes the user to the next page in sequence when viewing a series of Web pages.

+ **Previous.** Takes the user to the page that precedes the current page when viewing a series of pages.

+ **Up.** Takes the user to the page at the next level up in the hierarchy of pages.

+ **Help.** Takes the user to a help page.

+ **Site map.** Takes the user to a page that includes links to all the pages on the site.

A navigation bar can also contain links to major sections of your Web site, such as a Product Information section or an Online Catalog section.

Creating a text-based navigation bar

The easiest way to create a navigation bar is to use text links in a table. Each cell in the table contains a link. The following bit of HTML shows how to create a navigation bar with links to four pages (home, help, previous, and next). (For more information about the <TABLE>, <TR>, and <TD> tags, see the section, "Using Tables" earlier in this chapter.)

```
<TABLE BORDER="0" CELLSPACING="0" CELLPADDING="0" WIDTH=800>
<TR>

<TD BGCOLOR="SILVER" HEIGHT="25" WIDTH="160" VALIGN="TOP">
<IMG SRC="blank.gif">
</TD>

<TD BGCOLOR="SILVER" HEIGHT="25" WIDTH="100" VALIGN="TOP">
<A HREF="home.html">Home</A>
</TD>

<TD BGCOLOR="SILVER" HEIGHT="25" WIDTH="100" VALIGN="TOP">
<A HREF="help.html">Help</A>
</TD>

<TD BGCOLOR="SILVER" HEIGHT="25" WIDTH="100" VALIGN="TOP">
<A HREF="page3.html">Next</A>
</TD>

<TD BGCOLOR="SILVER" HEIGHT="25" WIDTH="100" VALIGN="TOP">
<A HREF="page1.html">Previous</A>
</TD>

<TD BGCOLOR="SILVER" HEIGHT="25" WIDTH="240" VALIGN="TOP">
<IMG SRC="blank.gif">
</TD>

</TR>
</TABLE>
```

This HTML table is set up so that the entire table is 800 pixels wide. The table has a single row, which has six cells. The first and last cells contain the image file blank.gif, which displays a blank cell; they provide the spacing necessary to precisely position the four middle cells, which contain the text links for the home, help, previous, and next pages.

Figure 3-8 shows how this navigation bar appears when positioned at the bottom of a blank page.

Remember that you have to modify the HREF attributes in the text links used for the Next and Previous links on each page.

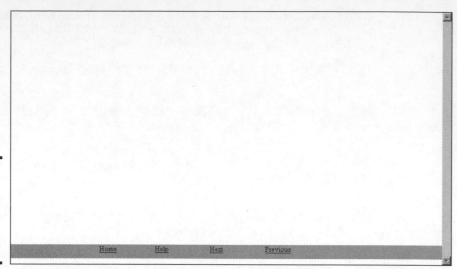

Figure 3-8:
A text navigation bar created using an HTML table.

Using images in a navigation bar

You can create a navigation bar using images of the buttons you would like the user to click to move from page to page. Here is the HTML for a simple navigation bar that uses two images of arrows, one facing left, the other right, to link to the next and previous pages, with a simple two-cell table to position the buttons. (The images in this navigation bar are created as links within the cells of a table. For more information about the <TABLE>, <TR>, and <TD> tags, see the section, "Using Tables" earlier in this chapter.)

```
<TABLE BORDER="0" CELLSPACING="0" CELLPADDING="0" WIDTH=50>
<TR>

<TD HEIGHT="25" WIDTH="25">
<A HREF="page1.html"><IMG SRC="larrow.gif" BORDER="0"
    HEIGHT="25" WIDTH="25"></A>
</TD>

<TD HEIGHT="25" WIDTH="25">
<A HREF="page3.html"><IMG SRC="rarrow.gif" BORDER="0"
    HEIGHT="25" WIDTH="25"></A>
</TD>

</TR>
</TABLE>
```

In this example, both larrow.gif and rarrow.gif are 25 x 25 GIF images that show a left and right arrow.

Introducing Frames

Frames enable you to divide a page into separate areas that each display the contents of a separate HTML file. The advantage of using frames is that the user can interact with each frame independently. For example, a frame that contains a long text document can have its own scrollbars so that the user can scroll through the document, and other elements of the page — such as a navigation bar — remain on the screen.

The use of frames is an advanced HTML technique that enables you to create several HTML files for each page. The first HTML file replaces the beginning and ending <BODY> tags with the beginning and ending <FRAMESET> tags that indicate the arrangement of frames on the page. Between the <FRAMESET> and </FRAMESET> tags, you use one or more <FRAME> tags to create the actual frames. Each <FRAME> tag includes an SRC attribute that names a separate HTML file that spells out the contents that will be displayed within the frame. The <FRAME> tag can also include additional attributes that indicate such things as whether the frame has a visible border, scrollbars, and so on.

A <FRAMESET> tag can include a ROWS attribute to create frames stacked one atop the other, or it can include a COLS attribute to create side-by-side frames. In the ROWS or COLS attribute, you list the pixel size of each frame you want to create. For the last frame, use an asterisk to indicate that the frame should fill the remainder of the page. For example, the following <FRAMESET> tag creates three frames side by side: The first is 150 pixels wide, the second is 20, and the third fills the remainder of the page:

```
<FRAMESET ROWS="150,20,*">
```

In the <FRAME> tags, use the SRC attribute to indicate the name of the HTML file that should be displayed in the frame.

The following examples show how you can use frames to set up a grid page layout that has four layout areas: a page header area, a page footer area, a left margin area, and a main text window that can be scrolled. Five HTML files are required. The main HTML file contains the following lines:

```
<HTML>
<FRAMESET ROWS="75, *, 50" FRAMEBORDER=0 FRAMESPACING=0>
  <FRAME SRC="frtop.html">
  <FRAMESET COLS="150, *">
    <FRAME SRC="frleft.html">
    <FRAME SRC="frright.html" SCROLLING="YES">
  </FRAMESET>
  <FRAME SRC="frbottom.html" SCROLLING="NO">
</FRAMESET>
</HTML>
```

The frtop.html, frbottom.html, frleft.html, and frright.html files contain the HTML used to display the content of each of the frames. Figure 3-9 shows how these frames appear in Internet Explorer 5 when each of the HTML files are empty except for a <BODY> tag that specifies a background color to be used for the frame.

Frames are a troublesome HTML feature where browser compatibility is concerned. The current versions of both Navigator and Internet Explorer both support the <FRAME> and <FRAMESET> tags, but each has several attributes that aren't supported by the other. In addition, Internet Explorer has a simpler method of creating inline frames by using an <IFRAME> tag. Inline frames are floating frames that you can place inside a Web page, similar to the way you can place images inside a Web page. Although the <IFRAME> tag is easier to deal with than the <FRAMESET> and <FRAME> tags, Navigator doesn't support the <IFRAME> tag.

Figure 3-9:
A frame containing four layout areas: page header, page footer, left margin, and scrollable main text area.

Chapter 4: Working with Graphics, Sounds, and Video

In This Chapter

✔ Understanding formats for image, sound, and video files

✔ Working with images

✔ Using image maps

✔ Adding sounds and video clips to a Web page

✔ Creating transparent GIF images

Adding images, sounds, and movie clips to your Web pages can make your pages come alive. Book 5, "Multimedia: Creating Graphics, Sound, Animations, Video, and Java Applets," describes how you create multimedia files. However, if you already have a few multimedia files and you want to incorporate them into your pages, this is the chapter for you. Here you find the guidelines and specific steps you need to add multimedia files to your Web pages like a pro.

Getting Familiar with File Formats for Image, Sound, and Video

You can choose from many different file formats for images, sounds, and videos. Fortunately, you can construct almost all Web pages by using just the formats I describe in the following sections.

Image file

Although dozens of different image file formats exist, only two are widely used for Web page images: GIF and JPEG.

GIF images

GIF, which stands for *G*raphic *I*nterchange *F*ormat, was originally used on the CompuServe online network and is now widely used throughout the Internet. GIF image files have the following characteristics:

✦ GIF images can have a maximum of 256 different colors.

✦ GIF files are compressed to reduce their size. The compression method GIF uses does not reduce the image quality.

✦ A GIF image can include a transparent color, which, when displayed in a Web browser, allows the background of the Web page to show through.

✦ GIF images can be interlaced, which allows the Web browser to quickly display a crude version of the image and then display progressively better versions of the image.

✦ GIF supports a simple animation technique that enables you to store several distinct images in the same file. The Web browser displays the animation by displaying the images one after the other in sequence.

✦ GIF files usually have the filename extension .GIF.

The GIF format is the best choice for most Web graphics that were created with drawing or paint programs and that do not contain a large number of different colors. It is ideal for icons, buttons, background textures, bullets, rules, and line art.

A format called PNG (*P*ortable *N*etwork *G*raphics) was developed in 1995 as a successor to the GIF format. PNG (pronounced *Ping*) supports all the features of GIF and then some, including support for more colors than GIF. PNG hasn't really caught on yet, though, so GIF remains the most widely used image format.

JPEG images

JPEG, a format developed by the *J*oint *P*hotographic *E*xperts *G*roup, is designed for photographic quality images. It has the following characteristics:

✦ JPEG images can have either 16.7 million or 2 billion colors. Most JPEG images use 16.7 million colors, which provides excellent representation of photographic images.

✦ To reduce image size, JPEG uses a special compression technique that slightly reduces the quality of the image while greatly reducing its size. In most cases, you have to carefully compare the original uncompressed image with the compressed image to see the difference.

✦ JPEG supports progressive images that are similar to GIF interlaced images.

✦ JPEG does not support transparent background colors as GIF does.

✦ JPEG does not support animation.

✦ JPEG files usually have the filename extension .JPG.

Other image file formats

Many other image file formats exist that *don't* work on the Web. (To use a graphic file saved in one of these non-Web-friendly formats, you must convert the file to JPEG or GIF using a graphics program such as PaintShop Pro.) Here are just a few non-Web-friendly graphics formats:

+ **BMP:** Windows bitmap
+ **PCX:** Another bitmap format
+ **TIF:** Tagged Image File
+ **PIC:** Macintosh picture file

Sound file formats

The following paragraphs describe the most commonly used sound file formats.

+ **WAV:** The Windows standard for sound recordings. WAV stands for *Wave*.
+ **SND:** The Macintosh standard for sound recordings. SND stands for *Sound*.
+ **AU:** The UNIX standard for sound recordings. AU stands for *Audio*.
+ **MID:** MIDI files, which are not actually sound recordings but are instead music stored in a form that a sound card's synthesizer can play. MIDI stands for *Musical Instrument Digital Interface*.

Don't confuse sound files with sound you can listen to in real time over the Internet, known as *streaming audio*. The most popular format for streaming audio is RealAudio. RealAudio enables you to listen to a sound as it is being downloaded to your computer, so you don't have to wait for the entire file to be downloaded before you can listen to it. To listen to RealAudio sound, you must first install a RealAudio player in your Web browser.

I show you how to play and record sound using RealAudio in Book 5, "Multimedia: Creating Graphics, Sound, Animations, Video, and Java Applets."

Video file formats

Three popular formats for video clips are used on the Web:

+ **AVI:** The Windows video standard. AVI stands for *Audio Video Interleaved*.
+ **QuickTime:** The Macintosh video standard. QuickTime files usually have the extension .MOV.
+ **MPEG:** An independent standard. MPEG stands for *Motion Picture Experts Group*.

Although AVI is known as a Windows video format and QuickTime is a Macintosh format, both formats — as well as MPEG — have become cross-platform standards. Both Netscape Navigator and Microsoft Internet Explorer can play AVI, QuickTime, and MPEG videos.

I show you how to play and create video files for the Web in Book 5, "Multimedia: Creating Graphics, Sound, Animations, Video, and Java Applets."

Inserting a Graphic Image

To insert a graphic image on a Web page, follow these steps:

1. **Obtain an image file you want to include on your page. If necessary, use a graphics program to convert the file to the format you want to use (GIF or JPEG). Store the image file in the same directory as the HTML document that displays the image.**

   To find out how to create images you can add to your Web pages, check out Book 5, "Multimedia: Creating Graphics, Sound, Animations, Video, and Java Applets."

2. **In the HTML file, add the `<IMG>` tag at the point in the document where you want the image to appear. Use the SRC attribute to provide the name of the image file. For example:**

   ```
   <IMG SRC="image1.gif">
   ```

Working with Graphic Images

Here are some guidelines for using graphic images wisely on your Web pages:

✦ Don't add so many images or such large images that your page takes too long to download. As a general rule, try holding your breath while your page downloads with a 28.8 Kbps modem. If you turn blue, the download takes too long.

   Use the ALT attribute with the `<IMG>` tag to provide text for users who view your page with images turned off. For example:

   ```
   <IMG SRC="chicken.gif" ALT="Picture of a chicken">
   ```

✦ Use the HEIGHT and WIDTH attributes with the `<IMG>` tag to preformat your pages for the correct image dimensions.

   ```
   <IMG SRC="chicken.gif" HEIGHT=100 WIDTH=50>
   ```

✦ Use the GIF format for most images created with drawing or painting programs. Use the JPEG format for photographic images.

✦ Use `BORDER=0` in the `<IMG>` tag to eliminate the border that appears around your images (unless you want the borders to appear):

```
<IMG SRC="chicken.gif" BORDER=0>
```

✦ Use transparent GIFs to create images that blend seamlessly with your page background.

For more information about transparent GIFs, skip ahead to the "Using Transparent GIF Images" section you find later in this chapter.

✦ If you want to make large image files available for download on your Web site, provide smaller, thumbnail versions of the images that people can preview before deciding whether to download the full-size image. Many graphics editing programs, including PaintShop Pro, enable you to create thumbnail versions of graphics files quickly and easily.

Keep in mind that many of the images you see displayed on the Web are copyrighted materials that you cannot simply copy and use on your own Web site without permission from the copyright holder. Similarly, photographs, artwork, and other images that appear in magazines and books are copyrighted. You cannot legally scan copyrighted images and post them on your Web site without the copyright owner's permission. For the skinny on U.S. copyright law, check out `www.loc.gov/copyright`. If you're not based in the United States, you may want to check out The Canadian Intellectual Property Office at `cipo.gc.ca`, the U.K. Patent Office at `http://www.patent.gov.uk/copy/index.htm`, or the Australian Copyright Council Home Page at `www.copyright.org.au`.

Carving Up Graphics with Image Maps

An *image map* is a graphic image in which specific regions of the image serve as links to other Web pages. For example, if you're creating a Web site about *The Wizard of Oz,* you could use an image map showing the Scarecrow, Tin Man, and Cowardly Lion to link to pages about these characters.

To create an image map, you must use several HTML tags: `<MAP>` and its companion `</MAP>`, `<AREA>`, and `<IMG>`. Here are the steps to follow to create an image map:

1. **Find or create a graphic image that can serve as an image map. The image should have distinct regions that will serve as the map's links.**

For example, the image you see in Figure 4-1 could be used for an image map that will provide two links: one for the chicken, the other for the egg.

Figure 4-1:
You can use
an image
with at least
two distinct
regions
as an
image map.

Which came first?

2. **Using your favorite graphic drawing program to display the image, determine the rectangular boundaries of each area of the image that will serve as a link. Write down the pixel coordinates of the top, left, bottom, and right edges of these rectangles.**

   The example shown in Figure 4-2 shows these coordinates: 0, 40 (width) and 30, 79 (height). (For suggestions on graphics programs you can use, check out Book 5, "Multimedia: Creating Graphics, Sound, Animations, Video, and Java Applets.")

   Most graphics programs display these coordinates in the program's status bar as you move the mouse around or when you use the selection tool to select an area. For example, Figure 4-2 shows an area selected in Microsoft Photo Editor.

   For the chicken-and-egg image, the following coordinates define the rectangular areas for the links:

	Top	Left	Bottom	Right
Chicken	40	0	109	79
Egg	0	40	39	79

3. **Type a set of <MAP> and </MAP> tags. In the <MAP> tag, use the NAME attribute to provide a name for the image map:**

   ```
   <MAP NAME="IMGMAP1">
   </MAP>
   ```

Coordinates: width always comes first, then height

Figure 4-2:
You use the
coordinates
a graphic
program
displays to
create an
image map.

4. **Between the <MAP> and </MAP> tags, type an <AREA> tag for each rectangular area of the image that will serve as a link. In the <AREA> tag, include the following attributes:**

   - SHAPE=RECT
   - COORDS="*top, left, bottom, right*"
   - HREF="*url*"

   For example:

   ```
   <MAP NAME=IMGMAP1>
     <AREA SHAPE=RECT COORDS="0,40,39,79" HREF="egg.html">
     <AREA SHAPE=RECT COORDS="40,0,109,79"
   HREF="chick.html">
   </MAP>
   ```

5. **Type an <IMG> tag. Use the SRC attribute to name the image file and the USEMAP attribute to provide the name of the image map listed in the <MAP> attribute:**

   ```
   <IMG SRC="chickegg.gif" USEMAP="#imgmap1">
   ```

   Be sure to type a pound sign (#) before the image map name in the <IMG> tag's USEMAP attribute. But don't use the # symbol when you create the name in the <MAP> tag's NAME attribute.

Putting it all together, here is a complete HTML document to set up an image map:

```
<BODY>
<H1>Which came first?</H1>
<MAP NAME=IMGMAP1>
  <AREA SHAPE=RECT COORDS="0,40,39,79" HREF="egg.html">
  <AREA SHAPE=RECT COORDS="40,0,109,79" HREF="chick.html">
</MAP>
<IMG SRC="chickegg.gif" USEMAP="#imgmap1">
</BODY>
```

Figure 4-3 shows how this page appears when displayed.

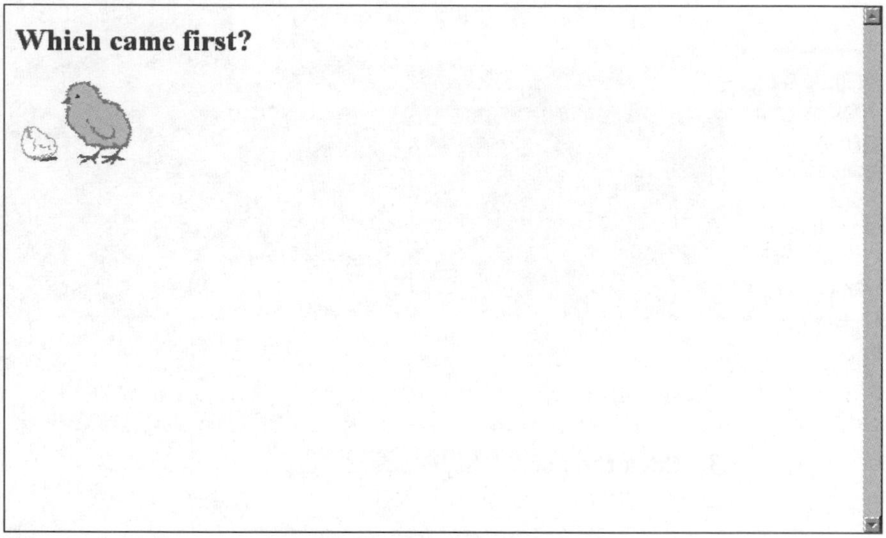

Which came first?

Figure 4-3:
An image
map
displayed in
a browser.

Use the `<TITLE>` attribute in the `<AREA>` tags to create ToolTips that are displayed when the user pauses the mouse pointer briefly over an image map area. For example:

```
<AREA SHAPE=RECT COORDS="0,40,39,79" HREF="egg.html"
   TITLE="The Egg">
<AREA SHAPE=RECT COORDS="40,0,109,79" HREF="chick.html"
   TITLE="The Chicken">
```

Remember that some people configure their browsers to not download and display images. Whenever you use an image map, be sure to also provide text links as an alternative to the image map. Otherwise, users who visit your page with images turned off won't be able to navigate your site.

Using Transparent GIF Images

Most graphics programs can create transparent GIF images, in which one color is designated as transparent. When the image is displayed on your page, the background color of the page shows through the transparent area.

The procedures for setting the transparent color are similar in most graphics programs. Follow these steps to set transparent color in the new version of Microsoft Paint that comes with Windows 98:

1. **Open the GIF file you want to create a transparent color for.**

2. **Choose Image➪Attributes.**

The Attributes dialog box appears, as shown in Figure 4-4.

Figure 4-4:
Use the
Attributes
dialog box
to set the
transpar-
ency
attribute for
an image.

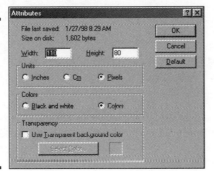

3. **Click the Use Transparent Background Color option.**

4. **Click the Select Color button.**

The Select Color dialog box appears, as shown in Figure 4-5.

Figure 4-5:
Use the
Select Color
dialog
box to
specify the
transparent
background
color of an
image.

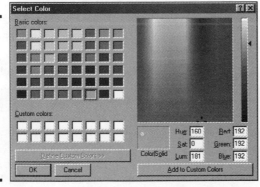

5. **Click the color you want to use as the image's transparent background color.**

6. **Click OK to return to the Image Attributes dialog box.**

7. **Click OK.**

8. **Choose File⇨Save to save the file with the transparent color information.**

To use a transparent background color, make sure the image's background consists of a single color and that the background color does not appear elsewhere in the image. You may need to fiddle with your paint program's painting tools to adjust the background of the image accordingly.

If you aren't one of the lucky owners of Windows 98, you can use other graphics programs, including Microsoft PhotoDraw or JASC PaintShop Pro, to create transparent GIF images.

Incorporating Sounds

You can insert a sound file on a Web page in one of two ways: as a link or as an embedded sound. The following sections show you how to use the HTML tags necessary for each method.

You can also insert a sound as a part of the page's background so that the sound is played automatically whenever the page is displayed. Flip to the section, "Creating a background sound," later in this chapter for more information.

To find out how to create sound files to include in your Web pages, check out Book 5, "Multimedia: Creating Graphics, Sound, Animations, Video, and Java Applets."

Inserting a link to a sound file

The advantage of linking to a sound file is that the sound file isn't downloaded to the user's computer until the user clicks the sound file link. To insert a link to a sound file, follow these steps:

1. **Obtain a sound file you want linked to your Web site.**

2. **Place the sound file in the same directory as the HTML document that will contain the link.**

3. **Add an <A> tag, some descriptive text, and an </A> tag to the HTML file as follows:**

    ```
    <A HREF="sound.wav">Click here to play the
    sound.</A>
    ```

    Be sure to type the name of your sound file in the HREF attribute.

Embedding a sound file

Embedding a sound file displays sound controls (stop, play, and start) on a Web page, allowing visitors to control when and how the sound file plays. You can embed a sound on a Web page by using an `<EMBED>` tag as follows:

```
<EMBED SRC="sound.wav">
```

The `SRC` attribute specifies the name of the sound file.

Be sure to specify a full-qualified filename if your sound file is located in a different directory than your HTML file. For example: `SRC="d:\mysite\ mysounds\sound.wav"`

Creating a background sound

A background sound plays automatically whenever a user displays your Web page. To add a background sound to a page, follow these steps:

1. **Obtain a sound file you want to use as a background sound.**

2. **Place the sound file in the same directory as the HTML file.**

3. **Add a `<BGSOUND>` attribute following the document's `<BODY>` tag. Use the `SRC` attribute to name the sound file you want to be played:**

```
<BODY>
<BGSOUND SRC="music.mid">
```

4. **If you want the sound to repeat several times, add the `LOOP` attribute:**

```
<BGSOUND SRC="music.mid" LOOP=3>
```

You can type any number you want in the `LOOP` attribute to indicate how many times the sound should be repeated. Or you can type `LOOP= INFINITE` to repeat the sound repeatedly as long as the page is displayed.

Some people — myself included — would rather listen to fingernails dragged across a chalkboard than annoying background sounds that play over and over again. If you want people like me to visit your site more than once, avoid `LOOP=INFINITE` like the plague.

Incorporating Video Clips

You can insert a video file on a Web page in one of two ways: as a link or as an embedded object.

To find out how to create a video clip to add to your Web page, see Book 5, "Multimedia: Creating Graphics, Sound, Animations, Video, and Java Applets."

Inserting a link to a video

Inserting a link to a video clip enables your visitors to decide whether and when to view your visual masterpiece. All your visitors need to do to view a linked video is click the link. (To view an embedded video, on the other hand, visitors need to click the embedded playback controls. Check out the next section, "Embedding a video," for details.)

Follow these steps to insert a link to a video file:

1. **Locate a video file you want to provide a link to from your Web page.**

2. **Add an <A> tag, some descriptive text, and an </A> tag to the HTML file as follows:**

```
<A HREF="movie.avi">Click here to download a movie.</A>
```

Provide the name of the video file in the <A> tag's HREF attribute.

When the user clicks the link, the Web browser downloads the file and plays the video.

Embedding a video

Embedding a video differs from inserting a link to a video — which I describe earlier — in one very important respect: Embedding a video automatically displays a video control panel your visitors can use to stop, start, and pause video playback.

Use the <EMBED> tag to embed a video on a Web page. Follow these steps:

1. **Locate a video file you want to embed on a Web page.**

2. **In the HTML document for the Web page, add an <EMBED> tag specifying the name of the video file in the SRC attribute:**

```
<EMBED SRC="movie.avi">
```

3. **If you want to change the size of the area used to display the video, add the HEIGHT and WIDTH attributes:**

```
<EMBED SRC="movie.avi" HEIGHT=200 WIDTH=200>
```

4. **If you want the video to play automatically as soon as it finishes downloading, add AUTOSTART=TRUE to the <EMBED> tag:**

```
<EMBED SRC="movie.avi" AUTOSTART=TRUE>
```

5. **If you want the video to repeat, add a LOOP attribute to the <EMBED> tag.**

You can set the LOOP value to a number to cause the video to repeat a specific number of times, or you can specify LOOP=INFINITE to cause the video to replay over and over again as long as the page is displayed.

Chapter 5: Building Your Web Workshop

In This Chapter

- ✔ Examining Web browsers
- ✔ Selecting an HTML editor
- ✔ Perusing Java, JavaScript, and multimedia tools
- ✔ Opting for office suites
- ✔ Choosing a graphics program

Whether you're cooking, building furniture, or creating Web pages, the right tool for the job can be a big help. Fortunately, there's an enormous selection of Web tools on the market today, ranging from free to pricey, from general, all-purpose tools to unbelievably specialized wizards. For every Web developer and every project, the perfect tool!

In this chapter I introduce you to some popular, useful tools you may want to consider adding to your Web toolbox. Some of these are commercial programs you must buy and others are programs you can download free from the Internet.

The CD that comes with this book contains trial versions of several popular commercial programs. I flag these with an icon so you can find them easily as you skim through this chapter.

Web Browsers

Two Web browsers are in widespread usage on the Internet. If you are a serious Web developer, you should have both of them so that you can make sure your Web pages work with both browsers.

Netscape 6.1

Netscape 6.1 is the complete package of Internet access tools from Netscape, including the following components:

- ✦ Navigator, for Web browsing
- ✦ Mail, for e-mail

✦ Instant Messenger, for instant messaging

✦ Composer, for creating Web pages

You can download Netscape free, or you can purchase one of several Netscape editions that includes additional software. You can also order Netscape on CD-ROM for $6.95.

Price: Free

Web site: `home.netscape.com/browsers`

Internet Explorer 5.5

Internet Explorer 5.5 features the latest Web technologies from Microsoft: Dynamic HTML (a combination of HTML, style sheets, and scripting tools that enables you to create Web pages that respond to user interaction) Visual Basic Scripting Edition (VBScript), channels, ActiveX (a language for creating and plugging self-contained programs — similar to Java applets — into Web pages), and more.

The complete Internet Explorer 5.5 suite includes the following components:

✦ Internet Explorer 5.5, for Web browsing

✦ Outlook Express, for e-mail and newsgroups

✦ MSN Messenger Service, for instant messaging

✦ NetMeeting, for online conferencing

All of these are available free to download from the Microsoft Web site.

Price: Free

Web site: `www.microsoft.com/windows/ie/default.htm`

Graphics Programs

Graphics programs are an essential part of your Web toolkit. You need a graphics drawing program that can create images in either GIF or JPEG format, and the program should be able to handle advanced features such as GIF transparent backgrounds, interlaced images, and animations.

The following sections describe several graphics programs you can use for creating Web pages.

CorelDRAW

CorelDRAW 10 Graphics Suite is one of the best suites of graphics programs available. The relatively stiff price makes sense when you realize that the comprehensive CorelDRAW 10 Graphics Suite package includes not just the CorelDRAW drawing program, but Corel PHOTO-PAINT, Corel R.A.V.E. (Real Animated Vector Effects), and a bunch of graphics utility programs, as well.

Price: $549.99

Web site: www.corel.com

Microsoft PhotoDraw

Microsoft PhotoDraw 2000 is a full-featured program for creating Web images designed to work with other Microsoft Office applications. It includes more than 20,000 customizable images and clip art.

Price: $109

Web site: www.microsoft.com

PaintShop Pro

PaintShop Pro, from JASC, Inc., is a powerful, yet inexpensive painting program you can download from the Internet to use free for a 30-day evaluation period. If you like it, you can purchase it after the trial period. PaintShop Pro has just about everything you could possibly want in an image drawing program. PaintShop Pro supports more than 30 graphic image formats, including, of course, GIF and JPEG, and it includes sophisticated features such as gradient fills, blur effects, and textured brush effects for creating stunning images. PaintShop Pro also comes with Animation Shop for creating GIF animations.

You'll find an evaluation copy of PaintShop Pro on the companion CD.

Price: $109 after free 30-day evaluation period

Web site: www.jasc.com

Windows 98 Paint

Paint is the free image drawing program that comes with Windows. With Windows 3.1 and Windows 95, Paint is hardly adequate for creating images for the Web. The only image formats supported by older versions of Paint are BMP and PCX, neither of which is widely used on the Web. With Windows 98, however, Microsoft has beefed up Paint to make it suitable for working with Web images by supporting the GIF and JPEG file formats. Paint can handle transparent background colors for GIF images, but it cannot create interlaced GIF images or GIF animations.

Price: Included with Windows 98

Web site: www.microsoft.com

HTML Editors

You can create HTML documents with a simple text editor such as NotePad, but for serious HTML work, you should invest in a more sophisticated HTML editor such as one of the programs described in the following sections. Most HTML editors let you work in two modes: graphical WYSIWYG (What You See Is What You Get) mode lets you create Web pages by dragging and dropping, like a cross between a word processor and a drawing program; HTML mode lets you work directly with HTML tags and attributes.

Dreamweaver

Dreamweaver 4, from Macromedia, Inc., combines a text editor with a visual development environment so you can choose the Web page creation style you're most comfortable with. A bonus for developers interested in creating animations for their Web sites: Dreamweaver is compatible with Flash (Macromedia's animation creation tool).

You'll find an evaluation copy of Dreamweaver 4 on the companion CD.

Price: $299

Web site: www.macromedia.com/software/dreamweaver

Composer

Composer is a free HTML editor that comes bundled with the Netscape Web browser. Nifty toolbar buttons let you quickly add lists, tables, images, links, colors, and font styles to your pages.

Price: Free download or $6.95 on CD

Web site: www.netscape.com

FrontPage 2002

FrontPage 2002 is the Microsoft full-featured Web site development tool. The FrontPage 2002 WYSIWYG HTML editor enables you to use advanced HTML features, such as frames and tables, and it enables you to directly edit HTML tags and attributes. In addition, FrontPage 2002 includes tools that let you manage and coordinate all the pages that make up your Web site, including a feature that maintains your hyperlinks automatically.

(At the time this book was published, Microsoft had not officially released FrontPage 2002. If you can't wait until FrontPage 2002 hits the streets, you can order a 30-day sneak-peek trial version for $9.95 USD by visiting www.microsoft.com/frontpage/evaluation/trial.htm).

Price: $149 (FrontPage 2002)

Web site: www.microsoft.com/frontpage

HotDog Professional

HotDog Professional, made by a company called Sausage Software, is a sophisticated code-based HTML editor that uses wizards to create HTML tags for your documents. Unlike most HTML editors, HotDog Professional lets you utilize advanced features such as style sheets, Java, and push channels using Microsoft, PointCast, or Netscape channel technologies. (*Push channels* work much like radio and television channels: They push (or broadcast) content to users, rather than waiting for users to request content. In contrast, traditional Web sites are considered *pull channels*, because users must take a specific action, such as clicking a link, to download content.)

Price: $99.95

Web site: www.sausagetools.com

Java, JavaScript, and Animation Tools

If you're interested in creating Java applets (self-contained programs written in the Java programming language), JavaScript scripts (short programs written in JavaScript that allow users to interact with your Web pages), or flashy animations to add to your Web pages, you want to invest in a top-notch development tool such as one of the following.

Visual Café for Java

Visual Café for Java, from WebGain, is a rapid development environment for creating Java-based Web sites. It is available in three editions: Standard, Expert, and Enterprise. If you are a serious Java developer, you want the Expert edition (or the Enterprise edition, if your boss is picking up the tab!). For casual or first-time Java users, the Standard edition is a great way to get started with Java.

Price: $99.00 (Standard Edition), $799.95 + $159.95 required one-year maintenance contract (Expert Edition), $2,995.95 + $719.95 required one-year maintenance contract (Enterprise Edition)

Web site: www.webgain.com/products/visual_cafe

JBuilder

JBuilder 5, from Borland Software Corporation, is another popular visual Java development environment for creating Java-based Web sites. It is available in three editions: Personal, Professional, and Enterprise. A free trial version of JBuilder is available for download at Borland's Web site.

Price: $99.95 (Personal Edition), $999 (Professional Edition), $2,999 (Enterprise Edition)

Web site: www.inprise.com

Visual J++ 6.0

Visual J++ is the complete development environment for creating Java applications from Microsoft. Visual J++ features support for ActiveX components (independent programs you can drop into your Web pages), database connectivity, and VBScript support.

Price: $109 (Standard Edition), $549 (Professional Edition)

Web site: www.microsoft.com/products/develop.htm

NetObjects ScriptBuilder

From NetObjects, Inc. comes NetObjects ScriptBuilder 3.0, which you can use to create scripts in JavaScript — as well as in other scripting languages — that allow your users to interact with your Web pages. NetObjects ScriptBuilder includes a clickable representation of the Web browser's document object model as well as a library of prebuilt scripts and script snippets to help you construct custom scripts quickly. (The *document object model* describes each of the objects that makes up a Web page — for example, HTML forms, input fields, and push buttons — as well as how you interact with those objects to create your own scripts.)

You'll find an evaluation copy of NetObjects ScriptBuilder on the companion CD.

Price: $149

Web site: www.netobjects.com

Flash 5

Macromedia Flash 5 has become the standard for any Web designer wanting to produce high-quality, high-impact animations for Web sites. This tool offers advanced drawing tools and interactive support you can use to create navigation bars (those cool rows of clickable buttons that enable users to visit other sections of a site) and presentations complete with synchronized sound.

You'll find an evaluation copy of Flash 5 on the companion CD.

Price: $399

Web site: `www.macromedia.com/software/flash`

Office Suites

All three of the popular Office suites — Microsoft Office, Corel WordPerfect Suite, and Lotus SmartSuite — include Web authoring features. These features enable you to use a word processor, spreadsheet, or desktop presentation program to create Web pages. One of the useful features is the ability to quickly convert an existing document, spreadsheet, or presentation to a Web page.

Corel WordPerfect Office 2002

The Corel basic office suite features these programs:

✦ Word processing: Corel WordPerfect 10

✦ Spreadsheet: Corel Quattro Pro 10

✦ Desktop presentations: Corel Presentations 10

You can use all these programs to create new Web pages or to convert existing documents or data to HTML. The Professional Edition also includes the database program, Paradox 9, which can publish database data to a Web page, and Corel WEB.SiteBuilder, a site-development tool that integrates with the other WordPerfect Suite applications to help you quickly create consistent and attractive Web sites.

Price: $389.99 (Standard Edition), $489.99 (Professional Edition)

Web site: `www.corel.com`

Lotus SmartSuite Millennium Edition

SmartSuite Millennium Edition 9.6 includes the following programs:

✦ Word processing: Lotus Word Pro

✦ Spreadsheet: Lotus 1-2-3

✦ Desktop presentations: Lotus Freelance Graphics

✦ Database: Lotus Approach

All the SmartSuite programs can be used for Web publishing. SmartSuite programs can automatically convert documents, presentations, and spreadsheets to HTML format and publish them on the Web. SmartSuite is especially adept at collaborative work by enabling you to electronically distribute documents to other Internet users and automatically consolidate multiple versions of a document to create a final, edited document.

Price: $449

Web site: www.lotus.com

Microsoft Office XP

Microsoft Office XP comes in several versions; the most popular are the Standard Edition and the Professional Edition. Office XP Standard Edition includes the following programs:

✦ Word processing: Word 2002

✦ Spreadsheet: Excel 2002

✦ Desktop presentations: PowerPoint 2002

✦ E-mail/organizer: Outlook 2002

The Professional Edition also includes the database program Access 2002, as well as Publisher 2002 and FrontPage 2002.

All the Office XP programs include features for creating Web pages. You can use Word 2002 as a simple WYSIWYG HTML editor, or you can convert existing documents to HTML pages. You can also use Access 2002 and Excel 2002 to publish database or spreadsheet data to the Web.

Best of all, the Professional Edition of Office XP comes with FrontPage 2002.

Price: $499 (Standard Edition), $599 (Professional Edition)

Web site: www.microsoft.com/office

Chapter 6: Publishing Your Web Site

In This Chapter

✔ Using Personal Web Server to test your Web pages

✔ Using ftp to publish your Web pages

✔ Using Microsoft's Web Publishing Wizard to publish your Web pages

✔ Rating your site using the RSACi rating service

✔ Submitting your site to search services

In Web parlance, *publishing* your Web site means taking the steps necessary to move your Web pages from your computer to a Web server — whether that Web server is maintained by an Internet service provider or a Web hosting company. After your pages are on a Web server, anyone with a Web browser and a working Internet connection can see them.

Because visitors won't exactly flock to your site just because it exists on a Web server, though, this chapter shows you not only how to transfer your files to a Web server but also how to test your site, rate it (an optional step you can take to announce to the world that your Web pages contain, for example, no sexually-explicit content) and submit it to search engines.

Testing Your Site with the Personal Web Server

To help test your Web pages before you transfer them to your Web server (where everyone else can see them!), Microsoft devised a program called the Personal Web Server. This program enables you to set up a Web server on your own computer so that you can view Web pages that reside on your hard disk as if they were on the Web. Personal Web Server was introduced with Internet Explorer 4 and was then included with Windows 98. A substantially improved version of Personal Web Server comes with Internet Explorer versions 5 and higher.

After you publish your Web pages, you can test your site by loading it into a Web browser.

Starting Personal Web Server

To start Personal Web Server, choose Start⇨Programs⇨Internet Explorer⇨ Personal Web Server⇨Personal Web Manager. Personal Web Manager launches, as shown in Figure 6-1.

Figure 6-1:
You can use the Personal Web Server to test your Web pages before you publish them.

Personal Web Manager enables you to control the operation of Personal Web Server. Notice that Personal Web Manager indicates the status of the Web server; in Figure 6-1, the message "Web Publishing is on" indicates that Personal Web Server is active.

You can disable the Personal Web Server by clicking the Stop button. When you do, the message changes to "Web Publishing is off," and the Stop button changes to a Start button. Click this Start button to reactivate the server.

For more information about using Personal Web Server, call up the Personal Web Manager and then choose Help⇨Personal Web Server Topics.

Publishing a Web page to Personal Web Server

To publish your HTML files to Personal Web Server so that you can view them using your Web browser, just copy the file to the folder named `Inetpub\wwwroot` on your C drive (or wherever you installed Personal Web Server). Personal Web Server uses this folder as the root directory for your Web pages.

Alternatively, you can use Personal Web Server's built-in Publishing Wizard to publish Web files to your PWS folders. Just click the Publish icon in the Personal Web Manager window and follow the instructions.

Accessing Personal Web Server Web pages

To access a Personal Web Server Web page, use your computer's computer name as the URL. The computer name is the name you gave your computer when you installed Windows 95 or Windows 98. For example, if your computer name is Frank, you would type `Frank` as the URL to access the Personal Web Server default home page (which is named default.html).

To access a page other than the default home page, type the computer name, a slash, and the name of the page you want to display. For example, to display a page named sample.html, use `Frank/sample.html` as the URL.

If you're not sure what your computer name is, double-click the Personal Web Server icon in the Control Panel to call up the Personal Web Manager window, which lists the Web address of your home page under Personal Web Server.

To change the computer name used by Personal Web Server, open the Control Panel and double-click the Network icon to summon the Network dialog box. Click the Identification tab, type a new computer name in the Computer Name field, and then click OK. Your computer restarts with the new name in effect.

Publishing Your Web Pages

Before anyone on the Web can see your Web pages, you must first *upload*, or transfer, them from your computer to a Web server. You have a couple of options for making this transfer:

✦ **File Transfer Protocol (FTP).** If your computer is running either Windows 95 or Windows 98, you can use the command-line program called `ftp.exe` to upload your pages to a Web server.

✦ **Web Publishing Wizard.** If your computer is running Windows 98 or if you have Internet Explorer Version 4 or higher installed, you can use the Web Publishing Wizard to walk you through the process of uploading your files.

Most Web page creation tools, such as FrontPage 2002 and Dreamweaver, come with their own built-in utilities to help you upload your Web pages.

FTP

FTP, or *File Transfer Protocol,* is a commonly used method of *uploading,* or transferring, your Web files to a Web server.

What you need to know to use FTP

To use FTP to transfer your Web files to a Web server, you need to obtain the following information from your Internet Service Provider:

✦ The host name for the FTP server. This usually, but not always, starts with ftp, as in ftp.yourwebserver.com.

✦ The user-id and password you must use to sign on to the FTP server. This is probably the same user-id and password you use to sign on to your service provider's Web, e-mail, and news servers.

✦ The name of the directory in which you can copy your Web files. On the server I use, the directory is named PUBLIC_HTML. (A directory on an FTP server is similar to a folder in Windows 95 or Windows 98.)

The Windows 95/Windows 98 FTP client

If you use Windows 95 or Windows 98, you already have the software you need to access an FTP server. The following steps describe how to transfer files to a Web server using the FTP program that comes with Windows 95 and Windows 98:

1. **Collect all the files required for your Web site in one folder.**

   (If you have a lot of files — for example, 50 or more — you may want to consider using several subfolders to organize the files. But if you do, keep the folder structure as simple as possible.)

2. **Make sure that you have the information you need to access the FTP server, as described in the previous section, "What you need to know to use FTP."**

3. **Open an MS-DOS command window by choosing Start⇨Programs⇨ MS-DOS Prompt.**

4. **Use the CD (Change Directory) command to change to the folder that contains the Web files you want to transfer to the Web server.**

   For example, if your Web files are stored in a folder named \Webfiles, type the following command into the MS-DOS command window:

```
cd \Webfiles
```

5. **Type** ftp **followed by the name of your FTP host:**

```
ftp ftp.yourwebserver.com
```

A line similar to User (ftp.yourwebserver.com) appears in the MS-DOS command window, followed by a colon.

6. **Type your user ID.**

The Password: prompt appears.

7. **Type your password.**

After you successfully log in to the FTP server, you see an FTP prompt that looks like this:

```
ftp>
```

This prompt indicates that you're connected to the FTP server, and any commands you type are processed by the FTP server, not by the DOS command prompt on your own computer.

8. **Use the CD command to change to the directory to which you want to copy your files. For example:**

```
cd public_html
```

You can verify your current directory at any time by typing in the command PWD (short for *print working directory*) at the FTP command prompt.

Remember that this command is processed by the FTP server, so it changes the current directory on the FTP server, not on your own computer. The current directory for your own computer is still set to the directory you specified in Step 4.

9. **Use the** ascii **or** binary **command to set the appropriate file transfer mode.** If you plan to upload non-text files such as GIF files, JPG files, or sound files — or a mix of both text and non-text files — type binary at the FTP command prompt and press Return. If, on the other hand, you plan to upload only plain text (HTML) files, type ascii (short for ASCII text) at the FTP command prompt and press Return.

Setting the file transfer mode to ascii and uploading non-text files causes your non-text files to arrive at the Web server in a horribly mangled form. When in doubt, always set the file transfer mode to binary.

10. **Use the following MPUT command to copy all the files from the current directory on your computer (which you set in Step 4) to the current directory on the FTP server (which you set in Step 8):**

```
mput *.*
```

You're prompted to copy each file in the directory:

```
mput yourfile.html?
```

11. **Type** Y **and then press Enter to copy the file to the FTP server. Type** N **and then press Enter if you want to skip the file.**

After all the files have been copied, the FTP> prompt displays again.

12. **Type** bye **to disconnect from the FTP server.**

Windows 95, Windows 98, and Macintosh use the terms *folders* and *subfolders*. FTP uses the terms *directories* and *subdirectories* to refer to the same concept. Throughout the following discussion, keep in mind that the terms *subdirectory* and *subfolder* mean essentially the same thing, except that folders and sub-folders exist on Windows 95, Windows 98, or Macintosh computers, whereas directories and subdirectories exist on the FTP server.

If you have files stored in subfolders on your computer, you must copy those files to the FTP server separately. First, though, you must create the subdirectories on the FTP server. Use the MKDIR command to do that. For example, to create a subdirectory named IMAGES, type a command:

```
mkdir images
```

Now you can copy files to the new directory. First, use the CD command to change to the new directory:

```
cd images
```

Then, use the MPUT command to copy the files. You must specify the name of the subfolder that contains the files on your computer in the MPUT command:

```
mput images\*.*
```

You are prompted to copy the files in the IMAGES folder one at a time.

Partial FTP command summary

The following table lists the FTP commands you're most likely to use when you store your Web files on an FTP server:

Command	Description
ascii	Sets the transfer mode to ASCII text (for plain text files)
binary	Sets the transfer mode to binary (for non-text files)
bye	Disconnects from the FTP server and exits the FTP program
cd	Changes the current FTP server directory
delete	Deletes a file on the FTP server
dir	Displays the names of the files in the current FTP server directory

Command	Description
get	Copies a single file from the FTP server to your computer
help	Displays a list of commands (help command displays instructions for command)
mget	Copies multiple files from the FTP server to your computer
mkdir	Creates a new directory on the FTP server
mput	Copies multiple files from your computer to the FTP server
put	Copies a single file from your computer to the FTP server
rename	Renames a file on the FTP server
rmdir	Removes (deletes) a directory on the FTP server

Web Publishing Wizard

The Microsoft Web Publishing Wizard simplifies the task of transferring files from your computer to your Web server. Web Publishing Wizard comes with Internet Explorer versions 4 and higher; it also comes with Windows 98. If you don't have the Web Publishing Wizard, you can download it from www.microsoft.com/downloads/release.asp?ReleaseID=22658

Follow these steps to set up the Web Publishing Wizard for your Web site and copy the Web files to your Web server for the first time:

1. **Choose Start⇨Programs⇨Internet Explorer⇨Web Publishing Wizard.**

The Web Publishing Wizard springs to life, as shown in Figure 6-2.

Figure 6-2: You can use the Web Publishing Wizard to publish your Web pages.

2. **Click Next.**

The wizard displays the Select a File or Folder dialog box shown in Figure 6-3.

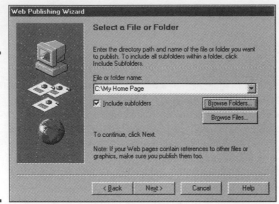

Figure 6-3:
You must
specify the
directory
that
contains the
files you
want to
publish.

3. **Type the name of the folder that contains the files you want to upload in the File or Folder Name field, or click the Browse Folders button to browse the folders on your hard disk.**

4. **If you want to include files from subfolders located within the folder you specify, click the Include Subfolders check box.**

5. **Click Next.**

6. **Type a name for your Web server in the Descriptive Name field.**

   You can use any name you want here.

7. **Click the Advanced button to summon the dialog box shown in Figure 6-4.**

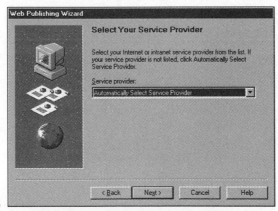

Figure 6-4:
To publish
your Web
pages, you
must specify
your
Internet
Service
Provider.

8. **Select the connection method your Internet Service Provider uses to upload files to the Web server.**

The caption associated with the dialog box is deceptive. The caption leads you to believe you use the dialog box to select a service provider (an ISP) — but the drop-down options pertain, instead, to the connection methods.

If you want the Web Publishing Wizard to determine automatically which type of server to use, leave the Service Provider field set to Automatically Select Service Provider. Otherwise, choose one of the options listed in the Service Provider drop-down list. The choices are FrontPage Extended Web, FTP, HTTP Post, and Microsoft Site Server Content Deployment. You'll have to ask your ISP which method to use. Most ISPs support FTP, so the rest of this procedure assumes that you select FTP in this step. If you select a different method, the information requested by the Web Publishing Wizard varies slightly from what this procedure shows.

9. **Click Next.**

The Specify the URL and Directory dialog box appears, as shown in Figure 6-5.

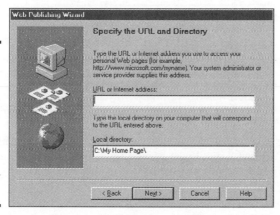

Figure 6-5: On this screen you specify your URL and the local directory where your Web pages are stored.

10. **Type the address of your Web page in the URL or Internet Address field. Then, in the Local Directory field, type the directory on your computer that contains your Web page files.**

11. **Click Next.**

The Specify the FTP Server and Subfolder dialog box appears, as shown in Figure 6-6.

Figure 6-6:
You must specify both an FTP server and the subfolder to which you want to transfer your files.

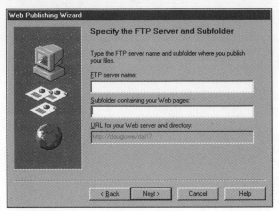

12. **Type the FTP server name and the name of the FTP server directory that will contain your Web files.** (Check with your ISP if you're unsure what to type in either of these fields.)

13. **Click Next.**

14. **Click Finish.**

The wizard asks you to enter a name and password in the dialog box that appears in Figure 6-7.

15. **Type a name and password.**

These fields contain the name and password to log onto your directory on the Web server. If you don't know this information (or have forgotten), ask your ISP.

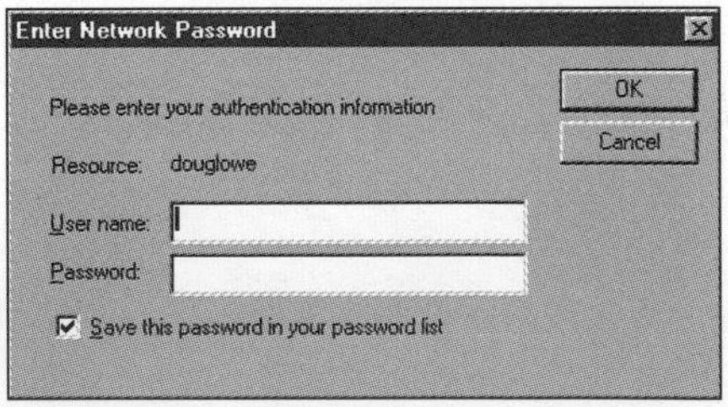

Figure 6-7:
On this screen you type in the user name and password for your FTP server.

Wait a moment while the Web Publishing Wizard connects to the FTP server and transfers your files. After the entire operation is finished, you see a dialog box like the one shown in Figure 6-8.

Figure 6-8:
The Web
Publishing
Wizard lets
you know
when it is
finished
publishing
your site.

16. **Click OK and celebrate.**

You're done.

The Web Publishing Wizard stores most of the information it gathers from you the first time you run it so that you don't have to type everything in each time you use the wizard.

Rating Your Site

Many Web users activate their Web browsers' content filtering features to ban access to sites that contain offensive material. For example, Internet Explorer includes a Content Advisor feature that enables users to prevent access to offensive Web sites.

Content Advisor uses a system of ratings similar to ratings used for movies, but the Web site ratings are more detailed. Web publishers voluntarily assign ratings to their Web pages for four categories: violence, nudity, sex, and language. The ratings are stored in special HTML tags that appear in the <HEAD> section of Web pages.

If you fail to provide a rating for your Web site, your site may be banned even if it doesn't contain offensive material. So it's a good idea to provide ratings for your site, even if your site is G-rated.

Internet ratings are overseen by an organization called the Recreational Software Advisory Council on the Internet, or RSACi. RSACi has an online service that simplifies the task of rating your site, and best of all, it's free. Just follow these steps:

1. Go to the RSACi home page at `www.rsac.org`.

2. Follow the links to register your site.

3. Type the site information requested by RSACi (your Web page URL, contact name, phone number, and so on).

   This information is kept private, so you don't have to worry about your address being sold to junk mailers.

4. Answer the questions about the content level of your Web site for language, sex, nudity, and violence.

   Answer truthfully so you can give your site an accurate rating.

   After you finish, the RSACi Web page displays a snippet of HTML that contains the appropriate tags to add to your Web page.

5. Use the mouse to highlight these HTML lines and then press Ctrl+C to copy them onto the clipboard.

6. Open your home page in your favorite HTML editor, switch to HTML view so you can see the actual HTML code, and paste the RSACi tags into the <HEAD> section of the page.

If you want to let people know that you have rated your site, flip back to the RSACi page that contains the HTML tags you copied in Step 5. On that page, you'll find a "We rated with RSACi" graphic. Save this graphic to your hard disk and then insert it into your Web page.

Submitting Your Site to Search Services

Submitting your site to the major search services (also known as *search engines*) is like taking out a Yellow Pages ad: doing so helps Web surfers find your site. You should try to get your page listed in as many search services as possible.

The following table describes how to add your site to several of the popular Web search services. To list your Web site in the search service, go to the URL and click the link indicated in the last column of the table.

Search Service	URL	Click This Link
AltaVista	www.altavista.com	Submit a Site
Excite	www.excite.com	Submit a Site
Open Directory	dmoz.org	Add URL
Lycos	www.lycos.com	Add Your Site to Lycos
MSN Web Search	search.msn.com	Submit a Site
Yahoo!	www.yahoo.com	How to Suggest a Site
Google	www.google.com	All About Google⇨Submitting Your Site

For more information about getting your Web site noticed, refer to Chapter 8 of *Creating Web Pages For Dummies,* 5th Edition.

Submitting your site to search services isn't something you can do once and then forget about. To avoid having your site dropped from a search service's database, you need to resubmit your site every six months or so.

Chapter 7: Publicizing Your Web Site

In This Chapter

- ✔ Springing for a domain name
- ✔ Understanding search services
- ✔ Optimizing HTML meta tags
- ✔ Getting other sites to link to yours
- ✔ Advertising your site
- ✔ Exploring site statistics

S ome folks mistakenly think that as soon as they publish a Web site, the world will beat a path to their cyberdoor. Unfortunately, getting Web surfers to visit your site isn't quite that easy! Registering your Web site with a bunch of search engines (as I describe in Chapter 6, "Publishing Your Web Site") makes it easier for people actively hunting for your site to find you on the Web. But to attract visitors to your site who don't already know who you are and what your site is all about, you must do more than just submit your site to search engines: you must publicize your site. This chapter shows you how.

Springing for a Domain Name

The single most effective thing you can do to promote your own Web site is splash out for your own domain name. For example, `janedoe.com` (if your name happens to be Jane Doe and you're creating a personal Web site) or `mnsoccer.org` (if you happen to be creating a Web site for a Minnesota-based soccer association).

Why spend extra money on a domain name? Because typing your domain name into a browser or search engine is the way most visitors will find your site. If you *don't* register your own domain name, you take pot luck: Web hosts assign you a domain name, which may be long and tricky to spell, like `www.someFreeWebHost.com/~community/janedoe23423.html` As you may expect, it's much easier for prospective visitors to remember (or guess) and type `www.janedoe.com` into their Web browsers than `www.someFreeWebHost.com/~community/janedoe23423.html`.

If you're planning to use your Web site for business-related reasons, springing for your own domain name helps demonstrate your commitment to a professional image, much the same as investing in nice letterhead or a well-written résumé.

Choosing a domain name

Registering a domain name is like getting a driver's license: it's good for a couple of years before you have to renew. To select a domain name you'll be happy with for awhile, consider the following suggestions:

✦ **Make it meaningful.** Popular choices include your name (or a short variation, if your name happens to be really long) and the name of your business or organization.

✦ **Keep it simple.** With domain names, the shorter and easier to spell, the better. And try to resist the temptation to use cute spellings. `FatTuesday.com`, for example, is a lot easier for Web surfers to remember and spell than `phatttuzeday.com`.

✦ **Think ahead.** If you select `joesDonuts.com` as your domain name and decide a few months from now to sell your donut shop and take up goat ranching, your domain name will be obsolete.

Domain names are going fast! To find out if the domain name you're considering is still available, visit `www.register.com` and type in your selection.

Registering a domain name

The cost of registering and hosting a domain name has dropped like a stone in the last couple of years. (Yeah!) The good news is that registration services and Internet Service Providers are currently engaged in a price war to get your business. The bad news is that you may find it difficult to figure out who offers the best deal because many companies bundle the price of domain name registration with other services. Here are a few options for you to explore:

✦ **Internet Service Providers.** These days, many Internet Service Providers register your domain name for you for a small additional charge. Fees vary widely, so if you haven't already found space for your Web site, make sure to compare prices carefully. (See Chapter 1, "Finding Space for Your Web Site," for tips on finding a company to host your Web site.)

✦ **Registration services.** If you're the type of person who enjoys doing things yourself (especially if doing so means saving a buck or two), you may want to look into a do-it-yourself registration service such as `www.register.com` or `www.dotster.com`.

Because some Internet service providers charge a domain name transfer fee, registering your domain name yourself and *then* selecting an Internet service provider could turn out to be more expensive in the long run than paying for a package deal.

Understanding Search Services

Registering your site with search services such as Yahoo! and AltaVista, as I explain in Chapter 6, "Publishing Your Web Site," is the first step of any successful site publicity campaign. To make the most of your search service listing, however, you need to make sure that you code your HTML properly — *before* you submit your site.

Over the last few years, the number of Web sites has mushroomed to titanic proportions, and search services have reacted by merging with one another and by tweaking the way they examine site submissions. The result? These days, submitting to search services has become both art and science — especially for those hoping to win a coveted high ranking.

Despite all these changes, the following are still the three most important things you can do to help search services classify your site properly, in order of importance:

1. **Specify a descriptive page title.** Search services first examine the title of your Web page. (By *title* I mean the text you place between the beginning and ending HTML <TITLE> tags, and which appears in the browser window's title bar when your page is loaded.)

2. **Include appropriate page content.** After the title, search services look at the text that appears on your Web page.

3. **Add meaningful HTML meta tags.** Finally, search services scan special HTML tags, called *meta tags*, to decide how to classify your site.

Although submitting your site to many search services is still free, more and more search services are beginning to charge a fee for listing your Web site.

Specifying a descriptive HTML title

A good Web page title lets readers know precisely what they can expect to find on that Web page. (A good Web page title also helps prospective readers find that Web page because search services use the words in the title to classify that page.)

Consider this example. If you're creating a Web site that describes your book, you might want to place a title of "When Computers Kill: A Technical Thriller by Novelist Jane Doe" in the browser window title bar, rather than "My Book."

You create a title for your Web page by placing text inside the beginning and ending TITLE tags:

```
<HEAD>
<TITLE>When Computers Kill: A Technical Thriller by
Novelist Jane Doe</TITLE>
</HEAD>
```

You always place the title of your Web page between the beginning and ending HEAD tags, as shown in the example in this section.

Optimizing Web page text

To help ensure that search services classify your Web site properly, you need to make sure that the text of your Web page includes your *keywords* (the words you expect prospective viewers to search for your site with).

You include text in your Web page using the beginning and ending BODY tags.

The following example shows you the text you might include in your Web page if you're a novelist who's just written a technical thriller:

```
<BODY>
In the tradition of Michael Crichton and Tom Clancy, novelist
    Jane Doe's latest critically acclaimed technical thriller,
    When Computers Kill, confronts the specter of total anni-
    hilation as the world's computers turn on their owners
    and ...
</BODY>
```

If you think that repeating keywords in the body of your Web page might help you achieve a higher search engine ranking, you're right — sort of. Most search services count the repetitions of keywords. If they count more than a few repetitions, they may assume the creator of the Web page is trying to pull a fast one and refuse to list the site at all! The best advice: don't intentionally overdo keywords. Just make sure you sprinkle keywords naturally throughout the text of your Web page.

Using HTML meta tags

HTML defines a special tag (the <META> tag) for search services and Web directories to scan for hints on what your site is all about. There are dozens of different ways you can define a <META> tag, but the following two, which define the description and keywords you want to associate with your site, are far and away the most useful.

Here's an example:

```
<META NAME="description" CONTENT="When Computers Kill is the
    latest novel from award-winning author and novelist Jane
    Doe.  Read an excerpt and order your own copy at www.
    janedoe.com.">
<META NAME="keywords" CONTENT="Jane Doe When Computers Kill
    technical thriller novel">
```

Adding the preceding code snippet to an HTML file (and then submitting the HTML page to search services, as I describe in Chapter 6, "Publishing Your Web Site") enables readers to search for Jane Doe's novel by typing `techni-cal`, `thriller`, `novel`, and so on, into a search engine or directory. Then, when a link to Jane's Web page appears in the result list of a search service, it appears next to the description "When Computers Kill is the latest novel from award-winning novelist . . ."

Exploring automated submission tools

Submitting your site to search services and Web directories can be time-consuming. Not only do some of these services change their submission criteria every two seconds (okay, maybe it just feels that often!), but after your site is listed, you need to resubmit occasionally to make sure your site doesn't drop off of the search services' gigantic (and growing) databases.

You can save yourself some time by submitting your Web site to a submission service such as Submit It (`www.submit-it.com`). This service can submit your Web site to more than 400 search engines for a modest fee (as I write this, the fee is $59 for five URLs).

Going Beyond Search Services

Getting your site listed with search services is a great first step in any site publicity plan. If you really want to pull in the visitors, though, you'll have to do more. Two of the best ways to publicize your site are:

✦ Getting other people to link to your site from theirs

✦ Advertising your site

After you get a few links and start advertising your site, you can use site statistics to examine and fine-tune your online publicity efforts.

Getting links

One of the most effective means of promoting your site online — getting related, high-traffic sites link to yours — is also one of the most time-intensive.

Here are steps you can take to get other sites to link to yours:

✦ **Research the Web and come up with a list of sites that are similar in content to yours.** For example, if your site is devoted to Australian shepherds, you might include the American Kennel Club and a couple of dog training sites on your list. The more compatible sites you can find, the better.

✦ **Send a note to each site requesting a link.** Some folks swear by formal press releases, but a brief, personalized e-mail request to the Webmaster should do the trick. For best results, word your request cordially and be sure to point out precisely what makes your site worth linking to (after all, you're asking someone to do you a favor!).

Advertising your site

Online or off, if you want somebody to know about something, what do you do? You advertise!

Many for-profit Web sites sell advertising much like newspapers and magazines do — by the inch. Beyond paid advertising, though, you can take the following free steps to get the word out about your site.

✦ **Add your domain name to your e-mail signature.** One of the easiest and most effective ways to advertise your site is to include your domain name, along with a short description, in your e-mail signature. Virtually all e-mail programs let you create and modify a personalized signature, or *sig,* file. Unfortunately, every e-mail program is different, so I can't give you the precise steps for changing your signature; instead, you need to check the documentation for your particular e-mail program.

✦ **Participate in newsgroups, lists, and chats.** Newsgroups, lists, and chat rooms are electronic gathering places where folks with a common interest get together to share opinions and information. By participating and sharing your expertise on a particular topic — for example, cheese making — you can become acquainted with other cheese lovers who, chances are, will be delighted to know about the personal Web site you just created, called All About Cheese.

Publicizing your site offline

Just because your Web site is online doesn't mean your publicity efforts have to be restricted to cyberspace. Some obvious choices for *meat-space* (real-world) publicity include adding your domain name to your business cards, letterhead, and résumé. Some folks get *really* creative with their site publicity, slapping their domain names on everything from t-shirts to cars!

Visit www.liszt.com or www.deja.com to find newsgroups, lists, and chat rooms on virtually every topic you can think of.

Don't hesitate to mention your site to an appropriate audience, but never, ever *spam*. *Spam* means sending unsolicited messages to inappropriate audiences; you can think of it as the electronic equivalent of junk mail. For example, posting a message containing news of your latest cheese creation to alt.collecting.beanie-babies, or to a chat room devoted to single parents, would be considered spam. If you're not sure whether your message is appropriate for a particular newsgroup, list, or chat room, *lurk* (read others' messages without contributing) for awhile to get the feel for the community — and *then*, if it seems appropriate, jump in.

Using site statistics

If you're serious about reaching readers with a Web site, you need to know what site statistics are — and how to use them.

Understanding site statistics

Site statistic software sits on the same Web server your Web site files sit on. (For help in finding a Web server, check out Chapter 1, "Creating a Successful Web Site.") Every time a reader loads or interacts with your Web page, statistic software logs the interaction. The kinds of statistics typically logged include:

✦ **How many *hits* each page of your site gets, and when.**

Each *hit* corresponds to a person loading one of your Web pages into his or her browser.

This statistic is useful because it lets you know which of your sites is the most popular — and, therefore, a good candidate for frequent updates. You can also use this statistic to figure out whether your publicity campaign is working. For example, if you spent all weekend telling everyone you know about your Web site, you can verify whether your time was well spent by checking this statistic to see whether your site logged more hits after your whirlwind campaign than before.

✦ **Which site *referred* the visitor to your site.**

This statistic lets you know which links your visitors follow to find you on the Web. You can use this information to concentrate your link-getting efforts on the types of sites that are leading the most visitors to yours. (For tips on getting links, see "Getting links" in this chapter.)

✦ **How many times surfers tried to view your site, but couldn't (and why).**

After you publish a site, you may think your site is always available for viewing. Theoretically, consistently available Web sites exist — but in the real world, power goes out, computer hardware crashes, and Internet service provider staff occasionally make mistakes.

This statistic gives you insight into just how often your Web host is unavailable. (You may find that free services tend to be unavailable just a tad more often than for-pay services.)

✦ **What country your site visitors are from.**

You can use this statistic to find out if your site is being visited heavily by readers in Germany, for example. If that's the case, you may want to consider translating your site copy into German.

✦ **Which make and model of browser surfers are using to view your site.**

Internet Explorer and Netscape aren't the only browsers in town, although they are the two most popular. Each browser offers goodies that the other doesn't (Internet Explorer, for example, supports a different Java Virtual Machine than Netscape supports).

You can use this statistic to determine whether the majority of your viewers are using one particular browser to view your Web pages. If this is the case, you can take full advantage of the extra goodies that particular browser provides.

Accessing site statistics

Site statistic software must be installed on a Web server; it doesn't work if it's installed on your computer. The company that hosts your Web site controls which statistics package you have access to and how you access it. All you have to do is contact them and ask for instructions.

Different software reports statistics different, so be sure to ask your Web host for an interpretation guide if you have any difficulty figuring out what all the different numbers and charts mean.

Index

Symbols

A

B

C

D

E

F

G

Notes

Book II

HTML

The 5th Wave   By Rich Tennant

"Give him air! Give him air! He'll be okay. He's just been exposed to some raw HTML code. It must have accidently flashed across his screen from the server."

Contents at a Glance

Chapter 1: Creating an HTML Page

In This Chapter

- ✔ Understanding how HTML works: Text and tags
- ✔ Using HTML structure tags
- ✔ Getting familiar with basic HTML tags

*W*hether you choose to create your HTML pages by hand or by using one of the many fine HTML editors on the market, you want to be familiar with the HTML basics I present in this chapter. Why? Because understanding the basics — which HTML tags are necessary to create a bona fide HTML file, which tags are the most common and why, and how tags work in general — helps you create your pages in record time. Being familiar with the tags you see in this chapter even helps you catch errors that your HTML editing tool may make!

If you haven't already, go ahead and open your favorite text editor and browser so that you can try out the examples that follow. The examples help you begin to put in tags and set up your first HTML document.

Understanding HTML Basics: Text and Tags

HTML documents basically contain the following three things:

- ✦ Text that you're working with
- ✦ Tags that determine document elements such as headings, lists, and paragraphs
- ✦ Tags that insert other objects, such as images, style sheets, sounds, little programs called applets, and movies (although many of these are outside the scope of this book)

You use most of the HTML tags described in this chapter in pairs — one tag goes before the text, and the other tag goes after the text, as in the following example:

```
<TAG>whatever your text is</TAG>
```

✦ The first tag *(the opening tag)* indicates the beginning of a tag that you're applying to some of the text in your document.

✦ The second tag *(the closing tag)* indicates the end of an effect that you're applying.

Not all HTML tags require a closing tag, although many do. An example of an effect that doesn't require a closing tag is `<HR>`, which displays an attractive separator called a *horizontal rule* on a Web page. No closing `</HR>` tag is required to display a horizontal rule.

The tags affect everything between the opening and closing tag.

Opening and closing tags are generally identical, except that the closing tag has a forward slash (/) before the tag name. The tag name is always exactly the same in the opening and closing tags.

Sometimes opening tags also include an *attribute,* which is just an additional bit of information that further specifies information such as color, alignment, or the text that should appear to describe an image. So, in such a case, an attribute appears in the initial tag, as follows:

```
<TAG ATTRIBUTE="More Info">whatever your text is</TAG>
```

HTML tags are *case-insensitive,* which means that you can type the tags by using either UPPERCASE or lowercase letters, or BoTh. Typing the tags in all caps is a good idea: doing so helps you differentiate between the tags and text, particularly after your HTML document becomes pages and pages long.

Formatting text

Browsers disregard all formatting that's not incorporated by using *markup tags.* For example, they ignore extra spaces in the HTML document or blank lines that you use to move things down the page. As a result, the extra spaces, lines, or tabs that you put in don't affect your document's appearance.

You, for example, can type your line as follows:

```
<TAG>hill of beans information</TAG>
```

Or even like the following example:

```
<TAG>
hill
    of beans information
</TAG>
```

The next generation of HTML: XHTML

Recently released as a recommendation by the World Wide Web Consortium (`www.w3.org`), XHTML 1.0 is the reformulation of HTML 4 as an XML application. XHTML tags and attributes are almost identical to those in HTML; the difference is that XHTML is a stricter, tidier version of HTML. (In other words, sloppy programming practices you can get away with in HTML don't fly in XHTML.) When XHTML is fully supported by Web browsers — which should be soon — you'll notice the following changes in how you code your Web pages:

- XHTML tags are all lowercase.
- All XHTML tags must be closed.

Note: for more information on XML, check out Book 9, "XML," in this reference guide.

Book II
Chapter 1

Creating an
HTML Page

Nesting tags

In many cases, you may want to nest tags inside other tags. *Nesting tags* simply means enclosing tags within tags. By nesting tags, you apply multiple tags to the same bit of text.

Suppose that you want to make text both bold and italic. You can't achieve this effect by using only one tag — there isn't a "BOLD-n-ITALICS HERE" tag. Instead, you nest one tag inside the other, as the following example shows:

```
<B><I>more hill of beans information</I></B>
```

Notice that the tag that appears first (in this case, the bold tag) also appears last. If a tag starts first, it ends last. If a tag is right beside the text on the front end, it's right beside the text on the back end as well.

Using HTML Structure Tags

This section introduces you to a group of HTML tags that you use in every HTML document that you create. The first tags in this group are *structure tags* (so named because they define and describe a document's structure). Although most structure tags do not generally affect the appearance of the document or the information contained within the document, they do help some browsers and HTML-editing programs identify document characteristics.

For most HTML documents, you use the five structure tags, listed in the following table and described in the following sections.

HTML Tag	Purpose	Use in Pairs?
`<!DOCTYPE HTML PUBLIC "-//W3C//DTD HTML 4.01 Frameset//EN" "http://www.w3.org/TR/html4/frameset.dtd">`	Identifies document as an HTML document and specifies HTML version. Mandatory in all HTML documents.	No
`<HTML>. . .</HTML>`	Defines the document as an HTML document.	Yes
`<HEAD>. . .</HEAD>`	Includes introductory information about the document.	Yes
`<TITLE>. . .</TITLE>`	Indicates the document title. Mandatory in all HTML documents.	Yes
`<META NAME="KEYWORDS" CONTENT=". . .">`	Indicates keywords that describe the document.	No
`<META NAME="DESCRIPTION" CONTENT=". . .">`	Provides a short summary or description of the document.	No
`<BODY>. . .</BODY>`	Encloses all elements within the main portion of the document.	Yes

The !DOCTYPE tag

The `!DOCTYPE` tag identifies the document as an HTML document. It appears at the top of HTML documents and notes that the document conforms to specific HTML standards — in this example, to the final HTML Version 4.01 standards. If you use HTML editing programs, they probably put the `!DOCTYPE` tag in automatically. If they don't, however, make sure that you type the `!DOCTYPE` tag at the top of all your documents.

Suppose that you want to create an HTML document about making a water balloon. Enter the `!DOCTYPE` tag as follows:

```
<!DOCTYPE HTML PUBLIC "-//W3C//DTD HTML 4.01
    Frameset//EN"
    "http://www.w3.org/TR/html4/frameset.dtd">
```

The <HTML> tag

The `<HTML>` tag encloses everything except the `!DOCTYPE` tag in every document. This tag, as the name suggests, indicates that the document is HTML. If you don't specify HTML, the browser might conceivably not read the tags as tags. Instead, the browser might read the tags as text, in which case, the document looks pretty much as it does in the text editor. Yuck!

In the water balloon page example, enter the <HTML> tags at the beginning and end of the document, as shown in the following example:

```
<!DOCTYPE HTML PUBLIC "-//W3C//DTD HTML 4.01
    Frameset//EN"
    "http://www.w3.org/TR/html4/frameset.dtd">
<HTML>
...all the stuff about making water
    balloons will go here eventually...
</HTML>
```

The <HEAD> and <TITLE> tags

The <HEAD> tag is part of what many browsers use to identify or reference the document. For many HTML developers, the <HEAD> tag seems completely useless. Keep in mind that although this tag doesn't have a visible application for creating an HTML document, it does have a technical application — it contains information about the document that does not actually appear within the browser window.

The <TITLE> tag, one of those about-this-document bits, goes within the <HEAD> tags. This tag is required by the HTML specification to apply a title of your choice to the document. Titles appear in the title bar of a browser window. Make your title as descriptive as you can so that people can find or identify your documents more easily on the Internet.

Furthering the example of the water balloon document, add the <HEAD> and <TITLE> tags as shown in the following example:

```
<!DOCTYPE HTML PUBLIC "-//W3C//DTD HTML 4.01
    Frameset//EN"
    "http://www.w3.org/TR/html4/frameset.dtd">
<HTML>
<HEAD><TITLE>Making Effective Water Balloons
</TITLE></HEAD>
. . .all the stuff about making water balloons
    will go here eventually. . .
</HTML>
```

Notice that the <HEAD> and <TITLE> tags appear immediately after the initial <HTML> tag.

The <META> tag

The <META> tag appears in dozens of permutations and combinations, only a couple of which will have any significant effect at all on most HTML developers. These tags, cleverly positioned right alongside the <TITLE> between the <HEAD> tags, provide more about-this-document information. This meta-information fuels Internet directories (such as Lycos at www.lycos.com)

and search services (such as AltaVista at `www.altavista.com`) because providing the information makes categorizing and finding your documents easier. Although you don't have to include these tags, you'll greatly improve your chances of being found by people "out there" if you do.

Taking the water balloon document one more step, add the `<META NAME= "KEYWORDS" CONTENT="...">` and `<META NAME="DESCRIPTION" CONTENT= "...">` tags, as shown in the following example:

```
<!DOCTYPE HTML PUBLIC "-//W3C//DTD HTML 4.01
    Frameset//EN"
    "http://www.w3.org/TR/html4/frameset.dtd">
<HTML>
<HEAD><TITLE>Making Effective Water Balloons
</TITLE>
<META NAME="KEYWORDS" CONTENT="water balloon
    surprise splash splat cat oops sorry
    ouch cold wet">
<META NAME="DESCRIPTION" CONTENT="This document
    provides basic instructions for developing and
    using water balloons.">
</HEAD>
. . .all the stuff about making water balloons
    will go here eventually. . .
</HTML>
```

The <BODY> tag

The `<BODY>` tag surrounds all the information that's actually supposed to be visible to your readers — the real heart of the document. Everything you want people to see must be contained between the `<BODY>` and `</BODY>` tags.

Place the `<BODY>` tag just before the information that you want to put into your HTML document and then just before the closing `</HTML>` tag. Technically, all other tags that you use are nested between the `<BODY>` and `</BODY>` tags.

You actually begin the water balloon project by adding the `<BODY>` tags, as follows:

```
<!DOCTYPE HTML PUBLIC "-//W3C//DTD HTML 4.01
    Frameset//EN"
    "http://www.w3.org/TR/html4/frameset.dtd">
<HTML>
<HEAD><TITLE>Making Effective Water Balloons
</TITLE>
<META NAME="KEYWORDS" CONTENT="water balloon
    surprise splash splat cat oops sorry
    ouch cold wet">
```

```
<META NAME="DESCRIPTION" CONTENT="This document
    provides basic instructions for developing and
    using water balloons.">
</HEAD>
<BODY>
. . .all the stuff about making water balloons. . .
</BODY>
</HTML>
```

And that's all, folks! Those are the main structure tags that you use to create all your HTML documents.

Getting Familiar with Basic HTML Tags

Basic HTML tags are the ones that enable you to create simple, functional effects in your HTML documents. This section describes the tags necessary for making headings, paragraphs, and lists and for emphasizing and setting off text.

Making headings

HTML offers you six choices in headings, labeled as <H1> through <H6>. <H1> is the largest and boldest of the headings, and <H6> is the smallest and least bold (most timid?) one. You can use these headings to show a hierarchy of information (such as the headings in this book).

HTML Tag	Effect	Use in Pairs?
<H1>. . .</H1>	Heading 1	Yes
<H2>. . .</H2>	Heading 2	Yes
<H6>. . .</H6>	Heading 6	Yes

And as with all other paired tags, the text that you want to include goes between the tags. For example: <H1>Here is my heading</H1>

Making paragraphs

By using HTML, you can separate information into paragraphs. The HTML paragraph tag, <P>, indicates the beginning and the end of a paragraph of text, respectively, as the following table shows.

HTML Tag	Effect	Use in Pairs?
<P>. . .</P>	Indicates a paragraph.	</P> is optional (but including it is good programming practice).

Emphasizing text

After you write something, you may want to make some of the words within the text stand out. HTML offers several options for doing this, including emphasizing text and adding bold and italics to text. The following table describes some of these options.

HTML Tag	Effect	Use in Pairs?
`<EM>. . .</EM>`	Adds emphasis (usually appears as italic).	Yes
`<STRONG>. . .</STRONG>`	Adds strong emphasis (usually appears as bold).	Yes
`<B>. . .</B>`	Adds boldface.	Yes
`<I>. . .</I>`	Adds italics.	Yes

Making lists

Often you may want to provide information in lists rather than in paragraphs. Providing information in lists is especially valuable in HTML documents because lists enable the reader to skim through information quickly without needing to wade through paragraphs of text. And for you, the writer, making lists is an easy way to help organize your information and provide easy links to other pages.

Making lists is a two-part process. First, you must add a pair of tags to specify that the information is to appear in a list. You can specify, for example, an ordered (or numbered) list, `<OL>. . .</OL>`; or an unordered (or bulleted) list, `<UL>. . .</UL>`.

Then, you must specify each line of the list, called line items. Just put the `<LI>` tag at the beginning of each line, where you want the number or bullet to be. No closing tag is required here.

The following table shows the tags you use to create lists.

HTML Tag	Effect	Use in Pairs?
`<LI>`	Identifies each item in a list.	No
`<OL>. . .</OL>`	Specifies ordered (numbered) lists.	Yes
`<UL>. . .</UL>`	Specifies unordered (bulleted) lists.	Yes

To add an unordered (bulleted) list of materials to the "Making Effective Water Balloons" page, place the following HTML code between the <BODY> and </BODY> tags as shown:

```
<BODY>
<UL>
<LI>Water
<LI>Big, big balloon
<LI>Balloon ties (optional)
<LI>Second-story window
<LI>Target below window
</UL>
</BODY>
```

The bulleted list in Figure 1-1 shows the results of adding these tags and text.

**Book II
Chapter 1**

**Creating an
HTML Page**

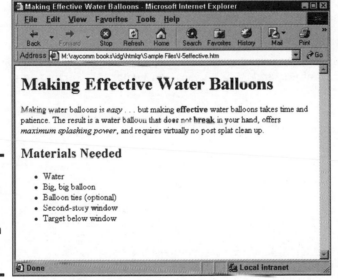

Figure 1-1:
You use the
<UL> and
</UL> tags
to create an
unordered
(bullet) list.

Notice that the list tags don't have <P> tags around them. If you have a list, you don't need a <P>.

To add an ordered list of instructions on how to make effective water balloons, you simply use the <OL> tags, as follows:

1. **Add opening and closing <OL> tags where the list appears, as in the following example.**

```
<H2>Instructions</H2>
<OL>
</OL>
```

2. **Add <LI> tags and text for each item, as follows:**

```
<H2>Instructions</H2>
<OL>
<LI>Fill balloon with water.
<LI>Tie balloon using a tie or by making a knot.
<LI>Go to second-story window.
<LI>Aim at spot below window.
<LI>Drop balloon.
</OL>
```

The result is a numbered list containing five items.

You can add attributes (extra information) to your list tags to control what the bullets look like, what kind of numbers (Roman, capital letters, regular Arabic numbers, and so on) appear, and what the starting number is for sequential lists.

Chapter 2: Setting Background and Text Characteristics

In This Chapter

- ✓ Applying a color background
- ✓ Applying an image background
- ✓ Setting document text colors
- ✓ Specifying text alignment
- ✓ Using font type specifications

*I*n this chapter you see how to set background and text characteristics, which can help you liven up your pages with various color and alignment options.

This chapter assumes you have a basic understanding of how HTML tags work. If you don't, check out Chapter 1, "Creating an HTML Page," then flip back here to continue. Before beginning to work through the examples in this chapter, make sure that you have your browser and text editor open and ready to create a new document.

Because the formatting attributes and tags in this chapter work with nearly all current browsers but are not recommended in HTML 4.0, consider using style sheets for all of your formatting needs. (For a more in-depth look at style sheets, see Chapter 8 in this book, "Developing Style Sheets.")

Applying a Color Background

To include a background color, all you need to do is insert the `BGCOLOR=` attribute in the opening `<BODY>` tag.

The following table shows the attribute used to specify background color in an HTML document.

HTML Attribute	Effect	Use in Pairs? (for the `<BODY>` tag)
`BGCOLOR="#rrggbb"`	Specifies the color name or number of the background.	No

Here's an example of how specifying a background color of sky blue might look:

```
<HEAD><TITLE>Fleabag Kitty</TITLE></HEAD>
<BODY BGCOLOR="#3399CC">With a scratcha scratcha here and a
    scratcha scratcha there...
</BODY>
```

#3399CC is an RGB value that translates to "sky blue," but you can substitute any RGB value. To get a black background, for example, you use #000000. (If you *do* specify a black background, look at the "Setting Document Text Colors" later in this chapter to find out how to set the text to a non-black color.)

Alternatively, you can specify some colors by name. The following colors work in most browsers: aqua, black, blue, fuchsia, gray, green, lime, maroon, navy, olive, purple, red, silver, teal, white, and yellow. The code would look something like BGCOLOR="purple".

So just where do you come up with the RGB values? Try one of the following two ways:

✦ **Find a list of RGB numbers provided on the Web.** If you browse enough on the Web, you're likely to find general sources of information that provide you with lists of commonly used Web page features, including RGB numbers, complete with samples. One to try: www.web-source.net/ 216_color_chart.htm

✦ **Look for RGB values in your image-editing or paint software.** Many of these packages offer you the option of altering the colors with which you're working and provide you with the RGB value for the colors that you choose. Look in the color-related screens for RGB values.

RGB stands for *red, green, blue.* RGB values string together three hexadecimal numbers representing the red, green, and blue components, respectively, of a color.

Applying an Image Background

In addition to using simple colors for backgrounds, you can use images as backgrounds. To do so, you specify a URL pointing to an image for the BACKGROUND attribute of the <BODY> tag. You can specify either a *relative* URL or an *absolute* URL:

✦ A *relative* URL is a URL that points to a file located in or below the same directory as the Web page: for example, `picture.gif`.

✦ An *absolute* URL is a URL that points to a file located anywhere on your computer: for example, `/mypictures/picture.gif`.

HTML Attribute (for <BODY> tag)	Effect	Use in Pairs?
BACKGROUND="..."	Places an image as a background.	No

Here's an example of specifying an image for the background. (See Chapter 1 for more information on the `<BODY>` tag.)

```
<HEAD><TITLE>Fleabag Kitty</TITLE></HEAD>
<BODY BACKGROUND="flea.gif">With a scratcha scratcha here and
    a scratcha scratcha there...</BODY>
</HTML>
```

Figure 2-1 shows the flea.gif image (one flea) tiled throughout the page.

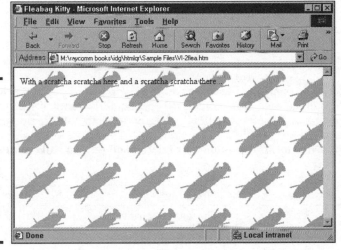

Figure 2-1: Using the BACKGROUND attribute of the <BODY> tag to specify a background image.

Background images, such as the flea.gif image, that do not fill the entire background are tiled to cover all the available space; that is, copies of the image are automatically placed together like a tile floor. The background image in the example is really only one flea — the copies are done automatically by the browser.

Finding Images to Use

Coming up with images to use for a background is about as easy as using simple colors. The only difference is that you use an image file rather than just a color number. Here are two ways to find background images:

+ **Design your own.** You may want to use a background image that's specific to the Web site you're creating. We strongly suggest doing so if you have any graphics talent at all. (If you do what we do and make fleas that look like roaches, check out the other options.)

+ **Look for image or background CDs or disks in your local software store.** Many CDs chock-full of cool stock images are available, at varying prices. Make sure the images you choose are, indeed, *stock* images, which are images you can freely use without obtaining additional copyright permission. Putting non-stock, copyrighted images on your Web site, by contrast, is immoral, illegal, and proven to cause hair to grow on your palms.

Make sure that you choose simple backgrounds — ones with no more than a few subtle colors or with only a few elements. Busy backgrounds make reading difficult for your users.

Setting Document Text Colors

In addition to changing the background of Web pages, you can also change the color of the text. This technique is particularly handy if you've used a background on which the default colors of text and links do not show up well.

The following table shows the attributes used to color text in an HTML document.

HTML Attribute	Effect	Use in Pairs?
TEXT="#RRGGBB"	Changes color of the body text.	No
LINK="#RRGGBB"	Changes color of the link.	No
ALINK="#RRGGBB"	Changes color of the active link.	No
VLINK="#RRGGBB"	Changes color of the visited link.	No

You fill in a color number where "#RRGGBB" is indicated, as shown in the following example in "Changing text colors."

Changing text colors

To change text colors on your Web page, you specify an RGB value for the TEXT attribute of the <BODY> tag:

```
<BODY BGCOLOR="#3399CC" TEXT="#FFFFFF">With a scratcha
    scratcha here and a scratcha scratcha there...
</BODY>
```

Changing link colors

To change link colors on your Web page, you specify an RGB color value for the ALINK (*active,* or normal) attribute of the <BODY> tag and the VLINK (visited) attribute of the <BODY> tag, as the following code shows:

```
<BODY BGCOLOR="#3399CC" TEXT="#FFFFFF"
    LINK="#FF0000" ALINK="#FFFF00"
    VLINK="#8C1717">With a scratcha scratcha here and a
    scratcha scratcha there...
</BODY>
```

Specifying Text Alignment

In addition to recoloring text and links, you can also move text around so that it's not all aligned on the left. You can align headings, paragraphs, other text, and images by using the attributes in the following table.

Keep in mind that although most browsers support these attributes, not all do, so your text may not be aligned correctly in some browsers. Always try out designs in more than one browser to make sure that your design works the way you think it should.

The following table presents the attributes used to control text alignment.

HTML Attribute	Effect	Use in Pairs?
ALIGN="CENTER"	Centers text within the left and right margins.	No
ALIGN="RIGHT"	Aligns text on the right margin.	No

You don't need to add an attribute if you want the element aligned left. Browsers align text to the left unless you tell them to do otherwise.

If you want to use center and right alignment for headings, paragraphs, and images, follow these steps:

1. **Start your HTML page, which should look similar to the following example:**

```
<!DOCTYPE HTML PUBLIC "-//W3C//DTD HTML 4.01
    Frameset//EN"
    "http://www.w3.org/TR/html4/frameset.dtd">
    <HTML>
<HEAD><TITLE>Birthday</TITLE></HEAD>
<BODY>
</BODY>
</HTML>
```

2. **Type a heading, as follows:**

```
<BODY>
<H1>Happy Birthday, Winchester</H1>
</BODY>
```

3. **Add the** `ALIGN="right"` **attribute to the heading, as in the following example:**

```
<H1 ALIGN="right">Happy Birthday,
    Winchester</H1>
```

4. **Insert a graphic on the left side of the heading, as follows:**

```
<H1 ALIGN="right"><IMG SRC="winch.jpg">Happy
    Birthday, Winchester</H1>
```

5. **Type the following paragraph information:**

```
<H1 ALIGN="right"><IMG SRC="winch.jpg">Happy
    Birthday, Winchester</H1>
<P>On March 3, Deb and Eric snuck up on their cat,
Winchester, and surprised him with a water balloon for
his birthday. It was lucky #13 for Winchester.</P>
</BODY>
```

6. **Add the** `ALIGN="center"` **attribute to the paragraph, as shown here:**

```
<P ALIGN="center">On March 3, Deb and Eric
    snuck up on their cat, Winchester, and
    surprised him with a water balloon for his
    birthday. It was lucky #13 for
    Winchester.</P>
```

Figure 2-2 shows the result.

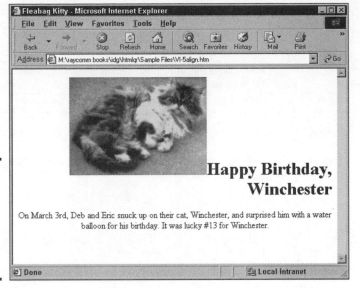

Figure 2-2:
Aligning
headings,
text, and
images with
the ALIGN
attribute.

Using Font Type Specifications

HTML was not designed to support specific formatting. HTML was conceived with the idea that authors would specify headings and lists, and readers (or the readers' browsers) would take care of applying fonts and sizes.

A generation of designers accustomed to desktop publishing and to being able to control every aspect of document design, however, sought out ways to control HTML design as well. In response, newer browsers and the most widely supported HTML specification provide some tags specifically to format text precisely.

The combination of "pure" HTML, without the formatting tags in this section, and style sheets (covered in Chapter 8) provides the best of both worlds — HTML coding simplicity and complete layout and design control.

If you choose to use the formatting commands in this section, remember that not all browsers support them. In particular, remember that a font you specify isn't necessarily installed on your readers' machines!

The following table shows the tags and attributes used to specify type characteristics.

HTML Tag or Attribute	Effect	Use in Pairs?
`<FONT>...</FONT>`	Changes the font.	Yes
`COLOR="#RRGGBB"`	Colors the text based on the RRGGBB number.	No
`FACE="..."`	Sets the typeface NAME. A list of font names can be specified.	No
`SIZE="n"`	Changes the font size n on a scale from 1 to 7.	No

To change the characteristics of a specific block of text, follow these steps:

1. **Start your HTML document, which should look something like the following example:**

```
<!DOCTYPE HTML PUBLIC "-//W3C//DTD HTML 4.01
    Transitional//EN"
    "http://www.w3.org/TR/html4/
    transitional.dtd"> <HTML>
<HEAD><TITLE>Making Effective Water
    Balloons</TITLE>
</HEAD>
<BODY>
<H1>Making Effective Water Balloons</H1>
<P>
Making water balloons is <EM>easy</EM>...
    but making <B>effective</B> water balloons takes
time and patience. The result is a water balloon that
does not break in your hand, offers <I>maximum splash-
ing power</I>, and requires virtually no post-splat
clean up.
</P>
</BODY>
</HTML>
```

2. **Add the `<FONT>` tags around the text you want to change, as follows:**

```
<H1>Making Effective Water Balloons</H1>
<P>
<FONT>
Making water balloons is <EM>easy</EM>...
    but making <B>effective</B> water balloons takes
time and patience. The result is a water balloon that
does not break in your hand, offers <I>maximum splash-
ing power</I>, and requires virtually no post-splat
clean up.
</FONT>
</P>
```

3. **To change the size, add the appropriate `SIZE=` attribute to the font tag, as shown in the following example.**

By default, the size is 4. (The number doesn't represent anything — it just is.) You can specify a size relative to the default (+1 for one size larger or –2 for two sizes smaller) or in absolute numbers such as 1 or 7.

```
<FONT SIZE=+2>
Making water balloons is <EM>easy</EM>...
    but making <B>effective</B> water balloons takes
time and patience. The result is a water balloon
that does not break in your hand, offers <I>maximum
splashing power </I>, and requires virtually no
post-splat clean up.
</FONT>
```

4. **To change the typeface, add the** FACE= **attribute, as the following example shows.**

You can name any font on your system (bearing in mind that the font also must be available on your reader's system to appear correctly). You can also list fonts in descending order of preference. If the first isn't available, your reader's browser moves along to the next and next.

```
<FONT FACE="Gill Sans, Arial, Courier"
    SIZE=+2>
Making water balloons is <EM>easy</EM>...
    but making <B>effective</B> water balloons takes
time and patience. The result is a water balloon that
does not break in your hand, offers <I>maximum splash-
ing power </I>, and requires virtually no post-splat
clean up.
</FONT>
```

Figure 2-3 shows the new typeface in a Web browser.

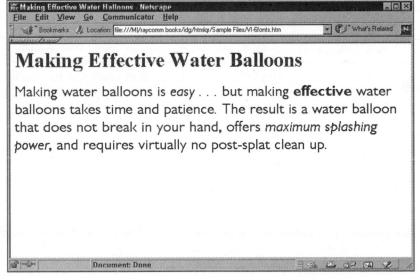

Figure 2-3:
Using the
<FONT> tag
to change
font size and
typeface.

**Book II
Chapter 2**

**Setting Background
and Text
Characteristics**

Reliable fonts for Windows include Arial, Times New Roman, and Courier New. Helvetica and Times are similar to Arial and Times New Roman and also are frequently available.

5. **To change the color, add the** COLOR= **attribute, as shown in the following example.**

As with other text color settings (described earlier in this part), you use an #rrggbb number to specify the color.

```
<FONT FACE="Gill Sans, Courier, Arial"
   COLOR="#000000" SIZE=+2>
Making water balloons is <EM>easy</EM>...
   but making <B>effective</B> water balloons takes
time and patience. The result is a water balloon
that does not break in your hand, offers <I>maximum
splashing power </I>, and requires virtually no
post-splat clean up.
</FONT>
```

Chapter 3: Adding Internal and External Links

In This Chapter

- ✔ Understanding links and anchors
- ✔ Making links between documents
- ✔ Making links within documents
- ✔ Using a link checker utility

*I*n this chapter, you see how to add anchors and links to your HTML documents. Anchors and links enable your readers to jump from place to place within your document or to other documents and files. Put another way, anchors and links are the sticky strands that connect your site to the rest of the Web.

You apply lots of tags in this section, so if initial tags, closing tags, and phrases such as "applying markup tags to your document" are unfamiliar, you may want to flip back to Chapter 1 in this book, "Creating an HTML Page," for more information about HTML basics.

Understanding Links

When you create HTML documents, you create documents that users can read by *linking* from topic to topic — that is, jumping from page to page and from topic to topic instead of reading linearly, as in a novel. *Links* (or *hyperlinks* or *hot spots*) are places that users can select to access other topics, documents, or *Web sites* (collections of HTML documents).

As you build your HTML documents, think about how you want your documents to link together. As a rule, you should create several short HTML documents rather than one long document. Short documents are easier for your readers to follow and are, therefore, more likely to be read. You can then link these shorter documents into a single cohesive set of documents (that is, a Web site).

To create a link, you need the following two things:

✦ **A URL (or Uniform Resource Locator):** This is just an address on the Web.

✦ **An anchor tag:** Marks the link in a Web page. (You read more about these later in this chapter.)

About URLs

A *URL* (pronounced You-Are-Ell), or *Uniform Resource Locator,* is a fancy way of saying an address for information on the Internet. If you hear URL, just think "address" or "location." URLs differ based on how specific you need to be.

URLs can be *absolute* (complete) or *relative* (partial), as described in the following list:

✦ If you're creating a document that you want to publish on the Internet, you use an absolute URL so that anyone — anywhere in the world — on the Internet can find the page.

✦ If you're creating links to other files within the same folder or on the same server, you need to provide only a relative URL. Remember that you're already in the same directory (or folder or general vicinity) as the file to which you're linking.

You'll find more about absolute and relative URLs in the section appropriately titled "Absolute and relative URLs," later in this chapter.

All HTML documents can use URLs to link to other information. URLs, in turn, can point to many different things, such as HTML documents, other sites on the Internet, or even images and sound files.

URLs are *case-sensitive.* On some computers, typing a filename such as `Kitten.html` is very different from typing `kitten.html`. If you create a filename that uses special capitalization (instead of, for example, using all lowercase characters), you must use this same capitalization the same way every time you link to the document. (Frankly, it's easier for you and your readers just to use lowercase.)

Anatomy of URLs

If you're not used to them, URLs can be pretty odd-looking. Each part of a URL has a built-in specific meaning, however, much like each part of your home address. The street address, "12 Fritter Lane, Apartment G, Santa Clara, CA 95051," for example, provides a postal carrier with essential and complete information — the specific apartment in a specific building on a specific street in a specific town in a specific state in a specific ZIP Code. Specifically.

URLs work the same way by providing a browser with all the parts it needs to locate information. A URL consists of the *protocol indicator,* the *hostname,* and the *directory name* and/or *filename*. The following (fictitious) URL is an example of an absolute URL:

```
http://cat.feline.org/fur/fuzzy.html
```

Here's a description of each URL part:

✦ `http://` **portion (protocol indicator):** Tells the server how to send the information. The `http://` protocol indicator is the standard used by Web servers and browsers that lets them talk to each other. The `http://` protocol indicator often is omitted by publications (like this one), both for space and because most URLs (at least those published in the media) tend to be `http://` type URLs.

   Note: Even though you can leave the `http://` off the URL in casual usage, you must include it when linking to another Web site, as described later.

✦ `cat.feline.org` **portion *(hostname)*:** Specifies a computer on the Internet. If you publish an HTML document, you're placing it on a computer that "serves" the document to anyone who knows the correct URL. The server thus "hosts" all these documents and makes them accessible to users.

   To obtain the hostname of the server on which you place your files, check with your system administrator.

✦ `fur` **portion *(directory name)*:** You may not need to show a directory name, or you may have several that represent directories inside directories (or folders inside folders).

✦ `fuzzy.html` **portion *(name of file located on the host computer)*:** Sometimes you don't need to provide a filename — the server simply gives out the default file in the directory. The default filenames are usually one of three: `index.html`, `default.html`, or `homepage.html`, depending on which kind of Web server the files are located. The filename is like many other files; it contains a name (`fuzzy`) and an extension (`.html`).

Sometimes URLs have a hostname with a port number at the end (for example, `cat.feline.org:80`). This number gives the server more precise information about the URL. If you see a URL with a number, just leave the number on the URL. If you don't see a number, don't worry about it.

Try to avoid creating directory names or filenames with spaces or other unusual characters. Stay with letters (lowercase is best), numbers, underscores (_), periods (.), or plus signs (+). Why? Because some servers have problems with odd characters and spaces.

Absolute and relative URLs

As I mention earlier in this part, links in Web pages use two different types of URLs: absolute URLs and relative URLs. Each of these types of URLs has a specific purpose and uses specific components, as the following list describes:

**Book II
Chapter 3**

**Adding Internal and
External Links**

✦ **Absolute URLs:** These give the full address of something on the Internet. They include the protocol indicator, hostname, and directory name/filenames. You use absolute URLs to indicate any location on the Internet.

Keep in mind that pointing people to Internet locations requires as much information as you can provide, just as you'd provide very detailed information to an out-of-town friend who's driving to your apartment. You'd provide, for example, the state, city, building number, and apartment number (unless, of course, you want that friend to get lost). Similarly, you need to provide as complete a URL as possible — including the protocol indicator — so that people around the world can find your Web site.

✦ **Relative URLs:** These don't contain a complete address, but they can still provide all the information you need to link to other documents. A relative URL usually contains only the last part of the absolute URL — the directory name (possibly) and the filename. You use relative URLs to link to locations within the same folder or same group of folders.

To go back to the postal address analogy, if you're giving a local friend directions to your apartment, you'd probably just provide the street address, building, and apartment. The city and state are implicit. In the same way, a relative URL implies the missing information based on the location of the file containing the relative URL. The browser infers the missing information from the location of the document containing the link.

Check out Figure 3-1, which shows how absolute URLs and relative URLs work.

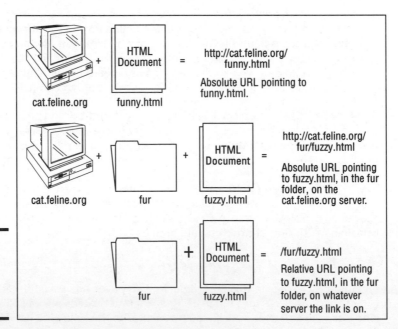

Figure 3-1:
Absolute
versus
relative
URLs.

Understanding Anchors

The linking process begins with anchors; this term is just a fancy way of saying links. (Folks call them anchors because the tag is ⟨A⟩.)

Anchor tags are generally used with one of the following two attributes:

✦ HREF: Enables users to jump from one bit of information to another — either to material within the same Web site or to other material out on the Internet. These tags create the hyperlinks.

✦ NAME: Labels a spot within a document. That spot can then be part of a URL so that readers can jump directly to it. The NAME anchor is useful in long documents that users must otherwise scroll through. If NAME anchors and links to them are present, users can jump to specific information and don't need to wade through pages of material.

**Book II
Chapter 3**

Adding Internal and
External Links

HTML Tag or Attribute	Effect	Use in Pairs? (attributes in italics)
⟨A⟩...⟨/A⟩	Marks anchor.	Yes
HREF="..."	Indicates where to jump.	No
NAME="..."	Identifies an internal label.	No

Making Links

Links are the connections to other material within or among HTML documents. Links are visible as (often blue) text that you select as you're surfing the Web. (After you've linked to a document, the link often appears in a different color to indicate that you've already been there.)

The next three sections show you how to link to other documents within your site, link to HTML documents "out there" on the Web, and link to other information on the Internet. For now, you work with the ⟨A⟩ tag's HREF attribute.

Linking to documents within your site

Here you start with plain text and build your first hypertext link. To make things easy on yourself, work with two (preferably small) HTML documents at first so that you can link from one to the other and back again. Practicing linking is much more difficult if you work with just one document.

Note: Before you begin the example in this section, open your text editor and browser. While you follow these examples, you should also have available a basic HTML document, such as the following:

```
<!DOCTYPE HTML PUBLIC "-//W3C//DTD HTML 4.01
    Frameset//EN"
    "http://www.w3.org/TR/html4/frameset.dtd">
<HTML><HEAD><TITLE>Cats</TITLE></HEAD>
<BODY>
</BODY>
</HTML>
```

Follow these steps to build your first hypertext link:

1. **Enter** Cats are funny. **between the** <BODY> **tags, as the following example shows:**

   ```
   <BODY>
   Cats are funny.
   </BODY>
   ```

2. **Apply the anchor tags to funny, as follows, to make that word the anchor (the part that your readers click to link to something else):**

   ```
   Cats are <A>funny</A>.
   ```

3. **Add an attribute** (HREF=, **in this case) to link to another document, as follows:**

   ```
   Cats are <A HREF="funny.html">funny</A>.
   ```

HREF= is the attribute that specifies which document appears after your readers click the anchor. And funny.html is the name of the document to which you are linking.

In this case, funny.html is a file in the same directory or folder as the document that you're building.

Linking to pages out on the Web

To create links to other documents on the Internet, follow the same procedure as with other links, but include the complete URL in the HREF attribute.

To make a link from the word cats to a completely different address on the Web, use the following example, starting with the following basic HTML document.

Note: Before you begin, open your text editor and browser.

```
<!DOCTYPE HTML PUBLIC "-//W3C//DTD HTML 4.01
    Frameset//EN"
    "http://www.w3.org/TR/html4/frameset.dtd">
<HTML><HEAD><TITLE>Cats</TITLE></HEAD>
<BODY>
</BODY>
</HTML>
```

Use the following steps to add a link to a document at another location:

1. **Type** Cats are funny. **between the** <BODY> **tags, as follows:**

```
<BODY>
Cats are funny.
</BODY>
```

2. **Add the following anchor tags:**

```
<A>Cats</A> are funny.
```

3. **Add the** HREF **attribute to link to a sample (fictitious) Web site about cats, as follows:**

```
<A HREF="http://cats.com/home.html">Cats</A>
    are funny.
```

Book II
Chapter 3

Adding Internal and
External Links

You can also link to non-HTML files from a regular http:// type address. If, for example, you have a Word document that you want people to be able to download from your Web site, you can put in a link such as the following:

```
<A HREF="catjokes.doc">Download original cat
    stories here</A>.
```

Or you could use an absolute URL, as follows:

```
<A HREF="http://cat.feline.org/furry/catpix.jpg">
    Download a picture of the cutest cat in history</A>.
```

Then all you need to do is upload the catjokes.doc and catpix.jpg files to the server at the same time that you upload your HTML document to the server.

Linking to other stuff on the Internet

Just as you can link to HTML documents or images or files on the Internet by including the right URL, you can also link to other types of information (such as discussion groups or file archives) on the Internet. All kinds of other protocols (the language that computers use to transfer information) are in use.

For example, if you see or hear of neat material on the Internet that's available through an FTP (File Transfer Protocol) site (a source for data on the Internet), you can link that material into your document.

Suppose that your best friend found a collection of cat jokes at an FTP site on the Internet. You can simply copy the URL from your friend. The URL may look something like `ftp://humor.central.org/jokes/animals/cats.zip`. You can put that URL into your document, as shown here.

```
A collection of <A HREF="ftp://humor.central.org/jokes/
    animals/cats.zip"> cat jokes</A> is good to have.
```

To create a hyperlink to an e-mail address, type this: `<A HREF="mailto:me@mycompany.com">E-mail me</A>`

Making Links within Documents

Making links to places within an HTML document requires a little more work than creating links to other documents. On regular links to other documents or to documents on other servers, you just point to a computer and a file. If you're going to point to a place within a document that you're creating, however, you must also identify the targets to which you intend to link.

Making internal links

An internal link points to a specific location within a document. Internal links work well if you have a long HTML document that really doesn't lend itself to being split into different files. If you're dealing with one of these long documents, you can use internal links to point from one place to another within the same document. As a result, readers don't need to scroll through pages of information; they can just link to a place (defined by a special anchor) within the document.

Within the `kitten.html` file, you may have a long list of favorite kitten names along with a description of the names' origins. You can enable readers to jump right to the "W" names without needing to scroll through the "A" through "V" names. The following URL points directly to the "w" anchor within the kitten.html file (I show you how to create the named "w" anchor in the next section, "Marking internal targets"):

```
kitten.html#w
```

The relative URL could also be written as follows:

```
fur/kitten.html#w
```

or

```
/fur/kitten.html#w
```

Or you could write the address as the following absolute URL:

```
http://cat.feline.org/fur/kitten.html#w
```

Marking internal targets

Developing anchors to permit links to points within a document is very similar to creating the links themselves. You use the NAME= attribute to create internal targets (also called *named anchors*).

(In the preceding — and hypothetical — example, the author of kitten.html inserted name anchors for all 26 A–Z headings, just so that you can link to them.)

For the following example, imagine that you have a heading within your document called "Funny Cats I've Known" as shown below:

```
<!DOCTYPE HTML PUBLIC "-//W3C//DTD HTML 4.01
    Frameset//EN"
    "http://www.w3.org/TR/html4/frameset.dtd">
<HTML><HEAD><TITLE>Cats</TITLE></HEAD>
<BODY>
<H2>Funny Cats I've Known</H2>
General information about the cats would be here.
</BODY>
</HTML>
```

Follow these steps to include the anchor:

1. **Include an anchor, as follows:**

    ```
    <H2><A>Funny</A> Cats I've Known</H2>
    ```

2. **Insert the NAME= attribute, as follows:**

    ```
    <H2><A NAME="funny">Funny</A> Cats I've
        Known</H2>
    ```

This anchor doesn't show up in the browser view of your document, but you know it's there.

If you want to link directly to the funny cats section of your document from within the same document, you include a link to `funny` by using the hash (#) sign, as follows:

```
<A HREF="#funny">Funny cats</A> are here.
```

The #funny anchor to which you want to link, for example, may be in the cats.html file on the server called cat.feline.org. You just create a URL that looks as follows:

```
http://cat.feline.org/cats.html#funny
```

Your friends and admirers can then set up links to your funny cats section:

```
Boy, you know, those <A HREF="http://
    cat.feline.org/cats.html#funny">funny cats
    </A> are something else.
```

Using a Link Checker Utility

As you've no doubt noticed if you've spent much time surfing the Web, Web sites come and go with lightning speed. Unfortunately, this volatility means that the links you create to other peoples' Web pages can be broken at any time. While broken links may not be a problem if you're creating a personal home page, it reflects poorly on a professional or business-related site.

The only way to prevent broken links is to check them periodically. Checking links yourself — by loading your own Web page into a browser, clicking on each link, and noting whether the linked site appears — can be awfully time-consuming, depending on how many links you've created. To automate the process, you can use a link checker utility. A link checker utility follows all the links in your Web page and then issues a report telling you which ones are broken. (It's up to you to decide whether to delete or change any links reported as broken.)

Not surprisingly, most HTML editing tools — including Dreamweaver, a trial version of which is included on the CD that comes with this book — include a link checker utility.

If you haven't decided on an HTML tool, however, you can still check your links by visiting an online link-checking utility such as the World Wide Web Consortium's Link Checker: http://validator.w3.org/checklink.

Chapter 4: Working with Images

In This Chapter

⊭ Adding images to your Web page

⊭ Controlling image alignment

⊭ Optimizing images for quick download

⊭ Creating clickable images

*I*f you're interested in incorporating images into your Web pages (and who isn't?) you're in luck: this chapter shows you everything you need to know. Here you find out how to add images, position them on the page attractively, and even make them *clickable*. (As you may be able to guess, clickable images are images that do something — for example, load another Web page — when someone viewing your page clicks on them.)

Note: if you want to create images that respond differently based on *where* users click them — in other words, if you want to create imagemaps — check out Book 5, "Multimedia: Creating Graphics, Sound, Animations, Video, and Java Applets."

Before working through the examples in this chapter, make sure that you have your browser and text editor open and ready to create a new document. You should also have an image available to use in the document.

Adding Images

Adding images to your HTML documents is just as straightforward as the basic link and text tags are. (An image can be a picture, drawing, diagram, or what-have-you.)

You can include images with either *GIF* (usually pronounced *jiff*), *JPG* (pronounced *jay-peg*), or *PNG* (pronounced *ping*) file formats. These formats are compressed, so they take up minimal disk space and downloading time. You choose which format to use based on the image itself:

✦ Choose GIF images for line drawings, images with only a few colors, images that should blend into the background, or animated images. GIF remains a popular file format because all graphical browsers can interpret and display them and because transparent images are far spiffier than the regular kind. (*Transparent images* contain see-through portions, so they can be any shape — unlike regular images, which are always square.)

✦ Choose JPG images for photographic images or images with fancy shading. JPG files are considerably smaller than GIF files in terms of disk space and, therefore, don't take f-o-r-e-v-e-r to download to your readers' browsers.

✦ Choose PNG images if you have photographic or complex images and you know your readers will be using newer browsers: Microsoft Internet Explorer 5.5 and Netscape Navigator 4.7 or newer.

Adding images isn't too complicated — just include an `<IMG>` tag and the `SRC="...  ."` attribute, pointing to a valid URL (either absolute or relative) for your image.

The following table shows some of the common image-related tags and attributes.

HTML Tag or Attribute	Effect	Use in Pairs?
`<IMG SRC="...">`	Inserts an image.	No
`ALT="..."`	Specifies text to display if image isn't displayed.	No
`BORDER=n`	Controls thickness of border around an image in pixels.	No

The following example shows you how to add an image to your document.

To include an image in your document, follow these steps:

1. **Start your HTML page.**

Start with the following sample of HTML code:

```
<!DOCTYPE HTML PUBLIC "-//W3C//DTD HTML 4.01
    Frameset//EN"
    "http://www.w3.org/TR/html4/frameset.dtd">
<HTML>
<HEAD><TITLE>Cat Gallery</TITLE></HEAD>
<BODY>
<H1>Cats in Our Lives (for Better or Worse) </H1>
<P>We've got several cats that figure prominently in
our lives, including:</P>
<UL>
<LI>Winchester
<LI>Lucy
<LI>Booker
</UL>
</BODY>
</HTML>
```

2. **Add the** <IMG> **tag wherever you want your image to appear, as in the following example:**

```
<P>We've got several cats that figure prominently in
our lives, including:</P>
<IMG>
```

3. **Add the** SRC= **attribute to provide the address of the image, as the following example shows.**

    The image we're using is called winchest.jpg, and it's located in the same folder as our HTML document.

```
<IMG SRC="winchest.jpg">
```

4. **Add the** ALT= **attribute to describe the image, just in case the viewer can't view (or chooses not to view) the image, as follows:**

```
<IMG SRC="winchest.jpg" ALT="Winchester the Cat">
```

The resulting Web page looks like what you see in Figure 4-1.

Technically, you don't *have to* provide the ALT= text (which stands for *alternative text*) with the image; however, doing so is a good idea. Sometimes people use browsers — including read-aloud browsers for the visually impaired — that can't display images.

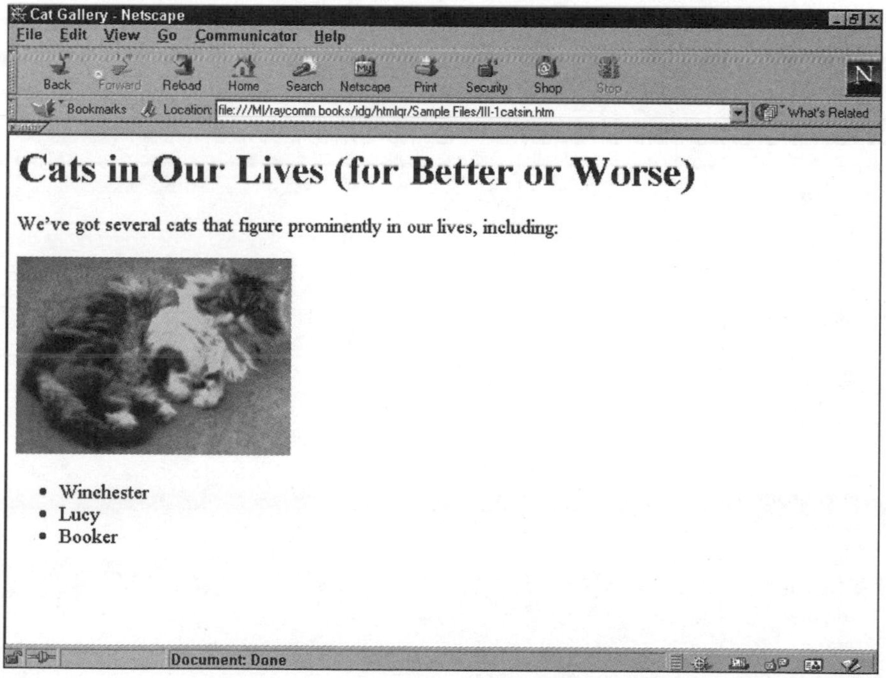

Book II
Chapter 4

Working with
Images

Figure 4-1:
Using the
<IMG> tag
to add an
image to
your Web
page.

Finding images to use in your Web pages

Unless clearly stated otherwise, all images are copyrighted. So don't even think about copying images from other peoples' Web sites and using them in your own pages. Instead, check out one of the hundreds of good sites on the Internet that offer clip art or Web art that's free for noncommercial use. Check out Yahoo! (www.yahoo.com) by typing and searching for clip art. You'll find all you could ever use.

Many people also commonly stop their browsers from showing images so that they don't need to wait for the images to copy to their computer over a slow modem connection.

By using alternative text, you tell them what they're missing instead of making them guess. As a bonus, many browsers use the alternative text for those cute little pop-up blurbs that appear when you hover your mouse over the image.

Figure 4-2 shows an example of how the alternative text may look to readers viewing the same page without the images.

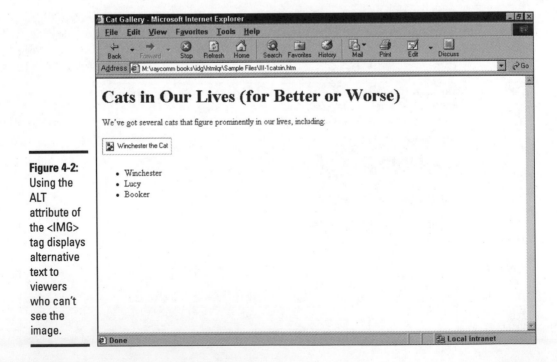

Figure 4-2:
Using the ALT attribute of the <IMG> tag displays alternative text to viewers who can't see the image.

Addressing Image Download Speed: Specifying File Size

Images take quite a while to download (particularly over a slow Internet connection), and your readers are likely to give up on your Web site and move on if the images take too long to appear on-screen. If you're on a fast Internet connection or if you're testing your HTML documents directly from your hard drive (as most of us do), you probably don't notice how long some images take to load, but 28.8 or 56.6 Kbps modems (which are still pretty common) take a long time to transfer images — sometimes up to several minutes.

Basically, you can shorten the time it takes for images to download in either of the following two ways:

✦ Reduce the image file size. You do this when you create an image, as described in Book 5, "Multimedia: Creating Graphics, Sound, Animations, Video, and Java Applets."

✦ Indicate image dimensions in the HTML document using the WIDTH and HEIGHT attributes associated with the <IMG> tag.

Thumbnail images, covered later in this chapter, can also be helpful in managing the "World Wide Wait" when you want to use large images.

You specify the dimensions of the image (generally displayed in the title bar or status bar of image-editing programs) by including height and width attributes in the <IMG> tag. When you do so, browsers leave space for the image, finish loading the text (at which point your readers can start reading), and then continue loading the images. The images don't actually load faster, but specifying image size can help readers *think* they're loading faster, which is almost as good. The numbers you specify for height and width specify the size in *pixels*, which are those itty-bitty dots on-screen that make up the image.

The following table shows the attributes used to specify image height and width.

HTML Attribute	Effect	Use in Pairs?
HEIGHT=n	Specifies the height of the image in pixels.	No
WIDTH=n	Specifies the width of the image in pixels.	No

The code for specifying HEIGHT and WIDTH attributes would look something like <IMG SRC="lucy2a.gif" ALT="Lucy Looking Right" WIDTH=200 HEIGHT="157">

Controlling Image Alignment

By default, browsers align images on the left side of the page. If you want, you can realign them so that the images appear aligned at the right or aligned vertically.

HTML 4.0 (and 4.01) recommends that you use style sheets to control image alignment, rather than using the attributes given here. However, using the following attributes can be useful if the folks visiting your site are using old browsers — for example, pre-5.5 Internet Explorer and pre-6.0 Netscape. See Chapter 8 for the lowdown on style sheets.

The following table shows the attributes used to control image alignment.

HTML Attribute	Effect	Use in Pairs?
ALIGN="bottom"	Aligns the bottom of the image with the baseline of the current line.	No
ALIGN="left"	Allows an image to float down and over to the left margin (into the next available space); subsequent text wraps to the right of that image.	No
ALIGN="middle"	Aligns the baseline of the current line with the middle of the image.	No
ALIGN="right"	Aligns the image with the right margin and wraps the text around the left.	No
ALIGN="top"	Aligns the text with the top of the tallest item in the line.	No
HSPACE=n	Controls the horizontal space (white space) around the image in pixels.	No
VSPACE=n	Controls the vertical space (white space) around the image in pixels.	No

All you need to do is include these attributes in the <IMG> tag in your HTML document. The order of the attributes within the <IMG> tag isn't important. You can put them in the order that you find most convenient. The following HTML code shows you how to align an image to appear on the right-hand side of the page.

```
<IMG SRC="lucy.jpg" ALT="Lucy looking Right" ALIGN="RIGHT">
```

Surrounding Images with Blank Space

You can include these alignment effects by adding vertical and horizontal space around the images.

Just add the HSPACE=n or VSPACE=n attributes (or both). The n is the number of pixels wide that the space should be on each side of the image; thus, the total width added is two times n. An example of what this looks like is shown below.

```
<IMG SRC="lucy.jpg" ALT="Lucy Looking Right" ALIGN="left"
    HSPACE=40>
<IMG SRC="lucyl.jpg" ALT="Lucy Looking Left" ALIGN="right"
    HSPACE=40>
```

Figure 4-3 shows the results of the extra space around the images.

Note: If most of your readers will be using HTML 4.0-compliant browsers such as Internet Explorer 5.5 (and higher) and Netscape 6 (and higher), consider achieving the same effects with style sheets, covered in Chapter 8.

Book II
Chapter 4

Working with Images

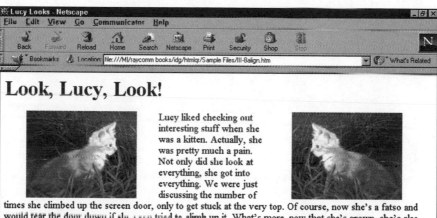

Figure 4-3:
Using the HSPACE attribute of the <IMG> tag to surround images with blank space.

Making Clickable Images

You can use images as your anchors for making links. Using images as anchors isn't any more complicated than creating a link and then adding an image.

Note: if you want to create images that respond differently based on *where* users click them — in other words, if you want to create *imagemaps* — check out Book 5, "Multimedia: Creating Graphics, Sound, Animations, Video, and Java Applets."

To use an image as the anchor to link to another document, follow these steps:

1. **Start your HTML document.**

   Your document may look similar to the following example:

   ```
   <!DOCTYPE HTML PUBLIC "-//W3C//DTD HTML 4.01
      Frameset//EN"
      "http://www.w3.org/TR/html4/frameset.dtd">
   <HTML>
   <HEAD><TITLE>Cat Gallery</TITLE></HEAD>
   <BODY>
   <H1>Cats in Our Lives (for Better or Worse)</H1>
   <P>We've got several cats that figure prominently in
   our lives, including:</P>
   <UL>
   <LI>Winchester
   <LI>Lucy
   <LI>Booker
   </UL>
   </BODY>
   </HTML>
   ```

2. **Add a link, as shown in the following example.**

   ```
   <P>
   <UL>
   <LI>Winchester
      <A HREF="winchbio.html">(Biography)</A>
   <LI>Lucy
   <LI>Booker
   </UL>
   ```

   For more information about links, take a look at Chapter 3.

3. **Add the** `<IMG>` **tag between the opening and closing link tags (between <A> and </A>), as follows:**

```
<P>
<UL>
<LI>Winchester <A HREF="winchbio.html">
<IMG>(Biography)</A>
<LI>Lucy
<LI>Booker
</UL>
```

4. **Add the** `SRC=` **attribute to the** `<IMG>` **tag, as follows.**

(***Remember:*** This attribute tells what graphic you're including in your HTML document.)

Book II
Chapter 4

Working with
Images

```
<P>
<UL>
<LI>Winchester <A HREF="winchbio.html">
    <IMG SRC="winchest.jpg">(Biography)</A>
<LI>Lucy
<LI>Booker
</UL>
```

5. **Add the** `ALT=` **attribute to the** `<IMG>` **tag, as shown in the following example.**

(***Remember:*** This attribute tells what text to display if the image isn't displayed.)

```
<P>
<UL>
<LI>Winchester <A HREF="winchbio.html">
<IMG SRC="winchest.jpg" ALT="Link to Winchester's
Biography">(Biography)</A>
<LI>Lucy
<LI>Booker
</UL>
```

The Web page looks something like what you see in Figure 4-4.

Notice that the image shown in Figure 4-4 contains a border. The border is the same color as other links in the document, which indicates to your readers that the image links to other information or files.

You can remove the border from around the linked image. To do so, just add the `BORDER=` attribute to the `<IMG>` tag with a value of `BORDER=0`, for example:
`<A HREF="winchbio.html"><IMG SRC="winchest.jpg" ALT="Link to Winchester's Biography" BORDER=0></A>`

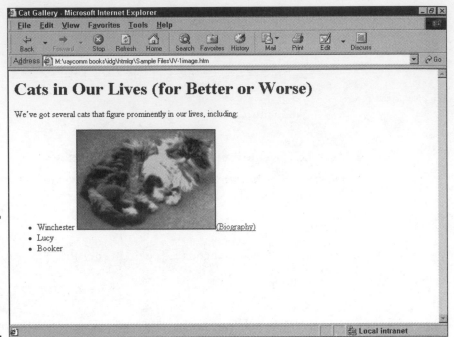

Figure 4-4:
This image
is also
a link,
courtesy of
the <A> and
<IMG> tags.

Making an image into a link is useful when you want to link a small *thumbnail* image file to a large, full-size version. (Using thumbnail images is a good idea if you have many images or very large images on your Web page because visitors get the idea of what the pictures look like but don't need to wait all day for the bigger image files to download.) To link a thumbnail image to a full-size version, follow the steps described in the preceding example, placing the name of the full-size image in the link and the name of the thumbnail image in the SRC attribute, for example: `<A HREF="big_img.jpg">` `<IMG  SRC="thumb_img.jpg" ALT="Thumbnail image"></A>`

Chapter 5: Controlling Page Layout

In This Chapter

- ✔ **Developing tables**
- ✔ **Embedding horizontal rules**
- ✔ **Forcing line breaks**

This chapter introduces you to some really nifty things you can do with HTML to format your pages attractively.

You need to be pretty familiar with the basic HTML tags before diving into this chapter. Most of the examples in this part include only the tags and attributes discussed under a particular heading and do not include structure or body tags. I assume that you know where structure and body tags go. If you don't, you may want to refer to Chapter 1, "Creating an HTML Page."

Developing Tables

Tables — not just for dinner any more. In the context of HTML, tables are very handy for the following purposes:

- ✦ Lining up material vertically and horizontally
- ✦ Making creative layouts
- ✦ Placing text next to graphics

The following table shows the tags and attributes used to create tables.

HTML Tag or Attribute	Effect	Use in Pairs?
`<TABLE>...</TABLE>`	Indicates table format.	Yes
`BORDER=n`	Controls table border width in pixels. 0 specifies no border.	No
`<TD>...</TD>`	Indicates table data cell.	Yes
`<TH>...</TH>`	Indicates table headings.	Yes
`<TR>...</TR>`	Indicates table row items.	Yes

These steps describe how to create a table, such as the one that follows with two rows and two columns. *Note:* Before you begin, make sure that you have your browser and text editor open and ready to create a new document. Or you can apply this information to an existing document.

Culprit	*Water Balloon Skills*
Deborah	Fair
Eric	Excellent

Follow these steps:

1. **Type text, row by row, using a space or two between row elements.**

```
Culprit Water Balloon Skills
Deborah Fair
Eric Excellent
```

2. **Insert** `<TABLE>` **tags before and after the text to indicate the** `<TABLE>` **information that goes in the table.**

```
<TABLE>
Culprit Water Balloon Skills
Deborah Fair
Eric Excellent
</TABLE>
```

3. **Add** `<TR>` **tags to show where the table rows go.**

(**Remember:** TR stands for *table rows*, and rows go across the page.)

```
<TABLE>
<TR>Culprit Water Balloon Skills</TR>
<TR>Deborah Fair</TR>
<TR>Eric Excellent</TR>
</TABLE>
```

4. **Add pairs of** `<TH>` **tags to show where the table heading cells go (in the top row).**

At this point, adding some spacing may help you more easily see what's going on.

```
<TABLE>
<TR><TH>Culprit</TH>
<TH>Water Balloon Skills</TH>
</TR>
<TR>Deborah Fair</TR>
<TR>Eric Excellent</TR>
</TABLE>
```

5. **Add pairs of <TD> tags to indicate the individual data cells of a table.**

```
<TABLE>
<TR><TH>Culprit</TH>
<TH>Water Balloon Skills</TH>
</TR>
<TR><TD>Deborah</TD> <TD>Fair</TD></TR>
<TR><TD>Eric</TD> <TD>Excellent</TD></TR>
</TABLE>
```

6. **Add the BORDER attribute to the <TABLE> tag to create lines around each table cell.**

```
<TABLE BORDER=1>
<TR><TH>Culprit</TH>
<TH>Water Balloon Skills</TH>
</TR>
<TR><TD>Deborah </TD> <TD>Fair</TD></TR>
<TR><TD>Eric </TD> <TD>Excellent</TD></TR>
</TABLE>
```

Figure 5-1 shows the result of all this work.

Figure 5-1:
Use the
<TABLE>
tag to
create nice,
even rows
and
columns.

Experiment with tables. You can come up with many creative layouts and page designs. Here are some ideas:

✦ Embed images in tables (to align graphics and text the way you want).

✦ Place text in table cells to make columns — like a newspaper.

✦ Place headings to the left (or right) of a paragraph of text.

If you find that your tables have problems — or don't seem to work at all — make very sure that your tags are paired correctly and that you haven't omitted any tags. Printing a copy of your HTML code and marking pairs of tags are sometimes necessary for troubleshooting tables. As you can see from the very small example in the text, getting confused is easy with all the different tags necessary for tables. Additionally, save yourself some trouble by liberally using white space and blank lines as you create the table. The extra white space can help you see what's going on.

Embedding Horizontal Rules

HTML allows you to break up Web pages by applying a horizontal rule, <HR>. This horizontal rule can serve not only as a visual break for long pages but also as an informational break. The following table illustrates the tag used to create horizontal rules and the attributes that let you format them.

HTML Tag or Attribute	Effect	Use in Pairs?
<HR>	Applies a horizontal rule.	No
SIZE="number"	Indicates how thick the rule is.	No
WIDTH="number"	Specifies an exact width in pixels or percent (%) of document width. A percentage value must appear in quotes, like WIDTH="50%".	No
ALIGN="LEFT", "CENTER", or "RIGHT"	Specifies the alignment; works only in combination with WIDTH.	No

To use horizontal rules, apply the following tags and attributes.

```
<P><EM><H1 ALIGN=CENTER>Lost
    Cat!</H1></EM></P>
<HR WIDTH=80% ALIGN=CENTER>
<HR WIDTH=60% ALIGN=CENTER>
<HR WIDTH=40% ALIGN=CENTER>
<P>Fuzzy tortoise shell Persian--lost in Big
    Lake area. Probably looks confused.</P>
<HR>
<P>Answers to:
<UL>
<LI>Winchester
<LI>Hairheimer
<LI>Fritter
<LI>Sound of can opener
</UL></P>
<P>Please call if you find him: 555-9999</P>
<HR WIDTH=200>
<HR WIDTH=400>
<HR WIDTH=200>
```

Figure 5-2 shows the effects of these tags.

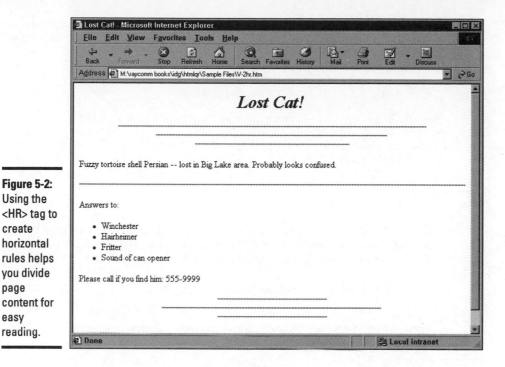

Figure 5-2:
Using the
<HR> tag to
create
horizontal
rules helps
you divide
page
content for
easy
reading.

Getting carried away with horizontal rules is easy. Figure 5-2 shows horizontal rules used to excess. You should use these rules only where they help readers find information more easily or help them wade through long passages of information.

You can also use style sheets (covered in Chapter 8) to format horizontal rules.

Forcing Line Breaks

HTML allows you to break lines of text so that you can determine exactly (or as much as possible) how they appear on the users' end.

The following table shows the tag used to force line breaks.

HTML Tag or Attribute	Effect	Use in Pairs?
 	Breaks line; new line begins after tag.	No
CLEAR="..."	Requires that LEFT, RIGHT, NONE, or ALL margins are clear before new line starts.	No

To break lines of text so that each line appears the way you want it to (for example, in a poem), use the <BR> tag as the following block of code shows.

```
<BODY>
<P>
I'm Hungry, I'm Hungry! I said with a
    sigh.<BR>
I want to cancel dinner and go straight to my
    pie.<BR>
I want cake and ice cream and toast with
    jelly,<BR>
And I don't care if I grow a big belly.<BR>
</P>
</BODY>
```

If you include a line break and want to make sure that the new line starts after an image, for example, add the CLEAR=ALL attribute to the <BR> tag. That forces the new line below all other objects on the line.

Figure 5-3 shows the effects of these line breaks.

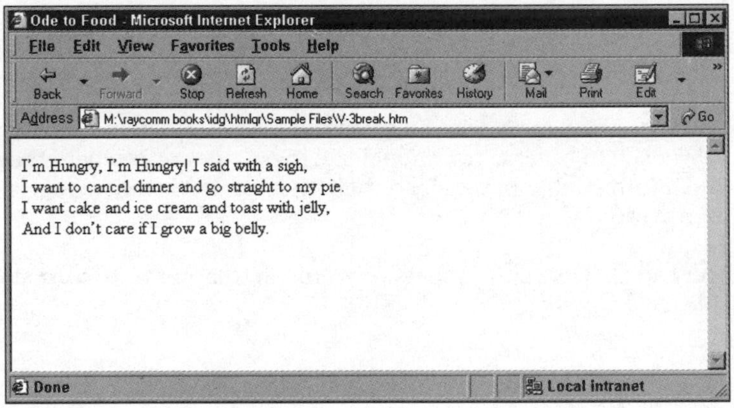

Figure 5-3:
Using <BR> to force line breaks helps you control the way your Web page text appears.

Chapter 6: Creating Forms

In This Chapter

✔ **Creating a basic form**

✔ **Including form components (buttons, checkboxes, radio buttons, selection lists, text fields, and more)**

This chapter introduces forms, which you may think of as online versions of hard-copy forms that have check boxes and blanks to fill in, among other possible features. These online forms can help you get feedback and information from the folks who visit your Web site.

To develop a fully functional form, you need the help of your server administrator. In this chapter, I tell you where you need to ask for help, as well as what information to request.

Creating a Basic Form

In HTML, forms are just what they are in real life — a fairly impersonal, pretty effective means of getting standardized information from other people. You may use forms to:

✦ Conduct a survey.

✦ Collect addresses or information about visitors to your site.

✦ Enable people to register for something.

The following table shows the basic `<FORM>` tags and attributes that you use.

HTML Tag or Attribute	Effect	Use in Pairs?
`<FORM...>` ... `</FORM>`	Encloses the entire form.	Yes
`ACTION="..."`	Identifies what should happen to the data after the form is submitted.	No
`METHOD="..."`	Identifies methods; valid options are `GET` or `POST`— one is required.	No

When you create forms, you need to make sure that the information gets back to you after the reader fills out the form and clicks Submit. Although form results can be processed and returned in various ways, your server administrator most likely has the server set up to e-mail form results directly to you.

The basic <FORM> tag is a two-parter, having both an initial tag and a closing tag. You can use the <FORM> tag to have information sent back to you directly or to a program that compiles the information for you.

The <FORM> tag has two primary (essential) attributes, ACTION and METHOD. The ACTION attribute tells the server what to do with the information after the server receives it. The METHOD attribute tells the server how to get the processed information back to you. Exactly what you fill in as values for these two attributes depends on what your server administrator tells you. So, before you get started creating your form, go ahead and contact your server administrator and tell her that you want to create a form that can be e-mailed to your personal address and ask what you should fill in for the ACTION and METHOD attributes.

For example, my administrator told me to use the following elements:

```
ACTION="http://www.raycomm.com/
    cgi-bin/email?raycomm"
Method=POST
```

Notice that the rest of the examples in this chapter are constructed based on this information. Just ask your server administrator exactly what to use (or where to look for instructions).

Before I outline how to create a form, I assume that the following information is true:

✦ You've already contacted your server administrator and gotten the ACTION and METHOD information.

✦ You have your HTML document open in an editing program.

✦ You've opened the HTML document in your browser so that you can view and test the document.

To include a form in your Web page, follow these basic steps:

1. **Start with a basic HTML document, similar to this one:**

```
<!DOCTYPE HTML PUBLIC "-//W3C//DTD HTML 4.01
    Frameset//EN"
    "http://www.w3.org/TR/html4/frameset.dtd">
<HTML>
<HEAD><TITLE>Survey: How to Get the
    Cats</TITLE></HEAD>
<BODY>
<H1>Survey: How to Get the Cats</H1>
<P>We've decided to take a survey about the best pranks
to play on the cats. Please complete the survey and
```

```
click the Submit button.</P>
</BODY>
</HTML>
```

2. **Add the** <FORM> **and** </FORM> **tags to show where the form goes, as follows:**

```
Please complete the survey and click the Submit
button.</P>
<FORM>
</FORM>
</BODY>
</HTML>
```

3. **Add the information that your server administrator gave you for the** ACTION **and** METHOD **attributes. (Remember, this is what my administrator told me to fill in.)**

```
<FORM METHOD="POST"
   ACTION="http://www.raycomm.com/
   cgi-bin/email?raycomm">
</FORM>
```

At this point, you can't see anything different about your page. Nor can you test the page to find out whether it works. Just forge ahead, finish up the form, and satisfy your curiosity.

Including Form Components

If you have the basics of the form under control, you now want to include some <INPUT> fields so that you can start collecting information. The basic form-input tags shown in the following table, in many permutations, should carry you through the next several sections.

HTML Tag or Attribute	Effect	Use in Pairs?
<INPUT...>	Identifies some type of input field.	No
CHECKED	Shows which item is selected by default (check box/radio button).	No
MAXLENGTH=n	Indicates the maximum number of characters in the field width.	No
NAME="..."	Indicates the name of the field.	No
SIZE=n	Displays field n characters wide.	No
TYPE="..."	Indicates the type of field. Valid types are TEXT, PASSWORD, CHECKBOX, RADIO, SUBMIT, RESET, FILE, IMAGE, BUTTON, and HIDDEN.	No
VALUE="..."	Indicates value of button (and the label for Submit and Reset).	No

Including Submit and Reset buttons

After you create a form, you need to add Submit and Reset buttons that the readers click to submit the form (or start over again if they goof up). The Submit button sends the information after your readers click it, whereas the Reset button just clears the input from the form.

To include Submit and Reset buttons, enter the following text and tags in your HTML document.

Remember: You need a functional form before you start adding Submit and Reset buttons.

```
<FORM METHOD="POST" ACTION="http://www.raycomm.com/
    cgi-bin/email?raycomm">
<INPUT TYPE="SUBMIT" VALUE="Submit">
<INPUT TYPE="RESET" VALUE="Reset">
</FORM>
```

To change the text that appears on the Submit and Reset buttons, change the values associated with the VALUE attributes of the Submit and Reset buttons, respectively. Here's an example:

```
<INPUT TYPE="RESET" VALUE="Forget it!">
```

Including check boxes, radio buttons, and more

Check boxes and radio buttons are the objects that users can click to select choices from a list. Check boxes allow you to select multiple options. Radio buttons are designed so that you can choose only one from a list — just like with pushing buttons on a car radio. Both check boxes and radio buttons are variations on the <INPUT> field. You see examples of both in the following sections.

Making check boxes

Making check boxes is not complicated — you use several tags, but the process is the same as creating anything else with HTML.

Note: You need to have a functional form, including Submit and Reset buttons, before you add check boxes. Start with the following example — just a section of a complete document — and build on it.

```
<FORM METHOD="POST"
    ACTION="http://www.raycomm.com/
    cgi-bin/email?raycomm">
<INPUT TYPE="SUBMIT" VALUE="Submit">
<INPUT TYPE="RESET" VALUE="Reset">
</FORM>
```

To use check boxes in your document, follow these steps:

1. **Enter** <INPUT TYPE="CHECKBOX"> **on the blank line after the beginning of the form, as follows:**

```
<FORM METHOD="POST"
    ACTION="http://www.raycomm.com/
    cgi-bin/email?raycomm">
<INPUT TYPE="CHECKBOX">
<INPUT TYPE="SUBMIT" VALUE="Submit">
<INPUT TYPE="RESET"VALUE="Reset">
</FORM>
```

Book II
Chapter 6

Creating Forms

2. **Insert the text that you want people to see behind that check box, as follows.**

   (Until you do so, they see a check box with no description.)

```
<FORM METHOD="POST"
    ACTION="http://www.raycomm.com/
    cgi-bin/email?raycomm">
<INPUT TYPE="CHECKBOX">Throw a balloon!
<INPUT TYPE="SUBMIT" VALUE="Submit">
<INPUT TYPE="RESET" VALUE="Reset">
</FORM>
```

3. **Identify the name of the** <INPUT> **field, as shown here.**

   (You see this field as you're reading the input from your form. Make the name something short and logical.)

```
<FORM METHOD="POST"
    ACTION="http://www.raycomm.com/
    cgi-bin/email?raycomm">
<INPUT TYPE="CHECKBOX" NAME="Throw">
    Throw a balloon!
<INPUT TYPE="SUBMIT" VALUE="Submit">
<INPUT TYPE="RESET" VALUE="Reset">
</FORM>
```

4. **Enter the text that you want to see if someone selects this option, as shown in the following example.**

```
<FORM METHOD="POST"
    ACTION="http://www.raycomm.com/
    cgi-bin/email?raycomm">
<INPUT TYPE="CHECKBOX" NAME="Throw"
VALUE="ThrowBalloon"> Throw a balloon!
<INPUT TYPE="SUBMIT" VALUE="Submit">
<INPUT TYPE="RESFT" VALUE="Reset">
</FORM>
```

5. **Enter a couple more lines to complete the list, as follows (because you probably don't want a check box list with only one thing to check).**

   (The <P> tag at the end forces a new line.)

   ```
   <INPUT TYPE="CHECKBOX" NAME="Throw"
   VALUE="ThrowBalloon"> Throw a balloon!
   <INPUT TYPE="CHECKBOX" NAME="Hurl" VALUE="HurlBalloon">
   Hurl a balloon!
   <INPUT TYPE="CHECKBOX" NAME="Lob" VALUE="LobBalloon">
   Lob a balloon!<P>
   ```

6. **Enter a** CHECKED **attribute in the check box that you want to have selected by default, as in the following example.**

   (Do so if you want to select a check box in advance to give a recommendation or to make sure that something gets checked.)

   ```
   <INPUT CHECKED TYPE="CHECKBOX" NAME="Hurl"
   VALUE="HurlBalloon"> Hurl a balloon!
   ```

Making radio buttons

Making radio buttons is similar to making check boxes — you use several tags, and the process is the same as that for using other HTML tags.

Note: Before you start making radio buttons, make sure that you already have your functional form completed.

To include radio buttons in your form, follow these steps:

1. **Insert** <INPUT TYPE="RADIO"> **and the text that people should see.**

   ```
   <INPUT>Do it--it'll be funny!
   <INPUT TYPE="SUBMIT" VALUE="Submit">
   <INPUT TYPE="RESET" VALUE="Reset">
   </FORM>
   ```

2. **Add the** NAME **and** VALUE **indicators.**

   (The NAME applies to the whole set of radio buttons, so we've chosen a less specific name.)

   ```
   <INPUT TYPE="RADIO" NAME="Prank" VALUE="Do" >Do it--
   it'll be funny!
   ```

3. **Add the** CHECKED **attribute again, as follows because this selection is the recommended choice:**

   ```
   <INPUT TYPE="RADIO" NAME="Prank" VALUE="Do"
   CHECKED>Do it--it'll be funny!
   ```

4. **Add as many more radio buttons to this set as you want, along with line breaks (
 or <P>) between them just to make them look nice.**

   (***Remember:*** Radio buttons are designed to accept only one selection from the group, so make sure that they all share the same NAME field. This way, the computer knows that they belong together.)

   ```
   <INPUT TYPE="RADIO" NAME="Prank" VALUE="Do" CHECKED>Do
   it--it'll be funny!<BR>
   <INPUT TYPE="RADIO" NAME="Prank" VALUE="DoNot">
       Don't play a prank, meanie!<BR>
   <INPUT TYPE="RADIO" NAME="Prank"
       VALUE="DoNotCare">I couldn't care less.
       They're your cats, and you'll have to live with
   yourself.<P>
   ```

Using other input types

Other input types, such as TEXT, can be very useful. TEXT allows visitors to insert a small amount of information (such as a name or an address) into your form.

Note: Before you start adding other input attributes, make sure that you already have your functional form completed.

To include text input areas in your form, follow these steps:

1. **Insert the <INPUT> tag and the text that people should see, plus a tag (
 or <P>) to force a new line.**

   ```
   <INPUT>Your Name<P>
   <INPUT TYPE="SUBMIT" VALUE="Submit">
   <INPUT TYPE="RESET" VALUE="Reset">
   </FORM>
   ```

2. **Add the TYPE indicator to show that it is a text input area.**

   ```
   <INPUT TYPE="TEXT">Your Name<P>
   ```

3. **Add the NAME indicator.**

   ```
   <INPUT TYPE="TEXT" NAME="name">Your Name<P>
   ```

4. **Add the SIZE indicator to tell the field how many characters wide it should be.**

   ```
   <INPUT SIZE=35 TYPE="TEXT" NAME="name">Your Name<P>
   ```

Including select lists

Select lists are lists from which your readers can choose one or more items. They're like the font selection drop-down list in your word processing program.

The following table shows the tags and attributes used to include select lists in your HTML document.

HTML Tag or Attribute	Effect	Use in Pairs?
`<SELECT...> ...` `</SELECT>`	Provides a list of items to select.	Yes
`MULTIPLE`	Indicates that multiple selections are allowed.	No
`NAME="..."`	Indicates the name of the field.	No
`SIZE=n`	Determines the size of the scrollable list by showing n options.	No
`<OPTION...>`	Precedes each item in an option list.	Yes, optionally
`SELECTED`	Identifies which option is selected.	No by default
`VALUE="..."`	Indicates the value of the field.	No

The following steps describe how to add a select list to your form. *Note:* Before you include select lists, make sure that you already have a functional form completed.

1. **Insert the** `<SELECT>` **tags into your document and a tag (`<BR>` or `<P>`) to force a new line.**

```
<SELECT>
</SELECT><P>
<INPUT TYPE="SUBMIT" VALUE="Submit">
<INPUT TYPE="RESET" VALUE="Reset">
</FORM>
```

2. **Add the** `NAME` **attribute to the** `<SELECT>` **tag.**

(The `NAME` should be appropriately broad to cover the spectrum of choices.)

```
<SELECT NAME="Method">
</SELECT><P>
```

3. **Add an** `<OPTION>` **that your readers can select.**

```
<SELECT NAME="Method">
<OPTION VALUE="single">Single Balloon
</SELECT><P>
```

4. **Complete your <SELECT> section by adding the other possible choices.**

```
<SELECT NAME="Method">
<OPTION VALUE="single">Single Balloon
<OPTION VALUE="multiple">Multiple Balloons
<OPTION VALUE="hose">Just Use the Hose
</SELECT><P>
```

Figure 6-1 shows the addition of the select list to your form.

Figure 6-1:
Adding a
select list to
your form
gives
visitors a lot
of options
without
taking up a
lot of space
on your
page.

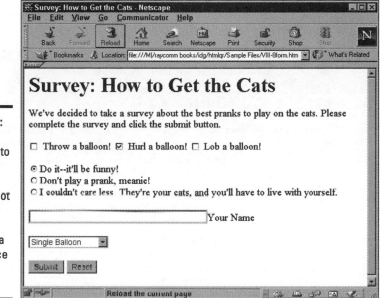

Including text areas

Text areas are open spaces in your form in which your readers can type comments or enter other information.

The following table shows the tags and attributes used to add text areas to your form.

HTML Tag or Attribute	Effect	Use in Pairs?
`<TEXTAREA ...>` `...</TEXTAREA>`	Encloses a multiline text field. The enclosed text is the value displayed in the field.	Yes
`COLS=n`	Indicates the number of columns in the field.	No
`NAME="..."`	Indicates the name of the field.	No
`ROWS=n`	Indicates the number of rows in the field.	No

To add a text area to your form, you include the opening and closing `<TEXTAREA>` tags, along with values for the `NAME`, `ROWS`, and `COLS` attributes as shown:

```
<TEXTAREA NAME="comments" ROWS=3 COLS=40>Enter your comments
    here.
</TEXTAREA><P>
<INPUT TYPE="SUBMIT" VALUE="Submit">
<INPUT TYPE="RESET" VALUE="Reset">
</FORM>
```

Check out Figure 6-2 to see the text area the preceding HTML code produces.

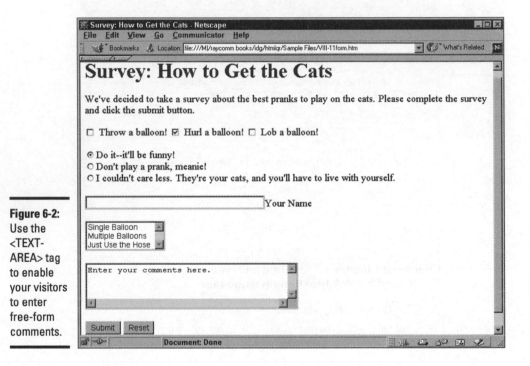

Figure 6-2:
Use the
`<TEXT-
AREA>` tag
to enable
your visitors
to enter
free-form
comments.

Chapter 7: Working with Frames

In This Chapter

✔ About frames

✔ Developing content

✔ Developing alternative content

✔ Establishing the frameset document

✔ Setting up the frames

✔ Setting up links and targets

✔ Testing your framed site

Frames let you place several different HTML documents within a single browser window, providing at least the possibility for visually interesting or easy-to-navigate sites. Of course, a framed site also makes you look like the HTML pro that you are.

The bad news: frames can get a little confusing at times, and the troubleshooting process isn't always the easiest. If you've gotten this far with HTML, however, nothing in this chapter should be a real problem. Just take things one step at a time.

In this chapter, I don't address tag basics — I just tell you to apply them. Check out Chapter 1, "Creating an HTML Page," for information about tags if you need a quick brushup on using tags.

About Frames

Frames divide a browser window into several parts, just as a window (the glass kind) can be divided into several panes. Each frame (or pane) consists of an individual HTML document. In effect, using frames lets you put multiple separate HTML documents on a single page, each in an individual box.

You can use frames to create a variety of layouts. For example, you may have seen frames used as a navigational aid, such as a frame with links on the left side of the browser window, as shown in Figure 7-1.

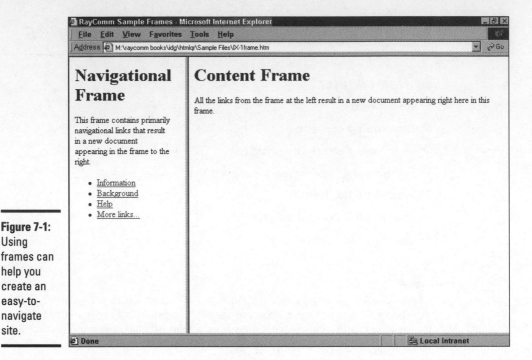

Navigational Frame

This frame contains primarily navigational links that result in a new document appearing in the frame to the right.

- Information
- Background
- Help
- More links...

Content Frame

All the links from the frame at the left result in a new document appearing right here in this frame.

Done   Local intranet

Figure 7-1: Using frames can help you create an easy-to-navigate site.

After readers click a link from the left frame, the linked document appears in the right frame — thus the navigational features stay visible at all times.

Or you may have seen frames used to help promote a corporate name or image. The logo and information, for example, appear in the top frame, and the linked documents appear in the bottom frame, as shown in Figure 7-2.

Think of these frames as being a two-column or two-row table. In these examples, the smaller of the two frames stays constant on the Web page (I refer to this as the *navigation* or *banner document*), whereas the larger frame changes to display various HTML documents in the site (called the *content documents*). The effect is that you can develop the banner or navigation document only one time, throw it in a frame, and then be done with it — not to mention that the frame can stay visible and fixed while other text within the same overall browser window moves.

You can provide more than two frames in a browser window, but that quickly becomes very complex for you, the author, and your readers. Two or (in extreme cases) three frames are plenty.

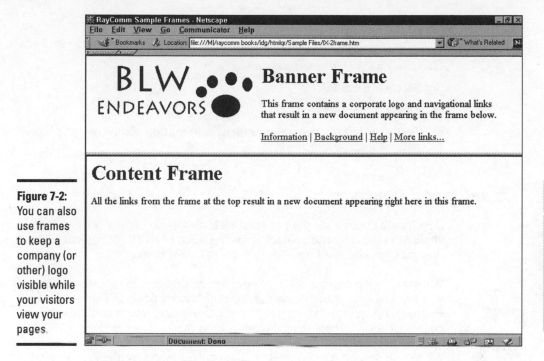

Figure 7-2:
You can also use frames to keep a company (or other) logo visible while your visitors view your pages.

Frames do have a few disadvantages. Whereas most browsers these days can display them, not all readers like them. If you do them well, however, most of your readers can at least tolerate them, and frames *are* quite widespread.

Creating a framed site requires planning above all else. First, sit down and sketch out where you want frames to go, and give them informative names, such as "banner" and "body" or "index" and "text." You should also note on your sketch which frame provides the navigation or banner page (and therefore stays constant) and which frame provides the content pages (and therefore changes). Planning this information now helps you develop content, set up the frames, and set up navigation between the frames.

The sample site you see in Figure 7-2 puts the corporate logo and some navigational links in the top frame, which should take only about 20 percent (about 100 pixels) of the total area of the window. The top frame acts primarily as a navigation tool; the bottom frame contains the new (changing) content of each link.

The following steps outline the process of creating frames after you finish planning and sketching. I discuss each step in more detail in the following sections.

1. Develop content for each frame.

2. Develop alternative content for browsers that can't accommodate frames.

3. Establish the frameset document.

4. Set up the frames.

5. Target the frames.

6. Test them extensively — in as many different browser/computer combinations as possible.

Developing Content

Developing content for your framed Web site doesn't really pose unique challenges because the content is just a bunch of HTML documents, just like the ones you see in all the other chapters in this book.

You start by developing an HTML document that includes text and images you want to appear on the navigational or banner page. In Figure 7-2, for example, I start with the content for the top frame, which contains the corporate logo and some navigational links.

When you develop the content for the content pages, remember a couple of items about the remaining content pages of your framed site:

✦ **On content pages, don't duplicate too much information that appears on the navigation or banner page.** If, for example, your top banner has the corporate logo, omit that item from the individual pages.

✦ **On content pages, include some contact and identification information.** Readers could possibly access content pages directly, without going through the frames (because the pages are just HTML documents, after all), and if you have no contact or identification information, nobody knows where the pages came from.

Remember the names of your content pages — you need them as you fill in your frames.

Developing Alternative Content

Because not all browsers accommodate frames (and not all readers choose to display frames), you need to provide alternative content. Alternative content is similar to alternative text you include with images; this text appears in place of images in case your readers can't or choose not to view your images. (See Chapter 4, "Working with Images," for information about alternative image text.)

In an ideal world, you could take the time to have two complete Web sites — one optimized for nonframed browsers and the other for framed browsers. Realistically, however, you're not likely to have the time for this luxury because having two sites doubles the time required to create and maintain them.

Instead, just make a single HTML document that includes all the corporate logos and links that your navigation and content documents contain.

Establishing the Frameset Document

After you develop the content — both for the frames and alternative content — you're ready to set up your *frameset document*. The frameset document tells the browser what frames are available and where they go, in addition to containing some content that only the nonframed browsers can see.

You use the tags listed in the following table to start developing a frameset document.

HTML Tag or Attribute	Description	Use in Pairs?
`<FRAMESET>...` `</FRAMESET>`	Establishes frame layout.	Yes
`BORDER=n`	Specifies width of border in pixels for all contained frames.	No
`BORDERCOLOR=#`	Specifies color (RRGGBB or name) for contained frames.	No
`COLS="n,n"`	Specifies column dimensions in pixels, percentage, or in terms of remaining space (`COLS="25%,100,*"`).	No
`FRAMEBORDER=n`	Specifies border (1) or no border (0).	No
`ROWS="n,n"`	Specifies row dimensions in pixels, percentage, or in terms of remaining space (`ROWS=25%,100,*`).	No
`<NOFRAMES>...` `</NOFRAMES>`	Specifies area of frameset document that is visible to frame-incapable browsers.	Yes

Follow these steps to set up your frameset document:

1. **Create a new HTML document.**

Don't use `<BODY>` tags; use `<FRAMESET>` tags instead.

```
<!DOCTYPE HTML PUBLIC "-//W3C//DTD HTML 4.01
    Frameset//EN"
    "http://www.w3.org/TR/html4/frameset.dtd">
<HTML>
<HEAD><TITLE>BLW, Inc.</TITLE></HEAD>
</HTML>
```

2. **Add a `<FRAMESET>` tag pair.**

```
<!DOCTYPE HTML PUBLIC "-//W3C//DTD HTML 4.01
    Frameset//EN"
    "http://www.w3.org/TR/html4/frameset.dtd">
<HTML>
<HEAD><TITLE>BLW, Inc.</TITLE></HEAD>
<FRAMESET>
</FRAMESET>
</HTML>
```

This example sets up two rows — and no columns — so you need to add a `ROWS=` attribute to the `<FRAMESET>` tag. The first (top) row is 100 pixels high, and the remaining row fills the remaining available space, so the complete attribute is `ROWS="100,*"`.

In more complex documents, you can have multiple `<FRAMESET>` tags to add frames within frames (such as a set of columns within a set of rows), but that's not necessary in this example.

3. **Add the `ROWS=` attribute.**

```
<FRAMESET ROWS="100,*">
</FRAMESET>
```

You can also specify something such as `ROWS="25%,*"` to make the first row take 25 percent of the window and the second row take the rest.

4. **If you want to remove the frame borders (kind of a neat effect), add the `BORDER=0` and `FRAMEBORDER=0` attributes to the tag.**

```
<FRAMESET ROWS="100,*" BORDER=0 FRAMEBORDER=0>
</FRAMESET>
```

Why do you need both `BORDER` *and* `FRAMEBORDER`? Well, you need one for most versions of Netscape Navigator, and the other for Microsoft Internet Explorer and other HTML 4.0-compliant browsers — dueling browsers require special accommodations.

5. Add a `<NOFRAMES>` tag pair under the `<FRAMESET>` tag to accommodate browsers that cannot display frames.

```
<FRAMESET ROWS="100,*" BORDER=0 FRAMEBORDER=0>
</FRAMESET>
<NOFRAMES>
</NOFRAMES>
```

6. Provide regular HTML code within the `<NOFRAMES>` tags for readers with frame-incapable browsers to see.

A brief identification and link to the extra content is plenty.

```
<FRAMESET ROWS="100,*" BORDER=0 FRAMEBORDER=0>
</FRAMESET>
<NOFRAMES>
<H1>Welcome to BLW Enterprises!</H1>
<A HREF="noframes.html">Please join us!</A>
</NOFRAMES>
```

Setting Up the Frames

Between the `<FRAMESET>` tags go the `<FRAME>` tags, which actually build the frames; one frame tag per column or row is called for in the `<FRAMESET>` tag. So, to set up frames, you need two `<FRAME>` tags plus the associated attributes. The following table shows the tags and attributes necessary to create frames.

HTML Tag or Attribute	Description	Use in Pairs?
`<FRAME>`	Establishes frame.	No
`BORDER=n`	Specifies width of border in pixels.	No
`FRAMEBORDER=n`	Specifies border (1) or no border (0).	No
`NAME="..."`	Provides frame name.	No
`NORESIZE`	Prevents reader from resizing frame.	No
`SCROLLING="..."`	Specifies whether the frame can scroll in terms of YES, NO, or AUTO(matic). Yes requires scrollbars; No prohibits them.	No
`SRC="URL"`	Identifies source file that flows into frame.	No

Note: At this point, I assume that you have a complete frameset document and need only to add the `<FRAME>` tags. The following block of code builds on the previous one:

```
<!DOCTYPE HTML PUBLIC "-//W3C//DTD HTML 4.01
    Frameset//EN"
    "http://www.w3.org/TR/html4/frameset.dtd">
<HTML>
```

```
<HEAD><TITLE>BLW, Inc.</TITLE></HEAD>
<FRAMESET ROWS="100,*" BORDER=0 FRAMEBORDER=0>
</FRAMESET>
<NOFRAMES>
<H1>Welcome to BLW Enterprises!</H1>
<A HREF="noframes.html">Please join us!</A>
</NOFRAMES>
</HTML>
```

Follow these steps:

1. **Add the first <FRAME> tag, corresponding to the top (banner) frame. (To see an example of a banner frame, take a peek at Figure 7-2 earlier in this chapter.)**

```
<FRAMESET ROWS="100,*" BORDER=0 FRAMEBORDER=0>
<FRAME>
</FRAMESET>
```

2. **Add the SRC= attribute, which uses a standard URL (absolute or relative) to point to the document that is to fill this frame.**

```
<FRAME SRC="banner.htm">
```

3. **Add the NAME= attribute to name the frame so that you can refer to it later within HTML documents.**

I call this one "banner" because it acts as a banner at the top of the page.

```
<FRAME SRC="banner.htm" NAME="banner">
```

4. **Add other attributes, if you want — for example, those that follow.**

The <FRAMESET> tag turned off the borders, but that can, optionally, also be done in each individual frame. Because the banner.htm document is primarily an image of a known size, turning off the scroll bars and preventing readers from resizing the frame is a good idea. This setup gives us a little extra layout control but could cause real problems for readers if you accidentally put more content in banner.htm than fits in the available space.

```
<FRAME SRC="banner.htm" NAME="banner" NORESIZE
SCROLLING=NO>
```

5. **Add the remaining <FRAME> tags and attributes.**

```
<FRAME SRC="banner.htm" NAME="banner" NORESIZE
    SCROLLING=NO>
<FRAME SRC="main.htm" NAME="content"
    SCROLLING=AUTO>
```

A good idea is not to restrict either scrolling or resizing for the content frame; readers may need to scroll to see all the text.

After your frames are complete, open up your frameset document in your browser and check out the frames. Figure 7-3 shows the frame I created.

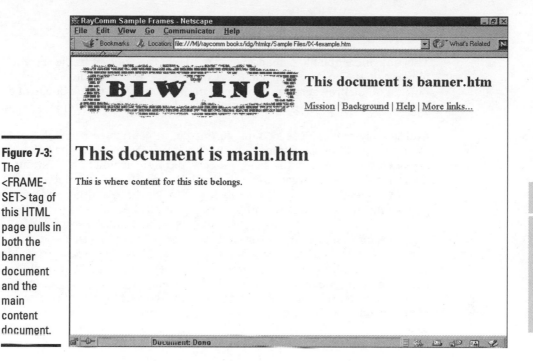

Figure 7-3:
The
<FRAME-
SET> tag of
this HTML
page pulls in
both the
banner
document
and the
main
content
document.

Setting Up Links and Targets

When you set up links in framed documents, you can make some links appear in a completely new window, some appear in the same frame, and some appear in different frames.

To control where links appear, you use an additional attribute, as shown in the following table, for the <A> tag.

HTML Attribute	Effect	Use in Pairs?
TARGET="..."	Specifies the default TARGET for links from framed pages.	No

Each of your links from a framed page should have the additional TARGET= attribute to name the frame in which the link should appear. The previous blocks of code named the top frame "banner" and the lower frame "content" so that links will be targeted accordingly.

To establish a link from the banner.htm document (contained in the banner frame) to the document called mission.htm (which appears within the content frame), add the following TARGET attribute to the existing link:

```
<A HREF="mission.htm" TARGET="content">Mission
    Statement</A>
```

This link opens the file named mission.htm in the content frame (as you may recall, the content frame in this example is the larger frame at the bottom of the browser window). If you omit the target, the link opens in the same frame as the anchor — the navigation frame, in this example.

Additionally, you can use a couple of "magic" target names: _top and _window are the most common and useful. If you target _top, the link replaces your frames in the same window and returns you to a nonframed environment. If you target _window, the link appears in a completely new window. Targeting _window is handy if you're linking to another site — your pages remain open while the others are also easily accessible.

Suppose, for example, that within your Web site you suggest that readers access the Dummies home page at www.dummies.com. You probably wouldn't want the Dummies page to appear within one of your frames; that would look silly. Therefore, you need to break out of the frames by using the _window magic target. Your framed site remains open and a new browser window appears with the Dummies home page in it. Just use code similar to the following:

```
<A HREF="http://www.dummies.com/"
    TARGET="_window">Dummies Home Page</A>
```

In addition to working in the <A> tag, the TARGET= attribute works in any other link, such as an imagemap or a form. (The form results appear in the targeted frame.)

Testing Your Framed Site

After you completely set up your framed site, you want to test the site extensively to make sure that all the pages and links work as you'd hoped. Beyond the obvious step of opening your frameset document in several different browsers and clicking all the links, a couple of tips may make the process a little easier:

✦ If you're sure that you've made and saved frameset document changes, but they don't seem to be appearing in the browser, exit from the browser and open it again.

✦ If you edited one of the documents within a frame and want to reload just that document, click inside the frame, and then click the Reload or Refresh buttons in your browser.

Chapter 8: Developing Style Sheets

In This Chapter

✔ **About style sheets**

✔ **Connecting style sheets to HTML documents**

✔ **Developing style sheets**

Style sheets, yet another standard from the World Wide Web Consortium, provide all the formatting capabilities you could ever want for your Web pages.

The bad news is that both Microsoft Internet Explorer and Netscape support style sheets, but that support isn't identical: Each browser displays style sheet code just a bit differently than the other. And readers who aren't using an HTML 4.0-capable browser won't be able to see the nifty formatting effects you add by using style sheets. This chapter gives you suggestions for accommodating those wood-burning browsers.

Throughout this chapter, I assume you're familiar with how HTML tags work. If you're not, brush up on Chapter 1 before diving into this chapter.

About Style Sheets

Style sheets provide formatting commands for Web pages in a more convenient and efficient manner than regular HTML offers.

Using style sheets, you can format practically any element of your HTML document and have that formatting applied to the same elements throughout your entire Web site. So, rather than manually change all those pesky headings, you can simply change the heading style and change the appearance of all of them in one fell swoop.

Accommodating browser differences

At the time of writing, browser support for styles sheets is still fairly unpredictable. Check out `www.webreview.com/style/css1/charts/mastergrid.shtml` for a comparative chart showing support for different browsers and different style sheet characteristics.

If you know that your readers are in the roughly 65 percent of the Internet population that uses style sheet-capable browsers, by all means, use style sheets, albeit with some care. If, as is more likely, your readers include some with style sheet-capable browsers and some with older browsers, you have three choices:

✦ Use style sheets exclusively and let readers with older browsers see the plain, mostly unformatted text.

✦ Use just regular HTML formatting commands and pretend that style sheets don't exist.

✦ Use both style sheets and regular HTML formatting options. It'll take twice as much effort on your part (and will be redundant and repetitive and format the same thing over and over again) but will accommodate a larger percentage of your readers more effectively than the other options.

A good compromise for using style sheets and accommodating browsers that do not reliably handle them is to do the following:

✦ Format the background and basic text colors (defined in the `<BODY>` tag of regular HTML documents) with HTML commands.

✦ Format the background and basic text colors with style sheets. (If necessary, these style sheet commands will override the analogous commands from the regular HTML document.)

✦ Provide any additional formatting commands through style sheets and, optionally, HTML markup tags.

Understanding inheritance

Inheritance means that a document takes on global basic characteristics, and each more specific formatting command that you define overrides the last (for most elements). For example, if you define the background of the whole page as red, the background of a table as blue, and the background of a table cell as green, the most specific formatting (green for the cell) takes precedence.

In general, here's the order of precedence:

✦ Document-wide formatting from HTML document (defined in the `<BODY>` tag) is the most basic.

✦ Document-wide formatting from a style sheet overrides document-wide formatting from an HTML document.

✦ Specific formatting in HTML overrides document-wide formatting.

✦ Specific formatting from a style sheet overrides specific formatting in HTML.

✦ Specific formatting from a style sheet overrides general formatting.

In general, if specific formatting is defined in the HTML document and the format for the same element is also defined in a style sheet, the style sheet formatting wins. If a more specific element (such as a table cell, rather than the whole table) is specified either in the style sheet or HTML document, the specific element wins.

Before you get started using style sheets, remember that the style sheet is not necessarily part of the HTML document. In fact, depending on how you do it (see the options in the next section), the style sheet can be a completely different document. So, the first step is to decide how you want to connect the style sheet to the HTML document. Then you can develop the style sheet, which specifies all the bells and whistles you want to include. Read on for details.

**Book II
Chapter 8**

Developing
Style Sheets

Connecting Style Sheets to HTML Documents

The first step in using style sheets is to decide how you want to connect them to your HTML documents. After you get the hang of using style sheets and know how you'll connect them, you might just dive in and start creating them. (You find the exact process later in this chapter.) For now, however, you need to get an idea of how style sheets and HTML documents can relate.

Basically, style sheets can connect to HTML documents in four ways. You can do any one of the following:

✦ Embed the style sheet in the HTML document.

✦ Link the style sheet to the HTML document.

✦ Import the style sheet into the HTML document.

✦ Add style sheet rules as attributes to regular HTML tags.

This chapter covers only the first two options — mainly because these are the most widely supported options and are the most practical ones to use. (Also, the latter two are somewhat more complicated, convoluted, and beyond the scope of the book.)

If you're interested in knowing how to use the latter two options, check out *HTML 4 For Dummies,* 3rd Edition, by Ed Tittel, Natanya Pitts, and Chelsea Valentine, published by Hungry Minds, Inc.

Embedding style sheets

The easiest way to handle style sheets is to embed them within the `<HEAD>` (technically, within `<STYLE>` tags within the `<HEAD>`) of the HTML document — easy because you don't have to create a completely different document for the style sheet. You can simply work with an HTML document you already have.

To embed a style sheet, use the tags and attributes listed in the following table.

HTML Tag or Attribute	Description	Use in Pairs?
`<STYLE>`...`</STYLE>`	Specifies style block.	Yes
`TYPE="text/css"`	Specifies type of style sheet.	No
`<!--` `-->`	Hides style sheet commands from older browsers.	Yes

The following steps show you how to add the `<STYLE>` tag and its attributes.

1. **Start with a functional HTML document.**

The top of the document should look something like the following block of code.

```
<!DOCTYPE HTML PUBLIC "-//W3C//DTD HTML 4.01
    Frameset//EN"
    "http://www.w3.org/TR/html4/frameset.dtd">
<HTML>
<HEAD>
<TITLE>Cats Galore</TITLE>
</HEAD>
<BODY>
</BODY>
</HTML>
```

2. **Add `<STYLE>` tags.**

```
<TITLE>Cats Galore</TITLE>
<STYLE>
</STYLE>
</HEAD>
```

3. **Add comment tags within the** <STYLE> **tags to hide the styles from older browsers.**

```
<STYLE>
<!--
-->
</STYLE>
```

4. **Add the** TYPE="text/css" **attribute to specify that you're using a Cascading Style Sheet.**

(Other style sheet formats exist, most notably JavaScript Style Sheets, but are less common and nonstandard, so this chapter doesn't address them.)

```
<STYLE TYPE="text/css">
<!--
-->
</STYLE>
```

That's it! You won't see anything different in the document, but you've found a home for your styles now. When you actually develop the style sheet and specify cool formatting, you add it between the <STYLE> tags, as shown in the section, "Developing Style Sheets," later in this chapter.

**Book II
Chapter 8**

**Developing
Style Sheets**

Linking style sheets

Linking style sheets can be a little more confusing than embedding them, mostly because the formatting information is in one location and the actual HTML code is in a completely separate document. That also, however, provides the biggest advantage of style sheets.

Here's why. Suppose that you have 17 documents in your Web site. You decide you want to add a background image to them all. If you're using embedded style sheets or traditional HTML coding, you have to open and edit every one of those 17 documents to add the appropriate code. If, however, you've linked a single style sheet to each of those 17 documents, you need to make only a single change in that style sheet and (voilà!) the change happens in each linked document.

You can use the following tags and attributes to link your style sheets:

HTML Tag or Attribute	Description	Use in Pairs?
<LINK>	Connects document to other information.	No
REL="StyleSheet"	Specifies that the link is to a style sheet.	No
TYPE="text/css"	Specifies type of style sheet.	No
HREF="..."	Indicates URL of linked style sheet.	No

In linking style sheets, you need to create the style sheet file (so that you have a filename to link *to*). Only then can you include a link to the style sheet file within your HTML document.

Creating the style sheet file

If you choose to link to a style sheet, you need to create a file that contains the style sheet. The file must be a plain-text file, just like regular HTML documents, and have an extension of .css (instead of .htm or .html). It contains the same style sheet rules you use in an embedded style sheet. Check out the section, "Developing Style Sheets," for help in creating a style sheet file.

Putting in the link

To link a style sheet to an HTML document, you use the <LINK> tag, including the REL, TYPE, and HREF attributes, as shown in the following block of code.

```
<LINK REL="StyleSheet" TYPE="text/css"
    HREF="newstyle.css">
```

You must specify the values for the REL and TYPE attributes as shown; for the HREF attribute, simply fill in the name (or address) of the style sheet file to which you want to link.

You can link and embed a style sheet in the same document. For example, you might have a generic style sheet that applies to most of your HTML documents — that one you'd link. Then, just below the <LINK> tag, you could embed another style sheet with exceptions or additions to the generic style sheet. Both style sheets affect your document, with the style definitions embedded in the document overriding the linked ones.

This capability of using multiple style sheets is the cascading part of the Cascading Style Sheet name. You could use a generic style sheet that applies to all of your documents and then a second (or third or fourth) style sheet with formatting specific to the particular document.

Developing Style Sheets

To develop a style sheet, you must get the hang of constructing style rules, which are the (unfortunately) cryptic pieces of code that make up a style sheet. In the next section, you see how these pieces fit together, and then you see how to use them to develop your own style sheets.

Constructing style rules

Style sheets are made up of rules which simply tell browsers how to format HTML elements. Just as HTML tags identify parts of a document — such as a paragraph, heading, table, or list — style rules specify formatting for those elements.

Style rules look a bit different from HTML. For example, instead of using angle brackets as you do with HTML code, you use curly braces ({ }). And instead of using HTML-like abbreviations, you get to use some spelled-out words and descriptions. After you get used to the differences, you may even find style sheets easier to read and work with than HTML code.

Style rules have two basic parts:

✦ The part that identifies which element the style applies to (technically called the *selector*)

✦ The part that tells browsers how to display that element (technically called the *declaration*)

Take a look at the following:

```
P { color: blue }
```

In this example, the P (called the selector) identifies which HTML element the style applies to, and the information within the curly brackets (the property and the value, respectively) tells browsers how to display the element. In this case, the style rule specifies that all paragraphs (P) in the document should be blue.

Also, note that you can string together style rules, if you find doing so easier. For example, instead of having two separate rules on two lines, like this:

```
P { color: red }
P { background-color: white }
```

you can put the rules together within the same set of brackets by using a semicolon, like this:

```
P { color: red ; background-color: white }
```

And, just as you can add multiple declarations and values within the brackets, you can specify multiple elements, like this:

```
H1, H2, H3, H4, H5, H6 { color: green }
```

Notice that when you string together elements, you separate them with commas (not semicolons, as you do between multiple declarations).

With these basic style rule construction concepts in mind, find out in the following sections how to bring them all together.

Applying style rules

The following table summarizes the various declarations and values you see in the next several sections.

Property	Selected Possible Values
font-family	Font names from reader's systems, plus generic choices of serif, sans-serif, or monospace
font-size	xx-small, x-small, small, medium, large, x-large, xx-large, smaller, larger
font-style	normal, italic, oblique
font-variant	normal, small-caps
font-weight	normal, bold, bolder, lighter
color	#RRGGBB number
background-color	#RRGGBB number or color name
background-image	url(. . .)
background-attachment	fixed, scroll
background-repeat	repeat, repeat-x, repeat-y, no-repeat
background-position	%,%
float	left, right

As you can see from this limited sample of declarations and values, the number of style combinations is endless.

Setting a font for an entire document

With just a few commands, you can apply formatting to the whole document. To set the font for the entire body (everything within the <BODY> and </BODY> parts of the HTML document), use the following steps:

1. **In the style sheet, add the** BODY **element to specify what the style rule applies to.**

```
<STYLE>
<!--
BODY
-->
</STYLE>
```

2. **Add { and } to contain the style declaration.**

```
<STYLE>
<!--
BODY { }
-->
</STYLE>
```

3. **Add the** `font-family` **property, followed by a colon (:).**

```
BODY { font-family: }
```

4. **Add the first choice font.**

```
BODY { font-family: Arial }
```

5. **Add other font choices if you want.**

```
BODY { font-family: Helvetica, Swiss }
```

6. **Add the closest generic choice from the preceding table.**

```
BODY { font-family: Arial, Helvetica,
        Swiss, sans-serif }
```

When this style sheet is applied to the document shown in Figure 8-1, the result is the niftily styled page you see in Figure 8-2.

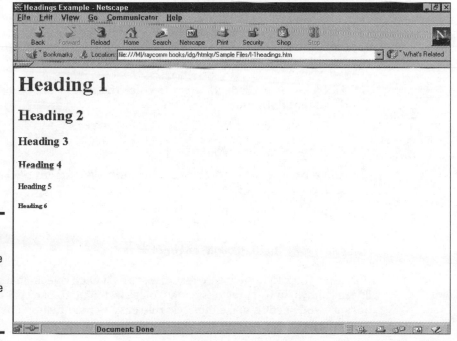

Figure 8-1:
This is how the example Web page looks before any styles are added.

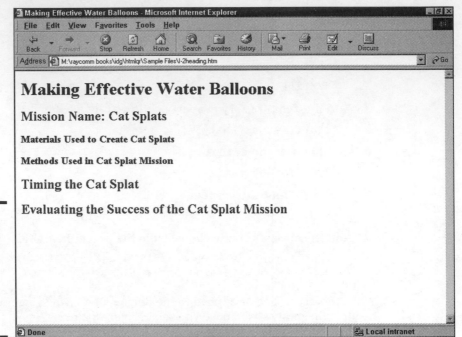

Figure 8-2:
Setting the
font for an
entire
document
using the
BODY
selector.

Specifying text and background colors

Another popular use of style sheets is to specify text and background
colors. The following steps describe how to do both within the same rule.

1. **Add a** `color` **style declaration to color the text in the body of the
   document dark blue.**

   ```
   BODY { font-family: Arial, Helvetica,
         Swiss, sans-serif ;
         color: #000066 }
   ```

2. **Add a** `background-color` **to set the entire document background to
   pale yellow.**

   ```
   BODY { font-family: Arial, Helvetica,
         Swiss, sans-serif ;
         color: #000066 ;
         background-color: #ffffcc }
   ```

Note that you can more easily read the styles if each one is on a separate
line, as shown in the previous code. You're welcome to use spaces or tabs
because you need to make the style rule easy to read by humans as well as
by computers.

To add other style rules, you need only put more rules on additional lines. Follow these steps:

1. **To color first level headings, you could add an H1 element.**

```
BODY { font-family: Arial, Helvetica,
    Swiss, sans-serif ;
    color: 000066 ;
    background-color: ffffcc }
H1 { color: #ff0000 }
```

2. **If you want the background of the first level headings — and only of the first level headings — to be white, you can set that, too.**

```
BODY { font-family: Arial, Helvetica,
    Swiss, sans-serif ;
    color: #000066 ;
    background-color: #ffffcc }
H1 { color: #ff0000 ;
    background-color: #ffffff }
```

Specifying background images

You can specify background images for the document as a whole, as you do in HTML, and for individual elements (which you cannot do in HTML). You can also control many aspects of the background image appearance as well. Here's how:

1. **Add a style declaration to set a background image.**

```
BODY { font-family: Arial, Helvetica,
    Swiss, sans-serif ;
    color: #000066 ;
    background-color: #ffffcc ;
    background-image:
    url(winchesterback.jpg) }
```

2. **Add another style declaration to keep the image from scrolling so that it looks like a watermark on the screen.**

```
BODY { font-family: Arial, Helvetica,
    Swiss, sans-serif ;
    color: #000066 ;
    background-color: #ffffcc ;
    background-image:
    url(winchesterback.jpg) ;
    background-attachment: fixed }
```

3. **Specify the location of the image on the background.**

The following code specifies background-position values of 50%, 0% to move the image horizontally halfway across the screen and position it at the top, respectively.

```
BODY { font-family: Arial, Helvetica,
       Swiss, sans-serif ;
     color: #000066 ;
     background-color: #ffffcc ;
     background-image:
     url(winchesterback.jpg) ;
     background-attachment: fixed ;
     background-position: 50% 0% }
```

4. **Set background images to repeat only horizontally, only vertically, both, or not at all.**

   To preserve the watermark effect, this case specifies "not at all."

```
BODY { font-family: Arial, Helvetica,
       Swiss, sans-serif ;
     color: #000066 ;
     background-color: #ffffcc ;
     background-image:
     url(winchesterback.jpg) ;
     background-attachment: fixed ;
     background-position: 50% 0% ;
     background-repeat: no-repeat}
```

The end result of the code in Steps 1 through 4 is a background image that remains in a specific location on a Web page — even when users scroll that Web page. I encourage you to experiment with specifying different values for the `background-attachment`, `background-position`, and `background-repeat` attributes until you create the perfect background effect for your site.

Using style sheets effectively

Although no "one right way" exists to develop and format style sheets, some techniques prove more effective than others. Here are a few tips to get you started:

✔ Take care of the document-wide formatting first — that is, specify the background image, background color, and font before you start specifying the nitpicky individual formatting.

✔ Add one or two styles at a time and test them. Troubleshooting just a few new styles is easier than troubleshooting a whole blob of new ones.

✔ Stay as simple as possible and expand gradually, as you need to. It's easier to add new styles one at a time than it is to back-track and remove styles.

✔ Remember not to get caught up in the apparent WYSIWYG-ness of style sheets. You still don't have absolute control of the final appearance of the document because your readers may not have style-sheet-capable browsers, may have their browsers set not to use style sheets, or may override your formatting with their own preferred formatting.

Index

Symbols

{} (curly braces), 179
/ (forward slash), 108
(pound sign), 136
+ (plus sign), 129
_ (underscore), 129

A

`<A>` tag, 131–133, 135–136, 171–172
ACTION attribute, 153–155
ALIGN attribute, 121–122, 142, 150
ALINK attribute, 120, 121
ALT attribute, 138, 139, 145
AltaVista, 112
alternative text, 139
anchors, 128, 131, 144–146

B

`<B>` tag, 114
background(s)
    color, 117–118, 180, 182–183
    images, 118–119, 180, 183–184
BACKGROUND attribute, 118–119
background-attachment attribute, 180, 184
background-color attribute, 180, 182, 183
background-image attribute, 180
background-position attribute, 180, 184
background-repeat attribute, 180, 184
BGCOLOR attribute, 117–118
blank space, around images, 143
`<BODY>` tag, 110, 112–113, 180–181
boldface font, 109, 114
BORDER attribute, 138, 145, 149, 167, 169
BORDERCOLOR attribute, 167

borders
    frame, 167, 169
    image, 138, 145
    table, 149
`<BR>` tag, 151–152
browser(s)
    differences, accommodating, 173–174
    style sheets and, 173–174
    XHTML and, 109

C

case-sensitivity, 108, 109
check boxes, including, 156–158
CHECKED attribute, 155, 158–159
`<CLEAR>` tag, 151–152
clip art, 140. *See also* graphics
colon (:), 181
COLOR attribute, 124, 126, 180, 182
color
    background, 117–118, 180, 182–183
    text, 120–121, 182–183
COLS attribute, 161, 162, 167
content documents, for frames, 164, 166
copyrights, 140
curly braces ({}), 179

D

declarations, 179
directory names, in URLs, 129
`<!DOCTYPE>` tag, 110
documents
    connecting style sheets to, 175–178
    links within, 134–136
    setting fonts for entire, 180–182
    within your site, links to, 131–132
downloading time, reducing, 141
Dreamweaver (Macromedia), 136

E

`<EM>` tag, 114

F

FACE attribute, 124, 125
file size, specifying, 141
File Transfer Protocol (FTP), 134
float attribute, 180
`<FONT>` tag, 124–125
font-family attribute, 180
font-size attribute, 180
font-style attribute, 180
font-variant attribute, 180
font-weight attribute, 180
fonts, 109, 123–126, 180–182. *See also* text
form(s)
    additional input types in, 159
    check boxes in, 156–158
    components, including, 155–162
    creating, 153–155
    radio buttons in, 156, 158–159
    select lists in, 160–161
    text areas in, 161–162
`<FORM>` tag, 153–155
forward slash (/), 108
`<FRAME>` tag, 169
FRAMEBORDER attribute, 167, 169
frames, 163–172
framesets, 167–169
`<FRAMESET>` tag, 167–169
FTP. *See* File Transfer Protocol (FTP)

G

GIFs. *See* Graphics Interchange Format
graphics
    adding, 137–140
    aligning, 142

Notes

Book III

FrontPage 2002

The 5th Wave   By Rich Tennant

"Maybe it would help our Web site if we showed our products in action."

Contents at a Glance

Chapter 1: Getting to Know FrontPage

In This Chapter

- ✔ Discovering the power of FrontPage
- ✔ Accessing the Views bar
- ✔ Using the FrontPage Editor

You don't need to be a whiz kid to churn out a quality Web page. By using FrontPage, you can join the ranks of Web page designers. FrontPage is a powerful program that enables you to create almost any type of Web page. This chapter covers the FrontPage basics and introduces you to some of the program's essential tools.

What Is FrontPage, and What Can I Do with It?

FrontPage is an all-in-one Web publishing tool for big-time Web companies (such as Yahoo! or ESPN), small companies, and personal users. By using FrontPage, you can create individual Web pages and publish them to the Internet, generate tracking reports about those Web pages, and effectively administer the Web site after it's on the Net . . . all from within the same program.

Of course, you may never want to administer an entire Web site and use all that functionality, and that's okay. If you just want to build ordinary HTML pages and put them up on the Internet or the company intranet, that's fine, too. FrontPage is exceptionally flexible and scalable; it can grow with you as your Web site needs grow.

How FrontPage Is Organized

FrontPage contains a multitude of features, mini-applications, and menus, all wrapped up in one tidy little package. Still, maneuvering around FrontPage can baffle anyone. So to better orient you, Figure 1-1 shows you a typical

FrontPage interface. You also see figure callouts for a number of features. Pay particular attention to the callouts, because you're going to find yourself using those features the most.

Formatting Toolbar

Standard Toolbar

Views bar

Figure 1-1:
Welcome
to the
FrontPage
Interface.

Picture Toolbar

Exploring the Views Bar

You need to work pretty hard not to notice the Views bar after you fire up FrontPage for the first time. The Views bar's big menu, with its icons running down the left side of the screen, makes accessing the vast majority of features in FrontPage easy.

Each Views bar icon represents a different feature in FrontPage. To jump to a FrontPage feature, simply click the icon. The new feature appears in the right three-quarters of the screen, below the menus and toolbars.

If you don't like the Views bar, you can turn it off by right-clicking the bar and choosing Hide Views Bar from the shortcut menu. Presto! The Views bar disappears. After you turn off the Views bar, you can still toggle your view within FrontPage by choosing one of the six views from the View menu. To see the Views bar again, choose View➪Views Bar.

If you want to change the size of the icons in the Views bar, right-click the Views bar and select Small Icons from the shortcut menu.

FrontPage features six key *views* to represent major components that you may or may not use, depending on your Web project. The following list describes these views:

✦ **Page view:** Where you build all your Web pages (refer to Figure 1-1).

   You can preview your Web site in Internet Explorer at any time by choosing File➪Preview in Browser.

✦ **Folders view:** Displays a typical Windows Explorer menu, making all your Web project's files and folders easily accessible within FrontPage (see Figure 1-2). From this view, you can also drag and drop files, which makes adding and deleting content easy.

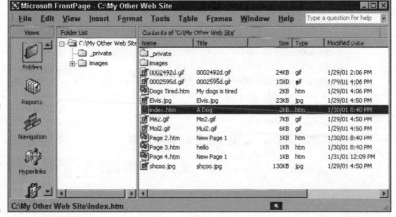

Figure 1-2: The FrontPage Folders view displays your folders.

Book III Chapter 1

Getting to Know FrontPage

A Folder List also appears in the Folders view. You can access the Folder List in other FrontPage views by choosing View➪Folders.

✦ **Reports view:** Gives you a Site Summary (see Figure 1-3), which provides a bird's-eye view of what's working within your Web site (or not working, if, for example, your site contains some broken hyperlinks). From the Reports view, you can also run a more detailed series of reports that give you immediate information on the status of various aspects of your Web site, such as load times or hyperlink status.

✦ **Navigation view:** Provides a visual representation of all the pages on your Web site and the pages' hierarchical order. By dragging around the pages, you can change the relationships of those pages to one another and organize the pages of your site more effectively.

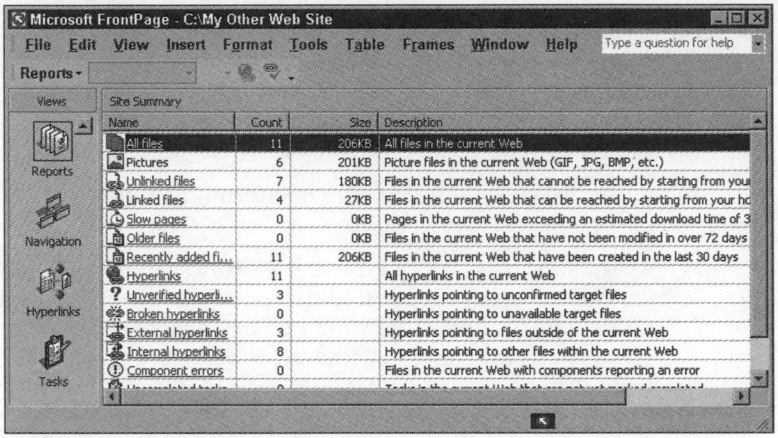

Figure 1-3:
Reports view enables you to manage your site at a glance.

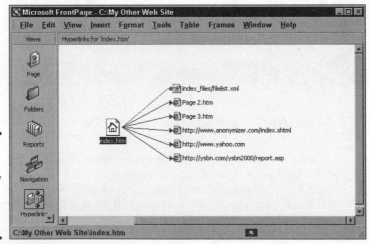

✦ **Hyperlinks view:** Gives you a graphical representation of how every Web page connects to every other page within your Web site (see Figure 1-4). This view can prove particularly useful if you want to see how your pages connect to one another. In addition, the Hyperlinks view provides a quick way to see which pages link to other sites outside your own.

Figure 1-4:
Check out your links by using the Hyperlinks view.

✦ **Tasks view:** Enables you to assign tasks to individuals on your team, check the status of tasks that are already underway, and manage the workflow and the publishing of new elements to the site. You can also use it to stay on top of tasks that you have to do yourself. Tasks view makes a very good to-do list. If you're going to use FrontPage in a multiuser environment, the Tasks view (which you display by clicking the Tasks view button, shown in Figure 1-3) no doubt becomes a common sight.

Introducing the FrontPage Editor

The FrontPage Editor is the program's built-in tool for creating and viewing Web pages. You can switch to Page view and then click a button at the bottom of the window — Normal, HTML, or Preview — to switch among the following modes:

✦ **Normal mode:** FrontPage's visual editor for Web development. In Normal mode, you can place elements — meaning text, graphics, applets, or whatever — on-screen in any location, and FrontPage automatically generates HTML to account for the location of every object on-screen.

✦ **HTML mode:** Enables you to edit raw HTML by hand, just as you did in the bad ol' days (for the purist).

✦ **Preview mode:** Enables you to see what your pages look like in a Web browser window before you put them up on the Internet. The FrontPage default browser is Internet Explorer.

As you become familiar with FrontPage, you may find yourself switching back and forth between modes when you create your Web pages. For example, many folks begin creating their pages in Normal mode, then switch to Preview mode to check their work and back again to Normal to adjust their layout and design, repeating as necessary. When they want to incorporate a bit of hand-coded HTML (for example, the HTML code necessary to incorporate a custom JavaScript script, which I cover in Book 7) they simply switch to HTML mode — then back again to Preview mode to view the finished product.

Book III
Chapter 1

Getting to Know FrontPage

Chapter 2: Getting Started with FrontPage: Your First Web

In This Chapter

- ✔ Creating a new Web yourself or with a template
- ✔ Creating a Web page yourself or with a template
- ✔ Naming (and renaming) your Web page
- ✔ Saving your Web page
- ✔ Opening files in odd formats with FrontPage

*O*h what a tangled Web you can weave — but FrontPage makes starting out and keeping track of what you're doing easy. Whether you plan to create a Web page on your own or use one of the Web templates that the program provides, this chapter shows you the basics. If you can figure out how to open, save, and close your Web pages, you're well on the road to Webmastery.

Creating a New Web

In FrontPage terminology, a *Web* is a Web site. As you create a Web site, FrontPage asks you to create a folder to store the files that make up the Web site.

FrontPage, if you let it have its way, names the folder *My Web*. Although this name may seem nice and homey, it isn't particularly effective in helping you remember what your Web contains. And after you name your Web site, changing the name can prove a hassle if you decide that you don't like the current name. Naming your Web, therefore, is one of the more important decisions that you can make. Before you save your Web for the first time, think of a good name for it.

Whenever you start FrontPage, the program creates a default HTML page, `new_page_1.html`, and then opens that page for you. Although FrontPage does some of this work for you, you want to create your own Web project. To do so, follow these steps:

1. **Choose File➪New➪Page or Web to open the New Page or Web task pane, as shown in the right side of Figure 2-1.**

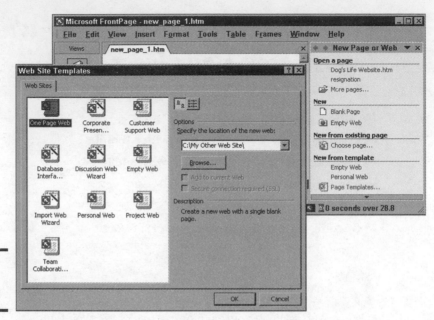

2. **Under New in the task pane, click Empty Web.**

   The Web Site Templates dialog box appears (refer to Figure 2-1).

3. **Enter a name for your Web site in the <u>S</u>pecify the Location of the New Web text box.**

   In fact — and this part is confusing — what you enter determines both the location *and* the name of your new Web. After you finish naming it, FrontPage creates a new folder with the name that you choose, and then FrontPage generates the Web contents in that folder.

4. **Select a type of Web from one of the available templates.**

   The templates appear in icon form in the Web Site Templates dialog box. Each has a descriptive name (refer to Figure 2-1).

   The templates make possible different kinds of Web sites that you may want to build. The default selection — the one that FrontPage loads on startup — is One Page Web, a simple, one-page-long Web site. But FrontPage comes with several Web templates that enable you to design a Web site that you can tailor to your business or personal needs. Choose the Personal Web template, for example, to create a Web site that describes your family and its adventures. Table 2-1 describes these Web templates.

5. Click OK or press Enter to create your new Web.

Note: As you create a Web, you notice that FrontPage creates a few extra items, including an Images folder and a Private folder. The Images folder is the default location for housing images in your Web. The Private folder (it's actually called _Private) is where FrontPage puts the majority of the code it generates automatically to create your Web site.

Table 2-1	Web Templates in FrontPage
Template	*Description*
One Page Web	Includes just a single Web page.
Corporate Presence Wizard	Includes pages for products and services, feedback, and a search page, as well as pages for mission statements and contact information.
Customer Support Web	Includes the tools necessary for building a compelling customer support site, including pages for discussion groups, FAQs, bug-list reports, a searchable database, and bulletin-board postings.
Database Interface Wizard	Includes tools for interfacing with a database so that you can view, add, and update records in the database.
Discussion Web Wizard	Includes search forms, a discussion area, and user registration.
Empty Web	Includes only the empty default folders.
Import Web Wizard	Walks you through the process of importing an existing Web into a new Web.
Personal Web	Includes a home page, plus pages for a photo album, your personal interests, and your favorite sites on the World Wide Web.
Project Web	Includes such things as schedules, task status, discussion pages, and team-member information.
Share-Point-based Team Web Site	Includes a calendar, library for documents that you share with others, and a task list so that you can build a Web site with your colleagues. (This Web template replaces the Team Collaboration Web Site found in earlier versions of FrontPage.)

Creating Web Pages

Creating new Web pages is perhaps the most common task that you perform in FrontPage, especially if you have a good-sized Web site. Not surprisingly, then, FrontPage offers you a plethora of options for generating new Web pages, whether you want to create merely an empty page or something as sophisticated as a page involving frames.

Creating an empty Web page

You can create a new, empty HTML page to add to your Web in several ways, but the following methods may prove the easiest:

✦ **From the New Page or Web task pane:** To create a Web page by using the task pane, choose File⇨New⇨Page or Web. Then choose Blank Page from the New Page or Web task page that appears.

✦ **From the toolbar:** Just below the File menu lies the New Page button. Click it (or press Ctrl+N) to create a new Web page.

✦ **From the Folder List:** Any time the Folder List is active, you can generate a new, blank Web page by right-clicking a blank part of the Folder List and choosing New⇨Page from the shortcut menu.

After you create a new page, a tab appears along the top of the window in Page View. Click a tab to go from page to page.

Saving an HTML file as a template

Suppose that you're working on a Web page and you suddenly realize, "Zoinks! All my other Web pages should have these same basic elements!" FrontPage enables you to save an HTML page as a template, which you can then load the same as other HTML templates. To save an HTML page as a template, follow these steps:

1. **Switch to Page view and make the pane active by clicking in it.**

2. **Choose File⇨Save As.**

   The Save As dialog box appears.

3. **Select FrontPage Template (*.tem) from the Save As Type drop-down list.**

   The dialog box opens to the C:\Windows\ Application Data\Microsoft\FrontPage\Pages folder, the folder where FrontPage keeps its templates. (Depending on which version of Windows you're running, the templates may

be in a different folder. You can look for the folder, however, starting in the C:\Windows path. Look in C:\Window*your name* to find the folder where FrontPage keeps its templates.)

4. **Click the Save button.**

   The Save As Template dialog box appears.

5. **Enter a title, name, and description for your template and click OK.**

   The title, name, and description that you enter appears in the Page Templates dialog box along with the titles, names, and descriptions of other templates.

After you save your file, you can see and choose your new template on the General tab of the Page Templates dialog box, which is the one that you see after you click Page Templates in the New Page or Web task pane.

Creating a Web page from a template

FrontPage gives you many more options for creating Web pages than just making an empty page. In fact, FrontPage includes 36 different Web page templates that make choosing a Web page for almost any of your needs easy. Table 2-2 lists some of these templates. To create a Web page from a template, choose File➪New➪Page or Web, click Page Templates in the New Page or Web task pane that appears, and double-click a template in the Page Templates dialog box that opens. The Preview box in the dialog box shows you what kind of Web page you get with each selection.

The fastest way to open the Page Templates dialog box is to open the New Page button drop-down list from the toolbar and choose Page.

Table 2-2	Web Page Templates
Web Page Template	*Features*
Bibliography	Creates a page with entries in the correct form for a bibliography.
Confirmation Form	Creates a customer-service reply page for users to submit a query.
Feedback Form	Provides a form for submitting and receiving feedback.
Form Page Wizard	Creates a customized page containing a form that Web surfers can submit.
Frequently Asked Questions	Includes a blank table of contents and links to major sections. (You get to fill them in, however.)
Guestbook	Creates a form that visitors can use to post comments to your Web site.
Narrow Left-aligned Body	Creates a page with a slender column along the left side.
Narrow Right-aligned Body	Creates a page with a slender column along the right side.
One-column Body	Creates a page with a column in the middle, a title at the top, and some default text down the middle of the page. Formatting options include:
	One-column Body with Contents and Sidebar
	One-column Body with Contents on Left
	One-column Body with Contents on Right
	One-column Body with Staggered Sidebar
	One-column Body with Two Sidebars
	One-column Body with Two-column Sidebar
Photo Gallery	Creates a page laid out for presenting photographs.
Search Page	Creates a search form with instructions.
Table of Contents	Creates a set of topics and built-in links for your Web pages.

(continued)

**Book III
Chapter 2**

**Getting Started
with FrontPage:
Your First Web**

Table 2-2 *(continued)*

Web Page Template	Features
Three-column Body	Creates three columns and a header at the top.
Two-column Body	Creates two text columns and a header at the top. Formatting options include:
	Two-column Body with Contents and Sidebar
	Two-column Body with Contents on Left
	Two-column Body with Contents on Right
	Two-column Staggered Body
	Two-column Staggered Body with Contents and Sidebar
User Registration	Includes a default set of text fields for registering new visitors to your Web site.
Wide Body with Headings	Creates a page with text in the middle and header at the top.

Creating framed Web pages

Ever see a Web page where you can scroll down the page, but the menu at the top never moves and the scrolling page seems to disappear underneath the menu? A feature known as *frames* controls these nifty tricks — and it's one of the great secrets of HTML. Frames aren't as popular as they once were, but you can still create frame pages with FrontPage by following these steps:

1. **In Page view, choose File⇨New⇨Page or Web to open the New Page or Web task pane.**

2. **Click Page Templates.**

   The Page Templates dialog box appears.

3. **Click the Frames Pages tab.**

4. **Select the frame style you want.**

   Be sure to glance at the Preview window — it shows precisely what your choice is.

5. **Click OK to generate the framed pages.**

After you select your framed page, you don't automatically see the page the way that it's eventually going to look. After you choose a frame page style, FrontPage creates a control page for the frame style, leaving the selection of the pages in the frame up to you. On-screen, you see borders breaking up the page according to the frame style that you select. Within each framed area on-screen, you find two buttons. You use these buttons to select the pages for each framed area in the style that you select. Figure 2-2 shows how these buttons look on-screen after you create a framed page.

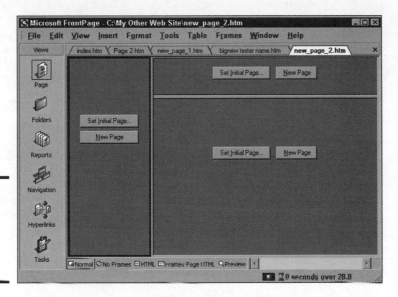

Figure 2-2: Select the pages for each framed area.

Here's when you use each button:

✦ **Set Initial Page:** If you have a page already made that you'd like to insert, click this button.

✦ **New Page:** If you want to make a new one up on the spot, click this button.

Click the Preview button along the bottom of the screen in Page View to see how a page with frames looks in real terms.

Changing a File Name

Sometimes you find that you want to change the name of a FrontPage file. For example, you may create a file named `page1.html` and later decide to give that file a more meaningful, easy-to-remember name, such as `ufo_ sightings.html`.

Keep those file names short

Although you live in the wonderful world of Windows, where you can have long file names that even include spaces between words, not all Web servers run Windows. Many non-Windows servers out there on the Internet can handle only filenames that are 8 characters long (not including the 3 characters allowed after the dot). So, to ensure that your files work fine on all types of servers, make sure that you give your files names that contain 8 characters or fewer.

If you're familiar with the way Windows enables you to rename files, FrontPage is sure to seem awfully familiar, because it works almost identically. To change the name of a file, follow these steps:

1. **If you don't already have the Folder List open, choose View⇨Folder List.**

   The Folder List area appears.

2. **Right-click the name of the file in the Folder List that you want to change.**

3. **Choose Rename from the shortcut menu that appears.**

   The file whose name you want to change is highlighted.

4. **Type the new name for the file.**

5. **Press Enter.**

If you change the name of a Web page, you break the links that connect the page to any other pages in your Web site. Fortunately, FrontPage knows exactly how all your Web pages link, so after you change the name of a file, FrontPage asks whether you want to automatically update your other pages as well.

Saving Your Web Pages

An old saying in software-development circles goes a little something like this: Save and save often. Well, saving and saving often is a great idea in FrontPage, too. The number of times that you save a file is directly proportional to how mad you get if you lose all the work you just finished. Keeping that in mind, use one of the following three easy ways to save a file in FrontPage:

✦ Choose File⇨Save.

✦ Click the Save button on the Standard toolbar.

✦ Press Ctrl+S.

If you haven't yet saved the file, the Save As dialog box appears.

From the Save As dialog box, you can give your file a name and choose where to save it. After you save the file the first time, you no longer see the Save As dialog box if you use any of the preceding three methods of saving.

Opening Files from Other Programs with FrontPage

Because FrontPage is part of Microsoft Office, the program can read and edit a large number of different file formats in addition to HTML. To open a file in FrontPage, follow these steps:

1. **Choose File⇨Open to access the Open File dialog box (see Figure 2-3).**

Figure 2-3:
The
Open File
dialog box.

You can also press Ctrl+O to access the Open File dialog box.

2. **Select the file type that you want to open from the Files of Type drop-down list.**

3. **Use the Look In drop-down list to find the file that you need.**

4. **Click the name of the file that you want from the list and then click the Open button.**

Chapter 3: Customizing FrontPage to Your Liking

In This Chapter

✔ **Getting to know the FrontPage Editor**

✔ **Setting up your toolbars**

✔ **Dealing with your folders**

✔ **Importing Web elements**

Before you get too far along into churning out Web pages like a well-oiled machine, take a step back and set things up in FrontPage to your liking. Get your toolbars just right because you may end up clicking lots of buttons during your Web creating. Organize your file folders so that you can at least remember where you're putting your masterpieces. And don't forget to use some of the Web stuff that you may have already lying around. With a little advanced thought, your future efforts don't seem so hard.

A Quick Guide to the Three Modes of the FrontPage Editor

As with most things in FrontPage, you can make the Editor as simple or as complex as you want. The Editor is designed to appeal to HTML editing newbies as well as to HTML masters and purists. It achieves this delicate balance between the new kids on the block and the veterans by enabling users either to use drag-and-drop tools for composing pages or to edit the HTML directly.

The FrontPage Editor is split into three basic modes, which you can access by clicking one of the following three tabs in the bottom-left corner of the editing window:

✦ **Normal mode:** This mode is the default for the Editor and undoubtedly the way Microsoft prefers that you create your Web pages.

In the Normal mode, shown in the Figure 3-1, you can create Web page elements on-screen and position them anywhere you want. As you do so, FrontPage autogenerates the necessary HTML to make the page that you're creating.

Figure 3-1:
FrontPage in
Normal
mode.

The idea is that FrontPage takes HTML editing out of the HTML creation process and replaces it with menus, toolbars, wizards, and other elements that Office users are accustomed to seeing.

✦ **HTML mode:** Prefer to do your own HTML editing? You can use HTML Mode, shown in Figure 3-2, to edit your HTML directly and bypass all the automated features that the Normal mode offers. This mode works the same as a more traditional HTML editor, but it also offers a number of handy features to make editing a little more user-friendly, such as HTML coloring and tag viewing.

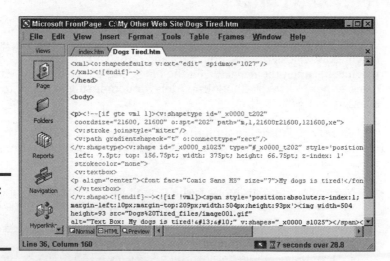

Figure 3-2:
The lovely
HTML
mode.

✦ **Preview mode:** Preview mode eliminates the need to open up a browser to see what your pages look like. This mode gives you an immediate idea of whether a page that you're creating is working correctly, because Preview mode shows what your Web page looks like in the Internet Explorer browser.

Preview mode is a good idea . . . almost. The downside is that it emulates Internet Explorer, which means that, if you use the Preview mode as the only method of previewing your work, you're neglecting the large number of Web users who use some form of Netscape Navigator.

Using FrontPage Toolbars

FrontPage comes with the requisite Office toolbars, including the Standard and Formatting toolbars. In addition to these two toolbars, FrontPage supports seven other toolbars that you can display and customize. If you get to know these toolbars, your life may become much easier later. Table 3-1 highlights the functions of each toolbar.

Table 3-1	FrontPage Toolbars
Toolbar	*Features*
Standard	Includes such general Office functions as Open, Save, and Print.
Formatting	Provides font-style and formatting functions.
DHTML Effects	Assigns Dynamic HTML events, allowing your Web page to respond to mouse clicks, mouse movement, and text input.
Drawing	Offers tools and buttons for drawing and formatting shapes and lines.
Drawing Canvas	Presents tools for expanding, collapsing, and cropping the drawing canvas.
Navigation	Enables you to control the layout and size of the Navigation view. You can also use this toolbar to add external links.
Picture	Gives you point-and-click access to all the image-editing tools built into FrontPage.
Positioning	Enables you to set locations and move the position of objects on a page.
Reporting	Makes all the FrontPage reports accessible through a drop-down list.
Style	Launches the Cascading Style Sheet dialog box.
Tables	Generates quick and easy HTML tables.
Task Pane	Opens the task pane. Click the down arrow in the task pane and select which pane you want from the drop-down list.
WordArt	Offers buttons and tools for creating and editing WordArt images.

Book III Chapter 3

Customizing FrontPage to Your Liking

To display a toolbar, choose View⇨Toolbars⇨*Name of the toolbar* or right-click a toolbar and choose a name from the shortcut menu that appears. After you choose the toolbar that you want, a check mark appears in the menu next to the name of the toolbar, and the toolbar that you choose either floats on-screen or sits next to the Standard and Formatting toolbars.

If a toolbar appears to be floating randomly on-screen, you can drag it up to the location of the other toolbars. After you get the toolbar up there, the toolbar area grows to accommodate the new toolbar. You can also double-click the title bar of a floating toolbar to mount it with the other nonfloating toolbars.

Creating Folders

Folders help you organize the files that make up your Web site. The larger your site — in other words, the more Web pages you create — the more important organizing your files becomes. (Just as in everyday life, hunting through a stack of disorganized files for that one single file you're looking for can be frustrating and time-consuming.)

FrontPage offers you two ways to create new folders for a Web project. The easiest way is to go to the Folders view and choose File⇨New⇨Folder. In this case, FrontPage generates the new folder in the directory that's currently selected in the Folders view.

Switching back over to the Folders view to create a new folder isn't always convenient. Fortunately, you can generate new folders in any view in which you can access the Folder List. Here's how you do it:

1. **If the Folder List isn't already open, choose View⇨Folder List to activate it.**

2. **Right-click the folder in which you want to place your new folder and then choose New⇨Folder from the shortcut menu that appears.**

   FrontPage creates the new folder and prompts you to enter a name for it.

3. **Enter a name for your new folder in the active text box next to your new folder.**

   The text box appears as a black box with a blinking white cursor at the end of the box.

4. **Press Enter to set the name of your new folder.**

Collapsing and expanding folders

If you use Windows, seeing your folders arranged in a hierarchy that you can collapse and expand may already be familiar to you. Such an arrangement makes grasping the overall structure of your folders easy. FrontPage also offers the capability to view data through collapsing and expanding folders. To expand and collapse folders, follow these steps:

1. **Activate the Folder List by choosing View⇨Folder List.**

2. **Click any folder with a plus sign next to its name to expand the folder and view the contents of that folder.**

   After you click the plus sign, it changes to a minus sign.

3. **To collapse the folder, click the minus sign.**

You can also copy and move files by using the Folder List, just as you can in the Windows Explorer. Simply right-click the file, drag it into the desired folder, and choose either Copy Here or Move Here from the shortcut menu.

Deleting Files and Folders

FrontPage offers a number of ways for you to delete files and folders. To delete any file or folder from your project, choose any of the following methods:

Book III
Chapter 3

✦ **Deleting from the Folder List:** Click an item and press the Delete key. The Confirm Delete dialog box appears to make sure that you're really serious about wanting to delete the file or folder (see Figure 3-3).

Customizing
FrontPage to
Your Liking

Figure 3-3:
FrontPage always checks to make sure that you really want to delete an item.

✦ **Deleting from the Folders view:** This procedure works just the same as the Folder List option that I describe in the preceding paragraph.

✦ **Deleting from the Reports view:** You can also delete various HTML pages on which you generate reports. Just click the HTML page in a report and press Delete. Again, the Confirm Delete dialog box appears to confirm that you want to delete the HTML page. You can't, however, delete a page from the Site Summary report.

✦ **Deleting from the Navigation view:** Deleting from this view is slightly different. Select the page that you want to delete and then press Delete. The Delete Page dialog box appears. Select the Remove Page from the Navigation Structure option to keep the page in the Web but delete all links to the file or select the Delete This Page from the Web option to eliminate the page entirely.

✦ **Deleting from the Hyperlinks view:** Select the page that you want to delete and press the Delete key. The Confirm Delete dialog box appears to make sure that you want to delete your selection.

After you delete a page from your Web, you can't undo the action. You're always better off eliminating the page from the active Web by stripping the page out of the Navigation view first and then removing the page. This method eliminates the file from use but keeps it in the Web. That way, you can check to see whether deleting it causes any unintended repercussions. The same rule applies for other kinds of files.

Importing Webs and Web Pages

If you're working with a number of different Web sites, you may want to import important Web pages, graphics, and even other Web sites into your current Web site. FrontPage enables you to import such accessories easily.

You always need to specify the destination into which you want to import files first! To do so, first activate the Folder List by choosing View➪Folder List. Then select the folder into which you want to import the data.

By the way, before you can use material that someone else created on your Web site, you *must* get the creator's permission. Presenting others' work without their permission is a violation of copyright laws.

Importing files that you created elsewhere

To import a file into FrontPage, follow these steps:

1. **Choose File➪Import.**

The Import dialog box appears, as shown in Figure 3-4.

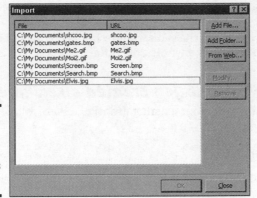

Figure 3-4:
You can
import a file
by using this
dialog box.

2. **Click the Add File button.**

   The Add File to Import List dialog box appears.

3. **Use the Look In drop-down list to tell FrontPage where you want to get the file(s), and then select the file(s) that you want to import from either your local drive or the network.**

4. **Click the Open button to add the file(s) to your Import List.**

   You return to the Import dialog box.

5. **Click OK to import the files into your Web.**

Importing folders that you created elsewhere

After you select a folder in the Folder List, follow these steps to import a folder into the folder you selected:

1. **Choose File⇨Import.**

   The Import dialog box appears.

2. **Click the Add Folder button.**

   The File Open dialog box appears.

3. **Select the folder you want to import by searching through the available local and network drives.**

4. **Click the Open button to add that folder and its contents to the Import List.**

   You return to the Import dialog box.

5. **Click OK in the Import dialog box to import the folder into your Web.**

You don't need to import files and then import folders separately. You can make a collection of files and folders by adding them to the Import List first. After you collect all the items that you want to import, click OK in the Import dialog box to import the whole collection.

Importing a Web that you created elsewhere

To import another Web into your existing FrontPage Web, follow these steps:

1. **Choose File⇨Import.**

   The Import dialog box appears.

2. **Click the From Web button.**

   The Import Web Wizard opens.

3. **Choose the location of the Web that you want to import.**

   The wizard provides two simple import options. If you select the From a Source Directory option, the Browse button appears on-screen. Click that button to search your local and network drives for available Webs. If you choose the From a World Wide Web Site option, the wizard provides a field for you to enter the URL from which you want to import the Web.

4. **Click Next.**

   The Choose Download Amount dialog box appears.

5. **Set the download options for the Web that you want to import.**

   You can limit the size of the Web you want to download by choosing from a series of check boxes. These check boxes enable you to specify the number of layers of the Web that you want to import, the size (in kilobytes) that you want to import, and the kinds of files that you want to import.

6. **Click Next.**

   The Finish dialog box appears.

7. **Click the Finish button to import the Web.**

Chapter 4: Laying the Groundwork for Your Web Pages

In This Chapter

✔ **Giving your Web a theme**

✔ **Editing your theme**

✔ **Setting up page properties**

*I*f you thought you could just jump right in and make a Web page, you've probably figured out that it's not that easy. To do a thorough job, you need to consider the elements that may seem secondary to you but that make a big difference — especially as you try to apply them later and realize that you should have done these things first! Before getting too far along, you need to consider whether you need a theme for your page, additional background images and colors, and page margins. To save yourself grief later, establish your Web groundwork today.

Applying a Theme to a Web

Themes are compelling graphics and varying text styles that help provide a common look and feel for your Web. FrontPage comes with more than 60 different themes that you can apply to individual pages, as well as to an entire Web. To add a theme to a Web or Web page, follow these steps:

1. **Choose Format⇨Theme.**

   The Themes dialog box appears (see Figure 4-1).

2. **Select the theme that you want from the list that appears.**

   The four check boxes in the bottom-left corner of the Themes dialog box give you the following additional options:

   • **Vivid Colors:** Uses more vibrant colors as you create your theme graphics and text.

   • **Active Graphics:** Creates more interesting and dynamic-looking graphics for such elements as a banner, the large heading that sometimes appears along the top of Web pages.

   • **Background Picture:** Adds a background image to the pages.

- **Apply Using CSS:** Uses Cascading Style Sheets instead of HTML to create your text and graphics styles.

  For the skinny on Cascading Style Sheets, check out Chapter 8 ("Developing Style Sheets") which you find in Book 2 ("HTML").

3. **Choose any of these options by clicking the check box next to the text that describes the option that you want.**

4. **Click OK to apply your chosen theme.**

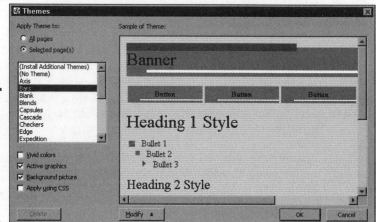

Figure 4-1:
What theme do you want to use today? Choose one in this dialog box.

Editing a Theme

What if you like the look of a theme, but the color just doesn't work for you? FrontPage enables you to modify any of the more than 60 themes in FrontPage, providing hours of fun for the entire family! To edit a theme, follow these steps:

1. **Choose Format⇨Theme.**

   The Themes dialog box appears.

2. **In the list of theme names, select the theme that you want.**

3. **Click the Modify button.**

   The new level of options that appear enables you to change the colors, graphics, and/or text of your theme.

4. **Click the Colors, Graphics, or Text buttons to edit the color, graphic, or text properties of your theme.**

   (You can click one, two, or all three of these buttons, so go hog wild!)

5. **Click the Save button to save any changes to the theme or click the Save As button to save your theme under a new name.**

If you click the Save As button, the Save Theme dialog box appears (see Figure 4-2). Type a new name for your theme and then click OK to save the new theme.

Figure 4-2:
The Save Theme dialog box enables you to save a new theme.

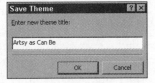

Editing Page Properties

Every Web page offers a number of options that you can modify to fit the needs of the site that you're building. These options range from choosing Web page background images to specifying the color of hyperlinks. FrontPage organizes these options in one convenient place so that accessing them is a snap.

In the Page view with the Normal Mode selected, you can right-click a Web page and choose Page Properties from the shortcut menu. The Page Properties dialog box appears, as shown in Figure 4-3. You can also choose File⇨Properties to access the same dialog box.

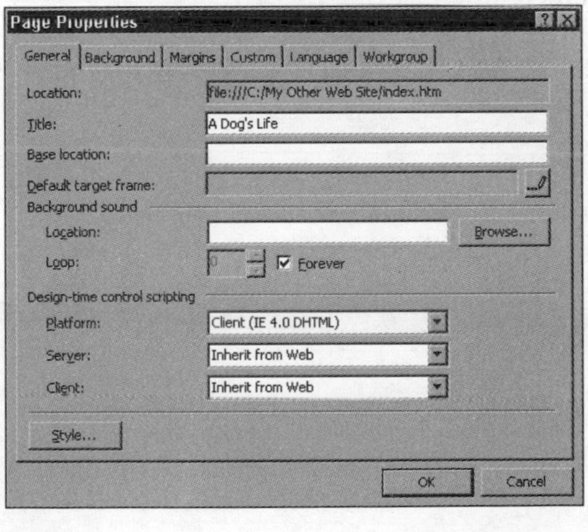

**Book III
Chapter 4**

**Laying the
Groundwork for
Your Web Pages**

Figure 4-3:
Choose your page options in this dialog box.

You can perform a number of detailed tasks in the Page Properties dialog box, most of which I describe in the following sections. Some of the simpler options that you can easily change include the following:

✦ **Changing a page title:** You can change a page title by typing a new name in the Title text box on the General tab.

✦ **Specifying a default page sound:** Also on the General tab, you can click the Browse button to place a sound in your Web. Unless you deselect the Forever check box and insert a value in the Loop text box, the sound loops continuously after the page loads. In other words, it keeps right on playing.

Sounds are platform-dependent, so if you specify a PC sound file (for example, a WAV file), Macintosh and Unix Web users can't hear it.

✦ **Specifying the page language:** On the Language tab, you can choose the language for both the page text and the HTML coding.

✦ **Assigning categories to the page:** You use categories to track a page as someone's working on it in a multi-user environment. On the Workgroup tab, you can specify the categories that a page falls under, as well as the current review status of the page and who's assigned to work on it.

Setting a background image

Click the Background tab of the Page Properties dialog box, as shown in Figure 4-4, to set a background image for a page. (You can access the dialog box by choosing File⇨Properties.) After you click the tab, follow these steps:

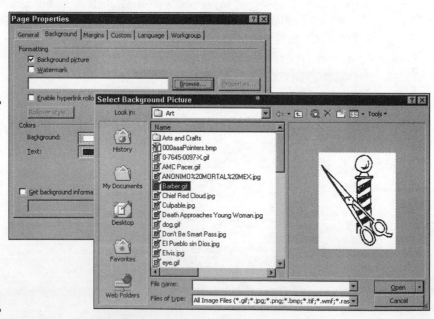

Figure 4-4: The Page Properties dialog box shows background options and enables you to add background images to your Web page.

1. **In the Formatting area of the Page Properties dialog box, click the Background Picture check box.**

2. **Click the Browse button to locate and select the background image that you want to use.**

   The Select Background Picture dialog box appears (refer to Figure 4-4). As does every other dialog box in FrontPage that requires you to find a file, the Select Background Picture dialog box defaults to enabling you to choose files from your Web only. By rooting around and going to different folders on your computer or a network, however, you can look for background images until you find the right one.

3. **Click OK.**

   After you click OK to close the Page Properties dialog box, the image that you choose is added to your page.

If you already set a background image for another page on your Web site, you can use the same background image for the page you're currently in by importing the page settings. To do so, start from the Background tab in the Page Properties dialog box, click the Get Background Information from Another Page check box, and then click the Browse button to find the page from which you want to import the background image.

If you choose to import a background image, you also import your background colors and hyperlink colors (see the following section).

If you're using a theme, you find that the Background tab in the Page Properties dialog box is missing. That's because you're using a theme, and themes require that all the pages using the theme also use the same background settings.

Setting background colors

On the Background tab in the Page Properties dialog box (right-click the page and choose Page Properties to see the dialog box), you can set the background colors and the various hyperlink colors for a Web page. For each option, a drop-down list (see Figure 4-5) enables you to choose from a series of default colors as well as specify your own Web-safe color by clicking the More Colors button and choosing a color in the More Colors dialog box.

Figure 4-5:
Specifying a
Background
color.

Click the Background tab of the Page Properties dialog box and choose from among the following options in the Colors area to set the colors of various parts of a Web page:

✦ **Background option:** If you didn't select a background image, the color that appears in the Background tab of the Page Properties dialog box appears on the page. You can click to open the drop-down list that appears next to this option and choose a new color.

✦ **Text option:** This menu sets the default color for text on your Web page, but you can open the drop-down list and choose a new color.

✦ **Hyperlink option:** The hyperlink color is the color that appears for either text that represents a link or the border around an image that's a link. This color appears only if no one has yet visited the link. Choose a new color from the drop-down list if you want.

✦ **Visited Hyperlink option:** Identical to the Hyperlink option, except that this color appears if the person who is visiting your Web page *has* previously clicked the link. You can choose a new color from the drop-down list.

✦ **Active Hyperlink option:** This color appears on a link if a visitor selects but does not visit the link. You can choose a new color from the drop-down list.

Setting page margins

Suppose that you want to indent an entire Web page, either from the top or from the left. What may otherwise prove a bear of an HTML problem, FrontPage makes an exceptionally trivial task. Here's how you do it:

1. **Choose File⇨Properties to access the Page Properties dialog box.**

The Page Properties dialog box appears.

2. **Click the Margins tab.**

3. **Click the check box of the margin that you want to indent.**

FrontPage enables you to indent only the top and left-hand margins.

4. **In the Pixels text boxes, type the desired margin sizes.**

All images on computer screens are constructed of pixels, the tiny dots that, taken together, form images. On a 640 x 480 screen — the one for which Web site designers typically plan their work — indenting by ten pixels on the right margin moves the page about a sixth of the way across the screen.

5. **Click OK to see how your new margins look.**

Chapter 5: Getting the Basics on Your Page: Text, Tables, and Links

In This Chapter

- ✔ Getting your text just right
- ✔ Making and modifying tables
- ✔ Creating and updating hyperlinks

During its infancy, pages on the World Wide Web offered only a few common elements. One constant was text on the page — nothing too fancy, but with a little bit of variety (maybe some color, a nice bulleted list, and so on). Some designers chose to present their text in columns and rows, so tables, which are a great way to arrange text on a page, became the rage. Finally, the Web would never have become the Web without its capability of enabling you to use hyperlinks — you click here and go there.

These concepts are still the fundamentals of the Web today and the focus of this chapter.

Changing Text Attributes

FrontPage, by and large, looks and feels like Microsoft Word if you're changing text attributes. In the Page view with the Normal button selected, creating text is as simple as placing the cursor where you want it on-screen and then typing away. Editing your newly-typed text is merely a matter of selecting the text and then choosing the appropriate text-editing feature.

You can change most of the basic attributes of a piece of text by highlighting it and then clicking the appropriate button on the Formatting toolbar, shown in Figure 5-1.

Figure 5-1:
The
Formatting
toolbar.

Changing font properties

To change the text attributes for text that you create in the Page view with the Normal button clicked, follow these steps:

1. **Highlight the text that you want to change.**

2. **Choose Format⇨Font.**

The Font dialog box appears, as shown in Figure 5-2. (You can also open the Font dialog box by pressing Alt+Enter or by right-clicking the selected text and choosing Font from the shortcut menu.)

Figure 5-2:
The Font
dialog box
gives you
complete
freedom to
change
your text
attributes.

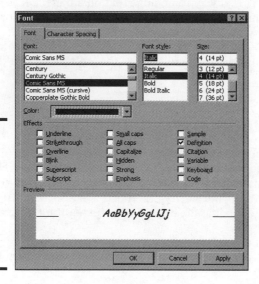

3. **Choose the new attributes for the selected text.**

On the Font and Character Spacing tabs, you can change the font type, style, color, and size, as well as modify things such as character positioning and spacing. You can also choose from a number of effects, which enable you to modify such aspects as the text's visibility and its emphasis.

One of the biggest problems with Web-site development involves fonts. If you change fonts by using the Font dialog box, you're changing to fonts that reside on *your* machine. Those fonts may not be installed on someone else's machine. As a result, what the user sees may look entirely different from what you see as you're creating the page. The two safest fonts to use, therefore, are Arial and Times New Roman, because those fonts are installed on everyone's computer.

Many of the items in the Effects category don't work with the older 3.0 browsers (Microsoft Internet Explorer 3.0 and Netscape Navigator 3.0) or with WebTV.

4. Click OK to activate your text changes.

Changing paragraph settings

You change paragraph settings in the same manner that you change font attributes, so if these steps seem familiar, that's because they *are* the same! (Well, almost.) To change the paragraph setting for a chunk of text, follow these steps:

1. Highlight the text that you want to change.

2. Choose Format⇨Paragraph or right-click and choose Paragraph.

The Paragraph dialog box, shown in Figure 5-3, appears.

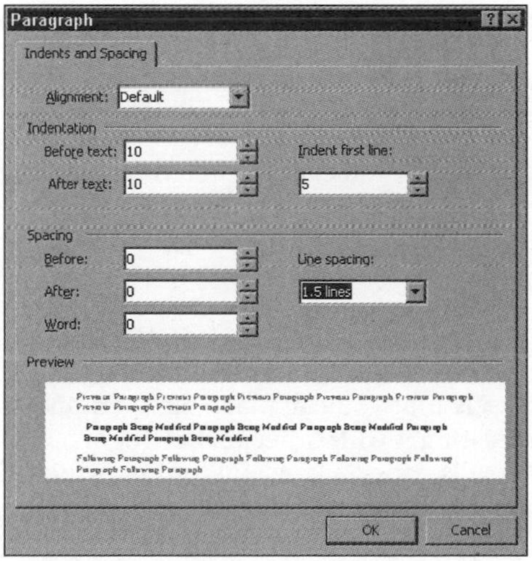

Figure 5-3:
You can change your paragraph settings with a few deft clicks in this dialog box.

Book III
Chapter 5

Getting the Basics on Your Page: Text, Tables, and Links

3. **Enter the new paragraph settings in the Paragraph dialog box.**

   You can change the alignment, line spacing, and indentation of the paragraph.

   As do font attributes, paragraph settings use Cascading Style Sheets and newer versions of HTML to set property values, making many of these settings nonfunctional for the 3.0 and earlier versions of Netscape Navigator and Internet Explorer, as well as WebTV.

4. **Click OK to save the paragraph settings.**

Creating bulleted and numbered lists

Bulleted and numbered lists are a simple, yet effective way to communicate an idea or concept with emphasis. And yes, FrontPage handles them just the same as the rest of the Microsoft Office programs. To turn a series of text items into a bulleted or numbered list, follow these steps:

1. **Highlight the text that you want to change.**

2. **Choose Format➪Bullets and Numbering.**

   The Bullets and Numbering dialog box appears.

3. **Click the appropriate tab for the kind of list that you want.**

   FrontPage provides three basic kinds of lists: picture bulleted, plain bulleted, and numbered.

4. **Select the bullet or number style that you want by clicking it in the dialog box.**

5. **Click OK to save the text to a bulleted or numbered list.**

You can click the Numbering or Bullets button on the Formatting toolbar to create a numbered or bulleted list. By going this route, however, you get plain numbers or bullets unless you chose a theme for your Web pages.

Changing borders and shading properties

FrontPage provides a number of text border and shading options. The value in changing these settings is that you can place more emphasis on a particular piece of text by contrasting it with other text elements. Putting emphasis on particular pieces of text is especially useful for important elements that you want visitors to your site to see, such as navigation menus, sidebars, and forms. To change borders and shading, follow these steps:

1. **Highlight the text that you want to change.**

2. **Choose Format➪Borders and Shading.**

   The Borders and Shading dialog box appears (see Figure 5-4).

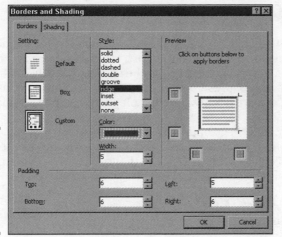

Figure 5-4:
Go wild with
the various
Borders and
Shading
options.

3. **On the Borders tab, specify the border style that you want for the text box. You can choose from the following options:**

- **Setting:** You can select one of three options: no border, a complete border around the text, or a custom border.

- **Style:** This box lists all the border styles that you can choose, including solid lines, dashed lines, and groove lines (my favorite), just to name a few.

- **Color:** You can select a color for your border from the many Web-safe colors that this option offers.

- **Width:** In this text box, you can specify how wide (in pixels) you want the border.

- **Padding:** You can set how much padding (in pixels) you want between all sides of the border and the text inside it by entering a value in this text box.

- **Preview:** In this area, you can see what your borders look like, as well as add or remove individual sides of the border. To add or remove sides, click one of the four buttons that surround the sample page.

4. **Choose your shading options.**

   On the Shading tab, you can set the foreground and background colors, as well as select an image as the background for the text box. To choose a background image, click the Browse button to find an image on your local drive, a network drive, or the World Wide Web. With each color selection, you get several default choices, but you can also specify any color from the Web palette.

5. **Click OK to set your border and shading options.**

Working with Tables

When it comes to laying out a Web page, tables are the backbone of nearly all Web-page development. The notion of a table with rows and columns was one of the first concepts introduced in the first version of HTML. Tables still offer the easiest way of presenting data within a Web browser. Instead of carefully laying out everything, you just plop each item in a table.

Not surprisingly, FrontPage offers a host of utilities that make generating and maintaining tables a reasonably easy task. The syntax and methodology for creating tables is, in fact, very similar to that of the other Office programs.

Creating a new table

To create a table in FrontPage, follow these steps:

1. **Choose Table⇨Insert Table.**

The Insert Table dialog box appears (see Figure 5-5).

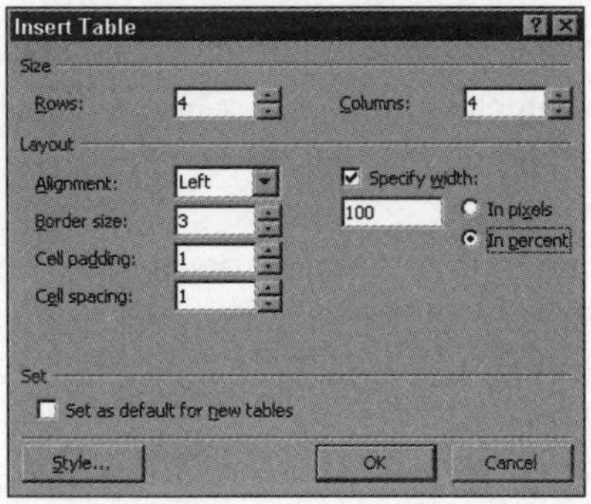

Figure 5-5:
You can use this dialog box to insert tables into your page the easy way!

2. **Type a number in the Rows and Columns text boxes to choose the number of Rows and Columns that you want for your table.**

Remember: If you need more rows and columns after you create your table, you can just right-click a cell and choose Insert Row or Insert Column from the shortcut menu.

3. **Set your layout options from the Layout area of the Insert Table dialog box:**

• **Alignment:** Determines how you want the table to be aligned on the page. You choices are left, right, and center. Choosing Left, for example, places the table against the left margin.

- **Border Size:** Establishes the thickness of the line border around both the cells and the outside of the table. Enter a number in this text box. If you don't want a border, set the value to 0.

- **Cell Padding:** Sets the distance, in pixels, between the borders of a cell and the text within the cell. Enter a number in this text box.

- **Cell Spacing:** Sets the distance, in pixels, between cells. Enter a number in this text box.

- **Specify Width:** Sets the width of the table. You can specify the width as a percentage of the page or as a set pixel width by choosing the In Pixels or In Percent option button.

4. **Click OK to insert the new table.**

After you create a table, you can go back and change the properties you just set by placing your cursor anywhere in the table and choosing Table⇨Table Properties⇨Table to open the Table Properties dialog box (see Figure 5-6). You can also right-click the table and choose Table Properties on the short-cut menu.

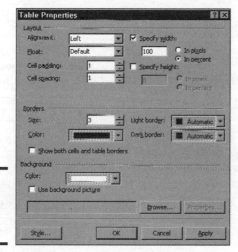

Figure 5-6:
The Table
Properties
dialog box.

You can also choose Table⇨Table Properties⇨Cell to change the properties you just set for individual cells. Make your changes in the Cell Properties dialog box that appears.

Modifying tables

In addition to generating tables, FrontPage offers a host of tools for modifying tables after you create them. The following list describes the ways in which you can modify a table:

✦ **Adding cells:** You can add individual cells, rows, or columns. In all cases, first place the cursor where you want to create the new cells, rows, or columns.

- To insert new cells, choose Table⇨Insert⇨Cell. FrontPage places a new cell directly to the right of the cell in which you placed the cursor.

- To insert new rows or columns, choose Table⇨Insert⇨Rows or Columns. The Insert Rows or Columns dialog box appears (see Figure 5-7). Choose the number of rows or columns that you want to insert, as well as their location, and then click OK to insert them.

Figure 5-7:
Use this
dialog box
to insert a
row or
column
wherever
you want.

✦ **Deleting cells:** Select a cell (or group of cells) and then choose Table⇨Delete Cells to eliminate the cell and its contents from the table.

✦ **Merging cells:** Select the cells that you want to merge and then choose Table⇨Merge Cells to collapse the two cells and combine their contents.

✦ **Splitting cells:** Select the cells that you want to split and then choose Table⇨Split Cells. From the Split Cells dialog box that appears, choose whether you want to split into rows or columns and how many rows or columns you want to split the cell(s) into and then click OK.

✦ **Distributing cells:** Select rows or columns of uneven size and then choose either Table⇨Distribute Rows Evenly or Table⇨Distribute Columns Evenly to make the rows or columns equal sizes.

✦ **AutoFit to Contents:** The AutoFit to Contents command tries to find the optimal size for the cells in the table based on their contents. This way, the table contains no wasted space. AutoFit to Contents is a good tool to use if you replace text or a graphic of a different size within a table cell. Select the cells and choose Table⇨AutoFit to Contents to set the optimal table.

Checking spelling on a Web page

Don't wait to check the spelling on your pages until they're up on the Web! Check your spelling before others find your mistakes. You can run a spell-check on a page to make sure that it doesn't contain spelling errors. You can also tell FrontPage to fix those spelling errors and track them so that you can see them in the Tasks View. To track spelling errors in FrontPage, follow these steps:

1. **Choose Tools➪Spelling.**

   The Spelling dialog box appears if FrontPage detects a spelling error. (As in other Office products, you can also press F7 to open the Spelling dialog box.)

2. **Click the correct spelling in the Suggestions list box or type it in the Change To box.**

3. **Click the Change button.**

4. **Continue correcting errors until you see the** `Spelling Check Is Complete` **message.**

You also find Ignore buttons for ignoring what FrontPage thinks are spelling errors, and an Add button for entering words in the dictionary and preventing the spell-checker from stopping on them in the future.

Creating and Using Hyperlinks

Hyperlinks sounds like such an impressive word . . . very futuristic . . . the kind of thing you'd expect Captain Kirk or Captain Picard to burst out with on any given episode of *Star Trek*. Truthfully, however, hyperlinks are just a way of jumping from location to location on the Web.

Hyperlinks are the navigational building blocks of any Web site. Without hyperlinks, you'd never get off the home page of a Web site. So, not surprisingly, FrontPage offers a vast array of tools for generating and maintaining hyperlinks. To create a hyperlink in a Web page, follow these steps:

1. **Highlight the text or image that you want to turn into a hyperlink.**

   (You can also create a link to a page without highlighting anything at all. In this case, the link uses the title of the page that you're linking to for a text description.)

2. **Choose Insert➪Hyperlink or press Ctrl+K.**

   The Insert Hyperlink dialog box appears (see Figure 5-8).

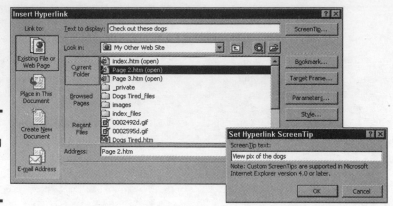

Figure 5-8: Hyperlinking has never been so easy.

If you're trying to cut down on using menus, you can click the Hyperlink button on the Standard toolbar to access the dialog box.

3. **Click the ScreenTip button.**

   The Set Hyperlink ScreenTip dialog box appears.

4. **Type a two- or three-word description of the hyperlink and then click OK.**

   When visitors to your Web site move their mouse pointers over the link, they see the description that you enter in a pop-up box.

5. **Create the link by choosing from the following options in the Insert Hyperlink dialog box:**

   A link to a Web page on the Internet: Under Link To, click the Existing File or Web Page button. Then type the address of the Web page by doing one of the following:

   - Type it in the Address text box.

   - Open the Address drop-down list and select it.

   - Click the Browse the Web button. Your Web browser opens. Go to the Web page that you want to link to. After you return to the Insert Hyperlink dialog box, the address of the page appears in the Address text box.

   - Click the Browsed Pages button, look for the address of the page, and select it.

   A link to another page in your Web: Click the Existing File or Web Page button. Then click the Current Folder button. The dialog box lists the files that make up your Web. Find the Web page that you want to link to and select it.

A link to another place in the same Web page you are on: Click the Place in This Document button. Then click the plus sign next to the Bookmarks label, if necessary, to see the bookmarks on the page; find the one that you want to link to and click it. To link to a place in the same document, you must have bookmarks in your document. To place a bookmark, click where you want the bookmark to go, choose Insert⇨Bookmark, enter a name for the bookmark in the Bookmark dialog box that appears, and click OK.

A link to an e-mail address: Click the E-mail Address button. Then enter your e-mail address, suggest a subject for the messages that others send you, and click the OK button.

After you create a hyperlink, make sure that you test it by pressing the Ctrl button and clicking it. If the hyperlink doesn't work, right-click it, choose Hyperlink Properties from the shortcut menu, and fix the link by typing the correct URL for the link in the Edit Hyperlink dialog box that appears. This dialog box works exactly like the Insert Hyperlink dialog box (refer to Figure 5-8). Click the Remove Link button to remove a hyperlink.

Working with the Hyperlinks view

One of the nice things about the Hyperlinks view is that you can choose any object in your Web site — including HTML pages and graphics — and see exactly what pages or other objects link into that object. You can also see where the object links. With the Folder List open, all you need to do is click an object, and the Hyperlinks view displays all the links to and from that page, as shown in Figure 5-9.

Book III
Chapter 5

Getting the Basics
on Your Page: Text,
Tables, and Links

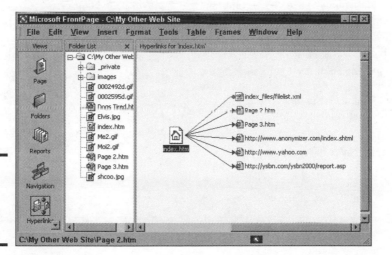

Figure 5-9: Hyperlinks view displays all your links.

FrontPage comes with a Web browser built into its editor, but sometimes you just can't beat the real thing. Check out the "So, what's your page looking like?" sidebar later in this chapter for hints on viewing your page live.

Recalculating a project's hyperlinks

Through the process of building pages, moving folders around, and generally doing the work that maintaining a Web site requires, some things are liable to get broken. Hyperlinks are usually the first things to go. To combat this problem, FrontPage depends on Hyperlinks view, which enables you to see the links to and from every page and graphic on your site.

Ah, but if a link's broken and you can't see it amid the links, how do you know that it's broken? That's where the FrontPage Recalculate Hyperlinks feature comes in handy.

To recalculate hyperlinks, choose Tools⇨Recalculate Hyperlinks. FrontPage warns you that recalculating may take a while and asks whether you really want to do it. Click Yes after you see the prompt, and you're off. Although a progress indicator doesn't appear, the bottom-left corner shows you that FrontPage is recalculating your hyperlinks. When the recalculation is complete, your pages are updated and broken hyperlinks are repaired.

So, what's your page looking like?

You probably don't like the idea of working on something that you can't see. Well, FrontPage doesn't keep you in the dark. To preview a Web page from any browser on your desktop, follow these steps:

1. **Switch to the Folders view by clicking the Folders icon in the Views bar or choose View⇨Folder List to open the Folder List from your current view.**

2. **Click the page that you want to preview in an external Web browser.**

3. **Choose File⇨Preview in Browser.**

   The Preview in Browser dialog box appears.

4. **Select the browser in which you want to preview the page.**

5. **Designate a window size by selecting one of the 640 x 480, 800 x 600, or 1024 x 768 options in the Window Size area.**

   FrontPage supports four viewing ranges: the browser Default size, 640 x 480, 800 x 600, and 1024 x 768.

6. **Click the Preview button to view your Web page in the specified browser.**

Chapter 6: Perking Up Your Pages with Buttons, Banners, and More

In This Chapter

✔ Adding ad banners, buttons, counters, and marquees

✔ Adding clip art and other graphics

*I*f people want to see black text on a white background, they can read a book. On the Web, people like to push things, watch things move, and see neat pictures. If you want to make your Web page a success, you need to make it visually pleasing. In this chapter, you find out how to add exciting graphics and navigation aids to your Web site.

Inserting Some Extra Effects

You may have admired some Web pages that feature moving messages, animated buttons, hit counters, and the like. These effects are easily within your reach, and this section shows you the way.

Adding a banner ad

So what is a banner ad? Well, mostly, it's how companies make their money on the Web — but that's a different story! Actually, a banner is a set of similarly-sized images, usually appearing at the top or bottom of a Web page.

Banners are commonly used as a method of promoting advertising messages as well as key pieces of information that you want users to know. Adding a banner in FrontPage is simple. To do so, follow these steps:

1. **Choose Insert⇨Web Component.**

   The Insert Web Component dialog box appears.

2. **Under Choose an Effect, double-click Banner Ad Manager.**

   The Banner Ad Manager Properties dialog box appears (see Figure 6-1). In this dialog box, you can specify all the different settings for your ad banner.

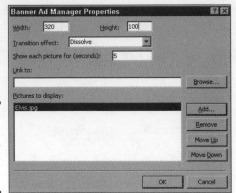

Figure 6-1:
The Banner
Ad Manager
Properties
dialog box.

3. **Choose the settings for your banner ad.**

   Table 6-1 explains the various settings.

4. **Click OK to insert the banner ad into your Web page.**

5. **Select the Preview view in the FrontPage Editor to preview your banner.**

Table 6-1	Banner Ad Settings
Setting	*What It Means*
Width/Height	The size of the banner. If your images are large, FrontPage crops them to fit. Enter the dimensions of your banner-to-be in the Width and Height text box.
Transition Effect	How the banner ads transition from one to the next. The more complicated the images are, the slower the page downloads. Choose an option from the drop-down list.
Show Each Picture For	The duration of time that users can view each image. Enter a number in the text box.
Link To	If you want the banner to link to another page, you can specify in this text box where you want it to link. Click the Browse button, and in Select Banner Ad Hyperlink, select the Web page (Chapter 5 explains how to establish a hyperlink).
Pictures to Display	By using the Add, Remove, Move Up, and Move Down buttons, you can specify from this area the number of images that you want to appear, as well as their viewing order.

Banner ads work by adding a Java applet to your Web. The advantage to using Java is that the ad transitions look nicer. But if you start using a lot of transitions, adding an applet makes your Web page run slower.

Adding a hit counter

A *hit counter* tracks the number of times people access a page and displays the number of "hits" on the Web page itself. It's a nice way of saying, "Hey, look how popular my Web page is!" (That is, unless nobody's visiting your Web site, in which case you probably don't want to include a hit counter.) To add a hit counter, follow these steps:

1. **Choose Insert⇨Web Component.**

   The Insert Web Component dialog box appears.

2. **In the Component Type area, click to select Hit Counter.**

   The right side of the dialog box offers different counters that you may choose for your Web page.

3. **Click to select the style and number of digits that you want in your hit counter.**

4. **Click the Finish button.**

   The Hit Counter Properties dialog box appears (scc Figure 6-2).

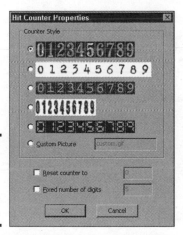

Figure 6-2:
The Hit
Counter
Properties
dialog box.

5. **Make any, all, or none of the following changes:**

- Change the counter style you set in Step 3 by clicking next to any of the styles you find in the "Counter Style" section

- Reset the counter to any number you want by checking the "Reset counter to" check box and specifying a corresponding number

- Specify a fixed number of digits other than the default, which is five, by checking the "Fixed number of digits" check box

6. **Click OK to finish.**

If you're editing an existing hit counter and you want to reset the counter, click the Reset Counter To check box and, in the text box next to it, type the number to which you want the counter to be reset.

Adding a hover button

Buttons that animate or highlight as you roll your mouse cursor over them are very popular. A number of methods exist for adding this kind of graphical quality to a Web page, including using JavaScript and Dynamic HTML. Not to be outdone, FrontPage offers you a way to use Java to create the same effect! To add a hover button (sometimes called a *rollover*), follow these steps:

1. **Choose Insert⇨Web Component.**

   The Insert Web Component dialog box appears.

2. **In the Choose an Effect area, double-click Hover Button.**

   The Hover Button Properties dialog box appears (see Figure 6-3).

Figure 6-3:
The Hover
Button
Properties
dialog box.

Hover Button Properties		? X
Button text:	My Books	Font...
Link to:	Books.htm	Browse...
Button color:		Background color: ■ Automa ▾
Effect:	Glow ▾	Effect color: ■ ▾
Width:	120	Height: 24
Custom...		OK Cancel

3. Specify the properties for the hover button.

You can set a number of different options for the button, including the size and color of the button, the *rollover effect* (what happens as the mouse cursor rolls over the button), and the page to which the button links after you click it.

4. Click OK to insert the hover button into your Web page.

Adding a marquee

Have you ever seen the stock listings whoosh by on a digital board or at the bottom of your television screen? Those are two examples of a marquee, which you can easily embed in your Web page. To add a marquee to a Web page in FrontPage, follow these steps:

1. Choose Insert➪Web Component.

The Insert Web Component dialog box appears.

2. In the Choose an Effect area, double-click Marquee.

The Marquee Properties dialog box appears (see Figure 6-4).

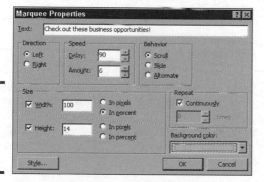

Figure 6-4:
The
Marquee
Properties
dialog box.

**Book III
Chapter 6**

**Perking Up Your
Pages with Buttons,
Banners, and More**

3. Specify the properties for your marquee.

Table 6-2 explains your options. In addition to these options, you can change the text style associated with the banner. To do so, click the Style button and then either select from the available styles or select Format to create a new style.

4. Click OK to insert the marquee into your Web page.

Table 6-2	Marquee Settings
Setting	*What It Means*
Direction	Specify the direction in which you want the text to move across the screen by selecting the Left or Right option.
Speed	Choose the speed at which you want the text to move. In the Delay text box, enter the amount of time in milliseconds that the marquee pauses before it starts moving. In the Amount text box, enter the distance in pixels that the marquee is to move.
Behavior	Indicate how you want the text to move on-screen by choosing the Scroll, Slide, or Alternate option. If you choose the Alternate option, the marquee alternates between scrolling and sliding.
Size	Choose the size of the banner by entering its dimensions in the Width and Height text boxes. By choosing an option, you can specify whether the dimension measurement you are entering is in pixels or a percentage. Percentage is the better option, because by choosing it, you can take into account the visitors' Web browser.
Repeat	Decide whether the banner repeats continuously or appears only once. Deselect the Continuously check box if you want it to appear once. To make it repeat, enter the number of times that you want it to repeat in the Times text box.
Background Color	Indicate the background color for the marquee by choosing a color on this drop-down list.

Adding Graphics to Web Pages

Now that FrontPage looks more like Word than anything else, the similarities between adding graphics to a Web page in FrontPage and adding graphics to a document in Word aren't surprising. In fact, adding graphics in FrontPage is very similar to adding graphics in Word. If, however, you don't choose to use the Word-like interface in FrontPage, you can still use the FrontPage HTML capabilities.

Although FrontPage supports a host of file formats for graphics, older browsers (3.0 and earlier) don't support many of the file formats that FrontPage supports. As a result, you're better off making sure that the graphic that you want to import is in either GIF or JPG format before you import it into FrontPage. (Besides, those graphics load faster than the others.)

If you're looking for graphics for your Web page, you can either get one from your computer or use one from the Microsoft Clip Organizer.

Adding a graphic on your own

To add a graphic that you're storing on your computer, follow these steps:

1. **Click the location on the active Web page where you want to put your graphic. (If your page is blank, your only choice is to place your cursor in the top-left corner.)**

2. **Choose Insert⇨Picture⇨From File.**

   The Picture dialog box appears (see Figure 6-5).

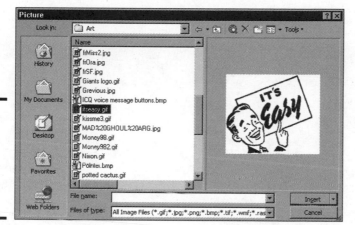

Figure 6-5:
If you can find it, you can insert it by using the Picture dialog box.

3. **Select the graphic that you want to insert.**

   From the Picture dialog box, you can browse your Web, the rest of your computer, or the Internet to find the graphic that you want to insert. FrontPage also provides thumbnail previews for each graphic that you click, so you can see what you're adding before you add it.

4. **Click the Insert button to add the graphic to your Web page.**

   You can also add graphics to a Web page via the traditional Windows drag-and-drop interface. To do so, go to the folder on your desktop that houses the graphic that you want to insert. Click and drag the graphic onto the active Web page and voilà! There it is . . . good to go!

If the graphic you're adding to your page was created by someone else, you need to ask permission to use that graphic — in other words, you need to secure copyright permissions. For more information on U.S. copyright and how it applies to Web, check out www.loc.gov/copyright.

Adding clip art from the Clip Organizer to a Web page

FrontPage comes with an extensive Clip Art gallery that helps you create buttons and banners, as well as communicate all kinds of different themes and emotions. To add clip art to your Web page, follow these steps:

1. **Click the Web page where you want the clip art to appear.**

2. **Choose Insert⇨Picture⇨Clip Art.**

The Insert Clip Art task pane appears on the right of your screen, as shown in Figure 6-6.

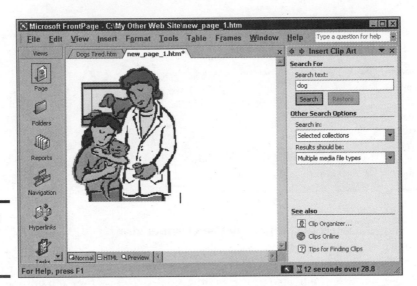

Figure 6-6:
The Insert
Clip Art
task pane.

3. **Tell FrontPage how and where to search for clip-art images.**

You use the Search Text field to search for clip-art images; you use the optional Search In and Results Should Be fields to limit (speed up) your search.

- **Search Text:** Type a word in this text box that describes what kind of clip art you want to look for. For example, to find images containing dogs, you might type in the word "dog."

- **Search In:** You can limit the search by clicking the drop-down list next to this option and selecting which directories you want FrontPage to search.

- **Results Should Be:** You can further limit the search by clicking the drop-down list next to this option and making choices to tell FrontPage what kind of files to look for. If you select All Media Types, for example, FrontPage searches for photographs, movies, and sounds as well as clip art. To limit your search to clip art only, click the plus sign (+) beside the All Media Types folder and then deselect Photographs, Movies, and Sounds.

4. Click the Search button.

If FrontPage can find clip-art images, they appear in thumbnail form in the Insert Clip Art task pane. If necessary, scroll down the list to examine all the images or click the small icon under the word *Results* to see the images in a box.

5. Click an image to insert it in your document.

The image is probably too large and you may need to make it smaller. To do so, drag a corner handle on the image toward the image's center. (Chapter 7 explains many techniques for changing the size of images.)

Book III
Chapter 6

Perking Up Your
Pages with Buttons,
Banners, and More

Chapter 7: Image Editing for Everyone

In This Chapter

✔ Using the Pictures toolbar

✔ Manipulating and editing your images

✔ Making an image map

Simply grabbing or creating an image and then plopping it as-is into your Web page doesn't enable you to take full advantage of the FrontPage editing capabilities. You may find a great image to use, but think about what else you can do to it. You can scale it, flip it, move it, bevel it, brighten it, and more! You may want to place some text over it or turn the image itself into a hyperlink. You can even turn different parts of the image into hyperlinks and make a clickable image map. This chapter walks you through the process of editing your images in FrontPage.

Activating the Pictures Toolbar

In FrontPage, you can't edit a graphics image without first activating the Pictures toolbar. Unlike a number of the other toolbars in FrontPage, the Pictures toolbar doesn't have any corresponding keyboard or menu options. To activate the Pictures toolbar, choose View➪Toolbars➪Pictures or right-click a toolbar and choose Pictures from the shortcut menu.

Working with Auto Thumbnails

An *Auto Thumbnail* is a handy tool that enables you to create a miniversion of a picture. This tool is particularly useful if you want to use an image as a button that then links to a larger version of the picture. To create an Auto Thumbnail, select an image and click the Auto Thumbnail button on the Pictures toolbar.

After you create a thumbnail and go to save the page, FrontPage prompts you to save the new thumbnail image. After you load the page in a browser, you see the thumbnail rather than the original image. Then, after you click the thumbnail, the larger version appears in the Web browser by itself.

Figure 7-1 briefly acquaints you with the buttons on the Pictures toolbar; the remaining sections in this chapter describe the buttons you're most likely to use most in greater detail.

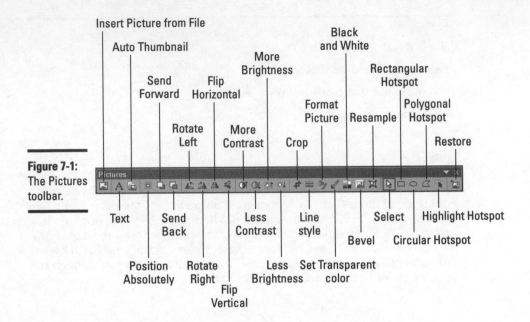

Figure 7-1: The Pictures toolbar.

Image Manipulation Made Easy

If FrontPage doesn't make image manipulation easy, it at least makes image manipulation easier than ever before. Although image editing in FrontPage isn't as powerful as in Photoshop or some of the other popular graphics software, you can't beat the convenience — and the price — of getting this editing capability already built into your Web-creation application.

Scaling an image

Scaling is the process of making an entire image either larger or smaller. (No cutting away of the image is involved here.) You can scale an image just by clicking it.

After you click an image, you see anchor points appear around the border of the image. To scale the image, click and drag one of these anchor points. The image resizes itself according to where you release the anchor point.

TIP

To scale an image and keep its proportions intact, choose one of the corner anchor points and then scale the image. Scaling in this manner keeps the *aspect ratio* (the height-to-width ratio of an image) consistent as the image gets bigger or smaller.

After you scale your image, you can resample it by clicking the Resample button on the Pictures toolbar. The Resample tool analyzes the image that you just scaled. If, for example, the image became bigger, the pixels that make up the image are stretched. The Resample tool then breaks up the stretched pixels into smaller pixels to create a crisper, cleaner image. Similarly, if you shrink the image, you end up with more pixels than are really necessary for a smaller image. In this case, using the Resample tool eliminates any unnecessary pixels without sacrificing image quality — a bonus for any image included in a Web page. (Small image files download to users' browsers faster than large image files.)

If you don't like how your newly-scaled image looks, you can click the Restore button to reset the image to its original size.

You can use the Restore button on a number of other Pictures toolbar features as well, including the Color, Brightness, Contrast, Rotate, and Flip tools.

Changing brightness and contrast

Changing a graphic's *brightness* makes the graphic appear lighter or darker. Changing a graphic's *contrast* makes the graphic's individual pixels either stand out more or become more muted. Usually, setting a graphic's contrast goes hand in hand with changing the graphic's brightness. So, for example, the brighter a graphic becomes, the more contrast you need to avoid it becoming washed out. To change an image's brightness and contrast, follow these steps:

1. **In the Page view, click the image that you want to modify.**

2. **Click any of the following four Contrast or Brightness options on the Pictures toolbar:**

   - **More Contrast:** This option increases the color distinctions between pixels.

   - **Less Contrast:** This option makes the colors blend together.

   - **More Brightness:** This option washes out the image.

   - **Less Brightness:** This option darkens the image.

   Every time that you click a button, the brightness or contrast either increases or decreases incrementally. The more times that you click the brightness button, for example, the brighter the image gets.

You can undo your work by pressing Ctrl+Z or clicking the Undo button on the Standard toolbar. In fact, FrontPage supports multiple undos, so if you're fiddling with an image and you want to return it to its previous condition, open the Undo button drop-down list and choose how many actions you want to undo. (To restore an "undone" action, press Ctrl+Y or click the Restore button.)

Setting an image's transparent color

GIF images support transparency, which means that you can choose to make a particular color on your image invisible. This feature is helpful if you have a square graphic and you want to display only the logo in the middle of the image. In FrontPage, setting the transparent color is a cinch! Here's what you do:

1. **In Page view, click the graphic that contains the color that you want to make transparent.**

2. **Click the Set Transparent Color button on the Pictures toolbar.**

3. **Click the color on the image that you want to make transparent.**

All instances of that color in the image become invisible, and you can see the Web page background through it.

Only GIF images can be made transparent, but all is not lost if you're using other image types in your Web page — a JPEG image, for example — because FrontPage turns images into GIF files after you click the Set Transparent Color button on the Pictures toolbar. In addition, you can set only one transparent color by using this tool. If you select the tool again and click another color, that color becomes the transparent color, and the preceding transparent color is no longer transparent.

Beveling an image

Beveling adds both a border and three-dimensional depth to a graphic. The most frequent reason to bevel an image is to create a button effect. To bevel an image in FrontPage, follow these steps:

1. **In Page view, click the image that you want to bevel.**

2. **Click the Bevel button on the Pictures toolbar.**

A bevel appears on the graphic, as shown in Figure 7-2.

3. **If you want to make the bevel darker and add more emphasis to it, click the Bevel button again.**

Click the Undo button on the Standard toolbar if you regret clicking the Bevel button too many times. (Click the Restore button to restore "undone" actions.)

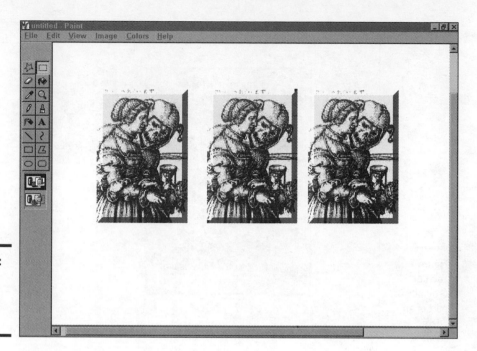

Figure 7-2:
An image
can have
a beveled
edge.

Cropping an image

Cropping reduces an image in size by lopping off portions of an image. Cropping images comes in handy if, for example, you have a picture of you and your mother-in-law and you want to eliminate your mother-in-law from the picture. To be honest, the FrontPage cropping features are limited in that you can crop only rectangular areas. To crop an image, follow these steps:

1. **In Page view, click the image that you want to crop.**

2. **Click the Crop button on the Pictures toolbar.**

A rectangular box appears inside the image's border.

3. **Click and drag a selection handle to form a rectangle around the part of the graphic that you want to keep (see Figure 7-3).**

You see eight selection handles, one at each corner and one in the middle of each side of the image. You can drag more than one selection handle in succession and in so doing form the rectangle around only the part of the image that you want.

4. **Press Enter to crop the image to the size of the rectangle.**

Figure 7-3:
You can crop any part of an image.

Cropping cuts away everything that remains outside the cropping rectangle. If you specify an area, you're specifying the area of the image that you want to keep and not the area that you want to cut.

If you decide that you don't want to crop an image, press the Esc key or click outside the image to disengage the cropping tool.

Flipping and rotating images

FrontPage makes flipping and rotating images easy. To do so, follow these steps:

1. **In Page view, click the graphic that you want to flip or rotate.**

2. **Click the Rotate Left, Rotate Right, Flip Horizontal, or Flip Vertical button on the Pictures toolbar, depending on the action that you want to initiate.**

   You get the following options with each button:

   - **Rotate Left:** This option rotates the image 90 degrees to the left.

   - **Rotate Right:** This option rotates the image 90 degrees to the right.

- **Flip Horizontal:** This option mirrors the image left to right.

- **Flip Vertical:** This option mirrors the image top to bottom.

Placing text over an image

FrontPage supports a clever little way of placing text in images to achieve a nice effect. To do so, follow these steps:

1. **In Page view, click the graphic over which you want to place text.**

2. **Click the Text button on the Pictures toolbar.**

A text box appears in the middle of your graphic (see Figure 7-4). To resize the text box, drag the box's anchor points by using your pointer.

3. **Type the text that you want in the text box.**

You can change the font or font size of text by selecting the text and choosing options from the Font and Font Size drop-down lists on the Formatting toolbar.

4. **Press Esc.**

Figure 7-4:
You can place text over an image.

To generate another text box on that image, click the image and then click the Text button again. If you want to move a text box around on the image, click and hold the mouse button while the cursor's in the middle of the text box and then move the text box to its new location.

Because this graphic is essentially an image map with text, you can also turn these text boxes into hyperlinks. Just choose Insert⇔Hyperlink from the main menu (or, alternatively, press Ctrl+K) to open the Edit Hyperlink dialog box after you create a text box in a selected image. Then enter the link location and click OK to add the link to the text on the image.

If you're using other image types in your Web page — a JPEG image, for example — FrontPage tries to turn the image into a GIF file after you click the Text button on the Pictures toolbar. In most cases, this change compromises the graphical quality of the image you're adding text to, because converting from a JPEG to a GIF reduces the number of colors in the image.

Adding a hyperlink to an image

Using images as hyperlinks can add pizzazz and flair to a Web site. To add a hyperlink to an image, follow these steps:

1. **With the Normal button selected in Page view, click the image that you want to make a hyperlink.**

2. **Choose Insert⇔Hyperlink or press Ctrl+K.**

    The Insert Hyperlink dialog box that appears may look familiar; it's the same dialog box that FrontPage uses to create text hyperlinks (see Figure 7-5).

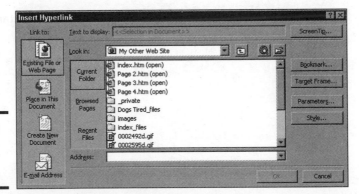

Figure 7-5:
The Insert Hyperlink dialog box.

See Chapter 5 for more information about creating text hyperlinks.

3. **Click OK.**

   You can now use the image as a hyperlink on your Web page.

Creating Image Maps

Image maps are great navigation tools that you see in many Web sites. You load a Web page, and a big graphic appears smack dab in the middle of the page. On the graphic are a host of hot links to various locations. How did the Web designers create such a helpful tool, you ask? The answer lies in *image maps*.

You create image maps by specifying regions of a graphic and then setting links for those regions. In the past, you needed to create image maps in a separate program and then load the map into your Web page. Times change. The following steps show you how to create an image map in FrontPage:

1. **In Page view, click the graphic for which you want to create an image map.**

2. **Select one of the Image Map shapes tools from the Pictures toolbar.**

   FrontPage provides the following shape tools for creating image maps:

   - **Rectangular Hotspot:** This button creates squares and rectangles. To create a square or rectangular link, click the image and then drag the mouse while holding the mouse button. FrontPage creates a square image from the point where you first click the mouse.

   - **Circular Hotspot:** This button creates circles and ovals. You create a circular link precisely the same as you do a rectangular hotspot.

   - **Polygonal Hotspot:** This button enables you to create multi-sided polygon areas. Click the image first to create a path and then click it again to specify each point for the linked area. You finish creating the polygon by selecting the first path point. Doing so encloses the polygonal image.

3. **Create the shape that you want.**

   The Insert Hyperlink dialog box appears.

4. **Create the hyperlink.**

   Chapter 5 explains in detail how to create a hyperlink.

5. **Click OK to set the hyperlink.**

You may want to move your link around on the graphic after you create it. To do so, click the Select button (the arrow) on the Pictures toolbar and then click and hold the mouse button on the link. As long as you continue to hold the mouse button, you can drag the link around on the graphic.

To change the size of the link, click and hold any of the link's *anchor points* — the square dots along the outline of the link area. Then drag the anchor to the desired location, and the link automatically scales according to where you move the anchor point. Releasing the mouse button changes the link's size.

Chapter 8: Publishing Your Web Pages

In This Chapter

✔ Publishing via HTTP

✔ Publishing via FTP

*E*ventually, you need to put your hard work on the World Wide Web for everyone to see. The process of publishing on the Web may seem difficult, but it's probably one of the easiest steps in creating a Web page (which may explain why so much junk is already out there! Ahem.). This chapter shows you how to join the fray.

Publishing a Web by Using HTTP

HTTP sounds new and nifty, but if you've ever loaded a Web page, you already know what HTTP does. HTTP, which stands for HyperText Transfer Protocol, is simply a way of transferring data from a server to your Web browser (and vice versa). In fact, HTTP is the preferred way of transferring files in FrontPage.

To use this method of file transfer, your Internet service provider must support the FrontPage server extensions. Use the FTP method of uploading files if your Internet service provider doesn't support the server extensions. (To find out whether your Internet service provider supports FrontPage server extension, you need to ask.)

To publish a Web by using HTTP, follow these steps:

1. **Choose File➪Publish Web.**

The Publish Destination dialog box appears.

2. **Type the URL where you want to publish your Web content in the Enter Publish Destination text box.**

Click the hyperlink in the dialog box if you're not sure whether your ISP provides the appropriate server extensions to support the FrontPage publishing features. Clicking the hyperlink sends you to the Microsoft Web site for the most current list of ISPs that support the extensions.

If you're not sure of the location to which you want to publish your Web, click the Browse button in the Publish Destination dialog box to search for FrontPage servers from the New Publish Location dialog box.

3. **Click OK to submit the new Web content.**

FrontPage tracks the progress of the upload and shows you which pages are transferring. After the upload is complete, an alert box appears, telling you so.

Web servers are typically password-protected, so the first time you see the Publish Web dialog box, you always see another dialog box prompting you for your user name and password. (Contact your ISP or Web host to find out your user name and password.) This safeguard is to prevent people from coming along and posting content on any Web site they want.

Publishing a Web by Using FTP

People were publishing Web sites long before Microsoft came along and tried to make the whole process transparent to the user. Now, by using FrontPage, you can finally connect to any server and publish your content on the Internet by using FTP. *FTP* (short for *File Transfer Protocol*) is a software interface that enables you to send (and also receive) files to a remote computer over the Internet. Thanks to the protocol, you don't have to enter detailed commands about which files you want to send. All you have to do is designate a folder on your computer.

If you're familiar with how the Web works, you may know that Web pages are transferred from Web servers to Web browsers using HTTP (HyperText Transfer Protocol). Why, then, the need for an additional protocol — FTP — to publish your Web pages? Simply this: FTP was designed to let you transfer all kinds of files (even large ones) quickly, with no browser involved.

Publishing by using FTP consists of two parts. The first is to set up your FTP connection, and the second is to publish the content.

Setting up an FTP connection

To set up an FTP connection, follow these steps:

1. **Choose File⇨Open Web to access the Open Web dialog box.**

Or, if you prefer, you can perform these same steps from the Open File dialog box, which you open by choosing File⇨Open.

2. **Open the Look In drop-down list and select Add/Modify FTP Locations.**

   The Add/Modify FTP Locations dialog box appears, as shown in Figure 8-1.

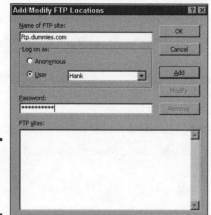

Figure 8-1:
Establishing
an FTP
connection.

3. **In the Name of FTP Site text box, type the name of the FTP site.**

   If you don't know the name of the FTP site you want to place your files on, ask your Internet service provider. For the *For Dummies* FTP site, for example, you type **ftp.dummies.com.**

4. **In the Log On As area, choose how you want to log on to the FTP site.**

   If you want to log on anonymously, select the Anonymous option. If you're a registered user, select the User option and then type your name in the text box to the right of that button.

5. **Type your password in the Password text box.**

   If you log on anonymously, most FTP sites either request or require that you use your e-mail address as your logon password.

6. **Click the Add button to add your FTP location to the FTP Sites area in the dialog box.**

   You can also change the particulars of a location by clicking in the FTP Sites area and then clicking the Modify button. Similarly, you can delete a location by selecting it and clicking the Remove button.

7. **Click OK in the Add/Modify FTP Locations dialog box to activate the connection and return to the Open Web dialog box.**

8. **Click Cancel to return to FrontPage.**

Publishing your Web

After you set up the FTP connection, you can publish your Web content by following these simple steps:

1. **Choose File⇨Publish Web.**

   The Publish Destination dialog box appears.

2. **Click the Browse button to access the New Publish Locations dialog box.**

   The following steps explain how to enter the publish destination by clicking the Browse button. But if you happen to know the location, you can type it in the Enter Publish Destination text box.

3. **Open the Look In drop-down list and select an FTP location.**

   You find FTP locations at the bottom of the drop-down list, below Add/Modify FTP Locations.

   The site that you select appears in the Web Name text box at the bottom of the dialog box.

4. **Click Open to return to the Publish Destination dialog box.**

   Your FTP location appears in the Enter Publish Destination text box.

5. **Click OK to FTP your content to the server.**

   If you see the Name and Password Required dialog box, type your user name and password there (contact your ISP or Web host if you can't remember your username and password) and click OK.

If you connect to the Internet through a *firewall* or *proxy server* (special computers whose job it is to intercept messages between your computer and the rest of the Internet as a security measure) you may run into a glitch or two when publishing your Web using FrontPage. If this is the case, contact your system administrator for instructions on how to proceed.

Index

Notes

Book IV

Dreamweaver

The 5th Wave   By Rich Tennant

Well, there's your Web page, Crypto. Designed like you asked. But personally, I think it has too many spinning spirals and blinking lights. It makes...hard reading. Make...tired... look...at...lose...all... con...cen...tra...tion...

Perfect!

CRYPTO THE HYPNOTIST

Contents at a Glance

Chapter 1: Getting to Know Dreamweaver

In This Chapter

- ✔ Discovering the power of Dreamweaver
- ✔ Getting familiar with the Document window
- ✔ Examining a site with the Site window
- ✔ Choosing between Standard and Layout views
- ✔ Exploring toolbar buttons
- ✔ Using panels and property inspectors
- ✔ Finding out how to get help

*I*f you're looking for a Web design tool that's both easy enough for beginners to use *and* sophisticated enough for Web design gurus, you've come to the right place. Dreamweaver 4, from Macromedia, is a powerful program that enables you to create almost any type of Web page. This chapter covers the Dreamweaver basics and introduces you to some of the program's essential tools.

What Is Dreamweaver, and What Can I Do with It?

Dreamweaver 4 is the industry standard for Web site design and production. Whether you're interested in creating a site for fun (such as an online photo album or a site devoted to one of your hobbies) or for business — say, an online store — Dreamweaver's flexible interface provides simultaneous graphical and HTML editing. In other words, using Dreamweaver, you can lay out pages like an artist, but also fine-tune the associated code like a programmer. And Dreamweaver's built-in FTP features let you upload your site to the Web in a snap, so that you can share your masterpieces with the world.

Introducing the Document Window

Your primary workspace in Dreamweaver 4 is the Document window, which appears automatically when you start Dreamweaver 4. In the Document window, you construct your individual Web pages using panels, inspectors, and dialog boxes to format your work. You can view the Document window full screen to work in a completely graphical environment (shown in Figure 1-1), or you can choose the Split View where you can view the Document window and the HTML source code for your page at the same time. (You display the Split View by choosing View⇨Code and Design from the main menu.)

When you have several documents open in a site, you can select which document you want to work on by clicking the icon's name in the Windows status bar at the bottom of the screen. You can also select the Site button to work on the entire site.

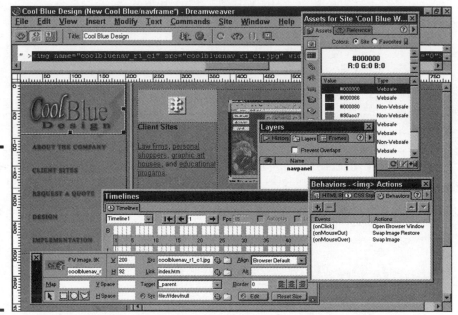

Figure 1-1: The Document window gives you many ways to view and work with your Web pages.

Examining Your Site with the Site Window

In the Site window, which you view by clicking the Map Only View button (described in Table 1-1), you can examine your entire site. As you can see in Figure 1-2, the Site window shows you a list of all files in your site and a map of how those files connect together. The Site window is also where you connect to the host server so that you can transfer, or *publish*, your site from your local computer to the Web. (You can find details for doing this in Chapter 9.)

The Site window is just one of the built-in tools you can use in Dreamweaver. To see more, check out the next section.

View buttons

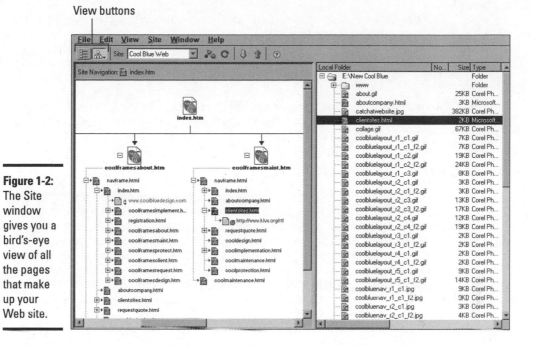

Figure 1-2:
The Site window gives you a bird's-eye view of all the pages that make up your Web site.

Choosing between Standard and Layout Views

You can work with content in your Document window using either the Standard View or the Layout View. If you've used a previous version of Dreamweaver, you'll recognize the *Standard View* as the familiar — and only — WYSIWYG ("what you see is what you get") graphical view through which you lay out pages in the Document window.

The *Layout View* is new to Dreamweaver 4 and is specifically geared toward helping you design your Web page using tables. The advantage of the Layout View is that it provides a simpler interface for drawing and editing tables and table cells. Two special tools are available only when working in Layout View: the Draw Layout Cell button and the Draw Layout Table button, both located in the Layout area of the Common Objects panel. (The Objects panel is indispensable during your Dreamweaver adventures. This handy panel contains "common" objects, such as tables, images, and e-mail links as well as form-related objects, character-related objects (such as the familiar copyright symbol), and other useful objects, all neatly organized into separate panels. You access the panels by using the drop-down box that appears at the top of the Objects panel. The Objects panel appears by default when you start Dreamweaver 4. For more information about the Objects panel, check out the "Panels" section later in this chapter.)

If the Objects panel doesn't appear, simply choose Window⇨Objects from the main menu to redisplay it.

 To work in Standard View: Select the document you want to work on. Click the Standard View button in the View area of the Common Objects panel.

 To work in Layout View: Select the document you want to work on. Click the Layout View button in the View area of the Common Objects panel.

Exploring Toolbar Buttons

Dreamweaver provides you with a number of other useful View buttons (shown in Table 1-1 and Table 1-2) that you can open to see different views of your site. You can easily switch among views to examine your site in different ways. Each Dreamweaver view offers specialized menus and tools to help you perform your work in that view. Certain views are available for an individual document or page, whereas other views are available for the entire site. At any time while you work, you can choose to preview your site in target Web browsers to see your site from the user's perspective.

 The buttons in the bottom-right corner of the Document window — Show Site, Show Assets, Show HTML Styles, Show CSS Styles, Show Behaviors, Show History, and Show Code inspector — are collectively known as the Mini-Launcher because you can click these buttons to open their respective panels. You can also display the full-size Launcher, a window for doing the same thing but that floats freely in the Document window, by choosing Window⇨Launcher from the Menu bar.

Table 1-1	Site-Related View Buttons	
Button/Tool	**Name**	**What You Can Do**
	Site Files button	View a list of all documents and dependent files in your site
	Map Only button	View a map showing icons representing all your documents and their relationships
	Connect to remote host button	Connects your local computer and your Web host, allowing you to transfer files between the two computers
	Get File(s) button	Download (retrieve) documents and files from the host
	Put File(s) button	Upload (send) documents and files to the host

Table 1-2	**Documented-Related View Buttons**	
Button/Tool	*Name*	*What You Can Do*
	Show Code View button	View HTML page code full screen
	Show Code and Design View button	View HTML page code and Document window at the same time
	Show Design View button	View Document window full screen
	File Management button	Click and then select Get to retrieve files from the Web site host or select Put to send files to the host
	Preview/Debug in Browser button	Click and select to preview or debug in IE or Navigator
	Reference button	Click to open the Reference panel for CSS, HTML, and JavaScript assistance
	View Options button	Click to select tools (such as Visual Aids and the Ruler) to assist you in viewing your site
	Show Site icon	Switch to Site View
	Show Assets icon	Open the Assets panel
	Show HTML Styles icon	Open the HTML Styles panel
	Show CSS Styles icon	Open the CSS Styles panel
	Show Behaviors icon	Open the Behaviors panel
	Show History icon	Open the History panel
	Show Code Inspector icon	Open a separate window showing HTML source code. HTML and JavaScript are color-coded

Using Panels and Property Inspectors

You can use Dreamweaver panels and property inspectors to enter details about all aspects of your Web site. These interfaces offer areas where you can add and format page features, set up navigation and behaviors, and manage your workflow.

Panels

A panel typically provides information about all instances of a particular page feature. For example, the Layers panel lists information about all the layers on the current page. One panel you may find very helpful is the Objects panel, which lets you add features, such as images, tables, and media, to your pages without accessing menus. You see an example of the Objects panel in Figure 1-3. The Objects panel is actually seven panels combined into one. To work with a different Objects panel, you simply click the Panel selector located at the top of the Objects panel and select a new panel from the pop-up menu.

You can open panels by choosing Window from the Menu bar and then selecting the desired panel name, such as Behaviors, Frames, or Layers, from the drop-down list. Panels can remain open in the Document window for as long as you want. To close a panel, simply click its Close (X) button.

Figure 1-3: The Objects panel lets you click to add images, tables, and other objects to your Web page.

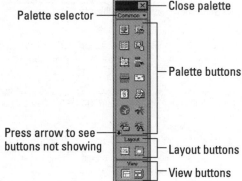

Palette selector ——————— Close palette

Palette buttons

Press arrow to see buttons not showing

Layout buttons

View buttons

Property Inspectors

A Property inspector is unique to the individual document object it represents and contains details on attributes of the object. For example, selecting text on a page opens the Text Property inspector where you can format the text size, font, color, link, and other information. To make certain that the Property inspectors are shown in the Document window, choose Window⇨ Properties from the Menu bar. You see an example of a Text Property inspector in Figure 1-4.

Figure 1-4:
You use Property inspectors, such as this one, to customize the char-acteristics, or *proper-ties*, of each document object.

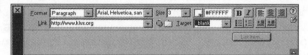

 Each Property inspector has a small down arrow in the lower-right corner, called an *Expander* button. Click the button to enlarge the Property inspec-tor to view additional formatting options. In an expanded Property inspector, click the small up arrow in the lower-right corner to collapse the inspector.

 The Pencil-and-Paper button at the right of each Property inspector pro-vides you access to the *Quick Tag Editor*. Click this button to open the Quick Tag Editor to open a work area where you can hand-code HTML for the selected object. When you're done, click outside the Quick Tag Editor work area to apply your edits to the HTML page code.

Getting Help

Dreamweaver offers a variety of tools to help you find the answer to virtu-ally any question you have about the program. The Help tools provide basic information for beginners as well as advanced references detailing HTML and JavaScript code.

 You can get help by clicking the Help button — the small question mark — in the top-right corner of any View window.

You can also access help using the Help menu located on the Menu bar. Just choose Help and then select one of the following options:

✦ **Using Dreamweaver:** Provides definitions and itemized steps in perform-ing routine Dreamweaver tasks. Opens in the Microsoft Internet Explorer browser and contains Help Contents, Index, and Search categories.

✦ **Reference:** Opens a panel offering a dictionary-style reference on CSS, HTML, and JavaScript. You can also access the Reference panel by clicking the Reference button in the Document window.

✦ **Dreamweaver Exchange, Dreamweaver Support Center, and Macromedia Online Forms:** Connects you to the Web where you can find constantly updated information on working with Dreamweaver, answers to Frequently Asked Questions, and program extensions. You can also join a developer's forum where you can chat with other Dreamweaver users to get (and give) help.

✦ **Extending Dreamweaver:** Provides assistance in performing more advanced Dreamweaver tasks, especially tasks involving the integration of adjunct programs, such as Flash, with Dreamweaver. This help option contains nitty-gritty information about application programming interfaces (APIs) — specific software interfaces that allow you to integrate Dreamweaver with databases, the C and Java programming languages, and much more.

Chapter 2: Getting Started with Dreamweaver: Your First Web Site

In This Chapter

✔ Starting Dreamweaver

✔ Creating a new site

✔ Creating a new document

✔ Adding content to your document

✔ Saving your document

✔ Previewing your document in a Web browser

Developing a Web page from scratch is an easy task with Dreamweaver. In this chapter, you see a five-minute procedure for creating a simple Web page.

Starting Dreamweaver

Each time you start Dreamweaver, a new Untitled document opens in the Document window. Starting Dreamweaver also opens the site you were working on when you last exited (Windows) or quit (Macintosh) the program. Follow these steps to start Dreamweaver:

In Windows: Choose Start⇨Programs⇨Macromedia Dreamweaver 4⇨ Dreamweaver 4 from the Status Bar at the bottom of Windows.

In Macintosh: Click the Application button on the Launcher and click the Dreamweaver program icon.

Don't get confused between the Macintosh Launcher and the Dreamweaver Launcher — they are not the same!

Creating a New Site

In Dreamweaver, creating a new site means specifying a location where you want your documents (Web pages) and dependent files (such as images and audio files) to be stored. You can create a new site in any view as follows:

1. **Create a new folder on your computer and name it.**

   For example, you can name the folder for your first site, `My First Site`.

2. **Start Dreamweaver and choose Site⇨New Site from the Menu bar.**

   A window similar to the one you see in Figure 2-1 appears.

3. **At the Site Definition dialog box, enter a name for your site at the Site Name text box.**

   The name can be the same as the site folder you created in Step 1.

4. **In the Local Root Folder area, click the folder button and browse to locate the site folder you created in Step 1.**

5. **Click OK.**

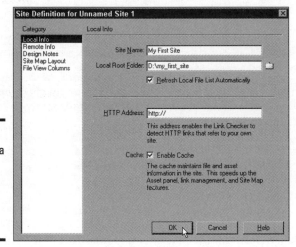

Figure 2-1:
You create a
new site
using the
Site
Definition
window.

Creating a New Document

Creating a new document means creating a new Web page to save in your site folder. (Dreamweaver refers to Web pages as *documents*.) Create a new document using either of these methods:

✦ In the Document window, choose File➪New from the Menu bar.

✦ In Site Files View, choose File➪New File from the Menu bar.

Adding Content to a Document

After you start Dreamweaver, create a new site, and create a new document, you're ready to add content, such as text, links, or images, to that document as shown in Figure 2-2.

To add content, follow these steps:

Chapters 2 through 7 show you how to add many different kinds of cool content, including tables, frames, and animations, to your pages.

1. Switch to the Untitled document. To do this in Windows, click the Untitled Document button in the taskbar. On a Macintosh, click the Untitled Document window.

2. Add content and color to your page by doing as many (or as few) of the following procedures as you want:

- **Choose a background color:** Choose Modify➪Page Properties from the Menu bar. Click the Background color swatch and then select a color from the palette. Click OK.

- **Specify a title:** Enter a title for your page in the Title text box at the top of the Document window. This title appears in the title bar of the browser window when your page is loaded.

- **Enter text:** Click your cursor in the Document window and enter something compelling, riveting, or insightful. (You can drag the object windows out of the way if you want.) Include the sentence, "I just bought this great book from Hungry Minds, Inc."

- **Create a link:** Select the text, "Hungry Minds, Inc." A Text Property inspector appears (if it doesn't, choose Window➪Properties from the Menu bar). In the Link text box, type http://www.hungryminds.com.

- **Add an image:** Click the Insert Image button on the Common Objects panel (if the panel doesn't show, open it by choosing Window➪Objects from the Menu bar). Browse to find a GIF or JPEG image on your computer and click Select.

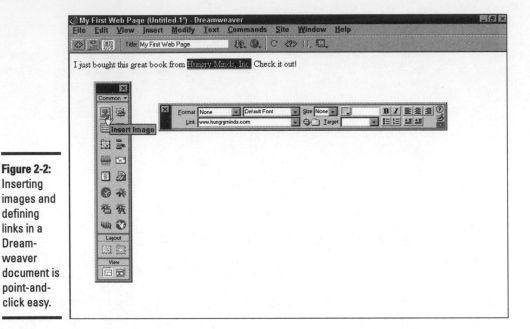

Figure 2-2:
Inserting
images and
defining
links in a
Dream-
weaver
document is
point-and-
click easy.

Saving a Document

After opening a new document or editing an existing document, you must
save your work. A document must be saved in your site folder before it can
be transferred from your computer to a host computer for display on the
Web. To save an open document, follow these steps:

1. **Choose File⇨Save from the Menu bar.**

2. **At the Save As dialog box, browse to your site folder at the Save In
drop-down list (this folder may already be selected).**

3. **In the File Name area, enter a name for your document followed by
the extension .html, as shown in Figure 2-3.**

4. **Click Save.**

To save a site, you simply save each document contained in the site. Also
save all dependent files, such as images, that you use in your documents.

Figure 2-3:
You save a
document to
a Web site
by browsing
to the site
folder and
specifying a
file name for
the
document.

Previewing a Document in a Web Browser

After you create or modify a document, preview it in a Web browser to see
how it appears after you publish it. (For the steps on publishing your document, check out Chapter 8.)

To preview a document:

1. **Click the Preview in Browser button in the Document window.**
   (Alternatively, you can choose File⇔Preview in Browser from the
   Menu bar.)

2. **From the menu, select an option for the browser you want to preview**
   the page in.

3. **If you go online, you can click any links you may have inserted to**
   check that they actually open the appropriate Web site. Click the
   Back button in your browser to return to your page.

If the browser you have installed on your machine doesn't appear in the
Preview/Debug in Browser list, click Edit Browser List to display the
Preferences dialog box; then click the + you see next to Browsers and type
the name and fully-qualified name of a browser-executable file in the Name
and Application fields, respectively. Choose either Primary Browser (if you
want Dreamweaver to open the browser by default) or Secondary browser
(if the browser is just one of many browsers you want Dreamweaver to work
with). When you finish, click OK to add the specified browser to the
Preview/Debug in Browser list.

**Book IV
Chapter 2**

**Getting Started
with Dreamweaver:
Your First Web Site**

Chapter 3: Creating Basic Web Pages

In This Chapter

✓ **Customizing what you see in the Document window**

✓ **Establishing page properties**

✓ **Entering text and line breaks**

✓ **Manipulating images**

✓ **Working with links and anchors**

✓ **Working with tables**

The most significant (and, fortunately, the easiest) process in building a Web site is creating the individual pages that convey the site's content. Even if you plan on creating an ultra-hip site chock-full of animation and interactive forms, the vast majority of your site-building efforts are spent constructing basic Web pages comprising words and images. This chapter shows you how to set up, color, and name individual Web pages. You also discover how to add basic elements, such as text, graphics, and tables, to your pages.

Customizing What You See in the Document Window

Dreamweaver offers you complete control over how you work in the Document window by providing two guide tools — rulers and a grid — to help you accurately lay out your work. You can customize a variety of guide tool attributes, such as ruler increments and grid snapping, to suit your personal preferences and speed Web page development.

You can customize almost all aspects of the Dreamweaver environment by specifying default settings in the Preferences dialog box. To open the Preferences dialog box, choose Edit⇨Preferences from the Menu bar.

Turning rulers on and off

Using rulers in the Document window can help you measure and numerically position page elements. Toggle the Ruler on and off by choosing View⇨Rulers⇨Show from the Menu bar.

Moving and resetting the origin

By default, the origin, or (0,0) coordinate, of a Dreamweaver ruler is set to the upper-left corner of the Document window. Reposition it to any coordinate in the Document window by clicking the origin cross hairs and dragging them to new coordinates. Reset the origin to its default position by choosing View⇨Rulers⇨Reset Origin from the Menu bar.

Changing ruler measurement units

You can change the ruler's measuring increment by choosing View⇨Rulers from the Menu bar and then choosing Pixels, Inches, or Centimeters from the pop-up menu.

Viewing the grid

Dreamweaver provides a Document window grid that can assist you in visually positioning and aligning page elements. You can toggle the grid on and off by choosing View⇨Grid⇨Show Grid from the Menu bar.

Activating and deactivating grid snapping

The Document window grid offers a snapping feature that causes a page element to automatically align precisely with the snap-to points you define. You can toggle grid snapping on and off by choosing View⇨Grid⇨Snap To Grid from the Menu bar.

Adjusting page size

When you design Web pages, you must consider how your target audiences will view them. People looking at your page may view it at any number of screen resolutions from 640 x 480 (the standard factory-set resolution for many computers) all the way up to 1024 x 768. Your audience may even view your pages using WebTV. Because pages appear differently at different resolutions, Dreamweaver offers you the ability to build your pages for a variety of monitor resolutions. The higher the resolution, the larger the workspace in your Document window.

To size your pages, click the Window Size Indicator in the middle of the Status bar (which, in turn, is located along the very bottom of the document window) and select a standard size — for example, 640 x 480 — from the pop-up menu. (The Selecting Edit Sizes option on the pop-up menu allows you to specify any height and width dimensions you want.)

You can adjust how the grid appears in the Document window through the Grid Settings dialog box. To do so, open the Grid Settings dialog box by choosing <u>V</u>iew⇨<u>Grid</u>⇨<u>E</u>dit Grid from the Menu bar and change any (or all) of the attributes that appear. When you finish, click Apply to view the effect of your changes. Click OK to accept the changes and close the dialog box.

Establishing Page Properties

The Page Properties dialog box provides you control over how several key page properties appear, including the title of the page, page background color, link colors, and page margins. Selections apply only to the current page, not the entire site. Open a Page Properties dialog box similar to the one you see in Figure 3-1 by choosing <u>M</u>odify⇨<u>P</u>age Properties from the Menu bar. Then make changes to any of the following:

✦ **<u>T</u>itle:** Enter a page title in the box. This title appears in the Title Bar area of the window both during construction in Dreamweaver and when the page is viewed through a Web browser.

✦ **Background <u>I</u>mage:** Click Browse (Windows) or Choose (Macintosh) to locate the image file that you want to appear as the Document window background. If the image is smaller than the available background area, it *tiles* (repeats in checkerboard fashion, like floor tiles) to fill the background.

✦ **Background, T<u>e</u>xt, <u>L</u>inks, <u>V</u>isited Links, and <u>A</u>ctive Links:** Click the Color box next to each property and select a color from the Web-safe color palette that appears. Alternatively, you may enter a hexadecimal color code directly in any Color Code box.

✦ **Le<u>f</u>t Margin and To<u>p</u> Margin:** These Property boxes set up margins that affect how your page appears in Microsoft Internet Explorer. Enter a whole number for the number of pixels of standoff space you want on the left and top sides of your document.

✦ **Margin <u>W</u>idth and Margi<u>n</u> Height:** These Property boxes set up margins that affect how your page appears in Netscape Navigator. Enter a whole number for the number of pixels of standoff space you want on the left and top sides of your document.

✦ **<u>D</u>ocument Encoding:** Choose a language for character encoding of text on your page. For example, if you want to create Web pages capable of displaying text in Korean, you can choose Korean (EUC-KR); if you want to display text in English, choose Western (Latin1). Click Reload to display the page with the changed encoding.

✦ **Tracing Image:** Click Browse (Windows) or Choose (Macintosh) to locate the image file you want to use as a guide for laying out your Web page in the Document window. This feature is handy for developers who prefer to "mock up" a portion of their Web page design in a graphics program, then recreate that design in their Web pages. Tracing images appear only in Dreamweaver, as a pattern to help guide you in creating an actual Web page design; tracing images never appear on the finished Web page.

✦ **Image Transparency:** Drag the slider to adjust the visibility level of the tracing image. At 0 percent the tracing image is invisible; at 100 percent the image is completely opaque.

Click Apply to view the effect of any property you change. Click OK to accept your changes and close the Page Properties dialog box.

Even if you choose to use a background image, select a complementary background color — the color shows while the background image is downloading.

Figure 3-1:
Use the
Page
Properties
window to
specify
settings that
affect your
entire
document
(such as
background
and title).

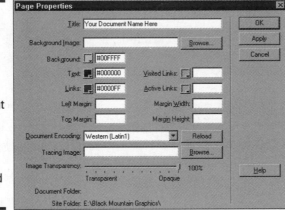

Entering Text

You can enter and manipulate text on a Web page in Dreamweaver by using similar procedures to those you use when working with a word-processing document.

Inserting text

To enter text on a page, click your mouse in the Document window and begin typing. Your mouse pointer appears as a blinking cursor that moves along with the text you enter. When you reach the end of a line, the text automatically wraps to the next line. Dreamweaver automatically adds the associated code for your new text in the HTML for the page.

Inserting a line break

When you want to start a new line in a word-processing program, you hit the Return key. In Dreamweaver, you create a line break by choosing Insert⇨Special Characters⇨Line Break from the Menu bar or by pressing Shift+Enter (Windows) or Shift+Return (Macintosh). Alternatively, you may click the Insert Line Break button from the Character Objects panel. If the panel doesn't show, open it by choosing Window⇨Objects from the Menu bar. Dreamweaver places the cursor at the start of the next line and creates the line break HTML code for the page.

Deleting text and line breaks

To delete text and line breaks from a page, in the Document window, select the item that you want to delete and press Backspace or Delete on your keyboard.

Modifying text

You can modify how text appears on a page by editing its font, size, color, alignment, and other attributes.

To modify text in the Document window, drag your mouse to select the text you want to modify. Doing this opens the Text Property inspector, as you see in Figure 3-2. (If the Property inspector does not show, choose Window⇨Properties from the Menu bar to open it.) On the Text Property inspector, modify any of the following properties:

✦ **Format:** From the first drop-down list, select a default text style. These styles are relative, not absolute. Heading 1 is the largest style and Heading 6 is the smallest, but none of the headings correlate with a specific pixel size. Select a text font from the second drop-down list. Browsers show your text formatted as the first font in your selection that resides on the user's computer.

✦ **Font:** Select a font face from the drop-down list. Choosing Edit Font List allows you to add additional fonts you may have installed on your computer to the font face drop-down list.

✦ **Size:** Select a font size from the drop-down list. The options include none (choosing this option displays text in the default size 3), 1 through 7 (smallest to largest), +1 through +7, and -1 through -7. Choosing a font size of -2 displays text 2 font sizes smaller than the previously specified font size. Alternatively, choosing a font size of +2 displays text 2 font sizes larger than the previously specified font size.

✦ **Color:** Click the color box and select a text color from the Web-safe color palette that appears. Alternatively, you may enter a hexadecimal color code directly in any color code box. (To set the default text color for a page, check out "Establishing Page Properties," earlier in this chapter.)

✦ **Bold or Italic:** Click the Bold button to bold your selected text. Click the Italic button to italicize your selected text. You can click either button or both.

✦ **Alignment:** Click an alignment button to align your text. Choices are Left, Center, and Right.

✦ **Link:** Type a URL in this field to transform text into a hypertext link.

✦ **Target:** From the drop-down list, choose one of the following: _blank (opens link in a new window), _parent (opens link in the parent of the currently opened window), _self (the default; opens link in the currently opened window), and _top (opens link in the top-level window, replacing frames, if any).

✦ **List:** Click the Unordered List icon next to the Target field to transform text into an unordered (bulleted) list; click the Ordered List icon to transform text into an ordered (numbered) list.

✦ **Placement:** Click the Text Outdent icon you find next to the Ordered List icon to outdent selected text; click the Text Indent icon to indent selected text.

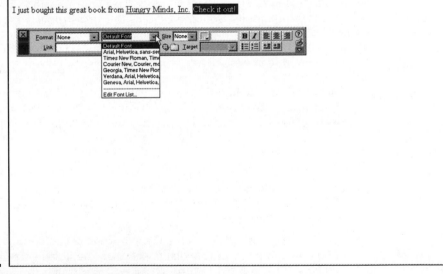

Figure 3-2:
You can change the format, color, and alignment of any text on your page using the Text Property inspector.

Manipulating Images

Next to entering text, manipulating images on a Web page is probably the most common Dreamweaver function you perform. You can add or delete an image and modify its properties to create an aesthetically pleasing layout that effectively conveys the information you want to deliver to the user.

To see how to place an image on the background of your page, check out "Establishing Page Properties," earlier in this chapter.

Inserting an image

To insert an image on a page, follow these steps:

1. **Choose Insert⇨Image from the Menu bar.**

   Alternatively, you can click the Insert Image button from the Common Objects panel. If the panel doesn't show, open it by choosing Window⇨ Objects from the Menu bar.

2. **At the Select Image Source dialog box (shown in Figure 3-3), click the image you want to insert.**

   If the image is outside the current folder, click the arrow tab beside the Look In box and browse to select the file you want.

Figure 3-3:
Clicking the Preview check box at the bottom of the Select Image Source window lets you preview an image before you add it to your page.

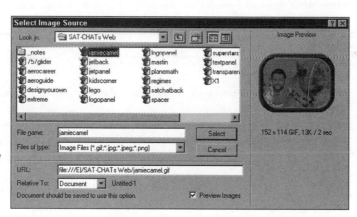

Book IV
Chapter 3

Creating Basic Web Pages

3. **Click the Select button to insert the image.**

   Note: Every image you want to include on a Web page must reside within the folder of the current site. If you attempt to insert an image from another location, Dreamweaver asks whether you want to copy the image to the current site root. Click Yes. At the Copy File As dialog box, you can enter a new name for the image in the File Name box, or you can accept the current name and click Save.

Put a check in the Preview check box at the bottom of the Select Image Source dialog box to view a thumbnail image before you select it for insertion. The preview area also tells you the size of the image and the expected download time.

Deleting an image

To delete an image from a page, click the image in the Document window and press the Delete key on your keyboard.

Modifying an image

You can modify how an image appears on a page by editing its size and alignment, adding a border, and changing other attributes.

To modify an image, click the image in the Document window to select it. If the Image Property inspector does not appear, choose Window⇨Properties from the Menu bar to open it.

To see all the options the Image Property inspector offers, click the down arrow in the bottom right-hand corner of the Image Property inspector. (Clicking the up arrow displays fewer options.)

As shown in Figure 3-4, you can modify any of the following properties:

✦ **Resize the image:** Click and drag a sizing handle to change the dimensions of the image. To resize the image maintaining the same proportions, hold down the Shift key as you drag a sizing handle.

✦ **Align the image:** On the Image Property inspector, click an Alignment button to position the image on the page (or within a cell if the image is located in a table cell). Alignment button choices consist of Left, Center, and Right. (To align an image with special word wrapping, choose one of the alignment options from the Align drop-down list that appears when you position your image near a bunch of text, as shown in Table 3-1.)

✦ **Add a border to the image:** On the Image Property inspector, enter a number in the Border box to add a border of that thickness to the image. Border thickness is measured in pixels.

✦ **Pad an image with spaces:** On the Image Property inspector, enter a number in pixels in the V Space (V for vertical) box for the space you want to appear at the top and bottom the image; then enter a number in pixels in the H Space (H for horizontal) box for the space you want to appear on either side of the image.

✦ **Make the image a link:** On the Image Property inspector, enter a URL in the Link box.

✦ **Specify alternative text for the image:** On the Image Property inspector, enter alternative text in the Alt box. (Specifying alternative text ensures that when viewers' browsers don't — or can't — display the image, some meaningful text appears instead.)

✦ **Name the image:** On the Image Property inspector, enter a name in the box next to the thumbnail image. (Naming an image is important if you want to refer to that image using a scripting language, such as JavaScript. You find out more about JavaScript in Book 6.)

✦ **Edit the image:** On the Image Property inspector, click the Edit button.

Dreamweaver doesn't enable you to edit images directly. Instead, clicking the Edit button opens the image-editing program that's installed on your computer. To specify a new image-editing program, choose Edit⇨ Preferences from the Menu bar. In the Preferences dialog box, choose File Types/Editors from the Category menu. Click an image extension (.gif, .jpg, or .png) in the Extensions menu. Then choose a program in the Editors menu and click the Make Primary button. You can add a new Editor by clicking the add (+) button. Click OK to apply your changes and close the dialog box.

✦ **Change the image file:** On the Image Property inspector, enter a different filename in the Src box (or click the file icon to browse for image files).

Table 3-1	Aligning an Image in Relation to Text
Alignment Option	*Effect on Image and Text Wrapping*
Browser Default	Same as Bottom alignment
Baseline	Same as Bottom alignment
Top	Aligns the image top with the highest other inline element
Middle	Aligns the image middle with the text baseline
Bottom	Aligns the image bottom with the text baseline
Text Top	Aligns the image top with the text top
Absolute Middle	Aligns the image middle with the text middle
Absolute Bottom	Aligns the image bottom with the bottom of the text descenders
Left	Aligns the image flush left
Right	Aligns the image flush right

Figure 3-4:
You use image sizing handles and the Image Property inspector to modify the way an image appears in your document.

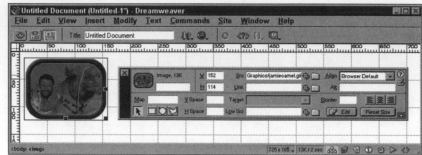

 Dreamweaver doesn't offer image-editing functions, such as recoloring or adding drop shadows; you have to use a program, such as Macromedia Fireworks or Adobe Photoshop, to accomplish these tasks.

Working with Links

Linking your page to other Web pages enables you to direct visitors to related content on the Web. To insert a link, you must specify an image or some text to serve as the link; you must also specify the link location to which you want to send your visitors. The link can go to a page within your site, or to a page elsewhere on the Web.

Inserting a link

To insert a link on a page, follow these steps:

1. Select the text or image you want to make a link.

Doing so opens the Property inspector for your text or image. If the Property inspector does not show, choose Window⇨Properties from the Menu bar to open it.

2. In the Link area of the Property inspector, enter the target of the link (text or image) you created in Step 1.

The URL you specify can be any valid URL, for example, a Web page on your computer (`somePage.html`), on the Web (`http://www.someSite.com/somePage.html`), or even an e-mail address (`mailto:somebody@somewhere.com`).

Alternatively, you may click the File Folder icon you see in the Property inspector to display the Select File dialog box. After you browse your computer using the Select File dialog box and select a file, click Select to make that file the target of a link.

To create an e-mail link quickly, click anywhere in your document and choose Insert⇨E-mail Link from the Menu bar. Specifying the same value for the Text and E-mail fields that appear allows folks who haven't configured their Web browsers to handle e-mail automatically to see the e-mail address on the page. Then, they can cut-and-paste the e-mail address information into their e-mail program of choice.

Deleting a link

To delete a link from a page, follow these steps:

1. **Select the text or image you want to remove the link from.**

   The Property inspector for your text or image opens. If the Property inspector doesn't appear, choose Window⇨Properties from the Menu bar to open it.

2. **In the Property inspector, delete the name of the link from the Link box.**

Using named anchors

When you want to create a navigational link that connects users not only to a page, but also to a specific location on the page, you need to create a *named anchor*. Named anchors are frequently used for jumping to exact positions within a large block of text so that users don't have to scroll through sentence after sentence to find the information they need. Setting up named anchors is especially useful when creating links from a directory or a table of contents to the content it presents.

Inserting a named anchor

Place an anchor anywhere on your Web page as follows:

1. **In the Document window, click your mouse cursor at the position you want to insert the named anchor.**

2. **Click the Insert Named Anchor button on the Invisible Objects panel or choose Insert⇨Invisible Tags⇨Named Anchor from the Menu bar. (If the Objects panel doesn't appear, open it by choosing Window⇨Objects from the Menu bar.)**

   The Insert Named Anchor dialog box appears.

3. **Type a name in the Anchor Name box.**

4. **Click OK.**

It's a good idea to insert the named anchor tag slightly above the actual position where you want the link to target. Doing so gives your targeted content a little padding on top. Otherwise, the top of your image or your first line of text appears flush with the top of the browser window.

Linking to a named anchor

To link to a named anchor, follow the procedure outlined in the "Inserting a Link" section above with the following modifications:

✦ **Linking to a named anchor on the current page:** In the Link box of the Property inspector, type a pound sign followed by the anchor name.

✦ **Linking to a named anchor on a different page:** In the Link box of the Property inspector, type the HTML page name followed by a pound sign and then the anchor name.

As of this writing, the latest version of Netscape Navigator (Version 6.0) supports linking to named anchors on the current page — not other pages.

Working with Tables

Adding a table to a Web page can help you lay out page elements more easily in the Document window. Tables consist of as many holding areas, or *cells,* as you want, and you can place virtually any Web element, such as text or an image, into a cell. Cells are organized horizontally into *rows* and vertically into *columns.* Dreamweaver provides you with complete control over the size, position, color, and other attributes of your table. And you can edit these attributes at any time via the Table Property inspector.

Inserting a table

To add a table, choose Insert⇨Table from the Menu bar to open the Insert Table dialog box shown in Figure 3-5. Alternatively, you may click the Insert Table button from the Common Objects panel. (If the panel doesn't show, open it by choosing Window⇨Objects from the Menu bar.) Enter the following information in the Insert Table dialog box:

✦ **Rows:** Enter a number in the box for the number of rows in the table.

✦ **Columns:** Enter a number in the box for the number of columns in the table.

✦ **Cell padding:** Enter a number in the box specifying how many pixels of padding you want between the inside edge of a cell and its contents.

✦ **Cell spacing:** Enter a number in the box specifying how many pixels separation you want between cells.

✦ **Width:** Select Percent from the drop-down list and then enter a number (0–100) in the box for the percent of page width you want the entire table to occupy. Or select Pixels from the drop-down list and enter a number of pixels for the width of the entire table.

✦ **Border:** Enter a number in the box for the width of the table borders in pixels. Entering 0 causes the borders to disappear.

Figure 3-5:
Use the
Insert Table
dialog box
to specify
what kind of
table you
want to add
to your
document.

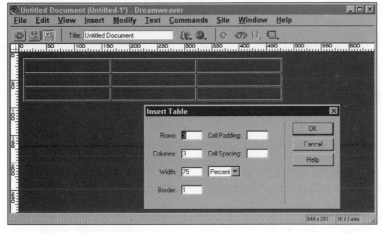

Deleting a table

To delete a table from a page, click the border of the table to select it and then press the Backspace or Delete key. Dreamweaver removes the table from your page and deletes the associated code in the HTML for the page.

Storing Information in Table Cells

After you insert a table on a page, you can add or delete elements, such as text and images, in the table cells.

Adding an image to a cell

To add an image to a table cell, click to position the cursor in a table cell and choose Insert➪Image from the Menu bar. Browse and select an image you want to add to the cell and then click Select. (For more information on inserting images, flip to "Inserting an image," earlier in this chapter.)

**Book IV
Chapter 3**

**Creating Basic
Web Pages**

Adding text to a cell

To add text to a table cell, click to position the cursor in a table cell and type the text you want placed inside the cell.

Deleting an image from a cell

To delete an image from a table cell, select the image and press Backspace or Delete.

Deleting text from a cell

To delete text from a table cell, select the text and press Backspace or Delete.

Chapter 4: Incorporating Interactive Images

In This Chapter

- ✔ Adding a link to an image
- ✔ Creating clickable hotspots
- ✔ Adding text rollovers (Flash text)
- ✔ Adding button rollovers (Flash buttons)
- ✔ Adding graphic rollovers
- ✔ Setting up a navigation bar

*I*mages are great — but if you really want to add pizzazz to your Web site, consider adding *interactive* images to your pages. Interactive images are more than just pretty pictures: They change appearance when users mouse over them. The most popular types of interactive images, called *rollovers* and *hotspots*, serve as navigation buttons that enable users to move through the site. Interactive images can be added in either Standard View or Layout View.

Creating a Link from an Image

You can make an image interactive by simply making it a link. Clicking an image that's set up as a link causes the user to jump somewhere else in the site or on the Web. Create a link from an image as follows:

1. **Select the image in the Document window.**

The Image Property inspector appears. (If the inspector does not appear, open it by choosing Windows⇨Properties from the Menu bar.)

2. **In the Image Property inspector, click the Link folder to open the Select File dialog box.**

3. **Browse to select the page you want to link to.**

If the link is outside the current folder, click the arrow tab beside the Look In box and browse to select the file you want. Alternatively, you can enter a Web address in the URL box at the bottom of the Select File dialog box.

4. **Click the Select button. The dialog box closes, and the link is activated.**

Creating Clickable Hotspots

You can designate certain areas of an image as *hotspots* — active areas that a user can click to open a link to another Web page or activate some other behavior. Hotspots can be shaped like rectangles, circles, or polygons (irregular objects).

Creating a hotspot

Use the following procedure to create a hotspot:

1. **Select the image that you want to add a hotspot to.**

   The Image Properties inspector you see in Figure 4-1 appears. If the inspector does not appear, open it by choosing <u>W</u>indow⇨<u>P</u>roperties from the Menu bar.

   If the bottom half of the Image Properties inspector is not visible, click the Expander button (the down arrow in the bottom-right corner).

2. **In the Map area of the Image Properties inspector, click a Hotspot button for the shape you want to draw.**

   You can choose among a rectangle, a circle, and a polygon. Your mouse pointer becomes a cross hair cursor when you move it over the image.

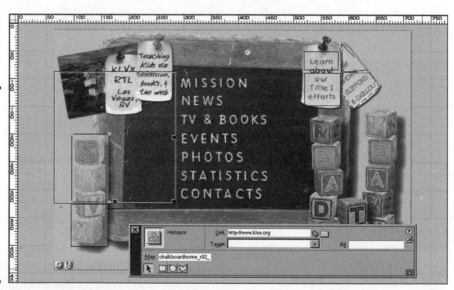

Figure 4-1:
You can create hotspots anywhere on your image using the circle, rectangle, and polygon drawing tools.

3. **Draw the hotspot according to the shape you select:**

- **Circle or rectangle:** Click your cross hair cursor on the image and drag to create a hotspot. Release the mouse button when your hotspot reaches your desired dimensions. The area you draw is highlighted light blue, and the Hotspot Property inspector appears.

- **Polygon:** Click your cross hair cursor on the image once for each point. Click the Arrow tool in the Image Properties inspector to close the shape. The area you draw is highlighted light blue, and the Hotspot Property inspector appears.

4. **In the Hotspot Property inspector, supply the following information:**

- **Map:** Enter a unique name for the hotspot.

- **Link:** Enter a URL or the name of an HTML file you want to open when the user clicks the hotspot. Alternatively, you can click the folder and browse to select the link from your files.

  Completing this box is optional. Instead, you may choose to attach a different kind of behavior to the hotspot.

  To attach a behavior other than *link* to the hotspot, open the Behaviors panel by choosing Window⇨Behaviors from the Menu bar. Then click the add (+) button in the Behaviors panel, which opens a pop-up menu of available behaviors, including Check Plugin, Play Sound, Popup Message, Preload Images, and many others. Choose a behavior from the pop-up menu, complete the information in the dialog box that appears for your selected behavior, and click OK.

- **Target:** Complete this box if you entered a link in the Link box. Click the tab and select from the drop-down list a target window where your selected link will appear. You can select from the following choices: _blank (opens link in a new window), _parent (opens link in the parent of the currently opened window), _self (the default; opens link in the currently opened window), and _top (opens link in the top-level window, replacing frames, if any). If you have created frames, you can also select a frame name from this list. (See Chapter 6 for more information about frames.)

- **Alt:** Enter the text you want to show when the user moves the mouse over the hotspot.

Modifying a hotspot

Use the following procedure to edit a hotspot:

1. **On an image in the Document window or table cell, click the hotspot you want to modify.**

   The Hotspot Property inspector appears. If the inspector does not appear, open it by choosing Window⇨Properties from the Menu bar.

2. **Edit any information you want to change in the Hotspot Property inspector.**

3. **Reshape any hotspot by clicking the Arrow tool in the Hotspot Properties inspector and dragging your mouse.**

4. **Delete a hotspot by clicking it and pressing the Delete key on your keyboard.**

Adding Text Rollovers (Flash Text)

A *text rollover* is text that changes colors when a user mouses over it. (One color appears to "roll over" to the next color.) One way to create text rollovers in Dreamweaver is by adding *Flash text* to your pages, as described below.

Flash text (and Flash buttons) are so called because Dreamweaver implements these features using the same code that Flash — an animation program developed by Macromedia — uses.

Adding Flash text

To add Flash text, follow these steps:

1. **Click in the Document window or table cell where you want to add Flash text.**

2. **Select the Insert Flash Text button from the Common Objects panel to open the Insert Flash Text dialog box.**

   If the panel doesn't appear, open it by choosing Properties⇨Objects from the Menu bar.

   Alternatively, you can choose Insert⇨Interactive Objects⇨Flash Text from the Menu bar.

3. **In the Insert Flash Text dialog box, select a text font from the Font drop-down list.**

4. **Enter a point size for your text in the Size box.**

5. **If you want, format the text. You can click the Bold button and/or Italics button. You can also click an alignment button. Alignment choices are Left, Center, Right, and Justify.**

6. **Select a Color (initial color) and a Rollover Color (color that responds to mouse movement) by clicking the color swatch in each area and selecting a color from the color palette that appears.**

7. **Enter your text in the Text box. Click to check the Show Font check box if you want to view the Text box in your selected font.**

8. **In the Link box, enter a URL or the name of the page you want to appear when the user clicks the Flash text.**

   Alternatively, you can click the Browse button to select a page from your files.

9. **In the Target area, click the tab and select from the drop-down list a target window where the link will appear.**

   If you have created frames, you can select a frame name from this list, or you can select from the following choices: _blank (opens link in a new window), _parent (opens link in the parent of the currently opened window), _self (the default; opens link in the currently opened window), and _top (opens link in the top-level window, replacing frames, if any).

10. **Select a Background color by clicking the Bg Color swatch and selecting a color from the color palette that appears.**

    Your Flash text appears over the background color you choose.

11. **Enter a name for your Flash text component in the Save As box or click the Browse button to select a name from your files.**

    Note: You must save Flash text with an .swf extension.

12. **Click OK to create your Flash text and close the dialog box.**

Changing Flash text

You can change a Flash text object you already created by simply double-clicking the object in the Document window. Doing so opens the Insert Flash Text dialog box where you can change your text as I describe in "Adding Flash text," earlier in this section. After you make changes to the Flash text object, you must resave the object.

Playing (previewing) Flash text

To play Flash text, select the text in the Document window to open the Flash Text Property inspector. In the Property inspector, click the Play button to view your Flash text as it appears in the browser window. Click the Stop button when you finish.

Adding Button Rollovers (Flash Buttons)

Buttons that change appearance when a user mouses over them — called *button rollovers* — are so popular that Dreamweaver gives you a way to create them quickly and easily.

Adding a Flash button

To add a Flash button, follow these steps:

1. **Click in the Document window or table cell in which you want to add a Flash Button.**

2. **Click the Insert Flash Button button from the Common Objects panel to open an Insert Flash Button dialog box similar to the one shown in Figure 4-2.**

   If the panel doesn't appear, open it by choosing Properties⇨Objects from the Menu bar.

   Alternatively, you can choose Insert⇨Interactive Objects⇨Flash Button from the Menu bar.

3. **At the Insert Flash Button dialog box, scroll through the button selections in the Style list and click to select a style.**

   You can preview the style in the Sample area of the dialog box — just point to the sample with your mouse to see the Flash button play.

4. **If your selected button has a placeholder for text, enter the text that you want to appear on the button in the Button Text area.**

5. **Select a font for your Flash button text from the Font drop-down list.**

6. **Enter a point size for your text in the Size box.**

7. **In the Link box, enter a URL or the name for the page that you want to appear when the user clicks the Flash button.**

   Alternatively, you can click the Browse button to select a page from your files.

8. **In the Target area, click the tab and select from the drop-down list a target window where the URL will appear.**

   You can select from the following choices: _blank (opens link in a new window), _parent (opens link in the parent of the currently opened window), _self (the default; opens link in the currently opened window), and _top (opens link in the top-level window, replacing frames, if any). If you have created frames, you can also select a frame name from this list.

9. **Select a Background color by clicking the Bg Color swatch and selecting a color from the color palette that appears.**

   Your Flash button displays on top of the background color you select.

   Alternatively, you can enter a hexadecimal color code in the Bg Color box.

10. **Enter a name for your Flash button in the Save As box or click the Browse button to select a name from your files.**

You must save the Flash button with an .swf extension.

11. **Click OK to create your Flash button and then close the dialog box.**

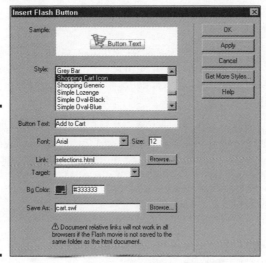

Figure 4-2: You can add over a dozen prebuilt rollover (Flash) buttons to your pages.

Get new Flash buttons on the Macromedia Dreamweaver Web site by clicking the Get More Styles button in the Insert Flash Button dialog box.

Changing a Flash button

To change a Flash button object you have already created, simply double-click the object in the Document window. Doing so opens the Insert Flash Button dialog box where you can change your button as I describe in "Adding a Flash button," earlier in this section. After you make changes to the Flash button object, you must resave the object.

Modifying Flash button features

You can add additional features to a Flash button as follows:

1. **In the Document window, click to select the Flash button object you want to enhance.**

The Flash Text Property inspector appears. If the inspector does not appear, open it by choosing Window➪Properties from the Menu bar.

2. **At the Flash Button Property inspector, modify any of the available Flash button attributes.**

Playing (previewing) a Flash button

To see what a Flash button looks like in action, select the button in the Document window to open the Flash Button Property inspector. In the Property inspector, click the Play button to view your Flash button as it appears in the browser window. Click the Stop button after you finish.

Inserting Image Rollovers

An *image rollover* (often just referred to as *rollover*) is an image that appears to change whenever the user rolls the mouse pointer over it. Rollovers add interactivity to a Web page by helping users know what parts of the page link to other Web pages.

A rollover is actually two images — one for normal display on a page (the original image) and one that is slightly modified for display when the image is rolled over (the rollover image). You can modify an image by changing the color or position, adding a glow or a shadow, or you can add another graphic — such as a dog changing from sleeping to wide-awake.

Insert a rollover by following these steps:

1. **Click either inside the Document window or inside a table cell in which you want to insert the rollover.**

2. **Click the Insert Rollover Image button from the Common Objects panel to open the Insert Rollover Image dialog box shown in Figure 4-3.**

   If the panel doesn't show, open it by choosing Properties⇨Objects from the Menu bar.

   Alternatively, you can choose Insert⇨Interactive Images⇨Rollover Image from the Menu bar.

3. **In the Insert Rollover Image dialog box, enter a name for the rollover in the Image Name box.**

   The rollover is referred to by this name in the HTML page code. Keep in mind that this rollover name refers to the combined original image/ rollover image pair.

4. **Enter the name of the original image file in the Original Image box or click the Browse button to select an image from your files.**

   The original image appears on the page when the user's mouse pointer is *not* over the rollover.

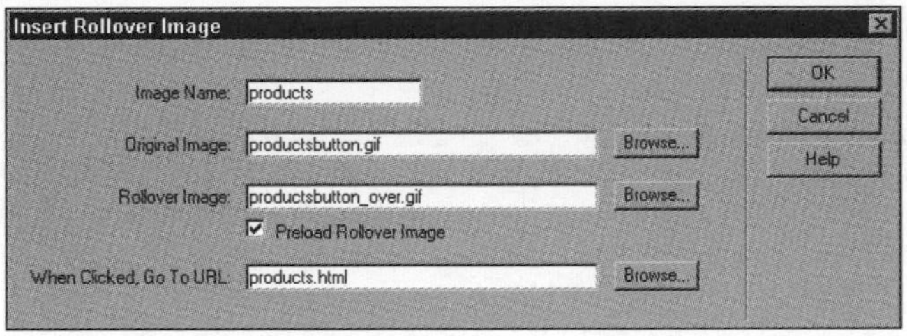

Figure 4-3:
Inserting an image rollover is as easy as using the Insert Rollover Image dialog box: Simply specify an URL and a pair of "on" and "off" images.

Insert Rollover Image

Image Name: products

Original Image: productsbutton.gif   Browse...

Rollover Image: productsbutton_over.gif   Browse...
☑ Preload Rollover Image

When Clicked, Go To URL: products.html   Browse...

OK
Cancel
Help

5. **Enter the name of the Rollover Image file in the Rollover Image box, or click the Browse button to select an image from your files.**

   The rollover image appears on the page when the user's mouse pointer *is* over the rollover.

6. **Check the Preload Rollover Image check box. This feature makes the rollover action appear without delay to users as they move the mouse pointer over the original image.**

7. **In the When Clicked, Go To URL text box, enter a URL or the name of the page you want to appear when the user clicks the rollover.**

   Alternatively, you can click the Browse button to select a page from your files.

8. **Click OK to accept your choices and close the dialog box.**

To check the rollover, preview your page in a browser by choosing File⇨ Preview in Browser from the Menu bar, or by clicking the Preview in Browser button and using your mouse to point to the original image.

As with all images, you can't create the original image or the rollover image directly in Dreamweaver; you must use an image-editing program, such as Macromedia Fireworks.

Setting Up a Navigation Bar

A *navigation bar* is a group of buttons that users can access to move throughout your Web site. Buttons within a navigation bar may present users with options, such as moving backwards, moving forwards, returning to the home page, or jumping to specific pages within the site.

Each button in a navigation bar possesses properties similar to a rollover in that the button *changes state* — or appears differently — based on where the user is positioning the mouse pointer. However, a navigation bar button can possess as many as four different states:

✦ **Up:** The original state of the button.

✦ **Over:** How the button appears when a user mouses over it.

✦ **Down:** How the button appears when a user clicks it.

✦ **Over While Down:** How the button appears when the user mouses over it after clicking it.

A navigation bar differs from individual rollovers in that clicking a navigation Bar button in the Down state causes all other buttons in the bar to revert to the Up state.

Creating a new navigation bar

Create a navigation bar as follows:

1. **Select the Insert Navigation Bar button from the Common Objects panel. (If the panel doesn't show, open it by choosing Properties⇨Objects from the Menu bar.)**

   Alternatively, you may choose Insert⇨Interactive Objects⇨ Navigation Bar from the Menu bar.

2. **At the Insert Navigation Bar dialog box (see Figure 4-4), enter a name for the first button in the Element Name box.**

   The new button appears in the Nav Bar Elements box.

3. **For each state of the button — Up Image, Over Image, Down Image, and Over While Down Image — enter the name of the image file that you want to use in the associated field.**

   Alternatively, you can click the Browse button for each field and select an image from your files. You must supply the Up Image. All other states are optional and can be left blank.

   You don't need to use all four navigation bar button states — creating only Up and Down works just fine.

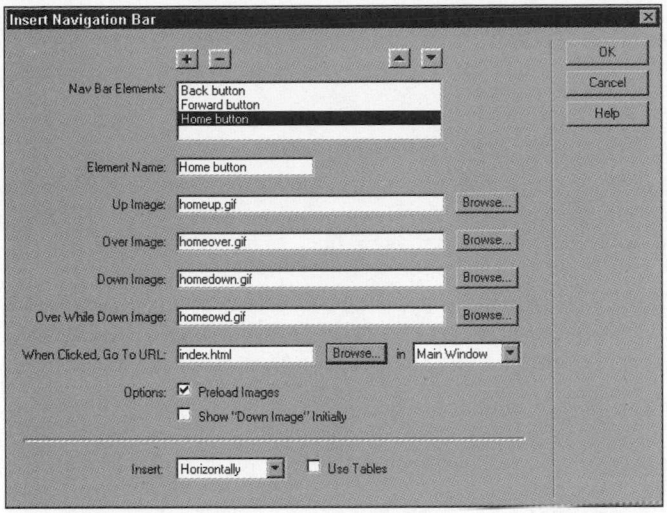

Figure 4-4:
You can create as many buttons for your navigation bar as you want in the Insert Navigation Bar window.

4. **In the When Clicked, Go To URL box, enter a URL or the name for the page you want to appear when the user clicks the navigation bar button.**

   Alternatively, you can click the Browse button to select a page from your files.

5. **Click the drop-down list tab and select a target window where you want the URL to appear. If you aren't using frames, the only option is to use the Main window.**

6. **Click the (+) button to add another navigation bar button.**

   Repeat Steps 2 through 5 to format the new button.

   Note: You can remove any button already created by clicking its name in the Nav Bar Elements box and clicking the Remove (–) button. Reorder the sequence of the buttons by clicking a button name in the Nav Bar Elements box and clicking the up or down arrow.

7. **In the Options area, select the Preload Images check box if you want the rollover effects to appear without delay as soon as the page loads.**

8. **To set the current button to appear in the Down state when the user first sees the navigation bar, select the Show "Down Image" Initially check box in the Options area.**

9. **In the Insert list box, click the tab and select from the drop-down list to position the navigation bar either horizontally or vertically.**

10. **To set up the button images in a table format, select the Use Tables check box.**

11. **Click OK to accept your choices and close the dialog box.**

To check the navigation bar, you must preview your page in a browser. Choose File⇨Preview in Browser from the Menu bar or click the Preview in Browser button and use your mouse to point to the buttons.

Modifying a navigation bar

To change elements of a navigation bar you already created, choose Modify⇨ Navigation Bar from the Menu bar, which opens the Modify Navigation Bar dialog box where you can make edits.

The Modify Navigation Bar dialog box is nearly identical to the Insert Navigation Bar dialog box shown in Figure 4-4, except that you can no longer change the orientation of the bar or access the Use Tables check box.

Chapter 5: Adding Multimedia Objects

In This Chapter

✓ **Adding audio**

✓ **Adding video**

✓ **Adding other media (ActiveX controls, Java applets, and Flash movies)**

*I*f you want to understand and appreciate the power of adding video — streaming or downloadable — to your Web site, just take a peek at sites, such as CNN (www.cnn.com). And for the talk-radio and music lovers among you, sites, such as National Public Radio (www.npr.org), demonstrate how you can effectively use audio on your pages.

This chapter shows you how to incorporate both video and audio — as well as other multimedia objects, such as Java applets, Flash movies, and ActiveX controls — into your sites using Dreamweaver. Keep in mind that Dreamweaver can't help you build the multimedia elements themselves; it can only make existing multimedia objects accessible to users who view your page.

Many different Web-friendly media formats exist. For a list of the most popular (along with tips for creating your own audio, video, and animation files), check out Book 5, "Multimedia: Creating Graphics, Sound, Animations, Video, and Java Applets."

Adding Audio and Video to Your Pages

You have two basic options for adding downloadable audio and video to your Web pages.

✦ **Embedding:** You embed an audio or video file to display a playback console on a Web page that users can use to play, rewind, and fast-forward the media file. (You can also embed an audio file and make it invisible to create a background audio effect.) Users must have an appropriate plug-in installed on their machines to play the embedded audio or video file.

✦ **Linking:** You link to an audio or video file to allow users the option of linking to that media file (or not).

The following sections describe the two options.

Keep in mind that most audio and video files are large — large enough that many folks impatiently click the Stop button on their browsers before a Web page chock-full of audio or video effects has a chance to finish loading. Two basic rules help you use audio and video effectively in your Web pages:

✦ Use audio and video only when plain text just won't do.

✦ Keep your audio and video clips as short (and corresponding file sizes as small) as possible.

Embedding an audio or video clip

You embed an audio file by using the following steps:

1. **In the Document window, click your page in the location where you want to add an embedded audio file.**

2. **Click the Insert Plugin button on the Special Objects panel or choose Insert⇨Media⇨Plugin from the Menu bar.**

   You see the result in Figure 5-1 below.

3. **In the Select File dialog box that appears, enter the path to the audio file you want to embed and click the Select button.**

   If the file is outside your current root directory, Dreamweaver asks whether you want to copy the file to your site root. Click Yes.

4. **In the Plugin Property inspector, size the Audio Plugin placeholder to any dimensions you prefer.**

   You can either enter a width and height in the W and H text boxes in the Plugin Property inspector, or you can drag a handle on the placeholder to manually resize.

   A width of 144 pixels and a height of 60 pixels ensure that users can view all the audio playback controls in both Netscape Navigator and Internet Explorer.

Click the Play button in the Plugin Property inspector to play your media file without previewing your page in a browser.

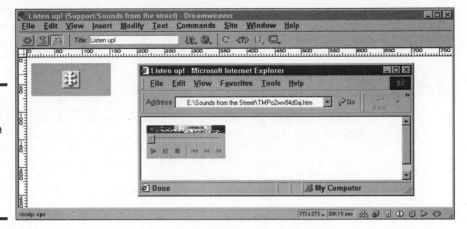

Figure 5-1:
Embedding a media file causes a player console to appear on your page.

To embed background music (music that plays automatically after the user opens a page) follow Steps 1 through 3 in "Embedding an audio or video clip." Then, enter a width and height of 2 in the W and H text boxes in the Plugin Property inspector. Click the Parameters button to open the Parameters dialog box; then, in the Parameters dialog box, click the Add (+) button to add a new parameter. Click in the Parameter column and type **hidden**. Then tab to the Value column and type **true**. (These last two steps hide the audio playback controls.) Finally, Click OK to complete the process and close the dialog box. That's it!

Linking to an audio or video clip

A simple and relatively trouble-free way to include audio and video clips on a Web page is to link the page to an audio or video file. Users can select the link if they want to hear the clip. This selection opens a player outside the browser where the user can control playback.

Book IV
Chapter 5

Adding Multimedia Objects

Streaming audio and video

RealPlayer, from RealNetworks, Inc., offers you the capability to stream audio and video files for user playback. *Streaming* files begin playing as soon as a browser transfers sufficient information to the user's computer to stay ahead of the remaining portion of the file as it downloads. Streaming enables the user to experience your audio or video clip much sooner than with a downloadable file. This option is especially useful for large audio files and all but the shortest video files. Book 5 shows you how to create streaming audio and video files with RealPlayer. For helpful details on including Real Media in your Web site, refer to *Dreamweaver 4 Bible*, by Joseph W. Lowery (Hungry Minds, Inc.).

You follow the same steps to create a link to an audio or video file as you do to create a link to a Web page; the only difference is the file format you choose as the link target. For help in creating a link, see Chapter 3.

Adding Other Media

Dreamweaver enables you to easily insert a number of other multimedia formats into your Web pages, including ActiveX, Java Applets, Flash, and Shockwave. After inserting any of the following media, you can set the control and playback features of the media in the Parameters dialog box. Additionally, you can fine-tune the media action on your page by using the Behaviors panel to create triggering actions that cause the media to play, stop, and execute other functions.

Follow these directions to insert other media:

1. **In the Document window, click your page in the location where you want to add a multimedia file.**

2. **In the Objects panel, switch to the panel containing the button of the media type you want to use and click that button. Or choose Insert⇨Media from the Menu bar and choose the media type that you want to use from the drop-down list.**

Media Type	Object Panel	Button
ActiveX	Special	
Java Applet	Special	
Flash	Common	
Shockwave	Common	

3. **Enter the name of the media file you want to insert.**

   For Applet, Flash, and Shockwave files: In the Select File dialog box, enter the path to the media and click the Select button. Your file is attached, and the associated Property inspector appears. You can change the selected file in the Plugin Property inspector by typing a new name in the Src text box or by browsing in the Src folder to select a file.

For ActiveX: An ActiveX placeholder is inserted, and the ActiveX Property inspector appears. Enter the name of the ActiveX file you want to play in the Class ID text box.

4. **In the Property inspector for your selected media, enter dimensions in the W and H text boxes to size the Media placeholder to any dimensions you choose.**

5. **In the Property inspector for your selected media, click the Parameters button to open the Parameter dialog box, where you can format the playback of your media file.**

See the reference materials for Flash and other multimedia programs for details on formatting and playing files on your Web pages that you create with these programs.

Chapter 6: Punching Up Your Pages with Forms and Frames

In This Chapter

✓ Incorporating forms

✓ Structuring your pages with frames

Two of the more popular Web page features, forms and frames, are also two of the most advanced. You use them for the following purposes:

✦ **Forms:** Enable you to gather information and feedback from the users who visit your Web pages.

✦ **Frames:** Enable you to construct sophisticated navigational schemes for your Web site.

In this chapter, you see how to work with these powerful features in Dreamweaver.

Incorporating Forms

Forms on the Web serve the same purpose as the paper-based forms you fill out — they provide a structured format for gathering specific information. The difference is that Web-based forms usually require less time for keyboard-savvy users to fill out (and using Web-based forms also saves a few trees otherwise destined for a paper mill).

Dreamweaver offers you a number of handy tools for creating Web-based forms that you can easily include on your Web pages. You can incorporate everything from text boxes to radio buttons, and you can create surveys, gather user data, and conduct e-commerce.

Creating Web-based forms requires two steps:

1. Creating the form that users see and interact with, which I demonstrate how to do using Dreamweaver in this chapter.

2. Creating the processing program that accepts and processes form input. These processing programs — typically written in Perl or C and connected to Web-based forms through a protocol called CGI (Common Gateway Interface) — must be installed on a Web server, and are beyond the scope of this book. For more information, check with your ISP (some allow you to use the simple form-processing programs on their Web servers for no extra charge) or check out a good book, such as *Perl For Dummies,* 3rd Edition, by Paul E. Hoffman (Hungry Minds, Inc.).

Adding a form

Before you can insert specific form objects, such as check boxes, on your Web page, you must first add a form to the page so that the appropriate code is written to the HTML page code. You can add a form directly to the Document window or in a table cell.

To add a form to a page, click in the Document window where you want to add the form and choose Insert⇨Form from the Menu bar or click the Insert Form button on the Forms Objects panel. (If the Forms Objects panel is not open, choose Window⇨Objects from the Menu bar to open the panel.)

Dreamweaver adds the form to the page as indicated by the red dashed lines and also adds the associated form tag to your HTML page code.

You can now insert form objects between the red dashed lines of the form.

If you attempt to add a form object without first adding a form, a dialog box appears, asking whether you want to add a form tag. Click Yes to add both the form tag and the object to your page.

Specifying form properties

A form has three properties that you can set using the Form Property inspector: Form Name, Action, and Method. Click the form to open the Form Property inspector. (If the Property inspector does not appear, open it by choosing Window⇨Properties from the Menu bar.) Then specify the following properties:

✦ **Form Name:** Enter an alphanumeric name in the empty text box. The advantage of naming your form is that you can use the name to reference the form in a scripting language that you use to retrieve, store, and manipulate the form data.

✦ **Action:** Enter the address of the location that processes the form data. Alternatively, you can browse to the location by clicking the folder and making a selection at the Select File dialog box.

You can select the following three common actions:

- Enter the URL of a Common Gateway Interface (CGI) program that runs after the user submits the form. The action resembles the following:

  www.server.com/cgi-bin/formhandler.pl

- Enter the JavaScript program that runs after the user submits the form. The action appears as follows:

  www.server.com/javascript:*function*()

  Here, function is your form handling function.

- Enter a mailto: address where the form data goes after the user clicks Submit. A mailto: address appears similar to the following:

  mailto:gruntworker@formhandling.com

✦ **Method:** Select a method from the drop-down list for how the form data passes to the processing entity that you specified in the Action field. Choices are Default, GET, and POST. (Default and GET are the same.) GET sends the form data by appending it to the URL that the Action specifies. POST sends the form data as a separate entity. GET limits the amount of data that can pass along, but POST does not.

Data received at the specified mailto: address is not formatted for easy reading: It appears as strings of code with the form data embedded within lots of ampersands and plus signs.

Labeling form objects

Dreamweaver enables you to provide labels for form objects and provide the user with directions about how to complete the information requested for each option. To label form objects, simply position your cursor in the form and begin typing. Then insert the form object you want.

Using text fields

Text fields are blank text boxes that you can insert in your form to hold alphanumeric information that the user types. You can set up a text field to hold a single line of text, multiple lines of text, or a password as follows:

✦ **Single line:** Provides space for the user to enter a single word or short phrase of text.

✦ **Multi line:** Provides space for the user to enter a longer string of text. Appropriate for a comment box.

✦ **Password:** Provides space for the user to enter a password. An asterisk (Windows) or dot (Macintosh) appears on-screen for each character that the user types.

To add a text field, do the following:

1. **In the Document window, click where you want to add the text and choose Insert⏐Form Objects⇨Text Field from the Menu bar or click the Insert Text Field button on the Form Objects panel. (If the Form Objects panel is not open, choose Window⇨Objects from the Menu bar to open the panel.)**

   Dreamweaver adds a text field to your form, and a Text Field Property inspector appears. If the Text Field Property inspector does not appear, choose Window⇨Properties from the Menu bar to open the inspector.

2. **Fill in the following fields of the Text Field Property inspector to format the text field:**

   - **TextField name:** Enter a name in the empty box. The field is referenced by this name in the HTML page code.

   - **Char Width:** Enter a whole number for the approximate visible width of the field. (The width is approximate because text characters in your form are displayed differently according to users' browser settings.)

   - **Max Chars:** (Applies to Single line and Password only.) Enter a whole number to indicate the maximum number of characters that the user can enter in the field. Max Chars can be equal to or greater than Char Width.

   - **Num Lines:** (Applies to Multi line only.) Enter a whole number for the maximum number of lines that the user can enter in the field.

   - **Type:** Click a radio button for Single line, Multi line, or Password.

   - **Init Val:** (Optional) Enter an alphanumeric word or phrase that occupies the text field when the user first encounters the field. The user can enter his own information over the Init Val.

   - **Wrap:** (Applies to Multi line only.) Select an option for text wrapping from the drop-down list. Options consist of Default, Off, Virtual, or Physical. Default and Off are the same and do not wrap text until the user clicks the Enter (Windows) or Return (Macintosh) key. The Virtual option wraps text on the user's screen but not when the form is submitted. The Physical option wraps text both on the user's screen and when the form is submitted.

Setting up buttons

After a user enters data into a form, the user must then perform some sort of task to transmit the data from his or her computer to another computer that can process the information. Dreamweaver offers you three buttons to use to activate your form: Reset, Submit, and Command:

✦ **Reset:** After the user clicks this button, it erases all data entered into the form, allowing the user to reenter data into a fresh, clean form.

✦ **Submit:** After the user clicks this button, the form data scoots off to another computer based on the specified Action. (You see how to set the Action of a form in "Specifying Form Properties," earlier in this chapter.)

✦ **Command:** After the user clicks this button, it executes the programming function that the Web designer assigned to it.

To insert a button, do the following:

1. **Click where you want to add the button in the Document window and choose Insert⇨Form Objects⇨Button from the Menu bar or click the Insert Button on the Form Objects panel. (If the Objects panel is not open, choose Window⇨Objects from the Menu bar.)**

   Dreamweaver adds a button to your form, and a Button Property inspector similar to the one in Figure 6-1 appears. If the Button Property inspector does not appear, choose Window⇨Properties from the Menu bar to open the inspector.

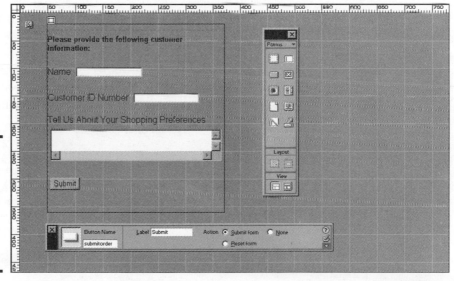

Figure 6-1:
You use the Button inspector to specify a name, label, and action for a form.

2. **Fill in the following fields of the Button Property inspector to format the button:**

   • **Button name:** Enter a name in the empty text box. This name identifies the button in the HTML code.

- **Label:** Enter a name for the button to appear on-screen.
- **Action:** Click a radio button to indicate the function of the button. Choices consist of Reset form, Submit form, and None (Command).

 You can create a graphical Submit button — a button created from a small image — by choosing Insert⇨Form Objects⇨Image Field from the Menu bar or by clicking the Insert Image Field button on the Form Objects panel. Then either browse to the image file on your hard drive or type the name of the image file directly into the File Name field. When you finish, click Select to create the graphical Submit button.

Adding form elements

In addition to the text fields and buttons I describe in "Using text fields" and "Setting up buttons," you can add a variety of form elements that help your users give you information. Table 6-1 shows some of the useful form elements you can add to your forms. To insert any of the elements you see in Table 6-1 follow these steps:

1. **Position your cursor in the area of the Document window where you want to add the element.**

2. **Click the appropriate button on the Form Objects panel. (See Table 6-1 for details.) If the Form Objects panel is not open, choose Window⇨Objects from the Menu bar to open the panel.**

   Dreamweaver adds the element to your form, and the appropriate inspector appears. (If the appropriate inspector does not appear, open it by choosing Windows⇨Properties from the Menu bar.)

3. **Fill in the fields of the inspector.**

4. **Click OK to apply your selections and close the dialog box.**

Table 6-1	Form Elements
Element	*Button on the Form Objects Panel*
Check box	
Radio button	
Scrolling list	
Jump menu (scrolling list of links)	

Structuring Pages with Frames

Frames are divisions of a Web page that enable you to load information independently into distinct regions of your page. Frames are useful if you want to display certain information on-screen while changing other information. You frequently see three-frame pages on the Web — the top frame shows the site's title graphic; the left frame shows the navigation bar; and the large body frame changes to show the content that you select.

A special HTML page called a *frameset* defines the structure and formatting of frames on your Web page. As you work with frames, be aware that you must always save the frameset page to lay out the size, position, and borders of your frames, along with the content that you want to display in each frame.

Adding frames

You can add a frame to a frameless Document window or to an existing frame within the Document window. Adding a frame to an existing frame divides the existing frame into two or more regions. The page describing the collective grouping of your frames is called a *frameset*.

To add a frame, click the Document window or existing frame in the area where you want to add the frame. Choose Insert⇨Frames and select an option from the drop-down list shown in Table 6-2.

Table 6-2	Options for Creating Frames
Frame Option	*What It Does*
Left	Creates a vertical frame down the left side
Right	Creates a vertical frame down the right side
Top	Creates a horizontal frame across the top
Bottom	Creates a horizontal frame across the bottom
Left and Top	Creates a square frame at the origin, a horizontal frame across the top, and a vertical frame down the left side
Left Top	Creates a vertical frame down the left side at the origin and a horizontal frame across the top
Top Left	Creates a horizontal frame across the top at the origin and a vertical frame down the left side
Split	Creates two frames of equal size and shape

**Book IV
Chapter 6**

**Punching Up Your
Pages with Forms
and Frames**

You can also add a frame by clicking the button on the Frames Objects panel corresponding to the frame type you want to create. The light-blue frame in each button represents where the content of the existing frame is placed after you add the new frame.

Modifying frames

You use the Frame Property inspector to select the source page that appears in a frame. You also use the Frame Property inspector to format the appearance of an individual frame. To modify a frame, follow these steps:

1. **Open the Frames panel by choosing Window⇨Frames from the Menu bar.**

The Frames panel appears and displays a miniature version of the frameset for your entire page. (See Figure 6-2.)

Note: You can't simply click a frame to open its associated Frame Property inspector. If you click a frame, you're actually clicking the source page that resides in the frame — a process identical to clicking in the Document window for that page.

2. **In the Frames panel, click the frame whose attributes you want to modify.**

A Frame Property inspector similar to the one in Figure 6-2 appears for the selected frame. If the inspector doesn't appear, open it by choosing Windows⇨Properties from the Menu bar.

3. **In the Frame Property inspector, enter a name for your frame in the Frame Name text box.**

This name is the name by which the frame is referenced in the Frames panel, Target drop-down lists, and the HTML page code. The frame name must start with a letter, and you cannot use hyphens, spaces, or periods. You must also avoid using JavaScript-reserved names, such as top.

4. **In the Src text box, enter the name of the source page whose content you intend to display in the frame.**

Alternatively, you can click the Src folder and browse to select the source page.

5. **Select a scrolling option for your selected frame from the Scroll drop-down menu. Options are:**

   - **Yes:** Adds a scroll bar to the frame, whether it's needed or not.

   - **No:** Doesn't add a scroll bar to the frame, even if needed.

   - **Auto:** Places a scroll bar in the frame if the frame contents exceed the frame boundaries.

   - **Default:** Places a scroll bar in the frame depending on the user's browser settings.

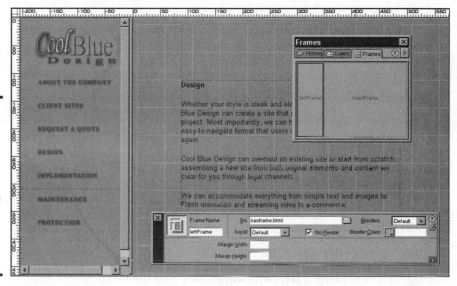

Figure 6-2:
The Frame Property inspector lets you set the attributes of each frame in the Frames panel.

6. **Click the No Resize check box if you don't want the user to be able to resize the frame.**

   If you do want the user to be able to resize the frame, leave the check box unchecked.

7. **Format the frame border appearance by selecting a choice from the Borders drop-down list box:**

   - **Yes:** Creates a three-dimensional look for the borders.

   - **No:** Creates a single-color flat look for the borders.

   - **Default:** Enables the user's browser to set how borders appear.

8. **Select a border color for the frame by clicking the Border Color swatch and selecting a color from the Color palette that appears.**

   Alternatively, you can enter a hexadecimal color code in the Border Color text box.

9. **Enter a number in pixels in the Margin Width and the Margin Height text boxes.**

   Margin Width specifies the horizontal standoff space between the frame content and the frame border. Margin Height specifies the vertical standoff space between the frame content and the frame border.

Deleting frames

To delete a frame, select the frame border and drag it to the edge of the parent frame or to the edge of the Document window — whichever is closer.

Saving frames

Saving a frame means that you're saving the HTML page from which the source content of the frame originates. To save a frame, follow these steps:

1. **Select the frame by clicking in it.**

2. **Choose File⇨Save Frame from the Menu bar.**

3. **On the first save, enter a name in the File Name text box of the Save As dialog box that appears and click Save.**

   Future saves require that you complete only Steps 1 and 2.

Saving framesets

Saving a frameset means saving the layout of frame positions, frame names, and border formatting on a page. Keep in mind that you must save individual frames to save the content contained in those frames. To save a frameset, follow these steps:

1. **Select the frameset by clicking one of its borders.**

2. **Choose File⇨Save Frameset from the Menu bar.**

3. **On the first save, enter a name in the File Name text box of the Save As dialog box that appears and click Save.**

   Future saves require that you complete only Steps 1 and 2.

If you also make changes to individual frames — not just the frameset — since your last save, Dreamweaver asks if you want to save individual frames. Make sure that you do so.

Setting no-frames content

Text-based browsers and many older browsers frequently don't support frames and can't correctly display pages that you create by using frames.

To help ensure that the maximum number of users can view your page correctly, Dreamweaver offers you a method for building *no-frames* pages as companions to your frame-enabled pages. To create a no-frames page for your current frameset, follow these steps:

1. **Choose Modify⇨Frameset⇨Edit NoFrames Content from the Menu bar.**

   A blank, NoFrames Content page appears in the Document window and replaces your frame-enabled page.

2. **On the NoFrames Content page, insert the information that you want to appear in No Frames browsers.**

3. **Return to your frame-enabled page by choosing Modify⇨Frameset⇨ Edit NoFrames Content from the Menu bar.**

Targeting content

You can set up a two-frame frameset in which you use the left frame for navigation and the main frame to display any link that the user clicks in the navigation frame. You need to set up only the link to target the main frame as the location where you want the selected HTML page to open.

Set up a target by following these steps:

1. **Select the text or image that you want to act as a link.**

   Doing so opens the associated Property inspector, as shown in Figure 6-3. If the inspector doesn't appear, open it by choosing Windows⇨Properties from the Menu bar.

Figure 6-3:
You use the Property inspector associated with a link to choose a target for your framed content.

2. In the Link box, enter the name of the HTML source page whose content will appear in the frame. Alternatively, you can click the Link folder and browse to select the source page.

3. From the Target drop-down menu, select the target frame where the link is to appear.

   All available targets are listed in the menu. As shown in Figure 6-3, these targets include the names of all frames that you set up and also the following system-wide targets:

   - **_blank:** Opens a new browser window and shows the link in that window. The current window remains open.

   - **_parent:** Opens the link in a window that replaces the frameset containing the current page.

   - **_self:** Opens the link in the current frame. The linked page replaces the page in the current frame. This setting is the default target.

   - **_top:** Opens the link in a window that replaces the outermost frame-set of the current page. (Same as _parent, unless you're using nested framesets.)

Chapter 7: Laying Out Pages with Layers

In This Chapter

✔ **Adding, selecting, and deleting a layer**

✔ **Placing objects in a layer**

✔ **Including a background image or color in a layer**

✔ **Naming a layer**

✔ **Nesting layers**

✔ **Aligning layers**

✔ **Changing the visibility of a layer**

✔ **Layering layers: Setting the z-index**

✔ **Moving and resizing a layer**

*T*o precisely lay out the content of your Web page, you can use tables (see Chapter 6), or you can use the latest and greatest layout aid: *layers.* Think of layers in Dreamweaver as separate pieces of paper that you fill with content (images, text, and so on) and shuffle, stack, position, and overlap until your page looks exactly the way you want.

Adding a Layer

Add a layer to the workspace of your Document window by using one of the following two methods:

✦ Choose Insert➪Layer from the Menu bar. A new layer appears in the upper-left corner of your Document window.

 ✦ Click the Draw Layer button from the Common Objects panel. (If the panel does not appear, open it by choosing Window➪Objects from the Menu bar.) Position the cross hair cursor anywhere in your Document window and click and drag until the layer obtains the dimensions you want. Release the mouse button.

For each layer you draw, Dreamweaver places a layer marker in the upper-left corner of the Document window. For Cascading Style Sheet, or CSS, layers (applicable to both Internet Explorer and Netscape Navigator), the marker appears as the letter *C* in a yellow box. For Netscape layers (the layer formatting unique to Navigator), the marker appears as the letter *N* in a yellow box.

Selecting a Layer

Selecting a layer enables you to identify which layer you want to affect when executing a layer operation, such as moving or naming the layer.

Use any of the following methods to select a layer:

✦ In the Document window, click on the boundary of the layer.

✦ In the Document window, click on the layer handle — the square enclosing a small grid located at the top-left corner of the layer.

✦ In the Document window, click on the layer marker that appears as the letter *C* or *N* in a yellow box.

✦ In the Document window, press the Shift key and click anywhere inside the layer.

✦ In the Layers panel, click on the name of the layer.

✦ Click on the layer's HTML tag in the tag selector of the Document window status bar.

Selection handles appear on the boundary of the layer to indicate that you have selected it.

Deleting a Layer

Deleting a layer removes the layer, the layer's contents, and the layer marker from the Document window. To delete a layer, select the layer and press Delete or Backspace.

Don't delete a layer if you want to remove it from one page and add it to another. Instead, cut the layer by choosing Edit⇨Cut from the Menu bar. Open the page where you want to add the layer and choose Edit⇨Paste.

Placing Objects in a Layer

To add an object to a layer, click inside the layer and follow the normal procedure for adding the object. For instance, add text to a layer by clicking inside the layer and typing text; add other objects to a layer by clicking inside the layer and selecting Insert from the main menu.

Including a Background Image or Color in a Layer

By default, an unnested layer has the same color or background image as the Document window in which it is drawn. (A nested *child* layer has the same color or background image as its *parent*. For more about nested layers, see the section "Nesting Layers" later in this chapter.)

You can change the background of any layer by including a background image or color in the layer by following these steps:

1. **Select the layer where you want to change the background.**

2. **If the Layer Property Inspector does not appear, open it by choosing Window⇨Properties from the Menu bar.**

3. **In the Layer Property inspector, change one of the following:**

   - **Bg Image:** Click the folder to the right of the box and browse to select a background image from the Select Image Source dialog box that appears. Click Select to accept your image choice and close the dialog box. The name of the background image appears in the Bg Image box, and the image is added to the background of the layer.

   - **Bg Color:** Click the color swatch and select a color from the color palette that appears. Alternatively, you can enter a color in the Bg Color box. The new color appears in the background of the selected layer.

Naming a Layer

The first layer you add to a page is automatically named Layer 1; the second layer you add is named Layer 2; and so on. You can change these default number names to other names that help you more easily distinguish layers when working with HTML and examining layers with the Layer Property inspector or Layers panel.

To name a layer using the Layers panel, follow these steps:

1. **Select the layer to open the Layers panel. If the Layers panel does not appear, open it by choosing <u>W</u>indow⇨<u>L</u>ayers from the Menu bar.**

2. **Double-click the Name column for the layer whose name you want to change. The current name is selected.**

3. **Enter a new name for the layer.**

Get in the habit of appropriately naming your layers as soon as you create them. The name *blueprint image map* helps you remember a layer's content much better than *Layer 15*.

Nesting Layers

A *nested* layer is a layer that has a dependent relationship with another layer. The nested layer is often referred to as a *child* layer, whereas the layer on which it depends is called the *parent* layer. A child layer can be drawn completely inside its parent (as shown in Figure 7-1) in an intersecting arrangement with its parent or completely unattached to its parent, depending on the effect you want to achieve. A nested layer has or *inherits* the same visibility of its parent and moves with the parent when the parent layer is repositioned in the Document window.

Figure 7-1:
A nested layer can be (but doesn't have to be) drawn inside its parent layer.

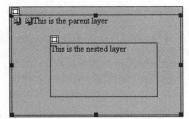

This is the parent layer

This is the nested layer

Enabling nesting

To create nested layers in the Document window, you must first enable nesting. To do so, follow these steps:

1. **Choose <u>E</u>dit⇨Preference<u>s</u> to open the Preferences dialog box.**

2. **At the Preferences dialog box, choose Layers in the category area.**

3. **Check the Nesting check box.**

4. **Click OK to banish the Preferences dialog box.**

5. **In the Document window, choose <u>W</u>indow⇨<u>La</u>yers to open the Layers panel.**

6. **In the Layers panel, make sure that the Prevent Overlaps box is unchecked.**

Creating a new nested layer

Use either of these methods to draw a nested layer:

✦ Click inside an existing layer and choose <u>I</u>nsert⇨<u>La</u>yer from the Menu bar. A child layer of default size appears inside the parent layer. If the dimensions of the parent layer are smaller than the dimensions of the child layer, the child layer will exceed the boundaries of the parent.

 ✦ Click the Draw Layer button from the Common Objects panel and drag it into the parent layer. A child layer of default size appears inside the parent layer. If the dimensions of the parent layer are smaller than the dimensions of the child layer, the child layer will exceed the boundaries of the parent.

Changing the nesting of an existing layer

To change the nesting of an existing layer, follow these steps:

1. **Open the Layers panel by choosing <u>W</u>indow⇨<u>La</u>yers from the Menu bar.**

2. **In the Layers panel, press and hold the Ctrl key (Windows) or Cmd key (Macintosh) while using the mouse to click and drag the intended child layer on top of its new parent.**

   The child is in the correct position when you see a box appear around its intended parent layer.

3. **Release the mouse button.**

   The new child-parent relationship is shown in the Layers panel.

Dreamweaver draws the new child layer and updates the associated code for changed layer-nesting in the HTML source code for your page.

Collapsing or expanding your view in the Layers panel

You can change how you view the names of nested layers in the Layers panel by collapsing or expanding your view, as shown in Figure 7-2.

✦ **To collapse your view:** Click the minus sign (-) in front of a parent layer. Names of nested child layers for that parent are hidden.

✦ **To expand your view:** Click the plus sign (+) in front of a parent layer. Names of nested child layers for that parent appear.

Figure 7-2:
You expand and collapse nested layer views by clicking the plus (+) and minus (–) sign, respectively, in front of the parent layer.

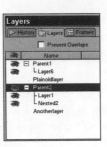

Aligning Layers

Aligning layers can help you precisely lay out visual content in the Document window. You can align layers with the top, left side, right side, or bottom.

To align layers, select the layers you want to align by pressing and holding the Shift key and then clicking each layer in the Document window. Choose Modify⇨Align from the Menu bar and choose one of the following options from the menu that appears:

✦ **Left:** Assigns the x-coordinate of the leftmost selected layer to all selected layers.

✦ **Right:** Aligns the right side of all selected layers with the right side of the rightmost selected layer.

✦ **Top:** Assigns the y-coordinate of the topmost selected layer to all selected layers.

✦ **Bottom:** Aligns the bottom of all selected layers with the bottom of the bottommost selected layer.

Changing the Visibility of a Layer

You can specify whether a layer is visible or hidden when a Web page *loads* —
first appears — and as a result of specific actions by the user. Visibility can
change as many times as you want. Visibility options consist of

✦ **Default:** The layer's initial visibility is the default setting. (To edit layer
default settings, choose Edit⇨Preferences from the Menu bar; then click
Layers on the Preferences dialog box that appears to display the layer
default settings you can change.)

✦ **Inherit:** For a nested layer, the layer's initial visibility is the same visibility of its parent. For an unnested layer, selecting the inherit option
causes the layer to appear as visible.

✦ **Visible:** The layer's initial visibility is visible.

✦ **Hidden:** The layer's initial visibility is hidden.

Layer visibility can be set by using either the Layer Property inspector or
the Layers panel. By setting layer visibility, you can create images that
appear (or disappear) in response to user interaction. For example, you can
create an image of a widget that appears on a Web page after a user clicks a
link marked, "Click here to see our top-of-the-line widget!"

To set the initial visibility of a layer via the Layer Property inspector, select
the layer in the Document window to open the Layer Property inspector. If
the inspector does not appear, open it by choosing Window⇨Properties
from the Menu bar. Click the down arrow tab at the Vis box and choose a
visibility option from the drop-down list.

Layering Layers: Setting the Z-index

The *z-index* of a layer indicates the layer's position in a stack of multiple
layers. Z-indices are useful when you have a handful of layers — some containing transparent portions, some of different sizes — stacked one on top of
the other. Changing the z-index of your layers lets you "shuffle" the layers —
much as you shuffle a deck of cards — to create interesting visual effects.

Z-indices are measured in whole numbers and do not have to be
consecutive — for instance, you can have three layers with z-indices of 1, 3,
and 7 respectively. The layer with the largest z-index sits on top of the layer
stack, and the layer with the smallest z-index sits on the bottom of the layer
stack. Layers with larger z-indices obscure those with smaller z-indices. You
can change the z-index of a layer in either the Layer Property inspector or
the Layers panel.

To assign the z-index of a layer by using the Layer Property Inspector, first select the layer to open the Layer Property Inspector. If the Layer Property Inspector does not appear, open it by choosing Window⇨Properties from the Menu bar. Then enter a new number in the Z-Index box of the Layer Property inspector.

To assign the z-index of a layer using the Layers panel (as shown in Figure 7-3), follow these steps:

1. **Select the layer to open the Layers panel.**

   If the Layers panel doesn't appear, open it by choosing Window⇨Layers from the Menu bar.

2. **Click the Z column for the layer whose z-index you want to change.**

   The current z-index is selected.

3. **Enter a new z-index for the layer.**

   The new number appears in the Z column for the selected layer.

Figure 7-3:
You can set the z-index for your layers using the Layers panel.

To assign relative z-indices to layers by reordering layers in the Layers panel, follow these steps:

1. **Open the Layers panel by selecting Window⇨Layers from the Menu bar.**

   The Layers panel lists layers in order of descending z-index.

2. **Click the name of a layer for which you want to change the z-index.**

3. **Drag the layer name into a new list position and release the mouse button. As you drag, the selected layer is indicated by a thick line.**

Dreamweaver reorders the list in the Layers panel and renumbers layer z-indices to reflect your change. Also, Dreamweaver updates the associated code for the layers' z-indices in the HTML source code for your page.

Because you don't have to number the z-index of layers consecutively, consider leaving gaps between indices in case you want to add new layers into the middle of the stack. For instance, use only even numbers for your indices so that you can easily sandwich a layer with an odd-numbered z-index in-between.

Moving a Layer

You may choose to move a layer to a place in another location in the Document window or to a position relative to the grid or to other objects.

To move a layer, select the layer in the Document window and then reposition your selection by using one of the following three methods:

✦ Click and drag the layer to a new location and release the mouse button.

✦ Press the arrow keys you find on the numeric keypad on your keyboard to nudge the layer up, down, left, or right one pixel at a time.

✦ In the Layer Property inspector, enter a new value in the T and L boxes to indicate the pixel coordinates of the layer's top-left corner.

When moving layers, you can choose to enable or prevent layer overlap, depending on how you want the final image montage to appear. You enable or prevent layer overlap as described in the following list:

✦ **To prevent layer overlap:** Open the Layers panel by choosing Window⇨Layers from the Menu bar and checking the Prevent Overlaps check box.

✦ **To enable layer overlap:** Open the Layers panel by choosing Window⇨Layers from the Menu bar and making sure that the Prevent Overlaps check box is unchecked.

Resizing a Layer

Resizing a layer means changing its height and width dimensions. To resize a layer, select the layer and perform one of the following tasks:

✦ Click and drag a selection handle — one of the large dots on the layer boundary — until the layer obtains the dimensions you desire.

✦ In the Layer Property inspector, enter a new width in pixels at the W box and a new length in pixels at the L box. If the Layer Property inspector does not appear, open it by choosing Window⇨Properties from the Menu bar.

**Book IV
Chapter 7**

Laying Out Pages with Layers

Resizing Multiple Layers at the Same Time

You can change the height and width dimensions of multiple layers at the same time as follows:

1. **Press and hold the Shift key while selecting each layer you want to resize.**

2. **If the Multiple Layers Property inspector does not appear, open it by choosing <u>W</u>indow⇨<u>P</u>roperties from the Menu bar.**

3. **In the Multiple Layers Property inspector, enter a new width in pixels at the <u>W</u> box and a new length in pixels at the <u>L</u> box.**

Chapter 8: Animating Your Pages

In This Chapter

✓ About timelines

✓ Creating a timeline

✓ Renaming a timeline

✓ Deleting a timeline

✓ Adding and deleting objects on a timeline

✓ Building a Web slide show

✓ Moving images across a page using paths

*U*sing Dreamweaver, you can play the role of animation director and add eye-catching motion and activity to any page in your site.

Creating animation in Dreamweaver hinges on manipulating the timeline. You use the timeline to define which objects show up on your page, how they are positioned, and what other media are playing anytime a user is viewing your Web page. The timeline enables you to change all these parameters from one second to the next, creating a motion-rich page — without the drudgery of generating true animation.

About Timelines

You can use the Timelines panel to record and play back Dreamweaver animation.

Attributes of the Timelines panel

Open the Timelines panel shown in Figure 8-1 by choosing Window⇨ Timelines from the Menu bar.

Playback head

Behavior channel

Timeline files

Playback controls

Figure 8-1:
You use the
Timelines
panel to
record and
play back
animated
effects in
Dream-
weaver.

Timelines	
Timelines	
Timeline1 ▾	I← ← 1 → Fps 15 ☐ Autoplay ☐ Loop
B	
1 5 10 15 20 25 30 35 40 45	
1 ○Layer1 ────────○	
2	
3	

Animation channels   Frames

The following features comprise the Timelines panel:

✦ **Timeline controls:** Enables you to select which timeline you want to view and to control the playback of the timeline. This area consists of the Timeline Name drop-down list, the Rewind button, Back button, Current Frame Number text box, Play button, Frame Rate (fps) text box, Autoplay check box, and Loop check box.

✦ **Behavior channel:** Enables you to attach behaviors to specific frames of animations in the timeline you select.

✦ **Frames:** Displays the frame numbers for your selected timeline. You can click any frame number to display that frame. The current frame is indicated by the pink playback head. Clicking and dragging the playback head plays the frames as you drag.

✦ **Animation channels:** Enables you to add layers and animate layers on a channel. You can create multiple channels that run simultaneously or start and stop at frames you choose.

You cannot animate the same layer on different channels simultaneously. For the scoop on layers, check out Chapter 7.

Functions of the timeline

Dreamweaver can't render animation like you see in the movies, but it can help you create motion on your Web pages without a lot of headache. Here's what the timeline can accomplish:

✦ *Simple animation* that displays in a Web browser at approximately 15 frames per second (fps). (Animation films show 24 fps.) Note that the display rate is approximate and is based on the capabilities of the user's system. See "Adding and Deleting Objects on a Timeline" later in this chapter for details.

✦ *Layer manipulation,* including the ability to change a layer's position, size, visibility, and z-index (stacking position).

✦ *Behavior triggering,* which enables you to set up a series of behaviors to execute at various points along the timeline.

I don't cover layer manipulation or behavior triggering in this chapter, but you can find out about these techniques by reading *Dreamweaver 4 For Dummies,* by Janine Warner and Paul Vachier, published by Hungry Minds, Inc.

✦ *Image revelation,* in which you can change the source of an image to show and hide several images over a period of time, effectively creating a Web slide show. (You don't need to use layers to create this type of animated effect — just images. See "Building a Web Slide Show" in this chapter for more details.)

Guidelines for applying the timeline

To generate timeline animations, you must consider these general rules:

✦ Only Web users with Internet Explorer 4.0 (or later) or Netscape Navigator 4.0 (or later) can view timeline animations.

✦ To create motion animation for an object on a timeline, that object must be contained within a layer. Without the absolute positioning of layers, motion animation is not possible. For more on layers, check out Chapter 7.

✦ You can use the Timelines panel to change the source attributes of images not enclosed in layers. Doing so enables you to cause images to appear and disappear on your Web page over a period of time.

✦ You can run multiple animations on a single timeline.

✦ You can run multiple timelines to animate different layers simultaneously.

✦ Multiple, simultaneous animations cannot be applied to a single layer in any way.

Creating a Timeline

To create a new timeline, choose Modify⇨Timeline⇨Add Timeline from the Menu bar.

Renaming a Timeline

You can rename a timeline at any time using Dreamweaver. To rename a timeline, follow these steps:

1. **Open the timeline that you want to rename by choosing Window⇨Timelines from the Menu bar and selecting the timeline you want to rename from the Timeline Name drop-down list.**

2. **Choose Modify⇨Timeline⇨Rename Timeline from the Menu bar.**

3. **Enter a new name in the Rename Timeline dialog box that appears and click OK.**

Alternatively, you can enter a new name directly in the Timeline Name box. The name must be a single word that begins with a letter and consists only of alphanumeric characters.

Deleting a Timeline

To delete a timeline, follow these steps:

1. **Open the timeline that you want to delete by choosing Window⇨ Timelines from the Menu bar and selecting the timeline you want to delete from the Timeline Name drop-down list.**

2. **Choose Modify⇨Timeline⇨Remove Timeline from the Menu bar.**

Adding and Deleting Objects on a Timeline

The first step in creating a timeline animation is to add the layer or image that you want to animate to a timeline. Added objects can be deleted at any time.

Adding an object to a timeline

To add an object to a timeline, follow these steps:

1. **Choose Window⇨Timelines from the Menu bar to access the Timelines panel, as shown in Figure 8-2.**

2. **In the Timelines panel, select the timeline you want to work on from the Timeline Name drop-down list.**

3. **In the Document window, select the layer or image you want to animate.**

4. **Add your selection to the timeline by using one of the following methods:**

   - Choose <u>M</u>odify⇨<u>T</u>imeline⇨<u>A</u>dd Object to Timeline from the Menu bar. Doing so adds an animation bar to one of the channels. The animation bar starts at the frame position of the playback head. The first animation bar you create is placed on Animation Channel 1, the second animation bar is placed on Channel 2, and so on.

   - Drag the layer or image to an animation channel on the timeline. You can drag the layer to any animation channel and any start frame.

   Regardless of the method you choose, a 15-frame animation bar is created with keyframes included on the first and last frames. The name of the layer or image labels the newly created animation bar.

5. **Repeat Steps 2 through 4 to add other layers and images to the timeline.**

Figure 8-2:
Adding an object (in this case, a layer) to an animation bar using the Timelines panel.

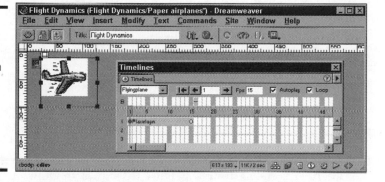

Name your layers and images something more descriptive than the default names (Layer 1, or Image 1) so that you can better distinguish animation bars in a timeline.

Deleting an object from a timeline

To delete an object from a timeline, simply select its Animation bar. Then choose <u>M</u>odify⇨<u>T</u>imeline⇨<u>Rem</u>ove Object from the Menu bar — or just press the Delete key.

Building a Web Slide Show

A Web slide show displays and removes images in the same position on your page over a period of time. You can set the slide show to play automatically when the user opens the page (select Autoplay in the Timelines panel), or you can add a behavior to the Behavior channel that causes the slide show to play. To build a Web slide show, follow these steps:

1. **Using an image-editing program of your choice, create the images you want to appear in your slide show.**

   All the images in a group will be placed on an animation bar together and must be the same size.

2. **Choose Window▷Timelines from the Menu bar to access the Timelines panel.**

3. **In the Timelines panel, select the timeline you want to work on from the Timeline Name drop-down list.**

   To create a new timeline, see "Creating a Timeline" earlier in this chapter.

4. **In the Document window, insert the first image from the same-size group of images.**

   You can insert the image directly into the window, in a table cell, or in a layer. Images from the group are displayed in this location during the animation.

5. **Click and drag the image to an animation channel in the Timelines panel.**

   A 15-frame animation bar is created with keyframes included on the first and last frames.

6. **Set the frame rate, Autoplay, and Loop options you see in the Timelines panel as desired. (Figure 8-3 shows you how the Timelines panel appears.)**

   Autoplay causes the slide show to play when the user opens the page, and Loop causes the slide show to play again when the end of the timeline animation is reached.

7. **Add a keyframe at the frame on the animation bar where you want the slide show image to change by selecting the frame in the Timelines panel and choosing Modify▷Timeline▷Add Keyframe from the Menu bar.**

   The added keyframe is now the selected keyframe.

Figure 8-3:
You can set the frame rate, Autoplay, and Loop options for your Web slide show using the Timelines panel.

Frame rate

Autoplay option

Loop option

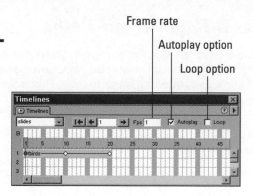

8. **In the Image Properties inspector, browse in the Src folder to select a new image from your group of same-size images. Figure 8-4 shows you how.**

   Note: If the Image Properties inspector does not appear, open it by choosing Window⇨Properties from the Menu bar.

   If you select image files of different sizes, Dreamweaver squishes all images to fit the smallest image dimensions.

Figure 8-4:
To select the next image for your slide show, specify a new image file name in the Src field.

9. **Repeat Steps 7 and 8 to add more images to your slide show.**

10. **After you finish building your slideshow, you can preview how it appears in a browser by choosing File⇨Preview in Browser from the Menu bar.**

Moving Images Across a Page Using Paths

You can move an image-containing layer across your Web page by recording a *path* in Dreamweaver. A path defines the starting and ending points for the movement you want an image-containing layer to take. Dreamweaver supports two kinds of paths: linear (straight line) paths, and freeform (curvy) paths.

Recording a linear path

Create an animation that moves a layer in a straight line as follows:

1. **Choose Window⇨Timelines from the Menu bar to access the Timelines panel.**

2. **In the Timelines panel, select the timeline you want to work on from the Timeline Name drop-down list.**

3. **In the Document window, select the layer you want to animate.**

    The current location of the layer is the starting point for the animation. If you want a different starting point, reposition the layer now.

4. **Drag the layer to the Timelines panel.**

    You can drag the layer to any animation channel and any start frame. By default, a 15-frame animation bar is created, with keyframes included on the first and last frames.

5. **Click the ending keyframe in the animation bar and drag it to create the duration of animation you want.**

6. **In the Document window, drag the selected layer to its ending position.**

    Dreamweaver draws a thin line that displays the animation path. For you caffeine junkies, you'll be happy to know that Dreamweaver automatically accounts for a shaky hand and makes your line straight.

    Dreamweaver adds the animation and updates the source code for your page.

Recording a freeform path

To create an animation that moves a layer around a Web page in a freeform path, use the following steps:

1. **Choose Window⇨Timelines from the Menu bar to access the Timelines panel.**

2. **In the Timelines panel, select the timeline you want to work on from the Timeline Name drop-down list.**

3. **In the Document window, select the layer you want to animate.**

   The current location of the layer is the starting point for the animation. If you want a different starting point, reposition the layer now.

4. **Choose Modify⇨Timeline⇨Record Path of Layer from the Menu bar.**

   Alternatively, right-click (Windows) or Control-click (Macintosh) the layer and choose Record Path from the pop-up menu.

5. **Click and drag the layer into the Document window, as shown in Figure 8-5, to create any path you want.**

   Doing so traces the path as you drag. The path follows the position of the top-left corner of the layer.

6. **Release the mouse button to end recording the path.**

   A new animation bar for the recorded path appears in the Timelines panel. The length of the bar corresponds to the time you spent dragging the layer. Intervals where you dragged slowly consist of more keyframes than those intervals where you dragged rapidly.

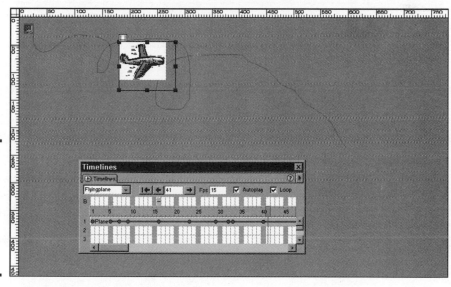

Figure 8-5: To record a freeform path, you click a layer and drag it around the page.

Playing a recorded path

To preview a recorded path in a Web browser, choose File⇨Preview in Browser from the Menu bar.

A quicker approach, however, is to use the playback controls provided on the Timelines panel. These playback controls enable you to preview your work directly in the Document Window. Table 8-1 explains the function of each control:

Table 8-1	Timeline Playback Controls
Timeline Control	*Function*
Rewind button	Moves the playback head backward to the first frame of the selected timeline.
Back button	Backs up the playback head by one frame; click and hold to play the timeline in reverse.
Frame indicator	Shows the position of the playback head. Enter a frame number to jump to that frame.
Play button	Advances the playback head by one frame. Click and hold to play the timeline start to finish.
Fps text box	Sets the frame rate in frames per second at which the animation plays. To change the default rate of 15 fps, enter a number and press Enter (Windows) or Return (Macintosh).
Autoplay check box	When checked, causes the selected timeline to begin playing when the page completely downloads in the browser.
Loop check box	When checked, causes the animation to repeat upon reaching the last frame.

Chapter 9: Publishing and Maintaining Your Site

In This Chapter

↙ Defining remote host settings

↙ Connecting to a Web server

↙ Transferring files

↙ Collaborating on site revisions

↙ Measuring download time, monitoring links, and updating metatags

To make your site available on the World Wide Web, you must sign up with a Web hosting service or have another method of accessing a Web server. You can then transfer a copy of your entire local site root to a folder on the Web server that hosts your site. You must transfer not only every HTML code page in your local site but also every image, video, and sound (and all other files you use in your site) to the remote host.

After your site is transferred, you and other collaborators can retrieve site pages, work on them locally, and upload the pages back to the host to keep the site updated. You can also fine-tune your site by setting up metatags, measuring the download time your site requires, and monitoring all the links on your site — quickly and easily — to ensure that users don't access any dead-end pages from your site.

Defining Remote Host Settings

Dreamweaver makes an easy task of transferring Web files from your local site to the remote host. But prior to transferring, or *uploading,* your first site to the host, you must tell Dreamweaver some basic information about the host, such as where it is located on the Web and what the access password is.

You define remote host attributes in the same dialog box that you use to define your local site — namely, the Site Definition dialog box — by following these steps:

1. **In Dreamweaver, choose Site⇨Define Sites from the Menu bar to open the Define Sites dialog box.**

2. **From the Site list, select the site you want to work on and click the** Edit **button.**

   The Site Definition dialog box for your site opens, as shown in Figure 9-1.

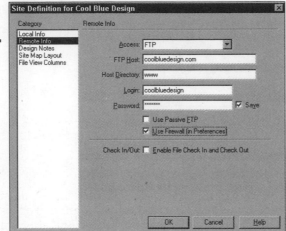

Figure 9-1:
You must define the settings for your remote host before you can transfer, or *upload,* your files using Dream-weaver.

3. **Select the Remote Info category.**

4. **At the** Access **drop-down menu, select a Web server access method from these options:**

   • **None:** Applicable only if you do not plan to upload your site to a remove server.

   • **FTP:** Select this option to transfer files to and from your server via File Transfer Protocol. Supply the requested information at the dialog box based on the information in Table 9-1.

Table 9-1	FTP-Related Settings You Can Set in Dreamweaver
Item	*Description*
FTP Host	Enter the name of the FTP connection for your server, such as www.domainname.com
Host Directory	Enter the name from which users will access your site, such as www/public/mccue
Login	Enter your login identification for accessing the server
Password	Enter your password for accessing the server and click the Save check box if you want Dreamweaver to remember your password

Item	Description
Use Passive FTP check box	Check this box if your firewall requires that your local software establish the server connection instead of the remote host (if you're not sure whether your computer configuration includes a firewall, ask your system administrator).
Use Firewall check box	Check this box if you connect to the host from behind a firewall

- **Local/Network:** Select this option if your local computer is also your Web server or if you connect to the Web server via a local area network. At the Remote Folder box, enter a folder name or browse to select the folder on the remote host where you store your site files. Click to check the Refresh Remote File List Automatically box if you want to see the Remote Files pane of the Site window updated automatically as you transfer files to the remote server.

- **SourceSafe Database:** Select this option if you want to access a SourceSafe database. Click the Settings button and complete the Open SourceSafe Database dialog box by typing (or browsing for) a Database Path, typing a Project Name, and providing your username and password.

- **WebDAV:** Select this option if you want to make a WebDAV connection. (WebDAV, which is short for *Web-based Distributed Authoring and Versioning,* allows you to edit and manage files on remote Web servers collaboratively — in other words, to share files with other developers. For more information, visit www.webdav.org). Click the Settings button and complete the WebDAV Connection dialog box by entering the server URL and providing your username, password, and e-mail address.

5. **Click OK to close the Site Definition dialog box.**

6. **Click Done to close the Define Sites dialog box.**

If you're confused about information regarding your Web server (and who isn't, at least at first?), contact your hosting service or your system administrator to find out the server name, directory, username, password, and other details you need to complete the Remote Info area of the Site Definition dialog box.

If you change hosting services or other remote server information, such as your password, you can edit your Remote Host attributes by returning to the Site Definition dialog box.

**Book IV
Chapter 9**

**Publishing and
Maintaining
Your Site**

Connecting to a Web Server

 To connect to your Web Server, simply click the Connect to Remote Host button in the Site window. Alternatively, you can choose Site➪Connect from the Menu bar. After you connect, your site files on the remote host appear in the *Remote Files pane* — the left pane of the Site window. Files of your local site root still appear in the right pane of the Site window.

 When you are done working with your Web server, simply click the Disconnect from Remote Host button in the Site window. Alternatively, you can choose Site➪Disconnect from the Menu bar.

Transferring Files

When you connect to the remote host, you can transfer files to and from the server. Just follow these steps:

1. **If you're not already at the Site window, switch to it by choosing Window➪Site Files from the Menu bar.**

2. **Select the files you want to transfer.**

To select files you want to send to the remote site: Click on one or more files in the Local Files pane.

To select files you want to retrieve from the remote site: Click on one or more files in the Remote Files pane.

3. **Transfer the files.**

 To send local files to the remote site: Click the Put button in the Site window or choose Site➪Put from the Menu bar. Dreamweaver presents a dialog box that asks whether you want to include dependent files in the transfer. *Dependent files* are files, such as images, that are included in your HTML code pages. Click Yes to include these files or No to transfer only your selected files.

 To bring remote files to the local site: Click the Get button in the Site window or choose Site➪Get from the Menu bar.

Your transferred files appear in the destination window pane. You can move files in and out of folders in their new location using standard Windows procedures.

 At any time, you can refresh your file lists to re-read a directory of files. To refresh the selected file directory, just click the Refresh button in the Site window.

Halt a file transfer in progress by clicking the Stop Current Task button in the Site window.

Collaborating on Site Revisions

Site maintenance can be an enormous task that you can accomplish best by giving multiple designers revision privileges for files on the site host. To simplify the maintenance task, Dreamweaver provides a Check In/Check Out system that enables you to work collaboratively with others in revising site files. This system helps you and your team keep track of who has which file currently checked out — so that revisers don't inadvertently duplicate editing efforts.

Enabling file Check In/Check Out

You can set up file check in/out for a site as follows:

1. **In Dreamweaver, choose Site⇨Define Sites from the Menu bar to open the Define Sites dialog box.**

2. **From the Site list, select the site that you want to work on and click the Edit button. Doing so opens a Site Definition dialog box for your site similar to the one you see in Figure 9-2.**

3. **Select the Remote Info category.**

Figure 9-2: You use the options in the bottom half of the Site Definition dialog box to describe who can check in (and out) Dream-weaver files.

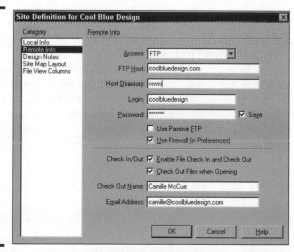

4. **The options you choose in this step depend on your access method.**

   If you select FTP or Local/Network for your Access method: Click the Enable File Check In and Check Out check box. After you do so, the additional options you see at the bottom of the Site Definition dialog box in Figure 9-2 appear.

   If you select SourceSafe Database or WebDAV for your Access method: Click the Settings button and complete the dialog box that appears.

5. **For all Access methods, click the Check Out Files When Opening check box.**

   The file is marked as checked out to you whenever you open it from the remote server.

6. **If you select FTP or Local/Network for your Access method, enter a Check Out Name and E-mail Address.**

   Any file you check out will show this name and address listed in the Check Out column of the Remote Files pane of the Site window.

Checking files in and out

Follow these procedures to check files in and out for collaborative site editing:

 To check files out: In the Remote Files pane of the Site window, select the files you want to check out. Then click the Check Out button at the top of the Site window or choose Site⇨Check Out from the Menu bar. The Checked Out By column in the remote pane of the Site window identifies the person checking out the file. A check mark appears in front of the filename to indicate that it is checked out.

 To check files in: In the remote pane, select the files you want to check in. Then click the Check In button at the top of the Site window or choose Site⇨Check In from the Menu bar. The Checked Out By column in the remote pane of the Site window removes the name of the person who had previously checked out the file. Also, the check mark in front of the filename indicates that its checked-out status is removed.

Maintaining Your Site

After you publish your site, you want to maintain and fine-tune it so that it always looks (and behaves) its very best. The maintenance tasks you find yourself performing most often include measuring download time, monitoring links, and updating metatags.

Measuring download time

Download time is an important measurement for you as a Web designer because it tells you how long users must wait to view your entire page on their computers. Download time depends on the connection speed, or *baud rate,* of a user's modem.

You can keep tabs on the expected download time for a page under construction by looking at the File Size/Download Time indicator in the Status Bar at the bottom of the Document window as shown in Figure 9-3.

Figure 9-3: File size and estimated download time appear at the bottom of the Document window as you work with a page in Dreamweaver.

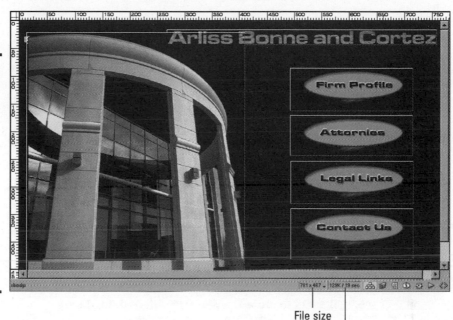

File size

Estimated download time

Dreamweaver computes the estimated download time based on the connection speed specified in the Preferences dialog box. To change the default connection speed, choose Edit⇨Preferences from the Menu bar to open the Preferences dialog box. At the Preferences dialog box, select the Status Bar category and then select a connection speed at the Connection Speed drop-down menu. Choices consist of 14.4, 28.8, 33.6, 56, 64, 128, or 1,500 Kilobits per second.

Book IV Chapter 9

Publishing and Maintaining Your Site

Try minimizing download time for a page — by optimizing or reducing the images on your page, for example — to the greatest degree possible prior to uploading it to the server. Then check the actual download time after the page goes online to determine whether additional file size reduction is needed.

Monitoring links

After constructing your site and putting it on the Web, you can monitor its currency by frequently checking that any absolute address links you set up still work as intended. URLs change frequently, and you don't want users to click on links that don't open their intended destinations.

Setting your HTTP address

To assist Dreamweaver in checking link accuracy, you must provide the actual URL for your site on the Web. Dreamweaver uses this information to check whether links in your site refer to other pages in your site root or to absolute addresses external to your site. Set your HTTP address as follows:

1. **In Dreamweaver, choose Site⇨Define Sites from the Menu bar to open the Define Sites dialog box.**

2. **From the Site list, select the site you want to work on and click the Edit button.**

   The Site Definition dialog box for your site opens.

3. **Select the Local Info category.**

4. **In the HTTP Address box, enter the URL for your site.**

   This URL is the actual Web address for your site, for example, `http://www.yoursite.com`.

5. **Click OK to close the Site Definition dialog box.**

6. **Click Done to close the Define Sites dialog box.**

Click to check the Enable Cache check box in the Local Info category of the Site Definition dialog box. Enabling cache causes file and assets information to be maintained in the site. This helps speed up site management tasks as you construct your site. You can rebuild the cache at any time by choosing Site⇨Recreate Site Cache from the Menu bar.

Updating links sitewide

The Dreamweaver Link Checker can tell you whether links in your site are functioning properly. If you do find an incorrect link, you can update the link throughout your site, whether it's a URL or a link to one of your own pages. Just follow this procedure:

1. **Choose Site⇨Change Link Sitewide from the Menu bar.**

The Change Link dialog box opens, where you can replace the name of an old link with its new name.

2. **In the Change All Links To box, enter the current URL or internal page name or address you want to change.**

3. **In the Into Links To box, enter the URL or internal page of what you want the links to change to.**

4. **Click OK.**

Setting up metatags

Your goal in putting a Web site online is probably to make a certain body of information accessible to the public. Search engines can help users track down your site, but you can improve the likelihood of search engines listing your site by including special HTML code on your pages. This special code is contained in metatags (tags defined using the ⟨meta⟩ keyword) and consists of keywords and descriptions that you create to help search engines match user queries with your Web pages. (For more information about meta tags, see Book 2, "HTML," Chapter 1.

Adding keyword <meta> tags

Set up keyword ⟨meta⟩ tags for a page as follows:

1. **In the Document window, click the Insert Keyword button from the Head Objects panel.**

Alternatively, you can choose Insert⇨Head Tags⇨Keywords from the Menu bar.

2. **In the Insert Keywords dialog box, enter individual words or phrases that describe the content of your page. Separate entries with commas.**

Search engines use these keywords to index the page.

3. **Click OK.**

The dialog box closes and inserts your entries into the ⟨meta⟩ keyword tag in the HTML page code.

Adding a description <meta> tag

Set up a description ⟨meta⟩ tag for a page as follows:

1. **In the Document window, click the Insert Description button from the Head Objects panel.**

Alternatively, you can choose Insert⇨Head Tags⇨Description from the Menu bar.

2. **At the Insert Description dialog box, enter a sentence or paragraph that describes the content of your page.**

   Search engines use this description to index the page.

3. **Click OK.**

   The dialog box closes and inserts your entry into the `<meta>` description tag and the HTML page code.

Index

Notes

Book V

Multimedia: Creating Graphics, Sound, Animations, Video, and Java Applets

The 5th Wave   By Rich Tennant

"What do you mean you're updating our Web page?"

Contents at a Glance

Chapter 1: Creating Images for Your Web Pages

In This Chapter

✔ **Choosing an image file format**

✔ **Understanding color restrictions on the Web**

✔ **Creating transparent images**

✔ **Using hotspots to create clickable images**

Creating images for your Web pages isn't really any more difficult than creating other images. You draw/format/edit/tweak the image by using an editing tool such as PaintShop Pro (a copy of which you find on the companion CD), and then save the image in a specific file format for use on the Web. After you have an image, you can help it blend into your Web page background by using transparent colors. You can also carve up your image into clickable hotspots that respond to your visitors' mouse clicks.

As you create images for your Web pages, keep in mind that some colors work better than others. Check the section "Choosing Image Colors" for information about choosing colors for use in Web pages.

Choosing an Image File Format

You need to know how to use a drawing or image-editing program to create images. You can use anything from Adobe Photoshop to PaintShop Pro to Microsoft PowerPoint to the drawing tools in your word-processing program to develop images. Whichever program(s) you choose, however, you need to make sure that at least one of them can save images in GIF, JPG, or PNG format. Why? Because these formats are supported by virtually all Web browsers.

To create images appropriate for use in Web pages, follow these steps:

1. **Create an image that you want to use in your Web page.**

2. **In the program you use to create the image, click File⇨Save As (or File⇨Export or something similar) to save the image as a GIF, JPG, or PNG image.**

   The Save As dialog box appears.

3. **Type a name and a location.**

   Make sure that the image type you select is GIF, JPG, or PNG and that the location is the same as your HTML documents (for ease of linking).

If your favorite image-editing program doesn't save in GIF, JPG, or PNG formats, you can try either of the following approaches:

✦ Save the image as a TIF image and import the file into a program that can save it in the format you want. PaintShop Pro for Windows, GraphicConverter for Macintosh, and xv for UNIX are some possible candidates.

✦ Copy the image from the image-editing program (by selecting the image and choosing Edit⇨Copy from the menu bar), and then paste the image into the other program — the one that can save in the correct format (by choosing Edit⇨Paste from that program's menu bar).

This second procedure also works well if you have an image-editing program such as Photoshop or PaintShop Pro (which can save in the right format) but you're more comfortable being creative in a different program, such as PowerPoint (which saves slides, but not individual images, in the correct format).

Choosing Image Colors

Good color choices are ones that look good in practically any browser and operating system and display resolution configuration. That is, they show up clearly, not splotchy or mottled. Unfortunately, color involves more than meets the eye.

As you're choosing colors, keep in mind that not all colors are created equal. Some colors don't show up at all in readers' browsers. If you choose a color from the 16.7-million-color palette, for example, and your readers' browsers are set to only 256 colors, the color you choose may not show up crisp and clear (unless it's one of the 256). For that matter, even if you choose a color from the 256-color palette, the color could show up splotchy (a condition technically called *dithered*) on many readers' screens.

To figure out which colors to use, you should first know how colors are described. For the Web, you specify colors with an RGB (Red-Green-Blue) number. By using three numbers (either three decimal numbers or three two-digit hexadecimal numbers), you can specify the amounts of red, green, and blue to create any one of about 16.7 million colors. By mixing the levels of RGB, you can create any color you want.

So which colors are best to use in HTML documents? Colors that are standard across all platforms and that look good even at lower color resolutions. How do you know which ones? Choose colors with the values from the tables in the following sections. By using these values to choose colors (pick one number from each column to create the RGB number), you stand the best chance of having the colors show up clearly in just about any browser.

If your image-editing software uses hexadecimal numbers: The *hexadecimal numbering system (hex)* provides you with the same values as the decimal system does, but hex uses 16 digits instead of 10. The digits for hex are 0–9 and the letters A–F in place of the numbers 10–15. By using two hex digits (##), you can specify a number between 0 (or 00 in hex) and 255 (FF in hex).

Table 1-1 shows values you can use if your image-editing software uses hexadecimal numbers. Use the following table as you would a Chinese restaurant menu (one from column Red, one from column Green, and one from column Blue) to choose six-digit color numbers.

You also use the hexadecimal numbers for specifying colors within your HTML documents (for example, for the background). For more information on specifying background colors for a Web page, see Book 1, "Web Page Basics."

Table 1-1	Hexadecimal RGB Values for Web-Safe Colors	
Red	*Green*	*Blue*
00	00	00
33	33	33
66	66	66
99	99	99
CC	CC	CC
FF	FF	FF

If your image-editing software uses decimal numbers: Table 1-2 shows values you can use if your image-editing software uses decimal RGB numbers to set colors. Again, think Chinese restaurant menu — take a number from column Red, then a number from column Green, and the final number from column Blue.

Table 1-2	Decimal RGB Values for Web-Safe Colors	
Red	*Green*	*Blue*
0	0	0
51	51	51
102	102	102
153	153	153
204	204	204
255	255	255

Reducing file size

One of the best ways you can help speed image download time is to reduce the image file size. The following techniques can help reduce image file size and make an incredible difference in how fast they load:

- **Reduce color depth.** Check your image-editing software for options such as Reduce Color Depth. For fairly simple graphics, reducing the color depth to 16 colors, instead of 256 colors or millions of colors, can make the image's file size much smaller with little or no visible difference in the image quality.

- **Use the JPG or PNG formats for photographs.** These formats compress photographs and complex images more effectively than the GIF format does. Also, programs that allow you to save files in these formats also usually offer a place to set compression options. Experiment with the compression and increase compression until you start to see a loss of quality; then back off a little.

Creating Transparent Images

A transparent image is one in which the background color doesn't show up — it's replaced by the background color that's visible in the browser. Consider making your images transparent if the background is likely to be a distraction or if the important part of your image is not rectangular. Take a look at Figure 1-1, which shows an image with a regular background (at top) and the same image with a transparent background (bottom).

If you want to use transparent backgrounds, you must save them as GIF images, Version *89a*. You should have selections in your Save As dialog box that let you select both GIF and the specific version number — Version 87a or 89a — as you're saving your GIF image. JPG images *cannot* be transparent.

Many graphics or photo-editing software packages allow you to easily make a background color transparent. If you don't have image-editing software and don't want to invest in it, you can check out freeware and shareware programs available on the Internet. Many of these programs offer menu options for choosing the background color (that is, the color that disappears in the browser).

To create transparent images, use a procedure similar to the following steps. I don't address the specifics for a particular software package; instead, I give you the general process for using any package.

Note: Before beginning, be sure that you have your image-editing software open and ready to use.

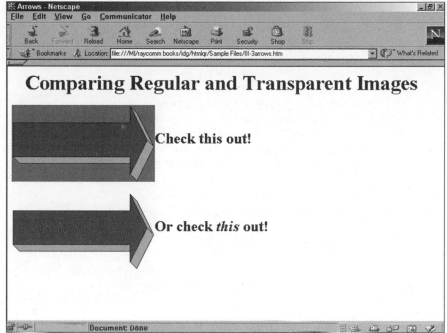

Figure 1-1:
The
difference
between
regular and
transparent
images is
easy to see.

Follow these steps:

1. **Open an image in your graphics software program.**

   The image must have a uniform background color.

2. **Locate your options for selecting a background color.**

   Many programs have a Background Color option under one of the menus, but this option varies greatly from program to program. (In PaintShop Pro, for example, select the Dropper tool, and then right-click the background color.)

3. **Select the existing background color (the one you want to be transparent).**

4. **Find the Save As dialog box (virtually all graphics programs include one of these), and type a name and a location.**

   (Make sure that you save the image as a GIF 89a image!)

5. **Look for Save As options (probably accessible by clicking an Options button), and select an option that specifies "Make Background Color Transparent" or something similar.**

6. **Click OK (to get out of the Options dialog box), and then click Save to — well — save the image.**

At this point, you don't see a change in the image background; you must open the image in your browser to see the results of your hard work. In any case, you should go ahead and view the image in your browser just to make sure that the image looks how you want it to look. In your browser, choose File⇨Open or File⇨Open Page; select Show All Files at the bottom of the dialog box that appears; find the image file you want to view; and then click Open.

Creating Clickable Images

You can use *clickable images* (also called *image maps*) to let readers click images or parts of images to link to other pages or images. The image map can provide a menu of selections for your reader, just as a set of regular links can provide a menu.

Image maps are good for making spiffy-looking menus — that is, menus arranged so that readers can click various parts of an image to link to different information. Image maps are also good for making geographic-related links (by letting people click the state or country of their choice) or for all kinds of orientation or training applications (by allowing people to click to get more information about whatever is pictured).

Keep in mind that some people choose not to (or cannot) view images, so image maps alone won't always work for navigation. Be sure to include text-based links to supplement your image map.

Including image maps in your HTML document is fairly easy. In the following sections, I describe in detail the process for including image maps:

1. Adding an image to your HTML document.

2. Defining clickable areas (a process called *mapping*).

3. Defining the map — that is, specifying which image map areas link to what information.

The following table shows the tags used to add an image map to an HTML document.

HTML Tag or Attribute	Effect	Use in Pairs?
`<IMG SRC="...">`	Inserts an image.	No
ISMAP	Specifies that the image is a server-side clickable image map.	No
USEMAP="#mapname"	Identifies the picture as a client-side image map and specifies a `MAP` to use for acting on the readers' clicks.	No

Note: Server-side imagemaps exist, but are not covered in this book. If you must delve into server-side imagemaps, consult your system administrator.

The `SRC="..."` attribute still points to a valid URL (relative or absolute) for your image. The remaining information points to an addition to the HTML document. Remember that all the other valid `<IMG>` attributes also apply to your imagemap.

Adding the image

The image you find or create to use in the imagemap should be as clear and small as you can make it. Stick to a few colors and think simple. Although your readers may be impressed with a graphical masterpiece the first time they see it, they quickly tire of waiting for it to load each time they view your page.

I created the simple image you see in Figure 1-2 to illustrate some of the possibilities of imagemaps.

Figure 1-2:
The best images for mapping are made up of clearly defined shapes. This image contains three distinct shapes.

To include an image in your Web page, follow these steps:

1. **Include the image in your document, along with the descriptive text you want to appear in non-image-supporting browsers, by adding the following tags and text to your HTML document:**

```
<H1>Making Imagemaps Can Be Fun!</H1>
<IMG ALT="This is a clickable map."
  SRC="imagemap.jpg">
The image above is an imagemap.<P>
```

2. **Include the** USEMAP= **attribute to indicate that the image is to be a client-side imagemap.**

The USEMAP= attribute points to a map by name — demomap, as you see in this example:

```
<H1>Making Imagemaps Can Be Fun!</H1>
<IMG ALT="This is a clickable map."
  SRC="imagemap.jpg" USEMAP="#demomap">
The image above is an imagemap.<P>
```

Note: The # before demomap indicates that you're using a map within the same document, just as the # in a <A> tag indicates a within-document link.

You just added the image into your document and indicated that it's an imagemap. You can't see much of a difference through your browser — the image looks like any other image that's a link in your document. You must define the map before the hot spots work, as I describe in the next section.

Mapping clickable areas

In mapping clickable areas, you divide the image into parts that eventually link to other information and pages. Mapping is sort of like taking a picture and carving it into individual pieces (like puzzle pieces) — each piece represents an individual area that you can then link to something else.

Many Web design tools allow you to map clickable areas on images with point-and-click ease. To see how to map clickable areas using Dreamweaver (a nifty Web design tool you also find on the CD) take a peek at the section "Creating Clickable Hotspots" in Book 4, Chapter 4. If you prefer mapping clickable areas by hand, as I describe in this chapter, you can use a trial version of image-editing program such as Paint Shop Pro (also available on the companion CD).

Mapping your image isn't too complicated. All points or coordinates are measured from the upper-left corner of the image, in x,y coordinates. The point at the upper-left corner of the image is 0,0 — zero pixels across by zero pixels down. Figure 1-3 shows the cursor pointing at (focused on?) that spot. Notice that you can see the coordinates (0,0) displayed at the lower left of the window.

This example identifies the coordinates for each of the three shapes in our sample image. These three shapes show you all you need to know to map all shapes. By identifying the coordinates of certain points in a figure, as described in the following list, you can describe any shape:

✦ Rectangular shapes require the upper-left and lower-right corners. The computer figures out the rest.

✦ Circles require the center and the radius length. (Yes, you must do the math to figure out the radius.)

✦ Polygons, such as our triangle, just require each corner. The computer connects the dots to finish the figure.

You can represent any other shape by using some combination of the rectangle, circle, and polygon. A sleeping cat, for example, can have a long rectangle for the tail, a fatter one for the body, a circle for the head, and a couple of triangles for the ears. Alternatively, you can just go point to point to point on the cat and call it a fancy polygon.

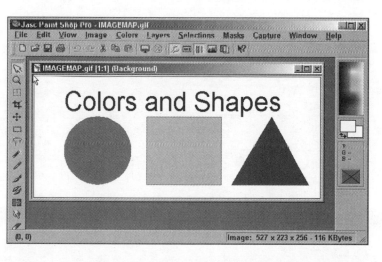

Figure 1-3:
In the lower-left-hand side of the screen you see the coordinates (in this case, 0,0) displayed.

Mapping a rectangle

To determine the coordinates that define a rectangle for use in an imagemap, follow these steps:

1. **Point the cursor at the upper-left corner of the rectangle, and write on a piece of paper the *x,y* coordinates (208,75), as shown in Figure 1-4.**

Figure 1-4: Begin by writing down the *x,y* coordinates of the upper-left-hand corner of the square — in this case (208, 75).

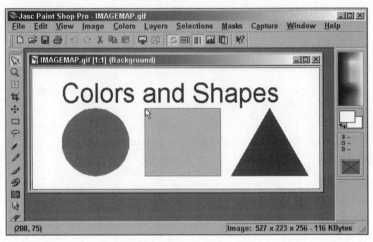

2. **Point at the lower-right corner and write the *x,y* coordinates (345,197), as shown in Figure 1-5.**

Figure 1-5: Next, write down the *x,y* coordinates of the lower-right-hand corner of the square — (345, 197) in this example.

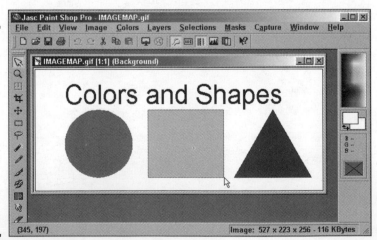

To see how to use the coordinates you gathered to define a map for the square, flip to "Defining the map" later in this chapter.

Mapping a circle

To determine the coordinates of a circle for use in imagemaps, follow these steps:

1. **Point the cursor at the center of the circle and write down the *x,y* coordinates that appear.**

2. **Move the cursor horizontally to the edge of the circle and note those *x,y* coordinates.**

3. **Subtract the first *x* coordinate from the second one to get the radius of the circle.**

To see how to use the coordinates you gathered to define a map for the circle, check out "Defining the map" below.

Mapping a polygon

To determine the coordinates that define the triangle (or any other polygon) for use in imagemaps, follow these steps:

1. **Pick a corner, point the cursor at it, and note the *x,y* coordinates.**

2. **Move to the next corner and note those *x,y* coordinates.**

3. **Continue moving around the edge of the shape, noting the coordinates of each corner. Make sure that you mark the corners in order — the computer connects the dots in the same order that you follow to figure out what the shape is.**

Don't lose the piece of paper with your notes. You need it to define your map, which I describe in the next section.

Defining the map

Defining the map simply tells the computer which areas readers may click and what link to follow after they click. The process looks more complex than it really is. The following table shows the tags and attributes used to define the map.

HTML Tag or Attribute	Effect	Use in Pairs?
`<MAP>...</MAP>`	Specifies a collection of hot spots for a client-side image map.	Yes
`NAME="..."`	Gives the MAP a name so that it can be referred to later.	No
`<AREA>`	Specifies the shape of a hot spot in a client-side image map.	No
`COORDS="x1,y1, x2,y2, ..."`	Specifies coordinates that define the hot spot's shape.	No
`HREF="URL"`	Specifies the destination of the hot spot.	No
`NOHREF`	Indicates that clicks in this region should cause no action.	No
`SHAPE="..."`	Specifies type of shape as `RECT` (for rectangle), `CIRC` (for circle), or `POLY`(for polygon).	No

The `<MAP>...</MAP>` tag tells the browser which areas in your image link to which URLs. The following block of code shows you how to include a map definition in your document along with the image map. You start with an HTML file similar to the following:

```
<!DOCTYPE HTML PUBLIC "-//W3C//DTD HTML 4.01
  Frameset//EN"
  "http://www.w3.org/TR/html4/frameset.dtd">
<HTML>
<HEAD>
<TITLE>Making Image maps</TITLE>
</HEAD>
<BODY>
<H1>Making Image maps Can Be Fun!</H1>
<IMG ALT="This is a clickable map."
  SRC="imagemap.jpg" USEMAP="#demomap"><P>
The image above is an image map.<P>
</BODY>
</HTML>
```

To include a map definition in your document along with the image map, follow these steps:

1. **Include the `<MAP>` tags in your document, as shown in the following block of code:**

```
<IMG ALT="This is a clickable map."
  SRC="imagemap.jpg" USEMAP="#demomap"><P>
The image above is an image map.<P>
<MAP>
</MAP>
</BODY>
</HTML>
```

2. **Add the** NAME= **attribute to the** <MAP> **tag, as the following block of code shows.**

   Note: The map is called demomap.

   ```
   <IMG ALT="This is a clickable map."
     SRC="imagemap.jpg" USEMAP="#demomap"><P>
   The image above is an image map.<P>
   <MAP NAME="demomap">
   </MAP>
   </BODY>
   </HTML>
   ```

3. **Add an** <AREA> **tag between the** <MAP> **tags, as follows.**

   You eventually have one <AREA> tag for each clickable area in your map, but the following examples build them one at a time.

   ```
   <IMG ALT="This is a clickable map."
     SRC="imagemap.jpg" USEMAP="#demomap"><P>
   The image above is an image map.<P>
   <MAP NAME="demomap">
   <AREA>
   </MAP>
   ```

4. **Add a** SHAPE= **attribute to the** <AREA> **tag, as follows.**

   I'm starting with SHAPE="RECT" because the square (rectangle) is the easiest one to do.

   ```
   <IMG ALT="This is a clickable map."
     SRC="imagemap.jpg" USEMAP="#demomap"><P>
   The image above is an image map.<P>
   <MAP NAME="demomap">
   <AREA SHAPE="RECT">
   </MAP>
   ```

5. **Add the** COORDS= **attribute to the** <AREA> **tag, as shown in the following block of code.**

   The coordinates for our square are 208,75 for the upper-left corner and 345,197 for the lower-right corner.

   ```
   <IMG ALT="This is a clickable map."
     SRC="imagemap.jpg" USEMAP="#demomap"><P>
   The image above is an image map.<P>
   <MAP NAME="demomap">
   <AREA SHAPE="RECT" COORDS="208,75,345,197">
   </MAP>
   ```

   Note: Don't include spaces between the coordinates.

6. **Add the** HREF= **attribute to the** <AREA> **tag, as follows.**

   You can use any valid URL for your client-side image map.

   ```
   <IMG ALT="This is a clickable map."
     SRC="imagemap.jpg" USEMAP="#demomap"><P>
   The image above is an imagemap.<P>
   <MAP NAME="demomap">
   <AREA SHAPE="RECT" COORDS="208,75,345,197"
     HREF="/shapes/square.htm">
   </MAP>
   ```

7. **Add more** <AREA> **tags as necessary.**

   Make sure that you include the correct SHAPE= and COORDS= attributes
   for each tag.

Chapter 2: Creating Audio, Video, and Animation Files

In This Chapter

✔ Understanding the difference between downloadable and streaming media

✔ Creating streaming audio files (RealAudio)

✔ Creating downloadable audio files (MP3)

✔ Creating video files

✔ Converting video files to streaming video (RealVideo)

✔ Creating animated effects

✔ Finding media files online

✔ Adding media files to your Web pages

*W*hereas text and images can convey an amazing amount of information, well-chosen multimedia effects such as audio, video, and animations can entertain and inform your visitors in a way that plain vanilla text and images can't. This chapter introduces you to the two main options you have when creating multimedia files — namely, *streaming* and *downloadable* — and shows you how to create both types. You also find tips for creating animated effects, as well as for adding audio, video, and animation files to your Web pages.

The Difference between Downloadable and Streaming Media

You can create two types of audio and video files:

✦ **Streaming media files.** A streaming media file, such as an audio file created using the RealAudio file format, begins to play immediately. The good news is that users don't have to wait for the entire streaming media file to download before they can begin listening. The bad news is that a slow modem connection can interrupt the streaming file transfer and make the listening experience less than perfect.

✦ **Downloadable media files.** Downloadable media files, such as MP3 audio files, sound just as their producers intend because playback isn't affected by modem connection speed. Unfortunately, users must download a downloadable media file in its entirety before they can begin playing it — and if the file is very large, users may have to wait awhile for the download to complete.

No matter which option you choose — streaming or downloadable — users must install special software players on their computers to enjoy your multimedia masterpieces.

Take a look at Tables 2-1 and 2-2 for an explanation of the most popular streaming and downloadable audio and video file formats around, as well as their associated players.

 Most media players are free, and many "plug in" to Web browsers easily — so installing media players isn't difficult for most folks. To make viewing your multimedia files even easier for your visitors, however, consider adding a link from your multimedia-laden Web page to a site on the Internet where users can download and install the appropriate player.

Table 2-1		Popular Web Audio Formats	
Audio File Format	*Extensions*	*Common Use*	*Streaming/ Downloadable*
AIFF	.aif, .aiff	Uncompressed files can be played in browsers but are slow to download.	Downloadable
Flash audio	.swf	Audio-only files can stream PCM or MP3-compressed audio.	Streaming
MIDI	.mid, .midi, .smf	Music files saved in the MIDI format. Plays in MIDI players (which are not well-standardized on the Web).	Downloadable
MP3	.mp3, .mp2	High-quality, compressed files with relatively speedy download times. Plays in numerous players, including QuickTime Player 4+, RealPlayer G2 6+, Windows Media Player 5.2+, and others that act as browser helper applications.	Downloadable

Audio File Format	*Extensions*	*Common Use*	*Streaming/ Downloadable*
QuickTime	`.mov`	Soundtrack-only QuickTime movies. Plays in the QuickTime Player.	Downloadable
RealAudio	`.ra or .ram`	Audio-only files in the streaming RealMedia format. Plays in RealPlayer.	Streaming
Rich Music Format	`.rmf`	Hybrid audio/music format. Plays in the Beatnik player.	Downloadable
Shockwave Audio	`.swa`	Audio-only Shockwave files that can be played by any MP3 player.	Downloadable
WAV	`.wav`	Uncompressed files can be played in browsers but are slow to download.	Downloadable
Windows Media	`.asf, .asx`	The Microsoft streaming media format. Plays in the Windows Media Player.	Downloadable

As you skim through Tables 2-1 and 2-2, notice that the file extension indicates the format in which you save the clip. For example, `song.ra` indicates a RealAudio clip; `video.mov` indicates a QuickTime clip.

Table 2-2		Popular Web Video Formats	
Video File Format	*Extensions*	*Common Use*	*Streaming/ Downloadable*
MPEG	`.mpg, .mpeg, .mpe`	High-quality, compressed files that play in Windows Media Player and on Macintosh via QuickTime.	Downloadable
QuickTime	`.mov`	QuickTime movies that play in the QuickTime Player on both Windows and Macintosh systems. Can include video and audio or just video-only.	Downloadable
RealVideo	`.ra or .ram`	Files in the RealMedia format. Plays in RealPlayer. Can include video and audio or just video-only.	Streaming
Video for Windows	`.avi`	Once-popular format is becoming less prevalent but still plays in most players.	Downloadable

Creating Streaming Audio Files

RealNetworks' RealAudio file format is the most popular choice for creating streaming audio files. In this section, I show you how to create audio files in RealAudio format using RealSystem Producer 8.5 Basic.

You can download and install your own (free) copy of RealSystem Producer 8.5 Basic from RealNetworks at `www.realnetworks.com/products/producer/index.html`.

To create a streaming audio file, follow these steps.

1. **Start RealProducer Basic, either by clicking the RealProducer Basic icon on your desktop or by clicking the Start button on the Windows task bar and choosing Programs⇨RealProducer Basic.**

The Recording Wizard dialog box, shown in Figure 2-1, appears.

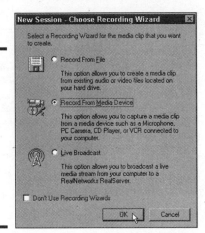

Figure 2-1: When you run Real-Producer Basic for the first time, the Recording Wizard dialog box appears.

2. **Choose a recording option from one of the following:**

- **Record From File.** Choose this option if you want to create a streaming audio file from another type of audio file — for example, a .wav file — you already have stored on your computer.

- **Record From Media Device.** Choose this option if you want to record a streaming audio file by speaking or singing into a microphone, or by recording an audio CD. (Before you choose this option, make sure your microphone or CD player is already hooked up to your computer.)

Virtually all commercial audio CDs are copyrighted, meaning that unless you ask for permission, you can only legally copy them for your own personal use. Because hundreds of thousands of folks all over the world can potentially visit you on the Web, your Web site — even a personal Web site — does *not* fall under "personal use." For more information on U.S. copyright law (including guidelines for incorporating multimedia into your Web pages) visit www.loc.gov/copyright.

- **Live Broadcast.** Choose this option if you want to set up a live streaming broadcast from a RealAudio-supporting Web server. (Before you choose this option, check with your system administrator to find out the name of your RealServer, username, and password.)

If you choose one wizard and then change your mind, you can select another wizard by choosing File➪Recording Wizards from the RealProducer Basic main menu.

The example you see in this section demonstrates selecting the second option — Record From Media Device — to create a streaming audio file from an audio CD. If you pick the Record From Media Device option, the dialog box shown in Figure 2-2 appears. Choosing either of the other two options (Record From File or Live Broadcast) causes slightly different windows to display than the ones I describe in the remainder of this section.

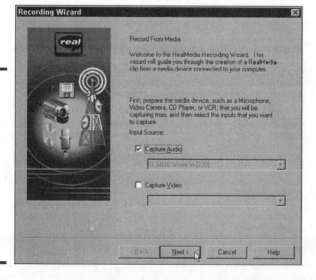

Figure 2-2:
The Recording Wizard dialog box allows you to choose whether to capture audio or video, or both.

Select Help from the main menu at any time when using RealProducer Basic to access commonly asked questions, product documentation, and online technical help.

3. **Click the Capture Audio check box you see in the Record from Media window and then click Next.**

   The RealMedia Clip Information window appears.

4. **Enter the values you want to associate with this media file's Title, Author, Copyright, Description, and Keywords designations; then click Next.**

   The File Type window appears.

5. **Select either Multi-rate SureStream for RealServer G2 (if you know your Web server supports this option) or Single-rate for Web Servers (if your Web server doesn't support SureStream or if you're not sure which option to choose). Then click Next.**

   The Target Audience window appears.

   To find out whether your Web server supports SureStream, ask your Web system administrator.

6. **Select the modem speed for which you want your streaming audio file optimized. (Options range from 28K modem to 512K cable modem.) Then click Next.**

   The Audio Format window appears.

7. **Select one of the following options; then click Next.**

   • **Voice Only:** Choose this option if you want to record spoken words.

   • **Voice with Background Music:** Choose this option if you want to record spoken words over background music.

   • **Music:** Choose this option if you want to record instrumentals and vocals.

   • **Stereo Music:** Choose this option if you want to record music from a player attached to your computer with a stereo input.

   The Output File window appears.

8. **Choose the filename and directory you want to associate with your streaming audio file. (Make sure the filename you choose contains the extension .rm which designates the file as RealMedia format.) Then click Next.**

   The Prepare to Record window appears.

9. **Double-check the values you entered on the preceding six windows. To make a correction, click Back; to begin recording your streaming audio file, click Finish.**

   The RealProducer Basic window appears.

10. **Begin playing the audio CD you want to record. To do this in Windows:**

1. **Insert the audio CD in the CD player attached to your computer.**

2. **Click the Start button on the Windows task bar and choose Programs⇨Accessories⇨Multimedia⇨CD Player.**

   The CD Player that comes bundled with the Windows operating system appears, as shown in Figure 2-3.

3. **Select the track you want to record from the Track drop-down list.**

   Figure 2-3 shows Track 1 selected.

4. **Click the Play button (the right arrow) you see in Figure 2-3.**

Figure 2-3:
To play an audio CD, click the Play button on your audio player (here, the CD Player that comes with Windows).

11. **When you're ready to begin recording your streaming audio file, click the Start button you see on the RealProducer Basic window. Click the Stop button when you want to stop recording.**

12. **To review your newly recorded streaming audio clip, click the Play button you see at the bottom of the RealProducer Basic window.**

To play RealAudio files, you must first download and install a RealAudio player such as RealPlayer Basic 8.5. You can download a free copy of RealPlayer Basic 8.5 at www.real.com.

Creating Downloadable Audio Files

Downloadable audio files are audio files that listeners must download completely (from your Web site to their computers) before playing. While many different types of downloadable audio files exist (refer to Table 2-1), by far the most popular format of downloadable audio file on the Web is a format called MP3. This section describes how to create MP3 audio files for including on your Web pages.

Many software programs exist that you can use to create downloadable audio files. In this section I demonstrate using RealJukebox Basic 2, from a company called RealNetworks, to create an MP3 file from an audio CD. You can download your own free copy of RealJukebox Basic 2 from www.realjukebox.com.

To create an MP3 file by using RealJukebox Basic 2, follow these steps.

1. **Start RealJukebox Basic, either by clicking the RealJukebox Basic icon on your desktop or by clicking the Start button on the Windows task bar and choosing Programs➪RealJukebox Basic.**

The RealJukebox interface shown in Figure 2-4 appears.

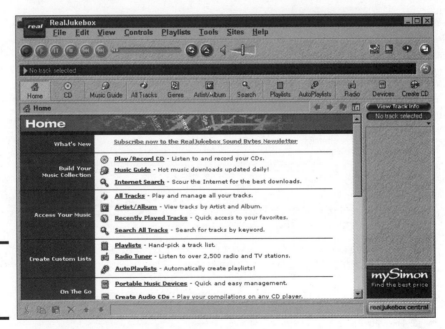

Figure 2-4:
The Real-
Jukebox
interface.

2. **Choose Tools➪Preferences.**

The Preferences dialog box appears.

3. **Click the Audio Quality tab at the top of the Preferences dialog box.**

The Audio Quality preferences page appears.

4. **In the Select a Format section, select MP3 Audio. Then click OK.**

5. **Select Tools➪Record from Mic/Line In...**

The Record from Analog Source dialog box appears.

6. **Select the audio source for the MP3 file you want to create, then click
Close. The options include:**

- **Line-in:** an audio input running from an audio source, such as a
  stereo, to your computer

- **Microphone:** a microphone hooked up to your computer

- **CD Audio:** a CD player hooked up to your computer

- **System Mixer:** an audio mixer attached to your computer

The example I use in this section demonstrates selecting the third
option, CD Audio, to create an MP3 file from an audio CD.

Virtually all commercial audio CDs are copyrighted, meaning that you
can only legally copy them for your own personal use.

7. **Insert the audio CD you want to record into the CD audio player
attached to your computer.**

The tracks on the audio CD appear in the main RealJukebox window, as
shown in Figure 2-5.

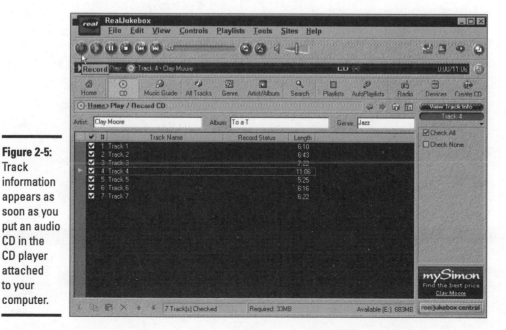

Figure 2-5:
Track
information
appears as
soon as you
put an audio
CD in the
CD player
attached
to your
computer.

8. **Select the track you want to record.**

   In Figure 2-5, track number four is selected.

9. **Click the record button you see on the upper-left-hand corner of the main RealJukebox window, shown in Figure 2-5. (Alternatively, you can choose Controls⇨Record.)**

   RealJukebox records the track you selected in Step 8.

To listen to an MP3 file, you must have an MP3 player, such as RealPlayer Basic, installed on your computer.

Creating Video Files for Your Web Pages

Video clips can add interest to your page by providing a television-like feel for the user. Because creating effective video is both art and science (heck, universities offer degrees in creating video) I don't discuss the soup-to-nuts video creation process in detail here. Instead, I cover how to convert an existing video clip into a streaming, Web-friendly video clip using the RealVideo format developed by RealNetworks.

Shooting for the Web

For the best results, keep the following tips in mind when shooting video for the Web:

✔ **Minimize camera movement:** Panning, tilting, and dollying (moving the camera sideways, up and down, and walking around with the camera) all add color and motion to the background, which makes the finished clip appear jerky when viewed on the Web. If you absolutely must move the camera, do so slowly and smoothly.

✔ **Zoom in close:** Because your finished video clip will appear in a relatively small frame on your Web site, close-ups work better than long-shots.

✔ **Don't include a time/date stamp:** A time/date stamp will be unreadable in the teeny-tiny video clip you end up putting on the Web. If the time and date are important, consider adding this information to the Web page where you link to the video clip.

✔ **Invest in an external microphone:** Video experts know that good video depends on good audio — and good-quality audio is especially important when creating video for the Web, because converting the audio portion of a video to a Web-friendly format compresses and degrades audio. External microphones usually produce better-quality sound than the microphones built into cameras.

Keep in mind that you can choose from many other options when creating video for your Web pages. For example, you can choose another video format, such as Microsoft Netshow (`www.microsoft.com/NetShow`), or QuickTime (`developer.apple.com/quicktime`). Or you can choose a video creation/editing tool, such as Adobe Premiere, that enables you to save your video file in any format you like. Whichever approach you take, the guidelines that follow help you understand the steps you need to incorporate video clips into your Web pages quickly and easily.

Gathering the hardware and software you need

To create a video clip for your Web page, you must have all of the following:

✦ **A video capture card:** Most PCs come with a video card, but that's not the same as a *video capture card* — so, chances are, you have to purchase a video capture card. Macintosh owners rejoice: Many Macintosh computers *do* come complete with a video capture card.

   To find out if you already have a video capture card, turn your computer around and look for a little round hole next to the words Video In. If you find this Video In port, you're in luck! If not, you must purchase and install a video capture card. A video capture card is a piece of hardware that fits into your computer, acting as a kind of adapter you use to hook up your computer to a video input device such as a video cassette recorder (VCR) or digital camera.

✦ **A video source device:** If you want to shoot your own video, you need a video camera . (You can create video for the Web by using any video camera, from a modest consumer model to a high-end professional digital video camera.) Alternatively, you can create video clips for your Web pages by converting prerecorded video tapes into Web-friendly formats — in which case, you need a VCR.

✦ **Cables:** You need to use video and audio cables to connect the video and audio ports of your source device (for example, a digital camera or a VCR) to the corresponding video and audio ports on your computer.

✦ **A powerful computer:** Creating and editing video files requires a powerful processor, as well as lots of memory and disk space. While the exact requirements depend on the video capture card and video creation and editing software you choose, at a minimum you want to invest in a 200-MHz Pentium with at least 32MB RAM running Windows, or a PowerMac G4.

✦ **Video capturing and editing software:** If you plan to create sophisticated video clips from scratch, you may want to invest in a full-featured video capturing and editing tool such as Abobe Premiere (`www.adobe.com/`

products/premiere) or Apple's Final Cut Pro (www.apple.com/finalcutpro). Most video capturing and editing tools — including the two I mention — let you choose among several Web-friendly format formats when it comes time to save your video file.

On the other hand, if all you want to do is convert a few seconds of that videotape of your daughter's first birthday party into digital format for presentation on your personal Web site, you may be able to get by with a free tool, such as RealProducer Basic.

Most commercial videotapes are copyrighted, which means that if you convert them to digital format and make them available from your Web site, you may be running afoul of the law. When in doubt, check with the copyright owner of the videotape you want to convert.

Converting a video file to RealVideo format

To create a streaming video file from an existing video file, follow these steps:

1. **Start RealProducer Basic, either by clicking the RealProducer Basic icon on your desktop or by clicking the Start button on the Windows task bar and choosing Programs⇨RealProducer Basic.**

   The Choose Recording Wizard dialog box appears.

2. **Select the Record From File option and click OK.**

   The Record From File window appears.

3. **Type (or browse and select) the name of the existing video file you want to convert to streaming video; then click Next.**

   The Real Media Clip Information window appears.

4. **Enter descriptive information in the Title, Author, Copyright, Description, and Keywords input fields; then click Next.**

   The File Type window appears.

5. **Select either Multi-rate SureStream for RealServer G2 (if you know your Web server supports this option) or Single-rate for Web Servers (if your Web server doesn't support SureStream or if you're not sure). Then click Next.**

   The Target Audience window appears.

6. **Select the modem speed for which you want your streaming audio file optimized. (Options range from 28K modem to 512K cable modem.) Then click Next.**

   The Video Quality window appears.

7. **Choose one of the video quality options that appears on the Video Quality window; then click Next.**

   The options include Normal Motion Video; Smoothest Motion Video; Sharpest Image Video; and Slide Show. (The default option is Normal Motion Video.)

   The Output File window appears.

8. **Specify the filename and directory you want to associate with your streaming video file. (Make sure the filename you choose contains the extension .rm which designates the file as RealMedia format.) Then click Next.**

   The Prepare to Record window appears.

9. **Double-check the values you entered on the preceding six windows. To make a correction, click Back; to begin recording your streaming audio file, click Finish.**

   The RealProducer Basic main window appears.

10. **Click the Start button you see on the RealProducer Basic window to convert the file.**

    RealProducer Basic creates a new streaming media file based on the information you provided in Step 8.

11. **To review your newly recorded streaming video clip, click the Play button at the bottom of the RealProducer Basic window.**

   To play RealVideo files, you must first download and install a RealMedia player such as RealPlayer Basic 8.5. You can download a free copy of RealPlayer Basic 8.5 from www.real.com.

Creating an Animated Effect

You create animated effects, or *animations,* by displaying a series of pictures (sometimes called *frames*) one after another to simulate movement. Two of the most popular forms of animated effects for Web pages are banner ads (animated advertisements you see on commercial Web sites) and slide shows.

Creating animated effects is a very broad subject — so broad I can't explain all the nitty-gritty details and artistic nuances in this book. Instead, I show you how to create a simple animated effect optimized for the Web. For more in-depth information on creating animated effects for your Web pages, you may want to check out *Web Animation For Dummies,* by Cynthia L. Baron and Renee Lewinter.

On a technical level, the process for creating animated effects is the opposite of creating video. To create animated effects, you take discrete images and put them together to create the illusion of continuous motion; to create video, you begin with continuous motion — then break it up into discrete images.

You can use any of a variety of animation tools to create animated effects for your Web pages. Flash 5 (the focus of Book 7) is one of the most popular. But Web page creation tools such as Dreamweaver (Book 4) also give you the ability to create animations. Some developers even create animations using a made-for-the-Web programming language such as JavaScript (Book 6) or Java (introduced in Chapter 6 of this book).

In this section, I demonstrate how to use Jasc Animation Shop to create a simple animated GIF file that is as easy to incorporate into your Web pages as a regular image.

You find trial copies of Flash 5, Dreamweaver, and Jasc Animation Shop on the companion CD.

To create an animated effect for a Web page using Jasc Animation Shop, follow these steps:

1. **Create or find the images you want to string together to create your animated effect.**

    To create a simple on/off animation, you need two images; to create a slide show or more complex animated effect, you may use two, three, or even dozens more.

    Two sample images, neutral.gif and surprised.gif, are located on the companion CD. For more information on creating (and finding) images for use in your animated effects, check out Chapter 1, "Creating Images for Your Web Pages."

2. **Start Animation Shop by clicking the Start button on the Windows task bar and choosing Programs⇨Jasc Software⇨Animation Shop 3.**

    The Jasc Animation Shop main window appears, as shown in Figure 2-6.

3. **Select File⇨Animation Wizard from the Jasc Animation Shop main menu. Or, alternatively, you can click the animation wizard icon on the far left of the toolbar.**

    The Animation Wizard dialog box shown in Figure 2-7 appears.

Animation Wizard icon

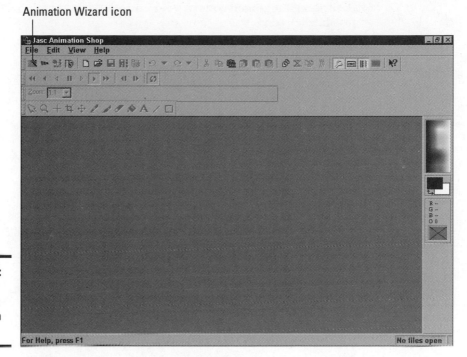

Figure 2-6:
The Jasc
Animation
Shop main
window.

Figure 2-7:
The
Animation
Wizard
walks you
through the
steps
necessary
to create an
animated
effect for
your Web
page.

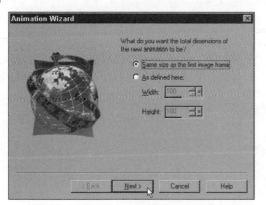

4. **To create an animated effect the same size as your first image, click
   Same size as the first image frame; to create a custom-size animation,
   click As Defined Here, then specify values for Width and Height**

describing the dimensions of your custom-size animation. When you finish, click Next.

In the example I use throughout these steps, I demonstrate selecting the first option.

The Animation Wizard screen appears, as shown in Figure 2-8.

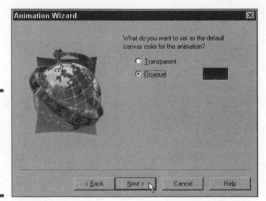

Figure 2-8:
Select a background for your animated effect.

5. **Select a default canvas color for your animated effect and then click Next.**

The options are Transparent (for a see-through background) and Opaque (for a colored background). If you choose Opaque, you can click on the color swatch you see next to the Opaque radio button to select the color background you want.

The Animation Wizard screen shown in Figure 2-9 appears.

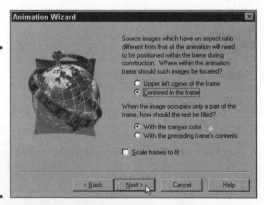

Figure 2-9:
Specify where (and how) your images appear in the finished animated effect.

6. **Specify where you want your images to appear in the finished animated effect by selecting either Upper left corner of the frame or Centered in the frame. Then specify how you want to fill blank portions of the animation frames to appear by selecting either With the canvas color or With the preceding frame's contents. If you want to scale the animation frames to fit your images (rather than crop the images), select Scale frames to fit. When you finish, click Next.**

The Animation Wizard screen shown in Figure 2-10 appears.

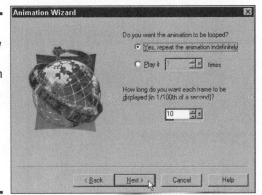

Figure 2-10: Specify how fast to display each image, and how many times to display the finished animated effect.

7. **Specify how many times you want the animated effect to repeat, or *loop;* then specify how long you want each image to appear onscreen before being replaced by the next. When you finish, click Next.**

The Animation Wizard screen shown in Figure 2-11 appears.

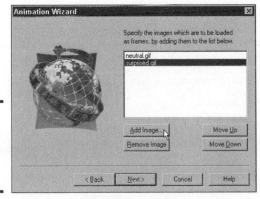

Figure 2-11: Add images to your animated effect.

8. Click the <u>A</u>dd Image button shown in Figure 2-11 to add as many images as you want to the animated effect. Then click <u>N</u>ext.

The final Animation Wizard screen appears.

9. Click the Finish button.

The Animation Wizard creates your animated effect.

10. Choose <u>V</u>iew⇨<u>A</u>nimation or click the View button to view the animated effect.

11. Choose File⇨Save to save the animated effect.

The Save As dialog box appears.

12. Enter a filename, select a file format from the Save as <u>t</u>ype drop-down box, and click <u>S</u>ave.

The Animation Quality Versus Output Size window, shown in Figure 2-12, appears.

Figure 2-12: You balance animation quality with file size to optimize your animated effect.

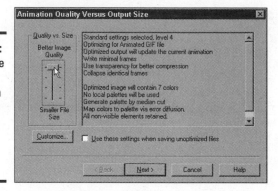

13. Drag the bar shown in Figure 2-12 according to whether you want the best-quality animation possible (the top of the bar) or the smallest possible file size (the bottom of the bar). Then click <u>N</u>ext.

The Optimization Progress dialog box appears.

14. Click <u>N</u>ext to continue.

The Optimization Preview dialog box appears.

15. Click <u>N</u>ext to continue.

The Optimization Results dialog box appears.

16. Click Finish.

Animation Shop saves the animation to the filename and directory you specified in Step 12.

To create a banner ad quickly and easily, choose File⇨Banner Wizard. (A *banner ad* is a standard-sized animated effect that typically incorporates text with motion.)

Editing your animated effect

You can add any of several visual effects to make your animated effect. Three basic types of effects exist:

✦ **Stretching or rotating individual images in your animation:** Choose Effects⇨Insert Image Effect and select any of the effects you see in the Effect drop-down box that appears in the Insert Image Effect dialog box. You see a preview of the effect you choose appear in the Effect section of the Insert Image Effect dialog box.

Click OK after you finish. Then choose Effects⇨Apply Image Effect to apply the effect to your animation file. To view your handiwork, choose View⇨Animation.

✦ **Wiping or dissolving the transitions between individual images:** Choose Effects⇨Insert Image Transition to display the Insert Image Transition window. Select a transition effect from the Effect drop-down box to preview the effect in the Transition area of the Insert Image Transition window.

Click OK after you finish.

✦ **Putting text in your animation:** Choose Effects⇨Insert Text Effect. Type the text you want to add to your animation in the Define Text field and select any of the effects you see in the Effect drop-down box that appears in the Insert Text Effect dialog box. You see a preview of the effect in the Effect section of the Insert Text Effect dialog box.

Click OK after you finish. Then choose Effects⇨Apply Text Effect to apply the effect to your animation file. To view your handiwork, choose View⇨Animation.

Optimizing your animated effect

Depending on the number of images and effects you add to your animation, you may find you end up with a very large file. Because keeping file size to a minimum is important on the Web, you may want to optimize your animation file — that is, choose to tweak the quality of the effect in order to reduce the file size.

Saving an animation file in Animation Shop automatically optimizes the saved file. To optimize an existing file (one you created with another program, perhaps, or got from a friend), choose File⇨Optimization Wizard.

Finding Media Files

If you want to add audio, video, or animated effects to your Web pages but don't want to create them yourself, you may be able to find what you want online. Many sources of stock media files exist on the Web. Most charge, although some offer free samples. Here are a few places to begin your online search for the perfect media file:

- ✦ **Eyewire** (`www.eyewire.com`): illustrations, photos, clip art audio, and video
- ✦ **Media Builder's Animation Factory** (`www.animfactory.com`): free and fee graphics and animations
- ✦ **ArtBeats WebStock** (`www.artbeats.com/artbeatswebtools/`): audio and video clips
- ✦ **Yahoo! Multimedia Guide** (`dir.yahoo.com/Computers_and_Internet/ multimedia`): directory listing includes links to graphics, audio, video, animations, and more

Adding Media Files to Your Web Page

When it comes to adding media files to your Web pages, you have two options. You can add a link to your media file, or you can embed your media file directly into your Web pages.

Adding a link to a media file

A simple and relatively trouble-free way to include audio, video, and animations on a Web page is to link the page to the media file. Users can select the link if they want to hear or view the clip (and not be forced to endure the clip if they're not in the mood). This selection opens a player outside the browser where the user can control the playback of the file.

To create a link to a media file, you use the HTMl `<A>...</A>` tags as follows:

```
<A HREF="mySong.ram">Click here to listen to my
song</A>
```

The preceding HTML code creates a link to the streaming audio RealAudio file `mySong.ram` file.

As you may know if you've read through the preceding "Creating Streaming Audio Files," RealAudio audio filenames contain the `.rm` extension. However, to create a link to a RealAudio file, you must link to a `.ram` file. Files with `.ram` extensions are special controller files, automatically created by the

RealProducer wizard, which pass the .rm file to the RealAudio player when a user clicks the link. For more information on Real file formats, take a look at the following sidebar, "RealMedia file formats."

For more information on linking in HTML, check out Book 2, Chapter 3.

 RealProducer Basic can generate the HTML code necessary to create a link to a media file. Choose Tools⇔Create Web Page and select Pop-up Player (Recommended) from the Playback Method window that appears; then follow the instructions on the remaining windows. RealPlayer Basic generates an HTML file containing the code necessary to link to your media file.

Embedding a media file

Another option for adding a media file to your Web page is to embed the playback controls directly into the page. (You can also embed invisible playback controls into a Web page. Doing so lets you create a Web pages with background sound or movement that plays automatically.)

You use either the HTML <OBJECT> or <EMBED> tags to embed a media file into a Web page. Because the attributes you must specify for the <OBJECT> and <EMBED> tags are fairly lengthy, complex, and closely tied to the specific media player you expect your site visitors to use, the best way to embed a streaming media file into your Web page is to let the media file creation tool you use generate the HTML code for you.

RealMedia file formats

In this chapter you see examples of creating audio and video files using tools from RealNetworks. The file formats created by RealNetworks are very popular; but because they span audio, video, audio-plus-video, and animation, they can be confusing. Here's a quick rundown of the formats you work with in RealMedia:

RealMedia File Format	Extensions	Function
Audio, video, animation files	.rm, .ra, .rp, .rt, .swf	Media file saved in the format required for RealPlayer playback
Metafile for linked media	.ram	The file that launches the independent RealPlayer
Metafile for embedded media	.rpm	The file that launches the RealPlayer plugin

Animated GIFs (such as the one I demonstrate how to create in the section, "Creating an Animated Effect," earlier in this chapter) are exceptions to the rule when it comes to embedding. Instead of using the <OBJECT> or <EMBED> tags, you use the <IMG> tag to embed an animated GIF in your Web page. For more information on using the <IMG> tag, see Book 2 (HTML), Chapter 4.

For example, to create HTML code that embeds an audio file using RealProducer Basic, follow these steps:

1. **Choose Tools⇨Create Web Page.**

   The Media File window appears.

2. **Type the name of the streaming audio file you want to embed in an HTML file and click Next.**

   The Playback Method window appears.

3. **Select Embedded Player and click Next.**

   The Player Control Layout window appears.

4. **Select the playback controls you want to embed on your Web page. (To create an embedded audio file that plays in the background and starts automatically, select Banner Ad. Then click Next and follow the instructions on the remaining windows.**

   RealPlayer Basic generates an HTML file containing the code necessary to embed your streaming audio file.

Other Web design tools, such as Dreamweaver, also generate the HTML code necessary for you to embed media files. For details on embedding media files into your Web pages using Dreamweaver, see Book 4, Chapter 5.

Chapter 3:
Getting to Know Java

In This Chapter

▸ Using Java-related HTML syntax

▸ Understanding applet security

*J*ava is a powerful object-oriented programming language you can use to develop:

✦ Standalone software *applications*, just as you can with any other programming language.

✦ *Java applets*, which are special applications that you embed inside Web pages. When users download a Web page that contains a Java applet, that applet is loaded onto their machines right along with the HTML code for the Web page. Java applets execute locally, right inside users' Web browsers. (Both Internet Explorer and Netscape Navigator provide support for running Java applets.)

In this chapter, I introduce you to the basic stuff you need to know to work with Java: specifically, how to incorporate Java applets into your Web pages using HTML tags. Because security is an important part of any Web-based development effort (including creating and using Java applets), I also give you the low-down on Java security.

Java-Related HTML Syntax

You use the HTML APPLET tag to embed Java applets in Web pages.

The World Wide Web Consortium — the good folks who define the HTML specifications — have *deprecated* the APPLET tag, which means they've suggested that browsers begin providing support for embedded applets (and other types of multimedia, such as plug-ins) through the OBJECT tag instead of the APPLET tag. However, support for the OBJECT tag has been slow to come. As I write this, only the latest version of Internet Explorer supports embedding applets with the OBJECT tag (which means that using the OBJECT tag to embed applets prevents users running any browser but the latest version of Internet Explorer from seeing that applet). So while in the future you may use the OBJECT tag to embed applets in Web pages, for now you can keep using the APPLET tag. For detailed information on the OBJECT tag, visit www.w3.org/TR/1999/REC-html401-19991224/struct/objects.html.

In this chapter, I show you the syntax for the APPLET tag, including an explanation of each tag element. The optional elements appear in regular typeface, and element values you must supply appear in italics. Mandatory elements appear in bold.

As a reminder, tags are HTML elements that appear after a less-than (<) character. Attributes are other elements that reside inside the less-than and greater-than characters (<>). Some attributes are mandatory. You understand why they are mandatory when you see them.

Looking at the complete APPLET tag syntax

Here is the complete syntax for the APPLET tag, followed by an in-depth look at each of the APPLET tag's attributes and a bare-bones example of the APPLET tag in action:

```
<APPLET
        CODEBASE = "codebaseURL"
        ARCHIVES = "archivesList"
        CODE = "appletFile" ...or... OBJECT = "serializedApplet"
        ALT = "alternateText"
        NAME = "appletInstanceName"
        WIDTH = "pixels"
        HEIGHT = "pixels"
        ALIGN = "alignment"
        VSPACE = "pixels"
        HSPACE = "pixels"
>
<PARAM NAME = "appletAttribute1" VALUE = "value">
<PARAM NAME = "appletAttribute2" VALUE = "value">
. . .
alternateHTML
</APPLET>
```

As you see in the HTML syntax above, the only required attributes associated with the APPLET tag are CODE, WIDTH, and HEIGHT. Read on for details about these and all the other, optional attributes.

CODEBASE = "codebaseURL"

This optional attribute specifies the base URL of the applet — the directory on the server that contains the applet's code. If you don't specify the CODEBASE attribute, the Web page's URL is used. You use CODEBASE = codebaseURL only when the applet does not reside in the same directory as the HTML file.

ARCHIVES = "archivesList"

ARCHIVES = archivesList is an optional attribute that describes one or more archives containing classes and other resources (images and sound, for example) that will be "preloaded." Archives provide a way of reducing download time.

CODE = "appletFile"

CODE = appletFile specifies the name of the compiled applet file you want to embed (the .class file). This file is relative to the CODEBASE base URL of the applet. Either CODE or OBJECT (see below) must be defined for every APPLET tag.

OBJECT = "serializedApplet"

This attribute specifies the name of a file containing a serialized representation of an applet. (Serialized files are non-executable files that have been "flattened" — in other words, reformatted and optimized for storing on disk and transferring across networks.) You must specify a value for either the CODE attribute (see above) or the OBJECT attribute. The serialized applet will be deserialized when it is downloaded. The applet's init() method will not be invoked, but its start() method will. This differs from the CODE attribute, in which the applet's init() method is called before the start() method. Attributes valid when the original object was serialized are not restored.

ALT = "alternateText"

This optional attribute specifies any text that should be displayed if the browser understands the APPLET tag but can't run Java applets. It's like the ALT attribute associated with an IMG tag, which you may be familiar with if you work with HTML.

NAME = "appletInstanceName"

This optional attribute specifies a name for the applet instance, which makes it possible for scripting code and other applets on the page to find (and communicate with) each other. You don't need to use this attribute unless you plan to communicate with an applet.

WIDTH = "pixels" and HEIGHT = "pixels"

These required attributes determine the width and height (in pixels) of the applet display area, not counting any windows or dialog boxes that the applet may create.

ALIGN = "alignment"

This optional attribute specifies the alignment of the applet. The possible values of this attribute are the same as those for the `IMG` tag: `left`, `right`, `top`, `texttop`, `middle`, `absmiddle`, `baseline`, `bottom`, `absbottom`. You can experiment with these values to see which combination works best with your applets.

VSPACE = "pixels" and HSPACE = "pixels"

These optional attributes specify the number of pixels above and below the applet (`VSPACE`) and on either side of the applet (`HSPACE`). You treat these attributes the same way as you do the `IMG` tag's `VSPACE` and `HSPACE` attributes.

The Applet parameter tag

You use the following syntax to specify one or more (optional) applet-specific parameters:

```
<PARAM NAME = "appletAttribute1" VALUE = "value">
<PARAM NAME = "appletAttribute2" VALUE = "value">
 . . .
```

Applets can retrieve their parameters with the `getParameter()` method. Remember that `PARAM` tags can appear only in between `<APPLET>` and `</APPLET>` tags. Also note that `PARAM NAME` attributes should be unique.

How do you know if you need to specify a parameter (or two or three) for any given applet? Simple: the creator of the applet tells you. Whether you download a free applet or purchase a commercial applet, the developer who created the applet describes the applet's specifications, or *specs* — how many parameters and what their names are; what methods the applet supports and how to call those methods; and so on.

alternate HTML

Java-enabled browsers ignore all other HTML tags that appear between the `<APPLET>` and `</APPLET>` tags. Non-Java-enabled browsers, however, ignore all the Java-related tags (because they don't understand the tags) and display any additional HTML tags. Adding additional HTML statements for display by non-Java-enabled browsers is good programming practice; you see an example in the next section.

Placing an applet on a page using the APPLET tag

The following HTML code places an applet on a Web page using the `APPLET` tag. The applet lists phone numbers which are stored in a file on the server. The width and height of this applet is 400 by 500 pixels, respectively. An applet parameter specifies the name of a file on the server containing the telephone numbers so that an HTML author can easily change the file name without bothering a Java programmer. Users who aren't running a Java-enabled browser (or who have Java support turned off in their Java-enabled browsers) see a helpful message in place of the Java applet.

```
<APPLET CODE = "PhoneBook.class" WIDTH = "400" HEIGHT =
    "500">
<PARAM NAME = "index" VALUE = "personal.dat">
<CENTER><H1>NOTICE</H1></CENTER>
<B>This page contains a Java applet. Your browser is either
    not capable of executing Java applets or you have that
    option turned off. Please obtain a Java enabled browser
    or turn on execution of Java.</B>
</APPLET>
```

Understanding Applet Security

Some of Java's critics have called applets a laboratory for viruses. Think of some of the obvious hacks that an unscrupulous Java programmer could perpetrate, these critics say: retrieving password files, deleting files, filling an unsuspecting surfer's hard drive with useless data, compromising a firewall. Yikes!

Fortunately, none of these security breaches (including other, more subtle hacks) is possible because untrusted applets — applets that are not digitally signed by a trusted source — are restricted by applet security. If applet security were not as tight as it is, Java would have died before it ever saw its first Web server.

Basically, this is how digital certificates work: imagine that Company X applies for, receives, and installs a digital certificate from a digital certificate authority, such as Verisign, Inc. (www.verisign.com). This certificate — software that uses a public key obtained separately at runtime from the granting certificate authority — identifies Company X's applets as originating from Company X's Web server. When users begin to download an applet, they're automatically informed (via their browsers) that Company X is on file with the digital certificate authority; then they're given the option of downloading the applet or banning it outright from their browsers.

An applet must overcome several hurdles before it can be executed on a remote machine. The class loader, the security manager, and the virtual machine itself (all of which are implemented in a Java-supporting Web browser) are what allow good to triumph over evil, order over chaos, the very survival of humanity! Well, maybe not the survival of humanity, but you get the picture.

The following list details operations that untrusted applets *can't* perform:

✦ Access the local file system, including reading, writing, deleting, renaming, or obtaining file information

✦ Execute native code on the local machine

✦ Create a network connection to any computer other than the machine from which the applet was loaded

✦ Listen for or accept socket connections from any port (in other words, transmit or accept data from some other computer)

✦ Create a frame or dialog box without a visible warning indicating the untrusted nature of the applet that created the frame or dialog box

✦ Define system properties

✦ Invoke `System.exit ()` (in other words, shut down the user's machine)

✦ Load dynamic Java class libraries using `load()` or `loadLibrary ()` (in other words, load and run other, malicious applets under the covers)

✦ Create or manipulate any thread that is not part of the same thread-group as the applet itself

✦ Create a `ClassLoader` or `SecurityManager` object (objects responsible for maintaining Java-related security)

✦ Define any of the "Factories," such as `ContentHandlerFactory`, `SockImplFactory`, or `URLStreamFactory`, responsible for creating data transmission mechanisms and thus bypass built-insecurity

Chapter 4:
Creating Java Applets: The Basics

In This Chapter

✓ Finding out what you need to begin programming Java

✓ Getting acquainted with Java language syntax

If you want to create your own Java applets, you need to be familiar with the Java language and how it works: In other words, you need to understand the Java language syntax. (You also need to know a bit about the Java API, which I describe in Chapter 5 of this book.)

Java is a rich, powerful, complex programming language, so I can't cover the entire Java language syntax in this short chapter. Instead, I describe the tools you need to use to create Java applets, some of which generate Java syntax for you.

I also introduce you to Java syntax basics. These basics come in handy as a quick reference guide when you begin programming in Java.

If you've programmed in C or C++, some sections in this chapter may seem familiar to you. That's because Java syntax is very similar to C and C++.

What You Need to Create Java Applets

If you have a Web browser such as Netscape Navigator or Microsoft Internet Explorer installed on your computer, you can execute Java applets; that's because a Java execution environment called the *Java virtual machine*, or JVM, is built into most Web browsers.

Before you can create Java programs of your own, however, you need more than just a browser. You need to have the following software installed on your computer:

✦ **A copy of the Java development kit.** The Java SDK (which stands for *Software Development Kit*) contains all of the following:

   • the Java class libraries (prebuilt Java *classes*, or APIs) and language support you need to create Java applets

   • the compiler (called `javac`) you need to turn Java source files into bytecode

- a Java runtime environment (called `appletviewer`) you use to turn compiled bytecode into machine language — in other words, to test the applet.

You can download a free copy of the Java 2 SDK, standard edition (the latest Java development kit at the time of this writing) from `java.sun.com/j2se`.

✦ **A text or graphical editor.** All Java programs begin as Java source code, which is plain text you save using the `.java` file extension. So, before you can create a Java program, you need to have a text editor installed on your machine. Depending on your preference, this can be a plain text editor (such as the Notepad application that comes bundled with Windows), a text editor designed specifically for programmers (such as TextPad), or an interactive development environment, or IDE, designed specially for Java programmers. IDEs combine a graphical, drag-and-drop editor with built-in code snippets, a Java compiler, and a code checker. Java development environments help you create Java applets much more quickly than you can by typing Java code into a text editor and compiling that code into executable applet form.

Dispelling the portability myth

One of the characteristics for which Java is often lauded is its ability to run unchanged on computers ranging from tiny handhelds to massive supercomputers; in other words, its portability. (Portability is often referred to as cross-platform capability, because portable code can execute on, or across, many different hardware/software platforms.)

But although it's true that Java strives to be a portable language in theory, if often falls short in practice. Here's why.

Java compilers and interpreters do their best to translate Java source code into bytecode, and bytecode into machine code, respectively. But how they do this is dependent on at least a couple of variables:

The target platform. IBM personal computers, Sun workstations, and Macintosh notebooks are different — period. As in human languages, some things just don't translate. So if you're

trying to accomplish a task using Java that the underlying operating system on one computer just can't handle, it doesn't matter what language you're developing in; you're out of luck.

The developers creating the compilers and interpreters. Different companies create and distribute different Java compilers and interpreters. Sun established a Java standard and makes that standard available to any companies who want to license it; but human nature being what it is, the end result — intentional or not — is that differences exist between Java compilers and runtime implementations.

The upshot? Whereas creating cross-platform programs using Java is easier than probably any other language out there, it's not a given. In other words, programming in Java doesn't guarantee portability; it just makes creating portable programs easier.

One popular Java IDE is VisualCafe, a trial copy of which you find on the companion CD.

From Source to Executable Code: A Look at the Applet Development Life Cycle

Good Java programming practice demands that you create an applet file, test it, and make changes as necessary until your applet executes error-free. Specifically, after you have the Java development tools I describe in the previous section installed on your computer, you must:

1. **Create an applet source file.** You can use the editor of your choice to create a Java applet source file; just be sure to and save that file using the .java extension. For example:

   ```
   myFirstProgram.java
   ```

2. **Compile the source file.** You compile a Java source file using the javac compiler. For example:

   ```
   javac myFirstProgram.java
   ```

   The compiler generates a new (compiled) file bearing the same filename, only with a .class file extension instead of the .java extension, like this:

   ```
   yourFirstProgram.class
   ```

3. **Execute, or test, the compiled file.** To test a compiled applet, you must create an HTML file and include the <APPLET> tag I describe in Chapter 3 to incorporate your compiled applet into a Web page. Then you must load that HTML file into a Java-supporting Web browser or into the special applet testing utility called appletviewer that comes with the Java SDK. For example:

   ```
   appletviewer myFirstProgram
   ```

   (Don't include the .class extension when invoking the appletviewer utility.) Figure 4-1 shows you an example of a simple Java applet executing inside the appletviewer utility.

Using the appletviewer utility to test your applets rather than testing your applets using a Java-supporting Web browser is a good idea. appletviewer displays a single navigation button, called Applet (which you see in Figure 4-1) that, when clicked, allows you to reload, start, stop, and otherwise test, or *exercise*, your applet.

Figure 4-1:
You can use the applet-viewer utility that comes bundled with the Java SDK to test your Java applets.

Java Language Syntax: The Highlights

You create Java source files by stringing together Java *statements*. A Java statement is analogous to an English statement: Both are complete, meaningful thoughts expressed using agreed-upon words and punctuation, arranged and ordered using agreed-upon syntax rules.

The following sections describe four important components of Java syntax: comments, operators, primitive data types, and reserved keywords.

This chapter doesn't provide you with an exhaustive description of Java syntax. For a complete rundown of Java syntax, surf to the Sun Microsystem online Java language reference, which you can find at java.sun.com/docs/ books/jls/second_edition/html/j.title.doc.html.

Looking at a syntax example

Before you dive into Java syntax, take a look at the following simple Java applet source file to get a feel for the structure of a typical Java statement. The file, FirstApplet..java, doesn't accept input or do any processing; all it does — after you compile it using the javac compiler and test it using the appletviewer applet testing utility, as described in the preceding section — is display This is my first Java applet! on the user's screen, (refer to Figure 4-1).

```
/* FirstApplet.java */
// This is a simple Java applet that
// displays a single line of text on the screen.

import javax.swing.JApplet;
import java.awt.Graphics;
```

```
public class FirstApplet extends JApplet {
    public void paint (Graphics g) {
        g.drawString("This is my first Java applet!", 25,
            25);
    }
}
```

As you look at the preceding Java applet code, pay particular attention to two very common Java syntax constructs:

✦ **import statements.** The import statements you see in the third and fourth lines of the code listing *import*, or include, two Java classes that come with the Java SDK: the JApplet class, and the Graphics class. (java.swing and java.awt are called *class libraries* because they contain many different classes each, not just the JApplet and Graphics classes, respectively; they are also referred to as application programming interfaces, or *APIs*.)

Import statements make all the capabilities of the imported classes available to you, the Java developer. For example, as shown in the code above, you can use the drawString() method (a *method* is a kind of function associated with a particular class) to display the "This is my first Java applet!" message on the screen *after* you import the Graphics class, which implements the drawString() method.

✦ **extends keyword.** The statement beginning with the public keyword and containing the extends keyword embodies Java's object-oriented approach. The previous Java code creates a new class called FirstApplet that extends, or derives from, a pre-built class called JApplet. What this means is that FirstApplet automatically contains all of the capabilities and behaviors of JApplet — all without your having to write a lick of code other than the statement containing the extends keyword!

I introduce you to the prebuilt classes and class libraries you can import into your Java applet files (and extend to create your own customized applets) in Chapter 5 of this book.

Commenting about comments

You use *comments* to insert human-readable messages in your Java code. As you see in the code listing in the previous section, properly worded comments can help a casual reader understand the purpose of a Java applet without having to know anything at all about Java syntax.

Java supports the same comments available in C and C++ (/*, */, and /, which you see in the code listing in the previous section), as well as special *javadoc comments*.

The compiler treats javadoc comments the same as any other comment; however, you can also extract these comments by using the `javadoc` tool. The `javadoc` tool, which comes free with the Java 2 SDK available from Sun Microsymstems (`java.sun.com/j2se`), automatically recognizes and pulls out, or *parses*, class, interface, method, and variable declarations from your javadoc comments and produces reference documentation in HTML format.

The `javadoc` tool is an extremely useful tool that creates consistent and professional-looking documentation for all your code. Because the comments are embedded in the actual source code, you can ensure that all your documentation is always up to date. Whenever the source code is modified, simply run `javadoc` again to produce a new set of documentation.

Constructing javadoc comments

You can place javadoc comments in your code by starting the comment with `/**` and ending the comment with `*/`. You must place javadoc comments immediately before a class, method, or variable declaration to allow you to supply documentation with a description.

The first sentence of each javadoc comment should be a summary sentence containing a concise but complete description of the item being discussed. This initial summary sentence ends at the first period, which is followed by a blank, tab, line terminator, or first `javadoc` tag.

The `javadoc` tool produces the documentation as HTML format files that can be viewed in any Web browser. You may include HTML tags in your javadoc comments, but you should not include HTML structural tags such as `<H1>` or `<HR>`. Because the documentation is in HTML format, you can add HTML tags to your comments that allow you to format the documentation.

Using javadoc tags

`javadoc` parses special tags, which begin with the at sign character (@). `javadoc` recognizes these special tags when they are embedded within a javadoc comment; the tags allow additional formatting for the documentation. You can also use them to add information, such as the author name and version number.

If you want your javadoc comment to contain such tags, you must place the tags on the first line of the comment. If you use more than one tag with the same name, you should put the tags together on subsequent lines so that javadoc can tell where the list ends.

Table 4-1 lists the available tags for javadoc.

Table 4-1	Javadoc Tags
Tag	*Function*
@see classname and @see classname(#)method-name	Adds a hyperlinked See Also entry to the class. You also can use the hash mark character (#) to separate the name of a class from the name of one of its fields, methods, or constructors. You can select an overloaded method or constructor by including a parenthesized list of argument types after the method or constructor name. A javadoc comment may contain more than one @see tag, which can appear before class, method, and variable definitions.
@version version-text	Adds a Version: entry to the documentation. A javadoc comment can contain only one @version tag, which can appear only before a class definition. Make use of any version entry you like to help you identify or describe the code.
@author name-text	Adds an Author: entry to the documentation. A javadoc comment may contain multiple @author tags, which can appear only before a class definition.
@param parameter- name description	Adds the specified parameter and description to the Parameters: section of the documentation. You can describe all input parameters to the method. This tag can be used only before a method definition. If you're feeling verbose, you can continue the description on the next line.
@return description	Adds a Returns: section, which contains the specified description of the return value. This tag describes the value of the method, and you can use it only before a method definition.
@exception fully-qualified-class-name description	Adds a Throws: entry, which contains the name of the exception that may be thrown by the method. The exception is automatically linked to its class documentation. You can use this tag only before a method definition.

Here's an example of a javadoc comment you could place before a class definition:

```
/**
* A class representing an improved Date.
* For example:
* <pre>
*       MyDate today = new MyDate();
* </pre>
*
* @see        util.Date
* @version    2.1 Feb 26, 1997
* @author     Steve Lockwood
* @author     Madhu Siddalingaiah
```

```
*/
class MyDate extends Date {
// Body of class not shown
}
```

The following example demonstrates placing a javadoc comment before a method definition.

```
/**
* Converts a String value to a double
* For example:
* <pre>
*               double dvalue = stringToDouble(strvalue);
* </pre>
*
* @param        strvalue the String to convert
* @return   the converted double value
*/
public double stringToDouble (String strvalue) {
               // Method body not shown
}
```

Figure 4-2 shows the HTML page that you could generate using javadoc from the preceding two javadoc comment examples:

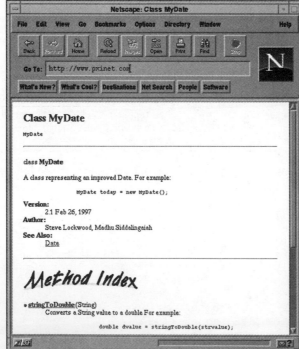

Figure 4-2: javadoc-generated HTML comments help you create consistent, professional-looking documentation.

Dealing with operators

If you're like most programmers, you find you use *operators* frequently when you create Java applets (or any other kind of program, for that matter.) Operators let you perform operations on data; for example, using the correct operator, you can add to a piece of data, subtract from a piece of data, inspect a piece of data to see if it meets a certain criterion, and so forth.

Table 4-2 lists all the operators Java supports in order of highest precedence to lowest. (Like regular math rules, the Java compiler evaluates operators using a standard order of precedence.)

Table 4-2	Java Operators in Order of Precedence (Lowest to Highest)		
Precedence	*Operator*	*Type(s)*	*Operation Performed*
1	++	Arithmetic	Pre or post increment
	-	Arithmetic	Pre or post increment
	+,-	Arithmetic	Unary plus and unary minus
	~	Integral	Bitwise complement
	!	Boolean	Logical complement
	(type)	Any	Cast
2	*,/,%	Arithmetic	Multiplication, division, and remainder
3	+,-	Arithmetic	Addition and subtraction
	+	String	String concatenation
4	<<	Integral	Left shift
	>>	Integral	Arithmetic right shift
	>>>	Integral	Logical right shift
5	<, <=	Arithmetic	Less than and less than or equal to
	>, >=	Arithmetic	Greater than and greater than or equal to
	instanceof	Object	Type comparison
6	==	Primitive	Equal
	!=	Primitive	Not equal
	==	Object	Equal
	!=	Object	Not equal
7	&	Integral	Bitwise AND
	&	Integral	Logical AND
8	^	Integral	Bitwise XOR
	^^	Boolean	Boolean XOR

(continued)

Table 4-2 *(continued)*

Precedence	Operator	Type (s)	Operation Performed
9	|	Integral	Bitwise OR
	|	Integral	Logical OR
10	&&	Boolean	Conditional AND
11	||	Boolean	Conditional OR
12	?:	Boolean, any	Conditional (ternary)
13	=,*=,/=,%=,+=,-=,<<=, >>=,>>>=,&=.^=,|=	Variable, any	Assignment with operator

For more information about operators, see *Java Programming For Dummies*, by David Koosis and Donald J. Koosis.

Referencing primitive data types

When you specify a data type in Java, you tell the Java compiler how to store a piece of data. For example, you may want to store data as a single character, a string of text, or an integer, all three of which are considered data types.

A *primitive data type* is a data type for which support is built into a language. (If you create your own data type for a particular applet — for example, the "customer identification number" data type — that new data type is not considered primitive because support for it isn't built directly into the Java language.)

Java supports the eight different primitive data types shown in Table 4-3.

The size of each data type isn't dependent on the execution environment as it is in other languages, such as C.

Table 4-3	Java-Supported Data Types			
Type	(Description)	Size	Default	Min Value/Max Value
boolean	(True or false)	1 bit	False	
char	(Unicode character)	16 bits	\u000	\u000 \uFFF
byte	(Signed integer)	8 bits	0	-128/127
short	(Signed integer)	16 bits	0	-32768/32767
int	(Signed integer)	32 bits	0	-2147483648/2147483647
long	(Signed integer)	64 bits	0	-9223372036854775808/ 9223372036854775807
float	(IEEE 754 floating-point)	32 bits	0.0	+/-3.40282347E+38/ +/-1.40239846E-45
double	(IEEE 754 floating-point)	64 bits	0.0	+/-1.79769313486231570E+308/ +/-4.94065645841246544E-324

Avoiding reserved keywords

Java reserves many words for various uses. You can't use any of these words as *variable* names (a variable is a programmer-defined data place-holder) , *method* names (a method name is the name of a function associated with a Java class), or any other identifier. For example, you can't declare a variable called `default`; you'd need to declare the variable using another name, like `defaultValue`.

Following are all the Java reserved keywords.

Items marked by an asterisk (*) — `byvalue`, `cast`, `const`, `future`, `generic`, `goto`, `inner`, `operator`, `outer`, `rest`, and `var` — are reserved but currently not used.

Reserved Keywords	Reserved Keywords	Reserved Keywords
abstract	float	protected
boolean	for	public
break	future*	rest*
byte	generic*	return
byvalue*	goto*	short
case	if	static
cast*	implements	super
catch	import	switch
char	inner*	synchronized
class	instanceof	this
const*	int	throw
continue	interface	throws
default	long	transient
do	native	try
double	new	var*
else	null	void
extends	operator*	true
false	outer*	volatile
final	package	while
finally	private	

Chapter 5:
The Java Core API

In This Chapter

✔ Getting acquainted with the Java API

✔ Understanding how to use the Java API to create Java applets

✔ Taking a peek at the core Java API

✔ Finding out where to get the latest Java API documentation

The whole point of an object-oriented language like Java is to prevent programmers from having to reinvent the wheel; in other words, to provide prebuilt components — called *classes* in Java parlance — which developers can combine, extend, and customize to create their own applets.

Sun Microsystems, the creators of the Java programming language, thoughtfully created the Java *Application Programming Interface,* or API, for that very reason.

The Java API represents all of the built-in classes you can use to construct your Java applets. You can choose from classes devoted to graphical user interface development, Java security, Java-to-database interaction, and much, much more. In this chapter, I introduce you to the Java *core* API — the API you find yourself using most often to create your Java applets — and show you where to find the latest documentation for the entire Java API.

What Is an API?

The Java API, or Application Programming Interface, consists of two separate items:

✦ **The API itself.** The Java API, which comes with the Java 2 SDK, is implemented as a collection of compiled Java *classes*, or object templates, packaged into neat little categories called *packages*. (Packages are sometimes referred to as *class libraries*). After you download the Java 2 SDK to your computer, you can begin to create Java applet source files that reference and build on the classes implemented in the API.

✦ **API documentation.** The Java API documentation is a monstrous document that describes all the classes implemented in the API, including nitty-gritty specifics such as the signature of each method contained in each class. (A *signature* is a complete description of a method, including the method name, a description of how you must call the method, and the value that the method returns, if any.)

To help you understand how the API relates to the API documentation, take a look at the following Java code, paying special attention to the bolded section:

```
import javax.swing.JApplet;
import java.awt.Graphics;

public class FirstApplet extends JApplet {
    public void paint (Graphics g) {
        g.drawString("This is my first Java applet!", 25,
            25);
    }
}
```

The first two lines in the preceding code import a class called JApplet located inside the javax.swing package, and a class called Graphics class located inside the java.awt package, respectively.

The third line defines a brand new class, called FirstApplet, which extends the built-in JApplet class. To customize the way this applet behaves, the fourth line redefines one of the methods associated with JApplet: the paint() method. (All Java-supporting browsers automatically invoke the paint() method associated with an applet to paint, or display, that applet on a Web page. When they do, they pass the paint() method an instance of the Graphics class.)

The preceding bolded line of code redefines the drawString() method associated with the Graphics class. When a Java-supporting browser attempts to display the FirstApplet applet on a Web page, the drawString() method causes the text string This is my first Java applet! to appear in a box 25 pixels down from the top-left-hand corner of the screen and 25 pixels to the right of the top-left-hand corner of the screen.

If you're not already familiar with Java programming (or a similar programming language, such as C++), you may find the above description a bit daunting. Programming in Java *can* be challenging; after all, Java is a rich, full-featured, powerful language, and the API contains literally hundreds of classes. However, with this reference book and a good how-to guide (such as *Java: How to Program,* by Deitel and Deitel, Prentice Hall) at your side, you may find you catch on sooner than you think.

The questions that immediately leap to mind (if you're like me) are:

✦ How do you know which classes to import — and which methods of those classes to redefine, or *override,* to customize your applet the way you want?

✦ How do you figure out how to override a particular method?

The answers to these questions can be found in the API documentation, which you find online by pointing your browser at `java.sun.com`. Take a peek at Figures 5-1 and 5-2 to see what I mean.

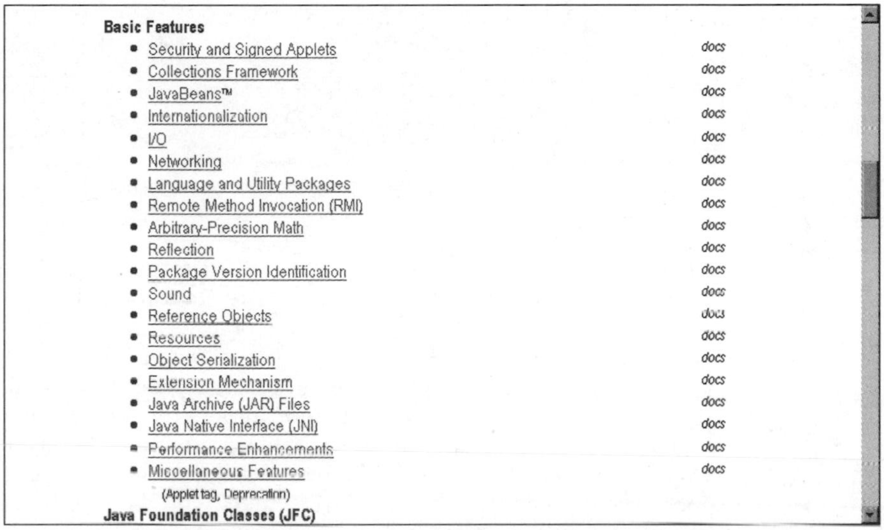

Figure 5-1:
You can find complete documentation for the Java API online at java.sun.com.

Basic Features
- Security and Signed Applets   *docs*
- Collections Framework   *docs*
- JavaBeans™   *docs*
- Internationalization   *docs*
- I/O   *docs*
- Networking   *docs*
- Language and Utility Packages   *docs*
- Remote Method Invocation (RMI)   *docs*
- Arbitrary-Precision Math   *docs*
- Reflection   *docs*
- Package Version Identification   *docs*
- Sound   *docs*
- Reference Objects   *docs*
- Resources   *docs*
- Object Serialization   *docs*
- Extension Mechanism   *docs*
- Java Archive (JAR) Files   *docs*
- Java Native Interface (JNI)   *docs*
- Performance Enhancements   *docs*
- Miscellaneous Features   *docs*
   (Applet tag, Deprecation)
Java Foundation Classes (JFC)

In Figure 5-1, you see just one of the many documents that Sun Microsystems makes available online. These documents describe every aspect of the Java programming language, as well as every method associated with every class implemented in the Java API.

Figure 5-2 shows you an example of "drilling down" from the broad list of topics shown in Figure 5-1 to find the specific information you need to override a method.

Packages	
java.applet	

(screenshot of Java API documentation three-frame display)

```
Packages
java.applet
java.awt
java.awt.color
java.awt.datatransfer
java.awt.dnd
java.awt.event

Event
EventQueue
FileDialog
FlowLayout
Font
FontMetrics
Frame
GradientPaint
Graphics
Graphics2D
GraphicsConfigTempl
GraphicsConfiguration
GraphicsDevice
GraphicsEnvironment
GridBagConstraints
GridBagLayout
```

abstract void **drawPolyline**(int[] xPoints, int[] yPoints, int nPoints)
      Draws a sequence of connected lines defined by arrays of *x* and *y* coordinates.

void **drawRect**(int x, int y, int width, int height)
      Draws the outline of the specified rectangle.

abstract void **drawRoundRect**(int x, int y, int width, int height, int arcWidth, int arcHeight)
      Draws an outlined round-cornered rectangle using this graphics context's current color.

abstract void **drawString**(AttributedCharacterIterator iterator, int x, int y)
      Draws the text given by the specified iterator, using this graphics context's current color.

abstract void **drawString**(String str, int x, int y)
      Draws the text given by the specified string, using this graphics context's current font and color.

void **fill3DRect**(int x, int y, int width, int height, boolean raised)
      Paints a 3-D highlighted rectangle filled with the current color.

abstract void **fillArc**(int x, int y, int width, int height, int startAngle, int arcAngle)
      Fills a circular or elliptical arc covering the specified rectangle.

Figure 5-2:
After you know what package contains the kinds of classes you want, you can drill down to specific method signatures.

In the three-frame display shown in Figure 5-2, you see the Java awt package listed in the upper-left frame; the Graphics class listed in the lower-left frame; and the signature, or description, of how you use the drawString() method in the right frame.

As you may have guessed, writing Java applets by hand using nothing more than a text editor, the Java SDK, and the API documentation, is mighty challenging — especially if you don't have a background in computer science. Most programmers (including programmers who *do* have backgrounds in computer science) prefer, instead, to use a graphical Java development environment such as Borland JBuilder or VisualCafe (a copy of which you find on the companion CD). These Java tools hide some of the complexity of the Java API, enabling you to design applets and generate Java applet code by simply pointing and clicking.

The Java Core API

A handful of API packages contain implementations of classes that are so basic to Java development that programmers refer to them as *core* APIs. I briefly describe these core APIs in the sections that follow.

To customize a Java class, you first *import* the class into your Java applet source code; then you must *override* selected methods associated with the class.

As you skim through the pictures of each package, pay particular attention to the solid and dashed lines that connect some of the classes: these lines show the relationships between the classes of one package, and the classes of another. (When you see these lines, you know you must work with all the packages involved.)

This book can only hold so many pages, so I can't give you details for every core package in the 1.4 Version of Java 2; instead, I give you an overview of the most commonly used packages and how they relate to each other (in other words, the "big picture.") For a full rundown of the Java Core API, including a list of all the classes, methods, variables, and fields contained in each package, visit java.sun.com/j2se/1.4/docs/api/index.html.

The java.applet package

If you're creating a Java applet, you need to take a look at the java.applet package, which contains the Applet class — the superclass of all applets. (A *superclass* is a Java class from which one or more related classes is derived.) Three interfaces are defined in conjunction with the Applet class. (In Java, an *interface* is similar to a class. The difference between the two is that when you extend a class to create your own custom class, you need only override the methods you want to override. When you extend an interface, you must override all the methods that interface defines.)

Figure 5-3 shows a quick sketch of the java.applet class hierarchy:

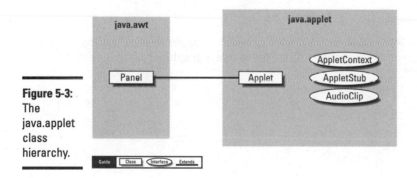

Figure 5-3:
The
java.applet
class
hierarchy.

If you want to create an applet that can run inside a Web browser, extend the Applet class and fill in the init(), start(), stop(), and destroy() methods. Take a look at *Java Programming For Dummies,* by David Koosis and Donald J. Koosis, for details.

The java.awt package

The java.awt package contains classes for developing graphical user interfaces (GUIs). (*awt* stands for Abstract Windowing Toolkit, in case you were wondering.)

Figures 5-4 through 5-6 show a partial class hierarchy of the java.awt package:

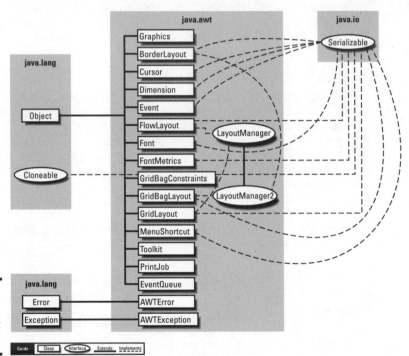

Figure 5-4:
One view of
the java.awt
package.

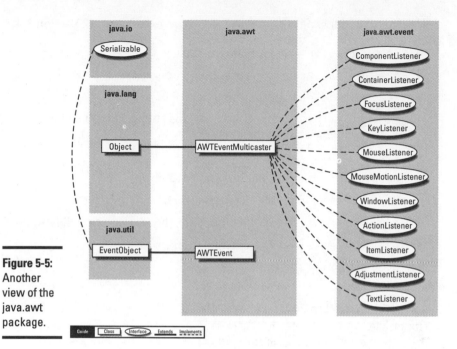

Figure 5-5:
Another
view of the
java.awt
package.

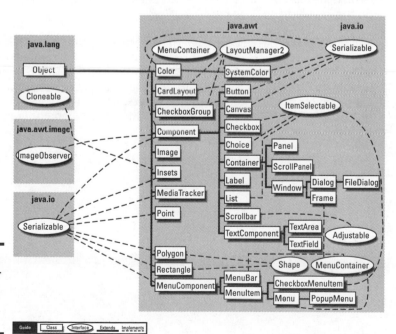

Figure 5-6:
Still another
view of the
java.awt
package.

Note that the following separate awt packages exist in Java 2 Version 1.4:

+ java.awt.color — color manipulation

+ java.awt.datatransfer — clipboard operations

+ java.awt.dnd — drag-and-drop operations

+ java.awt.event — event handling (This subpackage is so important I describe it separately in the next section.)

+ java.awt.font — display fonts

+ java.awt.geom — two-dimensional geometry

+ java.awt.im — input method framework

+ java.awt.im.spi — input methods for the Java Runtime Environment

+ java.awt.image — image manipulation

+ java.awt.print — printing

The java.awt.event package

The classes and interfaces in the java.awt.event package support Java's delegation event model. (An *event model* describes the way a system detects, recognizes, and responds to events — such as a user pressing a key on the keyboard.)

You find three types of objects in this package: events, adapters, and listeners. The events, such as ActionEvent or MouseEvent, contain information about events and are passed to event-handler methods. Adapters, such as WindowAdapter or ComponentAdapter, are abstract classes that you can extend in order to handle events. Listeners, such as MouseMotionListener or ActionListener, are interfaces that you can implement in order to handle events.

Figures 5-7 and 5-8 show the class hierarchy of the java.awt.event package:

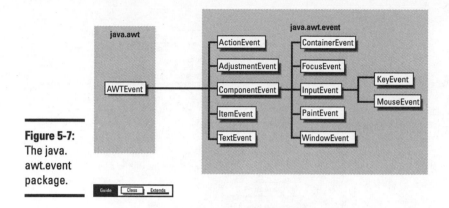

Figure 5-7:
The java.
awt.event
package.

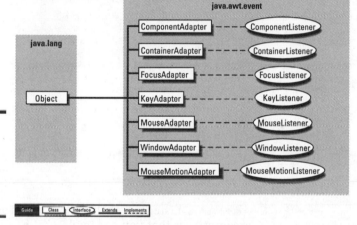

Figure 5-8:
Another
view of the
java.awt.
event
package.

The java.io package

What's a programming language without input/output functions? Not a very useful language, that's what! So here it is: the package that offers everything you ever wanted from an I/O library.

The java.io package looks really complicated, but it's not that bad. If you just want to read and write bytes, the java.io package offers a few simple classes to do just that. I don't mean to imply that the package only accomplishes simple functions: It also offers plenty of sophisticated classes.

Figures 5-9 through 5-11 show the hierarchy diagrams for the java.io package:

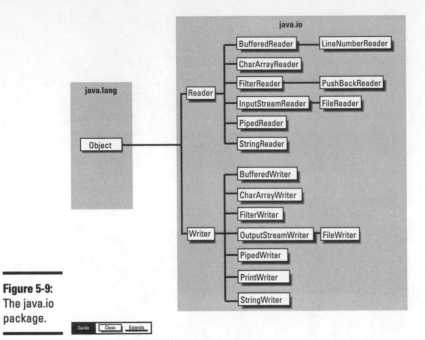

Figure 5-9:
The java.io
package.

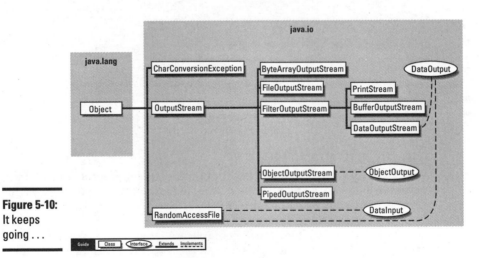

Figure 5-10:
It keeps
going . . .

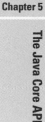

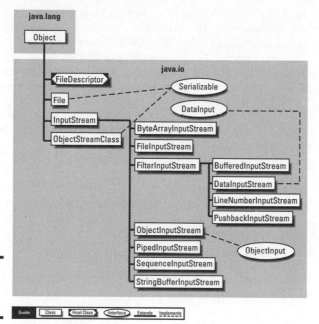

Figure 5-11:
And
going . . .

The java.lang package

The java.lang package contains all the fundamental classes that make up the Java language. This package contains classes that every program, no matter how simple or complex, needs to use. In fact, the java.lang package is the only package that doesn't require an explicit import statement; the classes that make up this package are always available to every Java applet.

In addition, the java.lang package contains the all-important Object and Class classes. Every class in Java must extend another class. If you create a class and do not explicitly extend a class, your class extends Object by default. Object is therefore the superclass of every class in Java. When a class is used, a Class object must be created at run time. Class represents Java classes at run time.

Frequently, you need to represent a value of a primitive type as if it were an object or a reference type. The *wrapper* classes, including Boolean, Byte, Character, Double, Float, Integer, Long, and Short, allow a primitive data type to be stored and referenced as an object, rather than a primitive data type. (You get some built-in goodies with objects — such as the ability to use certain operators — that you don't get when dealing directly with primitive data types.)

A primitive type is always passed to a method by copy, and an object is always passed by reference. The classes in this package are very helpful if you want to pass a primitive value to a method by reference.

Look in the wrapper classes for a number of methods to convert among the primitive types or from a `String`. For example, the `Integer` class contains a `parseInt()` method to convert a `String` to `int`.

The `Math` class provides commonly used mathematical functions, such as sine, cosine, and square root. The classes `String` and `StringBuffer` also provide commonly used operations on character strings.

The classes `ClassLoader`, `Process`, `Runtime`, `SecurityManager`, and `System` provide "system operations" that manage the dynamic loading of classes, creation of external processes, host environment inquiries (such as the time of day), and enforcing security policies.

The `Throwable` class encompasses objects that may be thrown by the throw statement. Subclasses of `Throwable` represent errors and exceptions (see Chapter 6 for more information on Java errors and exceptions).

Figures 5-12 and 5-13 show you the hierarchy of classes defined in the `java.lang` package:

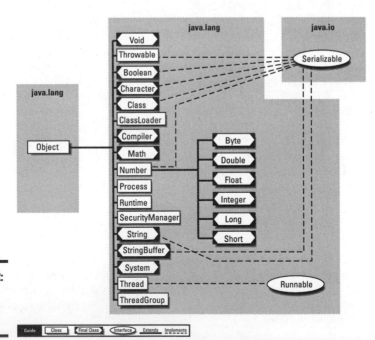

Figure 5-12:
The java.lang package.

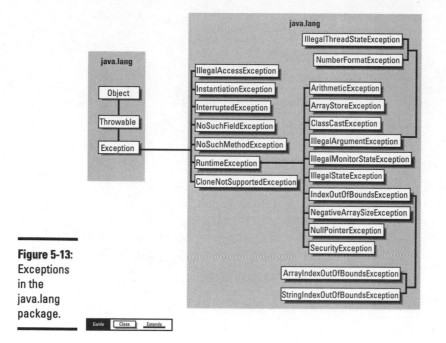

Figure 5-13:
Exceptions
in the
java.lang
package.

The java.net package

The java.net package contains classes that build a strong base for networking. The java.net package supports Transmission Control Protocol (TCP) and User Datagram Protocol (UDP) sockets that you can use to create any type of client/server you desire. In addition, java.net provides specific classes for URL connections and HTTP URL connections, which can take you to locations on the World Wide Web.

Check out the class hierarchy of this package in Figure 5-14:

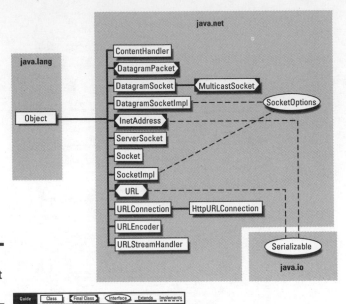

Figure 5-14:
The java.net
package.

The java.sql package

The creators of Java realized the power of using Java to access databases. To tap into that power, they developed a standard structured query language (SQL) database access interface called the JDBC (Java Database Connectivity) API. The JDBC API allows programmers to access SQL databases using object-oriented, platform-independent Java code.

All the classes associated with the JDBC API are grouped together in the java.sql package. Figure 5-15 shows the relationship of all of the classes in the java.sql package:

Using JDBC is not all that difficult. First you obtain a driver to supply the link between the JDBC driver manager and the underlying database. After you install the driver, you can get on with the Java programming!

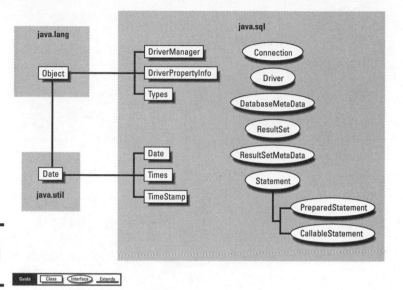

Figure 5-15:
The java.sql
package.

The java.util package

The "utility" classes in this package provide all kinds of useful miscellaneous services. For example, if you need classes to create data structures (such as hashtables), look no further. If you are interested in the date, this package offers a Date class as well as a Calendar class that you may find very helpful.

The java.util package also contains many tools to "internationalize" your Java programs in a snap. The worldwide reach of the Internet demands global software that can be developed independently of the nationality or language of its users, and Java inherently provides internationalization by supporting the Unicode character. (The Unicode character set is the 16-bit superset of ASCII that allows the use of international characters.)

Take a gander at the class hierarchy for java.util, shown in Figure 5-16:

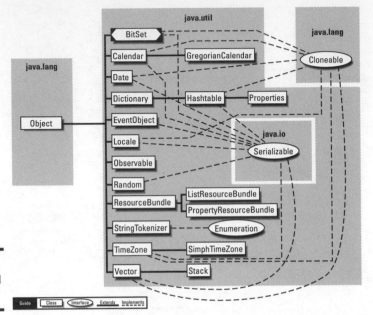

Figure 5-16:
The java.util
package.

If this book included all the details for every core package in the 1.4 Version
of Java 2, you wouldn't be able to lift it! (Not even with a forklift.) If you're
looking for complete, in-depth documentation for the Java Core API, check
out java.sun.com/j2se/1.4/docs/api/index.html.

Chapter 6:
Java Errors and Exceptions

In This Chapter

✔ Understanding Java exceptions

✔ Uncovering errors

Y ou, Java programmer extraordinaire, need to be familiar with core Java errors and exceptions so that you can *catch* and *handle* them. (In other words, so that you can create Java code that recognizes when an unexpected condition occurs and performs some intelligent action — such as displaying an appropriate error message to the user.)

This chapter uses hierarchy diagrams to show you the most common errors and exceptions associated with the Java Core API. The classes listed in this chapter are all subclasses of `java.lang.Error` or `java.lang.Exception`, but these subclasses are part of several different packages as well.

You will find the class hierarchy diagrams very useful tools. The Java compiler forces you to catch all exceptions that are not a subclass of `RunTimeException` or `Error`. From the diagrams, you can easily identify which exceptions you must catch in your Java code.

Figure 6-1, for example, shows `java.io` midway down the figure. Connected to `java.io` by a thin black line you see an exception called `IOException`; connected to that, `EOFException`. What this hierarchy shows you at a glance is that `EOFException` (which happens to be short for *end of file exception*) is derived from `IOException` (a more general kind of exception, relating to input/output), which in turn is thrown by classes in the `java.io` package. Armed with this knowledge, you can guess that you may have to implement an exception handler for `EOFException` if you're working with classes in the `java.io` package.

You may want to catch some of the exceptions defined in subclasses of `RunTimeException` as well, because these errors and exceptions will be fatal if not caught.

Looking at Java Exceptions

Figure 6-1 shows some common exceptions that occur in Java. All the classes in this diagram are subclasses of `java.lang.Exception`, but they show exception classes that are common to all packages.

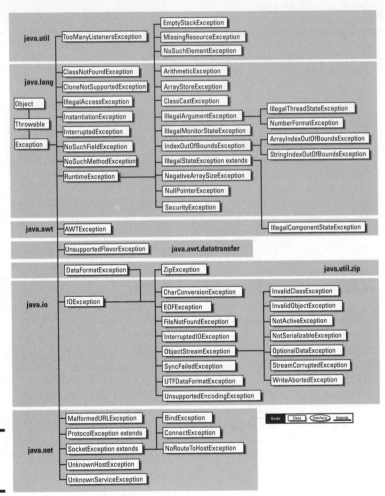

Figure 6-1:
Java
exceptions.

Picking Out Java Errors

Figure 6-2 shows some common errors that occur in Java. All the classes in this diagram are subclasses of java.lang.Error, but they show error classes that are common to all packages.

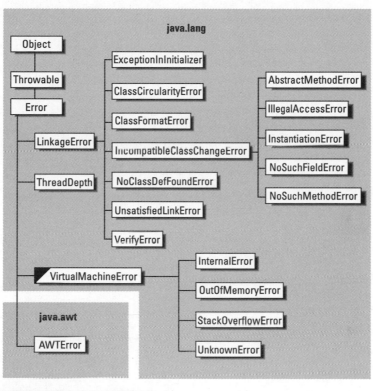

Figure 6-2:
Java errors.

Index

Notes

Book VI

JavaScript

The 5th Wave   By Rich Tennant

MIDTOWN

WHERE'S THE DANG DOOR?!

Website Design Co.

C'mon in!

OUR AWARDS

Contents at a Glance

Chapter 1: JavaScript Syntax and Keywords

In This Chapter

- Exploring JavaScript's role in Web development
- Understanding JavaScript security issues
- Getting acquainted with the document object model
- Unraveling JavaScript syntax and expressions

This chapter is like a JavaScript grammar book, dictionary, and thesaurus all rolled into one. In this chapter, you find the nuts-and-bolts mechanics of writing JavaScript statements — from syntax to keywords, from declaring variables to defining and calling functions. You also find an overview of all the Web page components, called *objects*, you can work with in JavaScript.

A Quick Overview of the JavaScript Scripting Language

Using JavaScript, you can create cool interactive features such as rollovers, clickable images, and smart forms to add to your plain old static HTML pages.

Like all scripting languages, JavaScript is a special kind of programming language designed to give folks easy access to prebuilt components. In the case of JavaScript, those prebuilt components are all the objects that make up a Web page (or, more accurately, a Web *document*): links, images, HTML form elements, browser configuration details, and so on. Together, these objects are referred to as the *document object model*. When you create a JavaScript script, you create lines of JavaScript code that access, change, and perform actions based on one or more of these objects.

Support for JavaScript, including the JavaScript interpreter that executes JavaScript code, is built into two Web browsers: Microsoft Internet Explorer and Netscape Navigator. If you have some kind of text editor and either of these two browsers installed on your computer, you have everything you need to create and run JavaScript scripts.

Web development tools such as Dreamweaver (included on the companion CD) help you begin creating JavaScript scripts quickly and easily — without having to learn nitty-gritty JavaScript programming details.

Technically, there are two versions of the JavaScript language: a client-side version that runs inside Web browsers, and a server-side version that runs inside Netscape Web servers. The client-side version, which is by far the most popular, is the version I describe in this book. If you're interested in finding out more about the server-side version, you can visit `developer.netscape.com/docs/manuals`.

Adding Scripts to HTML Files

You add JavaScript to HTML pages in one of two ways:

✦ By inserting JavaScript statements directly into HTML files: Use the HTML `<SCRIPT>...</SCRIPT>` tags, as shown in the following code:

```
<HTML>
<HEAD>
...
<SCRIPT LANGUAGE="JavaScript">
(Your JavaScript statements go here.)
</SCRIPT>
...
</HEAD>
</HTML>
```

✦ By assigning JavaScript statements to an event handler, such as `onClick` or `onChange`, as shown in the following code. (You find out all about event handlers in Chapter 6.)

```
<INPUT TYPE="TEXT" NAME="firstName" SIZE="25"
onBlur="if (!exists(this.value)) { alert('Please enter
a first name'); }">
```

About JavaScript Security

Because JavaScript runs entirely inside a Web browser (both Netscape Navigator or Microsoft Internet Explorer provide JavaScript support), JavaScript's ability to permit security breaches is extremely limited. Basically, JavaScript can only perform those functions that a Web browser allows it to perform.

Specifically, here's what JavaScript *can't* do:

✦ **Access your computer files.** Other than *cookies*, JavaScript can't write or delete files on your computer, which means JavaScript can't destroy data and can't plant viruses. (*Cookies* are special files that browsers can place on your computer when you surf the Web. The size of these tiny files — as well as how many, where they can be placed, and so on — is strictly controlled by the browser.)

✦ **Open its own direct connection.** Browsers control the receiving and sending of data from a client computer to a Web server, and JavaScript can't override this control. All JavaScript can do is trigger a few browser events. For example, you can use a JavaScript statement to load a Web page or send HTML form data to a Web server — but the actual receiving and sending is securely controlled by the browser, not JavaScript.

Security threats surrounding JavaScript have cropped up from time to time — usually when a brand-spanking-new version of a browser is released. Technically, these security threats aren't JavaScript-related at all; they're browser-related. And fortunately, these security "holes" are usually patched very quickly.

The only security threat JavaScript *can* pose is the insecure transfer of private data via signed scripts — and all signed scripts are administered and controlled by the Web browser. *Signed scripts,* which are supported in Netscape Navigator, allow a JavaScript developer to request certain privileges from the end user at run time — privileges such as the ability to send HTML form data without the end user's knowledge and other questionable (from a security standpoint) actions. These privileges can be exercised only with the end user's explicit permission, however. When Navigator attempts to run a signed script, a pop-up message appears asking the end user if he or she agrees to grant those special privileges.

For more information on script signing in Netscape Navigator, visit
developer.netscape.com/software/signedobj/jarpack.html

Internet Explorer takes a different approach to JavaScript security than Navigator. In Internet Explorer, users can turn scripting support on or off for certain specified "zones" but they can't grant specific privileges via signed scripts the way they can with Navigator. (To turn scripting support on or off in Internet Explorer, choose Tools⇨Internet Options and then click the Security tab.)

Document Object Model Basics

You can work with three main kinds of objects in JavaScript:

✦ Objects that make up a Web page (the *document object model*)

✦ Built-in data types

✦ Utility objects

Read on for a quick rundown of each object type and the differences among them.

You can also create your own custom objects by using the new operator, which you see at work later in this book.

The document object model

With the exception of custom objects you create using the JavaScript new operator (which I discuss in detail in Chapter 5, "Defining and Using Functions"), all the document objects you work with in JavaScript are created either by HTML statements or the browser itself. After the objects exist, you can use JavaScript to examine these objects, change them, perform calculations on them — whatever your heart desires.

The document object model is a hierarchy, which means that some objects contain other objects. For example, a Web page, or *document*, can contain an HTML form, which in turn can contain a text field. So, to access an object (such as a text field) in JavaScript, you must type in the entire hierarchy, from the top down, separated with periods like this:

document.someForm.someTextField

Table 1-1 describes all the objects you can work with in JavaScript.

Unfortunately, Internet Explorer's and Navigator's object models differ slightly. What's worse, these object models change a bit with each new browser release. The objects described in Table 1-1 are supported by both browsers at the time of this writing. To keep up to date with the latest information on Internet Explorer's and Navigator's document object models, respectively, visit msdn.microsoft.com/workshop/author/dhtml/reference/objects.asp and

developer.netscape.com/docs/manuals/js/client/jsref/partobj.htm

Table 1-1   **The Document Object Model**

Object	*Creating HTML Tag*	*JavaScript Syntax*
window	none (it's a given)	window (optional)
document	\<HTML\>...\</HTML\>	document
link	\<A\>...\</A\>	document.links[0]
anchor	\<A\>...\</A\>	document.links[0]
applet	\<APPLET\>...\</APPLET\>	document.applets[0]
area	\<MAP\>...\<AREA\>...\</MAP\>	document.*someArea*
form	\<FORM\>...\</FORM\>	document.*someForm*
button	\<INPUT TYPE="button"\>	document.*someForm.someButton*
checkbox	\<INPUT TYPE="checkbox"\>	document.*someForm.someCheckbox*
fileUpload	\<INPUT TYPE="file"\>	document.*someForm.someFileUpload*
hidden	\<INPUT TYPE="hidden"\>	document.*someForm.someHidden*
image	\<IMG\>	document.*someForm.someImage*
password	\<INPUT TYPE="password"\>	document.*someForm.somePassword*
radio	\<INPUT TYPE="radio"\>	document.*someForm.someRadioButton*
reset	\<INPUT TYPE="reset"\>	document.*someForm.someResetButton*
select	\<SELECT\>...\</SELECT\>	document.*someForm.someSelect*
submit	\<INPUT TYPE="submit"\>	document.*someForm.someSubmitButton*
text	\<INPUT TYPE="text"\>	document.*someForm.someTextField*
textarea	\<TEXTAREA\>...\</TEXTAREA\>	document.*someForm.someTextarea*
frame	\<FRAMESET\>...\<FRAMESET\>	frame
history	none (it's a given)	history
location	none (it's a given)	location
navigator	none (it's a given)	navigator

**Book VI
Chapter 1**

JavaScript Syntax
and Keywords

Both the `window` and `frame` objects have associated *aliases*. (An alias is an alternative way of referring to an object and should be used if doing so makes your code easier to understand.) For example, you can refer to a browser `window` by using any of the following identifiers: `parent` (if the window you're referring to is the parent of the window containing the reference); `self` (if the window you're referring to is the same window as the one containing the reference); or `top` (if the window you're referring to is at the top of the window hierarchy containing the reference). By the same token, you can refer to a frame by using either `parent` or `self`.

Built-in JavaScript data types

Numbers, *Boolean* values (`true` or `false`), and *strings* (a bunch of characters surrounded by quotes and treated as a single entity, like `"this"`) are such basic programming building blocks, or *data types*, that you don't even have to create special objects to use them in JavaScript. All you have to do is specify a numeric, Boolean, or string value, and the JavaScript interpreter takes care of the rest (see Table 1-2).

Table 1-2	JavaScript's Built-in Data Types	
Built-in Data Type	*JavaScript Syntax*	*Example*
Boolean	true, false	var lovesWork = true
null	null	var middleInitial = null
number	1, 2, 3...	var myAge = 20
string	*"someString"*	var fullName = "Kris Kringle"

The examples in Table 1-2 create four different variables to hold four different values, each associated with a different data type. The first variable, lovesWork, is assigned the Boolean value true; the second variable, middleInitial, is assigned the null value; the third variable, myAge, is assigned a number; and the fourth value, fullName, is assigned a string value.

The null data type means "nothing" (which is different from simply not assigning a value at all). The null data type is a valid value all on its own.

Utility objects

Utility objects are like data types in that you can use them to create your own variables. Unlike data types, however, you use the new operator when working with a utility object. Table 1-3 shows you examples.

Chapter 5 of this book shows you how to use the new operator to create variables using utility objects.

Table 1-3	JavaScript Utility Objects	
Utility object	*Description*	*Example*
Array	Lets you create a meaningful, ordered list of objects	var myPets = new Array ("Spike", "Zeke", "Fluffy")
Date	Lets you create and manipulate date and time values, including current date and time	var today = new Date()
Function	Lets you create a function definition programmatically	var salary = new Function ("base", "commission", "return base + (base * commission))"

Basic Punctuation and Syntax

As with English, the JavaScript language is made up words and punctuation which you, gentle JavaScripter, must combine with document object references (described at length in Chapter 2 of this book) to form meaningful statements.

Some JavaScript interpreters are a little more forgiving than others, but no guarantee exists that future versions won't tighten the screws a bit. What that means is that, while bending the punctuation rules in this section may work for now (for example, you may be able to get away with leaving off a piece of punctuation here or there), it probably won't work in all browsers, or for very long. To be on the safe side, always follow the guidelines in this section.

If you're familiar with C or C++ and have seen a bit of JavaScript code, you may immediately notice that JavaScript doesn't require a statement-ending semicolon. Punctuation is a little less rigorously enforced in JavaScript than in C or C++, but it's not a free-for-all! This section helps you avoid the annoying punctuation errors that cause you grief.

Top-down execution

The JavaScript interpreter reads from top to bottom, left to right. So, before you can access or refer to something, that something must first be defined. Case in point: In order to *call* (or use) a function, you must first define that function in an earlier statement. Likewise, if you want to access a variable, you must declare that variable first.

Spelling and capitalization (case)

All the words you use in programming JavaScript must be spelled correctly. For example, if you define a variable called *lastName* and then try to display it on your Web page but misspell it as *lastNam*, you get an error. As close as these two words may appear to human eyes, they look nothing alike to the JavaScript interpreter.

Character case is just as important as correct spelling. For example, the JavaScript interpreter won't recognize the variable named *lastName* if you type it *LastName*.

Pairs

JavaScript scripts are typically rife with pairs: pairs of parentheses, pairs of quotes, and pairs of curly braces. If you forget to add a closing bracket, brace, or whatever, the JavaScript interpreter complains. Sometimes the complaint takes the form of a syntax error; sometimes you get a goofy-looking page display.

Table 1-4 includes examples of pair mismatching to look out for.

Table 1-4	Mismatched Pairs in JavaScript
Statement with Mismatched Pair	*Explanation*
alert("Form processing complete."	Missing parenthesis())
firstName = "Barney	Missing quote (")
if (name == "") { alert("error")	Missing curly brace (})

Nested quotes

You use quotes in JavaScript — single quotes (') and double quotes (") — to surround string values. Why both kinds of quotes? Because you may run into a situation when you need to use two sets of quotes in a single JavaScript statement. If this happens, you need to use both single *and* double quotes, and alternate them in matching pairs, like this:

```
onClick="alert('This is an example of correctly nested
    quotes.')"
```

If you try to nest double quotes inside double quotes (or single quotes inside single quotes), you run into trouble. See the following block of code.

```
onClick="alert("Warning! This statement will produce an
    error.")"
onClick='alert('Warning! This statement will produce an
    error, too.)'
```

If you want a quote to appear in a string, precede the quote with a back-slash. This is called *escaping* the quote. The following code shows what it looks like.

```
alert("Did you see the movie \"Traffic\"?")
```

Chapter 2: Basic JavaScript Constructs

In This Chapter

✔ Documenting your script with comments

✔ Creating variables to hold temporary values

✔ Testing conditional expressions

✔ Constructing loops

✔ Getting familiar with JavaScript operators

*W*hen you create a script, you find yourself most often using a handful of basic JavaScript constructs: comments, variables, conditional expressions, loops, and operators. This chapter explains each of these constructs, including the specific JavaScript keywords you use to bring them to life in your scripts.

Documenting Your Script with Comments

Comments aren't processed by the JavaScript interpreter; they're ignored. Comments give script authors a free-form way to communicate with themselves — and with any other humans who read their scripts.

You may be tempted not to include comments in your scripts, but I urge you to do so as often as you need to. They take only a minute to type, and they may save you a lot of time later when you or someone else needs to update your script. You'd be surprised at how quickly you forget why you coded a script a particular way — and without a clear, concise comment, you may waste a lot of time trying to remember.

JavaScript supports two different kinds of comments: single-line and multiple-line. Either can appear anywhere in your script, as many times as you want.

You create a single-line comment by typing a double slash (//) at the beginning of the line, followed by your comment, like this:

```
// This is a single-line comment.
```

Create a multiple-line comment by beginning a line with /* and ending your comment with */:

```
/* This comment can span multiple lines.
Always remember to close it off, though; if you
forget, you'll get weird errors when your script runs. */
```

Nesting multiple-line comments is a bad idea. A block of code like the following can cause grief because the interpreter ignores the second /* when it gets to the first */:

```
/* This multi-line comment is fine by itself;
it causes no problems unless someone
/* This inserted comment will cause problems!*/
comes along later and inserts another
multi-line comment right in the middle of
this one. */
```

Creating Variables to Hold Temporary Values

A *variable* is a named placeholder for a value. You must do three things to a variable (if it is to be of any practical use): declare it, assign a value to it, and access it within its scope. The following sections show you how.

Declaring a variable

Before you can use a variable, you have to declare it. You declare a variable in JavaScript by using the keyword var, as shown:

```
var myNumberVariable
var streetAddress
var anArrayOfJobTitles
```

JavaScript is what's known as a *loosely typed* language, which means that you don't have to tell the interpreter what kind of value you're going to assign to a variable right up front. All that you need is the var keyword and a unique variable name of your choice. (A variable's type is determined by the value you assign to it, as you see in the next section.)

The name of your variable must begin with either a letter or an underscore. The variable name can contain numbers but no punctuation marks.

Assigning values to a variable

You can assign a value to a variable at the same time you declare it, or at any time after you declare it:

```
// Declaring and assigning all at once
var numberOfWineglasses = 6
```

```
// Assigning a value later in the program
numberOfWineglasses = 182
```

Accessing a variable

After you declare a variable, you can then access it. By *accessing* a variable, I mean you can modify, display, or use the variable's value in a computation. Here's an example:

```
// Variable declaration and assignment
var myTitle = "Princess of the Universe"

// Displaying the value on the screen in a browser alert box
alert("Here is my title: " + myTitle)

//  Adding to the value
myTitle += " and everywhere else"

// Comparing one value to another
if (myTitle == "dog catcher") {
    alert("Memo to myself: At least I won the election!")
}
```

Understanding variable scope

A variable is only valid when it's *in scope,* which means that the variable has been declared between the same curly brace boundaries as the statement that's trying to access it.

For example, if you define a variable named `firstName` inside a function called `displayReport()`, you can only refer to it inside `displayReport()`'s curly braces. If you try to use the `firstName` variable from inside another function, you get an error. Take a look at the following code example:

```
function displayReport() {

    var firstName = document.myForm.givenName.value
    alert("Click OK to see the report for " + firstName)

    /* Using firstName here is fine; it was declared inside
    the same set of curly braces as the alert() method. */

}
function displayGraph() {

    alert("Here's the graph for " + firstName)

 /* Error! firstName wasn't defined inside
this function's curly braces! */
}
```

As you can see from the comments in the preceding code fragment, it's perfectly okay to use firstName inside the displayReport() function; firstName is in scope anywhere inside displayReport(). It's *not* okay, however, to use firstName inside displayGraph(). As far as displayGraph() is concerned, no such animal as firstName has been declared inside *its* scope.

If you want to reuse a variable *among* functions (Eek! A *global variable*! Quick, call the cops!), you can declare it near the top of your script, before you declare any functions. That way, the variable's scope is the entire script, from the very first opening curly brace to the last — and all the functions defined within the script get to access it.

Testing Conditional Expressions: if...else

The if...else expression is called a *conditional* expression because you use it to test whether a certain condition is true. A condition can be a variable, a statement, or an expression — anything at all that can be resolved by the JavaScript interpreter to a simple true or false answer.

If the condition is true, the interpreter executes all the statements between curly braces that follow the if clause. If the condition is false, the interpreter executes all the statements between curly braces that follow the else clause. Here's the generic description of how to use if...else:

```
if (condition) {
statements
}
[  else {
statements
}]
```

The square brackets around the else clause mean that the else clause is optional — you can code just the if clause if you want. And no rule exists saying that an if...else expression can't have other statements nested inside of it, either (most do). Just remember to include the curly braces as shown for each if...else. There's no leeway here: They have to be curly braces, not parentheses, and they have to come in pairs, just like in the following example:

```
if (numberOrdered <= 100) {
    //calculate the order at retail cost
    calculateTotal(amount, 19.95)
}
else {
    // calculate the order at wholesale cost
    calculateTotal(amount, 11.00)
}
```

Constructing Loops

Loops are common programming constructs that you can use to perform a single task many times, in as compact a way as possible. JavaScript contains two basic kinds of loops: `for` and `while`. Both types of loops are explained in the following sections, along with some other keywords that you can use with `for` and `while` to create concise, powerful loops.

Other loops in JavaScript include `do while` and a variation of `for` (for working with objects) called `for...in`

for

The `for` loop comes straight from the C language — and because C is famous for its terseness, it won't come as a shock to you that in the wrong hands, `for` loops can be positively Byzantine.

First, have a look at the generic form:

```
for ([initial expression]; [condition]; [update expression])
    {
      statements
}
```

The preceding syntax introduces three terms that may be new to you:

✦ **Initial expression:** Think of the *initial expression* as the starting point — a snapshot of how things look right before the interpreter hops into the loop and gets down to business.

✦ **Condition:** The *condition* is the JavaScript expression to be tested each time the interpreter takes a pass around the loop.

✦ **Update expression:** If the condition tests true, the JavaScript interpreter performs the *update expression* before looping around to test the condition again.

Here's a short example that should help make the workings of the `for` loop crystal clear:

```
for (var i = 1; i <= 10; i++) {
    document.writeln(i)
}
```

The following steps describe what happens in the preceding `for` loop:

1. **The variable i is set equal to 1.**

2. **The JavaScript interpreter checks to see whether i is less than or equal to 10.**

3. i **is less than or equal to 10, so the body of the loop executes.**

4. i **is written to the screen (this one action,** `document.writeln(i)`, **forms the entire body of the loop).**

5. **The JavaScript interpreter adds** 1 **to** i; **now** i **is 2.**

6. **The JavaScript interpreter checks to see whether** i **is less than or equal to 10.**

7. i **is less than or equal to 10, so the body of the loop executes.**

8. i **is written to the screen via the** `document.writeln` **method (again, this one action comprises the entire loop body).**

9. **The JavaScript interpreter adds** 1 **to** i; **now** i **is 3.**

10. **Start again at Step 6.**

See the pattern? The interpreter begins at the top of the loop and performs the body of the loop once for each time that the loop condition is `true`. When the loop condition stops being true (in this case, when i = 11) the interpreter proceeds on to the first line of JavaScript code beneath the loop.

while

The `while` loop is similar to the `for` loop. First you set up a condition, and *while* that condition is true, the JavaScript interpreter executes the statements in the body of the loop. If the condition is *never* true, the statements never execute; if the condition is *always* true, well, those statements will execute for a long, long, long, long time. Obviously, then, you want to make sure that one of the statements in the body of your `while` loop changes the `while` condition in some way so that it stops being true at some point.

First, the generic syntax:

```
while (condition) {
    statements
}
```

Here's an example of `while` in action:

```
while (totalInventory > numberPurchased) {
    totalInventory = totalInventory - numberPurchased
    numberSales++
}
```

break

The `break` keyword can be used only inside a loop (such as `for` or `while`). When the JavaScript interpreter encounters a `break` statement, it breaks out of the loop and starts interpreting the script at the first line following the loop. For example:

```
for (var i = 1; i<= 20; i++) {
    ...
    if (i == 13) {   // Only go up to 12
        break
    }
    document.writeln(i) // print the value of i on the screen
}
// this is where the interpreter will pick up again
// after the break
```

Here's how the output will look:

```
1 2 3 4 5 6 7 8 9 10 11 12
```

continue

Like `break`, `continue` can be used inside `for` and `while` loops. When the JavaScript interpreter encounters a `continue` statement, it stops what it's doing and hops back up to the beginning of the loop to continue as normal. The following example may make it clearer:

```
for (var i = 1; i<= 20; i++) {
    if (i == 13) {   // Superstitious! Don't print #13
        continue
    }
    document.writeln(i)
}
```

The following output shows how `continue` works. You may want to compare the following output to the output generated by `break`:

```
1 2 3 4 5 6 7 8 9 10 11 12 14 15 16 17 18 19 20
```

In the output generated by `continue`, you can see that the number 13 is skipped — but then the loop continues and prints out the numbers 14 through 20 (unlike the example `break` command in the preceding section, which stops the loop dead in its tracks after printing the number 12).

The `continue` keyword is useful for handling exceptions to a rule. For example, you may want to process all the items in a group the same way except for one or two special cases.

Getting Familiar with JavaScript Operators

Operators are kind of like conjunctions in English: You use operators to join multiple phrases together to form expressions. The operators you're familiar with in everyday life include the plus sign (+) and the minus sign (–). JavaScript provides you with a lot more operators, however, as you can see in the following sections.

Assignment operators

Assignment operators let you assign values to variables. Besides being able to make a straight one-to-one assignment, though, you can also use some of them as a kind of shorthand to bump up a value based on another value. Table 2-1 describes how each operator works.

Table 2-1	Assignment Operators	
Operator	*Meaning*	*Value of x After Execution (Before Execution, x = 10 and y = 15)*
x = y	The value of y is assigned to x	15
x += y	x = x + y (addition)	25
x –= y	x = x – y (subtraction)	–5
x *= y	x = x * y (multiplication)	150
x /= y	x = x / y (division)	.6666666
x %= y	x = x % y (modulus)	10

Here's how the modulus operator works: x %= y means that the interpreter tries to divide y into x evenly. The result is anything left over. In the preceding example, x is 10 and y is 15. 15 won't go into 10 evenly at all, so 10 is what's left over.

Comparison operators

When comparing two values or expressions for equality, you have the choices shown in Table 2-2.

Table 2-2	Comparison Operators	
Operator	*Example*	*Meaning*
== (two equal signs)	x == y	x is equal to y
!=	x != y	x is not equal to y
<	x < y	x is less than y

Operator	Example	Meaning
>	x > y	x is greater than y
<=	x <= y	x is less than or equal to y
>=	x >= y	x is greater than or equal to y
?:	x = (y < 0) ? -y : y	If y is less than zero, assign -y to x; otherwise, assign y to x

A common mistake that beginning programmers often make is using a single equal sign in place of a double equal sign (and vice versa). JavaScript doesn't complain if you do that; after all, both (x == 6) and (x = 6) are legal expressions, and JavaScript has no way of knowing which expression you really want to state. The two examples are radically different, however, and interchanging them can wreak havoc on your logic. The first example *compares* 6 to x, and the second *assigns* 6 to x.

Logical operators

Logical operators work on logical values (also called *Boolean* values) and they also return Boolean values. A Boolean value can only be one of two things: It's either true or false. When you see two expressions separated by a logical operator, the JavaScript interpreter first computes (or *resolves*) the expressions to see whether each is true or false; then it computes the entire statement. If an expression resolves to a number *other than* zero, the expression is considered to be true; if the expression computes *to* zero, it's considered to be false. Check out Table 2-3 for examples of the logical operators available in JavaScript.

Table 2-3		Logical Operators	
Operator	Name	Example	Meaning
&&	logical "and"	if (x == y && a != b)	If x is equal to y AND a is not equal to b
||	logical "or"	if (x < y || a < b)	If x is less than y OR a is less than b
!	not	if (!x)	If NOT x (that is, if x is false, or zero)

Mathematical operators

Mathematical operators in JavaScript are just as you'd expect: addition, subtraction, multiplication, division, and modulus (the remainder operator). Unlike the assignment operators, which combined assignment with math operations, these operators don't automatically add in the value on the left-hand side of an equation. Take a look at Table 2-4 for examples of mathematical operators in action.

Table 2-4	Mathematical Operators	
Operator	*Example*	*Value of x After Execution*
Addition (+)	x = 1 + 3	4
Subtraction (−)	x = 100 − 75	25
Multiplication (*)	x = 6 * 7	42
Division (/)	x = 49 / 7	7
Modulus (%)	x = 11 % 5	1

String operators

Most of JavaScript's operators are designed to work with numeric values. A few, however, shown in Table 2-5, are also useful for manipulating strings. (In JavaScript, a *string* is a string of characters surrounded by quotes and treated — like a word — as a single item.)

In the following examples, stringA is "moo" and stringB is "cow".

Table 2-5	String Operators	
Operator	*Syntax*	*Result After Execution*
Addition (+)	myString = stringA + stringB	myString = "moocow"
Append (+=)	myString = "hairy " += stringB	myString = "hairy cow"
Equality (==)	if (myString == "moocow")	if myString is equal to "moocow"
Inequality (!=)	if (myString != "moocow")	if myString is not equal to "moocow"

Unary operators

Unary operators — operators that you apply to a single operand — look a little strange to the uninitiated eye. They're very useful, though, so it's worth spending a minute or two checking out Table 2-6 to get familiar with them.

(In the following examples, x is set to 11.)

Table 2-6		Unary Operators	
Unary	*Example (x = 11)*	*Result/Meaning*	
!	!(x == 5)	true (negation)	11 isn't equal to 5
−	x = −x	x = −11 (negation)	Turns positive numbers negative and vice versa
++	x = x++	x = 11 (increment by 1)	++ placed *after* a var increments x *after* assignment

Unary	Example (x = 11)	Result/Meaning	
	x = ++x	x = 12	++ placed *before* a var increments x *before* assignment
--	x = x--	x = 11 (decrement by 1)	-- placed *after* a var decrements x *after* assignment
	x = --x	x = 10	-- placed *before* a var decrements x *before* assignment

Operator precedence

Just as in regular (non-Web-page-oriented) math, an order of evaluation is applied to any JavaScript statement that contains multiple operators. Unless you set off phrases with parentheses, the JavaScript interpreter observes the precedence order shown in Table 2-7 (from the parentheses, which has the highest order of precedence, to the comma, which has the lowest):

Table 2-7	Operator Precedence in JavaScript (From Highest to Lowest)	
Operator	**Syntax**	**Explanation**
Parentheses	()	For calling functions and grouping math expressions
Unary	--, ++, --, !	Decrement, increment, and negation operators
Mathematical	%, /, *, --, +	Modulus, division, multiplication, subtraction, addition
Relational	>=, >, <=, <	Greater than/equal to, greater than, less than/equal to, less than
Equality	!=, ==	Not equal to, equal to
Logical "and"	&&	If *all* expressions in a statement meet some criteria
Logical "or"	||	If *at least one* expression in a statement meets some criteria
Conditional	?:	(y < 0) ? x : y If y is less than 0 (whatever is before the ? is true), then return x (whatever is *before* the :), else return y (whatever is *after* the :)
Assignment	%=, /=, *=, --=, +=, =	Assignment + mathematical
Comma	,	Used for separating parameters in a function call

So, how exactly does operator precedence work? Suppose that the JavaScript interpreter runs into the following statement in your script:

```
alert("Grand total: " + getTotal() + (3 * 4 / 10) + tax++)
```

The JavaScript interpreter knows that its job is to evaluate the statement — so the first thing it does is scan the whole line. When the interpreter finds the first set of parentheses, it knows that's where it needs to start. It thinks to itself, "Okay, first I'll get the return value from `getTotal()`. Then I'll evaluate (3 * 4 / 10). Within (3 * 4 / 10), I'll do the division first, then the multiplication. Now I'll add one to the *tax* variable. Okay, the last thing I have to do is add the whole thing up to come up with a string to display in a browser alert box."

If you don't want to go the trouble of memorizing the precedence order, that's okay. Just group expressions in parentheses. Because parentheses outrank all the other operators, you can effectively force JavaScript to override its default precedence order.

Other, more seldom-used JavaScript operators are `typeof` and `void` — `typeof` returns the data type of a JavaScript variable or object, and `void` enables you to create a "dummy" JavaScript function useful in certain situations.

Chapter 3: Working with the Document Object Model

In This Chapter

✔ **Accessing object properties**

✔ **Invoking object methods**

The two-bit definition of an *object* is "a software representation of some useful thing." The document objects you work with in JavaScript are no exception: Each of them is a representation of a thing that you need to build Web pages — push buttons, input fields, dates, and so on.

You create document objects by using HTML code. (Some browser-oriented document objects are created automatically for you by the Web browser.) After objects exist, you access their properties and invoke their methods using JavaScript.

This chapter first describes how you work with properties and methods, then contains, for each element, two separate sections:

✦ Which properties each object contains

✦ Which methods each object can perform

An exhaustive list of all objects supported by all browsers would make this book too heavy to lift. In this chapter I include the most common objects, properties, and methods you work with in JavaScript. To look up details for additional, more obscure objects not listed here, or to get detailed information and examples of any object, method, or property you see in this chapter, visit msdn.microsoft.com/workshop/author/dhtml/reference/objects.asp (for Internet Explorer-supported objects) or developer.netscape.com/docs/manuals/js/client/jsref/partobj.htm (for Navigator-supported objects).

Accessing Object Properties

Properties are values that describe objects. For example, an image object embedded in a Web page might include properties such as the image filename, the thickness of the border around the image, the dimensions of the image, and so on.

Most document objects are defined using HTML, which means that most document object properties are initially defined using HTML. However, after an object exists, you can access and, in some cases, change property values using JavaScript.

For example, suppose that you're working with an HTML document that includes the following HTML code snippet:

```
<BODY ALINK="cornflowerblue">...</BODY>
```

The previous HTML code sets the active link color for the Web page to a nice, soothing cornflower blue color. To access that color value in JavaScript, you type the following:

```
document.alinkColor
```

In the case of the JavaScript code above, the active link color is associated directly with the document. For objects embedded further down in the document hierarchy, however, you need to specify the entire dot-delimited hierarchy of the object. For example, suppose that you want to access the text displayed on a submit button named submitIt contained in a form called submitForm. Here's what you do:

```
document.submitForm.submitIt.value
```

Each of the object listings you find in this chapter contains a list of the properties associated with that object.

Technically, the example above could be written window.submitForm.submitForm.value, because all document objects — by definition — are contained within the browser window object. However, JavaScript makes specifying the browser window as part of hierarchical syntax optional, unless you're working with multiple browser windows. Because specifying the browser window is optional in most cases, I don't specify the browser window in this chapter unless doing so is required by JavaScript syntax.

Accessing Object Methods

A *method* is a special kind of function that operates on a specific object — the object with which the method is associated. A method's name is typically a verb that describes what the method does to its associated object. For example, the blink() method causes text to blink; the submit() method causes form data to be submitted; and the click() method causes a button to be clicked.

Because your Web page may contain several text elements, a couple of forms, and 23 buttons, JavaScript syntax provides a way for you to specify precisely which object's method you want to call. To call a method on a specific object, you include the entire dot-delimited hierarchy of the object, like this:

```
document.myForm.buttonOne.click()
```

The previous JavaScript code calls the `click()` method of the button named `buttonOne` — which is located in the form named `myForm`.

I devote the rest of this chapter to listings of the main objects you work with in JavaScript. Each of the object listings includes the hierarchical syntax you need to access that object's properties and methods. (If you look at the listings carefully, you also find useful comments I added using the JavaScript comment conventions I describe in "Documenting Your Script with Comments" in Chapter 2 of this book.)

anchor

An *anchor* is a piece of text that uniquely identifies a spot on a Web page. After you define an anchor for example, in the middle of a page, you (or anyone else for that matter) can set up a link so that when a user clicks the link, the page loads right where the anchor is located.

Accessing anchor properties

```
document.anchors.length  // list of anchors on the page
myAnchor.name // name of anchor
myAnchor.text // text of anchor
myAnchor.x // x coordinate of anchor
myAnchor.y // y coordinate of anchor
```

Invoking anchor methods

The `anchor` object has no associated methods.

applet

The `applet` object corresponds to a Java applet embedded in a Web page.

Accessing applet properties

The properties available to you depend on the specific Java applet you're working with.

```
document.applets[0] // list of applets embedded on a page
```

Invoking applet methods

The `applet` methods available to you depend on the specific Java applet you're working with. Ask the person who developed the Java applet that you're including in your Web page for a list of public methods that you can invoke on the applet.

area

The `area` object is used to make a specific area of an embedded image responsive to user events. You can make an area respond to a click event or to mouse events.

Accessing area properties

See the `link` object for details. (`area` objects are stored as `link` objects.)

Invoking area methods

See the `link` object for details. (`area` objects are stored as `link` objects.)

button

A `button` object represents a push button on an HTML form.

Accessing button properties

```
document.myForm.myButton.name // button name
document.myForm.myButton.type // button type ("button")
document.myForm.myButton.value // text value displayed on
    button
```

Invoking button methods

```
document.myForm.myButton.click() // clicks the button element
```

checkbox

A checkbox object represents a checkbox on an HTML form.

Accessing check box properties

```
document.myForm.myCheckbox.checked // true if checked; false
    if not
document.myForm.myCheckbox.defaultChecked // true if checked
    by default; false if not
document.myForm.myCheckbox.name // checkbox name
document.myForm.myCheckbox.type // checkbox type ("checkbox")
document.myForm.myCheckbox.value // value initially defined
    for this checkbox
```

Invoking check box methods

```
document.myForm.myCheckbox.click() // clicks
    (checks/unchecks) this checkbox
```

document

A document object defines characteristics of the overall body of a Web page, such as the background color of a page, the default text color, and so on.

Accessing document properties

```
document.alinkColor // color of activated links
document.anchors[] // array of this document's anchors
document.bgColor // background color for this document
document.cookie // cookie associated with this document
document.fgColor // foreground color
document.forms[index] // array of this document's forms
document.lastModified // document modification date
document.linkColor // link color for this document
document.links[index] // array of this document's links
document.location // URL of this document
document.referrer // URL of the linked-from document
document.title // title of this document
document.vlinkColor // "followed link" color for this document
```

Invoking document methods

```
document.close() // closes specified document
document.open("text/html") // opens new document
document.write(message) // writes message to document
document.writeln(message) // writes message to document
    (includes return)
```

fileUpload

A `fileUpload` object consists of a Browse button and a text field. To specify a file name, you can either click the Browse button and choose from the list of files, or enter a filename directly into the text field.

Accessing fileUpload properties

```
document.myForm.myFileUpload.name // name of fileUpload
    element
document.myForm.myFileUpload.type // type of element
    ("fileupload")
document.myForm.myFileUpload.value // value initially defined
    for this fileUpload element
```

Invoking fileUpload methods

The `fileUpload` object has no associated methods.

form

You use a *form* to gather input from users and to send data (including user input) to a server for additional processing.

Accessing form properties

```
document.myForm.action // value of the ACTION attribute
    initially defined for the form
document.myForm.elements[].name // array of form elements
    included in this form
document.myForm.encoding // value of ENCTYPE attribute
    initially defined for the form
document.myForm.length // number of form elements in the form
document.myForm.method // value of METHOD attribute initially
    defined for form
document.myForm.name // name of the form
document.myForm.target // value of TARGET attribute initially
    defined for form
document.forms[0] // first form defined in the document
document.forms.length //total # forms defined for this Web
    page
```

Invoking form methods

```
document.myForm.reset() // resets form data
document.myForm.submit() // submits form data to Web server
```

frame

A *frame* is a type of window. You can think of a frame as an individual pane of glass — that is, you can have several frames per regular window or just one. A user can scroll each frame independently.

Accessing frame properties
See the `window` object.

Invoking frame methods
See the `window` object.

hidden

A *hidden* element is an input text field that doesn't appear on-screen. (Some programmers use `hidden` elements to hold calculated values they don't want users to see.)

Accessing hidden properties
```
document.myForm.myHidden.name // name of hidden element
document.myForm.myHidden.type // type of element ("hidden")
document.myForm.myHidden.value // value initially specified
    for hidden element
```

Invoking hidden methods
The `hidden` object has no associated methods.

history

The `history` object contains an array of all the URLs that a user has visited from within a particular window. This object provides the list of URLs you see when you select the Go menu item in Navigator or Internet Explorer.

Accessing history properties
```
history.length // number of elements in history array
history.next // next URL in the history array
history.previous // previous URL in the history array
```

Invoking history methods

```
history.back() // reloads previous URL
history.forward() // reloads next URL
history.go(n) // reloads the URL specified by n (n can be
    either a negative or positive number)
```

image

The image object represents an image embedded into a Web page.

Accessing image properties

```
document.myForm.myImage.border // border width value set by
    BORDER attribute
document.myForm.myImage.complete // boolean value describing
    whether image has loaded completely (true or false)
document.myForm.myImage.height // height value set by HEIGHT
    attribute
document.myForm.myImage.hspace // horizontal padding value
    set by HSPACE attribute
document.myForm.myImage.lowsrc // alternate compressed image
    value set by LOWSRC attribute
document.myForm.myImage.name // name of image
document.myForm.myImage.src // filename value set by SRC
    attribute
document.myForm.myImage.vspace // vertical padding value set
    by VSPACE attribute
document.myForm.myImage.width // width value set by WIDTH
    attribute
```

Invoking image methods

No methods are associated with the image object.

link

A *link* is a piece of text (or an image) that loads another Web page when a user clicks it. (A link often loads a specific spot, or *anchor,* on another Web page.) The URL (or HREF attribute) associated with a link takes the following form:

```
protocol://hostname:port/pathname?search#hash
```

Accessing links (link array) properties

```
document.links[] // array of links in a document
document.links.length // number of links in a document
```

Accessing individual link properties

```
document.links[0].hash // hash (#) portion of the HREF of the
    0th link on the page
document.links[0].host // hostname and port portions of the
    HREF of the 0th link on the page
document.links[0].hostname // hostname portion of the HREF of
    the 0th link on the page
document.links[0].href // HREF of the 0th link on the page
document.links[0].pathname // path portion of the HREF of the
    0th link on the page
document.links[0].port // port portion of the HREF of the 0th
    link on the page
document.links[0].protocol // protocol portion of the HREF of
    the 0th link on the page
document.links[0].search // search portion of the HREF of the
    0th link on the page
document.links[0].target // target window defined for the 0th
    link on the page
document.links[0].text // text associated with the 0th link
    on the page
document.links[0].x // x coordinate associated with the 0th
    link on the page
document.links[0].y // y coordinate associated with the 0th
    link on the page
```

Invoking link methods

Neither the `link` object (for example, `document.links[0]`) nor the `links` array has any associated methods.

location

Instead of holding information on *all* the recently visited URLs, as does the `history` object, the `location` object contains information about just *one* URL — the one that's currently loaded. The URL of the currently loaded Web page is stored in the `location` object:

```
protocol://hostname:port/pathname?search#hash
```

Accessing location properties

```
location.hash // hash portion of the URL
location.host // host portion of the URL
location.hostname // hostname portion of the URL
location.href // entire URL
location.pathname // pathname portion of the URL
location.port // port portion of the URL
location.protocol // protocol portion of the URL
location.search // search portion of the URL
```

Invoking location methods

```
reload() // reloads the current URL
replace(newURL) // replaces the current URL with newURL
```

Math

The Math object contains properties and methods for all kinds of mathematical constants and functions, such as logarithms and square roots.

Accessing Math properties

```
Math.E // the constant e, the base of the natural logarithm
Math.LN2 // the natural logarithm of 10
Math.LN10 // the natural logarithm of 2
Math.LOG2E // the base-10 logarithm of e
Math.LOG10E // the base-2 logarithm of e
Math.PI // the constant ▼
Math.SQR1_2 // 1 divided by the square root of 2
Math.SQRT2 // the square root of 2
```

Invoking Math methods

```
Math.abs(x) // the absolute value of x
Math.acos(x) // the arc cosine of x
Math.asin(x) // the arc sine of x
Math.atan(x) // the arc tangent of x
Math.atan2(x, y) // the angle from the X-axis to the point
   (x, y)
Math.ceil(x.y) // x rounded up to the nearest integer
Math.cos(x) // the cosine of x
Math.exp(x) // e raised to the xth power, where e is the base
   of the natural logarithms
Math.floor(x.y) // x rounded down to the nearest integer
Math.log(x) // the natural logarithm of x
Math.max(x,y) // the larger of x, y
Math.min(x,y) // the smaller of x, y
Math.pow(x,y) // x to the yth power
Math.random() // a pseudo-random number
Math.round(x.y) // x.y rounded to the nearest integer
Math.sin(x) // the sine of x
Math.sqrt(x) // the square root of x
Math.tan(x) // the tangent of x
```

navigator

The navigator object contains information about the version of browser (Navigator or Internet Explorer) currently in use.

Accessing navigator properties

```
navigator.appCodeName // the code name of the browser
navigator.appName // the name of the browser
navigator.appVersion // version information for the browser
navigator.userAgent // the HTTP user-agent value (typically
     takes the form of navigator.appCodeName/navigator.
     appVersion)
```

Invoking navigator methods

```
navigator.javaEnabled()
```

password

A password object is a special text input field that displays asterisks on-screen in place of the characters that the user actually types, enabling users to type in sensitive information (such as a password or financial information) without fear that someone peeking over their shoulder will get a glimpse.

Accessing password properties

```
document.myForm.myPassword.defaultValue // default Value
     initially defined for the password element
document.myForm.myPassword.name // name of the password
     element
document.myForm.myPassword.type // type of the password
     element ("password")
document.myForm.myPassword.value // value for the password
     element
```

Invoking password methods

```
document.myForm.myPassword.focus() // switches focus to
     (selects) password element
document.myForm.myPassword.blur() // switches focus away from
     password element
document.myForm.myPassword.select() // selects contents of
     password element
```

radio

A *radio* button is a toggle switch, something like a check box. Unlike a check box, however, radio buttons are often grouped in sets to allow users to select a *single* option from a list.

Accessing radio buttons

```
document.myForm.myRadio.length  // # of radio buttons
document.myForm.myRadio[0] // 0th radio button in a group
```

Accessing individual radio button properties

```
document.myForm.myRadio[0].checked // true/false depending on
    whether 0th checkbox is currently checked
document.myForm.myRadio[index].defaultChecked // true/false
    depending on whether 0th checkbox was initially defined
    as default
document.myForm.myRadio[0].name // name of 0th checkbox
    element
document.myForm.myRadio[0].type // type of 0th checkbox
    element
document.myForm.myRadio[0].value // value associated with
    0th checkbox element (text passed to server on form
    submission)
```

Invoking radio methods

```
document.myForm.myRadio[0].click() // click (checks/unchecks)
    the 0th checkbox element
```

reset

When you click a *reset* button, the browser clears out all the user-input values in a form and resets each field to its default value.

Accessing reset properties

```
document.myForm.myResetButton.name // name of the reset
    button element
document.myForm.myResetButton.type // type of the reset
    button element ("reset")
document.myForm.myResetButton.value // value of the reset
    button element (text displayed on reset button)
```

Invoking reset methods

```
document.myForm.myResetButton.click() // clicks the reset
    button element
```

select

The select object is used to display both a single-selection list box and a scrolling multiple-selection list box.

Accessing select object properties

```
document.myForm.mySelect.name // name of select element
document.myForm.mySelect.selectedIndex // the selected option
document.myForm.mySelect.length // number of selectable
    options
document.myForm.mySelect.options[] // array of selectable
    options
```

Accessing individual selection properties

```
document.myForm.mySelect.options[0].defaultSelected //
    true/false depending on whether the 0th option was
    initially defined as the default option
document.myForm.mySelect.options[0].index // the index
    (position) of the 0th element in relation to other select
    elements
document.myForm.mySelect.options[0].selected // true/false
    depending on whether the 0th element is selected
document.myForm.mySelect.options[0].text // text that
    describes the 0th option
document.myForm.mySelect.options[0].type // type of element
    ("select")
document.myForm.mySelect.options[0].value // value associated
    with the 0th option (sent to server on form submit)
```

Invoking select methods

```
document.myForm.mySelect.focus() // Switches focus to the
    specified select element
document.myForm.mySelect.blur() // Switches focus away from
    the specified select element
```

Submit

The browser sends all of the user input values on a form to the server (based on the form's HTML ACTION attribute) when you click the *submit* button. The data is sent as a series of attribute-value pairs, each pair separated by an ampersand (&).

Accessing submit properties

```
document.myForm.mySubmitButton.name // name of the submit
    button element
document.myForm.mySubmitButton.type // type of the element
    ('submit')
document.myForm.mySubmitButton.value // text that appears on
    the submit button element
```

Invoking submit methods

```
document.myForm.mySubmitButton.click() // clicks the submit
    button element
```

text

The text object is a single-line input field. (If you want a multiple-line input field, see the textarea object, defined in the following section).

Accessing text properties

```
document.myForm.myTextElement.defaultValue // default value
    initially defined for the text element
document.myForm.myTextElement.name // name of the text
    element
document.myForm.myTextElement.type // type of element
    ("text")
document.myForm.myTextElement.value // value associated with
    the text element
```

Invoking text methods

```
document.myForm.myTextElement.focus() // switches focus to
    the specified text element
document.myForm.myTextElement.blur() // switches focus away
    from the specified text element
document.myForm.myTextElement.select() // selects the text
    contained in a text element
```

textarea

A textarea object is just like a text object, except that instead of defining one scrolling input line, the textarea object defines a multi-line scrolling text box.

Accessing textarea properties

```
document.myForm.myTextArea.defaultValue // default value
    initially defined for the textarea element
document.myForm.myTextArea.name// name of the textarea
    element
document.myForm.myTextArea.type// type of element
    ("textarea")
document.myForm.myTextArea.value // value associated with the
    textarea element
```

Invoking textarea methods

```
document.myForm.myTextArea.focus()// switches focus to the
    specified textarea element
document.myForm.myTextArea.blur()// switches focus away from
    the specified textarea element
document.myForm.myTextArea.select()// selects the text
    contained in a textarea element
```

window

The `window` object is the top-level granddaddy object for all `document` objects. You're given the first top-level window gratis, compliments of the HTML `<BODY>...</BODY>` tag pair; but you can create additional windows by using the `open()` method described as follows.

**Book VI
Chapter 3**

**Working with
the Document
Object Model**

Accessing window properties

```
defaultStatus // the default message associated with the
    specified window's status line
document // the document object contained in the specified
    window
frames[] // an array of frames associated with the specified
    window
history // the history object contained in the specified
    window
length // the number of elements in the frames[] array
location // the location object asociated with the specified
    window
name // the name defined for the specified window
navigator // the navigator object associated with the
    specified window
opener // the window that opened the specified window
parent // reference to the parent window/frame of the
    specified window (if any)
self // reference to the specified window
status // current contents of the specified window's status
    line
top // reference to the top-level window that contains the
    specified window
window // synonym for self
```

Invoking window methods

```
alert(message) // displays message in pop-up alert box
blur() // switches focus away from specified window
close() // closes specified window
confirm(message) // displays message in pop-up confirmation
    box
focus() // switches focus to specified window
```

```
moveBy(x, y) // moves specified window right x pixels and
    down y pixels
moveto(x, y) // moves specified window to the x, y
    coordinates
open(url, name, features, replace) // opens url in new window
    named name using comma-delimited features and boolean
    replace (true replaces currently opened window)
prompt(message) // displays message in pop-up prompt box
resizeBy(x, y) // increases window width by x pixels and
    height by y pixels
resizeTo(x, y) // increases window dimensions to x, y pixels
scroll(x, y) // scrolls specified window based on x, y
    coordinates
```

Chapter 4: Exploring Built-in Data Types

In This Chapter

✔ Understanding JavaScript's built-in data types: Array, Date, and String

✔ Creating variables based on built-in data types

Most of the variables you create in JavaScript are numbers, strings, dates, and arrays. Numbers are so basic that you don't need special objects to create them (A table in Chapter 1 shows you how to create a numeric variable). But strings, dates, and arrays are a bit more complex, so JavaScript provides special built-in *data types,* or *classes,* you use to create them.

JavaScript defines additional, less commonly used classes, including Function and Option. To get details on classes not listed in this chapter, visit msdn.microsoft.com/scripting/default.htm?/scripting/ jscript/default.htm (for Internet Explorer-supported classes) or developer.netscape.com/docs/manuals/js/client/jsref/partobj. htm (for Navigator-supported classes). *Note:* Although a technical difference exists between classes and objects, Netscape's documentation often refers to both classes and objects as *objects.*

In the sections that follow, I show you how to create variables of type Array, Date, and String, respectively. First I describe each built-in data type; then I outline the basic JavaScript syntax for creating a variable of that type. In each section you find an actual example — JavaScript code you can cut and paste into your own scripts. I finish off each section by describing how you can access the built-in properties and methods that you get free of charge when you create variables using a built-in data type.

Array

An array represents an indexed list of things called *elements.* Element values can be whatever you want them to be — numbers, strings, or even other objects. You can fill an array with elements when you create it by passing values to the array constructor, or you can create an empty array and fill it with elements later.

Arrays are useful whenever you want to keep track of a group of related items.

Syntax:

```
arrayName = new Array([element1, element2, ... elementN |
    arraySize])
```

Example:

The following line of JavaScript code creates an array named `listOfPets` containing three string elements, "dog" (index 0), "cat" (index 1), and "gerbil" (index 2).

```
var listOfPets = new Array("dog", "cat", "gerbil")
```

The following line of code adds a fourth string element to the `listOfPets` array.

```
listOfPets[3]="bird"
```

Accessing array properties:

```
myArray.length // number of elements in the specified array
```

Invoking array methods:

```
myArray.concat(value, ...) // Concatenates specified elements
    to array
myArray.join(optionalSeparator) // joins array elements
    (separated by optionalSeparator) to form a single string
myArray.reverse() // reverses index order of array elements
myArray.sort(optionalSortFunction) // sorts array elements
    based on optionalSortFunction; if no optionalSortFunction
    specified, sorts array elements in alphabetical order
```

Date

Any time you work with dates in JavaScript, you use the `Date` class. You can create dates based on the current time or on values that you provide. After a variable of type `Date` exists, you can modify and manipulate that variable by using the following `Date` methods.

Syntax:

```
dateName = new Date()
// if no parameters are passed to the constructor,
// the result is the current date/time
```

```
dateName = new Date("month day,
            year   hours:minutes:seconds")

dateName = new Date(year, month, day)

dateName = new Date(year, month, day, hours,
   minutes, seconds)
```

Example:

```
var today = new Date()
var birthday = new Date("October 21, 1973 01:40:00")
var graduation = new Date(1990, 8, 6)
var wedding = new Date(92, 07, 12, 10, 30, 21)
```

Accessing Date properties:

You access Date properties using special *getter* and *setter* methods, as shown in the following section.

Invoking Date methods

If you think about it, you can basically do only two things with a property after it's defined: You can *get* the value of the property to see what it is, and you can *set* the value of the property. Data types have predefined properties; you never have to define them yourself. All you have to worry about is getting values (which, for instances of Date, you do with what's affectionately known as *getter* methods, or *getters* for short) and setting values (using *setter* methods, or *setters*).

 The Date class supports many more methods than are shown here, many of which get and set time values based on different time zones. For details, visit msdn.microsoft.com/scripting/default.htm?/scripting/ jscript/default.htm (for Internet Explorer-supported classes) or developer.netscape.com/docs/manuals/js/client/jsref/partobj. htm (for Navigator-supported classes).

Date getters:

```
myDate.getDate() // returns the day of the month
myDate.getDay() // returns the day of the week
myDate.getHours() // returns the hours
myDate.getMinutes() // returns the minutes
myDate.getMonth() // returns the month, minus 1
myDate.getSeconds() // returns the seconds
myDate.getTime() // returns the date in milliseconds
myDate.getYear() // returns the year
```

Date setters:

```
myDate.setTime(milliseconds) // sets the time to specified
    number of milliseconds
myDate.setDate(dayOfMonth) // sets the day of the month where
    dayOfMonth is an integer between 1 and 31
myDate.setHours(hours) // sets the hours for a date where
    hours is an integer between 0 (midnight) and 23 (11 p.m.)
myDate.setMinutes(minutes) // sets the minutes for a date
    where minutes is an integer between 0 and 59
myDate.setMonth(month) // sets the month for a date where
    month is an integer between 0 (January) and 11 (December)
myDate.setSeconds(seconds) // sets the seconds for a date
    where seconds is an integer between 0 and 59
myDate.setTime(milliseconds) // sets a date to the specified
    number of milliseconds
myDate.setYear(year) // sets the year of a date where year is
    a four-digit value (such as 2005)
```

Other methods:

```
myDate.toString() // converts contents of date variable to a
    string
```

String

A String object is neither more nor less than a series of characters, usually surrounded by quotes, like this: "Ralph", "Henrietta and Bugsy", "123,456,789.00", or "1600 Pennsylvania Avenue". Using strings is the only way you can pass around pieces of text inside JavaScript. Unless you expect to do some arithmetic operations on a value, you probably want to work with the value in string form, which you can see exactly how to do in this section.

Syntax:

Two ways exist to create a string. One way is to use the built-in `String` data type, as shown in the first line of the following code; the other way is simply to surround the string value with double quotes ("like this") as shown in the second line of the following code.

```
var stringName = new String("stringValue")
var stringName = "stringValue"
```

Strings can be stored in variables but they don't have to be; when strings are not stored in variables, they're called *string literals*.

Example:

```
var stringName = new String("It was the best of times")
var stringName = "it was the worst of times"
```

Accessing String properties:

```
myString.length // number of characters in the string
```

The String class supports many more methods than are shown here, including match(), search(), and replace(). For details, visit msdn.microsoft.com/scripting/default.htm?/scripting/jscript/default.htm (for Internet Explorer-supported classes) or developer.netscape.com/docs/manuals/js/client/jsref/partobj.htm (for Navigator-supported classes).

Invoking String methods:

```
myString.blink() // Makes the string blink on and off
myString.bold() // Makes the string appear bold
myString.charAt(n) // Returns the character in the nth
    position
myString.fontcolor(fontColor) // Makes the string appear in
    color specified by fontColor
myString.fontsize(n) // Makes the string appear in the
    fontsize specified by n
myString.italics() // Makes the string appear in italics
myString.toLowerCase() // Makes the string appear in all
    lower case characters
myString.toUpperCase()// Makes the string appear in all upper
    case characters
```

Chapter 5: Defining and Using Functions

In This Chapter

✔ About functions

✔ Creating custom functions

✔ Using built-in functions

✔ Using functions to create your own custom objects

A *function* is a named group of JavaScript statements that, when called, execute all at once. Using functions is a powerful way to help you organize and streamline your JavaScript code.

About Using Functions

You can think of JavaScript functions as little "black boxes." When you call a function, that function:

+ Accepts optional input values, called *arguments*

+ Performs some kind of processing

+ Returns a result from all that processing, called a *return value*

Although JavaScript provides a handful of built-in functions, you're not nearly as likely to use them as you are to use the custom functions that you define. You can find a complete list of all the built-in JavaScript functions, as well as steps for how to create your own functions, in this chapter. Whether they're built-in or custom-designed, though, you call all functions the very same way.

Calling a function

When you want to call a function, it's essential that you know three things:

+ The correctly spelled name of the function

+ The number and type of arguments *(input parameters)* the function expects

+ What the function is supposed to return; for example, a number, a string, or whatever

The best way to find out the answer to these questions is to look at the function definition. If you created (or borrowed) the function, you probably have the function definition in front of you; if the function in question is one of the built-in JavaScript functions, you need to check out the JavaScript documentation, which you find by pointing your browser to `developer. netscape.com/docs/manuals/js/client/jsref/toplev.htm`.

For example, suppose that you want to call a function called `calculateTotal()` that

+ accepts two numeric arguments (one representing a number of items and one representing a purchase price), and

+ returns a number representing a total purchase price

Here's what the function call might look like:

```
var totalPrice = calculateTotal(3, 19.95)
```

The previous JavaScript code sends two numbers to the `calculateTotal()` function and places the numeric value returned by `calculateTotal()` into a variable called `totalPrice`.

You must define a function before you can call it; in other words, a function's definition must appear earlier in your script than a call to that function. (Built-in JavaScript functions are defined automatically; you can call them at the very top of your script if you want.)

Defining a function

Creating, or *defining*, a function is easy as pie. (Actually, whoever coined that phrase must have been better at rolling out pie crust than I am!) Here's the generic syntax for a function declaration:

```
function functionName([optionalArgument1][,
    optionalArgument2]
    [..., optionalArgumentN]){
    processing statements
return returnValue
}
```

Here's how the `calculateTotal()` function that was called in the preceding section may have been defined:

```
function calculateTotal(numberOrdered, itemPrice) {
    var result = numberOrdered * itemPrice
    return result
}
```

As you'd expect, this function multiplies the value for `numberOrdered` by the `itemPrice` and returns the result.

Returning values

The `return` keyword is used to hand a value from a function back to whatever line of code called the function in the first place. The calling line of code can then use the returned value for anything it wants (for example, display it or use it in further calculations). Technically, a function doesn't *have* to return a value but, in practice, most of them do. Here's the syntax for return:

```
return expression
```

You can see by the syntax that a function can return an expression, and an expression can be just about anything: a variable, a statement, or a complex expression. Check out these examples:

```
// returning a variable
return calculatedResult

// returning a statement
return (inputValue * 10)

// returning a complex expression
return (someValue / 100 + ((anotherValue * 55) % 9))
```

Make sure that the return statement is the very last statement in the body of your function. After all, return means just that — return. When the JavaScript interpreter hits the return statement, it returns to whatever line of code called it, right then and there, and continues interpreting the script. If you placed statements inside the function after the return statement, they'll never be evaluated.

Built-in Functions

The section, "Defining a function," earlier in this chapter, describes how to create your very own functions. The handful of functions you see in Table 5-1, though, are freebies — they've already been created and are ready and waiting for you if you ever want to call them.

For detailed instructions and examples on using the functions described in Table 5-1, visit `developer.netscape.com/docs/manuals/js/client/ jsref/toplev.htm`

Table 5-1	Built-in JavaScript Functions
Syntax	*Description*
escape(*string*)	Encodes a *string* containing special characters, such as spaces and tabs, so that they can be transferred safely between a Web page and a server-side program.
eval(*string*)	Evaluates a *string* containing a JavaScript phrase and returns the result.
isNaN(*value*)	Returns `true` if *value* is not a number; otherwise, returns `false`.
parseFloat(*string*)	Converts as many characters of *string* to a floating-point number as it can and returns this number; returns `NaN` if first character of string can't be converted.
parseInt(*string* [, *radix*])	Converts as many characters of *string* to an integer based on the specified base numbering system (*radix*) as it can and returns this integer. (If no radix is specified, a value of 10 is assumed.)
unescape(*string*)	Decodes a *string* into special characters, such as spaces and tabs, so that they can be transferred safely between a Web page and a server-side program.

Using Functions to Create Custom Objects

If you've had a chance to peek at "Document Object Model Basics" in Chapter 1 of this book, then you probably know that an *object* in JavaScript is a snippet of code that corresponds to a conceptual thing, such as a form, an input field, or a push button.

Objects are handy, no doubt: If you know you want to work with a form, for example, all you have to do is flip to the documentation for the `form` object (you find the latest at `msdn.microsoft.com/workshop/author/dhtml/reference/objects.asp` and `developer.netscape.com/docs/manuals/js/client/jsref/partobj.htm`) and bingo! In one neat little bundle you see what properties (characteristics) a form contains, what methods (behaviors) it contains, and how to access a form's properties and methods.

Objects are so handy, in fact, that the JavaScript language provides a way for you to create your own custom objects. In other words, you're not limited to the objects you find in a particular browser's document object model. If you're creating a script and feel the urge to create an `invoice` object, an `e-mail` object, a `customer` object, or any other kind of object, then you can by using the `new` and `this` operators in conjunction with a custom-built function. (*Operators* are special JavaScript keywords you use to perform operations, such as addition and subtraction, on objects. I give you an example below, but if you'd like to know more about operators right now, flip to Chapter 2. Don't worry — I'll wait!)

To get an idea of how to create your own object, first take a look at a function that defines how a customer object looks. You can see from looking at this function that every customer has an associated name, age, sex, and occupation:

```
function customer(inputName, inputAge, inputSex,
                  inputOccupation) {
     this.name = inputName
     this.age = inputAge
     this.sex = inputSex
     this.occupation = inputOccupation
}
```

In the JavaScript code you see above, the customer() function accepts four arguments and assigns these values to its own internal properties using the this keyword. (You see how these internal properties are accessed in the following block of code.)

C++ programmers refer to functions used this way as *classes,* and the objects that are created using the new operator, as demonstrated in the following code, as *instances.*

To create a new object based on the customer definition, you use the new operator, like this:

```
var firstCustomer = new customer("Junior Samples", 56, "M",
    "car dealer")

var secondCustomer = new customer("Margaret Martin", 38, "F",
    "contractor")
```

In the preceding JavaScript code, two variables containing customer objects are created: firstCustomer and secondCustomer. The properties associated with each customer object are different, because each was constructed using different data. To access the occupation of the second customer, you use the following line of code:

```
secondCustomer.occupation
```

To access the age of the first customer, you write the following:

```
firstCustomer.age
```

Working with custom objects can be complicated. (An entire programming discipline, called *object-oriented programming,* is devoted to the concept of creating and working with custom objects.) For more information on this topic, check out *JavaScript For Dummies,* 3rd Edition, by Emily A. Vander Veer.

Chapter 6: Adding Interactivity with Event Handlers

In This Chapter

✔ Getting familiar with the workings of the JavaScript event handling model

✔ Calling event handlers

In JavaScript, an *event* refers to some action (usually user-initiated) that affects a Web page element. Some examples of user-initiated events include

✦ Clicking — for example, clicking a radio button

✦ Checking — for example, checking a check box

✦ Selecting — for example, selecting an option in a drop-down list box

✦ Changing a value — for example, changing the text in a text field

You use an *event handler* to handle a specific event; in other words, to have the browser invoke a set of JavaScript statements automatically whenever the associated event occurs.

Calling Event Handlers

Typically, you add an event handler directly to the HTML definition of the associated object by using the following syntax:

```
<HTMLTAG onEvent="code you want the JavaScript interpreter to
    execute when the event occurs">
```

For example, in the following code snippet, the onAbort event handler is attached to an image object. When the user aborts image loading by clicking the browser Stop button, the message "Okay, but you missed a great picture!" appears in a pop-up alert box.

```
<IMG NAME="weed" SRC="thistle.gif" onAbort="alert('Okay, but
    you missed a great picture!')">
```

Alternatively, you can call event handlers outside of HTML statements, although doing so is somewhat less common. For details, visit `msdn.microsoft.com/scripting/default.htm?/scripting/jscript/default.htm` (for Internet Explorer support) or `developer.netscape.com/docs/manuals/js/client/jsref/partobj.htm` (for Navigator support).

Event Handlers Supported

Table 6-1 shows the event handlers that JavaScript supports, along with the associated events and the objects that support them.

Cross-browser, cross-platform support for JavaScript event handling is notoriously complicated. The event handlers you see in Table 6-1 work for the latest versions of Internet Explorer and Netscape Navigator, but may not work as expected on older browser versions (especially those on Macintosh and UNIX platforms). For the latest, definitive scoop on all the event handlers supported by the latest versions of both Internet Explorer and Netscape Navigator, check out `msdn.microsoft.com/scripting/default.htm?/scripting/jscript/default.htm` (for Internet Explorer support) or `developer.netscape.com/docs/manuals/js/client/jsref/partobj.htm` (for Navigator support).

Table 6-1	JavaScript Event Handlers	
Handler	*Event Handled*	*Associated with Which Object(s)*
onAbort	Loading interrupted	Image
onBlur	Element loses focus (element is deselected)	All elements
onChange	User chooses an option from a drop-down box (or enters text in a field) and then clicks somewhere else	Select, text input elements
onClick	User clicks once	Link, button elements
onDblClick	User clicks twice	Document, link, image, button elements
onError	Error occurs while loading an image	Image
onFocus	Element receives focus (element is selected)	Text elements, window, all other form elements
onKeyDown	User presses key down	Document, image, link, text elements

Handler	Event Handled	Associated with Which Object (s)
onKeyPress	User presses and releases key (combination onKey Down and onKeyUp)	Document, image, link, text elements
onKeyUp	User releases key	Document, image, link, text elements
onLoad	Loading finishes	Document, image
onMouseDown	User presses mouse button	Document, link, image, button elements
onMouseOut	Mouse moves off element	Link, image, layer
onMouseOver	Mouse moves over element	Link, image, layer
onMouseUp	User releases mouse button	Document, link, image, button elements
onReset	Form reset requested	Form
onResize	Resize requested	Window
onSubmit	Form submittal requested	(user clicks Submit button or programmer calls submit() method) Form
onUnload	Unloading finishes	Window

**Book VI
Chapter 6**

Adding Interactivity with Event Handlers

Chapter 7: Working with Forms

In This Chapter

✔ Validating user input with JavaScript

✔ Giving your users helpful feedback

*I*f you're familiar with HTML fill-in forms, you know how useful they can be. Adding an HTML form to your Web page lets your visitors communicate with you quickly and easily. Users can enter comments, contact information, or anything else into an HTML form. When users submit the form (usually by clicking a Submit button), the form data speeds directly to your Web server, where you can examine and process it.

JavaScript makes HTML forms even better. Using JavaScript, you can create intelligent forms — forms that instantly correct user input errors and provide helpful feedback. When you add JavaScript to your HTML forms, you create forms that are easy for your visitors to use — and that help you get the best quality data possible.

Data Validation Basics

To someone surfing the Web, few things are more annoying than typing a bunch of information into a form, clicking Submit, and then (after a lengthy wait while the form data travels all the way from their browser to a Web server and back again) seeing a generic error message that says something like, "You filled something out incorrectly."

JavaScript lets you check individual input fields and provides instant feedback to let your users know (before they tab clear down to the end of a long form) that they need to make a correction. Using JavaScript, you can also examine data after a user submits a form — but before the user's browser sends that form data off to your Web server. And instead of "You filled something out incorrectly," you can use JavaScript to give your users specific feedback such as, "You indicated you want us to contact you by phone, but you forgot to type your phone number in."

These two approaches are called *field-level validation* and *form-level validation*, respectively, and we discuss them in the following sections.

JavaScript For Dummies, 3rd Edition, by Emily A. Vander Veer, offers a more in-depth look at form validation than I can fit into this book. *JavaScript For Dummies* also includes sample validation scripts you can add directly to your Web pages.

Field-Level Validation

Independent fields are fields you can validate as soon as the user tabs away from them. An independent field is one that must be validated, regardless of what a user has typed in for any other field. The types of validation you want to perform on an independent field fall into the following three categories:

✦ **Ensuring a value exists.** Sometimes, you want to make sure a user enters a critical piece of information, such as a name. (In software parlance, this type of field is referred to as a *required field.*) Using JavaScript, you can detect whether a value exists after a user has clicked on the field and clicked away again, and if not, you can display a helpful reminder.

✦ **Ensuring a value is numeric.** When you expect users to type a number into a form field — for example, the number of products they want to purchase from you — you want to make sure they don't accidentally type in a word instead. (Performing mathematical calculations on a word is difficult, indeed!) Using JavaScript, you can detect whether a value is numeric, and if it's not, you can provide a message politely requesting your users to change their input.

✦ **Ensuring a value matches a pattern.** Sometimes you want your users to type in a common pattern, such as a phone number or e-mail address. Using JavaScript, you can examine the value your users type and make sure it conforms to the pattern you expect.

Ensuring a value exists

You can require that users provide a value for an HTML form field by attaching an *existence validation script* to one of that field's event handlers — typically, the `onChange` or `onBlur` event handlers. (Chapter 6 in this book gives you the lowdown on event handlers.)

Listing 7-1 shows you a JavaScript function, named `exists()`, that accepts a value, checks to see whether the value contains at least one character or number, and returns either `true` (if the value exists) or `false` (if the value does not exist).

Listing 7-1:   Testing for the Existence of an Input Value

```
function exists(inputValue) {

  ///////////////////////////////////////////////////
  // Assume the value doesn't exist until we know better
  ///////////////////////////////////////////////////
  var aCharExists = false

  ///////////////////////////////////////////////////
  // Step through the inputValue, using the charAt()
  // method to detect non-space characters.
  //
  // As soon as one character is detected, break out
  // of the loop.
  ///////////////////////////////////////////////////

  for (var i=0; i<=inputValue.length; i++) {
   if (inputValue.charAt(i) != " " && inputValue.charAt(i)
    != "") {
    aCharExists = true
    break
   }
  }

  return aCharExists
}
```

To call the function you see in Figure 7-1, you add an event handler to the text field for which you want to check existence. In the code snippet that follows, the text field is called firstName.

```
<INPUT TYPE="TEXT" NAME="firstName" SIZE="25" onBlur="if
    (!exists(this.value)) { alert('Please enter a first
    name'); }">
```

The ! operator you see in the JavaScript code above is the "not" operator — so called because when you see it, you whisper "not" to yourself. (For example, you read the code assigned to the onBlur operator as follows: "If the value of this text field does NOT exist. . .") This operator looks funny at first, but you get used to it quickly because it's so powerful — and so useful. For more information about the ! operator, check out Chapter 2 in this book.

For details on how the if. . .else conditional expression works, see Chapter 2 in this book.

When a user tabs away from the firstName text field, the field *blurs* (loses focus) and so the onBlur event handler passes the value of the firstName field to the exists() function. As soon as exists() receives this value, it begins stepping through the value one character at a time until it either detects a non-space character or comes to the end of the value. If it doesn't find a non-space character, it returns `false`, causing a pop-up alert dialog box to display the message "Please enter a first name," as shown in Figure 7-1.

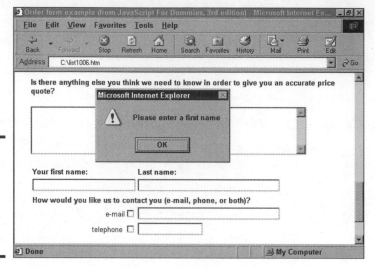

Figure 7-1: Using JavaScript, you can create a required field.

Ensuring a value is numeric

You can require that users provide a valid number for an HTML form field by attaching a *numeric validation script* to one of that field's event handlers — typically, either the `onChange` or `onBlur` event handler. (Chapter 6 in this book gives you the lowdown on event handlers.)

Listing 7-2 shows you a JavaScript function, named `isANumber()`, that accepts a value, uses the built-in JavaScript function `parseFloat()` to check whether the value contains any non-numeric characters, and returns either `true` (if the value is a valid number) or `false` (if it's not).

Listing 7-2: Testing an Input Value to See Whether It's Numeric

```
function isANumber(inputValue){

  // Assume everything is okay right off the bat
  var result = true

  // If parseFloat() returns false, a non-numeric
  // character was detected in the first position
```

```
if (!parseFloat(inputValue)) {
 result = false
}

// Otherwise, we still have to check all the
// rest of the digits, so step through
// the inputValue one character at
// a time and set result = false if any non-
// numeric values are encountered.

else {
   for (var i=0; i<inputValue.length; i++) {
   if (inputValue.charAt(i) != " ") {
    if (!parseFloat(inputValue.charAt(i))) {
     result = false
     break
      }
     }
   }
}

// Return true (inputValue is a valid number) or
// false (it's not).

 return result
}
```

To call the function you see in Listing 7-2, you add an event handler to the text field you want to validate. In the following code snippet, the text field is called numberOrdered.

```
<INPUT TYPE="TEXT" NAME="numberOrdered" SIZE="25" onBlur="if
   (isANumber(this.value)) {alert('Thank you for your
   order')} else {alert('Please enter the number of widgets
   you want to order');}">
```

When a user tabs away from the numberOrdered text field, the field *blurs* (loses focus) and so the onBlur event handler passes the value of the numberOrdered field to the isANumber() function. As soon as isANumber() receives this value, it begins stepping through the value one character at a time until it either detects a non-numeric character or comes to the end of the value. If it finds a non-numeric character, it returns false, causing a pop-up alert dialog box to display the message "Please enter the number of widgets you want to order."

If you need to brush up on the if...else conditional expression, check out Chapter 2 in this book.

Ensuring a value matches a pattern

You can require that users type in a value that matches a certain pattern, such as an e-mail address or a phone number, by attaching a *pattern-matching validation script* to one of that field's event handlers — typically, either the onChange or onBlur event handler. (Chapter 6 in this book gives you the lowdown on event handlers.)

Listing 7-3 shows you a JavaScript function, named isAValidEmail(), that accepts a value, uses the built-in JavaScript function charAt() to check for the existence of the At symbol (@) and a dot(.)in that order, and then returns either true (if the value contains both an @ and a .) or false (if it doesn't).

Listing 7-3:   A Script That Validates the E-mail Address Pattern

```
<SCRIPT LANGUAGE="JavaScript">

///////////////////////////////////////////////////
// Because all valid e-mail addresses contain a dot
// and the @ symbol, this function looks for these
// two characters. If they are found (and in the
// correct order, @ symbol first) the e-mail
// address is presumed valid; if not, the user
// is instructed to re-enter the e-mail address.
///////////////////////////////////////////////////

function isAValidEmail(inputValue) {

 var foundAt = false
 var foundDot = false
 var atPosition = -1
 var dotPosition = -1

 // Step through each character of the e-mail
 // address and set a flag when (and if) an
 // @ sign and a dot are detected.

 for (var i=0; i<=inputValue.length; i++) {
  if (inputValue.charAt(i) == "@" ) {
   foundAt = true
   atPosition = i
  }
  else if (inputValue.charAt(i) == ".") {
   foundDot = true
   dotPosition = i
  }
 }
```

```
// If both an @ symbol and a dot were found, and
// in the correct order (@ must come first)...

if ((foundAt && foundDot) && (atPosition < dotPosition)) {

  // It's a valid e-mail address

  alert("Thanks for entering a valid e-mail address!")
  return true
}
else {

  // The e-mail address is invalid

  alert("Sorry, you entered an invalid e-mail address.
  Please try again.")
  return false

}
}
```

To call the function you see in Listing 7-3, you add an event handler to the text field you want to validate. In the following code snippet, the text field is called emailAddress.

```
<INPUT TYPE="TEXT" NAME="emailAddress" SIZE="25"
    onBlur="isAValidEmail(this.value);">
```

When a user tabs away from the emailAddress text field, the field *blurs* (loses focus) and so the onBlur event handler passes the value of the emailAddress field to the isAValidEmail() function. As soon as isAValidEmail() receives this value, it begins stepping through the value one character at a time, looking first for the @ sign, and then for a dot (.). (This example assumes that a valid e-mail address contains both an @ and a ., in that order.) If both are found, isAValidEmail() displays a pop-up alert dialog box bearing the message "Thanks for entering a valid e-mail address!"; otherwise, the message that appears is "Sorry, you entered an invalid e-mail address. Please try again."

Fore more information on the if...else conditional expression, check out Chapter 2 in this book.

If you want to perform additional checks — for example, a check to ensure that at least one character precedes both the @ and the . or one to ensure that the last three characters are com, org, or edu — you can add the additional JavaScript statements to isAValidEmail() to do so. As a developer, the criteria that define a valid pattern are solely up to you. Whether the additional JavaScript statements necessary to catch all conceivable errors are worth the trouble and complexity is your decision, as well.

User feedback that helps, not hurts

Giving users appropriate, timely feedback can be the difference between a confusing Web site and one that is efficient and pleasant to use. Following are a few things to keep in mind as you decide when and how to interact with your users.

DON'T SHOUT!! Nobody likes being yelled at, and messages THAT ARE IN ALL UPPERCASE LIKE THIS AND END IN EXCLAMATION POINTS ARE YELLS! Say what you need to say; just use normal capitalization and punctuation.

Be specific. Sometimes, you don't particularly care what a user types (for example, if you're asking for freeform comments). At other times, what the user types is crucial. For the times when it's crucial, be sure to let the user know up front, right on the page, what format is expected. When you *do* need to include an error message, make sure that it tells users precisely what's wrong with their input. (`Invalid format. Please retry.` doesn't count!)

Give your users a break. Just because you're now a card-carrying expert at validating user input doesn't mean you have to include an error message *every* time you detect an error. In some cases, you may be able to *massage* (geek-speak for *modify*) the input data to suit yourself without bugging the user at all. For example, just because you'd like to see a value in uppercase letters doesn't mean the user has to enter it in uppercase letters. Instead of displaying an error and requesting that the user retype the entry, you can just as easily take the input and change it to uppercase yourself by using the `toUpperCase()` method of the `string` object.

Pat your users on the back. Don't reserve feedback for only those times when a user entered something incorrectly; reassuring users that things are proceeding as planned is just as useful. For example, let users know when a form passes all validation checks.

Test 'til you drop. Also (and this probably goes without saying, but you never know), make sure that you test your form carefully for every conceivable error (and series of errors) that a user might reasonably be expected to make. Few things are more frustrating to users than getting tangled in an endless loop of errors that refuse to go away, even *after* the user has figured out what's wrong and corrected it!

Form-Level Validation

You validate *dependent fields* when the user clicks the form's Submit button. A dependent field is one that may or may not need to be validated, depending on what a user has typed in for one or more other fields.

For example, suppose that you create an HTML form that requests, among other items,

✦ A preferred contact method (for which the user can check a radio button indicating either phone or e-mail)

✦ Two separate fields, one for a phone number and one for an e-mail address

Logically, you must wait until the user has had time to enter values for all of these fields before you can validate them. That's because the value for one field depends on the value for another. For example, you can't know that the e-mail address field is required until you know that users indicated they prefer to be contacted by e-mail.

You perform form-level validation by attaching a validation function to the onSubmit event handler associated with the form object:

```
<FORM NAME="quoteForm" onSubmit="return validateForm();">
```

In the previous code snippet, the JavaScript function validateForm() executes when the user clicks the Submit button associated with the quoteForm form.

If the form data passes the validation checks included in validateForm(), validateForm() returns a value of true, and the form data continues on to the Web server for further processing. If the form data fails the validation checks for any reason, validateForm() returns a value of false and the form data isn't transmitted.

The validation checks you include in your form validation function depend on your form, of course — what you name your text fields and how your text fields depend on each other. However, you may find the following tips helpful when creating your form validation function:

✦ **Access values through the document hierarchy.** To access field values from inside a script, you must follow standard object model syntax as described in Chapter 1 in this book. For example, to access a check box called emailChoice associated with a form named quoteForm, you type this: **document.quoteForm.emailChoice.checked**. To access a text field called emailAddr associated with the same form, you type this: **document.quoteForm.emailAddr.value**.

✦ **Use conditional expressions to validate form data.** You use conditional expressions, such as if...else, to determine whether user input meets the criteria you set. The listings in this chapter — Listings 7-1, 7-2, and 7-3 — contain examples of if...else. For more information about conditional expressions, check out Chapter 2 in this book.

✦ **Return a value of** true **or** false. Make sure the form validation function you create returns a value of true (if the data passes all your validation checks) or false (if it doesn't.) You may also choose to display a dialog box containing helpful feedback, as shown in Listing 7-3, but it's the return value that's responsible for determining whether the form data continues on to the server. (You can find out all about return values in Chapter 5 in this book.)

A common mistake new JavaScript programmers make is forgetting to include the return statement when defining the onSubmit event handler. If you forget to include the return statement, the form data continues on to the Web server, whether or not the validation function returns true or false.

Chapter 8: More Cool Things You Can Do with JavaScript

In This Chapter

✔ Hiding scripts from non-JavaScript-enabled browsers

✔ Generating pop-up messages

✔ Attaching scripts to clickable HTML elements

✔ Displaying a formatted date

✔ Reusing scripts with .js files

✔ Creating additional browser windows

✔ Creating automatically scrolling text

✔ Detecting browser versions and plug-ins

✔ Customizing Web page appearance based on user input

*O*ne of the most popular uses for JavaScript is form validation, which I demonstrate in Chapter 7. But you can do much more with JavaScript. In this chapter, I introduce you to a few more popular (and useful) ways to perk up your Web pages with JavaScript.

To use the JavaScript code in this chapter, you need to embed it in your HTML code by using the <SCRIPT></SCRIPT> tags. See Chapter 1 in this book to find out how.

Hiding Scripts from Non-JavaScript-Enabled Browsers

Users with non-JavaScript-enabled browsers who attempt to load your JavaScript-enabled Web page will be subjected to a frightfully ugly display: your JavaScript source code! (Because their browsers can't interpret JavaScript source code, the browsers assume it's text that's meant to be presented on-screen.) To keep this from happening (without affecting users running Navigator or Internet Explorer), all you have to do is add special comment characters just below the beginning <SCRIPT> tag and just above the ending <SCRIPT> tag:

```
<SCRIPT LANGUAGE="JavaScript">
<!--

(your JavaScript scripting statements go here)

// -->
</SCRIPT>
```

Note that these are special comments; they're neither standard HTML comments (which look like this: <!- ->) nor standard JavaScript comments (which look like this: //).

Generating Pop-up Messages

Pop-up messages are a great way to call users' attention to something (for example, when they enter a wrong value in a field). Generally, you want to assign one of these messages to the event handler of some input element — a button's onClick event handler, for example. (If you're interested, I cover event handlers in Chapter 6 of this book.) Be aware, though, that pop-up messages are fairly intrusive; users have to stop everything and deal with them before they can continue with what they were doing.

As you can see in Figures 8-1, 8-2, and 8-3, JavaScript supports three different kinds of pop-up messages, which you can create by using three different window methods: alert(), confirm(), and prompt(). To call any of these three methods, you must pass the string you want to display in the pop-up message, as shown in the following JavaScript code example. (You may specify an optional default value for the prompt() method, as shown.)

Figure 8-1:
You can use the Alert dialog box to let users know they typed an incorrect value.

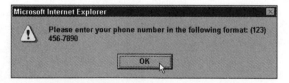

```
alert("Please enter your phone number in the
    following format: (123) 456-7890")

var answer = confirm("Do you really want to order 5,000
    toenail clippers?")

var numberOfOrders = prompt("Enter the number of orders you
    want to place", 1)
```

Figure 8-2:
The Confirm
dialog box
asks users
for their
okay.

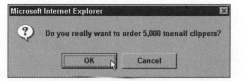

Figure 8-3:
The Prompt
dialog box
asks users
for input.

Attaching Scripts to Clickable HTML Elements

Just as Internet Explorer and Netscape Navigator recognize the http and
mailto protocols (special communication formats for Web pages and e-mail
messages, respectively), they also recognize the javascript protocol.

That means you can specify a JavaScript function as the value for the HREF
attribute associated with HTML tags such as <AREA> (a clickable area on an
image) and <A> (a hypertext link).

For example, the following line of code causes the JavaScript function
doit() to execute when a user clicks the link marked "Click here".

```
<A HREF="javascript:doit()">Click here</A>
```

Using the javascript protocol in this way enables you to execute a script
when a user clicks a link or a hotspot on an image.

Displaying a Formatted Date

When you create a variable of type Date, you get to use all the accessing methods that the Date class defines, as you see in Chapter 4. Unfortunately, the built-in Date methods only let you access the date a piece at a time, because that's how JavaScript stores data information — in discrete little chunks (hours, minutes, seconds, and so on). To display the current date on your Web page in a nice, attractive format, all you have to do is drop a few lines of JavaScript code similar to those in Listing 8-1 into your script.

Listing 8-1: Displaying a Formatted Date

```
// Get the current date
today = new Date();

// Get the current month
month = today.getMonth();

// Attach a display name to the month number
switch (month) {
    case 0 :
        displayMonth = "January"
        break
    case 1 :
        displayMonth = "February"
        break
    case 2 :
        displayMonth = "March"
        break

    <repeat for cases 3 through 8, April through November>

    case 11 :
        displayMonth = "December"
        break

    default: displayMonth = "INVALID"
}

document.writeln(displayMonth
    + " "
    + today.getDate()
    + ", "
    + today.getYear());
```

The result of the script is a date displayed in the following format:

```
June 21, 2001
```

For more information on the switch statement, which I don't discuss in this book, visit developer.netscape.com/docs/manuals/js/client/jsref/contents.htm.

Reusing Scripts with .js Files

You can separate your JavaScript statements from the rest of your HTML statements and put them in one or more special script files. Make sure you give your script files a meaningful names you can easily remember what each file contains. Also make sure you include the .js filename extension to your script files.

After you create a script file, you incorporate it into an HTML file by using the <SCRIPT>...</SCRIPT> tag pair, like so:

```
<SCRIPT LANGUAGE="JavaScript" SRC="myscript.js">
</SCRIPT>
```

In the example above, the myscript.js file is located in the same directory as the HTML document that includes the <SCRIPT> tag. If you want to place your script files in a directory other than the one in which your HTML documents are located, however, you can just assign the SRC attribute the fully qualified filename, like this:

```
<SCRIPT LANGUAGE="JavaScript" SRC="/myscripts/myscript.js">
</SCRIPT>
```

Organizing your JavaScript code into separate script files lets you reuse a single script file in multiple HTML files — without the hassle of cutting and pasting the script statements into each HTML file individually.

Creating Additional Browser Windows

One popular school of thought when it comes to Web design is to do everything you can to keep visitors at your site after they find it (within reason, of course!) For example, adding hypertext links to your site, while useful, may backfire by scooting your visitors off to other people's Web sites.

One remedy for this situation is to open HTML links in a new browser window. Visitors get to surf freely from your site to others, as appropriate — but without ever leaving your site. It's a win-win situation!

You create a new browser window using the open() method associated with the window object, as shown in the following code snippet.

```
open("newlink.htm", "secondWindow",
    "scrollbars,resizable,width=500,height=400");
```

As you can see, the `open()` method accepts three parameters:

✦ The URL you want to load into the new window (in this case, `newlink.htm`).

✦ The name for this new window (in this example, the name of the new window is `secondWindow`).

✦ A string of configuration options. In this example, the window created will have scrollbars, be resizable by a user, and appear with initial dimensions of 500 x 400 pixels.

To see a full description of the `open()` method, including all he configuration options supported, check out `developer.netscape.com/docs/manuals/js/client/jsref/window.htm#1202731`.

Creating Automatically Scrolling Text

For certain applications, scrolling text (either horizontal or vertical) can provide a sophisticated, eye-catching change from static text.

An option is to use the HTML `<MARQUEE>` tag, which allows you to create horizontally scrolling text effects. Unfortunately, the `<MARQUEE>` tag is only supported in Internet Explorer.

To create this effect, you

✦ Use the `scrollTo()` method associated with the `window` object to scroll the text to a specified spot on the screen.

✦ Use the `setTimeout()` and `clearTimeout()` methods associated with the `window` object to call `scrollTo()` over and over. (The repeated calling of `scrollTo()` creates the continuous scrolling effect.)

Listing 8-2 shows you an example.

Listing 8-2: Creating a Scrolling Text Effect

```
<SCRIPT LANGUAGE="JavaScript">

var position = 0

///////////////////////////////////////////////////
// Scroll vertically 1,000 pixels (which is enough
// times to display the content for a page when
```

```
// viewed in a standard-sized window.)
/////////////////////////////////////////////////

function scrollIt() {
    if (position != 1000) {
        position++;

        // Because you want to scroll vertically only
        // in this case, you continue to pass 0 to
        // the scrollTo() function but bump up the
        // value of the position variable each time
        // you call scrollTo().  This makes the
        // scroll effect appear to be very smooth.

        window.scrollTo(0, position);
        clearTimeout(timer);
        var timer = setTimeout("scrollIt()", 25);
    }
}
</SCRIPT>
```

**Book VI
Chapter 8**

When you attach the preceding scrollIt() function to the onLoad event handler associated with the HTML <BODY> tag, the document begins auto-scrolling vertically (as if a user were dragging the right scroll bar downward slowly) the instant it's loaded into a browser.

```
<BODY onLoad="scrollIt()">
```

For a detailed description of the scroll(), setTimeout(), and clearTimeout() methods, check out developer.netscape.com/docs/manuals/js/client/jsref/bklast.htm

Including scrolling text can be a good way to draw attention to something on your page, but misused, it can be very annoying! For maximum effectiveness, use scrolling effects sparingly.

Detecting Browser Version and Plug-ins

Sometimes you may find it useful to determine what version browser your users are running, or what browser plug-ins they have installed. For example, if you want to take advantage of a nifty HTML trick that only Internet Explorer supports, you may want to use JavaScript to check whether your users are running Internet Explorer — then display your Internet Explorer-optimized page for Internet Explorer users, and another for Netscape Navigator users.

Detecting browser version

You detect the make and version of a browser loading your Web page by adding a browser-detecting JavaScript code to the <HEAD> section of your HTML file. The JavaScript code you add must examine the `navigator` object, which is a built-in object created by the browser that stores all browser-related information.

For example, suppose you want to create a JavaScript-enabled Web page that

✦ Draws viewers' attention by scrolling a line of text

✦ Allows the user to stop (and restart) the scrolling action

The easiest way to implement this functionality is by using the <MARQUEE> tag, which is an HTML tag (and corresponding scripting object) supported by Internet Explorer (beginning with version 3.*x*). Trouble is, Navigator and many other browsers don't support the <MARQUEE> tag! When a non-marquee-supporting browser loads a Web page containing the <MARQUEE> tag, it may display the scrolling text statically, ignore your marquee-related JavaScript code, or generate a JavaScript error.

One way to ensure that your viewers see what you want them to see is by using JavaScript to detect whether the browser loading your script is Internet Explorer, version 3.*x* or higher. If it is, you can use the <MARQUEE> tag with confidence. If the browser *isn't* Internet Explorer version 3.*x* or higher, you can display the scrolled information in an alternate eye-catching fashion — for example, as a bolded, centered heading.

Listing 8-3 shows a snippet of code from a script that examines browser settings and displays a string of text either as a scrolling marquee, or as a bolded, centered heading (depending on whether the browser loading the script is Internet Explorer 3.*x* and higher).

The code in Listing 8-3 is excerpted from Netscape's "ultimate" sniffer script — so called because it "sniffs out" which browser a user is running. You can see Netscape's sniffer script in its entirety by going to

```
developer.netscape.com/docs/examples/javascript/browser_type_
oo.html
```

Listing 8-3:   An Excerpt from a Browser "sniffer" Script

```
function Is () {
    // convert to lowercase to simplify testing
    var agt=navigator.userAgent.toLowerCase();

    this.major = parseInt(navigator.appVersion);
```

```
    this.minor = parseFloat(navigator.appVersion);

    this.nav = ((agt.indexOf('mozilla')!=-1) &&
                (agt.indexOf('spoofer')==-1) &&
                (agt.indexOf('compatible') == -1) &&
                (agt.indexOf('opera')==-1) &&
                (agt.indexOf('webtv')==-1));

    this.nav2 = (this.nav && (this.major == 2));
    this.nav3 = (this.nav && (this.major == 3));
    this.nav4 = (this.nav && (this.major == 4));
    this.nav4up = (this.nav && (this.major >= 4));
    this.navonly = (this.nav && ((agt.indexOf(";nav") != -
1) ||
                    (agt.indexOf("; nav") != -1)) );
    this.nav5 = (this.nav && (this.major == 5));

    ...

    this.ie = (agt.indexOf("msie") != -1);
    this.ie3 = (this.ie && (this.major < 4));
    this.ie4 = (this.ie && (this.major == 4) &&
                (agt.indexOf("msie 5.0")==-1) );
    this.ie4up = (this.ie && (this.major >= 4));
    this.ie5 = (this.ie && (this.major == 4) &&
                (agt.indexOf("msie 5.0")!=-1) );
    this.ie5up = (this.ie && !this.ie3 && !this.ie4);

    ...

    this.aol = (agt.indexOf("aol") != -1);
    this.aol3 = (this.aol && this.ie3);
    this.aol4 = (this.aol && this.ie4);
    this.opera = (agt.indexOf("opera") != -1);
    this.webtv = (agt.indexOf("webtv") != -1);
...

} // end Is() function declaration

var is = new Is(); // create a new instance of the Is
    object

if (is.ie3up || is.ie4up || is.ie5up) {
    // the MARQUEE element is supported, so use it
    var builtInScroll = '<FORM NAME="myForm"><MARQUEE ID=abc
    DIRECTION=LEFT BEHAVIOR=SCROLL SCROLLAMOUNT=2>You are
    running IE 3,4, or 5, so the scrolling MARQUEE tag is
    supported.</MARQUEE><INPUT TYPE="button" VALUE="Start
    scrolling" NAME="startscroll"
    onClick="document.all.abc.start()"><INPUT TYPE="button"
    VALUE="Stop scrolling" NAME="stopScroll" onClick=-
    "document.all.abc.stop()"></FORM>';
        }
```

```
else {
    // display an attractive, non-scrolling alternative
    var builtInScroll = '<CENTER><H1>You are not running IE
    3, 4, or 5, so the scrolling MARQUEE tag is NOT
    supported.</H1></CENTER>'
}
document.write(builtInScroll)
}
```

The first half of the previous code snippet combs through the information stored in the navigator object to classify the executing browser as one of several different variables: ie3up (meaning Internet Explorer version 3 and later), ie4up (Internet Explorer version 4 and later), and so on.

Near the bottom of the listing, the information gleaned is used to make a presentation decision. If the executing browser is Internet Explorer 3, 4, or 5, the scrolling text element <MARQUEE> is supported. So in these cases, the write() method is used to implement an HTML document containing the <MARQUEE> tag.

In cases where the executing browser is not Internet Explorer 3, 4, or 5, the write() method is used to create an HTML document containing plain text.

As you can see from this section, detection scripts can be complicated to create. Not only do you have to know which properties of the navigator object to query, but also what the cryptic values you find there are supposed to represent — information that neither Netscape nor Microsoft makes readily available. So, to help you get started, I've included a browser "sniffer" script (list0803.htm) on the CD that comes with this book. Feel free to experiment with it and modify it to handle future browser versions.

Detecting browser plug-ins

A browser *plug-in* is a small add-on program that "plugs in" to a browser to enable users to view specially formatted content in their browser. An example of a popular plug-in is Macromedia Flash, which enables users to view cool animated effects in their browsers.

Sometimes you want to detect whether a user loading your Web page has a certain plug-in installed. For example, if you want to display a Flash animation on your Web page, you may want to determine, right up front, whether a user has a Flash plug-in installed — and, if not, either display an alternative Web page or display a message explaining where users can download the Flash plug-in.

You detect browser plug-ins in two ways:

✦ **Detecting plug-ins in Navigator.** As shown in Listing 8-4, you can access the `navigator.plugins[]` array, which contains a list of all of the plug-ins supported by Navigator. You can also access the `navigator.mimeTypes[]` array, which contains a list of all of the MIME types supported by Navigator. (MIME, which stands for *Multipurpose Internet Mail Extension*, refers to the file types that Navigator can understand and display. Examples of popular MIME types include Adobe's portable document framework (PDF) and Real.com's RealAudio (ram).

✦ **Detecting plug-ins in Internet Explorer.** Internet Explorer implements plug-ins as ActiveX objects. To detect these ActiveX objects, you access the `document.embeds[]` array as shown in Listing 8-5.

**Book VI
Chapter 8**

**More Cool Things
You Can Do with
JavaScript**

Listing 8-4:   Detecting Plug-ins in Netscape Navigator

```
if (navigator.plugins.length > 0) {
    alert(navigator.plugins.length + " plug-ins detected")
}
```

In Internet Explorer, the `navigator.plugins[]` and `navigator.mimeTypes[]` arrays are always null, because Internet Explorer implements embedded ActiveX objects in place of plug-ins. To detect embedded content in documents viewed in Internet Explorer, access the `document.embeds[]` array as shown in Listing 8-5.

Listing 8-5:   Detecting Plug-ins (ActiveX Objects) in Internet Explorer

```
if (document.embeds.length > 0) {
    alert(document.embeds.length + " embedded element(s)
    detected.")
}
```

Customizing Web Pages Based on User Input

Using JavaScript, you can offer your users the opportunity to view your Web site the way *they* want to view it.

How? By triggering a `prompt()` method on the `onLoad` event handler and using the user's response to build the body section of an HTML document. Listing 8-6 shows you a simple example.

Listing 8-6:   Customizing Page Appearance on the Fly

```
// Ask the user for a color preference (default is red)
var displayColor = prompt("What background color do you
    want?", "red")

// The default text color is black
var textColor = "black"

// If the user chooses a black background, change
// the text to white so it is visible

if (displayColor == "black" || displayColor == "#000000" ||
    displayColor == null) {
  textColor = "white"
}

// Display page content
document.writeln("<BODY BGCOLOR=" + displayColor + " TEXT="
    + textColor + ">You chose " + displayColor + "</BODY>")
```

When the script in Listing 8-6 is placed between the beginning and ending HTML <HEAD>...</HEAD> tags, the script statements execute right away — before the Web page loads. The prompt() method prompts the user to enter a favorite color; that color is then used to construct and display the document body. (If the user clicks Cancel, the default color scheme — white text on a black background — is used.)

You use the writeln() method of the window object to create a window on the fly. The argument you pass to the writeln() method, as shown in the example above, contains HTML tags, in string form, appended together into one long string using the addition (+) operator.

Index

Symbols

A

B

C

D

E

F

function(s)

H

I

J

Notes

Book VII

Flash 5

The 5th Wave By Rich Tennant

@RICHTENNANT

"FRANKLY, I'M NOT SURE THIS IS THE WAY TO ENHANCE OUR COLOR GRAPHICS."

Contents at a Glance

Chapter 1: Getting to Know Flash

In This Chapter

✔ Understanding the moviemaking process

✔ Starting Flash

✔ Working with movie files

✔ Tailoring your work environment with panels

✔ Setting Flash preferences

✔ Streamlining your workflow with keyboard shortcuts

✔ Getting help

Macromedia Flash 5 is one of the most popular tools around for creating cool, Web-friendly animations. (By *Web-friendly* I mean animations that are compact and run inside Web browsers with the help of a free, easily installed browser plug-in.) Using Flash, you can create animated effects, interactive interface elements (such as mouse rollovers that respond to a user's click), and even synchronize your visual masterpieces with sound.

This chapter begins with an overview of the moviemaking, or animation creation, process; then it introduces you to Flash. You see how to start Flash, work with movie files, and tailor your work environment by creating customized panels and setting preferences. You also see how to create keyboard shortcuts to cut down on your development time and get help when you need it.

Understanding the Moviemaking Process

Flash is a powerful animation tool, and the animation process itself is fairly complex — so creating animated movies can be confusing for first-time animators. Armed with the following overview of the moviemaking process, however, you can create animated movies with Flash with a minimum of muss and fuss.

Basically, an animated movie is nothing more than a series of *frames* displayed one after the other. Placing a different image in each frame of a movie creates the illusion of movement when the movie plays.

Don't confuse animation frames with HTML frames; the two are very different.

To create an animated movie in Flash, you first create a series of images. Figure 1-1 shows the drawing area (called the Stage) and drawing tools you use to create images in Flash. (Chapter 2 describes the Flash drawing tools in detail; for now, just be aware that you find all sorts of useful drawing tools in the Toolbar that stretches across the top of the Stage, and in the Tool panels you see on the left side of Figure 1-1.)

After you create a series of images, you use the Timeline shown in Figure 1-1 to associate each image with an animation frame. You can do this in one of two general ways:

✦ You can associate each image with a separate frame individually.

✦ You can associate two images — for example, an image of a puppy on the left side of a food dish and an image of the same puppy on the right side of a food dish — with a special kind of frame known as a *keyframe*. Then you can tell Flash to generate all the "in between" images and frames necessary to create an animation in which the puppy moves from the left side of the food dish to the right. (You find out about tweening in Chapter 6, "Making Movies.")

For more sophisticated animations involving several images stacked one on top of the other, you can associate individual images with separate layers by taking advantage of the Layers window in Figure 1-1. (Chapter 4, "Using Layers," is devoted to layers.)

You can also add many different effects to the individual images that make up your movie. For example, you can make text or images appear to fade, change color, or respond to mouse clicks. You can also add sound to your movies. (Chapter 6, "Making Movies," demonstrates applying these and other effects.)

Layers window   Timeline   Symbol Library

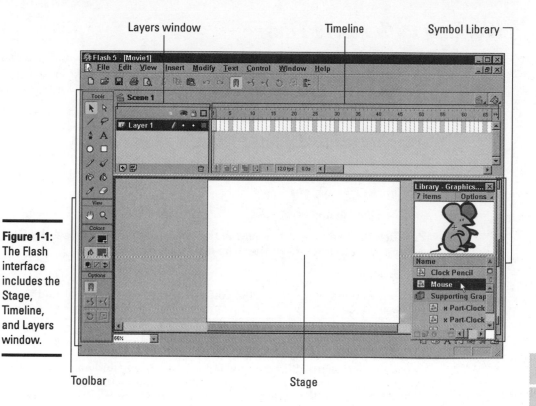

Figure 1-1:
The Flash
interface
includes the
Stage,
Timeline,
and Layers
window.

Toolbar   Stage

Starting Flash

Follow these steps to start Flash:

1. **Click the Start button on the Windows task bar.**

The Start menu appears.

2. **Choose Programs⇨Macromedia Flash 5⇨Flash 5.**

(Alternatively, find the Flash 5 icon on your desktop and double-click it
to start Flash.)

As soon as Flash launches, a new movie file like the one shown in Figure 1-1
appears, ready for your direction. You see an empty Stage, an empty
keyframe in the first position on the Timeline, and an empty Layer titled
Layer 1.

Working with Movie Files

You can create and work with movie files in Flash, of course — but you can also import movie files created in other programs (for example, Adobe Illustrator) and edit those imported movie files by using Flash tools. You use the File menu option to open and save files in Flash.

Opening a Flash movie file

To open an existing movie file, do the following:

1. **Choose File➪Open.**

The Open dialog box appears.

2. **Click the arrow you see next to the Look in: field and select the file you want to open from the drop-down list that appears.**

3. **Click Open.**

The contents of the movie file you selected in Step 2 appear on the Flash stage.

Importing a non-Flash file

You can import many different types of existing image and animation files into Flash. For example, you can import files created with Adobe Illustrator (.eps files) and Apple QuickTime (.mov) files into Flash.

To import a non-Flash file into Flash, follow these steps:

1. **Choose File➪Import.**

The Import dialog box appears.

2. **Click the arrow next to the Look in: field and select the file you want to open from the drop-down list that appears.**

3. **Select the type of file you want to import in the Files of Type drop-down list.**

4. **Double-click the desired file in the Import dialog box (or right-click the file and click the Open button).**

If you don't see the type of file you want listed in the Files of Type drop-down list, don't despair! If you have access to the authoring tool used to create the original file, try to use that tool's export function to export the file in a format — such as .fla or .gif — that *does* appear in the Files of Type drop-down list.

Saving a movie file

To save a movie file under its current name, choose File⇨Save; then click Save in the Save As dialog box that appears.

To save the movie with a new name and location, follow these steps:

1. **Choose File⇨Save As.**

The Save As dialog box appears.

2. **Type a new name for the movie in the File Name text box.**

3. **Navigate to the location where you want to save the movie by clicking the arrow next to the Save in: field and selecting the file you want to save from the drop-down list that appears.**

4. **Click Save.**

To close a movie file without saving it, choose File⇨Close and click No in the dialog box that appears.

Flash always saves movie files by using the .fla extension.

Tailoring Your Work Environment with Panels

Panels are floating boxes you use to modify selected movie-related items, such as color, text, images, and frames. You can display multiple panels at the same time, if you want. You can also resize and reposition panels to create a customized working environment.

By displaying and accessing the appropriate panel, you can easily work with every aspect of a movie, including colors, text, and frames.

Displaying panels

To display a panel, choose Window⇨Panels and select a panel option. The following list describes what you can do in each panel:

✦ **Info panel:** Edit the size and location of an object.

✦ **Fill panel:** Select a fill color and design linear and radial gradients.

✦ **Stroke panel:** Select stroke color, style, and width. (The options in this panel pertain to objects drawn with drawing tools that create strokes, such as the Pen and Pencil tools.)

✦ **Transform panel:** Rotate, skew, and scale an object, text, or a bitmap.

✦ **Align panel:** Align, distribute, and match size and spacing among selected groups of objects.

✦ **Mixer panel:** Select color in three modes: RGB, HSB, and Hex. Also set alpha transparency. Provides easy access to Stroke and Fill colors.

✦ **Swatches panel:** Manage color, save color sets, sort, and import color.

✦ **Character panel:** Edit a font's size, color, kerning, leading, and baseline shift. Also, set links.

✦ **Paragraph panel:** Align, indent, and set paragraph spacing.

✦ **Text Options panel:** Set parameters for text form fields (input fields) or dynamic text (regularly updated text; for example stock tickers, sports scores, or weather reports).

✦ **Instance panel:** Recall information of *symbols* (reusable templates, such as graphics, animations, and buttons) and *instances* (specific copies of symbols) in your movie.

✦ **Effect panel:** Create color tints and transparency effects for vector graphics.

✦ **Clip Parameters panel:** Add parameters to your movie clip. Adding parameters and an ActionScript script to a clip creates a *smart* clip — so called because the way it displays can vary based on user interaction. (For example, a smart clip may incorporate surveys, buttons, or pop-up menus.)

✦ **Frame panel:** Set Motion and Shape tweens.

✦ **Sound panel:** Set and edit sound, effects, and loops, and synchronize sounds.

✦ **Scene panel:** Control and manipulate scenes in your movie.

✦ **Generator panel:** Work with authoring templates that are extensions of the Flash authoring environment.

The Options menu in some panels enables you to select additional options when you work with a movie-related item. To display the Options menu for a panel, click the triangle in the panel's upper-right corner. (If the triangle is dimmed, no options are available for that panel.)

Closing panels

To close a panel, click the Close box you see in the upper-right corner of the panel.

To close *all* displayed panels, select Window⇨Close All Panels from the main menu.

Grouping panels

Grouping panels enables you to create a custom panel containing only panels that you access most often. For example, you may want to combine the Mixer, Fill, Stroke, and Swatch panels when you work with color.

To group panels, follow these steps:

1. **Position the cursor over the tab of a panel, as shown in Figure 1-2. Click and hold down the mouse button.**

2. **Drag the panel by the tab and drop it over the tab of another panel.**

3. **Release the mouse button.**

Align panel tab

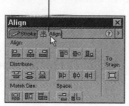

Figure 1-2: Click and drag a panel tab to group panels.

You can separate grouped panels by dragging a panel tag outside its panel and dropping it either on the work area (to create a separate panel) or on another panel tab (to regroup that panel).

To save your grouped panels, follow these steps:

1. **Choose Window⇨Save Panel Layout.**

The Save Panel Layout dialog box appears.

2. **Type a name you want to assign to this panel configuration.**

3. **Click OK.**

You can reset the default Flash panel configuration by choosing Window⇨Panels Sets and selecting Default Layout from the drop-down menu that appears.

Setting Flash Preferences

Setting preferences tells the Flash program how you want certain operations to be executed. Flash allows you to set preferences for three areas: General, Editing, and Clipboard.

Book VII Chapter 1

Getting to Know Flash

Setting General Preferences

General Preferences pertain to the way Flash operates overall. For example, by setting General Preferences, you can tell Flash to stop (or start) displaying Tooltips, the tips that appear when you move your mouse over a tool icon in the Tools panel. Follow these steps to set General Preferences:

1. **Choose Edit⇨Preferences.**

The Preferences dialog box appears.

2. **Click the General tab, as shown in Figure 1-3, and select the appropriate settings:**

- **Undo Levels:** Set the value from 0 to 200, depending on how many times you want to be able to undo changes you make to a Flash movie. (You undo a change to a Flash file by choosing Edit⇨Undo.) Remember that the higher the number, the more system memory Flash uses. This can cause a slowdown in response when working. The default setting is 100.

- **Printing Options:** Select to disable PostScript output when printing to a PostScript printer. (Disabling PostScript output helps you troubleshoot problems printing to a PostScript printer.) The default setting is off.

- **Selection Options:** Two options are grouped under this heading. Turning on the Shift Select feature means that you need to hold down the Shift key to select multiple items. Turning off Shift Select lets you select multiple items without bothering with the Shift key. Selecting the Show Tooltips feature prompts Flash to display tips when the cursor pauses over a tool button. Deselect Show Tooltips to turn off the tips.

- **Timeline Options:** You find three options under the Timeline Options heading. Selecting the Disable Timeline Docking feature prevents the Timeline from attaching to the application window after the two have been separated. Selecting the Flash 4 Selection Style feature lets you use the Flash 4 highlighting style in selected frames; selecting the Flash 4 Frame Drawing feature enables you to draw frames by using the Flash 4 frame drawing scheme.

- **Highlight Color:** You can choose Use this Color and pick a color to use as the highlight color (in other words, the color you want Flash to use to denote a selected item), or choose Use Layer Color to specify a highlight color from the currently selected layer.

- **Actions Panel: <u>Mode:</u>** Select one of two modes from the drop-down list. Normal Mode uses controls in the panel to create actions, which you associate with one or more frames. (An *action* is a specific action you want Flash to perform, such as "play the movie," "stop the movie," or "go to a specific frame number — such as frame #3).
" Expert Mode enables you to create actions by entering ActionScript code directly into the text box on the panel. (*ActionScript* is the scripting language Flash uses to allow you to add interactivity to a movie.)

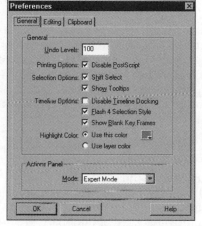

Figure 1-3:
The
Preferences
dialog box
enables
you to set
General,
Editing, and
Clipboard
preferences.

Setting Editing Preferences

In Flash parlance, *editing* means making a change to a movie file. So, every time you add an image, draw a shape, or change a line of text, you're editing.

However, the Editing Preferences Flash provides focus only on the changes you make to a movie file by using drawing tools. By setting the Editing Preferences, you can tell Flash to smooth your shakily-drawn arcs, connect almost-connected lines, and more, automatically.

To set the Editing Preferences, follow these steps:

1. **Choose <u>E</u>dit⇨<u>P</u>references.**

The Preferences dialog box appears.

2. **Click the Editing tab and choose the appropriate settings:**

   - **Pen Tool:** Under the Pen Tool heading, you can set three different options. The Show Pen Preview feature previews line segments as you draw, the Show Solid Points feature displays selected anchor points as hollow points and unselected anchor points as solid points, and the Show Precise Cursors feature displays the pen icon as a cross-hair icon, allowing for accurate placement.

   - **Drawing Settings:** The Drawing Settings heading brings together five separate options. The Connect Lines feature lets Flash automatically close ending points to beginning points of segments you draw by using the Pencil tool. The Smooth Curves feature enables you to determine how rough or smooth the curved lines as you draw should be. The Recognize Lines feature lets Flash automatically straighten any line segments you draw with the Pencil tool, whereas the Recognize Shapes feature lets Flash automatically identify the geometric shapes you draw and redraws them accurately. Finally, the Click Accuracy feature allows you to tell Flash how near the cursor must be to an item before Flash identifies it.

Setting Clipboard Preferences

You can cut, copy, and paste images to the Flash clipboard by choosing Edit⇨Cut, Edit⇨Copy, and Edit⇨Paste, respectively. To help you configure how you want Flash to store images on the clipboard — and, consequently, restore those images — Flash provides special Clipboard Preferences you can set.

To set the Clipboard Preferences, follow these steps:

1. **Choose Edit⇨Preferences.**

   The Preferences dialog box appears.

2. **Click the Clipboard tab and choose the appropriate settings:**

   - **Bitmaps:** The options under this heading include Color Depth (which sets the color depth parameters for bitmaps copied to the clipboard), Resolution (which sets the resolution parameters for bitmaps copied to the clipboard), Size limit (which sets limits for the amount of RAM being used to transfer a bitmap image to the clipboard), and Smooth (which lets you use the antialiasing feature to blur the image lightly).

   - **Gradients:** Sets the quality of gradient fills when pasting items into another application or outside of Flash. The default setting within the Flash application is always Normal.

   - **FreeHand Text:** Select Maintain Text as Blocks to ensure that you can still edit text in a pasted Macromedia FreeHand file.

Streamlining Your Work with Keyboard Shortcuts

For commands you enter repeatedly, using a keyboard shortcut can save you time and mouse clicks. Keyboard shortcuts enable you to click a simple key combination to perform an action (as opposed to selecting from a series of cascading menu options).

Most Flash commands come with keyboard shortcuts already assigned; however, by duplicating the built-in Flash keyboard shortcut set, you can add new shortcuts and modify existing shortcuts to your heart's content.

To modify a shortcut, follow these steps:

1. **Choose Edit⇨Keyboard Shortcuts.**

The Keyboard Shortcuts dialog box appears.

2. **Select the keyboard shortcut set you want to modify from the Current Set: drop-down list.**

Note: you can't create new shortcuts — or modify existing shortcuts — for the Flash built-in keyboard shortcut set. (And a good thing, too, when you think about it!) You can only create and modify shortcuts associated with your own custom keyboard shortcut set. To create your own custom keyboard shortcut set, select Flash 5 from the Current Set: drop-down list; then click the Duplicate Set icon you see directly to the right of the Current Set: drop-down list. In the Duplicate dialog box that appears, type the name of a custom set in the Duplicate Name: field; then click OK. After you create your own custom keyboard shortcut set, you can add, modify, and delete keyboard shortcuts at will.

3. **Choose one of the following from the Commands drop-down list: Drawing Menu Commands, Drawing Tools, or Test Movie Menu Commands.**

A list of commands associated with your choice appears in the scroll box you see beneath the Commands drop-down list. For example, choosing Drawing Tools from the Commands drop-down list displays a list of commands associated with Flash drawing tools.

4. **Scroll through the Commands list until you find a command for which you want a shortcut.**

A description of each command appears below the scrolling list of commands. The shortcut appears in the Commands scrolling list as well as the Shortcuts section. For example, the File⇨Open command appears next to the Ctrl+O shortcut.

5. **Select the shortcut text you want to change in the Shortcuts: field.**

Flash highlights the selected shortcut text.

6. **Select the text in the Press Key: field located just below the Shortcuts: field.**

   Flash highlights the selected text.

7. **Press the shortcut key combination you want to associate with the command.**

   Flash translates your key presses into shortcut text and displays that shortcut text in the Shortcuts: field.

   For example, if you want to change the shortcut for the File⇨Open command from Ctrl+O to Ctrl+Shift+O, you press those three keys — the Ctrl key, the Shift key, and the O — all at once.

8. **Click Change; then click OK.**

   Flash modifies the shortcut and the Keyboard Shortcuts dialog box disappears.

To add a new shortcut, perform Steps 1 through 5; then click the (+) button next to the Shortcuts: section. Doing so displays and highlights <empty> in the Press Key: field. Continue with Steps 7 and 8 to finish adding your new shortcut.

To delete a shortcut, perform the preceding steps to specify a shortcut; then click the (-) button next to the Shortcuts section and click OK.

Getting Help

Flash provides a comprehensive Help System that includes tutorials and online technical support. To access the Flash Help System, choose Help from the main menu and select one of the help options that appears:

✦ **What's New in Flash 5:** New features in the latest version of Flash.

✦ **Using Flash:** Contains basic information, tutorials, a search facility, and more.

✦ **ActionScript Reference:** Describes the ActionScript language, including syntax and examples.

✦ **ActionScript Dictionary:** Contains a list of all the ActionScript keywords and operators.

✦ **Macromedia Dashboard:** Allows you to organize links to Flash-related Internet sites.

✦ **Flash Support Center:** Loads the Flash technical support center Web site into a browser window.

✦ **Register Flash:** Allows you to register your purchased copy of Flash.

✦ **Flash Exchange:** Loads the Flash exchange center Web site into a browser window. (You can use this site to exchange Flash *extensions* — bits of code that extend the Flash application — with other developers.)

✦ **Manage Exchange Items:** Displays the Macromedia Extension Manager dialog box, which you can use to import and install Flash extensions.

✦ **Samples:** Displays several Flash movies you can examine, play, and modify.

✦ **Lessons:** Displays several step-by-step tutorials on Flash topics, including Drawing, Symbols, and Layers.

✦ **About Flash:** Displays the latest version number of Flash.

You can display the Help System interface at any time during a Flash session by pressing F1. Also, clicking the right mouse button while positioning the mouse cursor over the Stage, Timeline, or Layer window displays context-sensitive help menus.

Chapter 2: Creating and Modifying Images

In This Chapter

✔ Locating and using drawing tools

✔ Using tools to draw, paint, or otherwise modify images

*T*his chapter introduces you to the drawing tools that Flash offers. You can use drawing tools to create original artwork or modify existing images. Pens, Pencils, Erasers, and Paint Buckets are just a few of the tools you explore in this chapter.

Locating and Using Drawing Tools

To create, select, and modify artwork, you use the Tools window shown in Figure 2-1 to select and apply one or more tools to your Flash workspace, the Stage. The Tools window should appear automatically when you start Flash.

If you don't see the Tools window, choose Window⇨Tools to display it.

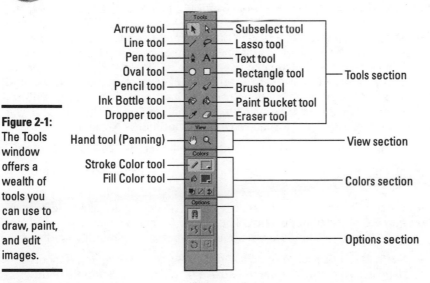

Figure 2-1: The Tools window offers a wealth of tools you can use to draw, paint, and edit images.

Arrow tool — Subselect tool
Line tool — Lasso tool
Pen tool — Text tool
Oval tool — Rectangle tool
Pencil tool — Brush tool
Ink Bottle tool — Paint Bucket tool
Dropper tool — Eraser tool
— Tools section

Hand tool (Panning) — View section

Stroke Color tool
Fill Color tool
— Colors section

— Options section

As Figure 2-1 shows, the Tools window contains four distinct sections:

✦ **Tools:** Contains the tools you use to draw, paint, and select. This chapter describes the tools in the Tool section.

✦ **Views:** Contains tools for repositioning and zooming images on the Stage.

✦ **Colors:** Contains the stroke and fill modifiers. (You use the *stroke* modifier to specify a color for stroke-related tools, such as the Line and Pen tools; you use the *fill* modifier to specify a color for fill-related tools, such as the Oval and Rectangle tools.)

✦ **Options:** Contains the options associated with the currently selected tool. Options (sometimes called *modifiers*) affect the way the selected tool behaves.

When you select a tool from the Tools, View, or Colors section, the Options section in the toolbox changes to reflect the options associated with that particular tool.

Arrow Tool

You select an object by clicking the Arrow tool, then clicking an object that appears on the Stage. After you select an object, the Arrow tool enables you to drag and reshape the object.

After you select an object and click the Arrow tool, the selection appears highlighted with a crosshatched pattern, and the following options appear in the Options section of the Tools window, shown in Figure 2-2:

✦ **Snap to Objects:** When turned on, the Snap to Object toggle aligns objects with the movie's grid lines automatically as you draw. (Grid lines exist although you can't see them. To display grid lines, choose View⇨Grid⇨ShowGrid.) To set the snap accuracy, choose View⇨Guides and select Edit Guides. Then, from the Snap Accuracy drop-down list, select from among Must be Close, Normal, or Can be Distant. The default setting for the Snap to Objects modifier is Normal.

✦ **Smooth:** Click this tool to smooth the selected line or shape outline.

✦ **Straighten:** Click this tool to straighten the selected line or shape outline.

✦ **Rotate:** Use this tool to rotate a selected object by dragging the corner handles of the bounding box. The Rotate tool also skews a selected stroke or fill if you grab and drag the bounding box by the middle handles.

✦ **Scale:** Use this tool to scale a selected object by dragging the corner handles. To distort a selected stroke or fill, drag the middle handles.

Make a mistake? Undo to the rescue!

Sometimes when you're drawing on the Stage, you want to undo an action (especially when you begin drawing in Flash!). To undo an action, simply choose Edit➪Undo or Ctrl+Z.

The number of actions you can undo is determined by the Undo levels set in the General Preferences, which you display by choosing Edit➪Preferences and clicking the General tab. (The default setting for Undo Levels preference is 100.)

To redo an undone action, choose Edit➪Redo or click Ctrl+Y.

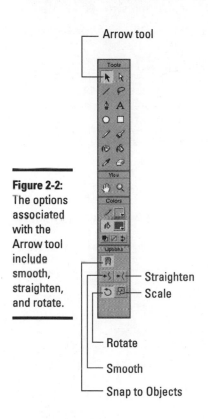

Arrow tool

Straighten

Scale

Rotate

Smooth

Snap to Objects

Figure 2-2:
The options associated with the Arrow tool include smooth, straighten, and rotate.

Brush Tool

 The Brush tool acts like a paintbrush, creating strokes of color. By varying the style of the brush and the brush stroke, you can create many interesting effects.

To use the Brush tool, follow these steps:

1. **Select the Brush tool from the toolbox.**

2. **Select a fill color by clicking the Fill Color pop-up menu located under the Colors section in the Tools window and dragging the eyedropper that appears to the color that you choose.**

3. **Select a paint mode by clicking the Brush Mode modifier located under Options in the toolbox and dragging the arrow that appears to one of the following paint modes:**

- **Paint Normal:** Paints over fills and strokes on the same layer.

- **Paint Fills:** Paints fills and blank areas, leaving strokes untouched.

- **Paint Behind:** Paints in blank areas, leaving fills and strokes on the same layer untouched.

- **Paint Selection:** Paints the currently selected fill.

- **Paint Inside:** Paints only the fill at which you begin your brush stroke. Starting at an empty point (or outside the fill area) paints nothing. In this mode, strokes are never affected.

4. **Select a brush size from the Brush Size modifier (see Figure 2-3).**

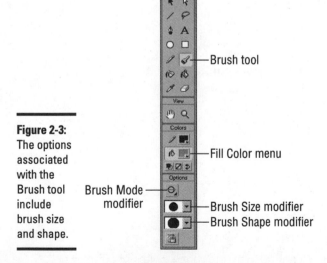

Figure 2-3:
The options associated with the Brush tool include brush size and shape.

Brush tool

Fill Color menu

Brush Mode modifier

Brush Size modifier

Brush Shape modifier

5. **Select a brush shape from the Brush Shape modifier (refer to Figure 2-3).**

6. **Press and hold down the mouse button and drag the cursor onto the Stage to paint.**

Shift+drag constrains brush strokes to horizontal and vertical directions.

Dropper Tool

The timesaving Dropper tool enables you to copy one object's color and apply it to another.

To use the Dropper tool, follow these steps:

1. **Select the Dropper tool from the toolbox.**

2. **Position the Dropper tool over an object on the Stage whose color you want to copy, and click.**

   Flash automatically copies the attributes from the object to memory. When you click on another object, you transfer the copied color to the new object.

Eraser Tool

You can use the Eraser tool to erase fills and strokes.

Dragging and erasing

To erase by using the dragging method, follow these steps:

1. **Select the Eraser tool from the toolbox.**

2. **Select an eraser mode by clicking the Eraser Mode icon under Options in the toolbox, and then dragging the arrow that appears to one of the following eraser modes:**

   * **Erase Normal:** Erases strokes and fills on the same layer.

   * **Erase Fills:** Erases fills but not strokes.

   * **Erase Lines:** Erases strokes but not fills.

   * **Erase Selected Fills:** Erases presently selected fills but not strokes, selected or not.

   * **Erase Inside:** Erases only the fill at which you begin your eraser stroke. Starting at an empty point (or outside the fill area) erases nothing. In this mode, strokes are never affected.

3. **Select an eraser shape and size by clicking the down arrow and selecting from the drop-down list that appears.**

4. **Make sure the Faucet modifier (see Figure 2-4) is not selected.**

   (Selecting the Faucet modifier works as kind of a reverse paint bucket, erasing all strokes and fills inside a shape with a single click. Selecting the Faucet modifier turns off the ability to erase portions of an image by dragging the mouse.)

5. **Position the pointer on the Stage and, while holding down the mouse button, drag to erase.**

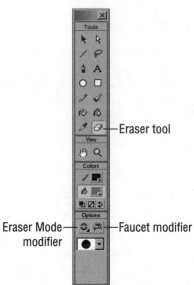

Figure 2-4:
You choose the size and shape of your Eraser tool.

Eraser Mode modifier ——— Faucet modifier

Eraser tool

 To erase an entire fill area or stroke segment at one fell swoop, select the Eraser tool. Then select the Faucet modifier and click once on the fill area or stroke segment you want to erase.

 Double-clicking the Eraser tool erases everything on the Stage.

Ink Bottle Tool

 You use the Ink Bottle tool to change the color, width, or style of lines or shape outlines.

To use the Ink Bottle tool, follow these steps:

1. **Select the Ink Bottle tool from the toolbox.**

2. **Choose Window➪Panels➪Stroke.**

   The Stroke panel appears.

3. **Select a stroke style, height, and color.**

4. **Move the pointer over the line that you want to change and then click.**

Lasso Tool

 The Lasso tool enables you to select an oddly-shaped object. To lasso an object, follow these steps:

1. **Select the Lasso tool from the toolbox.**

2. **Position the pointer on the Stage and, while holding down the mouse button, drag an outline around the object you want to select.**

TIP
When you select the Polygon mode by clicking the Polygon Mode icon (see Figure 2-5), you can outline an oddly shaped object by using a series of drags and clicks rather than straight freehand drawing. To finish an outline in Polygon mode, double-click your mouse.

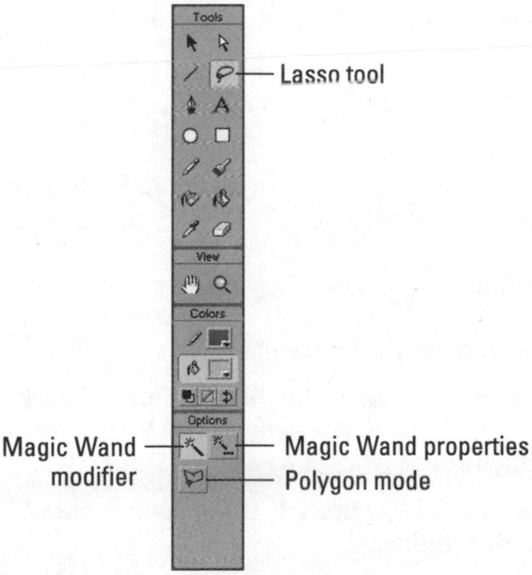

**Book VII
Chapter 2**

Creating and
Modifying Images

Figure 2-5:
The Lasso
tool lets you
select oddly-
shaped
objects.

Lasso tool

Magic Wand
modifier

Magic Wand properties

Polygon mode

While using the Lasso tool, you can access the Polygon mode on a temporary basis by simply holding down the Alt key.

You use the Magic Wand modifier and Magic Wand properties only if you want to modify or copy the color of a bitmap image. For more information, choose Help⇨Using Flash to display Flash help. Then click the search button and follow the prompts to search for detailed instructions on using the Magic Wand.

Line Tool

The Line tool enables you to create flawlessly straight lines. You can even connect these straight lines to form shapes, such as stars or octagons.

To create a straight line, follow these steps:

1. **Select the Line tool from the toolbox.**

2. **Select a stroke color by clicking the Stroke Color drop-down box in the Colors section of the Tools window or in the Stroke panel. (To display the Stroke panel, choose Window⇨Panels⇨Stroke.)**

3. **In the Stroke panel, select a Stroke Weight by using the slider. Also, select a Stroke Style by clicking the Stroke Style drop-down list.**

4. **Holding down the mouse button, drag the cursor onto the Stage.**

5. **Release the mouse button to complete the line.**

Oval Tool

The Oval tool enables you to draw ovals of all shapes and sizes, from a narrow cigar shape to a perfect circle.

To create an oval, follow these steps:

1. **Select the Oval tool from the toolbox.**

2. **Select a stroke color by clicking the Stroke Color Control in the Colors section of the Tools window or in the Stroke panel. (To display the Stroke panel, choose Window⇨Panels⇨Stroke.)**

3. **Select a fill color by clicking the Fill Color icon located in the Colors section of the Tools window.**

4. **Holding down the mouse button, drag the cursor onto the Stage.**

5. **Release the mouse button.**

The oval is complete.

To constrain the shape to a circle, use Shift+drag.

Paint Bucket Tool

 The Paint Bucket tool enables you to fill a closed shape with a solid color, gradients, and bitmapped patterns. If the shape is not fully enclosed or has a gap, you can ask Flash to ignore the gap and fill the shape anyway. The Paint Bucket tool also enables you to change the color of existing fills.

To fill a shape with color by using the Paint Bucket tool, follow these steps:

1. **Select the Paint Bucket tool from the toolbox.**

2. **Select a fill color from the Fill Color pop-up menu in the Colors section of the Tools window.**

3. **Select the desired mode from the Gap Close modifier located under Options, shown in Figure 2-6, if your shape has a gap.**

4. **Position the Paint Bucket tool over the fill, and click.**

The color you chose in Step 2 now fills your shape.

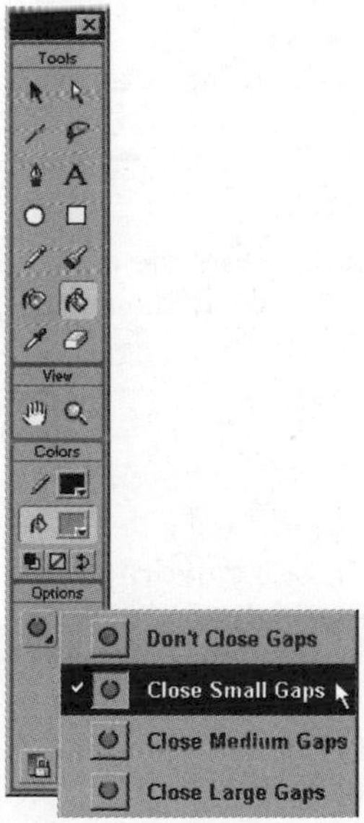

**Book VII
Chapter 2**

**Creating and
Modifying Images**

Figure 2-6:
Use the
Paint
Bucket tool
to fill shapes
with color.

If nothing happens when you click inside the shape, you may have an undetectable gap. Change your gap setting and try again.

Pen Tool

You can use the Pen tool to create straight lines and curves. The Pen tool works by filling in the end points you specify. (If you want to create straight lines and curves by dragging the cursor rather than by specifying end points, check out the Pencil tool in the following section.)

To create a line by using the Pen tool, follow these steps:

1. **Select the Pen tool from the toolbox.**

2. **Select a stroke color by clicking the Stroke Color Control in the Colors section of the Tools window or in the Stroke panel. (To display the Stroke panel, choose <u>W</u>indow⇨<u>P</u>anels⇨Stroke.)**

3. **Select a fill color by clicking the Fill Color icon located in the Colors section of the Tools window.**

4. **To draw straight-line segments with the Pen tool, click the Stage to create end points.**

   Flash automatically creates a straight line between the end points you create. When you connect the points to create a shape — a triangle, for example — Flash automatically fills that shape with the fill color you chose in Step 3.

5. **To create curved line segments, click the Stage and drag the Pen tool.**

   To reshape line segments, click the line and drag the Pen tool.

You can set Pen tool preferences (for example, how the end points appear on the Stage) by selecting Edit⌐Preferences from the main menu and clicking the Editing tab.

Pencil Tool

The Pencil tool acts much like a real pencil. You can draw lines, shapes, or objects freehand. Flash straightens or smooths lines according to the selected Pencil modifier.

To draw with the Pencil tool, follow these steps:

1. **Select the Pencil tool from the toolbox.**

2. **Select a drawing modifier, as shown in Figure 2-7.**

Figure 2-7:
You can
create
smooth or
straight lines
using the
Pencil tool.

3. **Select a stroke color from the Stroke Color pop-up menu located in the Colors section of the Tools window or in the Stroke panel. (To display the Stroke panel, choose Window⇨Panels⇨Stroke.)**

4. **From the Stroke panel, select a Stroke Weight by using the slider. Also, select a Stroke Style from the drop-down list.**

5. **Drag the cursor to draw on the Stage.**

Shift+drag constrains lines to horizontal and vertical directions.

Rectangle Tool

The Rectangle tool assists you in drawing rectangles of all shapes and sizes, from a narrow tube-like shape to a perfect square.

To create a rectangle, follow these steps:

1. **Select the Rectangle tool from the toolbox.**

2. **Select a stroke color from the Stroke Color Control in the Colors section of the Tools window or in the Stroke panel. (To display the Stroke panel, choose Window⇨Panels⇨Stroke.)**

3. **Select a fill color from the Fill Color pop-up menu.**

4. **Click the Round Rectangle modifier to display the Rectangle Setting dialog box shown in Figure 2-8, and then enter a corner radius value to round the corners of the rectangle.**

   A value of zero creates sharp corners.

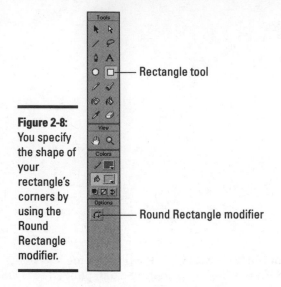

— Rectangle tool

— Round Rectangle modifier

Figure 2-8: You specify the shape of your rectangle's corners by using the Round Rectangle modifier.

5. **Hold down the mouse button and drag the cursor onto the Stage.**

   Release the mouse after you create the rectangle or square you want.

TIP

   To constrain the shape to a square, use Shift+drag.

Subselect Tool

Clicking the Subselect tool enables you to select, drag, and reshape your drawing by using anchor points and tangent handles, as shown in Figure 2-9.

Figure 2-9:
Clicking an
object
with the
Subselect
tool displays
anchor
points and
tangent
handles
you can
manipulate.

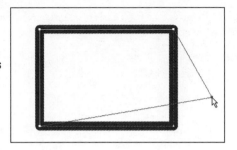

Text Tool

 The Text tool allows you to create text for your movies. You can manipulate text as an object or as basic shapes to create cool effects.

To create a single-line text element, select the Text tool, then click on the Stage and begin typing.

To create a multiline text element, select the Text tool; then click on the Stage, drag to create a rectangle, and begin typing.

 You can change the appearance of your text element by using the Character panel. To see the Character panel, choose Window➪Panels➪Character from the main menu.

Book VII
Chapter 2

Creating and
Modifying Images

Chapter 3: Using Layers

In This Chapter

✓ Viewing layers

✓ Creating and working with layers

✓ Using guide layers to position lines, shapes, and symbols

✓ Using motion guide layers to define a nonlinear motion path

✓ Using mask layers to show only selected portions of images

Do you remember those old overhead projectors and the clear plastic transparencies they used? To understand layers, imagine this scenario: You have a stack of 40 transparencies. Each one has an image on it, and you decide to change one of the images. You simply thumb through the transparencies to get to the one you want to change, change the image on the transparency, and return it to its place in the stack. When you stack the transparencies, you can see through them to view all the other images; you can change their order; you can draw on one transparency without affecting the others; you can omit some and add others; in fact, you can add as many as you want. Now you have a basic understanding of what layers are all about. However, Flash layers   which you manipulate by using the Timeline — are far more versatile. Guide layers, motion guide layers, and masking layers, all of which I explain in this chapter, are specialized types of layers you can use to create sophisticated graphic effects.

Flash displays all the layers contained in a movie in the Layers window (see Figure 3-1), which you find above the Stage and left of the Timeline. As you might expect, clicking on the name of a layer displayed in the Layers window selects that layer.

Working with numerous objects on multiple layers can be confusing. Flash brings order to the confusion by offering three viewing features located in the Layers window. Clicking the icons that represent these three features, as you see in the following list, allows you to manipulate the selected layer:

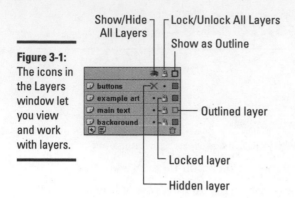

Show/Hide All Layers

Lock/Unlock All Layers

Show as Outline

Figure 3-1:
The icons in the Layers window let you view and work with layers.

Outlined layer

Locked layer

Hidden layer

✦ **Show/Hide All Layers:** Represented by an eye icon, this feature toggles between making all objects on the selected layer disappear or reappear.

A layer (and all the objects on that layer) are hidden when you see a red X in the Show/Hide All Layers column, and visible if a dot appears in the column.

✦ **Lock/Unlock All Layers:** Represented by a padlock icon, this feature disables/enables the editing of all objects while still allowing those objects to be visible.

A layer is locked when you see a padlock icon in the Lock/Unlock All Layers column and is unlocked when a dot appears in the column.

✦ **Show All Layers as Outlines:** Represented by a hollow square icon in the Show All Layers as Outlines column, this feature toggles between displaying all objects on a layer with a colored outline and displaying them normally.

The objects on a layer are displayed as an outline when a hollow square icon appears next to the layer's name. A solid square icon shows that all objects on a layer are being displayed normally.

Creating Layers

Creating a layer is a simple process. When you create a layer, Flash activates the new layer and displays it in the Layers window directly above the previously selected layer.

To create a layer, click the Insert Layer button located in the lower-left corner of the Timeline, as shown in Figure 3-2.

Alternatively, you can choose Insert⇨Layer from the main menu to create a new layer.

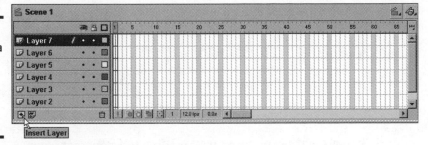

Figure 3-2: You create a new layer by clicking the Insert Layer button.

The total number of layers (no matter how many) doesn't affect the file size. You can insert as many layers as your computer's memory can handle.

Working with Layers

To manipulate a layer, you must first select it in the Layers window, making it the active layer and displaying the contents of the layer on the Stage. Flash lets you activate only one layer at a time — you can select multiple layers but not activate multiple layers. The active layer can be locked, unlocked, copied, deleted, or moved to a new location. A layer is active and available for editing when the Pencil icon appears next to the layer name inside the Layers window. When the pencil icon has a red line through it, the layer is active but cannot be edited — perhaps because the layer is locked.

Selecting a layer

Selecting a layer makes it *active,* allowing you to draw on it, paint on it, and otherwise modify it. The layer must be active to perform any modifications. Modifying includes renaming, locking, showing, hiding, copying, deleting, and reordering.

To select a layer, choose one of the following methods:

✦ Position the cursor on the Stage and click (select) an object on the layer you want to work with.

✦ From the Timeline, click a frame that's located on the layer you want to work with.

✦ Click the layer's name on the Timeline.

Selecting two or more layers

By selecting multiple layers, you can simultaneously unlock or lock layers, change layer order, show or hide layers, and turn layer outlines on or off.

To select two or more layers, do the following:

1. **Click a layer name on the Timeline to select that layer.**

2. **Shift+click another layer name to select all the layers between the initially selected layer and the shift-clicked layer.**

3. **Control+click a layer name in the selected block to deselect that layer.**

Copying a layer

Copying a layer can save you time because you don't need to re-create a complicated layer. For example, you would use the copy command to create multiple animated objects that are the same but that need to follow a slightly different path, such as a flock of flying birds.

To copy a layer, follow these steps:

1. **Select the layer you want to copy by clicking the layer name on the Timeline.**

2. **Choose Edit⇨Copy Frames.**

3. **Create a new layer by clicking the Insert Layer button in the lower-left corner of the Timeline.**

4. **Select the new layer and choose Edit⇨Paste Frames.**

Renaming a layer

When you create a layer, Flash gives that layer a generic name such as Layer 1, Layer 2, Layer 3, and so on. To give an existing layer a more descriptive name, do any one of the following:

✦ Select the layer name on the Timeline and choose Modify➪Layer. Enter the new name in the <u>N</u>ame text field of the Layer Properties dialog box.

✦ Right-click the layer name on the Timeline. From the context menu, select Properties. Enter the new name in the <u>N</u>ame text field of the Layer Properties dialog box.

✦ Double-click the layer name on the Timeline, delete it, and enter the new name.

Deleting a layer

Suppose that you're unhappy with what you created on a layer. No problem — just get rid of it. To delete a layer, choose one of the following methods:

✦ Right-click the layer name on the Timeline. From the context menu that appears, select Delete Layer.

✦ Select the layer name on the Timeline and, while holding down the mouse button, drag the layer to the Garbage Can icon on the Timeline.

✦ With the layer name on the Timeline selected, click the garbage can button on the Timeline.

Modifying layer properties

You can modify any of the properties associated with a layer by using the Layer Properties dialog box.

To do so, follow these steps:

1. **From the Timeline, double-click the layer's icon located to the left of the layer name.**

The Layer Properties dialog box appears.

2. **Modify one or more properties displayed in the Layer Properties dialog box.**

You can modify any or all of the following:

• <u>N</u>ame: Type a new name for a layer in this field to rename the layer.

• Show: Checking this option displays a layer's objects on the Stage. Unchecking this option hides a layer's objects.

• Lock: Checking this option disables editing for all the objects contained on a layer. Unchecking this option enables editing of all the objects contained on a layer.

- Type: You can choose one of the following layer types: Normal (the default type of layer), Guide (an "overlay" layer you use to align artwork on an underlying layer), Guided (a normal layer linked to a motion guide layer), Mask (a type of layer on which you create holes through which you expose the objects on one or more underlying layers), or Masked (a normal layer linked to a mask layer).

For details on the Guide and Guided layer types, see the "Guide Layers" section; for the skinny on the Mask and Masked layer types, see the "Mask Layers" section.

- Outline Color: Clicking the drop-down color swatch allows you to choose the color Flash uses to outline the selected layer.

- View layer as outlines: Checking this option tells Flash to display layer objects on the Stage as outlines. Unchecking this option tells Flash to display layer on the Stage normally.

- Layer Height: Clicking on this drop-down list allows you to specify the height of a layer as it appears in the Layers window. You can choose from 100% (the default), 200%, and 300%.

3. **Click OK to make the modifications.**

(The changes you make appear in the Layers window next to the layer's name.)

Guide Layers

You use *guide layers* to help position lines, shapes, and symbols on the Stage using horizontal and vertical *guides* (as you see in Figure 3-3, guides look like crosshairs). Guide layers don't actually show up in the final, published movie; they exist only during development.

A *motion guide layer* is a special type of guide layer that lets you specify a path along which motion-tweened animation sequences can be guided. (You find out how to create motion-tweened animation sequences in Chapter 5, "Creating Tweened Animation.")

You can link multiple layers to a motion guide layer to have multiple objects follow the same path.

Creating standard guide layers

To create a customized guide layer, you first create a standard guide layer; then you add guides and position them where you want them on your newly created guide layer.

To create a customized guide layer, click the Add Guide Layer button located in the lower-left corner of the Timeline, as shown in Figure 3-3. After you do, the newly created guide layer appears in the Layers window directly above the currently selected layer.

To add guides to your standard guide layer,

1. **Click on your guide layer in the Layers window to select it.**

2. **Select <u>V</u>iew⇨<u>R</u>ulers from the main menu.**

   Horizontal and vertical rules appear, as shown in Figure 3-3.

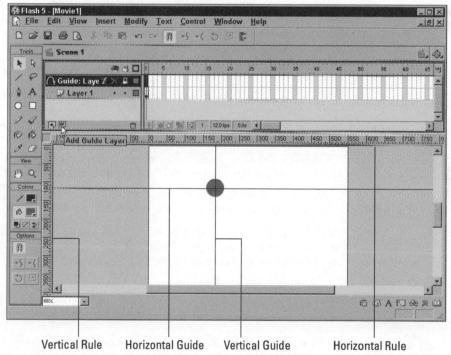

Figure 3-3: Click the Add Guide Layer button to add an invisible guide layer to your movie.

Vertical Rule   Horizontal Guide   Vertical Guide   Horizontal Rule

3. **Click on the horizontal rule and drag down to position one or more horizontal guides.**

    If you make a mistake, you can start over by dragging the guide back to the horizontal rule and releasing the mouse button.

4. **Click on the vertical rule and drag to the right to position one or more vertical guides.**

    If you make a mistake, you can start over by dragging the guide back to the vertical rule and releasing the mouse button.

To set preferences such as guide color, choose <u>V</u>iew➪Guid<u>e</u>s➪Edit Guides.

Creating motion guide layers

You use a motion guide layer to define a nonlinear path for a motion-tweened animation sequence.

For example, if you want to create an animation showing a mouse darting around in circles on the screen — as opposed to a mouse running in a straight line across the screen — you need to create a motion-tweened animation sequence, or tweened animation for short, that shows a mouse cavorting along a nonlinear path.

To create a motion guide layer, choose one of the following methods:

1. **Create a tweened animation. (To find out how to do this, see "Creating Tweened Animation" in Chapter 5, "Making Movies.")**

2. **Right-click the layer that contains the tweened animation sequence and select Add Motion Guide from the context menu that appears.**

3. **Use the Pen, Pencil, Line, Circle, Rectangle, or Brush tool to draw the desired path on the Stage.**

4. **Click the Arrow tool and choose <u>V</u>iew➪Snap to Ob<u>j</u>ects; then drag the tweened instance to the beginning of the path in the first keyframe, and to the end of the path in the last keyframe.**

    Checking the Snap to Objects option causes a black circle to appear when you correctly align the tweened instance with the ends of the path.

For additional details and help in creating motion guide layers and nonlinear paths, choose Help➪Lessons➪08 Animation.

Mask Layers

A *mask* layer works with a *masked* layer to create the *masking* effect. (Say *that* three times fast.) A simple explanation of a mask and masked layer is this: Take two pieces of paper, cut holes in one piece and leave the other untouched. Place the paper with holes on top of the untouched paper so that you can view the underlying paper through the holes. The piece of paper with holes in it is the mask layer, and the underlying piece of paper is the masked layer. Unlike plain paper, the masked layer in Flash can contain numerous transparent layers.

To create a mask layer, follow these steps:

1. **Select the layer that holds the images to be viewed through the mask.**

   Because it is intended to be covered by a mask layer, this underlying layer is referred to as the *masked* layer. The masked layer I demonstrate in this section is shown in Figure 3-4.

Book VII Chapter 3

Using Layers

Figure 3-4: A masked layer is designed to be displayed beneath a mask layer.

2. **Choose Insert⇨Layer from the main menu to create a mask layer.**

   The mask layer appears above the masked layer in the Layers window.

3. **From this newly created mask layer, which is now active, draw filled shapes or add type, symbols, or instances to create the mask.**

   Don't use gradients, transparencies, colors, bitmaps, or line style because Flash disregards these. You can see the mask layer I use in this section in Figure 3-5.

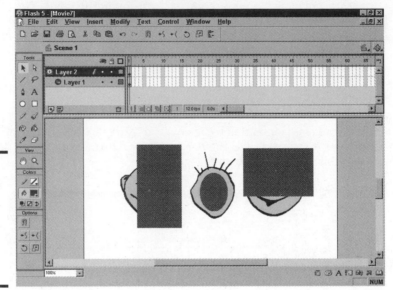

Figure 3-5: This mask layer will eventually be placed over a masked layer.

4. **Return to the Timeline after you finish drawing and position the cursor over the mask layer and right-click it.**

   A context menu appears.

5. **Select Mask.**

   The layers link together. You can see the masking effect in Figure 3-6.

After the masking is complete, the layers are locked (a padlock icon appears next to both layer names in the layer list). If you want to reposition the mask, follow these steps:

1. **Unlock the layers by clicking the Padlock icon next to the layer's name in the Lock/Unlock All Layers column of the Layers window.**

   The red slash on the Pencil Edit icon disappears to show you that you can now modify the layers.

2. **Drag the mask to the desired location on the Stage.**

3. **Relock the mask and masked layers by clicking the Padlock icon associated with each layer to display the Padlock icon.**

Figure 3-6:
Placing the mask in Figure 3-5 over the masked layer in Figure 3-4 creates this masking effect.

Chapter 4: Creating Reusable Symbols

In This Chapter

✔ Creating and working with symbols (buttons, graphics, and movie clips)

✔ Converting animations to symbols

✔ Adding instances of symbols to your movies

A *symbol* is a reusable element such as a button, bitmap image, animation, movie clip, or sound file. You store symbols in the Library so you can find them easily when you want to add them to your movies. (Flash comes with a handful of symbols to get you started.)

In this chapter, you see how to create and work with symbols. Because button symbols are so popular, I devote a separate section ("Working with Buttons") to their care and feeding. Finally, you also see how to make copies — called *instances* — of symbols and add them directly to your movies.

Working with Symbols

Using symbols speeds up development time because you don't have to reinvent the wheel. After you create an attractive image, you can designate that image as a symbol, copy it to the Library panel (which you can view by choosing <u>W</u>indow⇨<u>L</u>ibrary), and reuse it — with slight modifications, if you like — over and over again as many times as you like by creating instances of that symbol.

Using symbols reduces movie playback time because Flash needs to download a symbol only once, no matter how many instances you include in your movie.

Three basic types of symbols exist:

✦ **Graphic:** Graphic symbols work in sync with the Timeline of the main movie. These symbols are reusable fixed images or reusable animations. One fixed graphic symbol takes up one frame on the main Timeline, two fixed graphic symbols take up two frames on the main timeline, and so on.

✦ **Button:** Button symbols work with their very own four-frame Timeline. The four frames are displayed as one frame on the movie Timeline that is separate from the main Timeline. Each button on the Stage has its own set of four frames assigned to it, meaning that each button can have its own personality. (See "Working with Buttons" in this chapter for more information.)

✦ **Movie clip:** Movie Clip symbols work with a multiframe Timeline that plays separately from the movie's Timeline. They are basically tiny movies inside of the larger, main movie. Movie Clip symbols play separately from the main movie and can contain movie clip instances, sound, and even movie clip instances on a button symbol Timeline to create animated buttons.

When you edit a symbol, all of the instances associated with the symbol update automatically. Editing a specific instance of a symbol, however, does not cause the symbol to change.

Creating symbols

You can create symbols in two ways:

✦ Turn an existing graphic or graphics into a symbol by selecting it from the Stage and converting it.

✦ Make an empty symbol and either create the contents for it, or import the contents in symbol-editing mode.

Creating a symbol using selected objects

To create a symbol using existing graphics, follow these steps:

1. **Select the Arrow tool from the toolbox.**

2. **Position the arrow on the Stage and use the arrow to drag a rectangle around the graphic or graphics being converted to select them.**

3. **Choose Insert⇨Convert to Symbol from the main menu.**

   The Symbol Properties dialog box appears, as shown in Figure 4-1.

4. **Type a name for the symbol in the Name field.**

5. **Select the appropriate radio button for the symbol — Movie Clip, Button, or Graphic.**

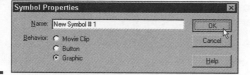

Figure 4-1:
The Symbol
Properties
dialog box.

6. Click OK.

Creating a new empty symbol

To create a new empty symbol, follow these steps:

1. Choose Edit⇨Deselect All from the main menu.

This is a precaution to ensure that nothing is selected on the Stage.
You should start with a clean slate.

2. Choose Insert⇨New Symbol from the main menu.

Alternatively, you can click the Options menu you see in the upper-right
corner of the Library window and scroll to New Symbol.

The Symbol Properties dialog box appears.

3. Type a name for the symbol in the Name field.

4. Select the appropriate radio button — Movie Clip, Button, or Graphic.

5. Click OK.

The screen changes to reflect the following alterations:

- The screen is now in symbol-editing mode.

- Small crosshairs appear in the middle of the screen. This is the
  symbol's *registration point*. (Flash uses the registration point for
  positioning and transformations, such as scaling and skewing. You
  can move the registration point for a selected symbol by choosing
  Modify⇨Transform⇨Edit Center and moving the registration point
  to the desired location.)

- The symbol is added to the Library window.

- You see the symbol name added above the Timeline in the upper-left
  corner of the window.

**Book VII
Chapter 4**

**Creating Reusable
Symbols**

6. **Create the symbol content by drawing with the drawing tool, creating instances of other symbols, or importing media.**

7. **Choose Edit⇨Edit Movie to return to movie-editing mode.**

Duplicating symbols

To duplicate a symbol, follow these steps:

1. **Choose Window⇨Library to display the Library window.**

2. **Select the desired symbol from the Library window.**

3. **Choose Options⇨Duplicate.**

   The Symbol Properties dialog box appears. Notice that the symbol name has the extension copy added.

4. **Use the default name or type in a new name for the copied symbol in the Name field.**

5. **Click OK.**

The duplicate symbol has no connection to the original symbol and each can be changed without affecting the other.

Converting animation into a movie clip symbol

Animation that contains a repeating or looping motion works best if you convert it to a movie clip because this reduces file size.

To change animation on the Stage into a movie clip, follow these steps:

1. **Choose File⇨Open to display the Open dialog box; then click the Look in: drop-down box and select the file you want to open. When you finish, click Open.**

2. **From the main Timeline, select all frames and all layers that contain the animation to be converted.**

3. **Choose Edit⇨Copy Frames or right-click the selection and select Copy Frames from the context menu that appears.**

4. **Deselect the selection by clicking outside of the selection with the Arrow tool or choosing Edit⇨Deselect All.**

5. **Choose Insert⇨New Symbol.**

   The Symbol Properties dialog box appears.

6. **Type a name for the symbol in the Name field.**

7. **Select the Movie Clip radio button.**

8. **Click OK.**

The screen is now in symbol-editing mode, and a new symbol is ready for editing.

9. **Select Frame 1 on Layer 1 from the Timeline and choose Edit⇨ Paste Frames.**

The frames you copied from the main Timeline in Step 3 are now pasted to the Timeline of the movie clip symbol and can be reused throughout the movie. All of the elements from the copied frames are now a stand-alone movie.

To return to movie-editing mode, choose Edit⇨Edit Movie.

10. **From the main Timeline, select all frames and all layers that contain the *original* animation (the preconversion version) and delete them by choosing Insert⇨Remove Frames.**

Placing a movie clip symbol on the Stage

To work with an instance of a movie clip, follow these steps:

1. **Open a movie by choosing File⇨Open to display the Open dialog box; then click the Look in: drop-down box and select the file you want to open. When you finish, click Open.**

2. **Choose Insert⇨Scene.**

Flash displays an empty Stage, a new Timeline with a single layer, and a blank keyframe in frame one.

3. **Choose Window⇨Library to display the Library window if it's not already on the screen.**

4. **Click the name of the movie clip you want to add to your movie and drag it from the Library window onto the Stage.**

Viewing movie clip animation

To view a movie clip animation in a movie, follow these steps:

1. **Place a movie clip onto the Stage (see the previous section for details) and then choose Control⇨Test Scene.**

A progress bar displays while the movie is being exported. (The movie is being exported to a Shockwave format and is renamed with the SWF extension.) When the export finishes, the Flash Player appears.

2. **Choose Control⇨Play to view the movie.**

3. **Click the Close icon in the upper-right corner of the Flash Player to return to the Stage.**

Working with Buttons

Buttons are a special class of symbol — special because they do something useful in response to a user's mouse click. (In other words, buttons are *interactive*.)

Buttons are also very popular among Web design folk; virtually every Web site contains at least a handful. Buttons can be very elaborate, using movie clips and sound, or they can be very straightforward, using simple graphics that change modestly when a mouse pointer rolls over them. In Flash, a button is a symbol associated with a *behavior*. When you create an instance of a button and assign a behavior to that instance (as I describe in the next section), Flash creates a Timeline containing four keyframes.

✦ **Up state:** The status of the button's appearance whenever the cursor lies outside the active zone of the button. Frame 1 stores the Up state.

✦ **Over state:** The status of the button's appearance whenever a user's cursor rolls over the button. A graphic change typically happens here, alerting users that they have encountered the active zone. Frame 2 stores the Over state.

✦ **Down state:** The status of the button's appearance when it's selected. For example, most buttons appear depressed or highlighted in this state so that users know they've clicked successfully. Frame 3 stores the Down state.

✦ **Hit state:** The surface area of the button that you want to respond to mouse movement and clicks. The area must be the same size or larger than the images in the Up, Over, and Down frames. It must be solid. Failing to define the area forces Flash to use the image in the Up state frame as the Hit frame. Frame 4 stores the Hit state.

Creating a button symbol

To create a simple button, follow these steps:

1. **If the Timeline isn't visible, choose View⇨Timeline.**

The Timeline appears.

2. **Choose Edit⇨Deselect All.**

This is a precaution to ensure that nothing is selected on the Stage. You should start with a clean slate.

3. **Choose Insert⇨New Symbol.**

The Symbol Properties dialog box appears.

4. **Type a name for the button in the Name field.**

5. **Select the Button radio button and click OK.**

   As shown in Figure 4-2, the Timeline changes to symbol-editing mode. The Timeline header holds titles for the Up, Over, Down, and Hit frames I describe in the preceding section, "Working with Buttons."

Figure 4-2:
To create
a button,
specify the
way you
want the
button to
appear in
each of four
distinct
states: Up,
Over, Down,
and Hit.

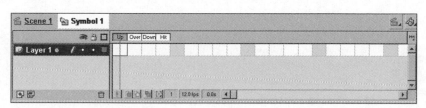

6. **From the Timeline, select the first blank keyframe titled Up.**

7. **Create an Up state button image by using the drawing tools, placing a graphic symbol, or importing a graphic, or create an animated button using the movie clip symbol.**

   By default, the first keyframe is blank, designating the Up state. You must add keyframes for Over, Down, and Hit.

8. **From the Timeline, select the second frame titled Over, and then choose Insert⇨Keyframe.**

   Flash duplicates the contents of the Up keyframe into the Over frame. The graphic on the Stage is highlighted and ready for modification. An exact duplication of the preceding keyframe enables you to precisely align the button images so that they don't appear to jump around when they change states.

9. **From the Stage, modify the graphic in the Over frame by using any drawing tool to reflect a change (for example, a size change or rotation).**

10. **From the Timeline, select the third frame titled Down, and choose Insert⇨Keyframe.**

    Flash duplicates the contents of the Over keyframe into the Down frame. The graphic on the stage is highlighted and ready for modification.

**Book VII
Chapter 4**

**Creating Reusable
Symbols**

11. **From the Stage, use one or more drawing tools to modify the graphic in the Down frame to reflect a change (for example, create a color shift that appears to cast a shadow).**

12. **From the Timeline, select the last frame titled Hit, and choose Insert⇨Keyframe.**

    This fourth frame defines the area that responds to mouse movement. The zone must be the same size or larger than the images in the Up, Over, and Down frames. (In other words, don't crop the image area Flash suggests, which is the area defined by the Up State frame you created in Step 6.)

    When defining the Hit zone for an elusive image, such as a block of text or a line drawing, use a filled geometric shape — such as a circle or square — that totally covers the image. That way, the user doesn't have to position the cursor with tedious precision to activate the button.

13. **Choose Edit⇨Edit Movie to exit the symbol-editing mode.**

Testing your button symbol

To test a newly created button symbol, create an instance of that button and interact with it by following these steps:

1. **Choose Window⇨Library.**

    The Library window appears.

2. **Drag the button symbol you're interested in out of the Library and onto the Stage to create an instance of the button.**

3. **Choose Control⇨Enable Simple Buttons.**

4. **Manipulate the enabled button with the cursor. As you drag your mouse onto and off of the button, notice how it changes.**

    The Up State defined for the button should appear initially; after you drag your mouse over the button, the Over state should appear; and so on.

Sometimes having buttons enabled is annoying. To disable buttons, choose Control⇨Enable Simple Buttons from the Flash main menu so that the check mark next to Enable Simple Buttons disappears.

To move a button (or any other object) on the Stage, select the object by clicking it; then use the arrows on your keyboard to nudge the object up, down, left, or right as desired.

Working with Instances

An *instance* is a copy of a symbol. Instances have their own sets of properties, all of which you can change without affecting the original symbol. For example, when you scale, rotate, or skew an instance, the symbol from which that instance was taken remains untouched.

Creating a new instance of a symbol

To create a new instance, follow these steps:

1. **Choose a layer on the main Timeline.**

2. **Choose <u>W</u>indow⇨<u>L</u>ibrary or <u>W</u>indow⇨<u>C</u>ommon Libraries to display a Library window if one isn't already on the screen.**

   The Library window appears.

3. **Drag the desired symbol onto the Stage.**

4. **Choose <u>W</u>indow⇨<u>P</u>anels⇨Instance.**

   The Instance panel appears.

5. **Pick color effects, add sound, or change the behavior of the instance (for example, you can change a plain image into a button).**

Animated graphic symbols comprise a series of framed images. So, depending on the effect you want to produce, you may have to modify several image frames (or keyframes) to modify an animated graphic symbol. To create gradual changes, you may have to tween your modified frames. See Chapter 5, "Making Movies," for more information on keyframes and tweening.

Inspecting instance properties

You can inspect and modify any of the properties of an instance to change how the instance looks and behaves. To inspect instance properties from the Stage, follow these steps:

1. **Select the Arrow tool from the toolbox.**

2. **Position the arrow on the Stage and use the arrow to drag a rectangle around the instance to select it.**

3. **Decide on a panel and open it by using one of the following methods:**

   - **Instance panel:** Shows the instance's behavior and settings. Choose <u>W</u>indow⇨<u>P</u>anels⇨Instance or click Ctrl+I.

   - **Info panel:** Shows the exact location and size of the instance symbol. Choose <u>W</u>indow⇨<u>P</u>anels⇨Info, or type Ctrl+Alt+I.

- **Movie Explorer:** Shows all the instances and symbols that make up the selected movie, in hierarchical order. Choose W̲indow⇨ M̲ovie Explorer.

- **Actions panel:** Shows all actions associated with a graphic, button, or movie clip. Choose W̲indow⇨A̲ction.

Changing the color and transparency of an instance

To change the color of an instance, follow these steps:

1. **Select the Arrow tool from the toolbox.**

2. **Position the arrow on the Stage and use the arrow to drag a rectangle around the instance to select it.**

3. **Choose W̲indow⇨P̲anels⇨Instance or just press Ctrl+I.**

4. **Click the Effect tab and click the drop-down list displayed there to choose one of the following options:**

- **None:** Applies nothing.

- **Brightness:** Adjusts lightness and darkness of the selected instance where –100% is black, 100% is white, and 0% is the instance's original color. Use the slider to adjust lightness and darkness.

- **Tint:** Changes the color of the selected instance. Change the color using the Color Picker or the RGB Value windows, as shown in Figure 4-3. In the RGB Value windows, enter the value numerically or use the sliders attached to the individual colors. Another way to change the color is to use the Percentage Value window located above the RGB Value windows. Key in a numeric value or use the slider to saturate or desaturate the instance with the selected color (100% being total saturation).

Figure 4-3:
The options associated with the tint effect let you change the color of an instance several different ways.

- **Alpha:** Adjusts transparency, where 0% is completely transparent and 100% is completely opaque.

- **Advanced:** Adjusts red, green, blue, and transparency values of the instance individually. As shown in Figure 4-4, the left column of numbers enables you to adjust individual percentages; the right column enables you to adjust values by using a constant value.

Figure 4-4:
The Advanced effect enables you to control the transparency of the individual RGB components of a color.

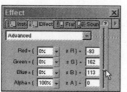

Chapter 5: Making Movies

In This Chapter

✔ **Creating frame-by-frame animation**

✔ **Creating tweened animation**

✔ **Making your movies interactive**

✔ **Adding sound to your movies**

lash provides a "one-stop shopping" application for creating multimedia-rich Web sites. As you see in this chapter, producing animated movies that contain wild morphing effects, synchronizing sound with movement, bringing logos to life, and setting up effective interactive navigational controls has never been easier.

Creating Animation

Frame-by-frame animation and tweened animation are the two forms of animation that you can create. The following list describes how each works:

✦ **Frame-by-frame:** Places slightly different images on individual frames.

✦ **Tweened:** Places images in two frames — in the beginning and ending keyframes — and lets Flash generate all the frames "in between" the starting and ending points.

Creating a frame-by-frame animation

In frame-by-frame animation, the contents of the Stage change in every frame — in other words, every frame is a *keyframe*. Frame-by-frame animation is a good choice for complex animation.

Frame-by-frame animation increases file size because Flash stores the values for each complete frame.

To create a frame-by-frame animation, follow these steps:

1. **Using the Arrow tool, click a layer displayed in the Layers window (to the left of the Timeline) to select it.**

If you're working with a new file, Flash automatically creates a layer (called Layer1) for you to use. If you're working with an existing file, additional layers may appear in the Layers window. For more information on creating layers, check out Chapter 3, "Using Layers."

2. **Select the frame on the Timeline where you want the animation to begin.**

3. **Choose Insert⇨Keyframe to turn the frame into a keyframe.**

4. **Create an image on the Stage by importing a file, pasting a graphic from the clipboard, or using the drawing tools.**

5. **Select the next frame on the Timeline after the image is complete; then add a new keyframe with the same contents as the previous keyframe by right-clicking the frame to open the context menu and selecting Insert Keyframe.**

6. **Using the newly created frame, vary the image slightly on the Stage using one or more drawing tools.**

7. **Repeat Steps 5 and 6 until you achieve the animation effect you want.**

8. **Test the animation by using one of the following methods:**

   - Choose Control⇨Play.

   - Choose Window⇨Toolbars⇨Controller and click Play on the Controller that appears.

Creating tweened animation

Motion tweening and *shape tweening* are the two types of tweened animation that Flash creates. Both types have the same guiding principle. Here is a general description of a tweened animation:

1. Give Flash a beginning and an ending point of a sequence by placing objects in keyframes on the Timeline.

2. Tell Flash to spread out the change over time by placing a number of in-between frames between the keyframes.

3. Sit back while Flash calculates the incremental changes, creating a series of images that completes the animation in the allotted number of frames.

Tweening a shape

You use *shape tweening* to create cool morphing effects, where one shape changes, or *morphs,* into another gradually.

To tween a shape, follow these steps:

1. **Select a layer by clicking the name of a layer in the Layers window.**

2. **In the Timeline, select the first empty keyframe.**

3. **On the Stage, create a shape by using any of the drawing tools.**

4. **Select a second frame on the Timeline where you want the animation to end.**

5. **Choose Insert⇨Keyframe or press F6 to turn the selected frame into a keyframe.**

6. **With the new, last keyframe selected, create a shape on the Stage using any of the drawing tools.**

Change the color and location if you want.

7. **Click the layer name that appears in the Layers window.**

Make certain that everything on the layer is selected.

8. **Open the Frame panel by choosing Window⇨Panels⇨Frame.**

9. **Choose Shape from the Tweening drop-down list in the Frame panel.**

10. **Select one of the following blend options in the Frame panel:**

- **Distributive:** Causes the intermediate shapes to be smoother.
- **Angular:** Causes the intermediate shapes to be sharper.

11. **Make a selection from the Easing slider you see in the Frame tab by dragging the slider in the Frame tab up and down or by entering a value in the text box. Choose one of the following:**

- A value between -1 and -100 begins the tween slowly and speeds it up toward the end. Dragging the slider down toward In has the same effect.
- A value of 1 through 100 begins the tween quickly and slows it toward the end. Dragging the slider up toward Out has the same effect.
- A value of 0 causes the movement to be constant. This is the default setting.

12. **Return to the Stage by clicking anywhere on the Stage. Press Ctrl+Enter on the keyboard to play back the animation.**

Tweening a motion

Two methods exist for creating a motion tween in Flash:

✦ **The Motion Tween option.** In this approach, you create the first and last keyframes — in other words, the starting and ending points for your motion tween — and instruct Flash to generate all the necessary frames in between. This is the approach you see demonstrated in this chapter.

✦ **The Motion Tween command.** In this approach, you create the first keyframe — the starting point for your motion tween. Then you drag the object in the first keyframe to another position on the Stage and instruct Flash to generate both the ending point of the motion tween and all the necessary frames in between. I don't demonstrate this approach here. If you're interested, you can find out all about the Motion Tween command by clicking F1 to display the Flash help interface.

To create a motion tween using the Motion Tween option, follow these steps:

1. **Select a layer by clicking the name of a layer displayed in the Layers window.**

2. **Select the first empty keyframe in the Timeline.**

3. **On the Stage, create an image by using one or more drawing tools.**

4. **Convert the image to a symbol by selecting the image and then pressing F8 (or, alternatively, by selecting the image and then choosing Insert⇨Convert to Symbol from the main menu).**

   In the Symbol Properties dialog box that appears, type a name for the symbol in the Name: field, click the radio button next to Graphic, and click OK.

   You must convert any drawn image into a symbol in order to use that image as part of a motion tween. Check out Chapter 4, "Creating Buttons, Instances, and Symbols," for more on converting drawn images to symbols.

5. **Select a second frame on the Timeline where you want the animation to end.**

6. **Choose Insert⇨Keyframe or press F6 to change the frame into a keyframe.**

7. **With the new, last keyframe selected, change the image by doing all or one of the following:**

   • Click and drag the image to relocate it on the Stage.

   • Change the size, rotation, or skew of the image by right-clicking the image and selecting one of the options (for example, Scale or Rotate) that appears on the pop-up menu.

8. **Click the layer name displayed in the Layers window.**

9. **Open the Frame panel by choosing Window⇨Panels⇨Frame.**

   The Frame panel appears, as shown in Figure 5-1.

10. **From the Frame panel, choose Motion from the Tweening drop-down list.**

Figure 5-1:
Setting the
Frame tab
options to
create a
motion
tween.

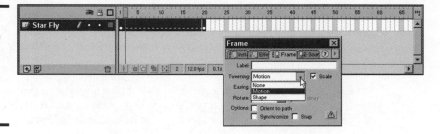

11. **Check the Scale check box in the Frame panel to tween the size if the size of the item was changed.**

12. **From the Frame panel, select one of the following rotate options:**

    - **None:** Nothing happens.

    - **Auto:** The item rotates once.

    - **CW:** The item rotates clockwise. Key in the desired number of rotations in the text box.

    - **CCW:** The item rotates counterclockwise. Key in the desired number of rotations in the text box.

13. **Make a selection from the Easing slider you see in the Frame panel by clicking the Easing slider and dragging the slider up and down or entering a value in the text box. Choose one of the following:**

    - A value between -1 and -100 begins the tween slowly and speeds it up toward the end. Dragging the slider down toward In has the same effect.

    - A value of 1 through 100 begins the tween quickly and slows it toward the end. Dragging the slider up toward Out has the same effect.

    - A value of 0 causes the movement to be constant. This is the default setting.

14. **Select Orient to Path in the Frame panel if you have created a motion path.**

    (You see how to create a motion path in the next section.)

15. **In the Frame panel, check Synchronize to match the number of frames in the animation to the number of frames the instance occupies in the movie.**

16. **Return to the Stage by clicking anywhere on the Stage. Press Enter on the keyboard to play back the animation.**

**Book VII
Chapter 5**

Making Movies

Creating a motion path

Associating a motion tween animation with a motion path causes an animated object on one layer to follow a created path on another layer known as the motion guide layer.

For example, if you want to create an animation showing a pen writing out the word HELP!, you create a pen image in one layer, and a path in the shape of the word HELP! in another layer — the motion guide layer.

To create a motion path, follow these steps:

1. **Create a motion tweened animation by following the steps in the previous section, "Tweening a motion."**

2. **Choose Insert➪Motion Guide.**

   A new motion guide layer is created directly above the selected layer. The old, selected layer now becomes a guide layer.

3. **Create a path on the Motion Guide Layer by using the Pen, Pencil, Line, Circle, Rectangle, or Brush tool.**

4. **Play back the animation by pressing Ctrl+Enter on the keyboard.**

The animation follows the path you created in Step 3.

 From the Frame panel, check Snap to attach the beginning and ending points of the path to the object's registration point. This assures that the animation starts at the exact beginning of the path and stops at the exact ending.

Making Your Movies Interactive

Assigning one or more *actions* to a movie element (such as a button) makes that element interactive — in other words, makes that element respond to user activity, such as mouse movement or a key press.

Working with actions: The Actions panel

You assign actions to buttons, frames, or movie clips by using the Actions panel, shown in Figure 5-2. Display the Actions panel by choosing Window➪Actions from the main menu.

Figure 5-2:
Use the
Actions
panel
(shown here
in Normal
mode) to
assign one
or more
actions to a
movie
element.

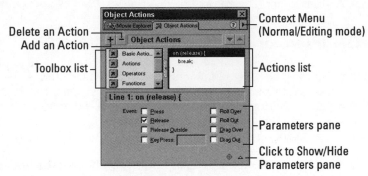

When you select a movie clip or button, the title in the text box of the Actions panel is Object Actions, and when you select a frame, the title is Frame Actions.

As Figure 5-2 shows, Flash provides dozens of built-in, or "prescripted," actions you can assign to a button, frame, or movie clip.

ActionScript is a scripting language, similar to JavaScript, that you can use to add interactivity to Flash movie elements. Flash provides a complete reference for the ActionScript scripting language, including detailed descriptions of each prescripted action. To view the ActionScript language reference, press F1 and click ActionScript Reference.

If you don't see the Basic Actions shown in Figure 5-2, check to make sure Normal mode is selected in the Actions panel context menu, described in the section, "Assigning an action to a movie element."

Normal mode

When you view the Actions panel in Normal mode, you see a list of pre-scripted actions you can assign to your movie elements. In this mode, you can point and click to add, delete, and rearrange the statements in the Actions list, but you're locked out from making any text changes.

To choose Normal mode, click the triangle in the upper-right corner of the Actions panel to display the context menu and check Normal mode.

Expert mode

Expert mode allows you to make text changes directly to the statements in the Actions list. If you're an advanced ActionScript programmer and feel comfortable entering script into the text box, choose Advanced mode.

**Book VII
Chapter 5**

Making Movies

Choose Advanced mode by clicking the triangle in the upper-right corner of the Actions panel. The context menu appears. Check Expert mode.

Assigning an action to a movie element

You can create interactive movies by adding actions to individual movie elements. One of the most popular actions is called On Mouse Event. This action, which I demonstrate adding to a movie element in this section, allows you to perform steps in response to a user's mouse activity.

To assign an action to a movie clip, frame, or button, follow these steps:

1. **Select a movie clip, frame, or button by clicking the item on the Stage.**

2. **Choose Window⇨Actions.**

   The Actions panel appears.

3. **Click the triangle in the upper-right corner of the Actions panel and check Normal mode.**

4. **In the Toolbox list in the left pane of the Actions panel, click Basic Actions to display a list of prescripted actions.**

5. **Scroll down the Basic Actions list and double-click the action that you want to add to the movie element.**

   In this example, I demonstrate double-clicking the On Mouse Event action.

   The Parameters pane shown in Figure 5-3 appears. By default, the Release event appears checked in the Parameters pane, and ActionScript *stub* (placeholder) code corresponding to the Release event appears in the Actions list to the right of the Toolbox list.

6. **In the Parameters pane, check the event (or events) to which you want to assign an action:**

   - **Press:** Action occurs when the user depresses the mouse button as the pointer is covering the button.

   - **Release:** Action occurs when the user releases the mouse button when the pointer is covering the button.

   - **Release Outside:** Action occurs when the user releases the mouse button when the pointer is not covering the button.

   - **Key Press:** Action occurs when the user presses a designated key. (You enter the name of the designated key in the text box.)

   - **Roll Over:** Action occurs when the pointer rolls over the button.

   - **Roll Out:** Action occurs when the pointer rolls outside the button.

- **Drag Over:** A series of actions occurs when the user depresses the mouse button while the pointer is covering the button, drags the mouse off the button, and then drags the mouse back onto the button.

- **Drag Out:** A series of actions occurs when the user depresses the mouse button while the pointer is covering the button and then drags the mouse button off the button.

7. **Double-click an action displayed in the Toolbox list in the left pane of the Actions panel to assign that action to the selected event.**

   (Alternatively, you can click the Add button [marked with a +] you see in the upper-left corner of the Actions panel and select an action from the cascading list.)

   The ActionScript stub (placeholder) code for the double-clicked action appears in the Actions list.

8. **Repeat Steps 5 through 7 to add actions for additional events.**

   When you finish, the Actions list contains ActionScript stubs (placeholder ActionScript functions) for all the actions you selected in Step 7. You need to define the actual steps you want Flash to take in response to a mouse event by fleshing out the ActionScript stubs you see in the Actions list with custom ActionScript code. The following section, "Editing an action," describes how to do that.

**Book VII
Chapter 5**

Making Movies

Figure 5-3:
Use On
Mouse
Event to
attach one
or more
actions to
mouse or
keyboard
activity.

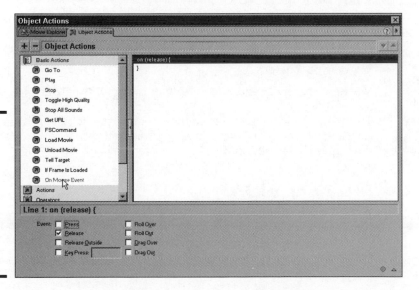

Editing an action

You need to edit an action to specify — using ActionScript code — what steps you want Flash to take when the action occurs. Flash provides two different methods for editing an action: Normal mode and Expert mode.

Normal mode is useful for generating ActionScript stubs (snippets of ActionScript code). Expert mode allows you to flesh out these ActionScript stubs by typing in the ActionScript statements that define an action.

Editing in Normal mode

When you assign an action to a movie element, ActionScript stub code appears in the Actions list on the right side of the Object Actions window as shown in Figure 5-3. (See the section, "Assigning an action to a movie element," earlier in this chapter for more details.)

After an action appears in the Actions list, edit that action in Normal mode by following these steps:

1. **Click the Parameters button (small down arrow) in the lower-right corner of the Actions window, if necessary, to display the Parameters pane.**

2. **Click to select the first line of ActionScript code you see in the Actions list.**

3. **Enter values in the Parameters pane to change the parameters of the selected action.**

   Flash modifies the ActionScript code in the Actions list to reflect the new parameters.

4. **Repeat Steps 2 and 3 to enter values for all the desired actions.**

To add or delete an action from the Actions list, click the Add an action (marked with a +) or Delete an action (marked with a -) buttons you see in the upper-left corner of the Actions panel, respectively.

Editing in Expert mode

When you assign an action to a movie element, ActionScript stub code for that action appears in the Actions list, shown in Figure 5-3. (See the section, "Assigning an action to a movie element," earlier in this chapter for more details.)

After an action appears in the Actions list, you can edit that action in Expert mode by following these steps:

1. **In the Actions list, click the ActionScript statement you want to edit.**

2. **Type the changes you want to make to the ActionScript statement.**

ActionScript is a fairly complex language. For help in creating ActionScript statements, choose Help⇨ActionScript Reference.

Testing an action

To test an action, press Ctrl+Enter on the keyboard or choose Control⇨ Test Movie.

Working with Sound

Besides the cool visual effects that Flash offers, audio can be added to movies and buttons. Flash handles two ways to incorporate sounds into your movies:

✦ **Streaming sound:** Streaming sound is designed to be used over the Web. As soon as the first few frames have been downloaded and enough data is available, streaming sound starts to play in synchronization with the movie Timeline. (In general, this option is useful for large sound files.)

✦ **Event sound:** Before an event sound starts to play, it must be downloaded completely. Event sound has its own Timeline and plays separately of the Timeline. (In general, this option is useful for short sound files and sounds you want to connect with a specific event, such as a user clicking a button.)

Importing a sound file

Before you can add sound to your movie, you must import a sound file into Flash. To import a sound, follow these steps:

1. **Choose Window⇨Library to open the Library window; then choose File⇨Import.**

The Import dialog box appears.

2. **Locate and open an AIFF, WAV, or MP3 file in the Import dialog box.**

3. **Make sure the name of the sound you imported in Step 2 appears in the Library Name list.**

Adding sound to buttons and movies

The steps you follow to add sound to a button are a bit different from the steps you follow to add and synchronize sound with a movie. In the sections that follow, I demonstrate both approaches.

Adding sound to a button

To add a sound to a button, follow these steps:

1. **Open the Library window by choosing Window⇨Library.**

2. **Right-click the desired button in the Library Window list and choose Edit from the pop-up menu that appears.**

   If the Library window list isn't expanded, expand it by clicking the Options menu you see in the upper-right corner of the Library window and and selecting Expand All Folders from the pop-up list that appears.

3. **Insert a new layer on the button's Timeline by choosing Insert⇨Layer.**

4. **In the Timeline, select the button state you want to assign the sound to and insert a keyframe by pressing F6.**

   Your button state choices are Up, Over, Down, and Hit.

5. **On the Stage, click the button to which you want to add sound.**

6. **Choose Window⇨Panels⇨Sound.**

   The Sound panel appears.

7. **Select a sound from the Sound drop-down list.**

   Only sounds you import into Flash appear in the Sound drop-down list. If you don't see any sounds in the drop-down list on the Sound panel, import a sound file by following the steps in the section, "Importing a sound file."

   If desired, continue selecting and assigning sounds to the other button states by following Steps 4 through 7.

8. **Choose an effect from the Effects drop-down list you see in the Sound panel.**

   Examples of effects you can apply to a sound include fade in, fade out, left channel, and right channel.

9. **Choose Event from the Sync drop-down list on the Sound panel.**

   Other synchronization options include Start, Stop, and Streaming. You choose Event when you want to associate a sound with a specific event. Choosing Start forces a sound to play when the associated event occurs, even if another sound is already playing. Choosing Stop causes a currently playing sound to stop when the associated event occurs. Choosing Streaming is useful if you want to associate a long sound file to a series of frames, as opposed to a button: the Streaming option causes an associated sound to stop playing when the movie stops playing.

10. **Press Ctrl+Enter on the keyboard to start a playback.**

Adding sound to a movie

To add sound to a movie, follow these steps:

1. **Follow the steps in the previous section, "Importing sound," to import a sound file into Flash.**

   After you import a sound file into Flash, that sound file is available to add to a movie.

2. **Insert a new layer on the movie's Timeline by clicking the Insert Layer icon in the lower-left corner of the Layers menu or by choosing Insert⇨Layer.**

3. **Open the Sound panel by choosing Window⇨Panels⇨Sound.**

4. **Select a sound from the Sound drop-down list located in the Sound panel.**

5. **Choose an effect from the Effects drop-down list.**

   Examples of effects you can apply to a sound include fade in and fade out (to cause the sound to get louder and softer, respectively).

6. **Choose one of the following synchronization options for the Sync drop-down list:**

   • **Event:** Synchronizes the sound to an event, such as a button click.

   • **Start:** Creates a new instance of a sound even though a sound is already playing.

   • **Stop:** Mutes a particular sound.

   • **Stream:** Synchronizes the sound with the animation for playback on the Web.

Streaming sound plays in harmony with the animation. If the animation can't keep up with the sound, Flash drops frames from the animation, causing the animation to look jerky. To correct this, use a technique called *scrubbing*. Drag the playhead through the Timeline, watching to see if the images and sound match. Add and delete frames as necessary.

7. **Decide how many times the sound should loop, and enter the value in the Loops text box you find on the Sound panel.**

   To play the sound for the entire animation, enter a value large enough to accommodate the length. For example, 20 seconds of sound needs to loop 15 times to accommodate a 5-minute animation.

8. **Press Ctrl+Enter on the keyboard to start a playback.**

You can place sounds on multiple layers. You have no limit to the amount of layers that can contain sound, and each layer can stand on its own. However, multiple sound layers that overlap play sounds at the same time.

Customizing a sound wave

You can edit a sound by clicking the Edit button in the Sound panel to display the Edit Envelope dialog box. Editing a sound is useful if you want to create a custom fading or channel effect.

To edit a sound wave for customization, follow these steps:

1. **Add a sound to a frame, or select a frame with sound already present.**

2. **Choose Window⇨Panels⇨Sound.**

3. **Make certain that the sound file is present in the Sound text box and click the Edit button.**

   The Edit Envelope dialog box, shown in Figure 5-4, appears, displaying a map of the sound wave.

4. **Edit the sound wave by dragging the envelope handle up and down, and left and right.**

5. **Click the triangular Play button in the lower-left corner to play and test the edited sound.**

Envelope handle

Envelope handle

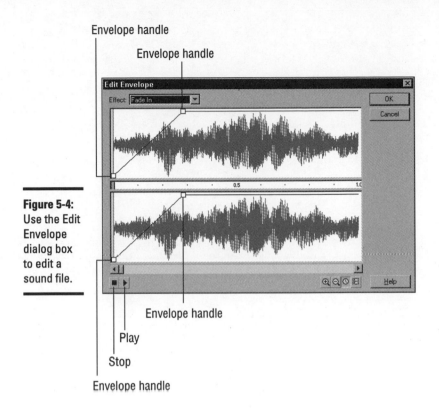

Figure 5-4:
Use the Edit
Envelope
dialog box
to edit a
sound file.

Envelope handle

Play

Stop

Envelope handle

Chapter 6: Optimizing Movies

In This Chapter

✔ **Getting familiar with general rules for optimization**

✔ **Using color efficiently**

✔ **Streamlining download performance**

✔ **Generating performance reports**

✔ **Optimizing lines and objects**

✔ **Optimizing text**

*I*f you surf the Web a lot, you know that few things are more frustrating than trying to download a site with a large movie file. You feel put upon, sitting, listening to the hard drive wheeze, watching the hourglass flicker, and waiting, and waiting, and waiting. And when the wait is over, playback is slow. Although the technology is not yet perfect, you can take steps to optimize download time and playback for your site visitors — to trim the fat, so to speak — by configuring the built-in optimization settings Flash provides.

General Rules for Optimization

Here is a list of optimization strategies to remember. Putting the following rules in place from the onset eliminates frustrations for both you and your audience.

✦ **Use tweened animation:** Using this animation type instead of frame-by-frame animation reduces file size because Flash needs to store significant information in just two frames (the keyframes that begin and end the animation) instead of every single frame.

✦ **Avoid animating bitmaps:** Instead, save bitmap images for use as backgrounds or fixed images. Why? Because bitmaps are like a mosaic. Each tile in the mosaic is known as a pixel, and each pixel contains information. When you animate a bitmap image, Flash must store all the information associated with thousands of pixels — causing playback to be slow. Instead, choose images in other file formats, such as Adobe Illustrator (.eps), GIF (.gif), JPG (.jpg), PNG (.png), and, of course, Flash (.swf).

✦ **Use symbols:** Use symbols for elements that appear more than once. Symbols reduce file size because Flash stores the symbol in the file only once, despite the number of instances of that symbol Flash encounters. (Chapter 4 is devoted to creating and using symbols.)

✦ **Group elements:** Use the Group command to group elements together instead of using numerous, separate graphic elements. (Flash compacts grouped elements, resulting in a smaller file size.) To group elements, select the elements on the Stage you want to group and choose Modify⇨Group.

Using Color Efficiently

Color can increase a file's size tremendously. You can work around this by using the following strategies:

✦ **Change the color of numerous instances of a symbol by changing the symbol (as opposed to changing the color of each individual instance).** To change the color of a symbol, choose Window⇨Panels⇨ Effect panel and then click the Effect tab to set the color for a symbol (and, therefore, all the instances of that symbol).

✦ **Coordinate the Color palette of the movie to the Web-safe Color palette.** Choose Window⇨Panels⇨Swatches, click the down arrow in the upper-right corner, and scroll through the menu to Web 216. Web 216 is a browser-safe palette that uses 216 colors to produce good image quality and the fastest processing on a Web server. When you modify the Color palette to the Web-safe Color palette from another Color palette, the colors associated with existing movie elements "snap" to the closest Web-safe alternative color automatically.

✦ **Limit the use of gradients.** Use solid fills instead whenever possible.

✦ **Limit the use of alpha transparency.** Use solid fills instead whenever possible.

Streamlining Download Performance

Because Flash movie files can be large — and because large files download agonizingly slowly over most users' Web connections — testing and optimizing a movie's download time is very important.

How important? Well, many users (including yours truly!) choose to surf away from slow-loading Flash animations rather than wait around for them to load. So, the more you streamline your movie, the greater the chance potential users will see your movie.

Typically, streamlining (or *optimizing*) a movie's download performance is an iterative process: First you test the movie's download performance; then — based on a report you can tell Flash to generate — you tweak specific frames of your movie; then you begin all over again by testing the download performance, making additional adjustments, and so on.

Testing download performance

To test a movie's download performance, follow these steps:

1. **Open a movie for testing.**

Choose File➪Open and select the SWF file of the movie you want to test.

2. **Select one of the following methods:**

- Choose Control➪Test Movie.
- Choose Control➪Test Scene.

Test Movie and Test Scene export the movie using the Exporting Flash Player and open the file as an SWF file. The exported file has its own window, and the movie begins to play immediately.

3. **In the main menu bar that appears in the Flash Player, select Debug and scroll to the desired modem setting.**

Flash can simulate modems running 14.4 kilobits per seconds, 28.8 kilobits per second, 56 kilobits per seconds, and a customizable speed.

4. **To simulate a non-standard modem speed, choose Debug➪Customize to display the Customize Modem Settings dialog box (see Figure 6-1). Then type a descriptive name in the Menu Text text box that appears in the Customize Modem Settings dialog box. In the Bit Rate text box, type the bit rate you want Flash to simulate. When you finish, click OK.**

5. **Choose Control➪Play from the Flash Player menu.**

Figure 6-1:
Simulating different modem speeds is easy using the Custom Modem Settings Flash provides.

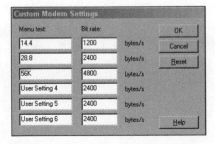

Custom Modem Settings		
Menu text:	Bit rate:	OK
14.4	1200 bytes/s	Cancel
28.8	2400 bytes/s	Reset
56K	4800 bytes/s	
User Setting 4	2400 bytes/s	
User Setting 5	2400 bytes/s	
User Setting 6	2400 bytes/s	Help

6. **Choose <u>V</u>iew⇨<u>B</u>andwidth Profiler from the Flash Player main menu to view the performance graph.**

Figure 6-2 shows an example of the performance graph Flash generates after you test a movie.

To see more of the graph, click on the bottom graph frame and drag downward.

Figure 6-2:
The Bandwidth Profiler displays statistics you can use to determine how optimized your movie file is.

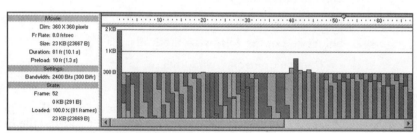

7. **Read the following guidelines to understand the graph you see in Figure 6-2:**

- The right window displays the Timeline and graph. A single bar represents a single frame of the movie. The bars that extend past the red line represent large frames that cause your movie to download slower. The bars under the red line stream in real-time in relation to the current setting. The height of the bar relates to the frame's byte size indicated to the left.

- The left window displays statistics about the movie, its settings, and state. The Movie header shows dimensions, frame rate, size both in kilobytes and bytes, duration, and preloaded frames in seconds. The Settings heading shows Bandwidth. The State header shows the number of the selected frame, and the Loaded header shows the percentage of the movie that loaded on export.

8. **Choose <u>V</u>iew⇨<u>S</u>how Streaming from the Flash Player main menu to simulate downloading the movie over the Web.**

This shows you how the movie appears when it is streamed over the Web, as opposed to when it plays directly from a file on your computer. (Be patient; this may take a few seconds.)

The movie stutters when it reaches any frames that extend above the red line. When Show Streaming is selected, a green progress bar runs along the top of the window. This *streaming bar* indicates the number of frames loaded in conjunction with the frame currently playing. The streaming bar only makes one pass. To rerun the streaming bar, toggle by pressing Ctrl+Enter.

9. **Click any of the bars to obtain information about a particular frame.**

The left window displays the statistics. When a bar is selected, the movie stops play.

10. **Choose either of two views of the graph to determine the type of information displayed:**

- **Choose View⇨Streaming Graph.** Displays all frames that cause problematic slowdowns on download. The bars display in light and dark gray. A single bar represents a single frame. As Figure 6-3 shows, the first bar is usually very tall and extends past the red line because it contains symbol information.

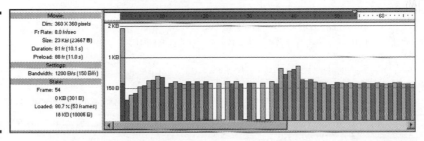

Figure 6-3: Viewing movie download statistics as a streaming graph.

- **Choose View⇨Frame by Frame Graph.** Displays the size of each frame (see Figure 6-4). The bars display in light and dark gray alternating shades. When a frame is selected, it turns green. A single bar represents a single frame. The bars that extend past the red line represent large frames that cause Flash to stutter on playback.

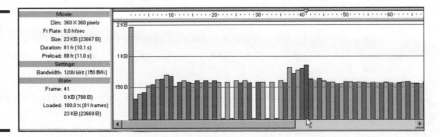

Figure 6-4: Viewing movie download statistics frame by frame.

11. **Click the Close icon in the upper-right corner to close the window.**

You return to the movie editing environment.

Improving download performance

After you test the movie's download performance, you have an idea of which frames may be causing your movie to download slowly. By deleting these frames (deleting frames shortens animation sequences) or editing the frames to reduce image size, you can improve your movie's download performance. (For more tips on optimizing your movie's download performance, check out "General Rules for Optimization," "Using Color Efficiently," and "Optimizing Lines and Objects" elsewhere in this chapter.)

To help you pinpoint specific frames which need to be optimized, you can generate a report that outlines test results and simulation settings used in the test. Flash puts the report file in the same location as the Flash movie file and gives it the extension TXT. The TXT file remains in this location until you overwrite or delete it.

You may find it helpful to run two different tests, generate two different reports, and compare the two reports to determine how different settings affect your movie's download performance.

To generate a report, follow these steps:

1. **Return to the movie editing environment by clicking the Close icon in the upper-right corner of the Flash Player.**

2. **Choose File⇨Publish Settings.**

The Publish Settings dialog box appears, as shown in Figure 6-5.

3. **Click the Flash tab.**

4. **Check the Generate Size Report check box.**

5. **Click the Publish button.**

6. **Click OK.**

The report generates.

To view the report, use your favorite text editing program to open the plain text file having the same main name (`yourMovieReport.txt`) and folder location as your original movie file.

If you follow the previous steps but don't find the generated report, check to make sure the movie file is saved somewhere on your hard drive.

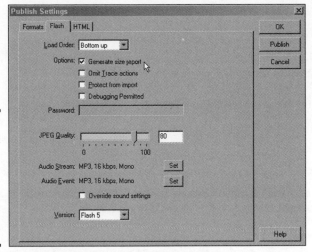

Figure 6-5:
You use the
Publish
Settings
dialog box
to generate
a perform-
ance report.

Optimizing Lines and Objects

The more information that Flash has to keep track of, the larger the file size. You can tweak several areas to help your playback performance. Keep these optimization techniques in the back of your mind when creating line drawings and images:

✦ Brush strokes require more memory than pencil strokes because more information needs to be calculated.

✦ Solid lines require less memory than specialty lines such as dashed and dotted lines.

✦ Flash describes shapes using lines. More lines equal more memory. Limit the number of separate lines by choosing Modify⇨Optimize and adjusting the slider in the Optimize Curves dialog box.

✦ Group elements whenever possible. Grouping elements allows Flash to reduce overall file size.

Optimizing Text

To help shrink file size, you can configure Flash to use the closest font match it can find installed on your visitors' computers — in other words, to use the device font setting. (The alternative is to embed fonts in your movies. While embedding fonts ensures that users see the fonts you select, it also causes movie file size to balloon.)

To select the Use Device Font setting, follow these steps:

1. **Using the Text Tool, select text block(s) on the Stage.**
2. **Choose <u>Window</u>➪<u>P</u>anels➪Text Options.**

   The Text Options dialog box appears.
3. **Click the Text Options tab in the Text Options dialog box.**

   A drop-down list appears.
4. **Choose Static Text.**
5. **Check the Use Device Fonts check box.**
6. **Close the Text Options dialog box by clicking the close icon in the upper-right corner of the Text Options dialog box.**

Fonts can quickly increase a movie's file size — especially when you use a variety. So, to help improve your movie download performance, don't use too many font sizes or font styles.

Chapter 7: Publishing and Printing Your Movie

In This Chapter

✔ Publishing your movie in Flash format

✔ Exporting your movie in a non-Flash format

✔ Printing frames and thumbnails of your movie

You've shot your last scene, your movie is done, and you're ready to wow your audience. Don't plan the premiere yet, however; you have a few more production details to attend to.

You must *publish,* or export, your movie to one of several formats for playback. *Printing* your movie provides you with a hard copy you can use for meetings (or just to show a friend who may not have a computer). This chapter shows you how.

Publishing Your Movie

When you create and edit your movie file, you work with an editable FLA file. When you finish editing and want to send your movie out into the world for all to see, however, you must tell Flash to convert that editable FLA file into a non-editable file for playback. In other words, you must *publish* your movie.

You can use either of the following options to publish your movie:

✦ **Publish command.** Converts your FLA file into a noneditable file for playback:

- Inside a Flash player (SWF)
- Inside a Flash-enabled Web browser (SWF, HTML)
- Using Macromedia Generator, a Flash site production and management tool, on a Web server (SWT)
- Inside an Apple QuickTime player (MOV)
- Inside a RealPlayer player (SMIL)
- As a standalone application, or *projector* (EXE, HQX)
- As an image file (GIF, JPG, PNG)

✦ **Export command:** Converts your movie into a file format suitable for viewing in non-Flash applications, such as Adobe Premiere. (You can find a complete list of the export file formats supported in Table 7-1.)

The sections that follow introduce you to the Publish and Export commands; you also see publishing settings for the most popular file formats.

Publishing your movie

To publish your movie, follow these steps:

1. **Choose File⇨Open and click the Look in: drop-down box to select the movie you want to publish. When the name of the movie file you want to publish appears in the File name: text box, click OK.**

   Flash opens the movie on the Stage.

2. **Choose File⇨Publish Settings from the Flash main menu.**

   The Publish Settings dialog box appears.

3. **Click the Formats tab.**

4. **Check the file formats you want Flash to generate.**

   By default, two formats are checked: Flash (.swf) and HTML (.html). Checking these two formats tells Flash to generate the Flash Player (SWF) file and an HTML document that includes that Flash Player file. However, you may check additional formats. For each file format you check, Flash displays a tab containing settings for that specific file format. (You find setting details for the most popular file formats later in this chapter.)

   If you want to create a standalone player that runs a movie automatically, select Windows Projector from the Publish Settings dialog box.

5. **To specify your own filenames for each file format selected, uncheck the Use Default Names check box at the bottom of the Filename list; then, in the text box to the right of each file format you choose, type a distinctive filename.**

   Flash automatically adds the proper extension for the selected format.

6. **Set the publishing settings for each file format you select by clicking the appropriate tabs.**

   (You find setting details for the most popular file formats later in this chapter.)

7. **Click Publish.**

   This generates the files in the formats you selected in Step 4.

Exporting your movie

Exporting a movie allows you to convert a Flash movie to another file format for editing in another application, such as an image-editing or animation-editing application.

To export a movie, follow these steps:

1. **Choose File⇨Open and click the Look in: drop-down box to select the movie you want to export. When the name of the movie file you want to export appears in the File name: text box, click OK.**

   Flash opens the movie on the Stage.

2. **Choose File⇨Export Movie.**

   The Export Movie dialog box appears.

3. **Choose a file format from the Save As Type drop-down list located at the bottom of the Export Movie dialog box.**

4. **Enter the name for the output file in the File Name text box.**

5. **Click Save.**

6. **Set the options for the selected format, if necessary.**

   For certain file formats, extra information is required. If this is the case, an Export dialog box will appear and ask for it. For example, to export a movie using the Adobe Illustrator file extension, the Export Adobe Illustrator dialog box you see in Figure 7-1 appears, asking for a version number. For example, click the radio button next to the version of Adobe Illustrator to which you want to export the movie and click OK.

Figure 7-1:
Customized
Export
dialog boxes
walk you
through the
export
process.

7. **Click OK.**

   Flash exports movies into the file formats listed in Table 7-1.

Table 7-1	Export File Types Supported by Flash
File Type	*Extension*
Adobe Illustrator	.ai
Animated GIF, GIF Sequence, and GIF Image	.gif
Bitmap	.bmp
DIX Sequence and AutoCAD DXF Image	.dxf
Enhanced Metafile	.emf
EPS (version 6.0 or earlier)	.eps
FutureSplash Player	.spl
Generator Template	.swt
JPEG Sequence and JPEG Image	.jpg
PNG Sequence and PNG Image	.png
QuickTime Publish Settings	.mov
WAV Audio	.wav
Windows AVI	.avi
Windows Metafile	.wmf

Flash publish settings

The following list describes the settings in the Publish Settings dialog box associated with the Flash tab:

✦ **Load Order:** Controls what displays first when the movie downloads. Used for the first frame only.

✦ **Generate Size Report:** Generates a text report so that the user can maximize download playback by manipulating frames. The report is saved as a file with the same name as the movie but with the .txt extension.

✦ **Omit Trace Actions:** Omits trace statements (statements you insert into your movie to track down bugs in your ActionScript code) in the current movie. When this is checked, Flash doesn't open an output window for displaying trace statements.

✦ **Protect From Import:** Prohibits the movie from being imported back into Flash. Prevents the access of your SWF file so that someone else cannot edit it.

✦ **Debugging Permitted:** Starts the debugger so that you can debug a file remotely. This command has a Password protection text box.

✦ **Password:** Allows you to key in a password if the Debugging Permitted option is checked.

✦ **JPEG Quality:** Sets the compression applied to bitmap images. Setting the compression value helps you optimize images — a good thing when creating movies for delivery over the Web. (The higher the compression value, the lower the file size.) Use the slider, or key in a value. This option only affects the bitmaps in the file.

✦ **Auto Stream:** Sets the compression and export stream rate for all movies. From the Sound Properties dialog box, set the Compression, Preprocessing, Bit Rate, and Quality.

✦ **Auto Event:** Sets the compression and event sound rate for all movies. From the Sound Properties dialog box, set the Compression, Preprocessing, Bit Rate, and Quality.

✦ **Override Sound:** Deals with the settings for individual sounds. These settings override the settings made in the Sound Properties dialog box.

✦ **Version:** Sets the playback for lower versions. Various features in version 5 don't work in movies exported with an earlier version.

HTML publish settings

The following list describes the settings in the Publish Settings dialog box associated with the HTML tab:

✦ **Template:** Directs Flash to use a specific template when creating the HTML document. For example, selecting Flash Only (Default) tells Flash to generate an HTML file containing <OBJECT> and <EMBED> tags — the most common option. Selecting Java Player, on the other hand, instructs Flash to generate an HTML file that incorporates the Flash Java player instead. For a description of each template, select the name of the template and click the Info button to the right.

✦ **Dimensions:** Sets the width and height of the movie in the browser. From the Dimensions drop-down list, select Match Movie, Pixels, or Percent. For Pixels and Percent, key in a value for width and height. The default setting is Match Movie.

✦ **Playback: Pause At Start:** Pauses the movie until your audience clicks a button or chooses Play from the shortcut menu. The default setting is off.

✦ **Playback: Loop:** Repeats the movie at the final frame when checked and stops the movie at the final frame when the box is not checked. The default setting is on.

✦ **Playback: Display Menu:** Offers a shortcut menu to users when they right-click the movie. The default setting is on.

✦ **Playback: Device Font:** Substitutes antialiased system fonts for fonts not found on the audience's system. The default setting is off.

**Book VII
Chapter 7**

**Publishing and
Printing Your Movie**

✦ **Quality:** Determines the degree of tradeoff between download time and applying antialiasing for playback appearance. Choose from among Auto Low, Auto High, Medium, High, and Best. The default setting is Medium.

✦ **Window Mode:** Makes the most of layering, positioning, and transparent movies in Internet Explorer 4.0. This option is only available to users with Windows Internet Explorer with the Flash ActiveX control on their systems. Choose from among Window, Opaque Windowless, and Transparent Windowless. The default setting is Window.

✦ **HTML Alignment:** Aligns the movie within the Flash browser window. Choose from among Default, Left, Right, Top, and Bottom. The default setting is Default.

✦ **Scale:** Aligns the movie within the specified boundary after a change has been made. Choose from among Default (Show All), No Border, or Exact Fit.

✦ **Flash Alignment:** Sets the horizontal and vertical dimensions of the movie in the movie window. Some cropping may occur. Choose from among Horizontal: Left, Center, and Right and Vertical: Top, Center, and Bottom. The default settings are Horizontal: Center and Vertical: Center.

✦ **Show Warning Message:** Tells Flash to generate an error message when you attempt to publish the movie and Flash detects an error that may affect its ability to publish your movie correctly.

Printing Your Movie

In Flash, you can print a single frame from a movie, a series of frames on one page using various storyboard layouts, or even the entire movie. This capability comes in handy if you ever need to present your movie as a hard copy — for example, when discussing a project with a client or colleague and no computer is readily available.

Printing designated frames

To designate a frame or frames for printing, follow these steps:

1. **Choose File⇨Open and click the Look in: drop-down box to select the movie from which you want to print frames. When the name of the movie file appears in the File name: text box, click OK.**

Flash opens the movie on the Stage.

2. **Choose Modify⇨Frame.**

The Frame dialog box opens.

3. **From the Timeline, click to select the frame or frames to print.**

To select multiple frames, use Shift+click. If you don't designate frames, Flash prints all frames.

4. **Type #p in the Label text box that appears in the Frame dialog box.**

When you return to the Timeline, the #p indicator you see in Figure 7-2 is placed on the selected frame.

5. **Choose <u>F</u>ile⇔<u>P</u>rint.**

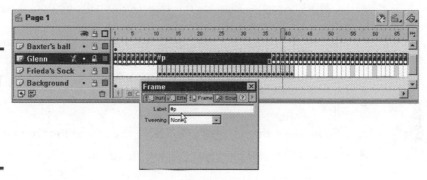

Figure 7-2: Designating which frames to print by using the #p Label.

Printing a storyboard filled with thumbnails

A *storyboard* is a printout containing small pictures of each of the frames in your movie. Storyboards are very helpful when you want to view, at a glance, all the frames that make up your movie. Printing a storyboard allows you to share a hard copy of your movie with other folks — other developers, friends, and family — without having to kill a bunch of trees printing one frame per page.

To print a storyboard, follow these steps:

1. **Choose <u>F</u>ile⇔<u>O</u>pen and click the Look <u>i</u>n: drop-down box to select the movie from which you want to print a storyboard. When the name of the movie file appears in the File <u>n</u>ame: text box, click OK.**

Flash opens the movie on the Stage.

2. **Choose <u>F</u>ile⇔Page Set<u>u</u>p.**

The Page Setup dialog box appears.

3. **Select one of the following from the Frames drop-down list you find in the Layout section of the Page Setup dialog box:**

• **All Frames:** Prints every frame in the movie.

• **First Frame Only:** Prints only the first frame of each scene.

4. **Select one of the following from the Layout drop-down list that appears in the Layout section of the Page Setup dialog box:**

- **Actual Size:** Prints the full frame. To reduce or enlarge the frame, enter a percentage in the Scale text field to the right.

- **Fit On One Page:** Adjusts the frame to fill the print area of the page by reducing or enlarging the frame.

- **Storyboard — Boxes:** Prints the thumbnails with borders.

- **Storyboard — Grid:** Prints the thumbnails with a grid pattern.

- **Storyboard — Blank:** Prints the thumbnails without a border.

When you apply the Storyboard option, you need to address several features. Type a value for the number of thumbnails viewed per page into the Frames Across text box. Set the spacing between thumbnails in the Frame Margin text box. To label each thumbnail, check the Label Frames check box.

5. **Click OK.**

6. **Choose File⇨Print Preview to check the layout before you print.**

7. **Choose File⇨Print to print the storyboard.**

Chapter 8: Using Flash with Other Programs

In This Chapter

✔ Importing a non-Flash file into Flash

✔ Importing a file sequence into Flash

✔ Pasting a non-Flash file into Flash

✔ Compressing imported bitmaps

Flash is a great program for creating images and animations. The more heavily you get into electronic graphics, however, the more you realize that many other cool tools exist, each with its own particular strength. You may want to create bitmap and vector images in other programs because they do things for you that Flash doesn't; Corel Painter, for example, creates impressive natural-media effects — effects that mimic the look of "real" media, such as medium-tip markers, waxy crayons, or oils applied with a camel hair brush.

Also, you may have an existing library of graphics that you've created in other applications, but that you'd now like to use with Flash. If so, good news! As this chapter demonstrates, you can import art created in other programs directly into Flash.

Bringing a File into Flash

You have two choices if you want to bring a file from another application into Flash:

✦ **Importing:** Importing preserves file attributes better than pasting, and you can still edit the file in some cases.

✦ **Pasting:** Pasting is the easiest way to bring in a new file, but you may lose editability and image attributes. If you have a choice, choose importing over pasting.

Importing Non-Flash Files

In general, importing does a better job of preserving file attributes than pasting.

Whenever you import a non-Flash file, you risk losing some file attributes. Fortunately, some of those lost file attributes can be restored. For example, when you import a file in Adobe Illustrator or Windows Metafile (WMF) vector format, Flash interprets the file as a group of objects in the current layer; before you can manipulate the imported file in Flash, you must choose Modify⇨Ungroup from the main menu.

Importing a file into Flash

To import a file into Flash, follow these steps:

1. **Choose File⇨Import.**

   The Import dialog box, shown in Figure 8-1, appears.

2. **Navigate to the desired folder.**

3. **Select from the Files of Type drop-down list the type of file you want to import.**

4. **Double-click the desired file in the Import dialog box (or right-click the file and then click Open).**

Flash opens the file you want to import and places it on the Stage.

File types that Flash can import

The following table lists importable bitmap and vector file types.

File Types	Notes
Adobe Illustrator 6.0, 5.0, 3.0, and 88 (*.EPS, *.AI)	
AutoCAD Release 10 (*.DXF)	ASCII format only, no binary; font mapping unpredictable; no fills are recognized; no 3-D files allowed
Bitmap (*.BMP)	
Enhanced Metafile (*.EMF)	
Flash (*.SWF)	
Freehand (*.FH9, *.FT9, *.FH8, *.FT8, *.FH7, *.FT7)	
Futuresplash (*.SPL)	
GIF (*.GIF)	Both still and animated

File Types	Notes
JPEG (*.JPG)	
MacPaint (*.PNTG)	Requires QuickTime 4 or higher
Photoshop (*.PSD)	Requires QuickTime 4 or higher
PICT (*.PCT, *.PIC)	Macintosh-style vector format; bitmap format requires QuickTime 4 or higher
PNG (*.PNG)	
QuickTime image (*.QTIF)	Requires QuickTime 4 or higher
QuickTime movie (*.MOV)	Requires QuickTime 4 or higher
Silicon Graphics (*.SAI)	Requires QuickTime 4 or higher
Targa (*.TGF)	Requires QuickTime 4 or higher
Tagged Image File Format (*.TIFF)	Requires QuickTime 4 or higher
Windows Metafile (*.WMF)	

Many of these file types are not the most current version of their associated application; some are downright outdated. You may be able to work around the problem by opening your non-Flash application and using the Save As command to specify compatibility with an earlier revision of the program.

If you need to import a file that says, "Requires QuickTime 4 or Higher" in the preceding list, point your browser to www.apple.com/quicktime/download and follow the instructions. You'll probably want the "Pro" version, for which Apple charges a nominal fee.

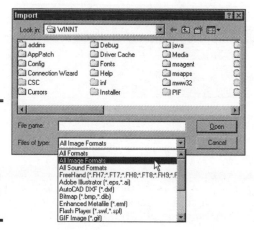

Figure 8-1:
You can import several different file formats into Flash.

Importing a file sequence

You may have created a *sequence,* or series, of images that you want to bring into Flash as successive frames to create an animated effect. To import a file sequence into Flash, follow these steps:

1. **Name your images sequentially: for example, pic01.tif, pic02.tif, and so on.**

Make sure the number part of the filename comes at the end; also make sure that you have enough digits so that Flash can order the files correctly.

2. **Choose File⇨Import.**

The Import dialog box appears.

3. **Navigate to the folder where your sequence of files resides.**

4. **Select from the Files of Type drop-down list the type of file you want to import.**

5. **Double-click the first file in the sequence.**

Flash notices that the filename ends in a number and asks whether you want to import a sequence of files (see Figure 8-2).

6. **Click Yes.**

Flash imports all the files in the sequence. (You can choose <u>W</u>indow from the main menu to view the imported files.)

Figure 8-2:
Flash automatic-ally detects and imports file sequences.

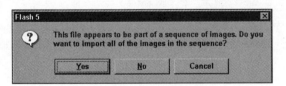

Pasting Non-Flash Files into Flash

Bringing artwork into Flash can be as simple as cutting and pasting. This method takes advantage of the operating system's built-in capability of copying and moving data between applications.

I don't recommend this method if the Import alternative is available (see the section, "Importing a file into Flash," earlier in this chapter). Pasting images from other programs into Flash can result in the loss of editability, image attributes, or both. For example, a cut-and-pasted bitmap image may lose its transparency feature. You may also find to your surprise that Flash pastes your graphic as a mirror image of itself. (Nope, rotating doesn't help in that case.) But if Flash doesn't support importing the type of file you want to work with and you want to give loading the file one more shot, try this simple method instead.

To cut and paste a graphic into Flash, follow these steps:

1. **Open the graphic's native application.**

2. **Load the graphic file and select the portion you want to copy (or the whole image).**

3. **Choose File⇨Copy.**

4. **Open Flash, and then open your movie file by choosing File⇨Open and clicking the Look in: drop-down box to select the movie you want to open. When the name of the movie file you want to publish appears in the File name: text box, click OK.**

Flash opens the movie on the Stage.

5. **Choose Edit⇨Paste.**

Using drag-and-drop as a method of importing graphics into Flash is an iffy proposition at best. Flash doesn't fully support Object Linking and Embedding (OLE) technology, which is the underlying technology for drag-and-drop operations.

The Clipboard preferences that you can view by choosing Edit⇨Preferences and then clicking the Clipboard tab don't apply to importing art! They apply to artwork that you cut or copy *from* Flash for pasting into another program.

Compressing Imported Bitmaps

When you import a bitmap image, depending on the source format, Flash may or may not store the image internally in the most efficient format. The result can be a movie file that's larger than you want. Fortunately, compressing an imported bitmap is easy:

1. **Open the Library window (choose Window⇨Library) if it's not already open.**

2. **Right-click the bitmap's icon in the Library window.**

3. **Choose Properties.**

   The Bitmap Properties dialog box appears.

4. **Choose a compression setting from the Compression drop-down list that appears.**

   - Choose Photo (JPEG) for continuous-tone images that have color gradations.
   - Choose Lossless (PNG/GIF) for line art or clip art style images.

5. **If you chose Lossless (PNG/GIF) in Step 4, skip to Step 6. If you chose Photo (JPEG), select one of the following approaches:**

   - Click Use Document Default Quality (if the original file is a JPEG file, you instead see the message Use Imported JPEG Data) if you want to use the same compression setting that was present in the original document.
   - Clear Use Document Default Quality (or Use Imported JPEG Data, if that's what the check box label says), and enter a compression ratio in the Quality field, if you want to specify your own compression setting (larger numbers mean better quality).

6. **Click the Test button to see the effect of the compression setting on the image excerpt in the upper-left corner of the Bitmap Properties dialog box.**

   The effect of your setting on the image's file size appears at the bottom of the dialog box.

7. **Repeat Step 6 until you've achieved a happy compromise between image quality and file size.**

8. **Click OK to close the Bitmap Properties dialog box.**

Index

Notes

Book VIII

Adding E-Commerce Capability

The 5th Wave   By Rich Tennant

"Just how accurately should my Web site reflect my place of business?"

Contents at a Glance

Chapter 1: Getting to Know E-Commerce

*E*lectronic commerce, or *e-commerce,* is a fancy way of saying "buying and selling stuff over the Web." When you use your credit card to purchase books, music, software, or airline tickets, you're participating in an e-commerce transaction.

Not so long ago, adding e-commerce capability to a Web site was confusing, cumbersome, and costly. Fortunately, times have changed! These days, dozens of companies offer solutions you can use to sell goods and services from your Web site, from quick-and-dirty solutions appropriate for a mom-and-pop Web site to industrial-strength, specialized applications designed for high-volume online businesses. In this chapter, I introduce you to the ins and outs of e-commerce and describe the things you need to know to select and implement the e-commerce solution that's right for you and your company.

Understanding E-Commerce

Gone are the days when Web surfers were reluctant to type their credit card numbers into a form on a Web site. With the advent of secure data transmission and transaction processing systems supported by thousands of banks and retail stores all over the world, shopping online is rapidly becoming as popular as shopping by catalog.

This year, for example, American consumers alone purchased millions of dollars worth of goods and services over the Web — and industry analysts expect this trend to keep growing. By 2005, some say, we could be using our keyboards and mice to rack up online purchases worth $100 billion dollars a year.

If you have a Web site and something to sell, you can join in the e-commerce party by adding e-commerce capability to your Web site. The remaining chapters in this book describe how to do just that; but before you dash off to implement an e-commerce solution, take a few minutes to check out the e-commerce overview you find in the following section.

Speaking e-commerce like a native

Here's a handy primer you can use to get yourself up to speed on e-commerce-related terms.

acquiring bank: Sometimes called a *processor*, an acquiring bank is a bank that processes credit card transactions. You set up a *merchant account* with an acquiring bank.

application service provider (ASP): Not to be confused with *active server pages* (a server-side programming language created by Microsoft that's also known as ASP), an application service provider hosts expensive applications that you can rent — instead of having to buy and install the applications on your own computer. Some ASPs offer hosted e-commerce applications you can rent.

clicks-and-mortar: A business that operates both online, through a Web site, and off, in a traditional store setting. (*Bricks-and-mortar*, in contrast, refers to an offline-only business.)

credit card network: A special communication network that transmits credit information securely between banks.

discount: The percentage of each credit card order deducted by the acquiring bank. (In other words, a transaction fee.)

hosted e-commerce solution: E-commerce software offered by an *application service provider*. Typically, you access hosted software through your Web browser.

issuing bank: A bank that issues credit cards.

nexus: A legal term that translates roughly to "where you do business" — an important distinction for e-commerce taxation purposes.

merchant account: An account you set up to hold funds from your customers' credit card orders. You set up a merchant account with an *acquiring bank*. A merchant account can be relatively expensive, depending on the volume of sales your Web page attracts; fortunately, not all e-commerce solutions require you to set up your own merchant account.

merchant ID (MID): A unique identifying number for a *merchant account*. You need both a merchant ID and a terminal ID to accept credit card transactions directly into your merchant account.

microtransaction (micropayment): A tiny transaction — anywhere from a few cents to a dollar or two — typically associated with downloadable pictures, software, and reports. Pay-as-you-go microtransactions were supposed to revolutionize the world of e-commerce; but so far, merchants and banks have been reluctant to implement a consistent, workable microtransaction scheme, and surfers have been reluctant to pay for items they feel they should get for free on the Web.

secure sockets layer (SSL): A transmission protocol that creates a secure, encrypted connection between a browser and a Web server. URLs that begin with "https://" indicate that data is being transmitted using SSL. (The "s" stands for "secure.")

shopping cart: Software on an e-commerce site that displays all the items a customer has selected for purchase. A shopping cart typically lists information such as item name and description, model number, price, and order subtotal.

storefront: The part of the e-commerce process the customer sees. An e-commerce storefront typically includes a *catalog* (product images and descriptions) and a shopping cart.

terminal ID (TID): A number that uniquely identifies your terminal (the point of sale) for credit card transactions. You need both a merchant ID and a terminal ID to accept credit card transactions directly into your *merchant account*.

E-commerce overview

Although using a credit card to pay for a purchase is easy for Web-surfing customers, quite a bit of behind-the-scenes work must be done before that purchase price shows up in the e-commerce business owner's (your!) bank account.

The following steps give you an overview of the process; Figure 1-1 shows the steps in handy diagram form.

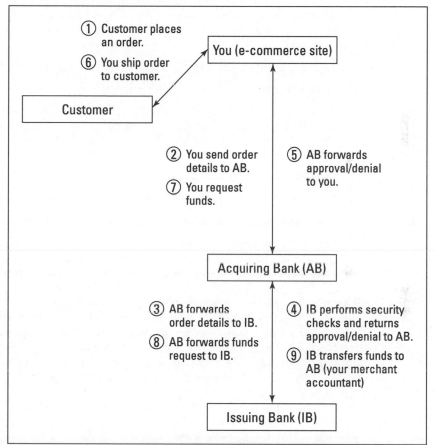

Figure 1-1:
An overview
of the
e-commerce
process.

1. **Purchase.**

The customer fills out and submits a Web-based order form, which sends the customer's credit card number, name, billing address, and other order-related details to you, owner of an e-commerce-enabled Web site.

2. Authentication.

You forward the transaction details and card number to the acquiring bank (a bank that specializes in managing credit card transactions, and with which you've set up a merchant account).

The acquiring bank forwards the information, via a credit card network (a bank-to-bank communication network such as CyberCash or Verifone), to the issuing bank (the bank that issued the credit card to the customer).

The issuing bank performs a variety of security checks, including address verification and card number validation, and then returns approval (or denial) details to the acquiring bank via a credit card network.

The acquiring bank forwards approval (or denial) information to you.

3. Order Fulfillment.

Assuming the credit card checked out, you ship the goods to the customer. (By law, just as with telephone or paper catalog orders, you can't charge a credit card until you've bundled up the order and dropped it in the mail.)

4. Settlement.

You send a request to the acquiring bank to secure the funds.

The acquiring bank forwards the request to the issuing bank.

Transactions are settled when the issuing bank pays the acquiring bank and the acquiring bank transfers the funds into your merchant account (and from there to your business checking account, if you like).

The previous steps give you a good idea of how e-commerce works — in theory. In practice, however, an e-commerce solution can be much simpler. For example, some simplified e-commerce systems, such as those I demonstrate in Chapter 2, take care of contacting the appropriate banks for authentication and fulfillment, so all you have to do is present your visitors with a "buy" button and stuff orders into big cardboard boxes.

On the other hand, doing high-volume business — online or off — typically includes such realities as returned merchandise and back orders, both of which *add* steps to the overview presented in Figure 1-1.

With so many options and possible scenarios, you're wise to begin your search for the perfect e-commerce solution by taking a look at a handful of successful e-commerce sites. The following section provides details.

Anatomy of a successful e-commerce site

Examples of successful e-commerce sites abound. (By *successful* I mean sites that attract not only traffic, but purchasers, as well.)

Amazon.com (see Figure 1-2) is probably one of the best-known e-commerce sites, but many more exist. Although these sites may differ in the particular software and services they use to implement their e-commerce features, the acquiring banks they do business with, and even the way they present their merchandise for sale, all of them address the same basic e-commerce issues I present in this section.

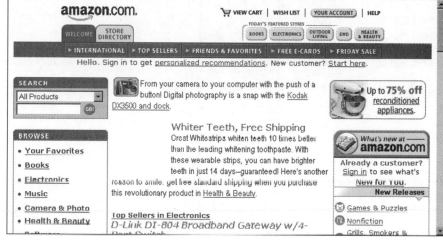

Figure 1-2: Amazon.com is one example of a successful e-commerce site.

Ease of use

Good e-commerce sites make finding and purchasing products easy.

Consider, for example, a popular e-commerce flower and gift shop. As Figure 1-3 shows, this site displays a list across the top of the page of the different kinds of items (flowers, plants, gourmet treats, and so on) available for sale. But the site doesn't stop there. To make shopping even easier for visitors, the site also offers an "In Season" category, listing seasonal gifts and best-selling items, and an "Everyday Celebrations" category, listing gifts appropriate for birthdays, anniversaries, and other major gift-giving occasions. Pictures of popular gifts — bouquets, snacks, and so on — are presented smack in the middle of the page, with prices and "click to buy" links prominently displayed.

Chapter 5 offers additional tips for making your e-commerce site easy for visitors to use, as well as for providing good customer service during and after the sale.

Figure 1-3: Giving your visitors a variety of ways to find items on your e-commerce site is a strategy for success.

Security blanket

Sending credit card information over the Internet has become practically hack-proof, thanks to beefy security mechanisms created for the banking and business-to-business industries. Communications protocols such as *secure sockets layer* (SSL), which protects data traveling between Web browsers and Web servers, and *secure electronic transactions* (SET), which encodes credit card numbers for access only by banks and credit card companies, are built into virtually every commercial e-commerce solution. You don't need to understand all the gory details of how encryption and secure protocols work; all you need to do is select an e-commerce solution (and provider) that you and your customers have confidence in. After you choose an e-commerce solution and incorporate it into your e-commerce Web site, you may want to follow the lead of popular e-commerce sites — such as the one you see in Figure 1-4 — that describe for their customers, in plain English, how Internet security works. Explaining the security policies you decide to implement helps potential customers feel more comfortable purchasing from you online.

Figure 1-4:
Many
e-commerce
sites ease
potential
customers'
concerns by
explaining
the security
policies in
place.

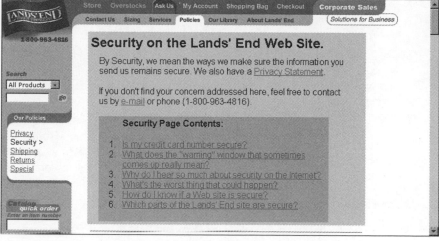

A taxing question

Every city, state, province, and country handles taxes a bit differently, of course, but in the United States, you must charge sales tax on any items you ship to a state in which your company has a physical presence, or *nexus*. Traditionally — in the days of catalogs, when customers would either mail or phone in their orders — that physical presence was a store, an office, or a warehouse. But what if you sell digital information such as software, medical reports, or downloadable music recordings over a Web site and don't need a store, an office, or a warehouse?

You may not be surprised to find that taxing authorities all over the planet are divided on this very issue: Does a Web server constitute a physical presence? The answer to this question affects whether you must charge your customers sales tax, and if so, how much tax to charge.

As the owner of an e-commerce site, it's your responsibility to check with an expert in such matters, such as a tax attorney, to find out how much tax to add to each order — and how to remit that tax to the proper authorities.

Most e-commerce solutions give you a way to display how much sales tax you collect as part of the order process. Doing so is a great idea, because it helps keep customers from being unfavorably surprised when they open their credit card statement and find out the amount of their total, tax-included bill.

The Taxman cometh

In 1998, the U.S. Congress passed the Internet Tax Freedom Act (ITFA), a three-year moratorium on Internet-related taxation. Although the three-year time period was subsequently extended, other legislation is in the works that may affect your e-commerce efforts. The Streamlined Sales Tax Project, for example, is a coalition of 38 U.S. states that hopes to simplify tax structures so that they may be applied uniformly to e-commerce. (In other words, this coalition hopes to ease the complexity of the current taxing structure that compelled the passage of the ITFA in the first place so that the government can begin taxing e-commerce sites in earnest.)

Other countries are busily working on similar rules and regulations. Tariffs, customers fees, and other charges may soon be imposed on products sold from a Web server based in one country to a customer living in another.

Order fulfillment

Unless the product or service you sell through your e-commerce site is digital (and, therefore, downloaded directly to customers' computers), you need to consider how you want to approach order fulfillment — in other words, shipping and handling. (*Shipping* refers to the price of packing materials and postage; *handling* refers to the time someone must spend stuffing that envelope, packing that box, and writing that label.)

You have two options when it comes to order fulfillment:

+ **Package and ship your own orders.** This option is fine for mom-and-pop or small businesses that don't expect a flood of orders — at least, not initially. (You can always select the following option later when that flood begins to arrive.) This option is also appropriate for established businesses that already have a fulfillment department.

+ **Select an order fulfillment company.** For a fee, some companies, such as Specialty Fulfillment Center (www.pickandship.com), process your orders for you.

Whichever option you choose, you may want to consider charging your customers an extra fee to cover the costs associated with shipping and handling.

International issues

Making your Web site open for e-business in another country is more than a matter of translating your site copy into another language. You must also account for international differences such as:

✦ currency conversion

✦ import tariffs

✦ national security and privacy restrictions

✦ cultural issues

✦ increased shipping fees

Few off-the-shelf e-commerce solutions offer customized help with these issues, so if you want to make your e-commerce site available to folks in other countries, you may need to consult an expert on international commerce and create your own custom e-commerce solution. (Chapter 4 gives you tips for doing just that.)

Choosing an E-Commerce Solution

Dozens of e-commerce products and services exist on the market today. These e-commerce products and services fall into one of the following four categories:

✦ **Simplified e-commerce solutions.** These pay-per-transaction solutions are easy and cheap (or even free) to add to your Web site. When a customer buys a product from your site using a simplified e-commerce solution, you pay the solution provider a small percentage of the total sale — usually somewhere between 1.5 percent and 9 percent.

> **The good news:** If you know a bit of HTML, you can have an e-commerce solution up and running in about half an hour, without any startup costs whatsoever. And because you only pay for the service when customers buy your products, you don't have to shell out a wad of cash only to find out nobody wants to buy your rhubarb-and-tofu breakfast bars.

> **The bad news:** Most of these solutions are fairly limited; for example, some don't support digital products (such as downloadable electronic books); most don't support international sales. Virtually none "hooks in" to back-end business processes, such as an accounting database.

> **Most appropriate for:** Small mom-and-pop businesses with one or two items to sell.

> I devote Chapter 2 to showing you how to find, evaluate, and implement simplified e-commerce solutions.

✦ **Hosted e-commerce solutions.** A slightly more expensive and time-consuming option is to rent space in an e-commerce network service such as Yahoo! Stores.

The good news: Hosted e-commerce solutions are relatively quick to implement (expect to spend a few hours using a point-and-click interface — no HTML knowledge necessary). These solutions also support more features than the previous option, including the ability to offer multiple products and, in some cases, the ability to handle international orders.

The bad news: You typically pay a fee for this service ($100 or more per month), whether or not customers buy your products; in addition, you pay a percentage of each sale to a credit card company. Also, the type of products and services you can offer on your own e-commerce Web site — when hosted through one of these hosting companies — is limited. For example, you may not be able to offer products or services the hosting company considers offensive, dangerous, or inappropriate.

Most appropriate for: Small to medium-size businesses.

You find out more about hosted e-commerce solutions in Chapter 3.

✦ **Off-the-shelf e-commerce software.** A variety of software vendors offer e-commerce software you can use to build and maintain your own e-commerce site. Just a few of the e-commerce software packages currently available are Microsoft's Commerce Server (`www.microsoft.com/commerceserver`), Open Market's ShopSite (`www.openmarket.com`), and Intershop's Enfinity (`www.intershop.com`).

The good news: Purchasing e-commerce software means you retain control of the software (unlike the hosted options I describe in **"Hosted e-commerce solutions,"** which are subject to the whims of the hosting service). Most off-the-shelf e-commerce software is configurable, so you can create a storefront with the look-and-feel you want.

The bad news: Prices vary, but these products typically cost several thousand dollars — and cutting through the hype and competing claims of these products (and multiproduct *suites*) to find the best, most cost-effective solution for your particular situation can be hairpullingly difficult.

Most appropriate for: Large to very large businesses.

✦ **Build-your-own e-commerce solutions.** If you have the expertise, you can build an e-commerce system from scratch using a programming language such as Perl, C++, or Java.

The good news: This option is the most customizable and, potentially, the most powerful. You retain complete control over any or all aspects of the system, such as security (you can add your own custom security features), presentation, and back-end integration. For example, you can choose to integrate your e-commerce solution directly into your existing invoice system.

The bad news: Building your own e-commerce software takes expertise, time, and a whole lot of money.

Most appropriate for: Medium- to very-large-size businesses.

Some companies offer e-commerce components you can add to your custom solutions. These components can help you build a custom solution more quickly than you could from scratch. You find out more about the types of e-commerce components available in Chapter 4.

Chapter 2: Simplified E-Commerce Solutions

In This Chapter

✔ The benefits and drawbacks of a simplified e-commerce solution

✔ Finding a simplified e-commerce solution

✔ Evaluating a simplified e-commerce solution

✔ Implementing a simplified e-commerce solution

Simplified e-commerce solutions let you begin processing credit card orders on your Web site within minutes.

For small, mom-and-pop businesses (folks who have only one or two products to sell on the Web), simplified, per-transaction e-commerce solutions are well worth looking into. These solutions typically require no up-front cost — you pay only a percentage of the sale price, if and when you make a sale — and you can set them up quickly and easily. (On the downside, these solutions aren't fit for high-volume sales or businesses that have huge catalogs of products to offer. I cover alternatives for those situations in Chapters 3 and 4 of this book.)

In this chapter, I introduce you to a handful of the most popular simplified e-commerce solutions and give you a few criteria you can use to choose the best solution for your particular needs. I also walk you through the process of incorporating a simplified e-commerce solution into a Web site.

What Is a Simplified E-Commerce Solution?

A simplified e-commerce solution is a quick-and-dirty way to add the capability of accepting credit card orders to your existing Web site. In a nutshell, here's how a simplified e-commerce solution works:

1. You register with one of the companies described in Table 2-1 (or some other simplified e-commerce solution provider).

2. You fill out a form on the company's Web site describing your products.

3. You cut-and-paste the HTML code the company's Web site generates into your own Web site.

4. Bingo! Your site can now accept credit card orders through the company's secure Web site.

These solutions are cheap — fees range from $0 to a small percentage of each sale, or *transaction;* startup fees are minimal — and getting them integrated into your Web site requires no more than an hour or two of your time. For small businesses, these solutions offer a great way to test the online waters without the time or expense involved in setting up a full-fledged merchant account. (A *merchant account* is a special bank account you set up with an acquiring bank to process credit card orders directly.)

Simplified e-commerce solutions aren't right for every business, however — or even every small business. Following are a few points to ponder when considering whether or not to choose a simplified e-commerce solution:

✦ **Control.** If the company you choose goes out of business or provides shoddy service, your customers may blame *you.* These solutions act as intermediaries between you and the banks. Although they insulate you from the nitty-gritty details (and expense) of merchant accounts, they can also add a layer of bureaucracy over which you have no control.

✦ **Volume.** These solutions aren't designed for high-volume sales or sales of, for example, hundreds of different items. If you sell (or expect to sell) many different items — and thousands and thousands of each one of them — you may want to investigate the alternatives I present in Chapter 3.

✦ **Tax compliance.** These solutions typically don't offer any way for you to calculate or display sales tax on your customers' orders. If you need to incorporate sales tax into your shopping cart (see Chapter 1 for more details on e-commerce-related taxes), you must either calculate the sales tax yourself and allow for it in your sales price, or choose another e-commerce solution, such as one of those I present in Chapters 3 and 4.

✦ **Integration.** Sales information can't be plugged in, or *integrated,* into back-end systems. If you run a small company that already has accounts receivable and tax software in use, for example, you can't plug that software directly into a simplified e-commerce solution. Instead, you must manually key orders into your existing system.

Finding a Simplified E-Commerce Solution

Many simplified e-commerce solutions exist. Some of the most popular are listed in Table 2-1. (You can find more by typing the terms "e-commerce" and "shopping cart" into your favorite search engine.)

The information I present in Table 2-1 is accurate as of the time of this writing, but may change by the time you read this. Always visit the URL listed in Table 2-1 to check with an e-commerce provider and get the latest rate information about any e-commerce solution.

Table 2-1	Popular Simplified E-Commerce Solution Providers		
Solution	*URL*	*Fee*	*Notes*
BuyIt! Button	buyit.beseen.com	No activation fee; $2.50 or 4% per sale	Only physical goods
CCNow	www.ccnow.com	No activation fee; 9% per sale	Only physical goods
ClickBank	www.clickbank.com	$50 activation fee; $1 + 7.5% per sale	Digital goods okay
Yahoo! PayDirect	paydirect. yahoo.com	No fees	Person-to-person payment service
PayPal	www.paypal.com	No activation fee; $0.30 + 2.9% per sale	Person-to-person payment service

Evaluating a Simplified E-Commerce Solution

When evaluating one of the solutions listed in Table 2-1 (or any other simplified e-commerce solution, for that matter) consider the following:

+ **Cost.** Some solutions charge small activation fees; some charge a percentage of every sale you make over your Web site. One of the options listed in Table 2-1 (paydirect.yahoo.com) charges no fees at all.

+ **Physical versus digital goods.** Some simplified e-commerce solutions only process tangible goods, such as candles and books and chocolate-chip cookies. Others enable you to sell digital products, such as electronic books (e-books), downloadable music files, electronic software subscriptions, and so on.

Most simplified e-commerce solutions place restrictions on the physical goods you can sell through their services; for example, most don't allow you to sell pornographic materials, live animals, or firearms through their services.

+ **Ease of use.** Adding e-commerce capability to your site using a simplified solution is — by definition — easy to do. Typically, as you see in "Implementing a Simplified E-Commerce Solution" later in this chapter, adding e-commerce capability to your site involves cutting and pasting a snippet of HTML code into your Web pages. Person-to-person payment services, however — because they were designed to be used for everything from paying your personal bills to auctioning off your old comic book collections — require a bit more work on your part. For example, person-to-person payment services don't typically offer a shopping cart template; other simplified e-commerce solutions do.

✦ **Reliability.** You need to have confidence in the solution you choose; after all, your customers' satisfaction depends in no small part on smooth, speedy credit card acceptance. One way to feel comfortable with a solution is to find out how long the solution provider has been in business; another is to ask folks using the solution you're considering if they're happy with their choice.

Implementing a Simplified E-Commerce Solution

After you've done your research, read the fine print, and determined the perfect simplified e-commerce solution for you, you're ready to turn your Web site into an e-commerce machine.

In this section, I walk you through the process of implementing your solution of choice. Here you see how to add e-commerce capability to your Web site using a simplified e-commerce solution called CCNow. Although all e-commerce solutions differ somewhat, you find that you follow the same general steps to add any simplified e-commerce solution to your Web site.

Signing up for the service

To begin implementing a simplified e-commerce solution, you must sign up for the service. Follow these steps:

1. **Surf to the solution provider's Web site.**

In this example, the provider is CCNow, and the URL is `www.ccnow.com`.

2. **Click the Sign Up link or button.**

(Figure 2-1 shows the CCNow Web site, with the Sign Up Now button on the left-hand side of the screen.)

A signup page, similar to the one shown in Figure 2-2, appears.

3. **Click the correct link for your country.**

The Create New Account screen you see in Figure 2-3 appears.

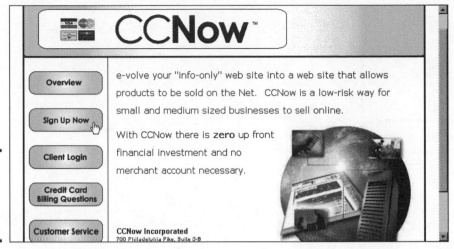

Figure 2-1:
Begin by
clicking the
Sign Up
Now button.

Figure 2-2:
The signup
page gives
you one
more
chance to
read the
client
agreement
before
signing up.

4. **Provide the information requested on the Create New Account screen.**

   You need to type the userid and password you want to use.

5. **Click the Create Account button at the bottom of the screen.**

   Be sure to write down the userid and password you choose on a slip of paper and keep it handy; you need this information to set up your shopping cart.

   The New Account Created screen you see in Figure 2-4 appears.

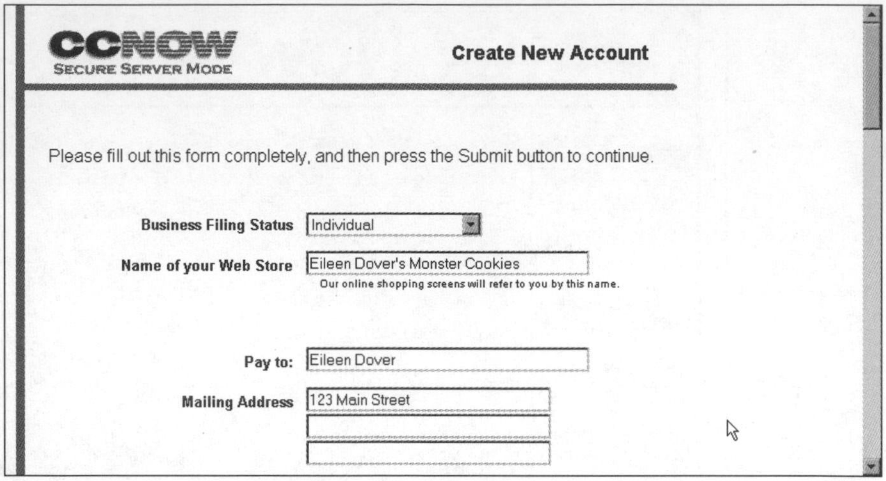

CCNOW
SECURE SERVER MODE   Create New Account

Please fill out this form completely, and then press the Submit button to continue.

Business Filing Status | Individual ▼ |

Name of your Web Store | Eileen Dover's Monster Cookies |
Our online shopping screens will refer to you by this name.

Pay to: | Eileen Dover |

Mailing Address | 123 Main Street |

Figure 2-3:
Creating a new account with CCNow is quick and painless.

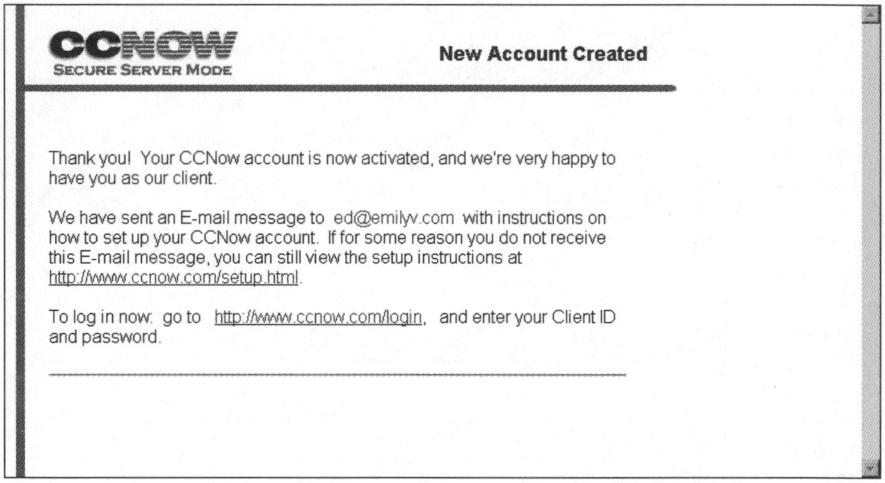

CCNOW
SECURE SERVER MODE   New Account Created

Thank you! Your CCNow account is now activated, and we're very happy to have you as our client.

We have sent an E-mail message to ed@emilyv.com with instructions on how to set up your CCNow account. If for some reason you do not receive this E-mail message, you can still view the setup instructions at http://www.ccnow.com/setup.html.

To log in now: go to http://www.ccnow.com/login, and enter your Client ID and password.

Figure 2-4:
Success! After your account is created, you can begin setting up your shopping cart.

When you create a new account with CCNow, you automatically receive an e-mail containing the latest detailed instructions on setting up your shopping cart.

Logging onto your CCNow account

To log onto your newly created CCNow account, follow these steps:

1. **Surf to** `www.ccnow.com/login` **and enter the userid and password you chose in Step 4 of the previous list.**

2. **Click the button marked I Have Read the Client Agreement and I Accept the Terms, shown in Figure 2-5.**

Setting up your shopping cart

After you establish an account with an e-commerce provider, you need to specify the way you want your shopping cart to look.

To customers, *shopping cart* means the list of items they've selected to purchase. But to you, the e-commerce site developer, *shopping cart* has a slightly broader definition: It refers to all the software features — features such as a product list and shipping calculations — that allow customers to view and purchase your products.

Here are some considerations when configuring your shopping cart:

✦ Descriptions of the products you want to sell

✦ The shipping you intend to charge for each product

✦ What image (if any) you want to display on the shopping cart

The following sections show you how to set up a shopping cart for a newly created CCNow account.

In this chapter, I demonstrate setting up a bare-bones shopping cart. CCNow offers many additional ways you can customize the way your shopping cart looks and behaves — as do most other simplified e-commerce solution providers.

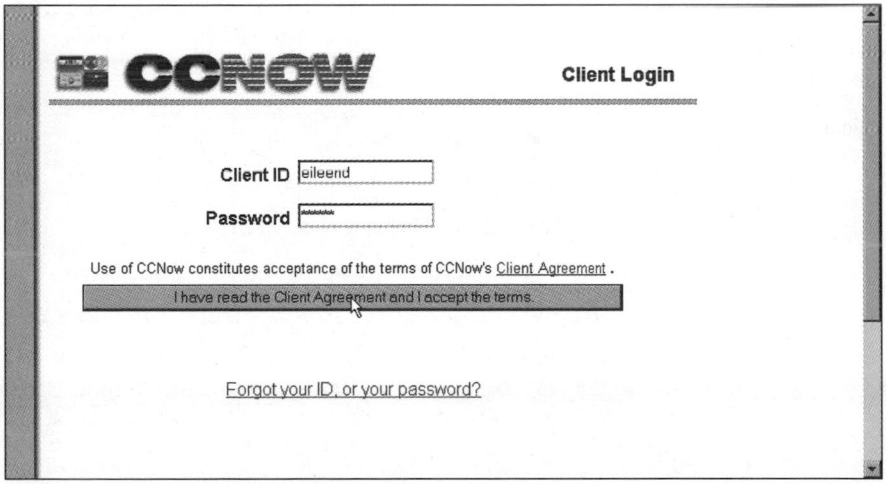

Figure 2-5:
To begin setting up your shopping cart, you need to log on.

> **CCNOW**
>
> Client Login
>
> Client ID [eileend]
>
> Password [••••••••]
>
> Use of CCNow constitutes acceptance of the terms of CCNow's Client Agreement .
>
> I have read the Client Agreement and I accept the terms.
>
> Forgot your ID, or your password?

The Account Summary for your newly created account appears (check out Figure 2-6 to see an example).

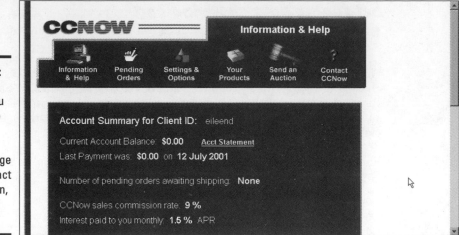

Figure 2-6:
From this screen you can set up your shopping cart, change your contact information, and much more.

Adding products to the shopping cart

A shopping cart is software that allows your customers to choose which of your products they wish to buy, and how many of each. Shopping carts usually include a description and pricing information for each available product.

Follow these steps to add products to your CCNow shopping cart:

1. **Log onto your CCNow account.**

(See the section, "Logging onto your CCNow account," earlier in this chapter, for details.)

2. **Click the Your Products icon at the top of the Account Summary screen (refer to Figure 2-6).**

The Your Products screen appears.

3. **Click the link marked Add a New Product.**

The Add Product screen shown in Figure 2-7 appears.

4. **Provide a description of the product (refer to Figure 2-7).**

Make sure you include values for the Product ID Number (choose any identifier you like), Product Name, Price, and Weight. Check Yes, available for immediate shipment if your product is in stock; if not, check No, product is backordered or temporarily unavailable.

5. **Click the Add Product button at the bottom of the screen.**

The Product Added screen appears.

You can add additional products to your shopping cart by clicking the Add Another Product link you see near the bottom of the Product Added screen.

Product ID Number | 1
Used when linking to CCNow.
Letters, numbers, and dashes are ok.

Product Name | 1 dozen homemade gingersnap cookies
For best results, use both upper- and lower- case letters.

Price US $ 13.50   **Weight** 1 lbs.
(O P T I O N A L)

Currently Available?
⦿ Yes, available for immediate shipment
○ No, product is backordered
or temporarily unavailable

Click Here To
Add Product

Figure 2-7: You use this screen to add a product to your shopping cart.

Specifying shipping charges

You may want to charge your customers for shipping and handling. To set shipping and handling charges in your shopping cart, follow these steps:

1. **Log onto your CCNow account.**

   (See the section, "Logging onto your CCNow account," earlier in this chapter for details.)

2. **Click the Settings and Options icon at the top of the Account Summary screen.**

   The Client Settings screen appears.

3. **Click the <u>Shipping Settings</u> link located near the top of the Client Settings screen.**

   The Shipping Settings screen appears.

4. **Click the <u>Basic Shipping</u> link on the Shipping Settings screen.**

   The Shipping Charges: Basic screen, shown in Figure 2-8, appears.

**Book VIII
Chapter 2**

**Simplified
E-Commerce
Solutions**

> **Will you take orders from international customers?**
>
> **What amounts will you charge for packaging and shipping?**
>
> You can decide whether you will ship to customers in the U.S. only, U.S. & Canada, or worldwide. When deciding on this option, you should consider the increased customer base that international customers represent vs. the higher risks involved in shipping to foreign countries.
>
> Basic Shipping supports only one flat-rate shipping charge per order, regardless of the order size. If you are selling a specific product that incurs a higher shipping cost, you will need to include that cost in the price of the product, or use Extended Shipping mode instead.
>
> **We will accept orders from customers:**   in the U.S. only ▾
>
> in the U.S. only
> in the U.S. and Canada only
> anywhere in the world
>
> **Our shipping charge per order is:**
>
> US $ [   ]   for U.S. orders
> US $ [   ]   for Canadian orders   *(if applicable)*
> US $ [   ]   for international orders   *(if applicable)*

Figure 2-8: You can specify separate shipping charges for domestic and foreign shipments.

5. **Click the "We will accept orders from customers" drop-down box and in the list that appears, specify whether you want to ship products to customers in the United States, United States and Canada, or anywhere in the world. Then specify the amount you want to collect for shipping each order.**

6. **Scroll down and click the Submit Changes button at the bottom of the screen.**

Adding an image to the shopping cart

You can customize your CCNow shopping cart by adding an image — for example, your company logo — to the top of the shopping cart. Here's how:

1. **Upload the image you want to add to the shopping cart to a directory on your Web server.**

   For tips on creating an image, check out Book 5, Chapter 1; for help in uploading an image from your computer to a Web server, see Book 1, Chapter 1.

   For best results, choose a logo in either GIF or JPG format. Your image dimensions should be 550 pixels wide by 36 pixels high or smaller. (For an overview of image formats and dimensions, check out Book 5, Chapter 1.

2. **Log onto your CCNow account.**

   (See "Logging onto your CCNow account" earlier in this chapter for details.)

3. **Click the Settings and Options icon at the top of the Account Summary screen.**

   The Client Settings screen appears.

4. **Click the <u>General Settings</u> link on the Client Settings screen.**

   The General Settings screen appears.

5. **Scroll down the General Settings screen until you see "Display your Logo on customer ordering screens," as shown in Figure 2-9.**

Figure 2-9:
You can add a customized image, such as a company logo, to your CCNow shopping cart.

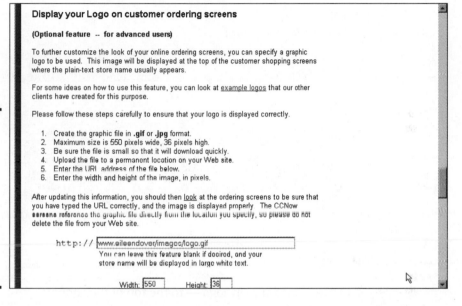

Display your Logo on customer ordering screens

(Optional feature -- for advanced users)

To further customize the look of your online ordering screens, you can specify a graphic logo to be used. This image will be displayed at the top of the customer shopping screens where the plain-text store name usually appears.

For some ideas on how to use this feature, you can look at example logos that our other clients have created for this purpose.

Please follow these steps carefully to ensure that your logo is displayed correctly.

1. Create the graphic file in **.gif** or **.jpg** format.
2. Maximum size is 550 pixels wide, 36 pixels high.
3. Be sure the file is small so that it will download quickly.
4. Upload the file to a permanent location on your Web site.
5. Enter the URL address of the file below.
6. Enter the width and height of the image, in pixels.

After updating this information, you should then look at the ordering screens to be sure that you have typed the URL correctly, and the image is displayed properly. The CCNow screens reference the graphic file directly from the location you specify, so please do not delete the file from your Web site.

http:// www.eileendover/images/logo.gif
You can leave this feature blank if desired, and your store name will be displayed in large white text.

Width: 550   Height: 36

6. **Type the URL of your image file as well as the width and height of your image, as shown in Figure 2-9.**

7. **Click on the window scrollbar to scroll down the page and click the Submit Changes button you find at the bottom of the General Settings page.**

Generating HTML

After you set up your shopping cart, you're ready to generate the HTML code that implements the e-commerce ability. (After you generate the HTML code, you must add this code to one or more of your Web pages. You see how to do this in the next section, "Adding HTML to your Web page.)

To generate HTML based on your CCNow account, follow these steps:

1. **Log in to your CCNow account.**

2. **Click the Your Products icon at the top of the Account Summary screen.**

    The Your Products screen appears.

3. **Click the <u>Generate HTML</u> link on the Your Products screen.**

    The HTML Setup: Page 1 screen shown in Figure 2-10 appears.

Figure 2-10:
Almost
done:
CCNow
generates
the HTML
you need to
add
e-commerce
capability to
your Web
site.

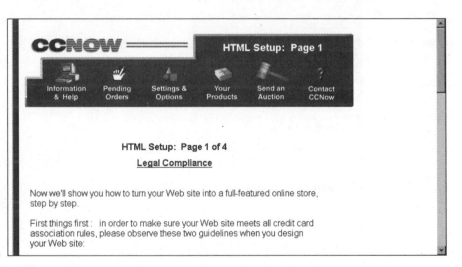

4. **Scroll through the HTML Setup pages until you find the generated HTML code for your products.**

    Figure 2-11 shows the generated HTML for the example I use in this chapter.

Your generated HTML may look different from the code you see in Figure 2-11, based on how you customize your own shopping cart in CCNow. You can generate a separate line of HTML code for each product you add to your shopping cart.

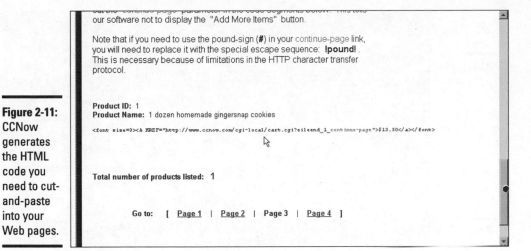

Figure 2-11: CCNow generates the HTML code you need to cut-and-paste into your Web pages.

Adding HTML to your Web page

The final step in implementing a simplified e-commerce solution is to add the e-commerce-solution-generated HTML code to your Web pages.

Adding generated HTML code to your Web page is simple. Follow these steps:

1. **Copy the generated code. (Select the code by clicking at the beginning of the code in your Web browser and dragging your mouse over the entire code selection.) Then press Ctrl+C.**

2. **Open your Web page (HTML file) in the text or graphical editor of your choice.**

3. **Paste the generated HTML code into your Web page by positioning the cursor between the `<BODY>` and `</BODY>` tags and pressing Ctrl+V.**

4. **Save your Web page and upload it to your Web server.**

(For help in uploading your Web page to your Web server, check out Book 1, Chapter 1.)

Testing your new e-commerce-enabled Web site

Follow these steps to make sure you set up your shopping cart and added your generated HTML to your Web site correctly:

1. **Surf to the Web page to which you added your generated HTML code.**

In the example shown in Figure 2-12, a single CCNow Buy It Now button appears on a musician's Web page.

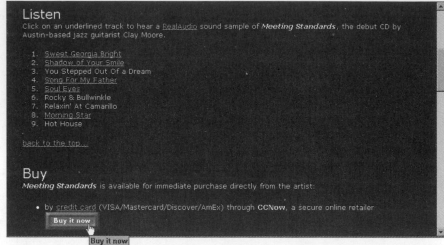

Figure 2-12:
Test your
new
e-commerce
capability by
clicking the
"Buy"
button
displayed by
the CCNow-
generated
HTML.

2. **Click the Buy It Now button (or link, depending on how you customized your shopping cart) on your Web page.**

   A shopping cart similar to the one shown in Figure 2-13 appears.

Figure 2-13:
When you
see this
shopping
cart, your
e-commerce
site is up
and ready
for
business!

If you have any problems setting up your shopping cart, generating your HTML
code, or adding your generated HTML code to your Web pages, contact your
e-commerce solution provider. For example, you can contact CCNow directly
by clicking the Contact CCNow icon at the top of the Account Summary screen.
(Figure 2-6 shows an example of the Account Summary screen.)

Chapter 3: Hosted E-Commerce Solutions

In This Chapter

✔ The benefits and drawbacks of a hosted e-commerce solution

✔ Finding a hosted e-commerce solution

✔ Evaluating a hosted e-commerce solution

✔ Implementing a hosted e-commerce solution

Hosted e-commerce solutions offer point-and-click Web building tools, e-commerce plug-ins such as shopping carts and catalog builders, and Web hosting — all in one neat package.

For small or medium businesses, hosted e-commerce solutions are well worth looking into. You can use their Web building wizards and templates to create an entire e-commerce-enabled Web site in a matter of hours, and at a reasonable cost, too: typically a few hundred dollars or less in up-front fees and about $50 USD or so per month.

In this chapter, I introduce you to a handful of the most popular hosted e-commerce solutions and give you a few criteria you can use to choose the best solution for your particular needs. I also walk you through the process of created a Web store using a hosted e-commerce solution.

What Is a Hosted E-Commerce Solution?

A hosted e-commerce solution is an all-in-one package that includes:

✦ Point-and-click Web-building tools, including templates and wizards

✦ E-commerce capability, including credit card acceptance, shopping cart templates, reports, and more

✦ Web hosting

The companies that provide hosted software are sometimes called *application service providers,* or ASPs for short.

Unlike a simplified e-commerce solution (which you find out about in Chapter 2 of this book), a hosted e-commerce solution requires you to set up a *merchant account* with an *acquiring bank*. (A merchant account is a special bank account you can use to hold funds from credit card orders; an acquiring bank is a bank that processes credit card orders.) The good news is, hosted e-commerce solutions typically walk you through the process of applying for a merchant account; some even have partner relationships with acquiring banks to make getting a merchant account quick and easy.

Hosted e-commerce solutions are very popular for small and medium-sized businesses because they offer more features than simplified e-commerce solutions (Chapter 2), yet are simpler and cheaper to set up than custom e-commerce solutions (which I introduce in Chapter 4 of this book).

Finding a Hosted E-Commerce Solution

Many hosted e-commerce solutions exist; I list a handful of the most popular ones in Table 3-1. (To find more, try typing a related phrase, such as "e-commerce solution" or "hosted e-commerce," into your favorite search engine.)

The information in Table 3-1 is accurate as of the time of this writing, but may well change by the time you read this. Always visit the URL listed in Table 3-1 to get the latest rate information about any e-commerce solution.

Table 3-1		Some Hosted E-Commerce Solution Providers	
Solution	*URL*	*Fee**	*Notes*
BigStep	www.bigstep.com	$50/month plus $0.20/transaction plus 2.4%/transaction	Price reflects "professional" Web site hosting; other pricing schemes available
Microsoft Commerce Manager	www.bcentral.com	$45/month plus $0.20/transaction plus 2.5 -3.5%/transaction (depending on the credit card)	Annual subscription brings the cost down
GoEmerchant	www.goemerchant.com	$50/month plus $0.30/transaction plus 2.3%/transaction	Minimum monthly transaction charge of $15
MerchandiZer	www.merchandizer.com	$150 setup fee, $95/month plus $0.20/transaction plus 2.5 - 3.5%/transaction (depending on the credit card)	Offers custom Web page design for additional price

Solution	URL	Fee*	Notes
Yahoo! Store	`store.yahoo.com`	$100/month plus $0.20/transaction plus 2.5 - 3.5%/-transaction (depending on the credit card)	Available to folks living in U.S., Canada, Australia, and New Zealand

* Fee includes the cost of obtaining and operating a merchant account

In addition to the options listed in Table 3-1, keep in mind that many Internet Service Providers — such as XO (`xo.com`) and Earthlink (`www.earthlink.com`) — provide hosted e-commerce solutions, as well. So if you already have a Web site, check with your Internet Service Provider to see if it offers an e-commerce solution you can use. Check with your favorite bank to see if it offers an e-commerce solution; many banks do. Wells Fargo (`www.wellsfargo.com`), for example, offers a hosted e-commerce solution called eStore.

Evaluating a Hosted E-Commerce Solution

When you evaluate one of the solutions listed in Table 3-1 (or any other simplified e-commerce solution, for that matter) consider the following:

✦ **Cost.** Most hosted e-commerce solution providers offer a large variety of pricing options based on how many features you want — so it pays to do your homework and determine, ahead of time, which features are most important to you. (For example, BigStep offers a lower price for its Web page services if you don't mind other people's banner ads appearing on your site.) Keep in mind, too, that in addition to the e-commerce solution provider fees, you must pay credit card companies separate processing fees. Contacting the acquiring bank associated with the e-commerce provider to make sure you understand how much it charges, both per transaction and per month, is a good approach.

✦ **Ease of use.** All of these solution providers give you Web-based tools you can use to set up your Web site, your shopping cart, and so on. Many, including Yahoo! Stores, offer 30-day trials for you to test the tools and make sure you find them easy to use. Take advantage of these trials. (After you set up your e-commerce-enabled Web site, you may want to change it occasionally to add a product or change the price of an existing product — so if the tools are hard to use, you may find yourself frustrated over and over again.)

✦ **Reliability.** You need to have confidence in the solution you choose; after all, your customers' satisfaction depends in no small part on smooth, speedy credit card acceptance. One way to feel comfortable with a solution is to find out how long the solution provider has been in business; another is to ask folks using the solution you're considering if they're happy with their choice.

✦ **Integration with other e-commerce-related applications.** Some solutions are designed to work with other useful software you may already have installed, such as tax calculation, accounting, or banking software. MerchandiZer, for example, offers integration with an off-the-shelf sales tax calculation component as well as with Microsoft's Commerce Manager, and Finance Manager accounting software.

✦ **Extras.** To make their offerings more attractive, e-commerce solution providers often add services such as customized Web page design (MerchandiZer), an online shopping mall for Web stores created using their products (Yahoo! Store), and so on. While these extra goodies may not add up enough to outweigh the other four factors in this list, they may help you decide between two close choices.

Implementing a Hosted E-Commerce Solution

After you've done your research, read the fine print, and determined the perfect hosted e-commerce solution for you, you're ready to begin implementing that solution. (*Implementing* is shorthand for installing and configuring.)

In this section, I walk you through the implementation process. Here you see how to create an e-commerce site using the popular Yahoo! Store. Although all e-commerce solutions differ somewhat, you find that the steps in the next section are similar in many ways to those that you follow to create an e-commerce Web site using any hosted solution. Basically, you need to do the following:

✦ Sign up for the hosted service

✦ Set up a merchant account

✦ Build your e-commerce Web site

In this section, you see how to set up a free trial e-commerce site using Yahoo! Store. This trial site is operational on Yahoo! Store servers for 10 days. At the end of those 10 days, Yahoo! Store e-mails you details on signing up for the real, nontrial version of the service (for a fee).

Signing up for the e-commerce service

Most e-commerce hosts require you to register or sign up for their service before you can begin putting together your Web store. To sign up for Yahoo! Store, follow these steps.

1. **Surf to the Yahoo! Store home page at** `store.yahoo.com`.

   The Welcome page shown in Figure 3-1 appears.

Figure 3-1:
Yahoo!
Store is a
popular
hosted
e-commerce
solution.

2. **Click the <u>Get Started Now!</u> link on the left-hand side of the screen.**

   A Sign In screen similar to the one shown in Figure 3-2 appears.

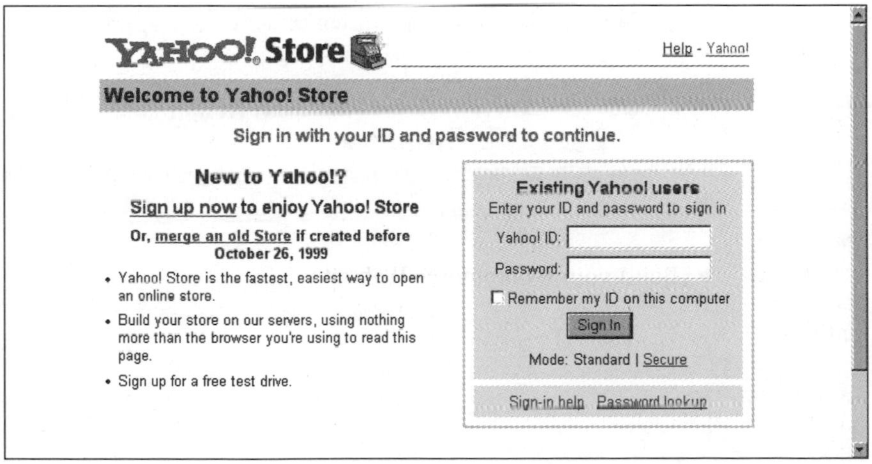

Figure 3-2:
The Yahoo!
Store signup
page.

3. **Click the <u>Sign Up Now</u> link in the middle of the Sign In screen.**

   The form you see in Figure 3-3 appears.

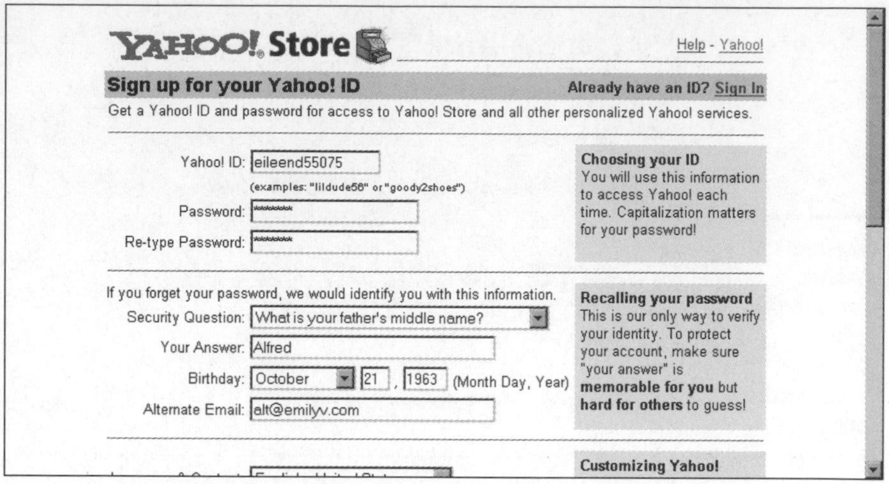

Figure 3-3:
Fill out a form to register for the Yahoo! Store service.

4. Scroll down the form and enter all the requested information, including a userid and password.

5. Click the Submit This Form button at the bottom of the page.

The confirmation screen shown in Figure 3-4 appears.

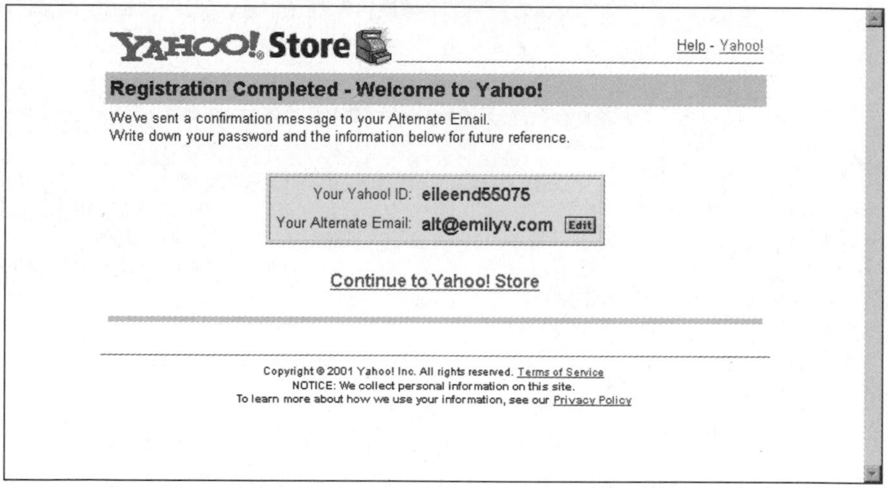

Figure 3-4:
The confirmation screen lets you know you've successfully registered for the Yahoo! Store service.

Each Yahoo! Store userid must be unique, and thousands of folks use this service — so you may find that you need to change your userid before Yahoo! accepts your registration. (The registration form displays an error message if you enter a userid someone else has already chosen.) Specifying a userid containing numbers or dashes, as shown in Figure 3-4, helps differentiate your userid from others.

After Yahoo! Stores accepts your registration information, be sure you write down the userid and password you specified. You need to refer to this information when you want to build, add to, or change your e-commerce site.

Building your e-commerce Web site

Most e-commerce hosts — Yahoo! included — offer *wizards,* or point-and-click graphical instructions that walk you through the process of building your e-commerce Web site.

To build a simple e-commerce Web site using the Yahoo! Store service, you need to create an account and then create the Web site itself.

Creating your account

For each e-commerce site you create with Yahoo! Store, you must create an account. (As you soon see, Yahoo! Store incorporates the account name you specify into the Web site URL that Yahoo! Store generates for you.) The following steps show you how to create an account with Yahoo! Store.

Before you create your account, you need to sign up for the Yahoo! Store service. See the section, "Signing up for the e-commerce service," earlier in this chapter for details.

1. **Surf to** `store.yahoo.com`.

The Yahoo! Store manager screen appears.

2. **Enter your userid and password in the Yahoo! ID: and Password: fields, respectively; then click the Sign In button.**

The Yahoo! Store welcome screen reappears.

3. **Click the <u>Get Started Now!</u> link on the Yahoo! Store welcome screen.**

The Yahoo! Store screen you see in Figure 3-5 appears.

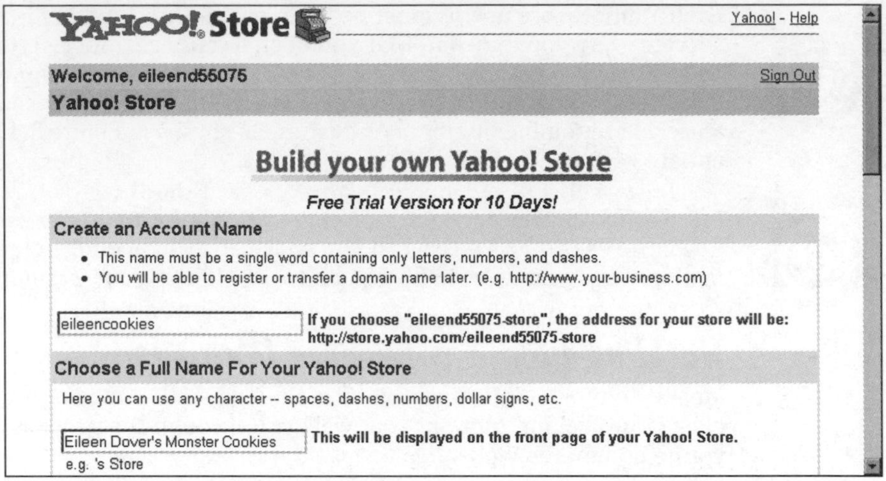

YAHOO! Store 　　　　　　　　　　　　　　　　　　　　　　　Yahoo! - Help

Welcome, eileend55075　　　　　　　　　　　　　　　　　　　　　Sign Out
Yahoo! Store

Build your own Yahoo! Store

Free Trial Version for 10 Days!

Create an Account Name

- This name must be a single word containing only letters, numbers, and dashes.
- You will be able to register or transfer a domain name later. (e.g. http://www.your-business.com)

eileencookies　　　　　　　　　**If you choose "eileend55075-store", the address for your store will be:**
　　　　　　　　　　　　　　　　http://store.yahoo.com/eileend55075-store

Choose a Full Name For Your Yahoo! Store

Here you can use any character -- spaces, dashes, numbers, dollar signs, etc.

Eileen Dover's Monster Cookies　　**This will be displayed on the front page of your Yahoo! Store.**
e.g. 's Store

Figure 3-5:
Specify an account name and contact information for your Yahoo! Store account.

4. **Provide the account and contact information requested.**

   Keep in mind that Yahoo! Store uses the account name you enter in the Create an Account Name section to generate the URL for your e-commerce site (in other words, you might want to specify an account name that's both meaningful and short).

   You can specify a longer, more descriptive name in the Choose a Full Name For Your Yahoo! Store field.

5. **Click the Create my Yahoo! Store button at the bottom of the screen.**

   Make sure you write down the account name you specify; you need it later.

   To create your Yahoo! e-commerce site, you must check the check box that says you've read through the service and test drive agreements. Make sure you click the links next to the check box to read and print each of these agreements for future reference. (You print a Web document by choosing File⇨Print from your browser main menu.)

Creating your e-commerce Web site

In a nutshell, the steps you must take to create your e-commerce Web site — your online store, in other words — include:

✦ Adding product or service descriptions to your site

✦ Choosing a "look and feel" for your site

✦ Publishing your Web site (opening your online doors for business)

In the following steps, I tell you how to construct a simple e-commerce site using theYahoo! Store tool.

1. **Surf to** `store.yahoo.com`.

   The Yahoo! Store welcome screen appears.

2. **Enter your userid and password in the Yahoo! ID: and Password: fields, respectively; then click the Sign In button.**

   A page containing a link to your Yahoo! Store account name appears.

3. **Click the link to your Yahoo! Store account name.**

   The My Store Manager screen shown in Figure 3-6 appears.

Figure 3-6:
Create and edit your e-commerce site from the My Store Manager screen.

4. **Click the link marked <u>Simple</u> under the Edit heading.**

   An online store template similar to the one shown in Figure 3-7 appears.

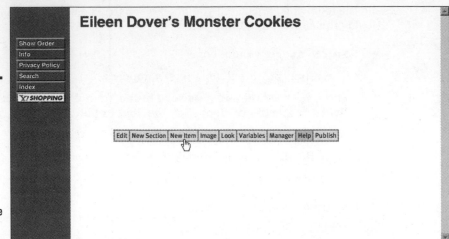

Figure 3-7:
Use the
menu bar at
the bottom
of the page
to add
elements to
your
e-commerce
site.

Clicking the Help button on the menu bar displays descriptions of each of the other buttons.

5. **Click the New Item button on the menu bar near the bottom of the online store template.**

   The form shown in Figure 3-8 appears.

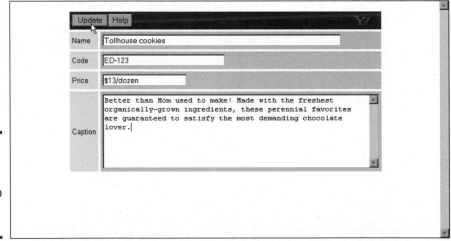

Figure 3-8:
Use this
form to add
sale items to
your Web
site.

6. **Enter the name of your product, a corresponding product code (if any), price, and description in the Name, Code, Price, and Description fields, respectively.**

7. **Click Update to finish.**

   The modified Web page appears. Notice in Figure 3-9 that in addition to the newly entered product data displayed on the Web page, the Yahoo! Store tool also added a navigation button — in this case, a button marked Tollhouse cookies — to the left-hand side of the page. The Yahoo! Store tool adds one button to the site navigation bar for each product you specify.

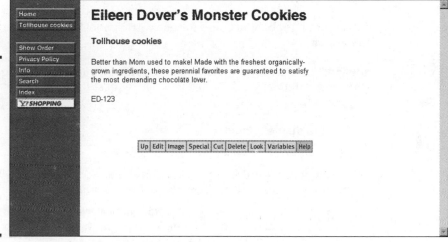

Figure 3-9: The Yahoo! Store tool converts your text fields into HTML and displays the result automatically.

8. **Repeat Steps 5 and 6 to add additional sale items to your site.**

9. **Surf to `store.yahoo.com/yourAccountName` to test your site.**

You can configure your site by adding images of your products (click the Image button on the menu bar), selecting a graphic look-and-feel (click the Look button), and much more. For detailed help on the Yahoo! Store building tool, take a look at the Yahoo! Store reference manual online at `store.yahoo.com/vw/refman.html`.

Signing up for a merchant account

Simplified e-commerce solutions, which I introduce in Chapter 2, shield you from the details and expense of setting up a merchant account. Hosted e-commerce solutions, however, don't; you need both a merchant id and a terminal id (both of which you get when you set up a merchant account) in order to accept credit card orders using a hosted e-commerce Web site.

Already have a merchant account for your bricks-and-mortar widget store? Unfortunately, you need to set up an additional merchant account for your e-commerce site. That's because e-commerce — referred to in the banking biz as a "card not present" or "MO/TO" (mail order/telephone order) business — carries different rules for approval than a traditional, offline business.

You can phone or visit your favorite bank to set up a merchant account; you can also set up a merchant account online. Many e-commerce hosts, including Yahoo! Store, work with one or more banks to make setting up your merchant account quick and easy.

To set up a merchant account for use with Yahoo! Store, for example, follow these steps:

You must have a prototype e-commerce Web site up and running — complete with lists of items for sale — before your request for a merchant account can be approved.

1. **Surf to** `store.yahoo.com`.

   The Yahoo! Store welcome screen appears.

2. **Enter your userid and password in the Yahoo! ID: and Password: fields, respectively; then click the Sign In button.**

   A page containing a link to your Yahoo! Store account name appears. (You specify this account name in Step 4 in the section, "Creating your account," earlier in this chapter.)

3. **Click the link to your Yahoo! Store account name.**

   The My Store Manager screen shown in Figure 3-10 appears.

Figure 3-10: Configure your e-commerce site at the My Store Manager screen.

YAHOO! Store   Yahoo! - Site - Shopping - Help

Welcome, eileend55075   Sign Out
Yahoo! Store: eileencookies
My Store Manager

Your demo account will expire after 10 days. Open your account soon.

Edit	**Process**	**Statistics**	**Order Settings**	**Site Settings**
Simple	Orders	Page Views	Order Form	Access
Regular	Requests	Sales	Fax/Email	Preferences
Advanced	NetLedger Accounting	References	Shipment Status	Domain Names
		Searches	Configure Inventory	Email
		Shopping Searches	Pay Methods	Customer Access
		Graphs	Ship Methods	Ratings
		Click Trails	Ship Rates	
		Reports	Tax Rates	
		Repeats	Foreign Orders	
			Test	
			Auctions Checkout	
			Published	

4. **Click the link marked <u>Pay Methods</u> beneath the Order Settings heading.**

   The Payment Methods screen shown in Figure 3-11 appears.

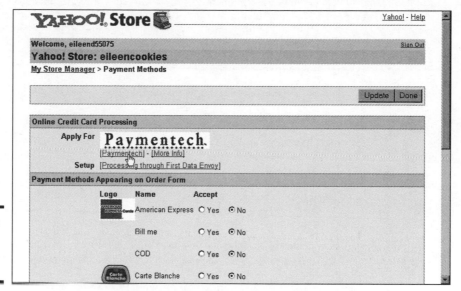

Figure 3-11:
Apply for a merchant account.

5. **Click the <u>Paymentech</u> link on the Payment Methods screen.**

   (Paymentech is the name of the bank that provides merchant accounts to Yahoo! Store e-commerce customers.)

   The merchant account terms and conditions screen appears.

6. **Read the information and click the I Agree button at the bottom of the screen; then follow the instructions to work through the merchant application process.**

7. **Click the radio buttons shown in Figure 3-11 to decide which credit cards you want to accept on your site.**

8. **Click the Update button at the top of the screen.**

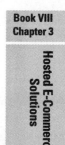

**Book VIII
Chapter 3**

**Hosted E-Commerce
Solutions**

No such thing as a free lunch

The price of a merchant account varies from bank to bank. Typically, you pay a monthly fee in addition to a per-transaction fee; often, you pay setup fees, too. At the time of this writing, the price of a merchant account through Paymentech is about $25 a month, plus 20 cents per credit card order. Technically, Paymentech charges no setup fee, but you must sign up for at least six months worth of monthly payments up front.

Chapter 4: Create-Your-Own E-Commerce Solutions

In This Chapter

✔ The benefits and drawbacks of creating your own e-commerce solution

✔ Getting acquainted with popular e-commerce programming languages

✔ Finding storefront components

✔ Taking security measures

✔ Exploring credit card processing options

*I*f you're an individual or small-business owner looking for a quick and easy way to sell stuff online, you may find one of the approaches I describe in Chapters 2 and 3 to be just what the doctor ordered. But what if neither of these options works for your particular situation? For example, what if you work for a big pet food company that needs an industrial-strength solution, one that can be completely customized and plugged into all the groovy financial and inventory software already installed on your company's computers?

Create-your-own e-commerce solutions were made for just such circumstances. Using this approach, you (or, more likely, your company's software development department) construct an e-commerce application from the ground up based on your particular requirements.

In this chapter, I describe the pros and cons of going the custom route. I also introduce you to the features you need to implement to create your own custom e-commerce solution.

By definition, a custom e-commerce solution is unique, so I can't describe how to create the perfect solution for you and your company here any more than I can describe how to cook the perfect dinner for your company party. (After all, I don't know your company's budget, how many folks your company employs, what your preferences are, and so on.) Instead, I describe the programming languages and e-commerce components you need to consider — along with a list of questions you may find helpful when evaluating the custom approach.

What Is a Custom E-Commerce Solution?

Figure 4-1 shows an overview of a custom e-commerce solution. As you can see, a custom solution consists of a server-side application that connects customers with banks and *back-office* applications, (applications such as accounting or accounts receivable, so called because they were traditionally handled by clerks hidden away in some dingy, ill-lit back office). A custom e-commerce solution must handle all the necessary security and transaction details associated with processing electronic orders.

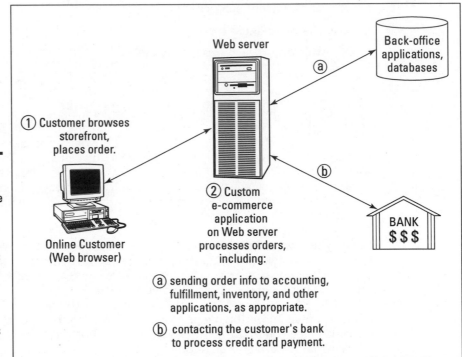

Figure 4-1:
Custom e-commerce solutions use server-side applications to connect customer input to back-office applications and banks.

(Figure labels:)

Web server

Back-office applications, databases

ⓐ

① Customer browses storefront, places order.

Online Customer (Web browser)

② Custom e-commerce application on Web server processes orders, including:

ⓑ

BANK $ $ $

ⓐ sending order info to accounting, fulfillment, inventory, and other applications, as appropriate.

ⓑ contacting the customer's bank to process credit card payment.

A custom e-commerce solution is one you build yourself, from the ground up. Often, this means using a programming language such as C, C++, or Java — but it can also mean selecting one or more software components, such as the ones I describe in "Standard e-commerce components" later in this chapter, and incorporating these components into your from-scratch code.

As with any other transaction-based software application, custom e-commerce solutions are expensive and time-consuming to build. You need a team of crackerjack coders who understand how to program for the

Web (no mean feat, when you consider all the security and browser issues involved) but also how to process Web orders, poke them into back-end databases, and integrate them into the company's back-office software applications as appropriate.

Why a custom solution?

While a custom solution isn't for everyone, some companies may find that all the time, money, and effort required to build an e-commerce system from scratch is well worth the investment.

To help determine whether a custom solution is right for you, consider the following:

✦ **Do you want complete control over your e-commerce site?** When you choose a simplified or hosted solution, you're subject to the rules and limitations imposed by that solution. For example, some simplified e-commerce solutions don't allow you to sell non-tangible goods, such as downloadable software; some hosted e-commerce solutions reserve the right to pull the plug on your e-commerce site at any time if, in their opinion, your products are "offensive" (whatever *that* means!). When you go the custom route, you don't have to use any specific tool or wizard, so you can make your e-commerce site look and behave precisely the way you want it to look and behave. You can also implement beefed-up security measures, if you choose, rather than relying on the security an e-commerce host offers — and you're never surprised by service price hikes because you own and control the software.

✦ **Do you expect a high volume of online sales?** Going through a simplified or hosted e-commerce service is fine for a handful of sales. But what if you work for an established retailer and expect sales of hundreds, or even thousands, every day of the week? When you work with an e-commerce service, such as those I describe in Chapters 2 and 3, you share hardware and software with all the other e-commerce customers. If the host you choose isn't set up to handle large sales volumes, your orders may take a long, long time to process. Creating a custom e-commerce site lets you incorporate a high-volume transaction server you don't have to share.

✦ **Do you need to integrate your e-commerce site into your existing back-end applications?** Most large companies already have accounting and inventory software in place and, naturally, want their e-commerce site to tie into that software, just as their regular retail operations do. For example, a company might want to:

• Automatically adjust inventory levels with every online order

• Route all online orders to an in-house fulfillment department

• Automatically send out invoices using its existing invoice system

You can't plug simplified and hosted e-commerce solutions into back-end software applications; to incorporate online orders using either of these two approaches, you must manually enter order information into your other software systems. But by creating your own custom e-commerce solution, you can pass online order information to your accounting, inventory, and other back-end applications automatically, with no human intervention required.

Popular e-commerce programming languages

Technically, you can use whatever programming languages you desire to create a custom e-commerce site. After all, as long as you can hook up a Web page or two to the front of your e-commerce site, your potential customers don't care what language you use any more than they care what kind of bricks and wallboard you use to build a retail shop.

Having said that, a handful of programming languages *are* becoming more and more popular for e-commerce application development. As you see in Table 4-1, these languages focus on Web development as well as Web-to-other-software-application integration.

Table 4-1	Popular Programming Languages for E-Commerce Development
Name	*Description*
ASP	Active Server Pages. Available on Microsoft Web servers, this scripting language — implemented as an HTML extension — lets you create Web pages on the fly, as browsers request them.
C, C++	These powerful (albeit cryptic) languages are the languages of choice for new server-side development.
CGI	Common Gateway Interface. Contrary to popular opinion, this isn't a language at all; it's a protocol that defines a way Web pages can pass information to server-side programs using CGI scripts. Popular CGI scripting languages include Perl, C, and C++.
CFML	ColdFusion Markup Language. Originally developed by Allaire (and now supported by Macromedia ColdFusion server), this server-side scripting language is equivalent to *ASP* and *PHP*.
HTML	HyperText Markup Language. HTML is often referred to as the "language of the Web" because all Web pages are written in HTML — whether that HTML is generated dynamically at runtime using a server-side tool like *ASP*, or coded the old-fashioned way, using a text or HTML editor.

Name	Description
Java	Originally developed by Sun Microsystems for embedded processors (think "smart toasters"), this C-like language has become very popular for delivering sophisticated applications inside Web pages. JDBC (Java Database Connectivity) lets you communicate directly with databases.
JavaScript	Created by Netscape with the help of Sun Microsystems, this client-side scripting language lets you add interactive features like mouse rollovers to your Web pages.
PHP	Pre-Hypertext Processor. Somewhat similar to *ASP*, PHP is a server-side, cross-platform, HTML-embedded scripting language.

Standard e-commerce components

All custom e-commerce applications are different. (If they weren't, they wouldn't be *custom,* now would they?) Still, you find that most e-commerce applications share the following standard components:

✦ Storefront

✦ Security measures

✦ Credit card processing

You can, of course, create these components from scratch If you have the time, expertise, and inclination — but you can also choose to purchase one or more. Doing so may help streamline the time and cost of developing your custom e-commerce site.

Storefront

A *storefront* refers to all the Web pages your customers interact with on your e-commerce site, from the time they begin browsing until they place an order. The storefront of a popular online bookstore is shown in Figures 4-2, 4-3, and 4-4.

As Figure 4-2 shows, storefronts typically include a store logo and a navigation bar, along with other items useful to potential customers, such as contact information and pricing policies; most also include an online catalog (Figure 4-3) and shopping cart (Figure 4-4), as well.

Store logo   Navigation bars

Figure 4-2: Online customers interact with an e-commerce site through its storefront.

Figure 4-3 shows an example of an online catalog. (Notice the Add to Cart button beside each catalog item.) Figure 4-4 shows an example of a shopping cart.

Catalog items   Click this button to add an item to a shopping cart.

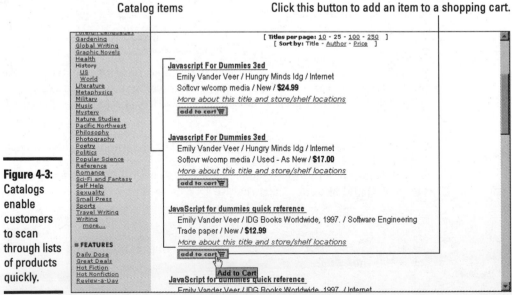

Figure 4-3: Catalogs enable customers to scan through lists of products quickly.

Chapter 5 introduces you to some sound design principles to keep in mind when you create your storefront.

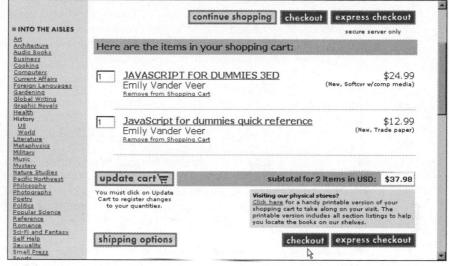

Figure 4-4: Shopping carts keep track of all the products customers select for purchase.

To create a storefront, you first build a Web site using the tips and tools you find in this book; then you create a catalog and shopping cart using one of the many shopping cart tools available — some of which are listed in Table 4-2.

Table 4-2	Popular Shopping-Cart-Creation Tools
Name	*For More Information*
ecBuilder Pro 6.0	`www.multiactive.com/smbiz/ecbuilder`
RealCart 2	`www.realcart.com`
Sales Cart (for FrontPage users)	`www.salescart.com`
ViaJCart	`www.vssd.com`
Web Genie Shopping Cart Pro v2.07	`www.webgenie.com`

Shopping cart tools vary in price (from free to several hundred dollars and more), ease of use, and how the end result looks and behaves — so make sure you take the time to try out a few before settling on one.

A quick way to assess a shopping cart tool is to take a look at a few e-commerce sites built with that tool. Most tool providers are happy to give you a list when you ask.

Security measures

Customers don't buy from e-commerce sites they don't trust. One way to earn customer trust is to implement one or more security measures and describe your approach to security on your e-commerce site where potential customers can easily find it. (Just as those little Mastercard and Visa symbols on a bricks-and-mortar storefront make us whip out our credit cards more readily, the display of a nice, reassuring electronic security policy makes online customers more comfortable.)

Security on the Web covers an awful lot of territory — so much territory I can only graze the surface here in this chapter. For more information on Web-related security, I suggest *Internet Lockdown: Internet Security Administrator's Handbook,* by Tim Crothers, published by Hungry Minds, Inc.

When you use a simplified or hosted e-commerce solution, data security is the responsibility of the e-commerce host. When you build your own e-commerce solution, however, it's up to you to protect the sensitive information your customers type in while that data is en route between the customer's browser and your Web server — and en route between your Web server and the bank.

One commonly used approach is to encrypt data customers type into your e-commerce site by using a data transmission protocol named *SSL* (short for *Secure Sockets Layer*). Supported by virtually all Web browsers and Web servers, SSL is an industry standard that works by using *digital certificates* to a) encrypt data transferred over an SSL connection and b) authenticate servers. (In other words, to protect data in transit and to make sure that protected data isn't siphoned off to a thief's server.)

Package deals

Customizable e-commerce software packages are beginning to appear on the market. Created for large corporations (and priced to match), these software packages include all the end-to-end components you need to create your own high-volume e-commerce site. They also include *hooks*, which are ways to hook the packages up to your own back-end systems using one or more standard programming languages.

Some of the e-commerce packages on the market today include:

Intershop's Enfinity - www.intershop.com

Microsoft Commerce Server 2000 - www.microsoft.com

IBM WebSphere Commerce Suite - www.ibm.com

To set up SSL, you need to purchase a digital certificate from a trusted source such as VeriSign, Inc. (You can find VeriSign on the Web at www.verisign. com.) After you install your digital certificate on your Web server, all communications between your visitors and your Web site are safe and secure.

Credit card processing

When you use a simplified or hosted e-commerce solution, the e-commerce host transmits data to the acquiring bank and issuing banks as necessary. (For an overview of the e-commerce process, see Chapter 1.) When you build your own e-commerce solution, however, it's up to you to set up your own merchant account and configure the hardware and software necessary to communicate with acquiring and issuing banks.

I explain how to do both in the following list.

✦ **Setting up a merchant account.** You can phone or visit your favorite bank to set up a merchant account; you can also set up a merchant account online with an e-commerce service such as those listed in "Communicating with acquiring and issuing banks."

✦ **Communicating with acquiring and issuing banks.** As you may expect, banks don't grant just anybody access to their systems. (And it's a good thing, too; if they did, we'd have to stay up nights worrying about our savings accounts!) To communicate with a bank, you need to get access to a *certified network* — a special line into a bank that's guaranteed to be safe and secure. (An example of a certified network is First Data Merchant Services — FDMS, for short.) Some banks share certified networks; some maintain their own individual certified networks. To get access to a certified network, you need to sign up for one of the following:

   • Access to a payment gateway such as Authorize.Net (www. authorize.net), Skipjack (www.skipjack.com), or CyberCash (www.cybercash.com)

   • A leased line, such as those provided by ClearCommerce (www. clearcommerce.com) and Open Market (www.openmarket.com)

   • A dial-up line, such as those provided by ClearCommerce (www. clearcommerce.com) and CyberSource (www.cybersource.com).

Chapter 5: Online Marketing: The Key to a Successful E-Commerce Site

In This Chapter

✔ Understanding the basics of online marketing

✔ Designing a credible storefront

✔ Making it easy for customers to buy from your site

✔ Offering top-notch customer service

At the end of the day, e-commerce isn't about technology; it's about selling stuff online. Obvious, right? Well, yes — and no. E-commerce solution vendors, such as those introduced in Chapters 2, 3, and 4, may try to dazzle you with acronyms and buzzwords in an attempt to get your hard, cold cash. But although it's true that secure protocols and high-volume transactions are essential to the success of any e-commerce site, they aren't enough to build a successful online business. You can think of these e-commerce technologies as articles of underwear: necessary, of course, but hardly sufficient all by themselves!

What's missing?

In a word, *marketing*. Often-overlooked features like carefully planned site navigation, an easy ordering process, and carefully outlined customer service policies can mean the difference between a successful e-commerce site — and one that gathers virtual dust.

In this chapter, I introduce you to the basics of online marketing. Here you find tips and tricks that help your customers find and buy from your e-commerce site.

Online Marketing: The Basics

Roughly translated into English (from business-ese), *marketing* means "presenting yourself and your products to the world." The colors you choose to add to your Web site, the products you offer, the prices you charge, and the way you choose to promote or advertise your business — all of these choices are marketing choices.

The marketing choices you make can (and should) be different from the decisions another e-business owner makes. A discount store, for example, might choose to offer inexpensive products through a no-frills e-commerce site. A purveyor of luxury items such as fine jewelry and imported chocolates, on the other hand, might choose a very different approach in terms of Web site copy, design, pricing — even color scheme.

The term *online marketing* can also refer to getting the word out about your site; for example, registering your site with search engines and getting other sites to link to yours. Because this aspect of online marketing isn't specific to e-commerce sites, I don't discuss it here in this chapter. Instead, you find it covered in Book 1, Chapter 7.

Figure 5-1 shows an e-commerce site that sells fine home furnishings. Notice how the graphic image the Web designer chose to display on the home page, the copy (Web page text), and even the fonts and subdued colors contribute to the genteel, upscale image of this company?

Figure 5-1:
The fonts, colors, layout, and copy all contribute to the upscale image of this e-commerce site.

Figure 5-2 shows another, very different example of an e-commerce site. In that figure, the logo, copy, and other design elements combine to form a relaxed, fun storefront appealing to this company's customers.

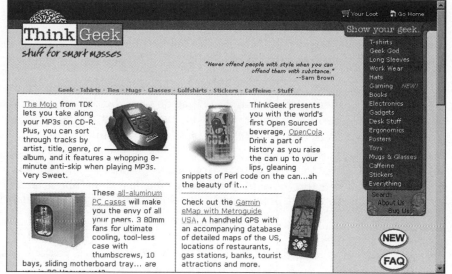

Figure 5-2:
This playful
e-commerce
site is
designed to
appeal to
a "geeky"
audience.

The approaches these e-commerce sites took differ because their businesses, inventory, and customers differ. All successful e-commerce sites, however, share the handful of core marketing strategies I outline in this chapter:

✦ Designing a credible storefront

✦ Making it easy for customers to buy products or services

✦ Offering top-notch online customer service

The art and science of marketing is a tad too broad for me to describe completely in these few pages. If you'd like to know more about marketing than I have room to describe in this chapter, I suggest you check out *Marketing For Dummies,* by Alexander Hiam.

Designing a Credible Storefront

To online shoppers, your e-commerce Web site *is* your store. Just as they do offline, shoppers online rely on visual cues and gut feelings when deciding whether or not to turn over their hard-earned money to a storeowner.

What this means is that you must pay close attention to Web site design. You must make sure that your site not only projects the marketing image you desire (such as upscale, funky, or dependable) but that it also projects an image that is credible, reputable, and trustworthy.

The following sections outline ways you can do just that.

Book VIII
Chapter 5

Online Marketing:
The Key to a
Successful
E-Commerce Site

Sticking to sound design principles

The Web has been around for a few years now, and during that time Web surfers have learned to expect the following basic features from professional e-commerce sites (like yours!):

✦ **Easy navigation.** If customers can't find your products, they can't buy them — it's as simple as that. So consider offering several different ways a potential buyer can zero in on a product, including clearly defined categories, catalog listings, and a search utility.

The music e-commerce site shown in Figure 5-3, for example, lets customers search by artist name, album title, and song title; customers can also browse recordings by musical style (blues, jazz, classical, and so on), by popularity (best sellers), and by release date.

Figure 5-3:
This site lets customers search as well as browse by musical style, popularity, and release date.

✦ **Professional graphics, layout, and color choice.** Like brochure or television advertisement design, Web design is largely a matter of taste. Although you may not have the budget to hire a professional Web designer, avoiding the following amateurish no-no's can go a long way toward boosting your site's professional image:

- Hard-to-read text and background combinations

- Cheesy, unnecessary graphics

- Cluttered layout

- Animations that aren't directly related to your marketing efforts

Cash, check, or money order?

While you can certainly offer alternative forms of payment on your e-commerce — personal checks and money orders, for example — many customers feel more comfortable making purchases with credit cards. Why? Because many credit card companies offer to pick up any charges over $50 that are associated with a lost or stolen credit card. Online shoppers know they're only liable for $50 if the unthinkable happens and their credit card information is stolen off the Internet (which is highly unlikely, by the way), so they prefer paying by credit card over paying by less convenient methods.

You can find more design tips in Chapter 1 of Book 1.

Creating professional copy

The text on your Web site — the *copy,* in marketing parlance — is one of the most critical (yet most often overlooked) components of a successful e-commerce Web site. Clear, informative, appropriate copy doesn't just describe your products and services; it also creates an image of credibility and entices customers to place an order.

Bad copy, on the other hand, makes your e-commerce site look amateurish and untrustworthy. If you can't make it through a paragraph without misspelling three words and breaking five basic grammar rules, a customer might reasonably question how you can process an order correctly.

Whether you pay a professional copywriter or write your own site copy, make sure you consider the following:

✦ **Style and tone.** Web site copy can be humorous, cheeky, stuffy, knowledgeable, friendly, or crisp, depending on the audience you're trying to reach. The style and tone of copy for a Web site selling $40-a-pound gourmet chocolates, for example, should be very different from the copy for a site selling bulk crocheting supplies.

✦ **Grammar.** Your customers may not be language experts, but they *do* notice blatant grammar gaffes — and the impression these mistakes make isn't favorable. Be sure you run your copy past a professional editor (or, at the very least, a grammar-geeky friend) before you put it on your Web site.

✦ **Punctuation and spelling.** The spelling and punctuation checking utilities that most text and HTML editors provide make this problem one of the easiest to fix.

**Book VIII
Chapter 5**

Online Marketing:
The Key to a
Successful
E-Commerce Site

Including contact information

Customers like to know that they're trading with a real person working for a real company; they're much less likely to purchase from a nameless, face-less "we" they can contact only through the Internet.

So, successful e-commerce sites include a contact link, such as the one shown in Figure 5-4, on their navigation bars that customers can click to view the company's physical (street) address, and the names of company officers, including phone numbers and e-mail addresses.

By convention, contact links are usually placed at the far right of a horizontal navigation bar, such as the one shown in Figure 5-4 (called "Ask Us" instead of "Contact" in this case), and at the bottom of a vertical navigation bar.

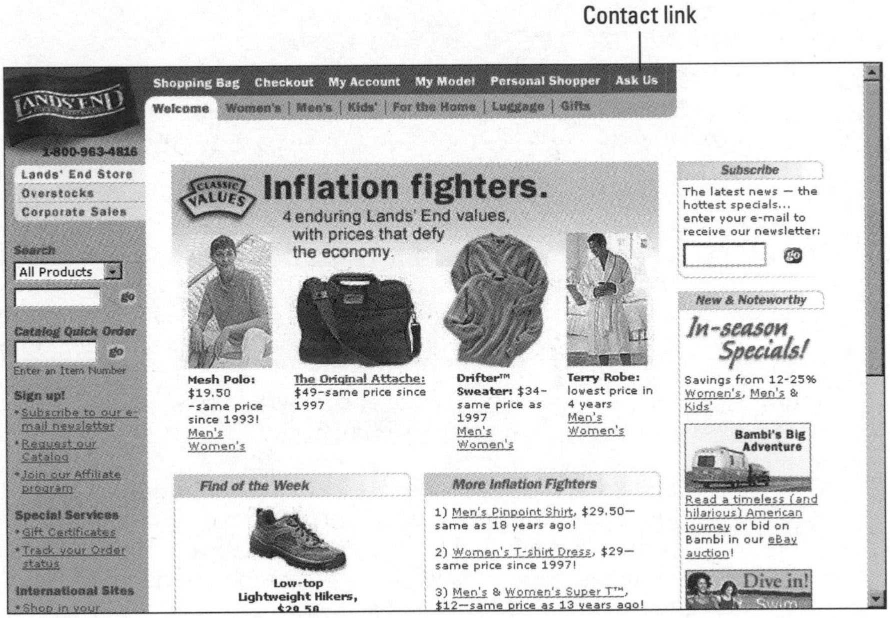

Contact link

Figure 5-4:
Successful
e-commerce
sites always
list contact
information
such as
street
address,
phone
numbers,
and e-mail
addresses.

Keeping your site up-to-date

Remember those "under construction" messages, complete with a little graphic that looked like a roadside sign, that used to appear on Web sites in the good old days?

Well, it's the twenty-first century, and everyone knows that the Web is a dynamic medium. (In other words, we all know that *all* Web sites are *always* "under construction"!)

For an e-commerce site, the correct approach isn't to apologize for not keeping your site up-to-date; it's to spend the time and effort required to keep your site up-to-date. Why? Because potential customers surfing an outdated e-commerce site may well assume that the company is no longer in business; at the very least, they assume that the company isn't particularly detail-oriented — not a good perception when you're trying to get their money!

Keeping Web copy current can be a time-consuming task. If you're a small mom-and-pop store, consider leaving nonessential information that must be maintained on a regular basis off your Web site altogether. Leaving off the details of your newest offline store expansion, for example, is far better than putting them up — and then never updating those details.

Streamlining the Purchase Process

If you've ever tried to buy something online, you may know how frustrating it can be to pull out your credit card; select an item; then become lost in a maze of shopping cart back buttons, incorrectly calculated totals, and errors, only to give up minutes later in disgust.

According to industry analysts (whose job it is to examine these things), if you've had this experience you're not alone: A huge percentage of sales — up to a whopping 50 percent — are lost after e-commerce customers begin to make a purchase, but before those purchases can be completed. It's enough to make an e-business owner cry! You finally get visitors to your site, finally get them sufficiently interested in your products to place an order, and then — bam! — like a fish wriggling off the hook, your customers disappear, most likely with a bad taste in their mouths and a keen distrust of your business.

To help keep *your* customers from going away empty-handed, apply the strategies in the following sections.

Adding a Click to Buy button

Conventional e-commerce wisdom cautions that most customers begin to rethink their decision to order a product after just three clicks. Put another way: If customers have to click more than three times in succession to order one of your products, they probably *won't*.

The solution? Add a Click to Buy button or link next to every description of every product, on every page that product description appears. Figure 5-5 shows you an example.

**Book VIII
Chapter 5**

**Online Marketing:
The Key to a
Successful
E-Commerce Site**

Figure 5-5:
A "click to buy" button lets shoppers in a hurry place their orders — fast.

"Click to buy" button

Price included in description

When you add a Click to Buy button next to each product description, customers aren't forced to click over here to view color options, or over there to view size options. They can cut to the chase and begin the order process immediately. (This approach is extremely popular with impulse buyers and shoppers who've already spent time shopping and come to your Web site knowing exactly what they want.)

Telling your customers the damage — in advance

Ever notice how, when you go to purchase something expensive, finding out the price of the item in advance is difficult? Companies that sell big-ticket items, such as health club memberships and expensive software, often hide pricing information until they have you hooked. They do this on purpose, knowing they're more likely to make the sale if they don't scare you off with a whopper of a price tag.

While this strategy may work for some products and some industries, it's not appropriate for most e-commerce sites. Why? Because many online shoppers are faced with enough surprises, thank you very much — from their browsers crashing, to shopping carts not working as they expect. They don't want to have to click through several screens just to find out the widget they want is five times more expensive than they think it should be.

So, because the name of the game is helping your customers purchase your products with a minimum of muss, fuss, and guesswork, make sure you include the price of each item next to that item's description (refer to Figure 5-5).

After your customers finish shopping and are ready to check out, make sure you display the correctly calculated total order price as well, including any shipping and handling charges and taxes due.

Guiding customers through the buying process

Ironically, one of the biggest causes of confusion among online shoppers is the feature that's supposed to streamline the buying process: the shopping cart.

A shopping cart is a piece of software that mimics a real-life shopping cart. When customers purchase an item online, they add that item to their virtual shopping cart; when they're ready to check out, the shopping cart software calculates the total of all the items placed in the cart, asks for billing and credit card information, and finishes processing the order.

Unfortunately, not all shopping carts are created equal. Some display the contents of the cart in terse, cryptic language; some contain "checkout" buttons that are hard for customers to find; some make customers jump through hoops to view their order total.

When evaluating a shopping cart tool (software you use to customize a shopping cart and add that cart to your e-commerce site) or when building your own shopping cart from scratch, make sure you pay attention to how easy the resulting shopping cart is for customers to use.

I introduce you to several shopping cart tools in Chapter 4 of this book.

The most user-friendly shopping carts walk customers through the process, such as the one shown in Figure 5-6.

Figure 5-6 shows the contents of the shopping cart in the upper-right-hand corner of the screen. (Actually, the e-commerce site in Figure 5-6 refers to its shopping cart as a *shopping basket* — same thing.) Displaying the contents of a shopping cart at all times during the purchasing process reassures customers that their order is proceeding as expected; it also lets customers know immediately if they accidentally delete an item from their cart, order 2000 widgets instead of 20, or otherwise goof.

Book VIII
Chapter 5

**Online Marketing:
The Key to a
Successful
E-Commerce Site**

Telling customers where they are in the process lets them know what to expect.

Shopping cart items are displayed at all times.

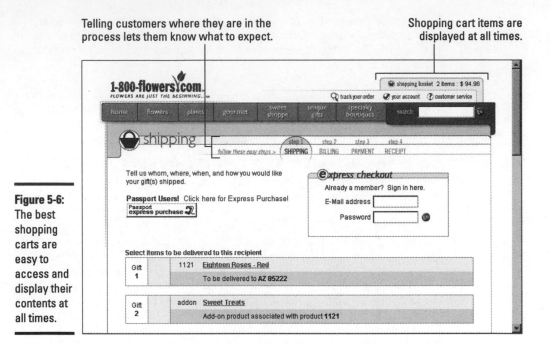

Figure 5-6: The best shopping carts are easy to access and display their contents at all times.

Near the top of Figure 5-6 you also see a four-step description of the purchasing process: Step 1 is Shipping, Step 2 is Billing, Step 3 is Payment, and Step 4 is Receipt. This handy guide lets customers know at a glance how many steps they have left to complete, which encourages antsy shoppers to hang in there. (The four-step guide also lets customers know they can expect a receipt at the end of the process — an important feature I describe in a bit more detail in the following section.)

Providing order confirmation and tracking information

In real life, when customers make a purchase, they get a receipt they can use for tax purposes or product returns. Shopping online should be no different. In fact, receipts are even more important in cyberspace, because they're all customers have to go on if their orders don't arrive as expected.

So, consider generating a receipt after every completed online transaction that includes:

✦ **Order confirmation.** This can be as simple as a Web page, pop-up window, or e-mail message containing a message such as "Thank you! Your order was successfully processed."

If you choose not to provide order confirmation, be prepared to handle a mountain of returns: Many online shoppers assume their order didn't go through properly if they don't receive confirmation, and so repeat the order process several times.

✦ **Tracking information.** A unique tracking number gives you the ability to pinpoint any problems that occur during fulfillment. Suppose, for example, that a customer's order doesn't arrive on time. That customer can call and read the tracking number located on the receipt. If you've incorporated that tracking number into your fulfillment system, you can use the tracking number to track down the order, determine that the order was shipped to the wrong address, and begin taking steps to satisfy the customer.

Offering special sales, promotions, and incentives

Many online shoppers are impulse buyers. To take advantage of this quirk of human nature, many e-commerce sites highlight a few products up front, on their home pages.

In Figure 5-7, for example, you see a handful of products, complete with nice color graphics, on the right-hand side of the screen.

Special offers

Figure 5-7: Highlighting special offers and promotions helps draw in the impulse buying crowd.

The site shown in Figure 5-7 offers a complete line of goods accessible through the search utility and catalog on the left-hand side of the screen. However, surfers whose attention is captured by the color graphics, short descriptions, or the promotions (in Figure 5-7 one of the products comes with free arrows) need click only once to begin the order process.

Offering Top-Notch Online Customer Service

When it comes to dropping wads of cash online, many shoppers prefer to stick with a bricks-and-mortar store that expanded its business to the Web rather than take their chances on an e-commerce startup they've never heard of before. The reason is simple: An established business has already built up a reputation for quality, price, or customer service — else it wouldn't still be in business. An e-commerce startup, on the other hand, is an unknown quantity.

While no magic bullet exists that can make your e-commerce site become a known (and well-respected) quantity, superior customer service is certainly the next best thing. And fortunately, the Web's 24/7 availability, two-way communication, and practically limitless space for content makes providing superior customer service easier than ever.

The three customer service strategies I describe in the following sections give you the most bang for the buck in terms of establishing your online reputation.

+ Providing product information
+ Communicating company policies
+ Offering order-related support

Providing product information

Compared to a brochure, a newspaper ad, or just about any other traditional medium, the Web offers a wealth of space you can use to describe your products and help your customers make informed choices. This is your chance to go wild! Think beyond simple product descriptions and full-color images. On the Web, you can present

+ Side-by-side charts comparing your products to your competitors'
+ Specifications and in-depth reports
+ Diagrams and blueprints
+ Animated slide shows
+ Movie clips of your products in action
+ Links to favorable reviews in online magazines

✦ Customer testimonials

✦ Related articles (for example, an e-commerce site selling organic foods might offer articles on health and nutrition, recipes, and so on)

✦ A list of product-related questions and answers called *FAQs* (Web-ese for *frequently asked questions*)

Another way you can provide potential customers with product-related information is to add an *online community* to your e-commerce site. An online community is an interactive feature — such as a bulletin board, online forum, or chat room — that allows your customers to share information with each other.

For more information on adding an online community to your e-commerce site, check with the company that hosts your Web site (your Internet service provider or Web host).

If you choose to add an online community to your e-commerce site, consider appointing yourself or a coworker as a community *monitor.* Monitors help kick-start discussions, answer customers' questions, and funnel important feedback (such as "all of our customers are complaining that widget X's left wing falls off after just four days in the field") to the appropriate company official.

Communicating company policies

As a seller of stuff, you need to think through some important policies that affect your customers. As the owner of an e-commerce site, you need to post those policies — prominently — so that potential customers can make informed decisions when it comes time to whip out their credit cards. Figure 5-8 shows an example of how one e-commerce site displays its no-nonsense company policies.

Here are three policies that most often affect e-commerce sites:

✦ **Your returns policy.** How do you plan to handle the inevitable customer returns? Do you refund the purchaser's money? Offer a replacement? Neither?

✦ **Your security policy.** Does your site use Secure Sockets Layer (SSL) to encrypt data from your customers' browsers to your server? Do you implement any additional security measures? How can customers tell that the security measures are in place?

✦ **Your privacy policy.** How much personal information do you collect from you customers? Do you retain this information after the sale? Sell the information to other companies? Does your site use cookies? Track visitors as they surf from page to page?

Book VIII
Chapter 5

Online Marketing:
The Key to a
Successful
E-Commerce Site

Figure 5-8:
Prominently
displaying
your
business
policies
helps online
shoppers
feel
comfortable
doing
business
with you.

Offering order- and product-related support

One of the most important services you can offer online shoppers is top-of-the-line customer support — access to a real, live human being through e-mail, telephone, or both. A good customer support line gives potential customers the chance to ask product-related questions that might close a sale; it gives existing customers the chance to clarify expectations (why the juicer they bought from you last Tuesday stalls out every time they try to feed spinach through the little hole thing-y, for example) and follow-up on orders they haven't received.

Here is a handful of the most popular types of e-commerce support:

✦ **An order tracking database.** Using a tracking number you provide at the time of purchase, customers can use an order tracking database to find out whether their order has been shipped — or is still sitting on your dock.

✦ **A product information or technical support database.** Databases, such as the Support Knowledgebase shown in Figure 5-9, allow online shoppers to look up product details at their own pace.

✦ **An FAQ.** FAQs allow you to address the questions most commonly asked about your products and services.

Constructing an FAQ, or frequently asked question list, is easy: Just sift through the product-related e-mails and phone calls you receive and type them up.

✦ **A list of e-mail addresses.** Offering several separate e-mail addresses helps route questions to the correct department quickly; for example, sales@companyXYZ.com, service@companyXYZ.com, and so on.

Don't offer e-mail support unless you're committed to a 24-hour (or less) turnaround; anything longer is likely to frustrate your customers.

✦ **A list of phone numbers.** Sometimes the old ways are the best ways! For the ultimate in support, prominently display a phone number customers can call to ask product-related questions and resolve their problems.

Figure 5-9:
The more complex your products are, the more varieties of support you need to offer.

**Book VIII
Chapter 5**

**Online Marketing:
The Key to a
Successful
E-Commerce Site**

Index

Notes

Book IX

XML

Contents at a Glance

Chapter 1: Getting to Know XML

In This Chapter

✔ Becoming familiar with the basic concepts of XML

✔ Understanding XML's strengths and weaknesses

✔ Taking a peek at the kinds of applications you can create using XML

✔ Getting an overview of the software you need to develop in XML

*I*f you've been working with a variety of document formats and data-management systems, you may have wished for a tool or a standard to bridge the differing technologies. XML has the potential to become such a bridge. XML combines the power of a markup language with the network optimization of HTML to create a new standard for document exchange. XML is also compatible with a variety of programming languages, Web data formats, and Internet protocols.

Although XML has been developed only recently, the interest from the Internet and programming communities has been phenomenal. This chapter offers an introduction to XML and a sneak peek at some of the XML-creating tools and software available.

What Is XML?

XML stands for *Extensible Markup Language*. XML's great claim to fame is that it can be used to encapsulate and transmit not just Web page, but *any* kind of structured information between any two computer systems.

A standard way to exchange documents over the Web

Unlike HTML, which defines specific, standard tags that allow Web pages (technically, Web *documents*) to be exchanged between any Web server and any Web browser, XML defines rules you can use to create your *own* document exchange language and exchange any kind of documents you want — not just Web pages.

Using XML, for example, you can package up data (for example, corporate data) into a specially structured XML document and then publish your own tag language specification that explains how your document is structured.

Standard practice

XML was developed by an international industry consortium called the World Wide Web Consortium — a group that has defined standards for many Web-related languages, including SGML (Standard Generalized Markup Language, the granddaddy of both HTML and XML) and, of course, HTML (HyperText Markup Language). If you're interested in taking a peek at the XML standard, point your browser to `www.w3.org/xml`. Unfortunately, the standard itself is written in hard-to-translate geek-ese, but the World Wide Web Consortium has added a helpful FAQ, which you can find at `www.w3.org/XML/1999/XML-in-10-points`, to help you make sense of it all.

After you do these two steps, anyone who wants to interpret your data — your retailers, distributors, branch offices, and customers, for example — can use your tag language specification to access, interpret, and process that data over the Web, no matter what kind of computer systems they're running.

Exchanging data between one computer system and another is nothing new; client/server applications have been doing it for decades. In the old days, developers exchanged *database extracts,* which required both sender and receiver to use the same database application; or they exchanged text files and *keys,* or detailed maps of those text files — similar to XML in theory. XML, however, offers a standard approach to data exchange built around Internet protocols, making it the approach of choice for many Web developers.

A standard way to separate data from presentation

If you're familiar with HTML, you know that a single HTML document contains text and tags, which represent two different conceptual components:

✦ **Data.** Data refers to the text, images, and other elements you want to display on a Web page.

✦ **Processing logic.** *Processing logic* refers to the way you want to process and present your data on the Web page; for example, you may want to display text in italic or display a big red border around your images.

HTML's approach is great, as far as it goes; but what if you want to create a single document that can be viewed in French, German, and Italian? Or a single document that can be viewed by folks using personal computers, hand-held computers, and special text-to-speech systems?

In other words, what if you want to separate data (the content of your document) from presentation (the language in which that content is presented)? In that case, you need to use a language such as XML, which defines a clear separation between data and processing logic.

A "family" of related standards

Power and flexibility don't come without a price: XML is considerably more complex and more difficult to learn than, for example, HTML. One of the reasons XML is relatively challenging to wrap your arms around is that XML application development includes not just XML files, but a handful of different files — each of a different type.

To develop an XML-based application, you need to create the following three basic items:

✦ **One or more XML files containing marked-up data.** Listing 1-1 shows you an example of a syntactically correct, or *well formed,* XML file created by using a simple text editor.

Listing 1-1:   A sample XML document

```
<?xml version="1.0"?>
<!DOCTYPE product_info SYSTEM "dtd_task.dtd">
<product_info>

    <item>
      <name">huckleberry jam</name>
      <price per_unit currency="USD">6.50</price_per_unit>
      <ingredient_list>
          <ingredient>huckleberries</ingredient>
          <ingredient>sugar</ingredient>
      </ingredient_list>
    </item>


    <item>
      <name>orange marmalade</name>
      <price_per_unit currency="USD">5.00</price_per_unit>
      <ingredient_list>
          <ingredient>orange juice</ingredient>
          <ingredient>orange peel</ingredient>
          <ingredient>sugar</ingredient>
      </ingredient_list>
    </item>

    <item>
      <name>amaretto spread</name>
      <price_per_unit currency="USD">8.25</price_per_unit>
      <ingredient_list>
          <ingredient>honey</ingredient>
          <ingredient>almonds</ingredient>
          <ingredient>amaretto</ingredient>
      </ingredient_list>
    </item>

</product_info>
```

As you scan through Listing 1-1, you may notice that the code looks similar to HTML code with all the beginning tags (such as ⟨item⟩) and ending tags (such as ⟨/item⟩). This similarity is no accident! HTML was designed using the rules outlined in a metalanguage called *SGML* (Standard Generalized Markup Language), and so was XML.

✦ **Rules for ensuring that data contained in your XML file is semantically valid (DTDs).** A *DTD,* or document type definition, is a set of rules that describes what kinds of values are acceptable for a given XML document. I introduce you to DTDs, which are sometimes referred to as *vocabularies,* in Chapter 3; in Listing 1-2, you see an example of a DTD designed to match the XML document shown in Listing 1-1.

You don't need to worry about the details right now (you find out more about XML syntax in the remaining chapters in this book), but if you're the curious type, you may be interested to know that the DTD you see in Listing 1-2 imposes the following rules on the XML document data you see in Listing 1-1:

- The product_info element can contain zero or more item elements.

- Each item element must contain one or more name elements, one or more price_per_unit elements, and one or more ingredient_list elements.

- Each name, price_per_unit, and ingredient element must contain *parsed character* (text) data.

- Each ingredient_list element must contain one or more ingredient elements.

If you're familiar with relational databases, you can think of an XML document as *table data,* an XML element as a *field,* and a DTD as a *database schema.*

Listing 1-2:   A sample DTD

```
<!-- Sample DTD -->
<!ELEMENT product_info (item*)>
<!ELEMENT item (name+, price_per_unit+, ingredient_list+)>
<!ELEMENT name (#PCDATA)*>
<!ELEMENT price_per_unit (#PCDATA)*>
<!ELEMENT ingredient_list (ingredient+)>
<!ELEMENT ingredient (#PCDATA)*>
```

In addition to DTDs, XML *schemas* can be used to describe a set of constraints, or rules, to apply to an XML document at runtime. For more information on XML schemas, visit www.w3.org/XML/Schema.

✦ **An application to access valid XML data, process it, and display it.** You can create an application that accesses valid XML data, processes, and displays it. Some popular approaches (not demonstrated in this book due to lack of space) include:

- **Cascading style sheets (CSS):** For displaying XML data in a simple format

- **XML style sheets (XSL):** For displaying XML data in a more sophisticated format than with CSS

- **The document object model (DOM):** For incorporating XML data into HTML-based applications

In addition to these three conceptual components, however, many more XML-related standards are currently being developed that may affect your future XML development efforts. Table 1-1 shows an accurate listing at the time of this writing.

For more information on any of the standards listed in Table 1-1, visit the World Wide Web Consortium at www.w3.org.

Table 1-1	XML-Related Standards in Progress
(Proposed) Standard	*Description*
XML Base	URIs for XML documents.
XML Encryption and XML Signature	Encryption and security.
XML Protocol	Standard peer-to-peer networking protocol using XML as an encapsulation language.
XLink/XPointer	Links among/between XML data elements.
XPath	Language for addressing parts of an XML document, designed to be used by XSLT and XLink/XPointer.
XML Query	Query facilities to integrate XML documents with relational database applications.
XML Schema	Schemas are similar to DTDs, but define rich data types such as integers, dates, and so on.
XSL/XSLT	Extensible Stylesheet Language — similar to cascading style sheets, but designed to be more flexible and dynamic.

Why Develop XML Applications?

One of the easiest ways to understand the benefits XML was designed to provide is by imagining how much simpler Web surfing would be if all HTML documents were XML documents containing semantic tags. (A *semantic* tag is a tag that specifies a category, classification, or other human-understandable — as opposed to computer-understandable — meaning.)

For example, if you wanted to find a wholesale distributor for a particular size of wing nut, you might type the word *nut* into a search engine. Because HTML documents don't include a standard way for Web page designers to provide semantic meaning for the word *nut,* for example, you likely have to wade through dozens of documents from pecan pie recipes to fan pages for a band called the Squirrel Nut Zippers before you find the information you want.

Sophisticated search capability can help ease this situation, but because no way exists for a search engine to classify documents beyond straight text matching, even an advanced search string like *"+wing nut"* will result in bad matches; documents describing the sleeping habits of "burro**wing nut**rias" or the "gro**wing nut**rition needs of infants" will be retrieved as readily as documents about wing nuts. Web sites containing non-English text, which are becoming more and more prevalent, only add to the confusion.

XML provides developers a way to describe document content semantically; in other words, to assign meaning to each of the *elements,* or pieces of information, a document contains. For example, using XML, online hardware manufacturers could associate every occurrence of "wing nut" on their pages with a special tag called <HARDWARE>. Search engines could then be directed to display only those *wing nut*-containing Web pages associated with a <HARDWARE> tag — resulting in far more efficient document retrieval.

The Downside of XML

Although XML offers tremendous potential for developing sophisticated Web applications, it also poses four formidable challenges.

✦ **XML requires cooperation between data producers and data consumers.** For the scenario I describe in the previous section to be realized, all hardware manufacturers on the Web would have to agree to support the XML tag named <HARDWARE>. A tag named <hardware>, <HardWare>, <METALWARE>, or something else entirely wouldn't work. The creators of the XML standard, the World Wide Web Consortium, proposed a set of rules, or *vocabulary,* called *RDF* (resource description format) to realize the above scenario, and many industry groups are working to establish additional, domain-specific vocabularies. To be useful, however, all of these vocabularies will have to be widely adopted and supported. If you've spent any time on the Web, you know that getting companies to agree to support a single standard can be harder than finding a white blackbird. (This little quirk of human nature means XML development is most suited for intranet development, as you see in the following section.)

XML isn't ready for prime time yet. Many developers have begun experimenting with XML, and many commercial products proclaim they're "XML-compliant." However,

- The standards that define how XML and XML-related languages, such as the Extensible Style Sheet Language (XSL), work are relatively hot off the press.

- At the time of this writing, no commercial XML tools are available. If you want to define a relational database and populate that database with data, you use standard, stable, easy-to-use graphical tools to create a *table definition* (which fields you want in your table; whether you want each field to hold text, numeric, currency, date, or some other type of data; how you want each field to relate to the other fields). Then you use other standard, stable, easy-to-use graphical tools to enter test records into the database, query the database, and display the contents of the database on the screen. Although XML is very similar to a database application, no such tools exist to help you create XML documents, DTDs, or XML processors.

✦ **XML is relatively difficult to learn.** XML isn't just an ordinary, garden-variety markup language; it's a *metalanguage* — a language that allows you to design your own markup language — and this flexibility is what makes understanding XML tricky for non-computer-science steeped folks. Books like this one, of course, help speed you on your way to becoming an XML developer. Compared to a straightforward, well-defined language like HTML, however — for which many point-and-click development tools exist — most casual and beginning programmers find creating XML applications fairly challenging.

✦ **XML poses special challenges for large data stores.** Markup languages are not exactly known for their terseness, and XML is no exception. The size of XML data files can balloon quickly — and the larger the file, the slower the XML-based application runs. Although improvements in file transfer and processing speed will no doubt evolve over time, for now, applications that involve large amounts of structured, validated data are best implemented with other technologies.

Applications Tailor-Made for XML

Despite what you may hear at geek cocktail parties, XML isn't right for every application. XML is a tool; and like a hammer, a hand mixer, or any other tool, it may be right for some jobs — but completely wrong for others.

Because it allows developers to separate data from the presentation and processing of that data, XML shines in the one-to-many data delivery scenarios so common among the following types of Web-based applications:

✦ **Internal development.** A company can store the content of its Web site in XML files, separate from the HTML, JavaScript, and Java code it uses to present that content. In this way, content updates can be performed independently — and thus more safely.

✦ **Intranet applications.** An international company based in the United States can publish its product specifications as XML files; using independently developed XML processors, its Japanese, French, and German divisions can identify the portion of the content that needs to be translated and process it accordingly.

✦ **Extranet, or business-to-business, applications.** Businesses in a specific industry — for example, the financial industry — can agree on a single standard vocabulary, making it possible to exchange data easily over the Web among all financial institutions and home banking applications.

✦ **End user applications.** A company can create the content for its site in XML. To meet the needs of its diverse customer base, it can then create three separate XML processors to perform such actions as

• Displaying a graphics-intensive version for viewers with high-end PCs

• Presenting an audio version for sight-impaired viewers

• Offering a printable version

Several commercial XML applications are in the works. For a rundown of the latest, including applications targeted for healthcare, financial, publishing, and many other industries, check out The XML Cover Pages at xml.coverpages.org.

Is It Soup Yet?

Although the automobile, healthcare, financial, and other industries have already begun developing domain-specific XML vocabularies, calling XML a mature technology is still a stretch. Whereas the second edition of the XML 1.0 specification was released in late 2000, related specifications (such as XLL, the XML linking language, and XSL, the XML style sheet language), have only recently been completed at the time of this writing.

As XML matures, tools that allow you to generate XML and related files are expected to appear on the market. Until then, creating XML-based applications is largely a do-it-yourself project using mix-and-match tools.

An excellent source of general information about XML is the XML FAQ, or Frequently Asked Questions list, which you can find at www.ucc.ie/xml.

XML Development Tools

In Table 1-2, I list some of the tools currently available you can use to create XML-based applications, many of which are in the prototype stage.

Table 1-2	XML Development Tools	
Product	*Manufacturer/Author*	*Description*
Ælfred XML Parser	Open Text	A Java-based XML parser
DAE SDK and DAE Server SDK	Copernican Solutions	An XML processor for building groves from XML documents
DataChannel XML	DataChannel Development Environment (DXDE) and DXP XML Parser	XML development tool and a validating XML parser
docproc	Sean Russell	An XML and Extensible Style Language (XSL) document processor
EditML Pro	NetBryx Technologies	XML editor
IBM XML for Java	IBM	A validating XML processor for Java
Jumbo	Peter Murray-Rust	A Java-based XML browser designed for the Chemical Markup Language (CML)
Lark	Tim Bray	A nonvalidating XML processor
Larval	Tim Bray	A validating XML processor built on the same code base as Lark
LT XML	The Language Technology Group at the University of Edinburgh	An XML developer's toolkit
MSXML	Microsoft	A validating XML parser written in Java
RXP	Richard Tobin	A nonvalidating XML parser written in C
SAX	Open Text	A Simple API for XML
SAXDOM	Open Text	An implementation of the World Wide Web Consortium (W3C) Document Object Model (DOM) API using Simple API for XML (SAX)

(continued)

Table 1-2 *(continued)*

Product	Manufacturer/Author	Description
SP Parser	James Clark	An object-oriented toolkit for SGML parsing and entity management that includes support for XML
SX	James Clark	An application of SP that converts SGML into normalized XML
TclXML	Steve Ball	A validating XML parser written in Tcl
XMetal	SoftQuad	An XML editor
XML Editing Mode in PSGML	Lennart Staflin (PSGML), David Megginson, Open Text (XML version)	XML patches for PSGML, an SGML mode for Emacs
XML Styler	ArborText	A tool for creating and modifying XSL style sheets
XMLTok	James Clark	An XML parser written in C
XP	James Clark	A nonvalidating XML parser written in Java
Xparse	Jeremie Miller	A JavaScript XML Parser
XSLJ	Henry Thompson	An XSL-to-DSSSL (Extensible Style Language to Document Style Semantics and Specification Language) translator
XSV	Henry Thompson	Validator for XML Schema

You can find information on all the tools listed in Table 1-2 by visiting `www.oasis-open.org/cover/xml.html#xmlSoftware`. This page is updated frequently, so new tools are added as they become available.

To create the different files that go into an XML application — the XML files, the DTD files, the schema files — and to process or test those files, you may need to use more than one of the tools you see listed in Table 1-2.

The following sections describe the basic categories of XML tools.

Editors

To create an XML document, a DTD document, or a schema document, you need to use one of the following:

✦ A plain text editor, such as Notepad. As you may guess, this authoring environment is probably the most time-consuming and has the least support in terms of error-checking, automation, and so on.

✦ An editing, or *authoring,* tool designed especially for XML. Such a tool is considered to be an *XML editor.* Examples of XML editors include EditML Pro and XMetal.

✦ A standard word processor that includes an XML filter or plug-in.

Parsers and processors

As I describe in the section, "A 'family' of related standards," earlier in this chapter, in addition to XML files and language rules (DTDs and schemas, which you find out about in Chapter 3), every XML application must include processing software capable of accessing XML files based on those language rules.

This processing software is the logical heart of any XML application; and although every XML application is different, all XML applications must include a software component called a *parser.* A *parser* reads and interprets an XML document and checks it for validity (checks to see that an XML document contains no syntax errors) or well-formedness (well-formed documents contain no syntax errors; they also map correctly to a published specification called a *document type definition,* or DTD).

In a real-world situation, you have two choices:

✦ You can code your own XML parser by using C, C++, Java, or any other programming language you choose and include that parser code as part of your *XML processor* (the software that accesses, manipulates, and displays XML data).

✦ You can incorporate an existing parser, such as one of those I introduce you to in Chapter 6, into your XML processor.

The XML specification, which represents the official set of grammar rules for XML, provides a precise guide for how an XML processor must work — that is, how it must read XML data, check XML syntax, and send the appropriate pass/fail information to the XML application. By definition, an XML processor must conform to the rules of the XML specification.

Basically, an XML parser can operate on either of two levels:

✦ A *nonvalidating XML parser* checks XML documents for *well-formedness* — that the XML syntax is correct — but not for *validity.* In other words, a nonvalidating XML parser does not apply the semantic rules defined in DTDs or schemas to XML files.

✦ A *validating XML parser* does check XML documents for validity. A validating XML processor, therefore, requires not only an XML file, but a DTD or schema file as input.

You can find a free online XML validation service from the Scholarly Technical Group at www.stg.brown.edu/service/xmlvalid.

Why on earth would anyone bother with a nonvalidating XML parser? After all, DTDs and schemas are an essential part of XML applications — without them, an XML file is nothing more than a plain old delimited text file! The answer lies in the relative immaturity of XML. Although the XML specification was still being hammered out, eager tool developers created nonvalidating XML parsers as a way to understand the specification and help others do the same. As XML matures, standalone, nonvalidating parsers will likely become a thing of the past.

Web browsers

By definition, XML-compliant Web browsers, such as Microsoft Internet Explorer 5.5 and Netscape Navigator 6.1, include both XML parsers and rudimentary XML processors. When you load a syntactically correct XML document into either of these two browsers, the contents of the XML document appears on the screen, making these two browsers useful for checking your XML syntax.

To see what I mean, check out Figure 1-1, which demonstrates an example of loading a syntactically correct XML file into Internet Explorer.

Figure 1-1: Loading a valid XML document into Internet Explorer displays the XML document contents on the screen.

```
<?xml version="1.0" ?>
<!-- The following is a processing instruction. -->
<!-- someProgram will be defined in the DTD using the NOTATION tag.   -->
<?someProgram aRequiredParameter anotherRequiredParameter?>
<!-- Jamcracker, Inc. Product Information   -->
- <!--
    For detailed description of data and data type definitions, contact
        Sarah Bellum
        Lead XML developer
        Jamcracker, Inc.

-->
- <jamcracker_product_info download_program="C" xmlns="x-schema:first_schema.xml">
  - <item>
      <productCode>1</productCode>
      <name xmlns="dummyProductURI">huckleberry jam</name>
      <price_per_unit currency="USD">6.50</price_per_unit>
    - <ingredient_list>
        <ingredient>fresh huckleberries</ingredient>
        <ingredient>sugar</ingredient>
      </ingredient_list>
      <nutrition_info calories_per_tbsp="13" fortified="no" high_in="expandableData" />
    - <marketing_info dept_code="A20">
```

Trying to load an XML document containing a syntax error (such as a missing angle bracket at the top of the file), for example, causes the browser to generate a syntax error, as shown in Figure 1-2.

The XML page cannot be displayed

Cannot view XML input using style sheet. Please correct the error and
then click the Refresh button, or try again later.
_____

Invalid at the top level of the document. Line 1, Position 1

```
?xml version="1.0"?>
^
```

Figure 1-2:
A missing
angle
bracket
generates
an XML
syntax
message.

Using Internet Explorer or Netscape Navigator is of limited utility when it
comes to testing and executing real-world XML applications; you can use
these browsers only to check XML syntax and display the contents of an
XML document on the screen. Real-world applications, on the other hand,
rarely just access data and dump it to a screen; they typically process data,
maybe crunch a few numbers, and display the data intelligently. So, to test
a real-world XML application, you need to use (or create) a browser built
specifically to process and display the type of XML and DTD/schema
combination that XML application defines.

API kits

At press time, the few companies that produce SGML conversion and application development engines are all working on XML API (application programming interface) kits. An *API kit* allows developers working in a
programming language, such as C, to make calls to prebuilt functions that
perform useful tasks, such as generating XML or DTD code.

One currently available tool that can be classified as an XML developer's API
kit is the C-based LT XML Toolkit, produced by The Language Technology
Group. The LT XML Toolkit includes a variety of modules for processing
well-formed XML documents, such as tools for

✦ Searching and extracting data

✦ Formatting data

✦ *Tokenizing* (breaking apart) and sorting data

Another API is Open Text Corporation's SAX: The Simple API for XML. SAX is a draft of an event-based interface for XML parsers. You can use it with Java and other object-oriented languages. SAX is designed to be compatible with any SAX-conformant XML *parser*. (I describe parsers in "Parsers and processors," earlier in this chapter.)

For more information on The Language Technology Group and its LT XML Toolkit, check out `www.ltg.ed.ac.uk/software/xml`. For more information on Open Text SAX, check the SAX Home Page at `www.opentext.com/ services/content_management_services/xml_sgml_solutions. html#aelfred_and_sax`. You can keep up with new developer's API kits in the XML Industry Support section of the SGML/XML Web page at `www. oasis-open.org/cover/xmlSupport.html`.

Chapter 2: The XML Specification

This chapter introduces you to the XML specification, which is the official definition of how you should compose XML documents and design DTDs. The XML specification itself is long and detailed and lends little assistance to someone actively using XML. Understanding how the specification works, however, is key to creating correct DTDs and working documents — hence the tips, explanations, and examples you find in this chapter.

Logical and Physical Structures

You structure XML documents based on the organization, syntax, and other rules outlined in the XML specification. XML documents have two types of structure:

- ✦ **Logical structure:** This type includes elements, attributes, and the rules and specifications associated with elements.

- ✦ **Physical structure:** This type involves *entities* (named sections contained in an XML document), types of characters, and the rules and specifications associated with entities.

Any rule that addresses logical structure as a whole is a *single logical structure;* similarly, rules that apply to the physical structure of one or more documents are *individual physical structures*.

For XML documents to work properly, you must order the logical and physical structures properly.

Logical structures

If you were to take an XML document apart, you would see that it involves two ingredients: materials (made up of text) and the way in which the materials are organized. The way in which the materials are organized is referred to as the *logical structure* of the document. Individual logical structures, then, are the technical rules that dictate how the text in XML documents are to be organized.

XML documents are specifically organized by logical structures, such as *declarations, elements, comments, character references,* and *processing instructions.* The way you denote which component is which is by including special markup tags within your XML documents. More examples of logical structures include

+ Definition of symbols

+ Logical order of items within an expression

+ Number of occurrences for each item

+ Other relevant instructions

In particular, logical structures involve *elements,* which are small instructions that you either delimit by start tags and end tags or specify as an empty-element tag. Each XML document must contain at least one element.

Each element has a type, which is identified by name — or the element's *generic identifier* (GI). Elements often have a set of attribute specifications, but not always. Of the elements that have attribute specifications, each attribute specification must have a name and a value.

The XML specification provides a very generic example of an element:

```
element ::= EmptyElemTag | STag content ETag [ wfc: Element
   Type Match ]
```

In the preceding logical structure, a named `element` offers a choice of using either `EmptyElemTag`, an empty element tag, or `STag content ETag`, which indicates content text sandwiched between a start tag preceding the content and an end tag following it. The `wfc:` code refers to a *Well-Formedness Constraint.* In this case, the `Element Type Match` constraint indicates that the name of an element's end tag must match the element type in the start tag.

Here's how a well-formed pair of matching element tags could appear in a document:

```
<tag>content</tag>
```

Notice that the element type tag matches on both sides of content; the end-tag is marked by the slash (/) at the beginning of the element type name.

Chapters 5 and 6 of *XML For Dummies,* 2nd Edition, by Ed Tittle and Frank Boumphrey (Hungry Minds, Inc.), contain extensive discussions of XML structure and markup notation.

Beyond using the correct syntax, you may use any element type or attribute you want, with the exception of names that begin with XML itself, including any combination of uppercase and lowercase letters of XML, such as xml, Xml, or xMl. Names beginning with anything that matches (('X'|'x') ('M'|'m')('L'|'l')) are reserved for standardization in the current or future World Wide Web Consortium XML specification.

Physical structures

Physical structures involve *entities,* which are virtual storage units found in XML documents. These virtual storage units contain content — or text found between start tags and end tags — and are identified by name. A few examples of physical structures include

✦ Allowed character sets

✦ Constraints for document well-formedness and validity

✦ Rules for character encoding

✦ The textual content of a document

Each XML document must have at least one entity. If a document contains only one entity, it must be the document entity, which serves as the starting point for the XML processor. The document entity may include the entire document.

Entities may be either *parsed* or *unparsed.*

✦ **Parsed:** A parsed entity's contents contain text that is an integral part of the document. This *replacement text* replaces the name of the parsed entity. You invoke parsed entities by name by using entity references. (An *entity reference* is the name of an entity prepended with an ampersand. For example, if you create an entity named Copyright, you invoke that entity by using the entity reference &Copyright.)

✦ **Unparsed:** If you need to use content that involves both text and nontext, or text that is not XML, you should use an unparsed entity. Like a parsed entity, you do identify an unparsed entity by name. Unlike a parsed entity, though, an unparsed entity has an associated notation for a file format rather than replacement text. You can set any content to unparsed entities, except for the name of a notation and associated identifiers required by the XML processor. You invoke unparsed entities by a name that you provide in the value of ENTITY or ENTITIES attributes.

Here are two types of parsed entities:

+ **General entities:** Used within the document content.
+ **Parameter entities:** Used within the DTD.

General entities and parameter entities each use a different syntax and are recognized in different contexts.

To find details of entities and entity processing, flip to Chapter 5.

Notation in XML Rules

XML rules — each complete line of the XML specification — indicate instructions for DTDs and documents. XML rules make up the grammar of XML; essentially, they define the legal syntax and sets of allowed codes or sequences of characters for DTDs and documents, as well as describe instructions for XML processors and applications.

In order for XML documents to be well-formed or valid, DTDs and documents must follow these rules of grammar. The syntax of the rules themselves is referred to as *notation*.

Don't confuse my use of the word *notation* in this section with the term *notation* as used in discussions on unparsed entities and notation declarations.

Here is the form of a standard rule of XML grammar:

```
symbol ::= expression
```

This notation contains the following parts:

+ `symbol` refers to the name given to a particular rule.
+ `::=` is the delimiter. Roughly translated, `::=` means "is equal to" or "is represented by."
+ `expression` refers to the definition of the symbol, or what the symbol is instructed to do. An expression is treated as a unit, and it may carry the *% prefix operator* (an operator you stick on the front of an expression) or one of the suffix operators: ?, *, or +. (A *suffix operator* is an operator you stick at the back of an expression.)

A sample notation looks like this:

```
PCData ::= [^<&]*
```

The notation breaks down like this:

✦ PCData is the symbol for character data.

✦ ::= is the delimiter, which separates the symbol from the expression.

✦ [^<&]* is the expression. The square brackets ([ ]) indicate that the characters inside are part of a set — a set that must be examined first and then operated on by a suffix operator, if one is present.

This notation indicates a rule for character data.

Chapter 9 of *XML For Dummies,* 2nd Edition, by Ed Tittel and Frank Boumphrey, contains several tables of special characters that you can use in your markup.

Expression code syntax and meaning

The expression (the part of a rule on the right-hand side of the ::=) contains one or more specific codes. Each code provides an important piece of information in determining the instructions and definition assigned to the symbol. Table 2-1 shows the syntax of expression codes and the meaning of each one.

Table 2-1	Expression Code Syntax and Meaning
Expression Code	*Meaning*
#xN	An expression that matches a character in the Unicode character set. The number of leading zeros in #xN is insignificant; N is a hexadecimal integer.
[a-zA-Z], [#xN-#xN]	Represents any character with a value in the range(s) indicated. This range includes every consecutive item within that range.
[^a-z], [^#xN-#xN]	The ^ means *not.* This code represents any character with a value outside the indicated range.
[^abc], [^#xN#xN#xN]	Represents any character with a value not among the characters given.
"string"	Represents a literal string matching that given inside the double quotes.
'string'	Represents a literal string matching that given inside the single quotes (called *apostrophes* in programming, even though technically only the closing single quote is an apostrophe).
a b	*a* followed by *b.*
a | b	*a* or *b* but not both. (One item from the list at most.)
a - b	The set of strings represented by *a* but not represented by *b.*

Expression extensions

The following codes that you find in the notation of the XML specification, shown in Table 2-2, are used to append information or instructions to expressions.

Table 2-2	Expression Code Extension Syntax and Meaning
Expression Extensions	*Meaning*
/* . . . */	A comment. (For insight into how rules work within the XML Specification, read the comments written by the developers of the XML Specification. You can find useful comments next to rules throughout the specification.)
[WFC: . . .]	Well-formedness check, identified by name.
[VC: . . .]	Validity check, identified by name.

Here's an example of a rule that contains a comment:

```
PCData ::= [^<&]* /* Typical rule for character data */
```

The text within the /* . . . */ code is a comment, which is not technically part of the rule; the comment was included by the XML specification authors to help you understand how the rule works.

The following example of a rule contains both validity and well-formedness checks:

```
Attribute ::= Name Eq AttValue [ VC: Attribute Value Type ]
[ WFC: No External Entity References ]
```

The expression, or right-hand side of the : : = delimiter, is as follows:

✦ In the expression, the VC: within square brackets ([ ]) means "validity check" or "validity constraint." This particular validity constraint refers to the Attribute Value Type, which means that you must have declared the attribute; the value must be of the type declared for it. (For more information about attributes, check out Chapter 4.)

✦ In the next line of the expression, the WFC: within square brackets ([ ]) means "well-formedness check" or "well-formedness constraint." This particular well-formedness constraint refers to No External Entity References. This constraint means that attribute values can't contain entity references to external entities.

Check out Chapter 5 of *XML For Dummies,* 2nd Edition, by Ed Tittel and Frank Boumphrey, to get the details on validity and well-formedness in XML markup. For more information about validity and well-formedness checks in this book, see Chapter 3. For more information about entities, see Chapter 5.

Prefix operator

If you have an expression unit a, the prefix operator (%) specifies that in the external DTD subset a parameter entity may occur in the text at the position where a may occur.

The prefix operator % has lower precedence than any of the suffix operators ?, *, or +; so %a* and %(a*) mean the same thing. The result of including a parameter entity reference at the indicated location must match a*.

For more information about parameter entities, see Chapter 5 of this book.

Suffix operators

Expression codes may be accompanied by suffix operators: the question mark (?), the plus sign (+), and the asterisk (*).

Table 2-3 explains each suffix operator as it applies to the expression code a:

Table 2-3	Suffix Operator Syntax and Meaning
Suffix Operator	*Meaning*
a?	*a* or nothing; *a* is optional
d+	One or more occurrences of *a*
a*	Zero or more occurrences of *a*

In this notation:

```
PCData ::= [^<&]*
```

The expression, or right-hand side of the ::= delimiter, is as follows:

+ In the expression [^<&]*, the square brackets ([ ]) must be examined first and then operated on by the suffix operator *.

+ Inside the square brackets, the ^ indicates "not any of the following characters or range of characters." Because only two characters follow the ^ < and & and no dash is present to indicate a range of characters, the notation ^<& means "neither the less-than nor the ampersand character may be used."

+ The * means that there can be any number of occurrences of the previously defined character set.

Putting it all together, [^<&]* means that there can be any number (including zero) of characters other than < and & present.

Syntactic Constructs

Some of the symbols that you find in XML grammar follow a specific syntax, which is referred to as a *syntactic construct.* Some common syntactic constructs include literals, names, and tokens — all of which I explain in upcoming sections.

In an XML rule, the expression may include letters, digits, or other characters. The full sets of letters, digits, and other characters belong to character classes. Each character within a character class is denoted by a hexadecimal code.

White space is an example of a common syntactic construct using characters in the expression.

```
S ::= (#x20 | #x9 | #xD | #xA)+
```

This rule indicates that S, the symbol for white space, may consist of one or more of the four choices listed in the expression. Each of these four choices in the expression is a code from the standard Unicode character database:

+ The first code, #x20, denotes a space character.

+ The second code, #x9, denotes a carriage return.

+ The third code, #xD, denotes a line feed.

+ The fourth code, #xA, denotes a tab.

So, according to this syntactic construct, white space is made up of one or more space characters, carriage returns, line feeds, or tabs.

Literals

If you need to define an exact string of characters to use in a document, or if you need to define a set of characters that must not be used, you may do this by specifying literal data. *Literal data,* or a set of literals, is any character string inside quotes — but the quotation marks themselves that are used as delimiters for the string aren't part of the character string defined by the literal.

You use literals to specify content in

+ **Internal entities.** An *internal entity* is a bit of replacement text you define and reference in the same document. For example, you may define an internal entity named Copyright that contains a page and a half of long, complex, copyright-related legalese. At runtime, every time the XML processor encounters a reference to `Copyright`, it replaces `Copyright` with the page-and-a-half of legalese — saving you time and cutting down on the potential for typing errors.

✦ **Attribute values**. An *attribute* value is a data value you associate with an attribute. For example, you may associate a value of "partTime" for an attribute named "employeeStatus."

✦ **External identifiers**. An *external identifier,* such as the PUBLIC or SYSTEM identifier, is an XML keyword that tells the XML processor whether to look for the associated file.

One rule specifying an internal entity is:

```
EntityValue ::= '"' ([^%&"] | PEReference | Reference)* ' |
    "'" ([^%&'] | PEReference | Reference)* "'"
```

This rule may initially seem complex, but it can easily be broken down.

✦ The symbol, `EntityValue`, denotes that this rule applies to an internal entity.

✦ What follows the `::=` delimiter is the expression, or definition, of the internal entity. The entire expression is `'"' ([^%&"] | PEReference | Reference)* ' | "'" ([^%&'] | PEReference | Reference)* "'"`.

✦ This expression can be broken down into two parts: `'"' ([^%&"] | PEReference | Reference)* '` and `"'" ([^%&'] | PEReference | Reference)* "'"`, divided by the logical "or" (`|`).

✦ Each of the two main parts of the expression can be broken down further. The first part, `'"' ([^%&"] | PEReference | Reference)* '`, indicates that a choice exists between the character set excluding the percent sign, ampersand, and quotation mark; the parameter-entity reference; and the entity reference. This part is proceeded by an asterisk, indicating that zero or more occurrences of this definition can occur.

✦ Similarly, the second part, `"'" ([^%&'] | PEReference | Reference)* "'"`, indicates that a choice exists between the character set excluding the percent sign, ampersand, and apostrophe; the parameter-entity reference; and the entity reference. This part is also proceeded by an asterisk, indicating that zero or more occurrences of this definition can occur.

Putting it all together, this means that the internal entity is defined by zero or more occurrences of any character but %, &, or either the quotation mark or the apostrophe, depending on which of the two parts is relevant; or a parameter-entity reference; or an entity reference.

Here's a similar rule that specifies the value of an attribute:

```
AttValue ::= '"' ([^<&"] | Reference)* '"' | "'" ([^<&'] |
    Reference)* "'"
```

The way this rule works is very similar to the way the internal entity works in the prior example. Two differences exist between these two examples. First, the attribute value excludes the less-than sign (<) instead of the percent sign. Also, no parameter-entity references are present in the expression as there are in the expression of the internal entity.

To make sure that no quotation marks or apostrophes are used in external identifiers, the literal data is defined by these two rules:

```
SystemLiteral ::= SkipLit
SkipLit ::= ('"' [^"]* '"') | ("'" [^']* "'")
```

Here's how these two rules break down:

✦ `SystemLiteral`, or the literal data for the external identifier, is defined as `SkipLit`.

✦ `SkipLit` is merely a pointer to another set of instructions — basically, a rule whose expression says `('"' [^"]* '"') | ("'" [^']* "'")`.

✦ Breaking down `('"' [^"]* '"') | ("'" [^']* "'")`, you can see that `SkipLit` indicates that either `('"' [^"]* '"')` or `("'" [^']* "'")` must be observed.

  • The first set within the expression of `SkipLit`, `('"' [^"]* '"')`, indicates that zero or more occurrences of the quotation mark may not be used.

  • Similarly, the latter set, `("'" [^']* "'")`, indicates that zero or more occurrences of the apostrophe may not be used. (Note that when referring to quotation marks in literal data, quotes inside apostrophes are used to delimit the literal; conversely, apostrophes inside quotes are used to delimit the literal containing an apostrophe.)

✦ Putting together the entire `SkipLit` expression means that any number of occurrences of quotation marks or apostrophes may be used.

✦ The expression of `SkipLit` is then applied to `SystemLiteral`.

✦ Because `SkipLit` is basically a generic rule for a literal that excludes quotes and apostrophes, it can be applied elsewhere. It basically means that the entire literal can be skipped without scanning for markup within it.

Names and tokens

In XML, the labels representing distinctive units of information within rules are called *tokens*. A *name* is a token that begins with a letter, an underscore, or a colon. After the first character, other letters, underscores, or colons, as well as digits, periods, or standard Unicode combining characters or extenders can exist. The characters that follow the initial character may appear in any combination.

This XML rule describes the composition of a Name:

```
Name ::= (Letter | '_' | ':') (NameChar)*
```

Analyzing the expression of this rule is simple:

- ✦ `(Letter | '_' | ':') (NameChar)*` can be divided into two parts. `(NameChar)*` must follow `(Letter | '_' | ':')`.

- ✦ The first part, `(Letter | '_' | ':')`, indicates that only one of the following can begin a Name: a letter, an underscore, or a colon.

- ✦ The second part, `(NameChar)*`, indicates that NameChar can occur zero or more times after the first character.

But how do you know what `NameChar` is or does? In order for the rule described above to work properly, it exists in conjunction with the `NameChar` rule:

```
NameChar ::= Letter | Digit | '.' | '-' | '_' | ':' |
    CombiningChar | Extender
```

The expression of `NameChar` indicates that you have a choice between using a letter, digit, period, hyphen, underscore, colon, or standard Unicode combining character or extender. Because the `Name` rule includes a reference to `NameChar`, the `NameChar` rule thus completes the `Name` definition.

Take this one step further, and you can have multiple Names. A multiple version of `Name`, or `Names`, can be composed of a single Name or a Name followed by a series of white spaces and Names. This rule defines `Names`:

```
Names ::= Name (S Name)*
```

Just like a Name, a name token is made up of any mixture of name characters. In rules, name tokens are abbreviated as `Nmtoken`.

`Nmtoken` rules are very similar to `Name` rules:

```
Nmtoken ::= (NameChar)+
Nmtokens ::= Nmtoken (S Nmtoken)*
```

The major difference is that the set of characters that can make up a name token is less restrictive than the set of characters for Names; name tokens can start with any name character, not just a letter or an underscore.

As long as the syntax is correct, you may use any Name or name token that you want, except for ones that begin with `XML` itself. This includes any combination of uppercase and lowercase letters of `XML`, such as `xml`, `Xml`, or `xMl`. Names beginning with anything that matches `(('X'|'x')('M'|'m') ('L'|'l'))` are reserved for standardization in the current or future World Wide Web Consortium XML Specification.

Chapter 3: Designing a DTD

In This Chapter

✔ Understanding the role of DTDs

✔ Incorporating DTDs into XML documents with document type declarations

✔ The difference between external and internal DTDs

✔ Character references

✔ Comments

✔ CDATA section delimiters

✔ Processing instructions

*I*f the flesh of XML is the XML document, then the heart and soul of XML is the description of how the document works — in other words, the *document type definition,* or DTD, associated with that XML document. Much of DTD design focuses on creating efficient and useful markup, which you see demonstrated in this chapter. I also show you examples of both internal and externally declared DTDs.

What is a DTD?

In a generic sense, an XML document consists of two types of information: a variety of textual content and the instructions for those pieces of content. The instructions appear as markup.

One reason why XML is so flexible is that you can define most of your own markup and create a variety of tags that perform a wide range of functions. How the tags work and what they do is up to you; to get them to work properly requires an understanding of markup rules and syntax — in essence, knowing how to program them.

Therefore, you must somehow define the markup itself. This is where the rules of the *document type definition* come in; these rules define the various types of markup that you may have in your document. In other words, the document type definition contains instructions for the instructions for your document's content.

Consider this section of an XML document:

```
<section><cooltext>This is the first sentence in this
     section, and it is cool.</cooltext>
This text is no longer cool.</section>
```

As far as XML is concerned, this document is correct: The markup tags are syntactically legal, and the two sets of markup tags are nested properly. Without a definition of the markup tags, however, you can't tell how the content within the tags appears and functions. For XML to be effective, you must define the markup by document type definition rules.

Prolog and document type declarations

Sometimes, the rules of a document type definition are called *document type declarations,* or simply *declarations.* These declarations define the technical instructions for markup. Among other things, defining the markup imposes constraints on how you should sequence and nest tags, such as those in the previous example. Because you can have many types of declarations in the document type definition, many of the rules in the XML specification are devoted to declarations.

Four kinds declarations exist in XML:

- ✦ **Element declarations,** which make up the logical structure of a document.

- ✦ **Attribute-list declarations,** which define and constrain elements.

- ✦ **Entity declarations,** consisting of parameter entities and general entities, which make up the physical structure of a document. (You can think of an entity as a kind of pointer, or shorthand notation, you define once and refer to over and over again.)

- ✦ **Notation declarations,** which define formats for referring to external binary, non-XML entities, such as executable files and graphic files.

Technically, the set of rules you want to apply to a given XML document is called a *document type definition;* the <!DOCTYPE> tag you use to associate that set of rules to an XML document is referred to as a *document type declaration.* Because the difference between the two is slight in practice, programmers often use these terms interchangeably.

These declarations describe how the document and its markup function. It makes sense, then, that you place them before the textual content of the document. The section that occurs before the textual content, or document proper, is called the *prolog.*

Take a look at this short XML snippet to see what I mean:

```
<?XML version="1.0"?>
<!DOCTYPE coolstuff SYSTEM "coolstuff.dtd"[
<!--comment about coolstuff-->
<!Element cooltext (#PCDATA)>
]>
<coolstuff><cooltext>This is the beginning of the cooltext
    document proper.</cooltext></coolstuff>
```

All the bolded code — everything you see between the first line, which is the initial processing instruction, up to and including the line containing just]> — is the *prolog* of the document.

You can include any of the following in the prolog:

+ An XML declaration (optional, but encouraged)

+ A document type definition that may contain one or a number of rules

+ Comments

+ White space

+ Processing instructions

To strictly conform to good XML style, you should begin XML documents with an *XML declaration,* which specifies the version of XML you're using.

For example:

```
<?XML version="1.0"?>
```

The XML declaration begins with a left angle bracket and a question mark (<?) and ends with a question mark and a right angle bracket (?>). Inside these opening and closing tags, the XML declaration tag contains the type of document it is (XML) and the version number of XML.

Note that the preceding example refers to XML version 1.0. Currently, every XML declaration should contain this statement, along with this version number, because the XML Working Group — the committee that oversees the development of the XML Specification — decided that the current specification is the first complete draft of XML. Including the version number 1.0 indicates to the XML processor that your document conforms to this version of the specification; if a document uses the value 1.0 when it doesn't conform to this version, you get an error.

You should include this or a similar XML declaration (when appropriate) in even your simplest XML documents. This is a good habit to form while you learn to use XML.

Here's another XML declaration:

```
<?XML version="1.0" encoding="UTF-8"?>
```

Again, this XML declaration contains all the necessary information — the type (XML) and the version number (version="1.0"). The only additional information is the character encoding (UTF-8), which the XML processor uses to read the characters in the document correctly. Note that the entire XML declaration appears within question marks and the appropriate left- and right-angle brackets, respectively.

The prolog should also contain a document type declaration. Although not required, the document type declaration often includes one or a number of rules that

✦ Define markup — technically, the constraints on the logical structure.

✦ Associate attributes with the markup. (For more information about attributes, flip to Chapter 4.)

A document type definition doesn't always have to contain rules, as in these cases:

✦ The document refers to a separate, external DTD, and that DTD contains all pertinent instructions. (I show you an example of this in the section, "Associating a DTD with an XML Document," later in this chapter.)

✦ The document just plain doesn't include rules. (Technically, no rules are necessary, although declaring none is rare — and a bit pointless, because XML documents require DTD rules to be of any real use.)

The document type declaration must appear before the first element — or the first markup tag — in the document.

Document type declaration examples

An example of a simple document looks like this:

```
<?XML version="1.0"?>
<!DOCTYPE simpledocument SYSTEM "simpledocument.dtd">
<simpledocument>This is a simple document, and it is
    correct.</simpledocument>
```

In this example, the XML declaration comes first. The next line is the document type declaration, which doesn't contain any rules (instead, this line refers to an external DTD; I discuss this approach in another section in this chapter, "Associating a DTD with an XML Document," later in this chapter.) The final line is the first element of the document; this marks the end of the prolog. The prolog in this example includes only the first two lines.

A slightly more complex document may look like this:

```
<?XML version="1.0"?>
<!DOCTYPE complexdoc SYSTEM "complexdoc.dtd" [
<!ELEMENT complexdoc (#PCDATA)>
]>
<complexdoc>This document is a bit more complex, and it is
    also correct. </complexdoc>
```

This document type declaration contains one rule. This rule, an element declaration, describes the appropriate type of content for complexdoc. When you include one or more rules in the document type declaration, place each one on a separate line and delimit the first rule with the left-square bracket ([) on the right-hand end of the line just above it and with the right-square bracket (]) and right-angle bracket (>) on a separate line just below the last rule.

You can find detailed information about DTDs in Chapter 5 of *XML For Dummies,* 2nd Edition, by Ed Tittel and Frank Boumphrey (Hungry Minds, Inc.).

Declaring the root element

The document type declaration identifies the *root element* of the document. The root element is the markup that contains the content of the entire document. All XML documents must have one, and only one, root element.

For example, in this example of an XML document

```
<?XML version="1.0"?>
<!DOCTYPE book [
<!ELEMENT book (text)>
<!ELEMENT text (#PCDATA)*>
]>
<book>
<text>This is text within the book.</text>
</book>
```

book is the root element of the document, so all of the XML content within the document proper must appear within the start tag <book> and end tag </book> respectively. The DTD content, too, must begin with the root element, as you see in this line taken from the previous code snippet:

```
<!DOCTYPE book [
```

The `<text>` markup tags identify content that complies with the rule for the `text` element. Remember, in order for the document to be valid, you must always include the markup of any existing nonroot elements (in this example, the `<text>` tags) and document content (such as `This is text within the book.`) within the root element markup tags (in this case, the `<book>` tags).

Chapter 6 of *XML For Dummies,* 2nd Edition, by Ed Tittel and Frank Boumphrey, covers markup in detail.

Associating a DTD with an XML Document

You have two choices when it comes to associating (attaching) a DTD with an XML file: You can include the text of a DTD directly in an XML document, or you can reference an external DTD file from inside an XML document. Whichever approach you choose, you use the `<!DOCTYPE>` tag to associate a DTD with an XML document, as you see in the following sections.

Typically, you choose the first option — including an internal DTD — during the testing phase of your XML application development; you choose the second option — referencing an external DTD — when you want to apply a single DTD to multiple XML documents.

Including an Internal DTD

The bolded XML code you see below incorporates a DTD (a short one, declaring just one element) into an XML document. All DTD statements must be placed inside the beginning and ending square brackets ([]) inside the `<!DOCTYPE>` tags, as shown.

```
<?xml version="1.0"?>
<!DOCTYPE form [
<!ELEMENT form (#PCDATA)>
]>
<form> The content of the form is located here.</form>
```

Referencing an External DTD

The syntax for the reference to an external subset within an XML document's document type declaration looks like this:

```
<!DOCTYPE rootElementName SYSTEM "filename.dtd">
```

In the document type declaration shown in the previous lines of code, the *system identifier* `filename.dtd` provides the *uniform resource identifier (URI),* which is the filename and necessary path or URL, immediately following the `SYSTEM` keyword.

To reference a *public external DTD* (a DTD located on a computer system other than the computer system where the XML document resides), add the `PUBLIC` keyword directly after the `rootElementName`.

At press time, much confusion exists on the meaning of (and even the necessity of) the `SYSTEM` and `PUBLIC` keywords. On a broader note, much confusion exists about how folks should refer to non-XML files from within XML. You can find more information about this topic at `www.w3.org/Addressing`.

DTD Markup

DTD markup provides the instructions for the XML processor. Much of the design of XML DTDs focuses on creating efficient and useful markup.

The components of markup include:

+ **Start and end tags.** Start and end tags start and end XML declarations, respectively. Examples of start tags include `<`, `<!--`, and `<?`. Examples of corresponding end tags include `/>`, `-->`, and `?>`.

+ **Empty elements.** An empty element is an element purposely associated with no data.

+ **Entity references.** An entity reference is a reference to a predefined entity (placeholder).

+ **Character references.** A character reference is a reference to one or more characters.

+ **Comments.** A comment is one or more lines of human-readable text inserted into XML code.

+ **CDATA section delimiters.** A CDATA section delimiter defines a section of code — often full of special characters that might confuse an XML parser — that the XML parser doesn't attempt to parse, but instead passes on to the XML processor.

+ **Document type declarations.** A document type definition (DTD) is a set of restrictions that define which values can be associated with the elements in an associated XML document at runtime.

+ **Processing instructions.** A processing instruction is a "passthrough" construct that lets XML developers pass executable files and other non-XML processing instructions to an XML processor.

For an explanation of start tags, end tags, and empty elements, see Chapter 4.

Characters

The smallest and most basic unit of an XML document is a *character*. Regarding the content of elements, *character data* is any string of characters that does not contain the start tag of any markup.

For example, if an element for a first name is defined in a DTD like this:

```
<!ELEMENT firstname (#PCDATA)>
```

a corresponding XML document may contain this string of characters:

```
<firstname>Mariva</firstname>
```

The DTD #PCDATA directive you see above stands for *parsed character data*.

Check out Chapter 4 for detailed information about elements.

CDATA sections

Sometimes, you may need to include a whole bunch of special characters, such as the ampersand or less-than sign (& or <, respectively) in your markup. To do this without confusing the XML parser, you need to use a CDATA (short for "character data") section.

The syntax for specifying a CDATA section looks like this:

```
<![CDATA[ a literal string containing wacky characters ]]>
```

You can include a CDATA section anywhere you see regular character data in the text of the document.

CDATA sections can't nest; in other words, you can only use one CDATA section at a time, and you can't include one CDATA section within another.

Comments

In some cases, you may need to include text in your DTD or document that human beings looking at the code can read, but that is invisible to an XML application. You can use the comment tag to do this.

The syntax of a comment looks like this:

```
<!--comment-->
```

You can include any character data, including characters normally reserved for markup purposes, in the text of a comment except for the literal string.

Processing instructions

Sometimes, you may need to include a *processing instruction,* or PI, in a DTD or XML document. A PI is the name of an application or other processing instruction that your XML processor knows how to execute.

A PI looks like this:

```
<?name pidata?>
```

The `name` identifies a particular PI within the DTD or XML document; `pidata` is the name of the processing instruction.

As long as the syntax is correct, you may use any name of a PI target you want, except for one that begins with `XML` itself.

Chapter 4: Logical Structures

In This Chapter

✔ **Using tags**

✔ **Declaring elements**

✔ **Adding attributes to elements**

✔ **Understanding content models, element content, and mixed content**

✔ **Making your documents more efficient by using conditional sections**

XML documents consist of two complementary types of information: the data that makes up a document and the way in which that data is organized and structured. The latter type of information forms the *logical structure* of the document. The logical structure is in turn composed of a variety of forms — defined as elements and attributes — all of which follow strict syntax rules. These forms are generically referred to as *logical structures*. After you learn the syntax of each logical structure, you're well on your way to producing your own XML documents.

Using Tags

You use tags to specify structure — in other words, to indicate markup — within a document. (Not all markup appears in the form of tags, however; entity references, processing instructions, and comments are all forms of markup that don't use tags.)

All tags are delimited by left-angle (<) and right-angle (>) brackets.

The two types of tags are:

✦ **Empty-element tags.** An example is `<EmptyTag/>`. All empty-element tags must contain a backslash (/) directly before the closing angle bracket (>).

✦ **A pair of nonempty element tags: one start tag, and one end tag.** An example is `<NonEmptyTag>Some data</NonEmptyTag>`. Start and end tags are identical, with one exception: end tags must contain a backslash (/) directly after the opening angle bracket (<).

You can nest tags inside each other, like this: `<TagOne><TagTwo></TagTwo></TagOne>`.

Elements

An XML document consists of two essential parts: data or information, and the logical units that contain the data or information. If you think of the data or information as items that you organize and store, then the logical units are the storage containers for those items. In XML, each logical unit is referred to as an *element*.

```
<element>This sentence represents a string of data. It is
    surrounded by "element" tags, which represent this data's
    storage container.</element>
```

All documents must contain at least one element, which is the root element of the document. The root element contains all other elements. Here's an example of a root element containing a couple of nonroot elements:

```
<rootelement>
    <nonrootelement>
        <nonrootelementchild>
        <nonrootelementchild>
    </nonrootelement>
</rootelement>
```

Elements can contain a number of things:

✦ **Character data.** You may find that most of the elements you define contain character data: for example, `<from>Mariva</from>`.

✦ **Other elements, known as subelements or *child elements (children)*.** You can organize elements into logical hierarchies by creating subelements within elements. For example, you can create an element called `Employee` that contains subelements called `PartTime`, `FullTime`, and `Contract`.

✦ **CDATA sections.** A CDATA section is a section of text that XML parsers don't access or attempt to process.

✦ **Processing instructions.** A processing instruction is unique to the system on which an XML application runs. An example of a processing instruction is the name of an executable program.

✦ **Comments.** A comment is one or more lines of human-readable text.

✦ **White space.** White space refers to the spaces, tabs, and returns that separate the characters that make up an element declaration.

✦ **Entity references.** An entity reference is a reference to a predefined entity, or expandable placeholder; for example, %Copyright is a reference for an entity named Copyright.

Elements can also be associated with one or more attributes. (See "Assigning Attributes to Elements," later in this chapter, for details.)

For more information about character data, CDATA sections, processing instructions, or comments, see Chapter 3.

Declaring elements

You specify, or *declare,* an element by including an *element declaration* in a DTD.

Element declarations enable you to constrain the content of an element; that is, decide what content is allowed for a given element and what is prohibited. For example, you can use the #PCDATA keyword to constrain an element to character data.

According to the rule in the XML specification, the syntax for an element declaration looks like this:

```
elementdecl ::= '<!ELEMENT' S Name S contentspec S? '>' [vc:
    Unique Element Type Declaration]
```

To understand how this works, you can break down each piece of this rule:

✦ All element declarations must begin with <!ELEMENT.

✦ A white space, S, follows <!ELEMENT.

✦ The Name of the element follows the white space. The Name indicates the element's *type.* Each element has such a type, which is sometimes called its *generic identifier (GI).*

✦ More white space must follow the Name.

✦ The next item in this sequence is contentspec, which I describe a little later.

✦ After the contentspec, you may either include exactly one white space or leave it out, which is an option indicated by the S?.

✦ Finally, close the element declaration with a right-angle bracket (>).

✦ The validity constraint (vc:), Unique Element Type Declaration, indicates that you may not declare an element type more than once; in other words, each element type must be unique.

According to a corresponding XML specification rule, the content specification, or `contentspec`, follows this syntax:

```
contentspec ::= 'EMPTY' | 'ANY' | Mixed | children [vc:
    Element Valid]
```

The rule for `contentspec` itself breaks down as follows:

✦ The logical "or" (|) indicates that any of the `contentspec` may contain any of the four options listed, `'EMPTY'`, `'ANY'`, `Mixed`, or `children`, but that you must use exactly one of the options.

✦ Using the `'EMPTY'` option, you include the literal string `EMPTY` in your element declaration. `EMPTY` means that the element has no content.

✦ As an inverse rule to `EMPTY`, an element declaration matching the literal string `ANY` indicates that the element may contain any type of content, such as character data, any other element types, or a mixture of both.

✦ `Mixed` enables you to include a mixture of elements and character data in your element declaration.

✦ `children` allows you to include `Names` of elements that are subelements, or children, of the element named in the element declaration.

✦ The validity constraint (`vc:`), `Element Valid`, indicates that an element is valid if you provide a corresponding element declaration for it. Strictly speaking — and this may seem obvious — the `Name` of the element must match the element type. In addition, you must properly observe all the points mentioned above for the element to be valid.

As long as the syntax is correct, you may use any element `Name` that you want, except for ones that begin with `XML` itself.

The following block of code shows examples of element declarations (in bold) placed inside a local, or internal, DTD:

```
<?xml version="1.0" encoding="UTF-8" ?>
<!DOCTYPE message [
<!ELEMENT message (from, to, subject, date, body)>
<!ELEMENT from (#PCDATA)>
<!ELEMENT to (#PCDATA)>
<!ELEMENT subject (#PCDATA)>
<!ELEMENT date (#PCDATA)>
<!ELEMENT body (p+)>
<!ELEMENT p (#PCDATA)>
]>
<message>
<from>Mariva</from>
<to>Reader</to>
<subject>Example</subject>
<date>December 31, 1999</date>
```

```
<body>
<p>Dear Reader,</p>
<p>This is an example of how you can declare a number of
    elements in a document type declaration, and how
    markup tags indicate how these elements are used in
    a document.</p>
<p>Does this make sense to you now?</p>
</body>
</message>
```

In this example, many of the elements declared in the document type declaration, such as from, to, subject, and date, are very simple because they just indicate that the element contains character data. The element body may contain one or more p elements (in this example, the p stands for "paragraph"), as indicated by the content specification (p+); body is thus the parent of p. (In other words, the body of the message may contain one or more paragraphs.) The root element, message, contains all the other elements and indicates that you must sequence these child elements in the specified order. In the document proper section, all of these elements appear in order, nest properly, and contain the correct types of content.

Declaring elements of type "mixed content"

If a content model for an element contains both subelements (or child elements) and character data, then the content model is *mixed,* or contains *mixed content.*

An element declaration that specifies mixed content is a *mixed-content declaration.* The rule for mixed content appears like this in the XML Specification:

```
Mixed ::= '(' S? '#PCDATA' (S? '|' S? Name)* S? ')*' | '(' S?
    '#PCDATA' S? ')' [vc: Proper Group/PE Nesting] [vc: No
    Duplicate Types]
```

Essentially, this rule states that you may supply any mixture of character data and child element Names. Specifically:

✦ To declare a mixed-content element properly, you must place the special symbol #PCDATA (whose moniker PCDATA stands for *parseable character data*), and then optionally include child element Names interspersed with other occurrences of #PCDATA.

✦ You must separate each element in the content specification list by the logical "or" (|).

✦ The entire group of listed child elements must be optional, as indicated by the asterisk (*).

✦ The validity constraint (vc:), No Duplicate Types, indicates that the same name must not appear more than once in a single mixed-content declaration.

Here are a few examples of mixed-content declarations:

```
<!ELEMENT p (#PCDATA|a|ul|b|i|em)*>
```

```
<!ELEMENT p (#PCDATA | %font; | %phrase; | %special; |
    %form;)* >
```

Assigning Attributes to Elements

Sometimes you want to associate additional information with an element. You can apply such information to an element by using an *attribute list* declaration, which in turn contains an *attribute declaration*.

Attribute-list declarations

To tell the XML processor which attributes you want to assign to elements and how they should be used, you include an *attribute declaration* in the DTD. Specifically, attribute declarations identify

✦ The elements that may have attributes

✦ The attributes, each specified by name, assigned to the elements

✦ The attribute types

✦ The value or set of values that may be associated with the attributes

✦ The default value for each attribute

You may specify more than one attribute for an element, or a *list* of attributes, by including an *attribute-list declaration* in the DTD. In XML, you use an attribute-list declaration to declare both a single attribute and a list of attributes. Whether you specify a single attribute or a list of attributes, you declare each attribute with three parts:

✦ A name

✦ A type

✦ A default value

The set of rules for attribute-list declarations appears like this in the XML Specification:

```
AttlistDecl ::= '<!ATTLIST' S Name AttDef* S? '>'
```

```
AttDef ::= S Name S AttType S Default
```

According to these rules for a) an attribute-list declaration, `AttlistDecl` and b) an attribute definition, `AttDef`:

✦ You must begin an attribute-list declaration with the literal string `<!ATTLIST`, followed by a white space (`S`).

✦ After the white space, indicate the type of element with its `Name`. (***Note:*** Some XML processors may issue a warning if you declare attributes for an element type that is itself not declared.)

✦ You may include zero or more attribute definitions, as indicated by the asterisk (`*`).

✦ An attribute definition must begin with a white space, followed by the `Name` of the attribute, the attribute type (`AttType`), another white space, and the attribute default (`Default`), respectively.

Here is an example of an attribute-list declaration:

```
<?XML version="1.0"?>
<!DOCTYPE account SYSTEM "account.dtd" [
<!ELEMENT account (#PCDATA)*>
<!ATTLIST BILL
NAME ID #REQUIRED
DATE CDATA #IMPLIED
STATUS (PAID | OUTSTANDING) 'OUTSTANDING'>
]>
```

In this example, the `BILL` element has three attributes:

✦ `NAME`, which is an `ID` attribute type and whose default is `REQUIRED`.

✦ `DATE`, which is a string of character data (`CDATA`) and isn't required, as denoted by the default `IMPLIED`.

✦ `STATUS`, which must be either `PAID` or `OUTSTANDING`, and defaults to `OUTSTANDING` if not specified.

Attribute declarations

The XML Specification rule for an attribute looks like this:

```
Attribute ::= Name Eq AttValue [vc: Attribute Value Type]
   [wfc: No External Entity References] [wfc: No < in
   Attribute Values]
```

In the expression of this rule, `Name` is the name of the attribute, `Eq` represents the equals sign (=), and `AttValue` is the attribute value, or the data description associated with the attribute name. An attribute, therefore, is essentially a *name-value pair* — in other words, two items: the name of an attribute, and the value of that named attribute — that is applied to an element.

This rule has one validity constraint (`vc:`) and two well-formedness constraints (`wfc:`). Each of the constraints means the following:

✦ The validity constraint `Attribute Value Type` indicates that you must declare the attribute in the DTD. Similarly, the value that you assign to the attribute name must be valid — that is, the value must conform to the type you had declared for it.

✦ `No External Entity References` means that you can't put direct or indirect entity references to external entities in your attribute values.

✦ The well-formedness constraint `No < in Attribute Values`, in technical shorthand, means that if you use replacement text for an entity referred to directly or indirectly in an attribute value, it must not contain a left-angle bracket (<). You may, however, use the escape character sequence for the left-angle bracket, which is `&lt;`.

The XML Specification rule for an attribute value reads like this:

```
AttValue ::= '"' ([^<&"] | Reference)* '"' | "'" ([^<&'] |
    Reference)* "'"
```

This rule indicates that you may use only literal data for an attribute value. *Literal data* is any quoted string that doesn't contain the double quotes (") or apostrophes (') as delimiters for that string.

Here are a few examples of what an attribute or an attribute value-pair could look like:

```
TERM="cat"
```

```
ID="156"
```

```
COLOR="black"
```

 Although the attribute names in this example are in all uppercase letters, you may use lowercase letters for your attribute names. You must be consistent in choosing one or the other, though, and remain consistent throughout your XML use. For example, the XML processor does not see `TERM` the same way it sees `Term`.

You place an attribute specification in the associated element's start tag. Here is the syntax:

```
<element attname="attvalue"></element>
```

You aren't limited to one attribute name-value pair; you may use as many as you need. Just make sure the attribute names are unique and include a space between each attribute:

```
<termdef ID="dt-cat" TERM="cat">
```

In XML, you cannot include any white space between the attribute name, the equals sign, and the attribute values. All three parts of an attribute butt up together.

Attribute default values

You can specify a *default value* for an attribute. When you specify default attribute values in an element's start tag (which you find in a DTD), the XML document inherits those default values from the DTD.

For each attribute, you may choose between one of four possible default values:

✦ #REQUIRED, which means that you must include the attribute in every occurrence of the element. If the attribute is missing, the document is invalid.

✦ #IMPLIED, which means that you don't have to include an attribute value, and that you didn't provide a default value. In this case, if you don't specify a value, the processor proceeds without issuing an error.

✦ A specific value consisting of any string of character data that you explicitly declare in quotes. If you leave out an attribute in an associated element, the element inherits the default value that you specified.

✦ #FIXED, which precedes a specific value consisting of any string of character data that you explicitly declare in quotes. In this case, any attribute value that you specify in an associated element must match the default value, or the document is invalid.

This is how the rule for default values appears in the XML Specification:

```
Default ::= '#REQUIRED' | '#IMPLIED' | (('#FIXED' S)?
    AttValue) [vc: Attribute Default Legal] [wfc: No < in
    Attribute Values ]
```

This rule involves the following two constraints:

✦ The validity constraint (vc:) Attribute Default Legal means that the declared default value must be legal; that is, it must meet the syntactic constraints of the declared attribute type.

✦ The well-formedness constraint (wfc:) No < in Attribute Values, in technical shorthand, means that if you use replacement text for an entity referred to directly or indirectly in an attribute value, it must not contain a left-angle bracket (<). You may, however, use the escape character sequence for the left-angle bracket, which is <.

This set of attribute-list declarations includes examples of each of the four types of attribute defaults:

```
<!ATTLIST termdef
    id        ID        #REQUIRED
    name      CDATA     #IMPLIED>
<!ATTLIST snack
    fruit     (orange|apple|banana) "banana">

<!ATTLIST form
    method    CDATA     #FIXED "POST">
```

In the attribute-list declaration for the element termdef, the value for the id attribute is required, but the value for name is optional. In the attribute-list declaration for the element snack, you can choose between specifying orange, apple, or banana, and if you do not specify one of these fruits, the fruit attribute of the snack element defaults to banana. Lastly, the attribute-list declaration for the element form indicates that if you specify a value for the method attribute, that the value must be POST, because the "POST" is declared above as the #FIXED value of the method attribute.

Attribute types

When you declare an attribute or an attribute list, you specify the function of each attribute with an *attribute type*. To produce a valid document, all of the values for each attribute must be the correct type; that is, they must match what you declared for them.

Many attribute types exist and can be classified into one of three categories:

✦ String types

✦ Tokenized types

✦ Enumerated types

String type

A *string type* accepts any literal string of text, or character data (CDATA), as its value. You declare string types with the literal CDATA. CDATA values are case sensitive; so they must match the declared values exactly. You may find that you use string type attributes more than any other attribute type.

In the XML Specification, this is the rule for a string type:

```
StringType ::= 'CDATA'
```

If this is your attribute-list declaration

```
<!ATTLIST BOOK
TITLE CDATA #IMPLIED
AUTHOR CDATA #IMPLIED>
```

both the `TITLE` and the `AUTHOR` attributes are string types. You may use any literal string as the value of these attributes, such as in this start tag for a `BOOK` element:

```
<book title="Creating Web Pages All-In-One" author="E. A.
    Vander Veer">
```

Be sure not to confuse `CDATA` *attributes* with `CDATA` *sections.* In `CDATA` *attributes,* the XML processor recognizes markup and expands entity references; `CDATA` *sections,* on the other hand, are sections of special-character-peppered text you can hide from XML parsers.

Tokenized type

A *tokenized type* is a type of data that can contain no white space (and so can be used for identifying purposes, much like a social security number or driver's license number). A tokenized type can be any of four specific types (with a total of seven type attributes):

✦ *IDentifier,* or `ID`, which uniquely identifies an individual element in a document, so each element can have only a single `ID` attribute. Because each `ID` is unique, all of the `ID` values in a document must differ. The value of an `ID` attribute must be a name. Also, you must declare an `ID` attribute with a default of #IMPLIED or #REQUIRED. You may find that the name of an `ID` attribute is usually `ID`.

✦ *ID reference,* or `IDREF` or `IDREFS`, which is a pointer or a set of pointers to an `ID` attribute value. An `IDREF` attribute's value is the value of a single `ID` attribute of an element in the document. If you need to include more than one `ID` reference, use `IDREFS` with multiple values separated by white spaces.

✦ *Entity name,* or `ENTITY` or `ENTITIES`, which is a pointer or set of pointers to an external entity. The value of an `ENTITY` attribute is the name of an entity, which is case-sensitive to match the name of an external binary general entity declared in the DTD. If you need to include more than one entity reference, use `ENTITIES` with multiple values separated by white spaces.

✦ *Name token,* or NMTOKEN or NMTOKENS, whose value is a mixture of name characters. Name token attributes are similar to string type attributes, but they are more restricted. In general, an NMTOKEN attribute consists of a single name, as opposed to the literal string of a CDATA attribute, which could contain white spaces and other characters. Other than this restriction, you may select any name you want for an NMTOKEN attribute, as long as it matches the NMTOKEN — although it doesn't have to match another attribute or declaration. If you need to include more than one name token, use NMTOKENS with multiple values separated by white spaces.

In the XML Specification, the set of rules for tokenized types looks like this:

```
TokenizedType ::= 'ID'
        [vc: ID]
        [vc: One ID per Element Type]
        [vc: ID Attribute Default]
    | 'IDREF'       [vc: IDREF]
    | 'IDREFS'      [vc: IDREF]
    | 'ENTITY'      [vc: Entity Name]
    | 'ENTITIES'    [vc: Entity Name ]
    | 'NMTOKEN'     [vc: Name Token ]
    | 'NMTOKENS'    [vc: Name Token]
```

I explain all you need to know about the associated validity constraints (vc:) in the earlier descriptions of tokenized types.

As an example, here are attribute-list declarations for two of the above-mentioned tokenized attribute types along with their corresponding start tags:

ID attribute type:

```
<!ATTLIST DATA
ID ID #REQUIRED>

<DATA ID="123">
```

ENTITY attribute type:

```
<!ATTLIST IMG SRC ENTITY #REQUIRED>

<IMG SRC="image.gif"/>
```

Enumerated type

The third group of attribute types, *enumerated attribute types,* enables you to specify a value taken from a list of names.

You can specify one of two kinds of enumerated types: *notation types,* which enable you to choose from a set of notations that you declare in the DTD, and *general purpose enumeration,* which consists of a set of NMTOKEN tokens.

Here is the syntax from the XML Specification:

```
EnumeratedType ::= NotationType | Enumeration

NotationType ::= 'NOTATION' S '(' S? Name (S? '|' Name)* S?
    ')' [vc: Notation Attributes]

Enumeration ::= '(' S? Nmtoken (S? '|' S? Nmtoken)* S? ')'
    [vc: Enumeration]
```

A notation type attribute looks like this:

```
NOTATION ( notationA | notationB | notationC | ... )
```

Where notationA, notationB, and notationC are names of notations declared in the DTD.

Enumeration attributes look like this:

```
( NmtokenA | NmtokenB | NmtokenC )
```

For example, in an attribute-list declaration, you'd include this notation type like this:

```
<!ATTLIST TEXT
FORMAT NOTATION ( DOC | TXT | RTF ) "TXT">
```

The values of notation type attributes must match one of the notation names DOC, TXT, or RTF.

Conditional Sections

A *conditional section* is any set of markup that you include in or exclude from the logical structure of the DTD.

To specify in the conditional section, whether you want to include or exclude a set of markup, you must provide a keyword with a value of either INCLUDE or IGNORE, respectively, as shown in the following examples.

You can only use conditional sections within an external DTD. For more information on external DTDs, check out Chapter 3.

The syntax for including a set of markup looks like this:

```
<![INCLUDE[
[included markup]
]]>
```

Similarly, this is the syntax for excluding a set of markup:

```
<![IGNORE[
[excluded markup]
]]>
```

Although technically you can nest conditional sections, an INCLUDE conditional section nested inside an IGNORE conditional section is ignored by the XML processor.

Chapter 5: Physical Structures

In This Chapter

- ✔ Selecting the most appropriate entity for each purpose
- ✔ Including non-XML components in your documents by using binary entities
- ✔ Using parameter entities to make your DTD modular
- ✔ Referencing characters and entities
- ✔ Specifying character encoding schemes
- ✔ Declaring notations

The building blocks that make up XML are called physical structures. Physical structures are composed of a variety of materials, including virtual storage units of data (known as entities), single characters, files, pointers to other sources of information, and whole documents. A physical structure can be as small as a bit of data or as large as an entire application. Taken all together, individual physical structures make up the general physical structure of an XML document. It may take some time and patience to learn how to define and use physical structures, but after you understand the concepts, you can master some of the most important and robust capabilities of XML.

Entities

You can break an XML document into one or more units, each of which contains data. Such virtual storage units of data are called *entities*. An entity is the essential building block of physical structure in XML. In fact, the reason physical structure is *physical* is that the data referred to by entities is physically located somewhere, such as in a file on a disk drive or in a field of a database.

Each entity consists of

- ✦ A *name*, which identifies the entity.
- ✦ A *value*, which is sometimes called the *content* of the entity. The value is either the data of the entity itself or it is a pointer to the data.

Each entity's name is mapped to its corresponding value or content. You can use entities to retrieve anything from a single character to a large file.

Each XML document has one essential entity called the *document entity* or the *root entity,* which serves as the starting point for the XML processor and which may contain the entire document.

Entities fall into two general classifications:

✦ **Parsed and unparsed entities.** A parsed entity is a named chunk of text; an unparsed entity is a named chunk of binary code.

✦ **Internal and external entities.** An internal entity is a reference to a chunk of text or binary code defined and referenced in the same document. An external entity is a reference to another document.

Both parsed and unparsed entities may be either internal or external entities.

In addition, here is another classification of parsed entities:

✦ Parsed entities used within the document content are called *general entities*. You reference general entities by the name of the entity beginning with an ampersand (&) and ending with a semicolon (;).

✦ *Parameter entities* are parsed entities used only within the DTD. You reference parameter entities by the name of the entity beginning with a percent sign (%) and ending with a semicolon (;).

General and parameter entities use different forms of reference and have different purposes.

You can use any of the entities that fall into the aforementioned classifications to refer to repeated or varying text and to include the content of external files.

The last classification of entities is predefined entities, which you use to represent special characters.

Document entity

All entities, no matter how large or small, are units of data. Some entities contain smaller entities. The largest entity, or the entity that contains all other entities, is the *document entity*.

If you created an outline of all the entities in your document, you may find that some entities contain smaller entities that contain still smaller entities. The largest entities in this case are like the branches of a tree, which yield smaller branches, and even smaller branches off those. The trunk of the tree is the starting point for all the branches. In XML, the tree trunk of a document — the document entity, which is also known as the *root* — serves as the starting point (as well as the ending point, if you will) for an XML processor. For this reason, the document entity is the first text entity you encounter when reading an XML document.

If you use entities to divide a large document into sections, you can use a document entity, in a separate file, to efficiently organize the sections.

Suppose that you have a screenplay with three acts: `act1`, `act2`, and `act3`. Each act is a unit of data, or an entity. You could set up entity references for each of the acts and refer to them within the root element of the screenplay (`screenplay`) like this:

```
<screenplay>
<characterlist>[list of characters]</characterlist>
<notes>[notes]</notes>
&act1;
&act2;
&act3;
</screenplay>
```

The preceding approach works quite well, and it presents a very clean way to organize the screenplay. But watch out for this: The embedded screenplay acts can only contain markup. In other words, an act file can't have its own document type declaration (`<!DOCTYPE`).

Entity declarations

An *entity declaration* defines the name of an entity and associates it with a corresponding replacement string or with data that is stored externally and identified by a URL. Like all other types of declarations, an entity declaration is located within the DTD.

You can use an entity declaration to associate a name with another fragment of the document, such as

✦ A string of regular text

✦ A section of the document type declaration

✦ A reference to an external file that contains either

• XML text

• Binary data, such as an executable program file

Here are some examples of entity declarations:

```
<!ENTITY CWPAIO "Creating Web Pages All-in-One">
```

The preceding code declares a simple internal entity, in which the entity Name `CWPAIO` is associated with the text string `Creating Web Pages All-in-One`.

```
<!ENTITY formletter SYSTEM "/standards/formletter.xml">
```

The preceding declaration is for an external entity named `formletter`, which refers to the XML file `formletter.xml` in the local `/standards/` directory.

Entity processing

The XML processor doesn't treat all physical structures in the same way. In fact, document entities, text entities, binary entities, character references, general entity references, predefined entities, and parameter entities are each processed in a unique way. This section describes the restrictions and unique processing treatment of each type of physical structure.

With external entities, providing an accurate and valid URL with the SYSTEM or PUBLIC identifier is important. If you declare an entity with a PUBLIC identifier, the XML processor may attempt to use that identifier to generate a URL for the declared entity. If the processor can't generate a URL, it uses the SYSTEM identifier that accompanies the PUBLIC identifier. The processor follows this routine to provide the application with an actual entity when possible; keep in mind, however, that you must provide at least one valid URL (either for the SYSTEM or the PUBLIC identifier) for the processor to do this.

The XML processor treats character and general entity references according to these rules:

✦ It informs the XML application of the presence of the entity reference and provides its name or number.

  • In the case of external entities, it provides the SYSTEM and PUBLIC identifiers.

  • In the case of binary external entities, it provides the notation name and its related data.

✦ When it passes a stream of textual data to the application, it removes the reference itself from that stream.

✦ In a related process, it replaces character references and internal entities with its character or textual data.

✦ Similarly, it interprets any markup within that text, except when the entity itself escapes markup characters.

✦ A validating processor inserts the content of an external text entity into the document. This rule is optional in nonvalidating processors. (In fact, the advantage of using a nonvalidating processor in this case is so that you have the option of saving time and system resources by essentially ignoring the content of an external text entity.)

The XML processor resolves, or expands, parameter-entity references and character references immediately. This expansion is not the case with general-entity references, because the processor first parses the replacement text for general entities, and then it resolves the reference.

Table 5-1 displays how the XML processor treats, and what it requires of, character references, entity references, and unparsed entities.

Table 5-1	XML Entities by Type				
Context	*Parameter*	*Internal General*	*External Parsed General*	*Unparsed*	*Character*
Reference in Content	Not recognized	Included	Included if validating	Forbidden	Included
Reference in Attribute Value	Not recognized	Included in literal	Forbidden	Forbidden	Included
Occurs as Attribute Value	Not recognized	Forbidden	Forbidden	Notify	Not recognized
Reference in Entity Value	Included in literal	Bypassed	Bypassed	Forbidden	Included
Reference in DTD	Included as PE	Forbidden	Forbidden	Forbidden	Forbidden

The labels in the left-hand column denote the contexts in which the processor recognizes the physical structures:

+ **Reference in Content:** Refers to a physical structure occurring after the start tag and before the end tag of an element.

+ **Reference in Attribute Value:** Means within either the value of an attribute in a start tag or the default value in an attribute declaration.

+ **Occurs as Attribute Value:** Means that it occurs as a single name (as opposed to a reference) that appears either as the value of an attribute that had been declared as type ENTITY, or as one of the space-separated tokens in the value of an attribute that had been declared as type ENTITIES.

+ **Reference in Entity Value:** Is a reference within the literal entity value of a parameter or an internal entity declaration.

+ **Reference in DTD:** Is a reference within either the internal or external subsets of the DTD, but outside the value of an entity or attribute declaration.

Each table field contains one of the following descriptions:

✦ **Not Recognized:** The processor does not recognize the structure in any meaningful way. For example, because the percent sign (%) character has no particular significance outside the DTD, the XML processor doesn't recognize parameter entity references as markup in content. Similarly, the processor doesn't recognize the names of unparsed entities except when they appear in the value of an appropriately declared attribute.

✦ **Included:** The processor includes an entity when it retrieves and processes its replacement text, as though the replacement text were an original part of the document. The replacement text may contain both character data and (except for parameter entities) markup.

✦ **Included If Validating:** To validate the document, the processor recognizes a reference to a parsed entity and includes its replacement text. This is an optional feature for external entities and nonvalidating processors, so that you can choose to view a visual indication of the entity's presence and retrieve it for display.

✦ **Forbidden:** This is a fatal error, which stops the processor from continuing to process the document normally. The following occurrences trigger a fatal error:

  • The presence of a reference to an unparsed entity

  • The presence of any character or general-entity reference in the DTD, except within the value of an entity or attribute declaration

  • A reference to an external entity in an attribute value

✦ **Included in Literal:** When an entity reference appears in an attribute value, or a parameter-entity reference appears in a literal entity value, the processor expands the reference immediately. One exception is that the processor always treats a single- or double-quote character (' or ", respectively) in the replacement text as a normal data character instead of as the delimiter of a literal.

✦ **Notify:** When the name of an unparsed entity appears as a token in the value of an attribute of declared type ENTITY or ENTITIES, a validating processor informs the application of the SYSTEM and PUBLIC (if any) identifiers for both the entity and its associated notation.

✦ **Bypassed:** When a general-entity reference appears in the value of an entity declaration, the processor bypasses — essentially, ignores — the reference.

✦ **Included as PE:** When the processor recognizes and includes a parameter-entity (PE) reference in the DTD, it enlarges the entity's replacement text by attaching a single leading space character (hexadecimal code #x20) and a single trailing space character. This is so that the replacement text of parameter entities contains an integral number of grammatical tokens in the DTD.

A well-formed set of entities looks like this:

```
<!ENTITY % C '"Correct"' >
<!ENTITY Answer "The answer is &C;" >
```

In the previous example, the value of the entity `Answer` is properly delimited by double quotes at the beginning and at the end. The fact that the replacement text of the parameter entity `C` itself contains two sets of quotes doesn't matter. `Answer` simply expands to the value `The answer is '"Correct"'`.

For more information about DTDs and well-formedness, see Chapter 3 of this book and Chapter 5 of *XML For Dummies,* 2nd Edition, by Ed Tittel and Frank Boumphrey (Hungry Minds, Inc.)

External entities

An *external entity* is an entity whose declaration doesn't contain the replacement data of the entity. Or, put another way, an external entity is mapped to data located outside its declaration.

You declare an external entity by associating its name with a *SYSTEM* or *PUBLIC identifier.* This identifier provides the XML processor with the *Uniform Resource Locator (URL)* to find the file containing the entity's data:

✦ The URL may point to a file found within your local disk drive or network drive; in this case, you identify the URL with the keyword `SYSTEM`.

✦ If the URL points to a public-domain file located in a publicly accessible place, you would identify the location and filename with the keyword `PUBLIC`.

An entity is either internal or external, so if the entity is not internal, you must declare it as a proper external entity.

Here are some examples of external entity declarations:

```
<!ENTITY chapter1 SYSTEM "chapter1.xml">
```

This entity declaration maps `chapter1` to the file `chapter1.xml`. This file is found locally (so locally, in fact, that it doesn't even require a path before the filename!), so it's identified with the keyword `SYSTEM`.

```
<!ENTITY systemfile SYSTEM "http://www.dummies.com/
    systemfile.xml">
```

This entity is very similar to the one in the first example; the only difference is that the SYSTEM identifier contains an entire URL and not just a filename.

```
<!ENTITY open-hatch PUBLIC "-//Textuality//TEXT Standard
    open-hatch boilerplate//EN"
    "http://www.textuality.com/boilerplate/OpenHatch.xml">
```

With the keyword PUBLIC, you can tell that this entity is mapped to an externally-located file.

```
<!ENTITY image SYSTEM "../graphics/image.gif" NDATA GIF>
```

The value of this entity is found locally, but it's not mapped to textual data. This unparsed, or binary, entity is associated with a GIF graphic image file. It's appropriately marked with NDATA, indicating that a notation declaration for GIF exists somewhere within the DTD.

Generally, external entities are unique to particular documents, so you might want to declare them within the internal DTD subset rather than in a class DTD.

Internal entities

An *internal entity* has a value that's included literally within its entity declaration. Or, put another way, an internal entity provides both the name of the entity and the data that the entity is mapped to in one convenient package.

Because including binary data within an internal entity declaration is impossible (or at least terribly inconvenient), all internal entities are parsed, or composed of textual data. The textual data that is mapped to an internal entity is always delimited by quotes.

A declaration for an internal entity looks like this:

```
<!ENTITY Name "Textual data">
```

Here are a few examples of internal entity declarations:

```
<!ENTITY rights "All rights reserved">
```

The preceding code declares an internal general entity. Whenever the document author includes the entity reference &rights;, the XML processor automatically replaces it with the literal string All rights reserved.

```
<!ENTITY % first "First Edition">
```

The preceding declaration is for an internal parameter entity. Remember, you can only use the parameter-entity reference %first; within the DTD, as follows:

```
<!ENTITY book "Creating Web Pages All-in-One: E. A. Vander
    Veer, &#xA9; 2001 %first;, &rights;">
```

This declaration for an internal parameter entity is a bit complex. You can expand it manually one step at a time:

✦ The entity `book` uses the entity reference `&book;`. The value of `book` is everything inside the quotes, `Creating Web Pages All-in-One: E. A. Vander Veer, &#xA9; 2001 %first;, &rights;`.

✦ The XML processor expands the character reference `&#xA9;` into its associated character, (©).

✦ The processor also expands the parameter-entity reference `%first;` into the string found in the example just above this one: `First Edition`.

✦ Similarly, the processor expands the reference `&rights;` into the literal string `All rights reserved`.

✦ Putting it all together, you have `Creating Web Pages All-in-One: E. A. Vander Veer, (©) 2001 First Edition, All rights reserved`.

The XML processor triggers an error if you refer to internal entities recursively; that is, if the value of an internal entity contains a reference to itself. Such an error protects the XML application from replacing an entity reference with the same text over and over again forever.

Parameter entities

A *parameter entity* is a text entity that's used and located only within a DTD. Besides being constrained to the DTD, a parameter entity functions just like a general entity.

For the XML processor to distinguish between a parameter entity and a general entity, you declare a parameter entity with a percent sign (%) and use the percent sign in its references instead of the ampersand (&) used in general-entity references.

You must include white space on either side of the % in the parameter-entity declaration to set it apart from the other components of the declaration. When you denote a parameter-entity *reference,* however, you must not allow any white space (or any other characters) in between the % and the name of the entity.

The syntax for a parameter-entity declaration looks like this:

```
<!ENTITY % Name "Value">
```

In this syntax, `Value` replaces any occurrence of `%Name;`, which is the parameter-entity reference for `Name`.

The XML processor immediately expands parameter-entity references so that their replacement text can be used in other parts of the DTD.

For example:

```
<!ENTITY % version "3.2">

<!ATTLIST document version CDATA #FIXED "%version;">
```

In the second declaration, the declaration for the element document's attribute version, the parameter-entity reference %version; is expanded into the literal string 3.2, which was determined by the entity declaration for the parameter entity version.

Parsed and unparsed entities

An external entity may contain one of two types of data:

✦ *Parsed* or *text.* Parsed data consists of XML-readable character data. Parsed data contains the textual content or markup that forms part of an XML document.

✦ *Unparsed* or *binary.* Unparsed data consists of code that is not XML-encoded. Unparsed data translates into nontext data, such as a graphic image, a sound file, an application, or even a non-XML plain-text file.

Parsed (text) entities

Text entities are called *parsed entities* because the XML processor parses all XML text. The content of a parsed entity is referred to as its *replacement text;* this text is an integral part of the XML document.

The syntax for a parsed entity looks like this:

<!ENTITY *EntityName* "*replacement text*">

The XML processor expands text-entity references immediately. In the following example

```
<!ENTITY XML "Extensible Markup Language">
```

the processor replaces the entity reference &XML; with the text string Extensible Markup Language. So this markup

```
<p>This is an example of &XML;.</p>
```

represents the same data as

```
<p>This is an example of Extensible Markup Language.</p>
```

Unparsed (binary) entities

An XML processor can't parse binary data, so *binary entities* are called
unparsed entities. The content of an unparsed entity may or may not be text;
even if it is text, it may not be XML-encoded text.

The syntax for a binary entity looks like this:

```
<!ENTITY EntityName [SYSTEM "URL" | PUBLIC "URL"] NDATA
    NotationName>
```

Here is an example of a typical binary entity:

```
<!ENTITY logo SYSTEM "graphics/logo.bmp" NDATA BMP>
```

The entity reference &logo; refers to the binary entity logo, as declared in
the preceding line of code. The file logo is found at the URL
graphics/logo.bmp. The notation BMP indicates that this file is a bitmap
file; of course, the DTD must contain a notation declaration for BMP in order
for this entity to be valid.

Referencing Characters and Entities

A *character* — in XML or any computer application — consists of a single
base-2 (8-, 16-, or even 32-bit) chunk of data. Because of how XML organizes
textual data, each character is significant in XML. Similarly, knowing how to
effectively use groups or sets of characters in your documents is crucial for
creating efficient and robust XML documents. Entities can identify characters,
character classes, or special characters, and so you can think of entities and
characters as partners in creating and organizing the single data chunks of
physical structure.

Character encoding in entities

XML uses the Unicode (ISO 10646) standard for encoding characters in text.
This standard offers a tremendous amount of flexibility within XML, because
you can choose one of several methods for encoding characters as bit
patterns. Such a method is called a *character encoding scheme*. The most
common character encoding schemes are the 8-bit scheme, known as *UTF-8,*
and the 16-bit scheme, known as *UTF-16.* Both schemes support the entire
Unicode range. However, UTF-8 can be mapped only to a 255-character
range at a given time. UTF-16 can support all the Unicode characters at once
without having to remap, but it uses more memory overhead. (You can use a
32-bit character encoding scheme, but you may not want or really need to
reference such a wide choice of characters in your document.)

For more information about the Unicode standard, check the Unicode Consortium home page at `www.unicode.org`.

You tell the XML processor which encoding scheme you need to use by using an *encoding declaration,* which is a processing instruction (PI) that is part of the XML declaration.

An encoding declaration looks like this:

```
<?XML encoding="[EncodingDescription]" ?>
```

You may use one of the following values for the `[EncodingDescription]`:

✦ Unicode/ISO/IEC 10646 encoding:

- `UTF-8`
- `UTF-16`
- `ISO-10646-UCS-2`
- `ISO-10646-UCS-4`

✦ ISO 8859 encoding: `ISO-8859-1` through `ISO-8859-9`

✦ JIS X-0208-1997 encoding:

- `ISO-2022-JP`
- `Shift_JIS`
- `EUC_JP`

Here are two examples of encoding declarations:

```
<?XML encoding="UTF-8"?>
```

```
<?XML encoding='EUC_JP'?>
```

Character references

You may need to use a character within the ISO 10646/Unicode character set that you can't enter directly via the computer keyboard or other input device. In fact, many such characters exist, and you may require some of them in your XML documents. You can include such a character in your document by using a *character reference,* which is an escape code for a single Unicode character. You do this by expressing a character reference with the numerical value of the character's bit string.

The rule for a character reference appears like this in the XML Specification:

```
CharRef ::= '&#' [0-9]+ ';' | '&#x' [0-9a-fA-F]+ ';' [wfc:
    Legal Character]
```

According to this rule, you can express a character reference with either

✦ A *decimal reference,* which is

- A number consisting of digits 0 through 9.

- Preceded by an ampersand and a pound sign (&#).

- Immediately followed by a semicolon (;).

✦ A *hexadecimal reference,* which is

- A base-16 number consisting of digits 0 through 9 and/or letters A (or a) through F (or f).

- Preceded by an ampersand, pound sign, and the literal string x (&#x).

- Immediately followed by a semicolon (;).

Both types of numbers refer to specific characters in the Unicode character set.

The well-formedness constraint (wfc:), Legal Character, indicates that the characters referenced must be legal according to the character range specified by the XML Specification in the rule char.

As an example, you denote the standard Rx prescription symbol (R_x) — represented by the Unicode character number U+211E — by the decimal reference ℞ and by the hexadecimal reference ℞. Although you couldn't tell just by looking at them, both of these numeric values refer to the same Unicode symbol.

Similarly, you denote the copyright symbol (©) by both the decimal reference © and the hexadecimal reference ©.

Here's an example of how a character reference may appear in a document:

```
Press the <key>less-than</key> key (&#x3C;) to invoke the
    macro.
```

Check out Chapter 9 of *XML For Dummies,* 2nd Edition, by Ed Tittel and Frank Boumphrey, to get an extensive list of special characters.

Entity references

An *entity reference* is a pointer — or an alias — to the content of a named entity. You may specify references for two types of entities:

✦ **General entities,** which are used inside XML documents and whose references use the ampersand (&) and the semicolon (;) as beginning- and end-delimiters, respectively.

✦ **Parameter entities,** which are used inside DTDs and whose references use the percent sign (%) and semicolon (;) as beginning- and end-delimiters, respectively.

General entities

The rule that defines a reference appears like this in the XML specification:

```
Reference ::= EntityRef | CharRef
```

This rule is quite simple: It says that a reference can be either an entity reference (EntityRef) or a character reference (CharRef), because the logical "or" (|) divides the two types of references.

The two rules immediately following this one define the syntax of an entity reference and of a parameter entity reference (PEReference).

Here is the rule for an entity reference:

```
EntityRef ::= '&' Name ';'
[wfc: Entity Declared]
[vc: Entity Declared]
[wfc: Parsed Entity]
[wfc: No Recursion]
```

This rule contains three well-formedness checks and one validity check.

First, the well-formedness constraint (wfc:), Entity Declared, indicates that the name given in the entity reference must match the name provided in the entity declaration in the following cases:

✦ In a DTD-less document

✦ In a document that only has an internal DTD subset and that doesn't contain any parameter entity references

✦ In a document with a standalone document declaration of "yes" (standalone='yes')

In addition, this constraint requires that you declare a parameter entity before referencing it. Similarly, you must declare a general entity before referencing it when it appears in a default value in an attribute-list declaration.

The exception to this constraint is that you don't have to declare any of these entities:

✦ amp (&)

✦ lt (<)

✦ gt (>)

✦ apos (')

✦ quot (")

The XML processor automatically recognizes the corresponding entity references for these special predefined entities. This is useful to, say, differentiate between a less-than symbol (<) in the textual content of your document and the delimiter that marks the beginning of markup.

For example, if you enter an ampersand (&) directly into the string Bonnie & Clyde, Inc. within the textual content of your document, the XML processor signals an error. The way to correct this is to use the amp entity, which inserts a literal ampersand into the document:

```
Bonnie &amp; Clyde, Inc.
```

Second, the validity constraint (vc:), Entity Declared, indicates that in a document with an external subset or external parameter entities with a standalone document declaration of "no" (standalone='no'), you must make sure the name in the entity reference matches the name you declared for the entity. And like the well-formedness constraint of Entity Declared, you must declare a parameter entity before referencing it; similarly, you must declare a general entity before referencing it when it appears in a default value in an attribute-list declaration.

Third, the well-formedness constraint, Parsed Entity, means that an entity reference must not contain the name of an unparsed entity, also known as a binary entity. You may only refer to unparsed or binary entities in attribute values that are declared of type ENTITY (or ENTITIES).

Finally, the well-formedness constraint, No Recursion, tells you that a parsed entity must not contain a recursive reference to itself, either directly or indirectly.

Consider the following entity:

```
<!ENTITY XML "Extensible Markup Language">
```

A legal reference for this entity would be &XML;.

As another example, here are two entity references that point to the entities docdate and security-level respectively:

```
On &docdate;, you will be given &security-level; security
    clearance.
```

Parameter entities

Here is the XML Specification rule for a parameter entity reference:

```
PEReference ::= '%' Name ';'
[wfc: Entity Declared]
[vc: Entity Declared]
[wfc: Parsed Entity]
[wfc: No Recursion]
[wfc: In DTD]
```

This rule contains four well-formedness checks and one validity check. The first four checks are the same as the ones in the rule for the entity reference. The last check, the well-formedness constraint, In DTD, specifies that parameter entity references may only appear in a DTD. Because parameter entities and parameter entity references can only appear in a DTD, entity references and character references are the types of references that you would see throughout an XML document.

So, for example, an entity declaration for a URL looks like this:

```
<!ENTITY % ISOLat2 SYSTEM "http://www.xml.com/iso/isolat2-xml.
   entities">
```

The parameter entity reference, as configured by this declaration, looks like this:

```
%ISOLat2;
```

To find more information on parameter entities, see the "Parameter entities" subsection of the "Entities" section, earlier in this chapter.

Notations and Notation Declarations

An external binary entity is stored in a particular type of file format. In XML, this format is known as the *notation* of the entity. A notation could indicate any legitimate file format, such as a BMP image, MPEG video, TXT plain-text file, or PL Perl script.

As you may expect, you declare a notation within a DTD subset with a *notation declaration*. A notation declaration identifies a specific type of external binary data to the XML processor so that you can reference the data type in your document.

After the notation declaration goes to the XML application, the application does what it's programmed to do with the data type, such as spawn an image viewer or a video player. An application that is spawned from the XML application this way is called a *helper application.* The name of the notation — which becomes its external identifier — helps the XML processor or application locate a helper application that is capable of processing the data described by the notation.

The set of three rules in the XML specification for a notation declaration looks like this:

```
NotationDecl ::= '<!NOTATION' S Name S (ExternalID |
    PublicID) S? '>'

ExternalID ::= 'SYSTEM' S SystemLiteral | 'PUBLIC' S
    PubidLiteral S SystemLiteral

PublicID ::= 'PUBLIC' S PubidLiteral
```

The rule for the notation declaration, NotationDecl, indicates that the literal string <!NOTATION must be followed by a white space (S), which is then followed by the Name of the notation, another white space, either an external ID or a public ID, an optional white space, and a right-angle bracket (>), respectively. When you substitute the expression for the ExternalID rule into the notation declaration rule, you find that you have a choice between using SYSTEM with the URL of a proprietary file or PUBLIC with the public ID of a public-domain file.

For more information about the XML Specification, see Chapter 2 of this book.

Here are a few examples of notation declarations:

```
<!NOTATION GIF87A SYSTEM "GIF">

<!NOTATION JPEG SYSTEM "/programs/viewjpg.exe">

<!NOTATION DOC SYSTEM "winword.exe">

<!NOTATION HTML PUBLIC "-//W3C//DTD HTML 3.2//EN">
```

After you declare the name of your notation, you may use that name in entity and attribute-list declarations and in attribute specifications.

Chapter 6: Converting, Publishing, and Serving XML

In This Chapter

✔ Converting non-XML documents to XML

✔ Publishing XML documents

✔ Serving XML

✔ Reading XML through a client

✔ Setting up server-side and client-side includes

✔ Maintaining an XML-based Web site or intranet

*I*n addition to creating XML documents and document systems from the ground up, you can also convert existing documents, such as HTML documents, to XML. After you have a set of documents, you want to serve them to your organization or to the public and possibly publish them in other formats, as well. In this chapter, I introduce you to each of these practical XML-related tasks.

Converting Non-XML Documents to XML

In addition to creating new XML documents from scratch, you can convert existing documents in other formats to XML. Theoretically, you can convert any document to XML — whether the original document is a 7-bit ASCII plain text file, a proprietary format, such as Microsoft Word, or a public standard like HTML or SGML.

Converting a document, formatted data, or a set of documents involves a process of massaging the textual formatting, markup, and instructions from one document format or standard to another. Usually, conversion requires using software or a script that automates the conversion process (useful for large numbers of documents), a person to make manual changes to the documents, or a combination of both.

If you need to convert a document format that's missing a lot of structural information — for example, a document format that contains no clear

descriptions of how the document's data fields relate to one another —
to an XML format that does contain a fair amount of structural information,
the conversion process may require several steps:

1. You can create a simple DTD based on the original document format.

2. Convert the documents from their original format to XML by using the
DTD.

3. Add markup definitions and instructions to the DTD as necessary. In
other words, the DTD can evolve over time to include more structural
information.

If you're interested in converting HTML documents to XML format, you're in
luck: The latest version of HTML, dubbed XHTML, redefines HTML as an
XML language — so all you have to do is edit your HTML files to conform to
XHTML. For more details on XHTML, visit `www.w3.org/MarkUp`.

Unfortunately, document conversion is beyond the scope of this book. If
you want more in-depth information on this topic, check out a good book
devoted exclusively to XML, such *XML For Dummies,* 2nd Edition, by Ed
Tittel and Frank Boumphrey. Or point your browser to an e-zine — a good
one is XML From the Inside Out, which you find at `www.xml.com` — that
covers tricky XML-related topics, such as document conversion.

Publishing XML

The output of XML documents is not limited to an XML client viewed via a
computer screen. As with SGML, HTML, and other document formats and
specifications, you can publish XML data to a number of venues.

Output of XML data can include

+ XML-compatible Web browsers

+ XML-aware databases

+ Printed publications, including

  • Newspapers

  • Newsletters

  • Brochures and advertising materials

  • Magazines

  • Books

  • Reference materials

  • Custom and personal publications

+ Computer help files
+ Software products, including
  • Multimedia products
  • Programming scripts that interpret XML data
+ CD-ROMs
+ Newsfeeds

You can probably think of other ways to use XML in addition to the ideas on this list. Theoretically, you can use XML in any form of data transfer or document exchange, which is a great reason to learn about and use it. For cutting-edge information about how other folks are publishing XML, check out a good XML portal such as `www.xml.org` (XML.org) or `www.xml.com` (XML From the Inside Out).

Serving XML

One of the main purposes of using XML is to create documents and data that conform to a technical standard, so that you can share your documents with others, and you can read their documents in the same format. Thus, when you work with XML, you probably want to set up a system that stores, manages, and shares XML DTDs and documents for more than one person. A system that works best is usually a client-server system, usually modeled after typical file-sharing servers and Internet servers. An ideal solution is a client-server system running over a TCP/IP-based network (that is, a network that uses standard Internet protocols) that includes both server and client XML-aware software.

Clients (and client-side includes)

Because XML is a specification that you can use on any platform and over a network, most developers of XML products focus on creating platform-independent, fully networkable XML-savvy systems. So, at this point, most XML clients are emerging in the form of Web browsers or Java applications, including Web browser plug-ins and products for Java-enabled Web browsers.

If you manage a Web site or an intranet that includes XML documents or you develop the technical aspects of the content for your organization, you may be interested in using client-side includes. A *client-side include* is an instruction or set of instructions embedded within a document that processes some type of data on or within the client.

You can use client-side includes in XML as long as any embedded code passed to a third-party engine or interface doesn't contain any characters that can be misinterpreted as XML markup. Third-party engines and interfaces include

✦ Structured Document Query Language (SDQL) inquiries

✦ Java input

✦ Netscape LiveWire requests

✦ Streamed data content

To prevent characters from being misinterpreted as XML markup, you have two options:

✦ Use CDATA sections to hold XML-specific code. CDATA sections provide a "safe zone" for XML code by telling the XML application to avoid parsing it. (You can find out more about CDATA sections in Chapter 3.)

✦ Use character and entity references instead of markup characters. For instance, substitute < for the left-angle bracket (<).

As long as you take these precautions, you can configure a powerful system that integrates XML with other types of data and data-processing engines.

Visit `www.oasis-open.org/cover/xmlSupport.html` to find a list of currently available and new XML-aware products, including clients.

Servers (and server-side includes)

After you have a number of XML files, you need a way to share them with others. An efficient way to share XML files is to store, organize, and serve them from a server on a network. In fact, an organization of people who need to effectively share XML files with each other must have access to one or more XML-enabled servers.

If you want to set up a system to host and serve XML documents, you may not have to purchase additional equipment and software if you already have an Internet or intranet server in place. You can serve XML files fairly easily by making a few changes to the server software settings.

To serve XML documents, which are usually identified as files with an `.xml` or `.XML` extension, you must add the correct Multipurpose Internet Mail Extensions (MIME) type to the MIME-types configuration file or list.

To configure your server to recognize an XML MIME type, add this line to the MIME-types configuration file or list:

```
text/xml xml XML
```

Your XML documents may reference one or several types of adjunct files, such as

✦ A DTD

✦ A schema

✦ A style sheet (cascading style sheet or XSL — Extensible Style Language — style sheet)

✦ An entity file containing either

- Parseable XML data

- Binary data

Each of these adjunct file types may require its own MIME entry in the MIME-types configuration file. Also, you must place each adjunct file in the appropriate directory referenced by the XML document.

For more about XSL, check out Chapter 8 of *XML For Dummies,* 2nd Edition, by Ed Tittel and Frank Boumphrey. For more on editing the MIME-types configuration file on your server, consult the manual for your server.

A *server-side include (SSI)* automatically and immediately parses and generates documents and sends them to client applications. If you have any SSIs running on your server, you may continue to use them with XML as long as the SSI scripts generate XML-conformant files that are either valid or well-formed.

For more information about validity and well-formedness, check out Chapter 3 of this book or Chapter 5 of *XML For Dummies,* 2nd Edition, by Ed Tittel and Frank Boumphrey.

An in-depth discussion of server-side includes is beyond the scope of this book, but you can find detailed information on SSIs in the NCSA HTTPd Server Side Includes (SSI) Tutorial at `hoohoo.ncsa.uiuc.edu/docs/tutorials/includes.html` or in Mark West's SSI Tutorial at `www.carleton.ca/~dmcfet/html/ssi3.html`. In addition, the official Web site for the popular HTTP server project Apache is at `www.apache.org`.

Managing and Maintaining XML

If you manage a Web site or intranet for your organization, you may consider transitioning from an entirely HTML-based Web site to a hybrid XML/HTML Web site. You can manage a Web site or intranet manually, but if the site grows, you probably want to use a software product to maintain all of your DTDs, documents, and data.

This type of product is often called a document management system. A *document management system* enables you to manage and serve a large number of documents as well as data that is classified in multiple ways.

Here are some important features and functions to look for in a document management system:

✦ You may configure a central repository or a directory in which you store documents.

✦ You may set access rights for users.

✦ It allows for library-style document checkout, and it locks documents when they're being accessed and edited to prevent the creation of multiple versions of the same document.

✦ It logs edits to documents and data.

✦ It automates publishing and report-generation from a set of documents or data.

✦ It accounts for both the physical structure and the logical structure of your documents and allows you to organize the entities and elements of a set of documents.

A number of software manufacturers are currently working on document management systems for XML. Some document management systems may support SGML, HTML, and other document types, as well.

 A list of currently available and new XML-aware products is posted to the XML Industry Support section of the SGML/XML Web page at `www.oasis-open.org/cover/xmlSupport.html`.

Index

Symbols

* (asterisk), 705, 725, 727
\ (backslash), 721
^ (caret), 705
: (colon), 709
" (double quotes), 706, 728
= (equal sign), 727
/ (forward slash), 701
< (less-than sign), 708, 718
@ (percent sign), 736, 740, 743, 748
? (question mark), 713
< (right-angle bracket), 715
; (semicolon), 736, 747, 748
[] (square brackets), 705, 715, 716
_ (underscore), 709

A

American Standard Code for Information Interchange (ASCII), 753
ampersand, 718, 736, 743, 747, 749
angle brackets (<>), 713, 721, 723, 728, 730, 756
APIs. See application program interfaces (APIs)
apostrophe ('), 728
application program interfaces (APIs), 697–698
ASCII. See American Standard Code for Information Interchange (ASCII)
asterisk (*), 705, 725, 727
attribute(s)
    assigning, to elements, 726–733
    declarations, 712, 727–733
    default values, 729–730
    types, 730–733

B

backslash (\), 721
Boumphrey, Frank, 701, 703

browsers, 696–697
business-to-business applications, 692

C

C programming, 695, 697
C++ programming, 695
Cascading Style Sheets (CSS), 689
case-sensitivity, 701
CDATA section, 717, 718, 722, 756
character(s)
    basic description of, 745
    encoding, in entities, 745–746
    parseable, 725
    referencing, 739–741, 745–750
client-side includes, 755
colon (:), 709
comments, 717, 718, 722
conditional sections, 733–734
CSS. See Cascading Style Sheets (CSS)

D

database(s)
    extracts, 686
    schemes, 688
decimal references, 747
document(s). See also document type definitions (DTDs)
    entities, 736–737
    management systems, 758
    object model (DOM), 689
    well-formed, 687, 695, 700–701, 747
document type definitions (DTDs)
    associating, with XML documents, 716–717
    basic description of, 695, 711–716
    document, 712–714
    examples of, 714–715
    external, 716–717
    internal, 716
    markup for, 717
    prolog, 712–714

public external, 717
referencing, 716–717
sample, 688–689
double quotes ("), 706, 728
DTDs. See document type definitions (DTDs)

E

element(s)
    assigning attributes to, 726–733
    basic description of, 700, 717, 722–726
    declarations, 712, 715–716, 723–726
    empty, 721
    root, 715–716
encoding declarations, 746
entities. See also entity references
    basic description of, 699, 701–702, 735–745
    declaring, 712, 737–738
    document, 736–737
    external, 741–742
    general, 747
    internal, 706–707, 742–743
    parsed, 701–702, 736, 744–745
    processing on, 738–741
    unparsed, 701–702, 736, 744, 745
entity references, 701, 717, 723, 738–741, 747–750
enumerated types, 732–733
equals sign (=), 727
eXtensible Markup Language (XML)
    advantages of, 689–690
    API kits, 697–698
    applications tailor-made for, 691–692
    basic description of, 685–690
    converting non-XML documents to, 753–754
    development of, 686
    disadvantages of, 690–691
    editors, 694–695
    expression code syntax, 703–704

Notes

Book X

Appendix

The 5th Wave   By Rich Tennant

"OK, I think I forgot to mention this, but we now have a Web management function that automatically alerts us when there's a broken link on The Aquarium's Web site."

Contents at a Glance

Appendix: About the CD

System Requirements

Make sure that your computer meets the minimum system requirements shown in the following list. If your computer doesn't match up to most of these requirements, you may have problems using the software and files on the CD. For the latest and greatest information, please refer to the ReadMe file located at the root of the CD-ROM.

+ A PC with a Pentium or faster processor; or a Mac OS computer with a 68040 or faster processor

+ Microsoft Windows 95 or later; or Mac OS system software 7.6.1 or later

+ At least 32MB of total RAM installed on your computer; for best performance, we recommend at least 64MB

+ A CD-ROM drive

+ A sound card for PCs; Mac OS computers have built-in sound support

+ A monitor capable of displaying at least 256 colors or grayscale

+ A modem with a speed of at least 14,400 bps

If you need more information on the basics, check out these books published by Hungry Minds, Inc.: *PCs For Dummies,* by Dan Gookin; *Macs For Dummies,* by David Pogue; *iMacs For Dummies* by David Pogue; *Windows 95 For Dummies, Windows 98 For Dummies, Windows 2000 Professional For Dummies, Microsoft Windows ME Millennium Edition For Dummies,* all by Andy Rathbone.

Using the CD with Microsoft Windows

To install items from the CD to your hard drive (and you have the Autorun feature enabled), follow these steps:

1. **Insert the CD into your computer's CD-ROM drive.**

2. **A window appears with the following options: HTML Interface, Browse CD, and Exit.**

3. **Choose one of the options, as follows:**

   - **HTML Interface: Click this button to view the contents of the CD in standard For Dummies presentation. It'll look like a Web page. Here you'll also find a list of useful Web links from the book.**

   - **Browse CD: Click this button to skip the fancy presentation and simply view the CD contents from the directory structure. This means you'll just see a list of folders — plain and simple.**

   - **Exit: Well, what can we say? Click this button to quit.**

If you do not have the Autorun feature enabled or if the Autorun window does not appear, follow these steps to access the CD:

1. **Insert the CD into your computer's CD-ROM drive.**

2. **Click the Start button and choose Run from the menu.**

3. **In the dialog box that appears, type** d:\start.htm.

   Replace *d* with the proper drive letter for your CD-ROM if it uses a different letter. (If you don't know the letter, double-click My Computer on your desktop and see what letter is listed for your CD-ROM drive.)

   Your browser opens, and the license agreement is displayed. If you don't have a browser, Microsoft Internet Explorer and Netscape Communicator are included on the CD.

4. **Read through the license agreement, nod your head, and click the Agree button if you want to use the CD.**

   After you click Agree, you're taken to the Main menu, where you can browse through the contents of the CD.

5. **To navigate within the interface, click a topic of interest to take you to an explanation of the files on the CD and how to use or install them.**

6. **To install software from the CD, simply click the software name.**

   You'll see two options: to run or open the file from the current location or to save the file to your hard drive. Choose to run or open the file from its current location, and the installation procedure continues. When you finish using the interface, close your browser as usual.

Note: We have included an "easy install" in these HTML pages. If your browser supports installations from within it, go ahead and click the links of the program names you see. You'll see two options: Run the File from the Current Location and Save the File to Your Hard Drive. Choose to Run the File from the Current Location and the installation procedure continues. A Security Warning dialog box appears. Click Yes to continue the installation.

To run some of the programs on the CD, you may need to keep the disc inside your CD-ROM drive. This is a good thing. Otherwise, a very large chunk of the program would be installed to your hard drive, consuming valuable hard drive space and possibly keeping you from installing other software.

Appendix

About the CD

Using the CD with Mac OS

To install items from the CD to your hard drive, follow these steps:

1. **Insert the CD into your computer's CD-ROM drive.**

   In a moment, an icon representing the CD you just inserted appears on your Mac desktop. Chances are, the icon looks like a CD-ROM.

2. **Double-click the CD icon to show the CD's contents.**

3. **Double-click** start.htm **to open your browser and display the license agreement.**

   If your browser doesn't open automatically, open it as you normally would by choosing File⇨Open File (in Internet Explorer) or File⇨Open⇨Location in Netscape (in Netscape Navigator) and select *CWP All In One DR FD*. The license agreement appears.

4. **Read through the license agreement, nod your head, and click the Accept button if you want to use the CD.**

   After you click Accept, you're taken to the Main menu. This is where you can browse through the contents of the CD.

5. **To navigate within the interface, click any topic of interest and you're taken to an explanation of the files on the CD and how to use or install them.**

6. **To install software from the CD, simply click the software name.**

What You'll Find on the CD

The following sections are arranged by category and provide a summary of the software and other goodies you'll find on the CD. If you need help with installing the items provided on the CD, refer back to the installation instructions in the preceding section.

Shareware programs are fully functional, free, trial versions of copyrighted programs. If you like particular programs, register with their authors for a nominal fee and receive licenses, enhanced versions, and technical support. *Freeware programs* are free, copyrighted games, applications, and utilities. You can copy them to as many PCs as you like — for free — but they offer no technical support. *GNU software* is governed by its own license, which is included inside the folder of the GNU software. There are no restrictions on distribution of GNU software. See the GNU license at the root of the CD for more details. *Trial, demo,* or *evaluation* versions of software are usually limited either by time or functionality (such as not letting you save a project after you create it).

BBEdit/BBEdit Lite

Demo version/freeware.

For Mac OS. Created by BareBones Software, BBEdit is a high-performance HTML and text editor designed from the ground up for the Macintosh.

BBEdit Lite, BBEdit's free "cousin," is a pared-down version of BBEdit that doesn't offer all the nice-to-have extras BBEdit contains, such as fancy formatting capabilities, graphics tools, and a thesaurus.

For more information, including ordering details, point your browser to www.barebones.com/products.

Dreamweaver

30-day trial version.

For Windows and Mac OS. From Macromedia comes this industrial-strength (yet user-friendly) Web site development tool.

For more information about Dreamweaver, visit Macromedia on the Web at www.macromedia.com/software/dreamweaver.

Fireworks

30-day trial version.

For Windows and Mac OS. You can use Fireworks 4, from Macromedia, to create, edit, optimize, and animate graphics for your Web pages.

For more information about Macromedia Fireworks 4, point your browser to www.macromedia.com/software/fireworks.

Flash
30-day trial version.

For Windows and Mac OS. You can use Macromedia's Flash to create graphics and nifty animations for your Web pages. (Flash also works with Dreamweaver, Macromedia's Web development tool.)

For more information about Flash, visit Macromedia on the Web at www. macromedia.com/software/flash.

GIF Movie Gear
Shareware.

For Windows OS. GIF Movie Gear is a professional-level development environment you can use to create animated GIF files for your Web site.

For more information, visit Gamani online at www.gamani.com.

HotDog Professional
Trial version.

For Windows OS. HotDog Professional is a Web development tool that supports not just HTML, but Cascading Style Sheets and JavaScript, as well.

For more information about this tool, visit Sausage Software online at www. sausagetools.com/professional/overview.html.

Internet Explorer
Commercial version.

For Windows OS and Mac. One of the two most popular Web browsers on the market, Internet Explorer provides support for both JavaScript and XML.

For more information, visit Microsoft's Internet Explorer Home Page at www. microsoft.com/windows/ie/.

Appendix

About the CD

NetObjects ScriptBuilder

Trial version.

For Windows OS. The focus of this Web develop tool is scripts — including JavaScript scripts. NetObjects ScriptBuilder contains a library of cut-and-paste scripts in addition to a point-and-click script building interface.

For more information, visit NetObjects on the Web at `www.netobjects.com`.

Paint Shop Pro

Evaluation version.

For Windows OS. With Paint Shop Pro , you can retouch photos and images and drop them into your Web pages. You can also use this tool's drawing and painting tools to create original Web-optimized graphics and even animations, through Animation Shop 3 (included).

For additional information about Paint Shop Pro, visit Jasc Software at `www.jasc.com`.

Photoshop

Evaluation version.

For Windows OS and Mac. From Adobe Systems, Inc. comes Photoshop, a top-of-the-line image editing program long used by print graphics professionals. Now updated to include Web graphics, Photoshop provides a wealth of goodies you can use to enhance digital photos — as well as slice-and-dice tools you can use to create multiple hotspots on a single image (great for creating navigation bars and rollovers).

To find out more about Photoshop, point your browser to `www.adobe.com/products/photoshop/main.html`.

Stuffit Expander

Commercial product.

For Windows and Mac OS. This drag-and-drop tool allows you to compress and uncompress large files for each transfer across the Net.

For additional details, visit Aladdin Systems on the Web at `www.aladdinsys.com/expander`.

Troubleshooting

I tried my best to compile programs that work on most computers with the minimum system requirements. Alas, your computer may differ, and some programs may not work properly for some reason.

The two likeliest problems are that you don't have enough memory (RAM) for the programs you want to use, or you have other programs running that are affecting installation or running of a program. If you get an error message such as `Not enough memory` or `Setup cannot continue`, try one or more of the following suggestions and then try using the software again:

Appendix

About the CD

+ **Turn off any antivirus software running on your computer.** Installation programs sometimes mimic virus activity and may make your computer incorrectly believe that it's being infected by a virus.

+ **Close all running programs.** The more programs you have running, the less memory is available to other programs. Installation programs typically update files and programs; so if you keep other programs running, installation may not work properly.

+ **Have your local computer store add more RAM to your computer.** This is, admittedly, a drastic and somewhat expensive step. However, if you have a Windows 95 PC or a Mac OS computer with a PowerPC chip, adding more memory can really help the speed of your computer and allow more programs to run at the same time. This may include closing the CD interface and running a product's installation program from Windows Explorer.

If you still have trouble installing the items from the CD, please call the Hungry Minds, Inc. Customer Service phone number at 800-762-2974 (outside the U.S.: 317-572-3994) or send email to techsupdum@hungryminds.com.

Index

Symbols

& (ampersand), 469, 718, 736, 743, 747, 749
<> (angle brackets), 37, 39, 713, 721, 723, 728, 730, 756
' (apostrophe), 728
\ (backslash), 37, 721
: (colon), 181, 709
{} (curly braces), 179, 443, 444
. (dot), 495
" (double quotes), 39, 441, 444, 706, 728
// (double slash), 445–446
= (equals sign), 727
/ (forward slash), 108, 445–446, 701
– (minus sign), 452
() parentheses, 444
% (percent sign), 736, 740, 743, 748
. (period), 129
+ (plus sign), 129, 241, 452
# (pound sign), 43, 49, 65, 136, 364
; (semicolon), 736, 747, 748
' (single quote), 444
[] (square brackets), 705, 715, 716

A

<A> tag, 48, 49, 441
 basic description of, 131
 frames and, 171–172
 internal targets and, 135–136
 linking to documents within your site with, 132
 linking to pages out on the Web with, 133
 JavaScript and, 501
 media files and, 68, 70, 390
About Flash option, 529
Absolute Bottom option, 285
Absolute Middle option, 285
Abstract Windowing Toolkit, 416–418
Access (Microsoft), 78

acquiring bank, 614, 640
ACTION attribute, 153–155
ActionEvent event, 418
actions
 assigning, to movie elements, 576–577
 editing, 578–579
 testing, 579
Actions panel, 525, 566, 574–577
ActionScript Dictionary option, 528
ActionScript Reference option, 528
activation fees, 627
Active Graphics option, 215
Active Hyperlink option, 220
Active Server Pages (ASP), 639, 656
ActiveX controls (Microsoft), 306–307
Actual Size option, 600
adapters, 418–419
Add File button, 213
Add File to Import List dialog box, 213
Add/Modify FTP Locations dialog box, 255–256
Adobe PhotoShop, 357, 770
Adobe Premiere, 381–382
Adobe Illustrator, 595–596, 602
advertisements, 15, 28, 98–99
ALIGN attribute, 45, 121–122, 142, 150, 396
Align panel, 522
aligning
 graphics, 142, 284
 layers, 326
 movies, 598
 tables, 226
 text, 39, 121–123, 282
Alignment option, 226
ALINK attribute, 120, 121
All Frames option, 599
Alpha option, 567
alpha transparency, 586
ALT attribute, 62–63, 138, 139, 145, 395
AltaVista search engine, 91, 112
alternative text, for graphics, 62, 139
Amazon.com, 617–620

H

M

N

P

U

Notes

Notes

Notes

Hungry Minds, Inc.
End-User License Agreement

5. **Limited Warranty.**

   (a) HMI warrants that the Software and Software Media are free from defects in materials and workmanship under normal use for a period of sixty (60) days from the date of purchase of this Book. If HMI receives notification within the warranty period of defects in materials or workmanship, HMI will replace the defective Software Media.

   (b) HMI AND THE AUTHOR OF THE BOOK DISCLAIM ALL OTHER WARRANTIES, EXPRESS OR IMPLIED, INCLUDING WITHOUT LIMITATION IMPLIED WARRANTIES OF MERCHANTABILITY AND FITNESS FOR A PARTICULAR PURPOSE, WITH RESPECT TO THE SOFTWARE, THE PROGRAMS, THE SOURCE CODE CONTAINED THEREIN, AND/OR THE TECHNIQUES DESCRIBED IN THIS BOOK. HMI DOES NOT WARRANT THAT THE FUNCTIONS CONTAINED IN THE SOFTWARE WILL MEET YOUR REQUIREMENTS OR THAT THE OPERATION OF THE SOFTWARE WILL BE ERROR FREE.

   (c) This limited warranty gives you specific legal rights, and you may have other rights that vary from jurisdiction to jurisdiction.

6. **Remedies.**

   (a) HMI's entire liability and your exclusive remedy for defects in materials and workmanship shall be limited to replacement of the Software Media, which may be returned to HMI with a copy of your receipt at the following address: Software Media Fulfillment Department, Attn.: *Creating Web Pages All-in-One Desk Reference For Dummies*, Hungry Minds, Inc., 10475 Crosspoint Blvd., Indianapolis, IN 46256, or call 1-800-762-2974. Please allow four to six weeks for delivery. This Limited Warranty is void if failure of the Software Media has resulted from accident, abuse, or misapplication. Any replacement Software Media will be warranted for the remainder of the original warranty period or thirty (30) days, whichever is longer.

   (b) In no event shall HMI or the author be liable for any damages whatsoever (including without limitation damages for loss of business profits, business interruption, loss of business information, or any other pecuniary loss) arising from the use of or inability to use the Book or the Software, even if HMI has been advised of the possibility of such damages.

   (c) Because some jurisdictions do not allow the exclusion or limitation of liability for consequential or incidental damages, the above limitation or exclusion may not apply to you.

7. **U.S. Government Restricted Rights.** Use, duplication, or disclosure of the Software for or on behalf of the United States of America, its agencies and/or instrumentalities (the "U.S. Government") is subject to restrictions as stated in paragraph (c)(1)(ii) of the Rights in Technical Data and Computer Software clause of DFARS 252.227-7013, or subparagraphs (c)(1) and (2) of the Commercial Computer Software - Restricted Rights clause at FAR 52.227-19, and in similar clauses in the NASA FAR supplement, as applicable.

8. **General.** This Agreement constitutes the entire understanding of the parties and revokes and supersedes all prior agreements, oral or written, between them and may not be modified or amended except in a writing signed by both parties hereto that specifically refers to this Agreement. This Agreement shall take precedence over any other documents that may be in conflict herewith. If any one or more provisions contained in this Agreement are held by any court or tribunal to be invalid, illegal, or otherwise unenforceable, each and every other provision shall remain in full force and effect.